Series Editors:
Steven F. Warren, Ph.D.
Marc E. Fey, Ph.D.
Alan G. Kamhi, Ph.D.

Communication
and Language
Intervention
Series

☞ **W9-DHM-198**

Treatment of Autism Spectrum Disorders

*Evidence-Based Intervention Strategies
for Communication and Social Interactions*

Also in the *Communication and Language Intervention Series:*

Dual Language Development and Disorders:
A Handbook on Bilingualism and Second
Language Learning, Second Edition
by Johanne Paradis, Ph.D.,
Fred Genesee, Ph.D., and
Martha B. Crago, Ph.D.

Interventions for Speech Sound Disorders in Children
edited by A. Lynn Williams, Ph.D.,
Sharynne McLeod, Ph.D., and
Rebecca J. McCauley, Ph.D.

Speech and Language Development and Intervention
in Down Syndrome and Fragile X Syndrome
edited by Joanne E. Roberts, Ph.D.,
Robin S. Chapman, Ph.D., and
Steven F. Warren, Ph.D.

Treatment of Language Disorders in Children
edited by Rebecca J. McCauley, Ph.D.,
and Marc E. Fey, Ph.D.

Communication and Language Intervention Series

Treatment of Autism Spectrum Disorders

Evidence-Based Intervention Strategies for Communication and Social Interactions

edited by

Patricia A. Prelock, Ph.D.
University of Vermont
Burlington

and

Rebecca J. McCauley, Ph.D.
The Ohio State University
Columbus

Baltimore • London • Sydney

Paul H. Brookes Publishing Co.
Post Office Box 10624
Baltimore, Maryland 21285-0624

www.brookespublishing.com

Typeset by Network Publishing Partners, Inc., Glenview, Illinois.
Manufactured in the United States of America by
Sheridan Books, Inc., Chelsea, Michigan.
Video finishing and DVD authoring by
MetaMedia Training International, Frederick, Maryland.

Cover image © iStockphoto.com/Christopher Futcher.

The individuals described in this book are composites or real people whose situations are masked and are based on the authors' experiences. In all instances, names and identifying details have been changed to protect confidentiality.

The Boardmaker™ symbols in Figure 13.2 are courtesy of DynaVox Mayer-Johnson, 2100 Wharton Street, Suite 400, Pittsburgh, PA 15203. http://www.mayer-johnson.com/pcs-sold/

The accompanying DVD contains a video segment for most of the interventions discussed in *Treatment of Autism Spectrum Disorders: Evidence-Based Intervention Strategies for Communication and Social Interactions* (see the DVD icons in the table of contents). The video clips were supplied by the chapter authors, and permission was obtained for all individuals shown in footage contained on the DVD.

Library of Congress Cataloging-in-Publication Data

Treatment of autism spectrum disorders : evidence-based intervention strategies for communication and social interactions / edited by Patricia A. Prelock and Rebecca J. McCauley.
    p.   cm. — (Communication and language intervention series)
  Includes bibliographical references and index.
  ISBN 978-1-59857-053-3 (pbk. : alk. paper)
  ISBN 1-59857-053-6 (pbk. : alk. paper)
  1. Autism spectrum disorders in children—Treatment. 2. Autism spectrum disorders—Treatment.
  I. Prelock, Patricia A. II. McCauley, Rebecca Joan, 1952–
RC553.A88T735 2012
618.92'85882—dc23   2012018831

British Library Cataloguing in Publication data are available from the British Library.

2016   2015   2014   2013   2012

10   9   8   7   6   5   4   3   2   1

Contents

||||||||||||||||||||||||||||||||||||||||||||||||||||||||||||||||||||||||||||||||||||||

About the DVD

||||||||||||||||||||||||||||||||||||||||||||||||||||||||||||||||||||||||||||||||||||||||||||||||||||||

CHAPTER 3: AUGMENTATIVE AND ALTERNATIVE COMMUNICATION STRATEGIES: MANUAL SIGNS, PICTURE COMMUNICATION, AND SPEECH-GENERATING DEVICES (WEGNER)

This video illustrates the use of aided language modeling and facilitative language strategies with a 12-year-old boy. The youngster uses a Palmtop 3 device. He and the student speech-language pathologist are completing a unit on the senses, which is something he was interested in and thus provides a meaningful context. The student therapist provides verbal and aided models, expands the boy's communication, interprets his behaviors as communicative, and is responsive to his communication. She has also provided contextual support in the form of pictures in the book and sounds and images on the iPod Touch.

CHAPTER 4: ELEMENTARY BEHAVIORAL INTERVENTION STRATEGIES: DISCRETE TRIAL INSTRUCTION, DIFFERENTIAL REINFORCEMENT, AND SHAPING (WILCZYNSKI, RUE, HUNTER, AND CHRISTIAN)

This video clip highlights the use of discrete trial instruction with both massed and varied trials to facilitate learning and understanding.

Massed trials: In order to make timely progress on a given skill, some children on the autism spectrum require a massed trial presentation of discrete trials. In her previous sessions, Natalya was unable to master shapes with a varied trial presentation. The interventionist elected to use a massed trial format so that she could gain the child's full attention to the relevant stimulus (i.e., triangle). Note that she provided the discriminative stimulus or instruction in multiple formats (e.g., "Where is the triangle," "Touch the triangle"), changed the presentation of the stimulus cards (i.e., they were sometimes in a vertical format and other times in a horizontal format), and increased the number of distracters to ensure that discrimination was occurring.

Varied trials: This child had been working on a number of novel skills. At the same time, it was important to ensure that she had maintained skills she had demonstrated in previous interactions. In this session, she was developing 1) her range of responses to the request to identify how stimuli differ and 2) learning how to request information (i.e., "What's in there?") and responding when offered choices. Her mastered task that was administered to assess for maintenance was color identification. Note how easily the interventionist was able to follow Natalya's interest and reinforce appropriate requesting within the context of varied trials.

CHAPTER 5: AN INTRODUCTION TO THE DEVELOPMENTAL, INDIVIDUAL-DIFFERENCE, RELATIONSHIP-BASED (DIR) MODEL AND ITS APPLICATION TO CHILDREN WITH AUTISM SPECTRUM DISORDER (GERBER)

This three-part video segment shows the nature of language intervention based on the principles of the DIR approach, used here with a 2-year-old child, Emma, who had a history of challenges in relating and communicating. The time span from the first segment to the last was approximately 2 months. Although Emma was capable of producing words, assessment of her speech, language, and communication suggested that her challenges in shared attention, affective engagement, reciprocity, and shared intentionality (*Diagnostic Manual for Infancy and Early Childhood;* Interdisciplinary Council on Developmental and Learning Disorders, 2005) should be considered the goals of intervention.

The strategies that were used with Emma were also derived from a developmental language perspective. They included the following:

- Share the focus of the child's attention.
- Maintain the child-directed focus by treating all behaviors as communicative.
- Interpret all of the child's behaviors as intentional.
- Use exaggerated and easily readable affective range.
- Maintain a reciprocal flow by consistently "giving" the child a turn in the interaction and then taking yours—keep the interaction going!

CHAPTER 8: IMPLEMENTING ENHANCED MILIEU TEACHING WITH CHILDREN WHO HAVE AUTISM SPECTRUM DISORDERS (HANCOCK AND KAISER)

This enhanced milieu teaching (EMT) session is with a therapist and a preschool-age boy whose language targets are one-word nouns, verbs, and requests. During this session, the therapist sits directly across from the child to facilitate social communication, centers her language on his focus of interest, and paces her talk at a rate that allows him time to both process her language and then imitate it. The therapist sets up opportunities for the child to functionally communicate and request in ways that are both fun and meaningful. The therapist also verbally responds to all of the boy's communicative attempts and expands any verbal utterance made by the boy, thus reinforcing his use of language. The EMT approach looks deceptively simple, but the power and effectiveness of this intervention lies in the adult's connecting with the child in a way that makes it possible for the adult to map the child's meaning into specific models of what the child would say and then providing the child with the time and space to practice this functional language.

CHAPTER 9: EARLY SOCIAL INTERACTION PROJECT (WOODS, WETHERBY, KASHINATH, AND HOLLAND)

This video clip depicts a little boy, Julius, with autism as he interacts with his dad and then with his mom. He first began early intervention at 18 months in the Early

Social Interaction Project. His intervention focuses on joint attention and building early language. The video depicts his interactions in four routines. In the first routine, Julius and his dad are engaged in a turn-taking game. You will notice Julius's vocalizations, movements, and gaze shifts. The father supports imitation and shared attention. The second activity is a dressing routine in which Julius has opportunities to follow directions and learn new words. During this activity, Julius initiates a social game, and the father follows his son's lead. In the next routine, the speech-language pathologist coaches Julius's father to extend pretend play. The final routine is book reading. Julius's mother pauses during the reading, allowing Julius to imitate and add words.

CHAPTER 11: PICTURE EXCHANGE COMMUNICATION SYSTEM (PECS) (SIMPSON AND GANZ)

This video presents an elementary-age boy with classic autism. The child is enrolled in a self-contained, public-school classroom for learners with autism and other developmental disabilities. The video illustrates the student using the Picture Exchange Communication System (PECS) in his classroom. The initial portion of the PECS video shows the boy working on PECS in a one-to-one learning situation with a speech therapist. Other classroom personnel, including the teacher and classroom paraprofessional, also use PECS.

CHAPTER 12: PIVOTAL RESPONSE TREATMENT (BRUINSMA AND McNERNEY)

This video clip shows a therapist working with a child with an autism spectrum disorder during a Pivotal Response Training one-to-one session. The child is 2 years, 8 months old and is learning her first words. The child is playing with the therapist on the floor of the family's living room. Expressive language targets in this video are "fish" and "tickle." The therapist uses the child's interest (an inset puzzle and tickling game) to target these words and varies his prompting level. He uses silly sounds to gain her attention and to keep her engaged and interested in the puzzle. The therapist also contingently reinforces her word attempts. The child's responsivity and affect are high, suggesting high motivation for the activity with the therapist. Finally, the therapist does an excellent job following the child's lead when she appears to be no longer interested in tickles at the end of the video clip, especially when reinforcing her initiation for "tickles."

CHAPTER 13: SOCIAL STORIES™ (HUTCHINS)

In this video segment, the clinician introduces a Social Story in a positive, non-threatening manner and in a relaxed and comfortable setting with a 17-year-old student. The student ("Jacob") is encouraged to read the story independently. In this example, the clinician repeats each sentence, as the sentences read by the student are often unintelligible. The Social Story is followed by brief comprehension checks to ensure that the images and key messages are meaningful to the student and accurately construed.

CHAPTER 14: VIDEO MODELING
APPLICATIONS FOR PERSONS WITH AUTISM (BUGGEY)

This video features a 3-year-old boy, Maverick, with childhood apraxia of speech. He is approximately a year behind in his expressive language development and slightly above average with his receptive language. The video was made with Apple's original iMovieHD software, which permits click-and-drag editing. The video begins with a brief introduction proclaiming that this is Maverick's movie and also labels the behavior. It is hoped that his interest will be piqued by announcing him in the starring role. The behavior is labeled to ensure that the child focuses on the targeted behavior. While on video, Maverick was asked to repeat individual words, including some verbs, so that the therapists could construct sentences from the video footage. He occasionally used longer utterances, and these were used even if the therapists were not sure what he was saying. Individual words were edited from the video clips, and iMovieHD allows frame-by-frame viewing, so the words could be cut very precisely. The individual words were dragged to a timeline and arranged into short sentences. The clips were scanned to find flattering images of Maverick, which were made into still frames that could be inserted in the movie. The narration was repeated at the end, with some reinforcement with children cheering and stating, "Good job talking!" Any footage depicting stuttering, adult prompts, or unintelligible words has been omitted from the movie. Maverick very much liked watching himself and would request to see the video. The self-recognition and interest as well as the ability to attend to the video have been recognized as prerequisites to the success of self-modeling.

Series Preface

‖‖

The purpose of the *Communication and Language Intervention Series* is to provide meaningful foundations for the application of sound intervention designs to enhance the development of communication skills across the life span. We are endeavoring to achieve this purpose by providing readers with presentations of state-of-the-art theory, research, and practice.

In selecting topics, editors, and authors, we are not attempting to limit the contents of this series to viewpoints that we agree with or that we find most promising. We are assisted in our efforts to develop the series by an editorial advisory board consisting of prominent scholars representative of the range of issues and perspectives to be incorporated in the series.

Well-conceived theory and research on development and intervention are vitally important for researchers, educators, and clinicians committed to the development of optimal approaches to communication and language intervention. The content of each book in the series reflects our view of the symbiotic relationship between intervention and research: Demonstrations of what may work in intervention should lead to analysis of promising discoveries and to insights from developmental work that may, in turn, fuel further refinement by intervention researchers. We trust that the careful reader will find much that is of great value in this book.

An inherent goal of the series is to enhance the long-term development of the field by systematically furthering the dissemination of theoretically and empirically based scholarship and research. We promise the reader an opportunity to participate in the development of this field through debates and discussions that occur throughout the pages of the *Communication and Language Intervention Series*.

Editorial Advisory Board

||||||||||||||||||||||||||||||||||||||||||||||||||||||||||||||||||||||||||||||||||||||||||

About the Editors

||||||||||||||||||||||||||||||||||||||||||||||||||||||||||||||||||||||||||||||||||||||||||||||||||

Patricia A. Prelock, Ph.D., Dean, College of Nursing and Health Sciences, and Professor, Department of Communication Sciences and Disorders, University of Vermont (UVM), Office of the Dean, College of Nursing and Health Sciences, University of Vermont, 105 Rowell, 106 Carrigan Drive, Burlington, VT 05405

Patricia A. Prelock's primary academic appointment is Professor of Communication Sciences and Disorders; she has a secondary appointment in pediatrics in the College of Medicine. Her primary research interests include collaborative, interdisciplinary practice and the nature and treatment of autism, including social perspective taking, peer play, emotion regulation, and the neural pathways involved in social discourse. She has served as Associate Editor for *Language, Speech, and Hearing Services in Schools,* was named an American Speech-Language-Hearing Association Fellow in 2000, and is President-elect of the American Speech-Language-Hearing Association. Dr. Prelock was the cochair of Vermont's statewide Autism Task Force for four years and is a member of the workgroup for the Autism Training Program through the Higher Education Collaborative. Dr. Prelock has more than 120 publications and more than 400 peer-reviewed and invited presentations in the areas of autism, collaboration, language assessment and intervention, and phonology. Dr. Prelock received the 1998 Friends Award through the Vermont Parent Information Center, UVM's Kroepsch–Maurice Excellence in Teaching Award in 2000, and the first annual Autism Society of Vermont Excellence in Service Award in 2000. She was named a University Scholar in 2003. In 2010, she was awarded the Puppet's Choice Award for Autism through the Kids on the Block Program. Dr. Prelock earned her bachelor's and master's degrees from Kent State University and her doctoral degree from the University of Pittsburgh. She is a board-recognized child language specialist.

Rebecca J. McCauley, Ph.D., Professor, Department of Speech and Hearing Science, Specialist in Child Language, The Ohio State University, 1070 Cermack Road, 105 Pressey Hall, Columbus, OH 43210

Rebecca J. McCauley joined OSU after 23 years at the Department of Communication Sciences, the University of Vermont, where she had at various times acted as Director of the Graduate Program and Chair. Her areas of scholarly interest encompass a wide range of topics in assessment and treatment of developmental communication disorders, with a special focus on childhood apraxia of speech. In addition to having served as an associate editor for the *American Journal of Speech Language Pathology,* she has coedited two previous books in the *Communication and Language Intervention Series: Treatment of Language Disorders in Children* (2006) with Marc Fey and *Interventions for Speech Sound Disorders in Children*

(2010) with A. Lynn Williams and Sharynne MacLeod. She has also published three other books and numerous articles related to developmental communication disorders, including the sole-authored *Assessment of Language Disorders in Children* (Lawrence Erlbaum Associates, 2001) and the coedited *Treatment of Stuttering* (Lippincott Williams & Wilkins, 2010). Dr. McCauley earned her bachelor's degree from Louisiana State University and her master's and Ph.D. degrees from the University of Chicago. She completed postdoctoral studies at the University of Arizona and the Johns Hopkins University before her first faculty appointment at the University of Vermont. She is a board-recognized specialist in child language and a Fellow of the American Speech-Language-Hearing Association.

About the Contributors

||||||||||||||||||||||||||||||||||||||||||||||||||||||||||||||||||||||||||||||||||||||||||||||||

Yvonne Bruinsma, Ph.D., BCBA-D, Executive Director, In STEPPS, 18008 Sky Park Circle, Suite 110, Irvine, CA 92614

Yvonne Bruinsma received a master's degree in developmental psychology in the Netherlands and a doctoral degree in special education, developmental disabilities, and risk studies from the University of California, Santa Barbara (UCSB). She studied Pivotal Response Treatment (PRT) with Drs. Robert and Lynn Koegel at the UCSB Autism Research and Training Center. She has published and presented internationally on PRT and early intervention and was instrumental in bringing PRT to the Center for Autism in the Netherlands. Dr. Bruinsma is a Board-Certified Behavior Analyst and has extensive experience working with children with autism spectrum disorders and other developmental disabilities and delays. She is founder and executive director at In STEPPS, a community service agency in California.

Tom Buggey, Ph.D., M.Ed., Professor and Siskin Institute Chair of Excellence, University of Tennessee at Chattanooga (UTC) Siskin Children's Institute, 6556 Joyful Drive, Hixson, TN 37343

In addition to conducting research at the Siskin Children's Institute in Chattanooga, Dr. Buggey also teaches courses as a faculty member in UTC's College of Health, Education, and Professional Studies. Before moving to Chattanooga, he was a professor at the University of Memphis for 14 years, serving as Project Director of Restructuring for Inclusive School Environments, Make a Difference, and Project Memphis. For the past 6 years, Dr. Buggey has worked as a consultant on the School Improvement Grant with the state's Department of Education, which has been spearheading the Response to Intervention initiative in Tennessee. He was a special education supervisor in Newfoundland, Canada, and taught for 10 years in Pennsylvania. He received his doctorate in early intervention from Pennsylvania State University in 1993.

Erik W. Carter, Ph.D., Associate Professor, Vanderbilt University, Peabody 228, 230 Appleton Place, Nashville, TN 37203

Erik W. Carter's research addresses peer relationships, self-determination, secondary transition services, and access to the general curriculum. He is the coauthor of four books, including *Peer Support Strategies for Improving All Students' Social Lives and Learning* (Paul H. Brookes Publishing Co., 2009) and *Peer Buddy Programs for Successful Secondary School Inclusion* (Paul H. Brookes Publishing Co., 2008).

Lauren Christian, M.A., Staff Clinician, National Autism Center, 41 Pacella Park Drive, Randolph, MA 02368

Lauren Christian is a staff clinician at the May Institute, providing clinical services to families managing distress associated with an autism spectrum disorder diagnosis.

Previous projects include involvement in the National Standards Project, conducting research on multicultural issues, and coauthoring and editing several articles and book chapters. She began at the May Institute in 2002, working in the classroom with children who had suffered traumatic brain injuries. She obtained her master's degree in clinical psychology from Bridgewater State University, Bridgewater, Massachusetts.

Yun-Ching Chung, Ph.D., Assistant Professor, Department of Special Education, Illinois State University, 516 DeGarmo Hall, Campus Box 5910, Normal, IL 61790

Yun-Ching Chung's research focuses on social and academic participation of students with complex communication needs in general education classrooms.

V. Mark Durand, Ph.D., Professor of Psychology, University of South Florida–St. Petersburg, 140 Seventh Avenue South, St. Petersburg, FL 33701

V. Mark Durand founded the Albany Center for Autism and Related Disabilities, Albany, New York. He has administered more than $4 million in federal grants. His published work includes numerous books and more than 100 other research publications. One book, *Severe Behavior Problems* (Guilford Press, 1990), is the product of 10 years of empirical research. He developed the Motivation Assessment Scale, a functional behavioral assessment instrument; has authored several best-selling textbooks, including *Essentials of Abnormal Psychology* (Wadsworth/Cengage Learning, 2010); and published the first book on sleep disorders for children with disabilities. Dr. Durand is on the Board of Professional Advisors for the Autism Society of America and the Board of the Association for Positive Behavior Support and is the coeditor of the *Journal of Positive Behavior Interventions.*

Danai Kasambira Fannin, Ph.D., CCC-SLP, Assistant Professor, Northern Illinois University, 360 Wirtz Hall, Allied Health and Communicative Disorders, DeKalb, IL 60115

Danai Kasambira Fannin received her doctorate from the University of North Carolina at Chapel Hill and was a postdoctoral fellow in Connie Kasari's lab at the Neuropsychiatric Institute at the University of California, Los Angeles. Her research interests include the development of evidence-based autism treatment, with a focus on providing appropriate evaluation and intervention for culturally and linguistically diverse families.

Jennifer B. Ganz, Ph.D., Associate Professor of Special Education, Texas A&M University, 4225 TAMU, College Station, TX 77845

Jennifer B. Ganz received her doctorate at the University of Kansas, with a concentration in autism spectrum disorders and behavioral disorders, and is a Board-Certified Behavior Analyst–doctoral level. Dr. Ganz works with general education and special education teachers, conducts research, and provides professional development relating to autism spectrum disorders and behavior difficulties. Dr. Ganz has authored or coauthored numerous articles, books, and chapters in related areas.

Sima Gerber, Ph.D., Professor, Department of Linguistics and Communication Disorders, Queens College, City University of New York, Kissena Boulevard, Flushing, NY 11367

Sima Gerber has more than 35 years of clinical experience, specializing in the treatment of young children with autistic spectrum disorders. Dr. Gerber is on the advisory board of the Interdisciplinary Council on Developmental and Learning Disorders

(ICDL), the faculty of the DIR Training Institute, the faculty of the ICDL Graduate School, and the board of directors of the Zero to Three network in New York City. Dr. Gerber has presented nationally and abroad on the topics of language acquisition and developmental approaches to intervention for children with challenges in language development. Dr. Gerber is the recipient of the award for outstanding service to the field of speech-language pathology given by the New York City Speech-Language-Hearing Association and of the Louis DiCarlo Clinical Achievement Award from the New York State Speech-Language-Hearing Association (NYSSLHA). Dr. Gerber was elected to fellowship by the American Speech-Language-Hearing Association in 2006. In 2010, she received the Distinguished Achievement Award from the NYSSLHA. Dr. Gerber is a board-recognized specialist in child language.

Kelly Stickles Goods, Ph.D., Postdoctoral Scholar, Semel Institute of Neuroscience and Human Behavior, University of California, Los Angeles, 760 Westwood Plaza, Semel Room 67-464, Los Angeles, CA 90095

Kelly Stickles Goods includes language and communication use and development in children with autism among her research interests.

Terry B. Hancock, Ph.D., Consultant, 113 Stone Hill Drive, Brenham, TX 77833

Terry B. Hancock, a Board-Certified Behavior Analyst and a licensed psychologist, was a research assistant professor at Vanderbilt University. She has been an investigator on nine federally funded research projects and has clinical expertise with assessment of and intervention with preschool children, including those with developmental, language, and behavioral issues. Her continued research interests include families of children with special needs, families of children who are high risk for developing special needs, language and communication interventions, mental health and behavioral issues, and treatment of dual diagnosis.

Renee Daly Holland, M.S., CCC-SLP, Speech-Language Pathologist and Clinical Coordinator, Florida State University Autism Institute, 625-B North Adams Street, Tallahassee, FL 32301

Renee Daly Holland is the intervention coordinator and lead clinician for the Early Social Interaction Project at Florida State University (FSU), funded by Autism Speaks and the National Institute of Mental Health. She also serves as project coordinator for the Autism Intervention Research Study in collaboration with the University of California, Los Angeles, and the Early Social Interaction Community Outreach Project with the University of Michigan. She completed her master's degree in speech-language pathology at FSU. Her nearly 20 years of clinical experience in both public and private sectors has focused on home- and community-based early intervention for autism spectrum and speech and language disorders. She has a special interest in the collaborative process of coaching families in parent-implemented intervention models. Current projects include supporting the development of culturally sensible interventions for families of children with autism spectrum disorders in South Africa and assisting in the development of web-based training tools for early intervention providers, families, and doctors.

Melissa Hunter, Ph.D., Licensed Psychologist, Clinical Director of Autism Services, Dickinson Center, Inc., Possibilities Autism Center, 20 Gillis Avenue, Ridgway, PA 15857

Melissa Hunter received her doctorate in school psychology from the University of Southern Mississippi. She completed her internship at the Munroe-Meyer Institute for Genetics and Rehabilitation in Omaha, Nebraska, and completed a postdoctoral fellowship in pediatric psychology, with an emphasis on autism and developmental disabilities, at the University of Oklahoma Health Sciences Center. She has provided services for individuals with autism and their families in several capacities, including therapy, consultation, and training.

Tiffany L. Hutchins, Ph.D., Assistant Professor, Department of Communication Sciences and Disorders, University of Vermont, 489 Main Street, 407 Pomeroy Hall, Burlington, VT 05405

Tiffany L. Hutchins has researched maternal belief systems and mother–child interaction strategies, as well as social-pragmatic instructional strategies to support the social, communicative, and behavioral functioning of children and adolescents with autism spectrum disorders (ASDs). Her recent work focuses on the development and validation of new measures of theory of mind. She is also investigating the efficacy of Social Stories™ to remediate the core impairments associated with ASDs. Dr. Hutchins teaches courses in the development of spoken language, cognition and language, language disorders, and measurement in communication sciences.

Ann P. Kaiser, Ph.D., Susan W. Gray Professor of Education and Human Development, Peabody College, Vanderbilt University, Box 228 GPC, Nashville, TN 37203

Ann P. Kaiser's primary area of research is early language interventions for children with developmental disabilities and children at risk because of poverty. Her research has investigated the effects of social communication interventions implemented by early childhood educators, parents, siblings, and peers. She has developed and researched a parent- and therapist-implemented communication program (KidTalk) to improve the language outcomes for young children with intellectual and developmental disabilities, children with autism, and children at risk because of behavior problems.

Connie Kasari, Ph.D., Professor, Psychological Studies in Education and Psychiatry, University of California, Los Angeles, 760 Westwood Plaza, Semel Room 78–222, Los Angeles, CA 90024

Connie Kasari is the principal investigator for several multisite research programs, including the Characterizing Cognition in Nonverbal Individuals with Autism Intervention network by Autism Speaks. She received her doctorate from the University of North Carolina at Chapel Hill and was a National Institute of Mental Health postdoctoral fellow at the Neuropsychiatric Institute at UCLA. Since 1990, she has been on the faculty at UCLA, teaching both graduate and undergraduate courses, and has been the primary adviser to more than 30 doctoral students. She is a founding member of the Center for Autism Research and Treatment at UCLA and has been actively involved in autism research for the past 25 years, leading projects under the Collaborative Programs of Excellence in Autism, Studies to Advance Autism Research and Treatment, and Autism Centers of Excellence programs from the National Institutes of Health. Her current research focuses on developing targeted interventions for early social communication development in at-risk infants, toddlers, and preschoolers with autism, and peer relationships for school-age children with autism. She is involved in several randomized controlled trials, with her most recent work involving multisite studies for interventions aimed at underserved and underrepresented populations of children with autism. She has published widely on topics related to social, emotional, and communication development and intervention in autism. She is on the treatment advisory board of the Autism Speaks Foundation and regularly gives presentations to both academic and practitioner audiences locally, nationally, and internationally.

Shubha Kashinath, Ph.D., CCC-SLP, Assistant Professor, Department of Communicative Sciences and Disorders, California State University, East Bay, 25800 Carlos Bee Boulevard, TR656B, Hayward, CA 94542

Shubha Kashinath completed her doctoral degree and postdoctoral training at Florida State University. Her research is informed by her extensive clinical experience in early intervention, autism, and service delivery for culturally and linguistically diverse families. She has served as project coordinator for clinical research and model demonstration intervention projects funded by the Office of Special Education Programs, including the Family-Guided Routines-Based Field-Initiated Research and Early Social Interaction Model Demonstration Projects, U.S. Department of Education. She also directed a personnel preparation project for training graduate students in speech pathology to better serve individuals with autism and their families. Current projects include a treatment acceptability study of parent-implemented interventions for young children with autism spectrum disorders and strategies to increase opportunities for communication within various types of daily routines.

Erin K. McNerney, Ph.D., BCBA-D, Clinical Director, In STEPPS, 18008 Sky Park Circle, Suite 110, Irvine, CA 92614

Erin K. McNerney received a master's degree in counseling psychology and earned a doctorate in clinical psychology from the University of California, Santa Barbara. She developed expertise in Pivotal Response Treatment (PRT) in working with Drs. Robert and Lynn Koegel at the Autism Research and Training Center. Dr. McNerney is a Board-Certified Behavior Analyst and has provided support in homes and community settings and consultation to schools across California. She has published research articles in the areas of early intervention, PRT, and positive behavior support, and has given presentations at numerous local and national conferences.

Hanna C. Rue, Ph.D., BCBA-D, Director of Evidence-Based Practice, National Autism Center; Vice President of Autism Services, May Institute, 41 Pacella Park Drive, Randolph, MA 02368

Hanna C. Rue is a licensed clinical psychologist and Board-Certified Behavior Analyst. Dr. Rue has worked with children and adults with developmental disabilities for 15 years. Currently, Dr. Rue is in the process of updating the National Standards Project.

Richard L. Simpson, Ed.D., Professor of Special Education, University of Kansas, Department of Special Education, JR Pearson Hall, University of Kansas, 1122 W. Campus Road, Lawrence, KS 66045

Richard L. Simpson has directed numerous demonstration programs at the University of Kansas and University of Kansas Medical Center for students with autism spectrum disorders (ASDs) and has coordinated a variety of federal grant programs related to students with ASDs and other disabilities. He has also worked as a special education teacher, school psychologist, and coordinator of a community mental health outreach program. He has authored numerous books, articles, and tests on the topic of students with ASDs. Dr. Simpson is the former senior editor of the professional journal *Focus on Autism and Other Developmental Disabilities.* His awards include the Council for Exceptional Children Research Award, the Midwest Symposium for Leadership in Behavior Disorders Leadership Award, the Autism Society of Kansas Leadership Award, and numerous University of Kansas awards and distinguished roles, including the Gene A. Budig Endowed Teaching Professorship of Special Education.

Lynn G. Sisco, M.S.W., University of Wisconsin–Madison, 1500 Highland Avenue, Madison, WI 53532

Lynn G. Sisco is a doctoral candidate in social welfare at the University of Wisconsin–Madison. Her areas of interest include autism, inclusion, school social work, and military families.

Jane R. Wegner, Ph.D., CCC-SLP, Clinical Professor and Director of the Schiefelbusch Speech-Language-Hearing Clinic, University of Kansas, 1200 Sunnyside Avenue, Lawrence, KS 66045

Jane R. Wegner directs the Pardee Augmentative and Alternative Communication Resource and Research Laboratory on the Lawrence campus of the university. Dr. Wegner has directed numerous personnel preparation projects funded by the U.S. Department of Education, Office of Special Education Programs, including the Communication, Autism, and Technology Project and the Augmentative Communication in the Schools Project. She has authored numerous articles and book chapters on augmentative and alternative communication. Dr. Wegner is a Fellow of the American Speech-Language-Hearing Association (ASHA) and has served on the ASHA Ad Hoc Committee on Autism Spectrum Disorders (ASDs) that developed the ASHA policy documents for practice with people with ASDs.

Amy M. Wetherby, Ph.D., CCC-SLP, Distinguished Research Professor, Department of Clinical Sciences, College of Medicine, Florida State University, FSU Autism Institute, 625B North Adams Street, Tallahassee, FL 32301

Amy M. Wetherby is Director of the Autism Institute in the College of Medicine, and the Laurel Schendel Professor of Communication Disorders at Florida State University. She has 30 years of clinical experience and is a Fellow of the American Speech-Language-Hearing Association. Dr. Wetherby has published extensively and gives presentations regularly at national conventions on early detection of children with autism spectrum disorders (ASDs) and intervention for children with ASDs using the SCERTS® Model. She is the project director of a doctoral leadership training grant specializing in autism funded by the U.S. Department of Education. She served on the National Academy of Sciences Committee for Educational Interventions for Children with Autism and is Executive Director of the Florida State University Center for Autism and Related Disabilities. Dr. Wetherby is Project Director of the FIRST WORDS Project, a longitudinal research investigation on early detection of autism spectrum and other communication disorders, funded by the U.S. Department of Education, National Institutes of Health, and Centers for Disease Control and Prevention. She is also the principal investigator of an early treatment study, funded by Autism Speaks and the National Institutes of Health, teaching parents of toddlers with ASDs how to support social communication and play in everyday activities.

Susan M. Wilczynski, Ph.D., BCBA, Plassman Distinguished Professor of Special Education and Applied Behavior Analysis, Ball State University, Teachers College, TC 702, Muncie, IN 27306

Before joining the faculty of Ball State University, Susan M. Wilczynski served as Executive Director of the National Autism Center. In her role there, she chaired the National Standards Project, the most comprehensive systematic review of the autism literature completed to date. She developed the first center-based treatment program in the state of Nebraska while on the faculty of the University of Nebraska Medical Center and was the first female faculty member with a research laboratory in the Psychology Department at the University of Southern Mississippi.

Dr. Wilczynski has edited several books and manuals on evidence-based practice and autism and has published scholarly works in the *Journal of Applied Behavior Analysis, Behavior Modification, Focus on Autism and Other Developmental Disabilities,* and *Psychology in the Schools.* She is a licensed psychologist and a Board-Certified Behavior Analyst.

Juliann J. Woods, Ph.D., CCC-SLP, Professor, School of Communication Science and Disorders, Florida State University, 107 Honors Way, Tallahassee, FL 32306

Juliann J. Woods is Director of the Communication and Early Childhood Research and Practice Center in the College of Communication and Information at Florida State University. Her three decades of experience in early intervention and preschool service delivery as both a speech-language pathologist and an early childhood special educator have informed her research, teaching, and professional development agenda. Her recent externally funded research and publications focus on parent-implemented interventions; early communication and social interaction for young children with autism spectrum disorders; family-guided, routines-based intervention; embedded instruction; and technology uses for professional development. She directs or codirects multiple state and federally funded personnel preparation, research, and demonstration projects, and she consults extensively with state agencies to support implementation of family-centered services in early intervention. She also gives presentations nationally, with an emphasis on research-to-practice strategies to improve service delivery.

Foreword

||||||||||||||||||||||||||||||||||||||||||||||||||||||||||||||||||||||||||||||||||||||||||||||||

This much-needed volume (and accompanying DVD) opens up the sometimes murky field of evidence-based social communication interventions for children and young people with autism spectrum disorders (ASDs). Its overriding aim is to make the research and clinical literature accessible to a wide range of audiences—parents and families of children with ASDs, frontline professionals working with children and families, and students and professors who are learning about or study ASDs.

The introduction by Prelock and McCauley (Chapter 1) summarizes the revolution that has occurred over the past decade and more in the recognition that social-pragmatic developmental interventions are appropriate—indeed even essential—for children and young people with ASDs, alongside the more traditional behavioral approaches. Given that difficulties with social communication are the core features that characterize children with ASDs, and in particular young children, including those who are nonverbal or who have minimal language skills, this might seem obvious, but it is only over the last 15 years that a secure evidence base has emerged for such approaches. The volume aims to translate the National Autism Center (NAC) report on the National Standards Project—a seminal but also very technical and very long review of interventions for children and young people with ASDs—into an accessible and practical manual. Each chapter not only explains the theoretical basis of a particular intervention approach and the evidence for its effectiveness but also highlights the practical requirements needed to implement it (time, training, expertise) and describes how practitioners and parents can evaluate whether the intervention is working for any particular child or young person. The use of case examples and the accompanying DVD to illustrate the different interventions makes this volume very much a manual for practice but one with an unusually close eye on evidence, which is as it should be to best serve children and young people with autism and their families.

The reader's guide by McCauley and Prelock (Chapter 2) provides a unique service and also shapes the rest of the volume by giving an accessible and readable introduction to the sometimes abstruse terminology that is used in the field. The summary tables decode the technical language (and acronyms!) of single-subject designs (SSDs) and randomized controlled trials (RCTs) into language parents can use in discussing the treatment plans with the team working with their child. The principle from the outset is that parents work *collaboratively* with professionals to develop the best program for their child, based on an understanding of what the child needs, the different foci of social communication interventions, and the evidence base behind these interventions.

Wegner summarizes the evidence for augmentative and alternative communication (AAC) strategies (Chapter 3). These are approaches used with children and young people who are nonverbal or minimally verbal—a significant minority of individuals with ASDs. Some of the most widely used systems are the Picture Exchange Communication System (PECS), graphic communication systems, sign language, and speech-generating devices. As with any successful intervention, but perhaps particularly so for AAC approaches, the fit between the communication needs of an individual child or young person and the particular intervention implemented is the key. Many of the interventions reviewed in the chapter use overarching frameworks such as the Participation Model, the Social Networks tool, or the Social Communication, Emotional Regulation, and Transactional Supports (SCERTS®) Model, all of which emphasize the need for AAC approaches to be person and family centered and place an emphasis on natural environments and meaningful contexts. By their nature, these approaches are time and labor intensive and require both considerable expertise (usually from a speech-language pathologist) and a team approach to ensure the consistency of approach that is critical for them to be successful.

Wilczynski, Rue, Hunter, and Christian summarize elementary behavioral intervention strategies (Chapter 4). They focus on the long-established but (as they discuss) sometimes misunderstood discrete trial instruction (DTI) approach. This method is based on behavioral approaches that date back to the original work of B.F. Skinner on operant conditioning. The fundamental principles of DTI are clearly laid out—a discriminative stimulus, a response, a consequence (reinforcement), and an intertrial interval. This approach has been applied to many aspects of development and behavior in children and young people with ASDs, including in broader, comprehensive programs, pioneered by Ivar Lovaas, which are sometimes called the applied behavioral analysis (ABA) approach or, more recently, early intensive behavioral intervention. The authors illustrate how DTI approaches can be used to promote prelinguistic skills, such as joint attention, as well as language in more formal verbal behavior programs. Perhaps more so with this approach than with many in the volume, a little bit of knowledge can be a dangerous thing, and the authors emphasize the need for such programs to include supervision by a senior, experienced consultant who has expertise both in behavioral approaches and in autism.

Gerber outlines the ASD-specific intervention developed by Stanley Greenspan, the Developmental, Individual-Difference, Relationship-Based (DIR) Model (Chapter 5). This approach emphasizes interpersonal development and draws on a wide range of theoretical foundations, most notably contemporary theories of developmental psychology. The functional emotional developmental levels characterize social communication and cognitive problem solving seen in typically developing children in the early years. Using the intervention strategy known as Floortime, the DIR approach emphasizes spontaneous interactions alongside semistructured and structured learning activities and includes sensory and perceptual-motor targets and activities that commonly present difficulties for children and young people with ASDs. Helpfully, the chapter also emphasizes the overlap between the DIR approach and other developmental social communication interventions such as the SCERTS® Model and the Hanen More Than Words program, which are also described as having an emerging evidence base in the NAC report.

In Chapter 6, Durand outlines the well-established behavioral approach known as functional communication training (FCT). This application of behavioral techniques is specifically designed to reduce challenging or problem behaviors such as tantrums, aggression, or self-injury. The author highlights that such difficulties are common and enduring in individuals with ASDs and have a significant impact upon them and their families. In common with other behavioral approaches, a functional behavioral assessment is the starting point for developing an individually tailored behavioral intervention. The principle of functional equivalence is central to the FCT approach in that an alternative, more adaptive behavior can serve the same function for an individual as the maladaptive, challenging behavior. Durand summarizes the close to 200 studies that have provided positive evidence for the benefits of FCT, most of which are single-case designs or small case series. In closing, the author raises an important caveat that also applies to all interventions covered by the volume: Some teachers and parents do not find FCT easy to carry out effectively. Not all interventions will suit all practitioners and families, and alongside consideration of the evidence base for any approach it is important to consider the "fit" between the approach and the individual implementing the intervention.

Kasari, Kasambira Fannin, and Stickles Goods summarize the evidence for joint attention interventions (Chapter 7) that specifically target a critical prelinguistic social communication skill that is a particular area of impairment for many young children with ASDs. Similar to the DIR approach, joint attention interventions have a theoretical foundation in developmental psychology. Joint attention, joint action routines (e.g., nursery rhymes), and symbolic play are interactive activities through which typically developing young children learn preverbal social communication and social interaction skills, typically in interactions with their parents and other caregivers. Kasari and colleagues summarize the findings from a landmark study that they conducted, a moderate-size RCT of a time-limited (6-week) focused intervention to teach joint attention (and symbolic play) skills. The intervention included techniques such as DTI but also more spontaneous play-based interactions. They found that joint attention and joint engagement skills improved in interactions both with therapists and with parents and, at a 12-month follow-up, language skills had improved. In common with all chapters in the volume, the authors include a section on considerations for children from culturally and linguistically diverse backgrounds. Specifically, they note that in some cultures, such as Latino, African American, and Asian cultures, sustained eye contact might be less acceptable than European American cultures, and therapists may need to take this difference into account, in particular when considering parent training in joint attention interventions.

Hancock and Kaiser introduce the enhanced milieu teaching (EMT) approach (Chapter 8). This approach is specifically tailored for young children with ASDs who have foundational verbal language skills. By using a combination of contemporary ABA and developmental pragmatic techniques, the therapist (who can be a parent) works on expanding and modeling the child's emerging language abilities. The four core components of EMT are 1) environmental arrangement, 2) responsive interaction, 3) specific language modeling, and 4) milieu teaching. The "milieu" around the child varies in the level of prompting, following a most-to-least support strategy, so that the child progresses from imitating language to independently initiating language interactions. In the Future Directions section of the chapter, the authors mention that they have recently started implementing EMT with a younger sibling of a child with an ASD diagnosis. Such developments stem from the recognition that the recurrence rate of ASD in families may be as high as 10%. Thus, the authors usefully highlight a new issue in the intervention field—working with "at-risk" individuals who may not themselves have a diagnosis.

Woods, Wetherby, Kashinath, and Holland describe the Early Social Interaction (ESI) Project, which is a large National Institutes of Health–funded RCT of a social communication intervention for toddlers as young as 18 months of age diagnosed with ASDs (Chapter 9). Although the outcomes of the trial are not yet known, the authors summarize the developmental foundations and evidence base for the ESI approach. In common with many of the modern approaches to intervention for children with ASDs covered in the volume (e.g., DIR, EMT), ESI combines elements from developmental-pragmatic and behavioral intervention approaches. It also emphasizes the importance of the family system around the child and the need for family-centered services and supports. In common with other parent-implemented social communication approaches, the intervention strategies are embedded in everyday caregiving interactions and family daily routines (e.g., mealtimes, bath time, bedtime). In using such approaches, the goal is to be able to deliver several hours per day of intervention with the child for only a few hours of direct, professional input per week. One emphasis throughout the volume is the need for programs to be both accessible and universally available across communities, and the ESI approach sets out to make this goal realizable.

Carter, Sisco, and Chung summarize the evidence base for peer-mediated interventions (Chapter 10). These are usually school-based programs that use behavioral and social learning theory approaches in which the assistance of nondisabled peers in inclusive education settings is engaged to promote social interaction and learning. The typically developing peers are trained and supported to prompt, model, and reinforce the social and academic learning targets for the child or children with ASDs. The authors systematically summarize the 29 published empirical studies that have used the peer-mediated model. Different programs use different approaches, ranging from peer interaction training and peer networks (for promoting social behaviors) to cooperative learning groups and peer tutoring (for promoting academic learning). General and special educators require training in how to implement such approaches, as the specific psychological theory that underpins peer-mediated approaches may not have been part of their original education training. In common with the previous chapter, although some input from expert professionals is required, the economic model behind peer-mediated approaches may allow the possibility of wide implementation.

Simpson and Ganz outline the evidence base for the augmentative Picture Exchange Communication System (PECS) approach for individuals with ASDs who are nonverbal or have limited verbal abilities (Chapter 11). The PECS system, developed by Frost and Bondy and based on behavioral principles, teaches individuals functional communication skills by requiring them to initiate self-motivated requests for desired objects. The individual gives the person with whom he or she is communicating a picture or icon of the object or activity and in return receives the object or activity depicted. Importantly, there is no requirement that they be able to label the object and no prerequisite communication skills, such as eye contact. The program moves through six demarcated phases, from exchanging pictures or icons of desired items (Phases I and II), through discriminating among pictures (Phase III) and expanding requests to phrases and sentences (Phase IV), to learning to ask questions (Phase V) and commenting (Phase VI). The authors systematically review the efficacy and effectiveness studies that have been conducted, including several RCTs. They illustrate how functional communication skills can be taught to adolescents and adults, as well as children, using the PECS approach.

Bruinsma and McNerney introduce another social communication intervention that draws both on behavioral and developmental principles—Koegel and Koegel's Pivotal Response Treatment (PRT; Chapter 12). In common with some other interventions covered in this volume, PRT emphasizes working within the child's natural environment and centrally involving parents as interventionists. The emphasis on "pivotal areas" in the child's behavioral repertoire is intended to take advantage of the cascading collateral effects on responding and functioning that can follow. These pivotal areas include identifying motivational strategies that engage the child, using multiple cues to overcome the "overselectivity" that characterizes some children with ASDs, promoting self-initiations and not prompted behaviors, and self-management—helping the child to monitor his or her own behavior. The authors highlight one collateral benefit from a parent training intervention such as PRT, which is that studies have shown reduced parental stress and increased parental confidence after having been through the training program.

Hutchins provides a comprehensive and up-to-date review of the evidence base for Carol Gray's Social Stories™ (Chapter 13). These are written-out, individualized stories that are aimed to facilitate social understanding by providing "direct access" to social information. This intervention addresses the difficulties in social cognition and social understanding that characterize individuals with ASDs. Gray's Social Stories approach draws on a wide range of contemporary psychological theories of ASDs, including impairments in "theory of mind" or mentalizing abilities and the cognitive style of weak "central coherence" or gestalt. The contextual approach that the Social Stories intervention takes emphasizes that social impairments in ASDs are located in the social space between people and not inherently located in the individual him- or herself. Alongside a thorough review of the evidence for the Social Stories approach, the author highlights two issues that apply to many of the interventions included in the volume. Although there is promising ("emergent") evidence for their effectiveness, we know much less about the generalizability and maintenance of treatment effects.

Buggey reviews the literature on the recently emerged technique of video modeling (Chapter 14). Its theoretical basis is learning theory and Bandura's social learning theory, and it builds on the notion that people with autism tend to be visual thinkers as opposed to language-based thinkers. The video modeling approach can be applied to a wide range of target behaviors, including social skills and behaviors, learning about emotions, perspective-taking skills, and language. Most programs have used adult or peer models, but more recently people have begun to use self-modeling (where the individual him- or herself acts as the model) and animations. The author usefully summarizes the practical advantages and disadvantages of these different formats in a table. In line with its relatively recent emergence, there is a limited but increasing literature on the effectiveness of video modeling approaches.

In their closing overview, the editors McCauley and Prelock set out future directions for the field of social communication intervention for individuals with ASDs (Chapter 15). Without repeating in full the thoughtful but also challenging directions that they outline for researchers, practitioners, and families, I will highlight some of the ideas that most strongly caught my attention. There is wide agreement, though disappointingly slower progress, that we need to develop better measures of meaningful outcomes against which to test different interventions. However rigorous the design and conduct of future research studies, if we are not measuring the right outcomes, we will not be doing the best for individuals with ASDs and their families. Another challenge is to find out more about *who* benefits from *which* treatments so that packages of interventions can be individually tailored to an individual's and family's needs. Finally, the authors emphasize the research-to-practice "gap": Even if research provides strong evidence for particular programs, how do we ensure that these programs are implemented correctly in the community and made accessible and acceptable to all members of the community? The modern practice of implementation science is only just emerging in the field of ASD intervention research. The authors end with another useful practical service by pointing out the increasing number of useful, balanced, and fair web sites where practitioners and family members can go to learn about the evidence base for interventions for individuals with ASDs. I am sure that readers of this excellent volume, once they have learned much from its contents, will use these resources as they continue their journey to improve the life outcomes for people with autism.

Tony Charman, Ph.D.
Centre for Research in Autism and Education
Institute of Education, London

Acknowledgments

‖‖‖

This book has taken its final shape as a result of the diligent and creative efforts of a large number of individuals. In particular, we would like to acknowledge the authors of the intervention chapters for their contributions. Through their writing, and the research and practice that led to it, they have demonstrated a remarkable dedication to recommended practices for individuals with autism spectrum disorders and their families, a dedication that is certain to guide others who share a similar desire to make a difference. The writing task they took on for this project asked them not only to offer their best insights into the interventions they wrote about but also to confine their writing within the boundaries of the framework we asked them to use. Without our authors, there would be no book.

We are especially grateful to all those at Brookes Publishing who have supported every step of the process involved in the making of this book—from its inception to its planning and preparation to its final editing and production. The resulting pages have benefited from their efforts, and the contributing authors and we as editors have benefited personally from their skillful advice, encouragement, and patience. As the series editor who has been most involved in this project, Marc Fey has contributed a wise perspective arising from his rich background in writing, editing, and treatment research, as well as a sense of continuity across the books in this series. Astrid Zuckerman has shepherded all of us toward our best work, with her extensive knowledge, steadfast belief in the value of the book, and good humor when the work progressed more slowly than one might have hoped. She is a gem! We also appreciate the good work of our production editor, Lynda Phung, and the help provided by Susan Hills.

In Vermont, Patty acknowledges the constant support of her husband and family, who gave up their time with her so she could write. In Ohio, Rebecca wants to offer special thanks to all of her colleagues and students at Ohio State University and to her friends and family in various locations, who might have wanted a bit more of her attention but understood that sometimes priorities need to shift. In addition, she would like to express her appreciation to members of the P3 writing group at Ohio State: Assistant Professors Monique Mills and Allison Bean and doctoral candidates Richa Deshmukh and Jing Yang. Their help demonstrates that mutual support and constructive criticism are always helpful for promoting productivity painlessly (or at least making productivity a bit less taxing).

Finally, we thank those individuals with autism spectrum disorders and their families who continually inspire us to understand more about how caring clinicians and others can assist them in their efforts to engage in more satisfying social interactions and communicate more effectively.

To the children, adolescents,
and adults with autism and their families from whom
we have had the privilege to learn over the years

1

Introduction to *Treatment of Autism Spectrum Disorders*

Patricia A. Prelock and Rebecca J. McCauley

This book is intended to introduce readers who are familiar with **autism spectrum disorders** (ASDs) and their core impairments to a group of interventions focused on communication and social interaction. Because ASDs represent a range of deficits in social interaction, verbal and nonverbal communication, and behavior, it is important to consider evidence-based interventions that address these core deficits. Therefore, the interventions selected for review in this book emphasize both established and emerging methods that are frequently used to support the communication and social interaction of individuals typically diagnosed with autism, Asperger syndrome, and pervasive developmental disorder-not otherwise specified (PDD-NOS).

BACKGROUND ON INTERVENTION STRATEGIES FOR COMMUNICATION AND SOCIAL INTERACTION

Over the last 15 years, thinking has evolved about which intervention approaches are most appropriate for supporting the social interaction and communication needs of children with ASDs. Although **traditional behavioral interventions** are well represented in the literature (e.g., Cooper, Heron, & Heward, 2007) and tremendously influential in a variety of settings (Downs, Downs, Johansen, & Fossum, 2007; Lafasakis & Sturmey, 2007; Taubman et al., 2001), **social-pragmatic developmental interventions** are gaining traction, at least in part because they emphasize opportunities for people with ASDs to establish positive social connections and generalize their skills in the natural environment. Interest in these approaches has also arisen in response to limitations identified in traditional behavioral approaches to ASDs, specifically in terms of generalization of targeted behaviors, particularly those related to the social use of communication and language (Wetherby & Woods, 2006, 2008). Social-pragmatic developmental interventions are the primary focus of this book because they offer a special promise in addressing communication and social interaction challenges at the core of ASDs and have the potential to minimize barriers to the functional application of learning.

1

In the traditional behavioral approach, skills are taught one to one with a pre-determined correct response (Karsten & Carr, 2009; Newman, Reinecke, & Ramos, 2009; Prelock & Nelson, 2011) and a highly prescribed teaching structure, such as that characterized by discrete trial instruction (Cooper et al., 2007). In contrast, in a social-pragmatic developmental approach, the interventionist follows the child's lead, fosters initiation and spontaneity, and reinforces contingent responses. Similar strategies have been implemented for more than 15 years as part of naturalistic communication and language interventions for children with a variety of communication and language challenges (Girolametto, Pearce, & Weitzman, 1996; Kaiser, Hancock, & Nietfeld, 2000; Kaiser & Hester, 1994) and have, in the last 10 years, been elaborated upon and modified to address the special challenges presented by ASDs.

Several of the interventions described in this book capitalize on the value of combining the best aspects of behavioral and developmental approaches to achieve functional and relevant social and communicative outcomes for children, adolescents, and adults with ASDs. For example, Prizant and Wetherby (1998) recognized the contributions of both traditional behavioral approaches to intervention and older developmental ones and proposed middle-ground **contemporary behavioral interventions** to support the communication and social interaction needs of children with ASDs. In particular, they described the value of giving children choices, sharing teaching opportunities between the interventionist and the child, and using preferred activities and materials—strategies that characterize Pivotal Response Training (Koegel, Koegel, Harrower, & Carter, 1999; Koegel, Koegel, Shoshan, & McNerney, 1999).

As intervention approaches have evolved, so too have comprehensive guidelines for best practices. In 2001, the National Research Council (NRC) offered a description of best practices for children with ASDs through the early childhood years. A number of intervention guidelines emerged from the NRC's comprehensive review of the literature, including

- Initiating treatment as soon as possible
- Ensuring active engagement during intensive instruction
- Using developmentally appropriate, goal-based, systematically planned activities
- Implementing planned teaching opportunities throughout the day
- Involving families and peers in the intervention to facilitate generalized skill learning

Many early intervention programs have used these best practices to design comprehensive educational programs for young children with ASDs.

As a follow-up to the NRC's work (National Research Council, 2001), Iovannone, Dunlap, and Kincaid (2003) proposed six educational practices as appropriate and effective for school-age children with ASDs. These practices included

- Providing individualized supports and services that match a student's profile, as defined through the individualized education program process
- Offering systematic, carefully planned, and defined instructional procedures to achieve valid goals, with a process for measuring outcomes
- Creating a structured learning environment

- Adding specialized curriculum content in the areas of social engagement and recreation and leisure skills
- Defining a functional approach to problem behaviors
- Engaging the family in the student's educational success

In spite of these defined best practices, challenges remained in determining the most effective instructional procedures for children of varying ages, language abilities, and cognitive levels with diagnoses of autism and subthreshold diagnoses, such as Asperger syndrome and PDD-NOS.

In 2009, to address the gaps in the intervention effectiveness literature for the large, heterogeneous group of children with ASDs, the National Autism Center (NAC) released the report of its National Standards Project, a comprehensive review of 775 intervention studies conducted from 1957 to 2007. Overall, behavioral treatments were identified as having the strongest support, and nonbehavioral approaches were identified as making a significant contribution but requiring more research. In its review, the NAC categorized the level of evidence for several interventions typically used in the treatment of individuals with ASDs. The interventions fell into one of four categories: established, emerging, unestablished, and ineffective/harmful. Table 1.1 lists the 12 interventions included in this book according to their level of evidence at the time of the report's publication (NAC, 2009).

Established treatments were those identified with sufficient evidence leading to positive outcomes. Emerging treatments were those with one or more studies yielding positive outcomes but for which study quality and results were inconsistent. Unestablished treatments offered little evidence and required additional research (e.g., academic interventions, auditory integration training, sensory integration package). No treatments were judged to be ineffective or harmful. The interventions described in this book fall primarily within the top two categories of evidence—established and emerging. Using the National Standards Project as a guide for evidence-based practice with children and youth affected by ASDs, this timely book emphasizes key established and emerging interventions used to facilitate the communication and social interaction of individuals with ASDs.

PURPOSE OF THIS BOOK

This book describes and critically analyzes specific treatment approaches used to address the communication and social interaction challenges of children, adolescents, and adults with ASDs. Although these challenges are of specific interest to speech-language pathologists, providers across disciplines have a stake in using evidence-based intervention to respond to these core areas of impairment for individuals with ASDs. Each approach in this book was selected for inclusion because of empirical evidence of its efficacy as established by systematic review or by the presence of at least two peer-reviewed articles indicating that the approach is a well established and probably efficacious or promising emerging intervention (e.g., Chambless et al., 1998; Chorpita et al., 2002; NAC, 2009).

Traditionally, randomized control trials have been considered the gold standard for evaluating treatment efficacy. However, such trials are rare in many clinical fields, including treatment for autism. Single-subject experimental designs have provided the majority of credible evidence in the intervention research in autism (Odom et al.,

Table 1.1. Levels of evidence for interventions included in this book, based on the National Standards Project

Level of evidence	Level description	Chapter in book	Intervention
Established (11 interventions identified[a])	Sufficient evidence that the intervention leads to positive outcomes	4	Discrete trial instruction
		6	Functional communication training
		7	Joint attention intervention
		8	Enhanced milieu teaching
		9	Early Social Interaction Project
		10	Peer mediation
		12	Pivotal Response Treatment
		13	Social Stories™
		14	Video modeling
Emerging (22 interventions identified)	One or more studies yielding positive outcomes, but study quality and results are inconsistent	3	Augmentative and alternative communication
		5	Developmental, Individual-Difference, Relationship-Based (DIR) Model/Floortime
		11	Picture Exchange Communication System (PECS)
Unestablished (five interventions identified)	Little evidence available; requiring additional research	—	—
Ineffective/harmful (no interventions identified)	Interventions that have been studied and found to be ineffective or to have negative outcomes	—	—

From National Autism Center (2009). *National Standards Project—findings and conclusions: Addressing the needs for evidence-based practice guidelines for autism spectrum disorders.* Randolph, MA: Author; adapted by permission.

[a]Number of interventions as identified in National Standards Project report. Only selected interventions are discussed in this book.

2003), yet they are underacknowledged in evaluating treatment efficacy (Barlow, Nock, & Hersen, 2009; Perdices & Tate, 2009). Single-subject designs make important contributions to the research on treatment when they are replicated across behaviors, participants, and contexts; measure change reliably and systematically; have established implementation fidelity; and are socially valid. In fact, results from many single-subject designs indicate that specific interventions are associated with positive learning outcomes for individuals with ASDs (Lord et al., 2005). Therefore, the effectiveness of the treatments included in this book has been established primarily through single-subject experimental designs.

To facilitate the reader's understanding of the similarities and differences among the interventions in this book—in terms of basic principles, techniques, teaching methods, treatment targets, and ages for which evidence has been established—a summary table has been provided (see Table 1.2). This table also identifies the evidence rating provided by the NAC (2009) for each of the included interventions.

Table 1.2. Characteristics of each intervention reviewed in the book

Intervention	National Standards Project rating[a]	Basic principles	Methods	Targets	Ages
Augmentative and alternative communication (AAC) strategies (Chapter 3)	Emerging	Social-pragmatic	Assessment of partner and environmental influence AAC system and target vocabulary selection Meaningful contexts Responsive partners Natural environment Family- and person-centered	Enhancement of existing communication skills Expanded language Substitute for inadequate speech Structure to support language development	Toddler through adult
Discrete trial instruction (Chapter 4)	Established	Behavioral	Adult-directed Individualized one-to-one instruction Predetermined correct responses Contingent or differential reinforcement Shaping behaviors Operant conditioning Massed trials Maintenance trials Mand-model techniques	Communication, social, and adaptive skills Use of verbal operants (e.g., mands, tacts, echoics, intraverbals)	3–21 years
Developmental, Individual-Difference, Relationship-Based (DIR) Model/Floortime (Chapter 5)	Emerging	Developmental	Family-based Child-directed Interpersonal development Individual differences Caregiver–child relationships Parent- and clinician-implemented	Shared attention and regulation Engagement and relating Two-way intentional communication Complex problem-solving Creative representations and elaboration Representational and emotional thinking	18 months to 9 years
Functional communication training (Chapter 6)	Established	Behavioral	Functional behavioral assessment Selection of an alternative behavior Fading prompts Response match, success, efficiency, acceptability, recognizability, and milieu Natural communities of reinforcement	Replacement of aggression, self-injury, elopement, and inappropriate sexual behavior with functional communication forms	3–21 years

(continued)

Table 1.2. *(continued)*

Intervention	National Standards Project rating[a]	Basic principles	Methods	Targets	Ages
Joint attention intervention (Chapter 7)	Established	Behavioral and developmental	Directed instruction Individualized Intensive Milieu teaching Parent- and clinician-implemented	Response to and spontaneous initiation of joint attention	3–5 years
Enhanced milieu teaching (Chapter 8)	Established	Behavioral and developmental	Environmental arrangement Responsive interaction Language modeling Milieu teaching Parent- and clinician-implemented	Productive, spontaneous, and meaningful use of new language forms Initiations and responses	3–9 years
Early Social Interaction Project (Chapter 9)	Established	Developmental	Family-based Child directed Environmental arrangement Responsive interactions Preferred activities and materials Routine-based Natural environment	Social communication from preverbal to multiword stage Gesture use Initiation of and response to joint attention Word knowledge Reciprocity	18 months to 3 years
Peer mediation (Chapter 10)	Established	Behavioral	Peer interaction training Peer network strategies Regular opportunities to interact within and outside instructional settings Adult coaching, guidance, and support Inclusive environment Communities of reinforcement Instructional arrangements (e.g., co-operative groups, peer support arrangements)	Initiating and maintaining conversation Exchanging compliments Taking turns Helping behaviors Sharing materials Collaborating on assignments Making introductions Conversing about shared interests	3–14 years
Picture Exchange Communication System (PECS) (Chapter 11)	Emerging	Behavioral	Systematic teaching Time delay Direct, natural reinforcement Shaping Modeling Prompting Visually based	Spontaneous initiation of requests Requests for reinforcing items/activities, help, break Rejecting offers for undesired items or activities Affirming offers for desired items or activities Following a direction to wait Responding to directions Following transitional cues and visual schedules	3–17 years

6

Intervention	Level of evidence	Type	Characteristics	Target areas	Age range
Pivotal Response Treatment (Chapter 12)	Established	Behavioral and developmental	Play-based Family-based Natural environment Routine-based Child choice Taking turns Shared control of teaching opportunities Direct and natural reinforcement Reinforcing communication attempts Preferred activities and materials Interspersing maintenance tasks within teaching sessions	First words Basic social skills Sophisticated language and social skills Pivotal behaviors (e.g., motivation, responsivity to multiple cues, self-management, self-initiations)	3–9 years
Social Stories™ (Chapter 13)	Established	Social-pragmatic	Visually based Situation-specific Individualized instructional strategy (e.g., determine topic, gather information, develop the story, consider additional supports, critical review, introduce story, generalization training, maintenance, fading)	Reduction of disruptive behaviors (e.g., tantrums, aggression, self-injurious acts) Establish routines Introduce changes in routines Understanding of a new or unfamiliar event Social skills (e.g., getting a peer's attention, making choices, playing independently, peer engagement, participation) Communication (e.g., reduction of echolalia, interrupting, loud talking)	6–14 years
Video modeling (Chapter 14)	Established	Behavioral and developmental	Visually based Viewing positive video models Adult and peer modeling Point-of-view modeling Self-modeling, including feed forward and positive self-review	Teach new skills or improve existing skills across developmental domains (e.g., self-help skills: dressing, feeding, washing) Cognitive skills (e.g., play, perspective-taking, attention) Social skills (e.g., conversation, prosody, taking turns) Language skills (e.g., question asking and answering, greeting, comprehending stories) Replace or extinguish maladaptive behavior	3–18 years

[a]From National Autism Center (2009). *National Standards Project—findings and conclusions: Addressing the needs for evidence-based practice guidelines for autism spectrum disorders.* Randolph, MA: Author; adapted by permission.

Each chapter in this book focuses on one treatment. To make the treatments more accessible to the reader and to facilitate their comparison, the chapters have been standardized using a structure similar to the one used in McCauley and Fey (2006), in which critical features of each treatment are consistently highlighted across chapters. Treatments in several of the chapters are illustrated in short videos provided on an accompanying DVD.

If a chapter offers a video example, a DVD icon appears next to the chapter title in the table of contents.

The interventions emphasize somewhat different principles, techniques, and teaching methods to foster communication and social development in children, adolescents, and adults with ASDs; therefore, there is not one "best" approach for all individuals. Instead, there are profiles of individuals with ASDs who are likely to benefit most from each intervention, as guided by the evidence. Early and intensive structured intervention and a collaborative approach to working in home, educational, and community settings appear to be critical features of effective treatment. Also emphasized is the importance of addressing the core impairments of social interaction and communication.

HOW TREATMENTS ARE DESCRIBED

As previously mentioned, each chapter in this book follows a consistent structure (see Table 1.3). Each chapter begins with a brief introduction in which the authors summarize the treatment and define the subgroups of individuals with ASDs for whom the treatment is designed. The authors also detail the age, developmental level, language level, and service delivery model the treatment entails, including the treatment's basic focus and methods. In describing the subgroups for whom the intervention is appropriate, the authors consider not only the specific diagnoses (i.e., autistic spectrum disorder, Asperger syndrome, PDD-NOS, Rett syndrome, childhood disintegrative disorder) but also the individual's level of verbal skills and cognitive abilities. Assessment methods used to establish the appropriateness of the treatment for an individual child, adolescent, or adult with an ASD are also presented.

The next section of each chapter provides the theoretical basis for the treatment approach. Here, the authors discuss four main components. The first component is the theoretical rationale for the treatment. The second component is the underlying assumptions regarding the nature of the communication and social interaction impairment being addressed by the treatment. The third component is the functional outcomes or desired consequences being addressed (e.g., increasing joint attention, facilitating social interaction, fostering communication, increasing symbol use). The final component is the treatment target (e.g., language or social functioning).

In the next section of each chapter, the authors summarize and interpret research studies that provide the evidence supporting use of the treatment. When possible, the authors distinguish among exploratory studies (e.g., observational or feasibility studies), efficacy studies (i.e., studies illustrating the usefulness of the treatment under conditions allowing for greater experimental control), and studies of effectiveness (i.e., studies illustrating the treatment's usefulness under the conditions of everyday practice) (Fey & Finestack, 2009; Olswang, 1998; Robey & Schultz,

Table 1.3. Description of content associated with chapter sections in this book

Section	Content
Introduction	Overview of the intervention, including the specific individuals for which it is designed, identified by age (i.e., infants/toddlers, children, adolescents, adults), developmental level, and language level. The service delivery model involved, the intervention's basic focus, and its primary methods are highlighted.
Target populations and assessments for determining treatment relevance and goals	Description of the subgroups on the autism spectrum (i.e., autistic disorder, Asperger syndrome, pervasive developmental disorder-not otherwise specified, Rett syndrome, childhood disintegrative disorder) for whom the intervention is primarily designed and for whom there is empirical support for its use. Addresses levels of verbal skills and cognitive abilities, and assessment methods used to establish the appropriateness of the treatment for an individual child, adolescent, or adult with an autism spectrum disorder (ASD).
Theoretical basis	Description of the dominant theoretical rationale for the treatment approach. Covers the underlying assumptions regarding the nature of the communication and social interaction impairment being addressed by the treatment, the functional outcomes being addressed, and the area of treatment being targeted.
Empirical basis	Comprehensive summary and interpretation of studies providing evidence that supports the use of the intervention. Describes the experimental design and treatment effects for both group and single-subject research, the nature of outcome data reported (e.g., standardized testing versus naturalistic probes), intervention fidelity, maintenance and generalization of treatment effects, and social validity.
Practical requirements	Description of the time and personnel demands for the primary clinician and other participants. Addresses whether or not a team approach is used, what training is required of personnel involved, and what materials are required.
Key components	Description of the goals addressed by the intervention, how multiple goals are addressed over time (sequentially, simultaneously, cyclically), the activities used to address the goals, and the participants beyond the clinician and child who are involved in the intervention (e.g., peers, siblings, teachers, primary caregivers).
Data collection to support decision making	Description of the data collection procedures used to make decisions within the intervention method, such as how data are collected, ways to evaluate progress, strategies for determining when and how adjustments should be made, and when to end the intervention approach.
Considerations for children from culturally and linguistically diverse backgrounds	Discussion of the applicability of the intervention approach to children from linguistically and culturally diverse backgrounds and of the ways in which the intervention might be modified to be more appropriate.
Application to a child	A description of a real or hypothetical case of a child that illustrates the implementation and effectiveness of the treatment.
Application to an adolescent or adult	A description of a real or hypothetical case of an adolescent or adult that illustrates the implementation and effectiveness of the treatment.
Future directions	Discussion of additional research needed to advance the refinement or ongoing validation of the intervention approach across populations of individuals with ASDs and related neurodevelopmental disabilities.
Suggested readings	Summary of a few readings of greatest use to readers who might want to know more about the specific intervention.
Learning activities	Topics for further discussion, ideas for projects, questions to test comprehension of the reading material, and possible writing assignments to facilitate the readers' learning.

1998). In many of the chapters, the authors provide tables that summarize key research examining the intervention. These tables highlight the following aspects:

- Participant characteristics (e.g., age, diagnoses, sample size), the experimental design, the treatment effects for both group and single-subject research
- Nature of the outcome data reported (e.g., standardized testing versus naturalistic probes)
- Intervention fidelity
- Maintenance and generalization of treatment effects
- Social validity

When possible, effect sizes are reported as originally published; otherwise, they were computed by the authors when means and standard deviations were provided.

To support practitioners' use of an intervention in their specific settings, the authors outline, in the next section of the chapter, practical requirements for implementing the treatment. They discuss time demands, training or expertise required by clinicians wishing to use the intervention, and any materials or equipment needed.

These practical requirements are followed by a description of the key components of the intervention approach. The goal of this section is to ensure that the reader has a strong preliminary understanding of the procedures. The authors provide information about the nature of the goals addressed by the intervention, how multiple goals are addressed over time (e.g., sequentially, simultaneously, cyclically), a procedural or operational description of activities within which the goals are addressed, and the nature of involvement of participants beyond the clinician and child (e.g., peers, siblings, teachers, primary caregivers). Several of the authors also reference training manuals that can be used to support a more thorough understanding of the procedures involved in the intervention they describe.

Recognizing the critical role of data in guiding practice, the authors next describe methods of collecting data to support decision making. The authors detail how data may be collected, ways to evaluate progress, strategies for determining when and how adjustments should be made, and when the intervention approach should be terminated. In addition, the authors explain how data collection is used to guide decision making in ongoing treatment and to assess immediate and long-term outcomes.

Next is a section that focuses on considerations for implementing the intervention for children from culturally and linguistically diverse backgrounds. The authors offer guidance in planning modifications related to the particular cultural and personal factors affecting an individual child, adolescent, or adult, while ensuring consistency in the treatment approach.

In the next two sections, the authors present specific examples of applications of the intervention to a child and to an adolescent or an adult. They offer a case study of a younger individual with an ASD for whom the treatment is considered appropriate and effective and a case study of an adolescent or an adult for whom the treatment is considered appropriate and effective (if, in fact, the intervention is appropriate for older individuals).

Each chapter concludes with a description of further research that is needed to advance the development or ongoing validation of the intervention across populations of individuals with ASDs and related neurodevelopmental disabilities. The authors then suggest three to five readings that they believe present important further details or background about the intervention, as well as learning activities to facilitate further discussion, generate ideas for projects, offer questions to test integration of the reading material, and serve as possible writing assignments. In addition to a comprehensive set of references at the end of each chapter, a glossary of key terms is provided at the end of the book; the first instance of each term is bolded in each chapter that discusses that topic.

SUMMARY COMMENTS

To enhance the usefulness of this book for as many readers as possible, two additional chapters have been included. Chapter 2 is a reader's guide that provides tutorial information tailored to the needs of individual audiences (i.e., students, clinicians, general and special educators, families). Readers from these various audiences are advised about chapters and sections of chapters that may prove of greatest interest to them, as well as where they can go for additional information to help them in their use of material addressed in the book. Chapter 15 provides a detailed discussion of the strengths and weaknesses of the treatment approaches covered in the book and includes tables summarizing shared characteristics and social communication outcomes of the treatments. Recommendations for future directions in treatment development and studies of treatment effectiveness also are provided. The book ends with a series of exercises and recommendations designed to encourage readers to use the book's content in their clinical decision making as well as in their design of future research studies.

REFERENCES

Barlow, D.H., Nock, M.K., & Hersen, M. (2009). *Single-case experimental designs: Strategies for studying behavior change* (3rd ed.). Boston, MA: Pearson/Allyn & Bacon.

Chambless, D.L., Baker, M.J., Baucom, D.H., Beutler, L.E., Calhoun, K.S., Crtis-Christoph, P.,... Woody, S.R. (1998). Update on empirically validated therapies, II. *The Clinical Psychologist, 51*(1), 3–16.

Chorpita, B.F., Yim, L.M., Donkervoet, J.C., Arensdorf, A., Amundsen, M.J., McGee, C.,... Morelli, P. (2002). Toward large-scale implementation of empirically supported treatments for children: A review and observations by the Hawaii empirical basis to services task force. *Clinical Psychology: Science and Practice, 9*(2), 165–190.

Cooper, J.O., Heron, T.E., & Heward, W.L. (2007). *Applied behavior analysis* (2nd ed.). Upper Saddle River, NJ: Pearson Merrill Prentice Hall.

Downs, A., Downs, R.C., Johansen, M., & Fossum, M. (2007). Using discrete trial teaching within a public preschool program to facilitate skill development in students with developmental disabilities. *Education and Treatment of Children, 30*(3), 1–27.

Fey, M.E., & Finestack, L.H. (2009). Research and development in child language intervention: A five-phase model. In R. Schwartz (Ed.), *Handbook of child language disorders* (pp. 513–531). New York, NY: Psychology Press.

Girolametto, L., Pearce, P., & Weitzman, E. (1996). Interactive focused stimulation for toddlers with expressive vocabulary delays. *Journal of Speech and Hearing Research, 39,* 1274–1283.

Iovannone, R., Dunlap, G., Huber, H., & Kincaid, D. (2003). Effective educational practices for students with autism spectrum disorders. *Focus on Autism and Other Developmental Disabilities, 18,* 150–165.

Kaiser, A., Hancock, T., & Nietfeld, J. (2000). The effects of parent-implemented enhanced milieu teaching on the social communication of children who have autism. *Early Education and Development, 11,* 423–446.

Kaiser, A.P., & Hester, P.P. (1994). Generalized effects of enhanced milieu teaching. *Journal of Speech and Hearing Research, 37,* 1320–1340.

Karsten, A.M., & Carr, J.E. (2009). The effects of differential reinforcement of unprompted responding on the skill acquisition of children with autism. *Journal of Applied Behavior Analysis, 42,* 327–334.

Koegel, L.K., Koegel, R., Harrower, J.K., & Carter, C.M. (1999). Pivotal response intervention I: Overview of approach. *Journal of the Association for Persons with Severe Handicaps, 24,* 174–185.

Koegel, L.K., Koegel, R.L., Shoshan, Y., & McNerney, E. (1999). Pivotal response intervention II: Preliminary long-term outcomes data. *Journal of the Association for Persons with Severe Handicaps, 24,* 186–198.

Lafasakis, M., & Sturmey, P. (2007). Training parent implementation of discrete-trial teaching: Effects on generalization of parent teaching and child correct responding. *Journal of Applied Behavior Analysis, 40,* 685–689.

Lord, C., Wagner, A., Rogers, S., Szatmari, P., Aman, M., Charman, T., Dawson, G.,...Guthrie, D. (2005). Challenges in evaluating psychosocial interventions for autistic spectrum disorders. *Journal of Autism and Developmental Disorders, 35,* 695–708.

McCauley, R.J., & Fey, M.E. (2006). *Treatment of language disorders in children.* Baltimore, MD: Paul H. Brookes Publishing Co.

National Autism Center. (2009). *National Standards Project—findings and conclusions: Addressing the needs for evidence-based practice guidelines for autism spectrum disorders.* Randolph, MA: Author. Retrieved from http://www.nationalautismcenter.org

National Research Council, Committee on Educational Interventions for Children with Autism, Division of Behavioral and Social Sciences and Education. (2001). *Educating children with autism.* Washington, DC: National Academy Press.

Newman, B., Reinecke, D., & Ramos, M. (2009). Is a reasonable attempt reasonable? Shaping versus reinforcing verbal attempts of preschoolers with autism. *Analysis of Verbal Behavior, 25,* 67–72.

Odom, S.L., Brown, W.H., Frey, T., Karasu, N., Smith-Canter, L.L., & Strain, P. (2003). Evidence-based practices for young children with autism: Contributions for single-subject design research. *Focus on Autism and Other Developmental Disabilities, 18*(3), 166–175.

Olswang, L. (1998). Treatment efficacy research. In C. Frattali (Ed.), *Measuring outcomes in speech-language pathology* (pp. 134–150). New York, NY: Thieme.

Perdices, M., & Tate, R.L. (2009). Single-subject designs as a tool for evidence-based clinical practice: Are they unrecognized and undervalued? *Neuropsychological Rehabilitation, 19*(6), 904–927.

Prelock, P.A., & Nelson, N. (2011). Language and communication in autism: An integrated view. *Pediatric Clinics of North America, 59*(1), 129–145. doi:10.1016/j.pcl.2011.10.008

Prizant, B.M., & Wetherby, A.M. (1998). Understanding the continuum of discrete-trial traditional behavioral to social-pragmatic developmental approaches in communication enhancement for young children with autism/PDD. *Seminars in Speech and Language, 19,* 329–352.

Robey, R.R., & Schultz, M.C. (1998). A model for conducting clinical outcome research: An adaptation of the standard protocol for use in aphasiology. *Aphasiology, 12,* 787–810.

Taubman, M., Brierley, S., Wishner, J., Baker, D., McEachin, J., & Leaf, R.B. (2001). The effectiveness of a group discrete trial instructional approach for preschoolers with developmental disabilities. *Research in Developmental Disabilities, 22,* 205–219.

Wetherby, A., & Woods, J. (2006). Effectiveness of early intervention for children with autism spectrum disorders beginning in the second year of life. *Topics in Early Childhood Special Education, 26,* 67–82.

Wetherby, A., & Woods, J. (2008). Developmental approaches to treatment of infants and toddlers with autism spectrum disorders. In F. Volkmar, A. Klin, & K. Chawarska (Eds.), *Autism spectrum disorders in infancy and early childhood* (pp. 170–206). New York, NY: Guilford Press.

Reader's Guide

Rebecca J. McCauley and Patricia A. Prelock

The purpose of this chapter is to prepare different groups of readers to make the best possible use of this book. We started work on the book with an assumption that a broad range of readers would be interested in learning more about current well-researched interventions aimed at the communication and social interaction needs of individuals with autism spectrum disorders (ASDs). We realized, however, that such readers would have different backgrounds, needs, and prior information on the topic. In particular, we anticipated at least three groups of readers: parents and families of individuals with ASDs, in-place professionals from a variety of fields, and students and professors. Although we recognized that adults with ASDs have a central claim to interest in our topic, we chose not to include them among the groups of readers. We made this choice because so many of the interventions we selected are for younger and less able individuals with ASDs and thus seemed less relevant to adults, except perhaps those who take on other roles, such as parent or professionals. This chapter, then, is included to help readers from a wide range of backgrounds prepare a plan for how they will approach the many pages that lie ahead.

Although this chapter is organized so that readers may head straight to the section they suspect is most closely aligned with their own perspectives and interests, we think all audiences will benefit from reading the entire chapter, to see relevant practice issues from several perspectives. For each group, we first offer key background information, then suggest questions that members of that group may want to keep in mind as they read further. Next, we indicate which particular chapters and chapter subsections may prove most helpful.

The first major section of this chapter addresses parents and families of children and adult children with ASDs, with the expectation that the other two groups of readers may benefit greatly from reflecting on the family perspective. Granted, there is increasing recognition in policies and research that parents must be at the core of all decision making about their children with ASDs (Iovannone, Dunlap, Huber, & Kincaid, 2003; National Autism Center [NAC], 2009; National Research Council, 2001). Nonetheless, professionals and those wishing to train or become professionals may understandably fall short when actually interacting with families of individuals with ASDs. They may fail to recognize the confusion their professional lingo creates or to consider just how complicated behavioral and communication issues really are when they shape one's entire life rather than just one's work life. Thus, the best possible strategy for all readers of the book may include reading both the next section and the section specifically focused on their role as a current or future provider or educator.

Subsequent sections of the chapter address the perspectives of in-place professionals and those of students and the professors who work with them. Here, too, there is an expectation that students and faculty would do well to be aware of the perspectives of in-place professionals. These two groups share interests and needs related to learning about recent developments in research and theories guiding intervention but are distinct in the background knowledge they bring to the task.

PARENTS AND FAMILIES OF PEOPLE WITH AUTISM SPECTRUM DISORDER

As a parent of a child with an ASD, you may feel as if you have been unwittingly enrolled in a never-ending crash course. This mandated course requires not just that you learn enhanced methods of parenting but also that you become an expert on the scientific understanding of your child's challenges, the interventions and systems available to help you address them, and the complex strategies required to access and manage that help. Compounding the immense difficulty of this crash course is the hard truth that remaining obligations—to job, spouse, other children and family members, and yourself—continue unabated. As a further complication (read *exasperation*), the "course" is poorly taught—with no syllabus, no regular instructor, and a reading list that is often perplexing, contradictory, and susceptible to grandiose claims masquerading as irrefutable evidence you *must* act on. Of course, no single book can help reduce the perils facing you in this challenge. Nonetheless, we hope that this book will help to fill in the syllabus for your crash course by offering structured accounts of 12 evidence-based interventions for addressing the communication and social interaction needs of individuals with ASDs, along with video clips demonstrating what the intervention actually looks like when it is used.

Prior to pointing you in the direction of chapters and sections that may be of special interest to you, we thought a review of—or introduction to—research terminology and research quality judgments seemed in order. In Chapter 1, we introduced you to the National Standards Project (NAC, 2009), in which interventions for ASDs were characterized as established (supported by sufficient evidence that the intervention leads to positive outcomes), emerging (supported by one or more studies yielding positive outcomes but with study quality and results that were inconsistent), unestablished (found to have little evidence and therefore in need of more), or ineffective/harmful (found to have evidence showing a lack of effectiveness or even harmful outcomes). Of the 12 interventions described in upcoming chapters, nine are rated as established and three are rated as emerging. For some of you, this project's endorsement may provide enough assurance of these interventions' quality to allow you to move on to the specific intervention chapters that interest you. If you would like a little more information about research and the factors that go into decisions such as those in the National Standards Project, the remainder of this background section is for you.

In your previous reading and other efforts to search for an appropriate intervention for your child, research terminology may have been used in passing or defined in terms that were hard to understand. Table 2.1 lists five terms that are used primarily by researchers and clinicians but that can also benefit research consumers who want to avoid accepting all research findings—or none—because the arguments for acting on them can seem so vague or confusing. For each term, the table provides a synonym or related term that touches upon a similar concept, an explanation that we hope gives you a firmer grasp of why it may be helpful to know the term, and a question you may have that relates to the term.

As you look over the terms in Table 2.1, note that researchers are usually interested in developing interventions that work for as many people with ASDs as possible. In addition, as researchers study an intervention, they want to be able to isolate the benefits of the intervention from other factors that could have resulted in the same benefits. Having these laudable goals means that researchers create studies that may seem somewhat distant from your child's needs. However, studies based on these goals allow researchers to be more certain of why the changes they see as part of intervention have happened and consequently which interventions appear likely to benefit more individuals with ASDs.

Table 2.2 describes four types of research designs used to study communication and social interaction interventions for ASDs: case study, single-subject design (SSD), randomized controlled trial (RCT), and systematic review. (Several of these were described briefly in Chapter 1.) These designs are listed in the order corresponding to how highly researchers rank the quality of their evidence. Sadly, that order also generally reflects the complexity of the research task—or, at least, the number of conditions that have to be in place before the study can be conducted. For SSDs and RCTs, the conditions that need to be in place (e.g., a greater ability of the researcher to exercise experimental control than in case studies, greater numbers of participants) mean that researchers require more resources, with RCTs being especially resource intensive. In contrast, the chief complexity limiting the number of systematic reviews that can be conducted relates to their use of already existing studies; if only a few studies have been done on a topic, a systematic review will not be feasible.

At a minimum, the designs in Table 2.2 are described in a way intended to clarify for readers why some are more highly regarded than others. Because you have a particularly strong justification for wanting the best possible evidence, we hope the table helps you appreciate that research designs differ in their strengths, weaknesses, and overall ability to provide high-quality evidence. Another application of this information is its utility in thinking about less formal sources of evidence. The constant barrage of intervention "evidence" available from the Internet and popular media sources and from well-intentioned friends and family can be scrutinized from the same perspective—in terms of the quality of the evidence. As you look over the research designs listed in Table 2.2, which one seems most similar to the personal accounts you hear in the form of testimonials and quasi advertisements? If you answered "case study," then review its description in the table. You may find that description a useful one to return to the next time you hear of a "great" new approach for your child's communication or social interaction difficulties. In short, we hope this table offers you a tool you can use in helping to shape your own "syllabus" into a more stable and manageable component of your crash course in ASDs.

Table 2.1.   Terms used in decision making by clinicians and in clinical research

Term	Synonym or closely related term	Explanation	Question that can be posed by parent
Decision making by clinicians			
Evidence-based practice (EBP)	Evidence-based medicine (EBM)	The view that clinical decisions should be informed by the best and most relevant scientifically based research findings, the clinician's expert judgment, and the child and family's values, interests, and choices.	How do professionals think about balancing family perspectives with their own and with the available research evidence?
Basic concepts in research			
Effect size	Treatment effect	A measure of the size of differences in skills before and after an intervention is used (to see how much skills have improved) or between treated and untreated groups (to see if one treatment results in bigger gains than another). Interventions with studies yielding larger effect sizes suggest they have more impact than those with studies yielding smaller effect sizes.	How much change was seen in the individual behaviors targeted by the intervention being studied?
Experimental control	Experimental rigor Internal validity	The care taken in research to make sure that the changes in a child's behavior during intervention are the result of the intervention and not due to other factors (e.g., chance, a child's development during treatment). This attribute of research is the reason research is thought to be an important basis for making decisions and more important than uncontrolled observations.	How likely is it that the intervention was the reason behaviors changed?
Generalizability	External validity	The likelihood that the treatment effect seen in a study would also be seen when the people being treated and/or the conditions under which treatment is given are somewhat different from those in the study. A study's generalizability is greater when a larger range of people are studied (with varying abilities and life situations) and when more everyday conditions are used in the study. However, as this greater variety of people and situations is introduced into a study's design, experimental control is usually diminished.	How confident can I be that this study's findings are relevant to people and conditions that are very different from those included in the study?
Statistically significant finding	Significant result	The finding that a treatment effect is unlikely to be due to chance; it does *not* mean that the associated changes in behavior are large (see *effect size*), nor does it mean they are important (what is being measured is more important for that decision).	How reliable are the results of this study?

Table 2.2. Description of research designs frequently used in autism spectrum disorder (ASD) intervention studies

Research design	Synonyms	Description
Case study	Case report Case series	A preliminary research method in which the researcher makes observations of a person's response to an intervention but exercises little or no experimental control. Case studies (such as stories from your neighbor) can be emotionally compelling and intellectually interesting. However, they are regarded as a very poor kind of evidence because 1) so many factors besides the intervention may have resulted in the changes seen and 2) the account relates to only one person with an ASD. Case studies have limited generalizability. Note: A neighbor's report of a great cure for an ASD in a distant cousin's child represents the crudest form of case study.
Single-subject design (SSD)	Single-subject experimental design (SSED) Single-case experimental design (SCED)	A research design in which the researcher observes a person's response to an intervention, similar to a case study. Unlike case studies, however, there are many observations of the behavior being studied, and SSDs are structured so that the effect of intervention can be more clearly separated from the possible effects of other factors. The value of SSDs is somewhat reduced because only a few people with ASDs are examined. Nonetheless, this is a very popular design that provides stronger evidence of treatment effects than a case study and is increasingly a valued type of evidence. An additional reason for the popularity of the SSD is that it is more feasible for ASD intervention because people with ASDs are so variable in their characteristics, strengths, and challenges.
Randomized controlled trial (RCT)	Controlled clinical trial	A highly valued research design in which a high degree of experimental control is possible and the benefits of one or more interventions can be examined for groups of people with ASDs. The RCT is less feasible than the SSD, however. The word *randomized* means that participants are randomly assigned to groups (e.g., treatment, delayed treatment) to avoid the influence of group differences that predate participation in treatment.
Systematic review	Meta-analysis Systematic overview	A relatively new type of research design in which precise methods are used for summarizing the findings of groups of research studies. This design is used to answer research questions by compiling more evidence, based on greater numbers of people with ASDs.

Questions to Bring to Your Further Reading

As you learned from Table 2.1, clinicians of all kinds (e.g., speech-language pathologists, physical therapists) involved in ASD interventions with children operate in a framework called evidence-based practice (or, in the case of physicians, evidence-based medicine). In that framework, clinicians are encouraged to join with families in using three sources of input as they work to devise an optimal plan for addressing a child's communication and social interaction challenges. Those three sources are 1) the clinician's expertise, 2) the most relevant scientifically based research findings, and 3) the family and child's own values, preferences, and circumstances. Ways of helping parents to best communicate their aspirations, challenges, and deeply held values in relation to their child's needs are still developing. Table 2.3 presents some questions that may help you reflect on these issues in relation to

Table 2.3. Questions to help families as they consider various interventions for their child's communication or social interaction challenges

Questions	Possible answers	Relation to intervention choice and planning
Who?		
Whom do you want involved in your child's intervention?	Professionals, other family members, peers, volunteers, yourself	Has implications for the type of intervention you might select and the setting in which the intervention would be implemented
With whom do you most want your child to be able to communicate?	You and your spouse, siblings, extended family members, teachers, peers	Helps determine the portability, accessibility, and utility needs of the communication system selected
Which social relationships are most important for my child?	Family, siblings, peers, friends, strangers	Guides the focus of social skills training and the context in which it would be implemented
What?		
What kinds of communications are most important?	Basic needs, education-ally relevant language, social communications, self-advocacy	Fosters the development of a range of communication strategies to support your child's needs across communicative contexts
What contexts for communication are most important?	Home, community, place of worship, school, recreational settings	Determines needs and planning for ensuring generalized use of skills
Where/when?		
What physical location for intervention would work best for my child? What location would work best for my family?	Home, school, clinic	Guides the selection of the most appropriate model for service delivery, recognizing that a particular location may facilitate your child's attention, comfort, and performance
When would intervention work most effectively for my child? be most workable for my family?	As part of our daily routine; at the time of day when my child is most likely to be able to participate fully; as infrequently as feasible, to allow all of the other needs of the child or the family to be met	Considers flexibility in scheduling, based on the family's other responsibilities, other valued activities, or preference for investing time in activities outside the family
How?		
How do I want clinicians and others conducting the therapy to interact with my child?	In a way that helps me raise a child who is socially appropriate in our culture; in a way that respects my child's role as a decision maker	Influences the likely approach to the intervention selected, recognizing that some families may be more comfortable with a behavior-based approach, whereas others may prefer a developmental or social-pragmatic approach
How do I want to provide input on the process and get feedback about progress?	Weekly, monthly, quarterly meetings; home-school journal; individualized education program (IEP) process	Influences responsibilities for material development, access, and use; for assessment of progress; and for modifications to intervention programming

the 12 interventions described in this book and perhaps help you identify which interventions you want to examine first because they seem a better fit for you and your child. They may also be useful points for discussion with the team involved in your child's care. Such discussions not only help the intervention team respond more effectively to your child and better understand your role and preferences in the process but also may help you learn more about how the team's perspectives or practices align with or diverge from your own. This process may clarify areas where compromises are possible and desirable, where they aren't needed because more information has led one party or another to change its view, or, less frequently we hope, where compromises cannot be reached and other partners should be sought. In the next section, we describe how you might decide to tackle the rest of this book, in terms of which chapters and sections of chapters may be most helpful to you.

Chapters and Chapter Sections of Special Interest

Identifying Chapters for Further Exploration You may find several different ways of deciding how to proceed. Perhaps you are coming to the book because you already have heard of some of the interventions it contains and you want more information about them. Or you may find that viewing all of the video clips illustrating interventions offers a straightforward method for gauging the relative fit of different interventions to your child's needs and your own views of what might help.

As yet another approach, we suggest that you consider your child's stage of development and areas of greatest challenge in communication and social relationships. For young children with ASDs and for older individuals who have not established early nonverbal communication and are not using vocal productions to communicate, the most relevant interventions are likely to be augmentative and alternative communication (AAC; Chapter 3), the Developmental, Individual-Difference, Relationship-Based (DIR) Model/Floortime (Chapter 5), joint attention (Chapter 7), enhanced milieu teaching (Chapter 8), Early Social Interaction (ESI) Project (Chapter 9), and Picture Exchange Communication System (PECS; Chapter 11). For a wide range of early to somewhat more advanced linguistic communicators with ASDs, appropriate interventions include AAC (Chapter 3), discrete trial instruction (Chapter 4), functional communication training (Chapter 6), peer mediation (Chapter 10), Pivotal Response Treatment (Chapter 12), and video modeling (Chapter 14). Finally, the intervention called Social Stories™ (Chapter 13) has been specifically developed for those children and adults with ASDs whose language may pose lesser or even minimal challenges but who have continuing pragmatic needs in the appropriate use of language and communication in social situations. Nonetheless, several of the already mentioned interventions also may be valuable for these older individuals—namely, peer mediation (Chapter 10), Pivotal Response Treatment (Chapter 12), and video modeling (Chapter 14).

Table 2.4 summarizes the developmental basis for the suggestions we have offered about which chapters to review first. In addition, it notes other intervention characteristics that may attract your attention—namely, the extent to which the intervention is considered useful for addressing problem behaviors that may interfere with social communication, the extent to which it emphasizes the visual modality, and, finally, whether it includes an emphasis on parent involvement.

Table 2.4. Interventions associated with different levels of communication development and different intervention needs

Chapter	Intervention	Student's existing level of communication and social interaction development			Other intervention characteristics		
		Early communication skills	Early language development	Later language development, social-pragmatic needs, or both	Emphasis on challenging behaviors that may interfere with social interaction	Emphasis on use of the visual modality	Emphasis on parental intervention
3	Augmentative and alternative communication	•	•			•	
4	Discrete trial instruction		•		•		
5	Developmental, Individual-Difference, Relationship-Based (DIR) Model/Floortime	•	•				•
6	Functional communication training		•	•	•		
7	Joint attention	•					•
8	Enhanced milieu teaching	•	•				•
9	Early Social Interaction Project	•					•
10	Peer mediation		•	•	•		
11	Picture Exchange Communication System		•			•	
12	Pivotal Response Treatment		•				•
13	Social Stories™			•	•	•	
14	Video modeling		•	•	•	•	

Identifying and Using Specific Chapter Sections   Because authors were asked to adhere to a specific structure for Chapters 3 through 14, readers should be able to find sections relevant to their needs and preferences. The sections that may be of greatest interest to you could be those that help you imagine what an intervention will entail. Thus, after determining—by reading the Introduction and the section Target Populations—that a particular intervention has been developed with children like yours in mind, you may want to read the sections Practical Requirements, Key Components, and either Application to a Child or Application to an Adolescent or Adult (depending on the age of your child). In connection with this reading, you may also want to examine (or reexamine) the video clip that illustrates the intervention. If you continue to be intrigued by the potential of the intervention, you may wish to go back to the section intended to explain the thinking behind it (Theoretical Basis) and also examine the research supporting it (Empirical Basis, Future Directions). Last of all, if your interest continues or—as we hope—grows, chapter authors have included suggested readings to point you in the direction of more in-depth information.

PROFESSIONALS WHO WORK WITH PEOPLE WITH AUTISM SPECTRUM DISORDERS

This category—professionals who work with people with ASDs—includes a broad range of readers! On the one hand, you may be a highly prepared professional in a specific discipline, such as pediatric medicine, speech-language pathology, special education, physical therapy, psychology, or social work—to name just a few. On the other hand, you may be a paraprofessional, a respite provider, or a volunteer who happens to be dedicated to working with children and adults with ASDs. Thus, we will proceed carefully in this section and try to be as clear as possible in our discussions so that you, the reader, can decide on the relevance and value of our comments.

Some of you may have a long history of study and experience with ASDs. As speech-language pathologists—working in a field whose core interest centers on communication and social interaction—we are members of a profession destined for involvement with ASDs, yet we recognize how new ASDs seem as an urgent professional demand, despite the seemingly long period of time since autism was first recognized by Leo Kanner (1943). For example, a broader perception of autism as a spectrum disorder did not arise until the late 1990s, and Asperger syndrome among adults, although identified about the same time that Kanner coined the term *autism* (Asperger, 1944), was not included in the *DSM-IV* until 1994. Furthermore, the stunning upsurge in diagnoses of autism both nationally and internationally has only recently fueled a dramatic sense of urgency—one echoed in the description of ASDs as an "urgent public health concern" by the Centers for Disease Control (2009, p. 6).

Because of the still-recent recognition of the scope of ASDs as a problem that professions must prepare to address effectively, we suspect not only that you (like us) are relatively new to this work but also that your education on important topics, including interventions for communication and social interaction, may be more limited in scope than you would like. Borrowing the analogy we used in considering the situation of parents—that is, being enrolled in a mandated crash course of dubious quality—we would suggest that you, too, may find yourself tackling a crash course with a barely more able instructor, perhaps one who is one chapter ahead in the book and not quite finished with the syllabus either. We hope that this book will provide some additional help as you piece together your own reading list and that you may even have learned something of value as you reviewed the preceding section.

For those of you with extensive professional training, much of the background information provided for parents in the previous section may have been review—for example, the descriptions of terms (Table 2.1) and research designs (Table 2.2). Even if that is the case, if your opinion is routinely sought on which interventions should be considered for a child, you may want to return to Chapter 1 for a discussion of the National Standards Project (NAC, 2009) recommendations concerning levels of research support for the various interventions described in subsequent chapters. Other information from the preceding section that was designed to help parents and family members reflect on their preferences and values for sharing with others may also be especially relevant if you participate in teams working with families affected by ASDs.

In the remainder of this section, we suggest questions you may want to bear in mind as you continue your progress through the book. We then make recommendations concerning which chapters and chapter sections may best serve your purposes.

Questions to Bring to Your Further Reading

The nature of specific questions we would ask you to consider as you read further about selected interventions probably depends on your level of involvement with individuals with ASDs. For example, are you working with these individuals as a lone professional and/or as a member of the child's multidisciplinary or interdisciplinary team? Also, will you be involved only as a contributor to the intervention selection process or will you be integrally involved in the implementation of the intervention? That you are tackling this book suggests that you have major involvement in one or more of these steps. As a contributor to the decision-making process, you may want to ask yourself if there are interventions you should investigate because you suspect they may not be considered by other members of the team but may be useful nonetheless. In addition, you may want to ask if there are interventions about which you have made assumptions that may or may not be accurate. Furthermore, you may recognize that you have a background that enables you to understand research findings better than other members of your team. In that case, you may want to consider questions or raise points that other team members will have insufficient background to consider or raise.

If you expect to play a significant role in the implementation of an intervention, you will need to consider whether you already possess the necessary skills to do so or can acquire them or whether you will need to refer to others while staying involved as a core member of the team. Finally, as you read each chapter, you may want to ask ongoing questions concerning the feasibility of an intervention given the context in which you and other team members work. By approaching the chapters that follow with questions such as these, you may find the chapters not only more interesting but also more readily usable.

Chapters and Chapter Sections of Special Interest

Chapters of Interest   As you read further, you will undoubtedly find that not all of the 12 interventions are of equal interest to you—either because they address individuals with levels of need that differ from those you serve or because your profession is infrequently involved directly in the selection or implementation of that intervention. To help you determine this quickly, two tables might be useful. Table 2.4 provides developmental information on the language level for which particular interventions are most appropriate. Table 2.5 lists each intervention, along with its NAC level of evidence and the professional groups most likely to be involved, the latter based on the authors' indications in the section Practical Requirements and on observations that certain professionals are typically included on most teams serving individuals with ASDs and their families (Blair, Lee, Cho, & Dunlap, 2011; Swiezy, Stuart, & Korzekwa, 2008; Woods, Wilcox, Friedman, & Murch, 2011).

Chapter Sections of Special Interest   For those readers who see themselves making a contribution that includes commenting on the evidential support for candidate interventions, the sections Target Populations, Theoretical Basis, and Empirical Basis offer excellent starting points. Later sections in each chapter will offer practical guidance in terms of training, physical and staff resources, and other details that will be required if the intervention is actually selected or as feasibility of implementation is addressed. For readers who expect to be deeply involved or only involved in implementation, those sections warrant reading or even deeper study, and the related video clips on the accompanying DVD should be viewed too. For both groups, the resources recommended by chapter authors can provide a direction for further investigation and study.

STUDENTS AND PROFESSORS INTERESTED IN AUTISM SPECTRUM DISORDERS

If you are a student reading this book, perhaps it was one assigned to you rather than one you chose to read yourself. Or perhaps you perceive the topic of ASDs as intriguing and are wondering how it might fit your long-range intentions. Perhaps you have chosen your career because you have been involved as a volunteer helping with interventions for people with ASDs or because you have an affected family member, friend, or neighbor; we think you will find a lot here to be enthusiastic about. Regardless of your perspective, this section helps clarify what value the chapters and their constituent sections can hold for you.

If you are a professor who has assigned all or parts of this book, this section is also intended to be helpful to you but in a less direct way, as you eavesdrop on our comments to students. In addition to providing information about how parts of the book may work for students, we hope this section and the book as a whole can provide information to supplement whatever store of information you possess on the topic. Our hope is that what you have read thus far and what remains of this chapter will help you to formulate the paths you will encourage your own students to take as they read one or more of the treatment chapters that follow.

Questions to Bring to Your Further Reading

As a student, the kinds of questions you might consider as you read through the interventions will depend in part on your interest in and likely contact with a population of individuals with ASDs. For example, will you be working in schools in which your caseload will include students with ASDs, or will you be in a pediatric outpatient or specialty clinic that primarily sees children with developmental disabilities,

Table 2.5. Professional and other groups involved in communication and social interaction interventions, along with intervention level-of-evidence ratings

Chapter	Intervention	National Standards Project rating[a]	Professionals with special involvement						
			Educators (special educators, classroom teachers)	Physicians (developmental pediatricians, other physicians)	Occupational therapists, physical therapists	Psychologists	Speech-language pathologists	Social workers	Other parties[b]
3	Augmentative and alternative communication (AAC)	Emerging	•						•
4	Discrete trial instruction	Established	•			•	•		•
5	DIR/Floortime	Emerging	•		•	•	•		•
6	Functional communication training	Established	•				•		
7	Joint attention	Established	•	•	•		•		•
8	Enhanced milieu teaching	Established	•		•				
9	Early Social Interaction Project	Established					•	•	•
10	Peer mediation	Established	•			•	•		
11	Picture Exchange Communication System	Emerging	•	•	•	•	•	•	•
12	Pivotal Response Treatment	Established	•			•	•		
13	Social Stories™	Established	•	•	•	•	•	•	•
14	Video modeling	Established	•		•	•			

[a]National Autism Center (2009).

[b]Other parties might include AAC specialists, nurses, guidance counselors, paraprofessionals, early interventionists or developmental educators, respite providers or personal care attendants, peers, siblings, parents, or other family members.

including autism? Because two of the core impairment areas in autism are social interaction and communication, you are likely to have a significant role as a member of the team and will be asked questions about best approaches to support students' communication and social engagement. You will also be a primary contributor to the decision-making process for ensuring effective social communication, so it will be important to ask yourself if there are interventions you should learn more about because they are likely not to be understood or considered by other team members. In preparation for playing a significant role in the implementation of an intervention, you will need to consider what additional training and support you will need in order to move beyond an understanding of the intervention and develop real skill in the delivery of it.

If you are a professor, you will want to determine how best to present the theoretical background of an intervention and the evolution of its use in special populations such as people with autism. You will also be challenged to support students in weighing the value of an intervention by posing questions to students that consider intervention goals, training needs, expected outcomes, and likely costs. You will need to ask questions about how best to help students understand evidence-based practice (EBP) in the context of service delivery for individuals with ASDs. You will also need to help students consider a family's values and beliefs, the available scientific evidence, and the clinician's experience when they are making critical intervention decisions.

Chapters and Chapter Sections of Special Interest

Chapters of Special Interest   Each of the interventions was included in this book because of its potential value for a group of children and/or adults with ASDs and therefore for future clinicians and their instructors. An explicit basis for the selected interventions was that they have some level of support—established or emerging, using the terminology of the National Standards Project (NAC, 2009). Depending on your interests and the guidance of your instructor, you may be best advised to begin with an intervention that particularly appeals to you so that you can gain experience with the template and the information it contains and then tackle chapters more widely. That appeal may rest upon the developmental levels of the group of people with ASDs for whom it is intended, your prior reading or actual exposure to it, or some other basis we cannot foresee. Your reading of subsequent chapters may be enhanced through the process. On the other hand, it may be that your instructor is having you read certain chapters in a certain order, to achieve ends essential to the course you are taking. That does not necessarily preclude you from following a truncated version of our suggestion, however.

Chapter Sections of Special Interest   For students who are just learning about the range of possible interventions for supporting the social communication needs of individuals with autism, it will be important to focus on the chapter sections Theoretical Basis and Empirical Basis. Understanding the theoretical underpinnings of an intervention as well as the science in support of using it is necessary if you are to become a successful future practitioner with evidence supporting what you do. Other sections, such as Key Components of the Intervention and Data Collection to Support Decision Making, will be critical to effective implementation of the intervention. These sections, as well as the video clips on the accompanying DVD, require your focused attention so that treatment fidelity (how accurately an intervention is followed) is ensured and expected results can be obtained.

CONCLUDING REMARKS

In this brief chapter, we have tried to acclimatize readers with different backgrounds to the terminology and perspectives they will encounter as they continue reading. We also included this chapter in order to whet readers' appetites for the main courses that follow—the 12 evidence-based interventions that are particularly designed to address the communication and social interaction challenges faced by individuals with ASDs. At the end of their reading, we hope that readers will join us in concluding that these interventions offer solid starting points for enriching the lives of individuals with ASDs and their social communities.

REFERENCES

Asperger, H. (1944). Die "autistischen Psychopathen" im kindesalter ["Autistic psychopathy" in childhood]. *Archiv für Psychiatrie und Nervenkrankheiten, 117,* 76–136. (English translation in Frith, 1991).

Blair, K-S.C., Lee, I-S., Cho, S-J., & Dunlap, G. (2011). Positive behavior support through family-school collaboration for young children with autism. *Topics in Early Childhood Special Education, 31*(1), 22–36.

Centers for Disease Control. (2009). Prevalence of the autism spectrum disorders (ASDs) in multiple areas of the United States, 2004 and 2006: Summary of the community report from the Autism and Developmental Disabilities Monitoring (ADDM) Network. *MMWR Sureill Summ.* 58(SS–10). Retrieved from http://www.cdc.gov/ncbddd/autism/states/ADDMCommunityReport2009.pdf

Iovannone, R., Dunlap, G., Huber, H., & Kincaid, D. (2003). Effective educational practices for students with autism spectrum disorders. *Focus on Autism and Other Developmental Disabilities, 18* (3), 150–165.

Kanner, L. (1943). Autistic disturbances of affective contact. *Nervous Child, 2,* 217–250.

National Autism Center (2009). *National Standards Project—findings and conclusions: Addressing the needs for evidence-based practice guidelines for autism spectrum disorders.* Randolph, MA: Author. Retreived from http://www.nationalautismcenter.org

National Research Council, Committee on Educational Interventions for Children with Autism, Division of Behavioral and Social Sciences and Education. (2001). *Educating children with autism.* Washington, DC: National Academy Press.

Swiezy, N., Stuart, M., & Korzekwa, P. (2008). Bridging for success in autism: Training and collaboration across medical, educational, and community systems. *Child and Adolescent Psychiatric Clinics of North America, 17,* 907–922.

Woods, J.J., Wilcox, M.J., Friedman, M., & Murch, T. (2011). Collaborative consultation in natural environments: Strategies to enhance family-centered supports and services. *Language, Speech, and Hearing Services in Schools, 42,* 379–392.

3

Augmentative and Alternative Communication Strategies: Manual Signs, Picture Communication, and Speech-Generating Devices

Jane R. Wegner

It is estimated that from one third to one half of children and adults with autism spectrum disorders (ASDs) do not develop speech sufficient enough to meet their daily communication needs (Light, Roberts, Dimarco, & Greiner, 1998; National Research Council [NRC], 2001; Wendt & Schlosser, 2007). Being able to understand and be understood is essential to quality of life and participation in activities of one's choice. Because augmentative and alternative communication (AAC) can be any mode of communication that supplements or replaces oral speech (American Speech-Language-Hearing Association [ASHA], 2004), it holds the promise of improving not only the communication but also the lives of many individuals with ASDs. In fact, AAC use has been shown to have positive effects for people with ASDs in the areas of behavior (Bopp, Brown, & Mirenda, 2004), social interaction (Garrison-Harrell, Kamps, & Kravits, 1997), and receptive language and comprehension (Brady, 2000) as well as in speech and expressive language (Millar, 2009; Mirenda, 2003). Cafiero (2001) described the roles AAC can play for individuals with ASDs as enhancing existing communication skills, expanding language, replacing speech, and providing structure to support language development.

It is thought that ASDs are the most common and fastest growing developmental disabilities in the United States today (Centers for Disease Control and Prevention, 2009). At the same time, technology and AAC applications are advancing, and we are learning more about instruction and AAC. This chapter will examine four frequently used AAC strategies: manual signs, the Picture Exchange Communication System (PECS), graphic communication systems, and **speech-generating devices** (SGDs) for children and adults with ASDs.

TARGET POPULATIONS AND ASSESSMENTS FOR DETERMINING TREATMENT RELEVANCE AND GOALS

The ASDs that are the focus of this chapter are autistic disorder (autism), pervasive developmental disorder-not otherwise specified (PDD-NOS), and Asperger syndrome. Because research concerning AAC and individuals with Rett syndrome (Van Acker, Loncola, & Van Acker, 2005) and individuals with childhood disintegrative disorder (Volkmar, Koenig, & State, 2005) has been minimal, these two groups will not be discussed.

Many individuals on the autism spectrum may benefit from AAC either temporarily or as a lifelong communication mode. Some require AAC for expression, whereas others need it to augment comprehension. Consequently, all individuals with ASDs should be considered potential candidates for AAC. That being said, it must be kept in mind that individuals with ASDs are a heterogeneous group and that it is not yet possible to predict which forms of AAC will be effective for specific individuals (NRC, 2001). Therefore, AAC interventions should always be "made for specific learners, in specific contexts, to meet specific needs" (Mirenda, 2009a, p. 16).

There is no standardized assessment for AAC, nor are there ASD-specific procedures for AAC assessments. Assessment should be an ongoing process and should be used to help the clinician provide a profile of the individual's social communication skills, identify learning objectives in the natural environment, and examine the influence of the partners and environments on the communication of the individual with an ASD (ASHA, 2006). Assessment for AAC should include descriptions of the individual's communicative forms and functions, as well as the influence of the communication partners and the learning environment on the individual's communicative competence (ASHA, 2004, 2006). The assessment should also include information about an individual's participation patterns and opportunities as well as his or her sensory, motor, literacy, and language capabilities. Only then can the features of an AAC system that support an individual's strengths, needs, and capabilities be identified (ASHA, 2004). Important features required for AAC use include symbol representation, lexical organization, and motor skills (Light et al., 1998). The overall goal of assessment is to identify the individual's current and future unmet communication needs and the supports and ways to address those needs (Beukelman & Mirenda, 2005).

To address this overall goal, the clinician collects information through interviews, surveys, and observations of the individual and his or her partners in daily activities and conducts assessments of the individual's specific skills. There are several assessment models that include tools useful in meeting AAC assessment goals for individuals with ASDs. Among these are the Participation Model (Beukelman & Mirenda, 2005), the SCERTS® Model (Prizant, Wetherby, Rubin, & Laurent, 2003; Prizant, Wetherby, Rubin, Laurent, & Rydell, 2006a), the Social Networks tool (Blackstone & Hunt-Berg, 2003), and the Augmentative and Alternative Communication Profile (Kovach, 2009).

Table 3.1 and the following paragraphs provide an overview of the models and tools discussed in this chapter. The Participation Model (Beukelman & Mirenda, 2005) focuses on AAC as a support to allow the AAC user to participate in daily activities in the same manner as same-age peers without disabilities. Using this model, information is gathered about the individual's current participation and communication patterns and how they differ from those of the individual's peers, as is information about barriers to participation, opportunities for communication, and capabilities. The assessment also includes preferences, attitudes, skills, and abilities of communication partners. The model is a comprehensive guide for assessment over time and across the life span.

The SCERTS Model (Prizant et al., 2006a) is also a life-span model, although it has been used more frequently with preschool and elementary-age children than with older individuals. It focuses on the person with an ASD and his or her communication partners as well as on the environment. The acronym SCERTS stands for social communication, emotional regulation, and transactional supports, the focus areas of the program. The model includes an assessment process, the SCERTS Assessment Process (SAP), that is criterion referenced and "designed for profiling relative strengths, needs, and priorities to inform program development and goal setting and to monitor progress" (Prizant et al., 2006a, p. 132). The assessment includes an initial determination of a language stage (social partner, language partner, or conversational partner), interviews, observations in daily environments, and behavior sampling. The SAP is ongoing, with quarterly updates. One important feature of the assessment and the SCERTS Model is the inclusion of interpersonal and learning support assessment and goal setting. Rubin, Laurent, Prizant, and Wetherby (2009) pointed out that relationships between AAC and reductions in challenging behavior, understanding of language, and expressive language can be investigated and monitored with the use of the SAP.

Table 3.1.   Augmentative and alternative communication (AAC) assessment models and tools

Model or Tool	Strategies	Characteristics	Environments	Age
Participation Model (Beukelman & Mirenda, 2005)	Observational data collection, interviews, inventories, and specific capabilities assessments leading to interventions for present and future	Provides systematic process of assessment based on participation requirements of peers without disabilities.	Daily living and learning environments	Life span
SCERTS® Model (Prizant, Wetherby, Rubin, Laurent, & Rydell, 2006a)	Questionnaires and interviews; observational data collection with person with an autism spectrum disorder (ASD), his or her environment, and communication partners; quantification of data to generate intervention goals	Focuses on the areas of social communication, emotional regulation, and transactional supports from partners and environment; is multidisciplinary in nature. Can be used to measure progress.	Social context of daily activities and experiences	Life span
Social Networks tool (Blackstone & Hunt-Berg, 2003)	Interview by trained professional with expertise in communication; interview with AAC user (if possible), family member, and support person	Supports Participation Model, captures multimodal nature of communication, delineates communicative competence (Light, 1989), supports person-centered planning. Is part of a comprehensive communication assessment. Can be used to measure progress.	Information obtained in interview reflects daily activities and experiences	Life span
Augmentative and Alternative Communication Profile (Kovach, 2009)	Observation and rating of operational, linguistic, social, and strategic communicative competence (Light, 1989)	Is multidisciplinary in nature. Can be used to measure progress specific to AAC use.	Any environment in which the AAC system is being used	Life span

The Social Networks tool (Blackstone & Hunt-Berg, 2003) is based on the Circle of Friends model (Falvey, Forest, Pearpoint, & Rosenberg, 1994). The Social Networks tool "helps identify communication goals that lead to successful interactions with diverse partners, across multiple environments, using tools appropriate to the situation" (Blackstone & Hunt-Berg, 2003, p. 15). Interviews used in this assessment involve the individual with an ASD (when possible), a support person, and a family member. Information is gathered in the areas of skills and abilities, communication partners, modes of expression used, representational strategies, strategies that support interaction, and types of communication. Data gathered with the Social Networks tool support the Participation Model (Beukelman & Mirenda, 2005).

The Augmentative and Alternative Communication Profile (Kovach, 2009) is an observational tool that rates an individual's performance in four areas of learning based on Light's (1989) definition of communicative competence with respect to AAC. These areas are operational, linguistic, social, and strategic competence. This tool focuses on assessing individuals who already use AAC. The profile can be used to compare different AAC modes as well as performance across partners and contexts. Given its descriptive nature, the profile has potential for individuals with ASDs.

THEORETICAL BASIS

The underpinnings of AAC use with individuals on the autism spectrum include the beliefs that all people have a right to communication (ASHA, 2004; National Joint Committee for the Communication Needs of Persons with Severe Disabilities [NJC], 1992), that behavior is communicative (NJC, 1992), that communication is multimodal in nature (Lonke, Campbell, England, & Haley, 2006), and that improved communication leads to more participation, increased self-determination, and improved quality of life (NJC, 1992).

Though individuals with ASDs are a heterogeneous group, their learning characteristics are a good match for AAC. Cafiero (2005) delineated the features that characterize AAC and how they correspond to the learning characteristics of individuals with ASDs. These are described in Table 3.2.

Assessment and intervention practices with individuals with ASDs are guided, as they are in AAC, by researcher-clinicians' beliefs about development, learning, social interactions, and etiology (ASHA, 2006). Consequently, interventions for individuals with ASDs have varied along a continuum including traditional behavioral, contemporary behavioral, and social-pragmatic developmental approaches (Prizant, Wetherby, & Rydell, 2000). Augmentative and alternative communication is more likely to be used in approaches that have an emphasis on social communication and social interaction (Mirenda & Erickson, 2000). Within a social interactionist or transactional perspective, the individual with an ASD, his or her communication partners, and environmental variables are considered within the intervention plan (Wetherby & Prizant, 2000). Prizant and Wetherby (1998) and Woods and Wetherby (2003) describe a social-pragmatic approach as family or person centered, occurring in the natural environment, embedded in meaningful contexts, and using transactional communication. Communication, from this transactional perspective, is dynamic and reciprocal; therefore, the intervention strategies to support communication development must be as well.

Table 3.2.   Augmentative and alternative communication (AAC) and autism: A good match

Autism	AAC
Visual learners	Uses visual cues
Interest in inanimate objects	Tools and devices are inanimate
Difficulty with complex cues	Level of complexity can be controlled so AAC grows with individual
Difficulty with change	Is static and predictable
Difficulty with the complexities of social interaction	Provides buffer and bridge between communication partners
Difficulty with motor planning	Is motorically easier than speech
Anxiety	AAC interventions don't apply pressure or stress
Behavioral challenges	Provides an instant means to communicate, preempting difficult behaviors
Difficulty with memory	Provides means for language comprehension that relies on recognition rather than memory

From Cafiero, J.M. (2005). *Meaningful exchanges for people with autism: An introduction to augmentative and alternative communication* (p. 26). Bethesda, MD: Woodbine House; reprinted with permission.

Initially, AAC was considered primarily for individuals who had severe expressive communication challenges but good language comprehension. As the field of AAC has grown, and as the view of which groups of people can benefit from AAC has expanded, the understanding of the importance of enhanced input has been realized (Cafiero, 2001; Drager, 2009; Drager, Postal, Carrolus, Catellano, & Glynn, 2006; Romski, Sevcik, Cheslock, & Barton, 2006). This is especially important with respect to individuals with ASDs because they experience challenges in both generating language and understanding it. Enhanced input has been termed augmented input (Romski & Sevcik, 2003), natural aided language (Cafiero, 2005), aided language stimulation (Goossens, Crain, & Elder, 1992), and aided language modeling (Drager, 2009; Drager et al., 2006). Although these strategies differ slightly from one another, each highlights the importance of communication partners' using the AAC system to provide input and a model for use in a meaningful context.

The application of AAC strategies to individuals with ASDs is based on the same foundation as AAC strategies for other individuals: maximizing communication. The Participation Model (Beukelman & Mirenda, 2005), the Social Networks tool (Blackstone & Hunt-Berg, 2003), and the SCERTS Model (Prizant et al., 2006b) all have this focus and include the elements important to social communication intervention—that is, family or person centeredness, natural environments, meaningful contexts, and responsive communication partners.

EMPIRICAL BASIS

The National Research Council (2001) and ASHA's Ad Hoc Committee on Autism Spectrum Disorders (2006) have recognized AAC as having an important role in supporting the social communication of individuals with ASDs. There is a growing body of evidence to support the use of AAC with individuals with ASDs (Mirenda & Iacono, 2009). Nevertheless, the use of AAC is at times not considered for individuals with ASDs because families and/or professionals fear that AAC will impede speech development despite the evidence to the contrary (Millar, 2009; Millar, Light, & Schlosser, 2006). Specifically, evidence collected by Millar shows that AAC has been effective in reducing challenging behavior and does not have negative effects on the development of natural speech in individuals with developmental disabilities, including ASDs.

There are four main AAC approaches that have been used with individuals with ASDs. These are manual signs, graphic communication systems, PECS, and SGDs.

Manual Signs

Manual **sign language,** an **unaided AAC** strategy, has been used with individuals with ASDs since the 1970s (Mirenda & Erickson, 2000; Nunes, 2008; Wendt, Schlosser, & Lloyd, 2004). Typically, manual signs are used in conjunction with speech, a method that is often referred to as "total communication" or "simultaneous communication" (Mirenda, 2003; Mirenda & Erickson 2000; Ogletree & Harn, 2001). Nunes (2008) reported that the use of signs is advantageous because signs are iconic, easily prompted and shaped, visual, and portable. Wendt (2009) pointed out that the reduced demand on memory and abstract understanding that signs place on the learner may help the individual overcome a negative history related to unsuccessful speech attempts. There have been several reviews of the research related to the use of manual signs with individuals with ASDs (Goldstein, 2002; Mirenda, 2003; Swartz & Nye, 2006; Wendt, 2009). In general, the results of the reviewed studies suggest that manual signing is an effective option for individuals with ASDs (Goldstein, 2002; Mirenda, 2003; Wendt, 2009). In contrast, however, Swartz and Nye (2006, p. 15) noted limited support in the evidence they reviewed and called for "high-quality" research that includes measures of intervention fidelity, sufficient detail of the interventions for replication, and group studies. Intervention fidelity refers to how well the implementation of the intervention followed the original design. The National Standards Project (National Autism Center [NAC], 2009) has designated sign instruction as an emerging treatment, indicating that there is some evidence of favorable outcome but citing the need for additional high-quality research with sign instruction.

In the four reviews of studies—Goldstein (2002), Mirenda (2003), Swartz and Nye (2006), and Wendt (2009)—there was both overlap and variety in the studies that were mentioned. However, most of the research focused on vocabulary rather than on functional, spontaneous communication, and none addressed the motor component of signing—two important issues to consider. With respect to functional, spontaneous communication, one disadvantage of manual signing is that communication is limited to partners who know sign language and can interpret the signs used, especially for users whose signs are approximations or idiosyncratic in nature (Mirenda & Erickson, 2000). With respect to the motor component of signing, Mirenda (2009a) summarized research that suggests that motor impairments are more common in ASDs than had been previously thought. If these motor impairments extend to the planning or execution of the movement patterns required for signing, limitations are placed on the individuals with ASDs who might benefit from their use. Despite these drawbacks and because of the supportive evidence reviewed here, signing may be part of a multimodal AAC system for some individuals with ASDs.

Graphic Communication Systems

Graphic communication systems, or **graphic symbols,** are aided forms of AAC in that they require something external to the communicator. The use of graphic systems for people with ASDs was introduced in the 1980s, and the systems appear to be a good fit for this population because of the static nature of the symbols and the relative strength of visual processing in people with ASDs (NRC, 2001; Wetherby & Prizant, 2000). Graphic communication systems are also described by many authors as visual supports because they can be used for comprehension as well as expression (Dettmer, Simpson, Myles, & Ganz, 2000; Hodgdon, 1995; Johnston, Nelson, Evans, & Palazolo, 2003). Such systems can be used in the form of a communication book, card, wallet, or board. The graphics themselves may consist of iconic photographs, line drawings, or written words (or other arbitrary symbols) that are generated for the user from commercially available software options.

Graphic communication systems vary in terms of their organization (Beukelman & Mirenda, 2005; Light & Drager, 2007; Porter & Cafiero, 2009). Display options typically include semantic-syntactic, taxonomic, and schematic organizations. Graphic communication systems include items that are usually arrayed in a grid format. *Semantic-syntactic organization* groups vocabulary according to grammatical categories, such as nouns, verbs, adverbs, and so forth. *Taxonomic organization* groups vocabulary items according to categories, such as people, places, and animals. *Schematic organization* groups vocabulary according to activity, such as lunch, bath time, or shopping. To date, little research is available on how display organization affects use by individuals with ASDs. Two organizational strategies described as "promising" by Mirenda (2009b, p. 112) are Pragmatic Organization Dynamic Display (Porter & Cafiero, 2009) and visual graphic language (Shane, O'Brien, & Sorce, 2009).

Some common uses of graphic symbols with individuals with ASDs are visual schedules (Mirenda & Brown, 2009), choice making (Sigafoos, O'Reilly, & Lancioni, 2009), expressive communication (Beukelman & Mirenda, 2005; Cafiero, 2005), and augmented communication input (Cafiero, 2005; Romski & Sevcik, 2003).

Wendt (2009) reviewed research from previous AAC systematic reviews and meta-analyses of the use of graphic symbols and signs (Schlosser & Wendt, 2008a, 2008b) and conducted an additional search relative to AAC and ASDs. He found a smaller research base for graphic symbols than for manual signs, a result that he construed as being due to the increasing use of graphic symbols rather than signs with individuals with ASDs. The majority of the studies related to AAC use focused on teaching the use of graphic symbols in requesting. Wendt found what he considered conclusive evidence for the use of graphic symbols to teach requesting. In contrast, he found mixed results for the use of graphic symbols to support transitions within and between activities and places. Wendt concluded that the research base is not sufficient to reliably inform clinical decisions. Not surprisingly, therefore, the National Standards Project (NAC, 2009, p. 57) designated AAC that includes graphic symbols as an "emerging" treatment.

Wendt (2009) suggested that practitioners and families consider the advantages and disadvantages of graphic symbols and of signs, as well as the universal benefits of each approach. Graphic symbols are easier for partners to interpret and are nontransient, whereas signs are portable and limitless in terms of access to vocabulary.

Picture Exchange Communication System

The PECS is a pictorial communication system that was developed by Bondy and Frost in 1985 for children with ASDs. It incorporates behavioral principles to teach young children with ASDs to request and describe what they see during typical activities (Sulzer-Azaroff, Hoffman, Horton, Bondy, & Frost, 2009). Consequently, PECS can be considered a hybrid approach that combines both AAC and behavioral methods—a strategy that is frequently applied in intervention strategies for ASDs but that is uniquely delineated in PECS.

Bondy and Frost (2009) indicated that PECS is beneficial for children who do not speak and for children who have some spoken language but who are being taught more complex language. The system consists of six training phases (each preceded by identification of potential rewards): 1) teaching the communicative exchange, 2) teaching persistence, 3) training discrimination, 4) teaching "I want..." sentences, 5) teaching a response to the question "What do you want?" and 6) teaching the use of additional sentence starters, such as "I have..." and "I see..." (Bondy & Frost, 2009). Several systematic reviews of research relative to PECS have been conducted (Schlosser & Wendt, 2008a; Sulzer-Azaroff et al., 2009), with positive results. An SGD well suited for use with PECS is available (http://www.proxtalker.com). For further description and discussion of PECS, see Chapter 11.

Speech-Generating Devices

As technology has advanced and our research base has expanded, SGDs are being considered more often as a viable option for individuals with ASDs (Cafiero, 2005; Light et al., 1998; Mirenda, 2009a). They are portable computerized devices that produce synthetic or digitized speech output when graphic symbols are activated and thus give a voice to those who use them. The devices vary in terms of their output (synthetic or digitized speech), written symbol systems, displays, and language capacity (Beukelman & Mirenda, 2005). Synthetic speech output is probably what most people think of when they think of computerized speech. Synthetic speech is text-to-speech synthesis, text that is converted to waveforms that correspond to spoken output (Beukelman & Mirenda, 2005). In contrast, digitized speech is natural speech that has been recorded and stored for playback once selected by the system user (Beukelman & Mirenda, 2005). Over the past decade, the quality and intelligibility of the voices in SGDs has improved, and more choices of voices are available.

Graphics used in SGDs include photographs, line drawings, and orthography. The organization of the graphics (also called symbols) varies in the same way graphic displays vary in visual communication systems. The devices also vary with respect to the number of symbols and messages available to the user. The displays of the symbols available can be fixed, dynamic, a combination of fixed and dynamic, or a visual scene display. Fixed-display selection sets are "fixed" in that they do not change and are the only symbols available to the user at that time. Dynamic displays, on the other hand, change when activated. Touching one button changes the selection set available to the user. Fixed and dynamic displays are typically in a grid overlay format. A **visual scene display** is a picture or photograph of an event or experience. In this type of display, messages are programmed onto specific parts of the scene. Drager, Light, and Finke (2009) pointed to the advantage of visual scene displays over grid displays in that they facilitate an understanding of the concept in context rather than the more isolated presentation associated with fixed and dynamic displays.

The use of SGDs with individuals with ASDs has not been extensively studied because it is more recent than the use of manual signs, graphic systems, and PECS. Schlosser, Sigafoos, and Koul (2009) reviewed the available research relative to SGD effectiveness for individuals with ASDs and concluded that "SGDs are viable options for individuals with ASDs who require AAC" (p. 162). The National Standards Project (NAC, 2009) designated AACs that include SGDs as an emerging treatment.

In summary, there is some evidence of positive outcomes when manual signing, graphic systems, PECS, and SGDs are used to support the communication of individuals with ASDs. The National Standards Project (NAC, 2009) deemed them emerging treatments because of the quantity and quality of the available research. Given the evidence available, clinicians and families making AAC decisions need to review the current best evidence in light of the goals and outcomes and the needs of the individual with an ASD and his or her family.

PRACTICAL REQUIREMENTS

By their very nature, AAC interventions are time intensive and labor intensive and require a collaborative team effort (Beukelman & Mirenda, 2005). Successful AAC intervention requires careful attention to a number of team activities: 1) system selection, 2) system acquisition, 3) system setup and maintenance, 4) instructional strategy selection, 5) training for families and professionals, and 6) ongoing support, collaboration, and monitoring of the intervention (Mirenda, 2005).

To address these requirements for AAC assessments and interventions, a successful team approach is imperative. Cumley and Beukelman (1992) suggested roles and responsibilities for team members based on Light's (1989) definition of communicative competence (linguistic, operational, social, and strategic) and areas of support (educational and/or vocational, home or residence, funding, and technical). Cumley and Beukelman proposed that once a team has been formed, team members be designated to take the lead in facilitating specific aspects of the AAC intervention. They suggested that various team members be assigned primary responsibility for the different categories, with assistance and consultation from other team members. For example, the speech-language pathologist would take the lead in the area of linguistic competence, with assistance from the educator, and the assistive technology specialist would provide technical support, with assistance from the paraprofessional educator.

Beukelman and Mirenda (2005) suggested formulating team membership around the individuals with the needed expertise, the individuals who will be affected by team decisions, and the individuals who have an interest in participating. It is clear that a coordinated, explicit effort involving many individuals is needed to initiate, develop, and support AAC strategies for individuals with ASDs.

KEY COMPONENTS

The key components for AAC use include the following: 1) selecting the AAC system, 2) selecting the initial vocabulary and planning for expansion, 3) identifying instructional strategies, 4) training communication partners on the system and strategies, and 5) monitoring and adapting.

Selecting the Augmentative and Alternative Communication System

In selecting an approach, AAC is best thought of as a system rather than a single entity (ASHA, 2004; Beukelman & Mirenda, 2005). The AAC systems can be aided or unaided. **Unaided AAC** components are those that do not require anything external to the user. These include signs, gestures, vocalizations, and speech. **Aided AAC** components require something external to the individual, such as communication books or SGDs (Beukelman & Mirenda, 2005). All AAC systems need a way to represent meaning, a means to select the message, and a way to send the message (McCormick & Wegner, 2003). As an early step, the AAC team will need to reach consensus on the AAC system.

Selecting Vocabulary

An important aspect of an AAC system is the vocabulary initially selected for the system and a plan for expanding it over time. If the appropriate vocabulary is not selected and later expanded, AAC will be ineffective. Beukelman, McGinnis, and Morrow (1991) described vocabulary selection as a dynamic process that reflects "changing experiences, interests, and knowledge" (p. 171). Cafiero (2005) suggested selecting a rich vocabulary and including more vocabulary than the user actually knows. Several strategies for selecting vocabulary have been documented in the literature. These include ecological inventories, communication diaries, vocabulary word lists, vocabulary generation useful to the communicator, word selection from specific categories, preselected vocabulary on devices or symbol sets, and use of informants such as family, peers, and the AAC user to generate items to include in the system's vocabulary (Beukelman et al., 1991; Fallon, Light, & Paige, 2001).

Beukelman and Mirenda (2005) described two types of vocabulary, core and fringe, both important to communication. **Core vocabulary** includes words and messages that occur frequently and are used by many individuals. **Fringe vocabulary** words and messages are unique to the individual user, and these need to be addressed during vocabulary selection in order to provide a fuller means of personal expression in the communication process.

Reviewing and expanding the vocabulary of the system should be done regularly. Zangari and Van Tatenhove (2009) stated that although all students with AAC needs require systematic instruction to learn new vocabulary, there is no research comparing approaches for such semantic instruction. Two approaches that may have potential for students with ASDs who use AAC is an adapted version of *Bringing Words to Life* (Beck, McKeown, & Kucan, 2002) and *The Bridge of Vocabulary* (Montgomery, 2007).

Identifying Instructional Strategies

The instructional strategies selected by the team are important to successful AAC use because just providing the AAC system is not enough. The focus of the instructional strategies should be on teaching communication rather than on use of a device, given that AAC is the means to functional, spontaneous communication, not an end in itself. Toward that end, instructional strategies that incorporate modeling have been found to be effective with individuals with ASDs (Cafiero, 2001; Drager, 2009; Drager et al., 2006; Drager et al., 2009; Romski et al., 2009). Modeling can help

AAC users learn the symbols and vocabulary and how to use them in communicative exchanges, much as children who are developing typically learn language and language use. In addition, AAC models may facilitate comprehension (Wood, Lasker, Siegel-Causey, Beukelman, & Ball, 1998).

Several modeling strategies have been described. Aided language stimulation was developed to teach AAC users to use graphic symbols (Goossens et al., 1992). The system for augmenting language is similar to aided language stimulation but uses SGDs (Romski & Sevcik 1992, 1996; Romski et al., 2009). Natural aided language (Cafiero, 2005) is based on aided language stimulation, with the use of graphic symbols such as pictures, icons, or written words. Aided input (Kelpin, 1995; Wegner, 1995) incorporates facilitative language intervention strategies, such as verbal models, expansions, event casts (running commentary about a situation), and focused contrasts (calling attention to speakers' contrasting statements; Bunce & Watkins, 1995) in natural settings combined with input using the SGD. Aided language modeling (Drager et al., 2006) is an instructional strategy based on the previously mentioned strategies. All of these instructional strategies provide input in the mode that the AAC user is expected to use, embed models in meaningful contexts, provide verbal and aided models, and involve communication partners.

Training Partners

Because communication partners are fundamental to social interaction and language learning, training the partners is an essential component of AAC interventions. Training is needed in two areas: in the AAC system itself and in the strategies to be used to teach its use. Training related to the system itself should cover general operation, maintenance, and programming. Responsibility for the training can be assigned through the process described previously. Several models for partner training in ASDs and AAC have been documented and can serve as examples (Culp & Carlisle, 1988; Kent-Walsh & McNaughton, 2005; Light, Dattilo, English, Gutierrez, & Hartz, 1992; McNaughton & Light, 1989).

Monitoring and Adapting

Because AAC teaching and learning are dynamic, the system needs to be frequently monitored and adapted. This is best accomplished within the team structure, with regular meetings to review data and changes in design. It is important for professionals to remember that the family is part of the team and that each family is different in terms of the extent of their participation.

DATA COLLECTION TO SUPPORT DECISION MAKING

Decisions about data collection depend on the desired outcomes and goals of the AAC user and his or her family or support system. Outcomes typically articulate the desired results of intervention, whereas goals are the specific steps needed to achieve the outcomes. Data related to the specific skills an individual needs to be an effective communicator can be one focus of data collection and evaluation (Beukelman & Mirenda, 2005). Hill (2009) described such data as performance data, which typically are obtained by quantifying specific language targets. Outcome measures include broader concepts, such as increased participation, enriched social networks, consumer satisfaction, and quality of life (Beukelman & Mirenda, 2005; Hill, 2009). Both types of data are needed to monitor progress and to consider in decision making.

Pretti-Frontczak and Bricker (2004) described guidelines for data collection in activity-based interventions that are applicable to AAC interventions. They suggested that collection methods should 1) be flexible and applicable across settings, events, and people; 2) yield valid and reliable data; 3) be shared by team members; and 4) be compatible with available resources. Data collection should also not interfere with the intervention process (Arthur-Kelly & Butterfield, 2006). This means that data are not collected during every session or teaching opportunity but during well-planned probes, videotaped interactions, or observations by a third party.

For some AAC users, performance data may focus on the use of specific vocabulary or language structure, whereas for other users, such data may focus on initiations or responses to peers. Data should also be collected on supports provided to the AAC user. For example, a support might be having a partner use aided modeling or providing the AAC user with access to the AAC system across the day. To ensure validity and representativeness, the data should be obtained from multiple sources in different environments. Data can be collected from live observations, video recordings, or electronic recordings of device use (Hill, 2009). The last of these is possible because some AAC devices are capable of tracking and printing out device use (AAC Institute, 2007; Hill, 2009; Binger & Kent-Walsh, 2009). Analysis of electronically collected data is possible with the use of a Performance Report Tool (PeRT) (AAC Institute, 2007). The PeRT software performs analyses on language samples collected from an SGD and includes transcripts, utterances, and word lists. Well-designed and carefully timed probes can ensure that ineffective strategies are reevaluated and changed or discontinued.

Teams should collaboratively decide what data will be collected, by whom, and when. Collected data should regularly inform team decisions. If teams meet weekly, weekly collection of data on at least some targets would be needed to facilitate meaningful comparison with baseline performance. If a team meets monthly, then monthly data on all targets could help guide decisions. The assessment tools previously described in Table 3.1 provide guidance to teams regarding progress monitoring and performance-based decision making as determined by predetermined outcomes measures (Beukelman & Mirenda, 2005; Blackstone & Hunt-Berg, 2003; Kovach, 2009; Prizant et al., 2006a).

CONSIDERATIONS FOR CHILDREN FROM CULTURALLY AND LINGUISTICALLY DIVERSE BACKGROUNDS

Considerations for children—and adults—from culturally and linguistically diverse backgrounds are important because of shifting demographics and the growing awareness of cultural diversity in the United States and how such diversity affects AAC services. In addition, there has been a growing awareness that cultural factors underlie all of our educational and clinical activities (Soto, 2000). Barrera and Corso (2003) pointed to the need for cultural competence, which they defined as "the ability to craft respectful, reciprocal, and responsive interactions across diverse cultural and linguistic parameters" (p. 34).

Issues that may influence the use of AAC by individuals from culturally and linguistically diverse backgrounds include the view of disability, differences in language form and functions, attitudes toward the use of technology, and child-rearing practices (Huer, 2008). Thus, cultural differences provide a critically important context for clinicians as they assess and plan for AAC interventions (Soto, Huer, & Taylor, 1997).

Roseberry-McKibbin (2008) highlighted the following considerations as important when collaborating about AAC with individuals and their families from culturally and linguistically diverse backgrounds: 1) understanding the social-pragmatic rules of a family's culture, 2) recognizing the family's perceived value of technology use, 3) determining the family's view of AAC use, 4) identifying the family's view of AAC as a priority, and 5) determining the most appropriate ways to teach families to use AAC. Another important consideration is the nature of the graphic elements (symbols) used in the AAC system with respect to bilingual students.

Roseberry-McKibbin (2008) delineated several aspects to consider regarding symbols and bilingual students. Do the symbols allow for communication at home and in mainstream environments? Are the symbols relevant to the cultural experiences of the student? For example, if a written language system is used, is it widely used in the individual's social network? Are the symbols arranged in sequences that are appropriate for the structure of the language? For example, is the array structured so that it conforms to the word order of the language? Is the family involved in vocabulary selection?

Robinson and Solomon-Rice (2009) suggested that the services can be made more culturally responsive by focusing on self-assessment and acquisition of cultural knowledge. Barrera and Corso (2003) proposed a particular method for achieving this, a method that they call Anchored Understanding and 3rd Space and describe as the skills needed to attain cultural competence with respect to early childhood education. Specifically, Anchored Understanding relates to knowing someone at an experiential level rather than just having information about that person's culture. Similarly, 3rd Space is the ability to take differing perspectives and reframe them to form an additional, third option. For example, if a parent of a child with an ASD disagrees with service providers on the use of a technological device at home, an option can be found (i.e., having the child use the device only to share what happened at school as soon as the child arrives home) that is not the parent's or service providers' initial preference.

It is clear that providing AAC services for individuals with ASDs from culturally and linguistically diverse backgrounds creates complicated demands on service providers and the researchers who support them. Thus, there is a need for more research in the area of AAC and multiculturalism (Bridges, 2004; Huer, 2008) and an even more focused need for research that can guide practices in the area of ASDs, AAC, and multiculturalism.

Application to a Child

Tait is a 12-year-old boy who was diagnosed with an ASD at 2 years of age. He began receiving speech-language services shortly after his diagnosis and has continued to receive them since that time. Tait is generally healthy, although he was recently diagnosed with rheumatoid arthritis and is sensitive to pain. He has difficulty with small spaces and "bottlenecks," areas in which many people are congregated. He has a keen interest in wood and carpentry and an excellent memory. Tait participates in special education at a local elementary school. He has a positive behavioral support team (Janney & Snell, 2008) and receives additional speech-language intervention at a university clinic.

Tait's strengths include being curious, social, and visually astute. His challenges include unconventional communication, impulsivity, and challenging behaviors that can consist of tantrums, aggression, and property destruction. These challenges have contributed to making peer interaction difficult for Tait.

Tait began using PECS at age 2 and used it until he was 3½, when he began to prefer using signs. He was introduced to his first SGD when he was 9 years old. He is now a multimodal communicator. He uses a Palm 3 (his second SGD), pictures, idiosyncratic signs, gestures, and some words to communicate. Most of his speech is unintelligible to those who do not know him. Tait can navigate through more than 200 pages and several levels on his SGD, which is programmed with both words and phrases. He uses his PECS materials as a backup when his SGD is not available, and he uses more than 100 signs, though many of them are difficult to read.

Tait's communication was initially assessed with the SCERTS Assessment Process (Prizant et al., 2006a) and was found to perform at the Language Partner Stage of communication. Goals for Tait generated from the assessment addressed increasing his skills related to commenting, expressing emotions with his SGD, and choosing among offered alternatives needed to calm him when he was upset. Goals for his communication partners included their using augmented input with Tait for purposes of redirection, expansion, and modeling; providing Tait with a binder including a schedule and Social Stories™ (Gray, 1995) to help him prepare for activities; making the SGD always available; and using an interactive diary developed for Tait by his mother.

Since the initial SCERTS assessment, Tait has made many communication gains. He independently expresses his feelings and engages in reciprocal exchanges. He also comments on shared objects or events of interest. To clarify messages, he has started to mark tense, using the "later" and "past" icons on his device. He is beginning to combine symbols. His dysregulation has decreased, as has the time it takes him to recoup from a period of dysregulation. He is able to let his partner know what he needs to calm himself when presented with alternatives. He also has more communication partners who are responsive and able to provide him with the learning supports he needs. Current goals focus on increasing his vocabulary, self-regulation, and literacy skills. During a recent SCERTS reassessment, Tait's performance was in the Conversational Partner Stage of communication.

 Readers can access a further introduction to Tait on the Internet (http://www2.ljworld .com/news/2009/jul/21/autistic-children-might-find-their-voice-ku-projec/#comments). For a video of Tait using his SGD, see the DVD that accompanies this book.

Application to an Adolescent or Adult

Joe is a 24-year-old man with a dual diagnosis of Down syndrome and an ASD. He recently moved into his own home, where he lives with support. Prior to that, he had lived with his parents. Joe owns and operates Poppin Joe's Kettle Korn and makes kettle corn to sell at fairs and crafts shows, in stores, and online (http://www.poppinjoes.com).

Joe has used an SGD for more than 10 years. He now uses a DynaVox V (DynaVox Technologies), which is his third SGD. Joe uses some speech, but it is difficult to understand him unless you know him well. His speech is less than 50% intelligible. In conversation, he is apt to repeat what his conversational partner is saying.

Joe received speech-language therapy from an early age, with most efforts directed toward improving his speech. Consequently, he did not receive an SGD until he was 14 years old. He began receiving speech-language services outside of the school setting when he was 15 years old. At that time, he was rarely using his SGD device, using it only for specific tasks. Joe received individual intervention focusing on vocabulary, SGD use, and literacy during the academic year, and he participated in group sessions as part of a summer camp for 5 years. Since then, he has participated in an AAC group 90 min per week, followed by an individual session. Joe's progress has been slow but steady.

Joe's most recent goals included using three- to five-word utterances with his SGD; making four to five unique utterances in his AAC group; creating and sending Facebook messages containing subjects, verbs, and objects, using his SGD interfaced with the computer; and completing lessons in the *WordMaker* (Don Johnston) phonemic awareness program. Direct instruction, aided modeling and expansion, and visual supports have been used to support Joe during his sessions. New vocabulary is introduced through AAC group activities and reinforced in individual sessions. Support personnel have attended Joe's sessions, and the speech-language pathologist provided training to support staff in Joe's home. Joe has made progress in his language development and use. He is using more multiword utterances with his SGD in conversation ("Joe is T-shirt white") and with his SGD interfaced with the computer ("Amber, Hi, Amber how are you?"). Joe has made several presentations to national organizations about his life and business and has testified at a congressional briefing using his SGD.

It is anticipated that Joe will continue in intervention for the near future. His goals will continue to focus on improving his literacy skills and on using longer and more complex novel utterances with his peers both in person and online.

FUTURE DIRECTIONS

As technology advances, so will the opportunities for people with ASDs, but we need more information for them to take full advantage of the opportunities. Future research needs to focus on three areas to support the communication needs of individuals with ASDs who are using AAC: system design factors, instructional strategies, and training partners to support AAC learning.

Drager and colleagues (2009) pointed to the need to investigate the impact of AAC designs on social interaction, language development, and effective communication for individuals with ASDs. The effect of different design strategies on partners' ability to provide aided language input is also an important area for future investigation (Porter & Cafiero, 2009). There is a need to investigate which instructional techniques are most effective for individuals with specific characteristics. Given the importance of literacy skills to AAC and quality of life, Light and McNaughton (2009) pointed to the need to compare the effectiveness of different interventions and instructional approaches to design technology so that communication and curricular content are more integrated and to evaluate different approaches to training parents and support personnel in using evidence-based practices. As new, less expensive technology such as Proloquo2Go (Sennott & Bowker, 2009) becomes available and easier for families to purchase, research will be needed to identify the advantages and disadvantages of different technologies in relation to individual characteristics.

Knowledge about AAC and ASDs is emerging, and there are many unknowns. In the meantime, Cafiero and Delsack (2007) have suggested that we assume that each "individual with ASD is able to receive and has the potential to generate communication" (p. 25). Certainly, AAC strategies play an important role in this "least dangerous assumption" (Donnellan, 1984, p. 141), which proposes that when there is no conclusive evidence, we make decisions that are likely to have the least harmful effect on the individual if we are wrong.

SUGGESTED READINGS

Beukelman, D.R., & Mirenda, P. (2013). *Augmentative and alternative communication: Supporting children and adults with complex communication needs* (4th ed.). Baltimore, MD: Paul H. Brookes Publishing Co.

This book provides extensive information about AAC assessment and intervention planning. The authors present pertinent information for professionals and students that will provide them with a basic understanding of AAC as well as information about individuals with complex communication needs.

Buron, K.D., & Wolfberg, P. (2008). *Learners on the autism spectrum: Preparing highly qualified educators.* Shawnee Mission, KS: Autism Asperger Publishing Co.

Written for use in university classrooms, this book is a good resource for educators, speech-language pathologists, and families. The text covers a wide range of current topics, including communication.

Cafiero, J. (2005). *Meaningful exchanges for people with autism: An introduction to augmentative and alternative communication.* Bethesda, MD: Woodbine House.

This book is a good introduction to AAC, with a focus on individuals with ASDs. Dr. Cafiero presents information about AAC and relates it to ASDs with meaningful examples. This is a book that families as well as professionals will appreciate.

Mirenda, P., & Iacono, T. (Eds.). (2009). *Autism spectrum disorders and AAC.* Baltimore, MD: Paul H. Brookes Publishing Co.

This resource presents the current research and practice in AAC as it applies to individuals with ASDs. The book is for readers who have some basic knowledge of AAC and ASDs because it is not an introduction to either area. The topics are comprehensive and timely.

Soto, G., & Zangari, C. (Eds.). (2009). *Practically speaking: Language, literacy, and academic development for students with AAC needs.* Baltimore, MD: Paul H. Brookes Publishing Co.

This book provides information about AAC and academic and social success for professionals and preprofessional students. Although it does not focus only on students with ASDs, there is much valuable information that can be applied to students with ASDs. Many practical examples are provided.

Learning Activities

1.   Try out some software.

Many manufacturers of SGDs have free downloads of the software that is used in their products. Go to the Prentke Romich (http://www.prentrom.com) or Dynavox Technologies (http://www.dynavoxtech.com) web site and download software for one of the devices. Try it out on your computer. Explore the software and then create a context in which you could provide aided input to a child. Write what you might say during the interaction and then try it. For example, interactive storybook reading could be the activity. Decide which book you would read and then try using aided input during the book reading to comment on the book. Reflect on your experience. What was difficult about it? What kind of preparation would you need to actually do this with an AAC user?

2.   Select vocabulary.

Using the same software as in the first activity, determine what vocabulary is available to use with a fourth or fifth grader with an ASD going on a nature hike. First make a list of the potential vocabulary that might be needed. Do not forget about peer interactions as well. If, after making your list, you find that the vocabulary needed isn't available on the software you have, explore the software to determine if there are other settings with more or different vocabulary. If so, change the settings. If not, try to program a few of the vocabulary words into the software.

3.   Interview an AAC user who has an ASD or the family of an AAC user who has ASD.

Possible questions you could ask to learn about the AAC user's life story are as follows:

a.   When did you (your child) obtain an AAC system? What difference has it made in your life (in your child's life)?

b.   What do you like and not like about the system?

c.   Describe the AAC system the individual is using. What kind of vocabulary was available? What kind was used?

d.   How effective was the individual's communication? If there were breakdowns in communication, why do you think they occurred? If there were no communication breakdowns, why was the person successful?

REFERENCES

AAC Institute. (2007). http://www.aacinstitute.org/

American Speech-Language-Hearing Association. (2004). Roles and responsibilities of speech-language pathologists with respect to augmentative and alternative communication: Technical report. *ASHA Supplement, 24.* Rockville, MD: Author.

American Speech-Language-Hearing Association. (2006). *Guidelines for speech-language pathologists in diagnosis, assessment, and treatment of autism spectrum disorders across the lifespan.* Available from http://www.asha.org/policy

Arthur-Kelly, M., & Butterfield, N. (2006). Monitoring progress. In J. Sigafoos, M. Arthur-Kelly, & N. Butterfield (Eds.), *Enhancing everyday communication for children with disabilities* (pp. 107–113). Baltimore, MD: Paul H. Brookes Publishing Co.

Barrera, I., & Corso, R.M. (2003). *Skilled dialogue: Strategies for responding to cultural diversity in early childhood.* Baltimore, MD: Paul H. Brookes Publishing Co.

Beck, I.L., McKeown, M.G., & Kucan, L. (2002). *Bringing words to life: Robust vocabulary instruction.* New York, NY: Guildford Press.

Beukelman, D., & Mirenda, P. (2005). *Augmentative and alternative communication: Supporting children and adults with complex communication needs* (3rd ed.). Baltimore, MD: Paul H. Brookes Publishing Co.

Beukelman, D., McGinnis, J., & Morrow, D. (1991). Vocabulary selection in augmentative and alternative communication. *Augmentative and Alternative Communication, 7,* 171–185.

Binger, C., & Kent-Walsh, J. (2009). *What every speech-language pathologist/audiologist should know about augmentative and alternative communication.* Boston, MA: Pearson Education

Blackstone, S., & Hunt-Berg, M. (2003). *Social networks: A communication inventory for individuals with complex communication needs and their communication partners.* Monterey, CA: Augmentative Communication.

Bondy, A., & Frost, L. (2009). The picture exchange communication system: Clinical and research applications. In P. Mirenda & T. Iacono (Eds.), *Autism spectrum disorders and AAC* (pp. 279–302). Baltimore, MD: Paul H. Brookes Publishing Co.

Bopp, K., Brown, K., & Mirenda, P. (2004). Speech-language pathologists' roles in the delivery of positive behavior support for individuals with developmental disabilities. *American Journal of Speech-Language Pathology, 13,* 5–19.

Brady, N. (2000). Improved comprehension of object names following voice output communication aid use: Two case studies. *Augmentative and Alternative Communication, 16,* 197–204.

Bridges, S. (2004). Multicultural issues in augmentative and alternative communication and language: Research to practice. *Topics in Language Disorders, 24*(1), 62–75.

Bunce, B.H., & Watkins, R.V. (1995). Language intervention in a preschool classroom: Implementing a language-focused curriculum. In M. Rice & K. Wilcox (Eds.), *Building a language-focused curriculum for the preschool classroom* (pp. 39–72). Baltimore: Paul H. Brookes Publishing Co.

Cafiero, J.M. (2001). The effect of an augmentative communication intervention on the communication, behavior, and academic program of an adolescent with autism. *Focus on Autism and Other Developmental Disabilities, 16,* 179–189.

Cafiero, J.M. (2005). *Meaningful exchanges for people with autism: An introduction to augmentative and alternative communication.* Bethesda, MD: Woodbine House.

Cafiero, J.M., & Delsack, B.S. (2007). AAC and autism: Compelling issues, promising practices, and future directions. *Perspectives on Augmentative and Alternative Communication (16)*2, 23–26.

Centers for Disease Control and Prevention. (2009). Autism Spectrum Disorders. Retrieved from http://www.cdc.gov/ncbddd/autism/faq_prevalence.htm#whatisprevalence

Culp, D., & Carlisle, M. (1988). *PACT: Partners in augmentative communication training.* Tucson, AZ: Communication Skill Builders.

Cumley, G.D., & Beukelman, D.R. (1992). Roles and responsibilities of facilitators in augmentative and alternative communication. *Seminars in Speech and Language, 13* (2), 111–119.

Dettmer, S., Simpson, R., Myles, B., & Ganz, J. (2000). The use of visual supports to facilitate transitions of students with autism. *Focus on Autism and Other Developmental Disabilities, 15*(3), 163–169.

Donnellan, A. (1984). The criterion of the least dangerous assumption. *Behavioral Disorders, 9,* 144–150.

Drager, K.D. (2009). Aided modeling interventions for children with autism spectrum disorders who require AAC. *Perspectives on Augmentative and Alternative Communication, 18,* 114–120.

Drager, K.D., Light, J.C., & Finke, E.H. (2009). Using AAC technologies to build social interaction with young children with autism spectrum disorders. In P. Mirenda & T. Iacono (Eds.), *Autism spectrum disorders and ACC* (pp. 247–278). Baltimore, MD: Paul H. Brookes Publishing Co.

Drager, K.D., Postal, V.J., Carrolus, L., Catellano, M., & Glynn, J. (2006). The effect of aided language modeling on symbol comprehension and production in two preschool children with autism. *American Journal of Speech-Language Pathology, 15,* 112–125.

Fallon, K., Light, J., & Paige, T. (2001). Enhancing vocabulary selection for preschoolers who require augmentative and alternative communication (AAC). *American Journal of Speech-Language Pathology, 10*, 81–94.

Falvey, M.A., Forest, M., Pearpoint, J., & Rosenberg, R.L. (1994). *All my life's a circle: Using the tools Circles, Maps and Path.* Toronto, Canada: Inclusion Press.

Garrison-Harrell, L., Kamps, D., & Kravits, T. (1997). The effects of peer networks on social-communicative behaviors for students with autism. *Focus on Autism and Other Developmental Disabilities, 12*, 241–254.

Goldstein, H. (2002). Communication intervention for children with autism: A review of treatment efficacy. *Journal of Autism and Developmental Disorders, 32*(5), 373–396.

Goossens, C., Crain, S.S., & Elder, P. (1992). *Engineering the preschool environment for interactive, symbolic communication.* Katya Hill, AL: Southeast Augmentative Communication Conference Publications.

Gray, C. (1995). Teaching children with autism to "read" social situations. In K. Quill (Ed.), *Teaching children with autism: Strategies to enhance communication and socialization* (pp. 219–241). New York, NY: Delmar Publishers.

Hill, K. (2009). Data collection and monitoring AAC intervention in the school. *Perspectives on Augmentative and Alternative Communication, 18*, 58–64.

Hodgdon, L. (1995). Solving social behavioral problems through the use of visually supported communication. In K. Quill (Ed.), *Teaching children with autism: Strategies to enhance communication and socialization* (pp. 265–286). New York, NY: Delmar Publishers.

Huer, M. (2008). Toward an understanding of the interplay between culture, language, and augmentative and alternative communication. *Perspectives on Augmentative and Alternative Communication, 17*, 113–119.

Janney, R., & Snell, M. (2008). *Teachers' Guides to Inclusive Practices: Behavioral support* (2nd ed.). Baltimore, MD: Paul H. Brookes Publishing Company.

Johnston, S., Nelson, C., Evans, J., & Palazolo, K. (2003). The use of visual supports in teaching young children with autism spectrum disorder to initiate interactions. *Augmentative and Alternative Communication, 19*, 86–103.

Kelpin, V.C. (1995). *The outcomes of augmented input and facilitative language strategies with children using augmentative communication devices.* (Unpublished master's thesis). University of Kansas, Lawrence.

Kent-Walsh, J., & McNaughton, D. (2005). Communication partner instruction in AAC: Present practices and future directions. *Augmentative and Alternative Communication, 21*(3), 195–204.

Kovach, T.M. (2009). *Augmentative and alternative communication profile: A continuum of learning.* East Moline, IL: LinguiSystems.

Light, J. (1989). Toward a definition of communicative competence for individuals using augmentative and alternative systems. *Augmentative and Alternative Communication, 5*, 137–144.

Light, J., Dattilo, J., English, J., Gutierrez, L., & Hartz, J. (1992). Instructing facilitators to support the communication of people who use augmentative communication systems. *Journal of Speech and Hearing Research, 35*, 865–875.

Light, J., & Drager, K. (2007). AAC technologies for young children with complex communication needs: State of the science and future research directions. *Augmentative and Alternative Communication, 23*, 204–216.

Light, J., & McNaughton, D. (2009). Addressing the literacy demands of the curriculum for conventional and more advanced readers and writers who require AAC. In G. Soto & C. Zangari (Eds.), *Practically speaking: Language, literacy, and academic development for students with AAC needs* (pp. 217–245). Baltimore, MD: Paul H. Brookes Publishing Co.

Light, J., Roberts, B., Dimarco, R., & Greiner, N. (1998). Augmentative and alternative communication to support receptive and expressive communication for people with autism. *Journal of Communication Disorders, 31*, 153–180.

Lonke, F., Campbell, J., England, A., & Haley, T. (2006). Multimodality: A basis for augmentative and alternative communication: Psychological, cognitive, and clinical/educational aspects. *Disability and Rehabilitation, 28*(3), 169–174.

McCormick, L., & Wegner, J. (2003). Supporting augmentative communication. In L. McCormick, D. Loeb, & D. Schiefelbusch (Eds.), *Supporting children with communication difficulties in inclusive settings* (pp. 435–459.). Boston, MA: Pearson.

McNaughton, D., & Light, J. (1989). Teaching facilitators to support the communication skills of an adult with severe cognitive disabilities: A case study. *Augmentative and Alternative Communication, 5,* 35–41.

Millar, D. (2009). Effects of AAC on the natural speech development of individuals with autism spectrum disorders. In P. Mirenda & T. Iacono (Eds.), *Autism spectrum disorders and AAC* (pp. 171–192). Baltimore, MD: Paul H. Brookes Publishing Co.

Millar, D.C., Light, J.C., & Schlosser, R.W. (2006). The impact of augmentative and alternative communication intervention on the speech production of individuals with developmental disabilities: A research review. *Journal of Speech, Language, and Hearing Research, 49,* 248–269.

Mirenda, P. (2003). Toward functional augmentative and alternative communication: A research review. *Augmentative and Alternative Communication, 16,* 141–151.

Mirenda, P. (2009a). Introduction to AAC for individuals with autism spectrum disorders. In P. Mirenda & T. Iacono (Eds.), *Autism spectrum disorders and AAC* (pp. 3–22). Baltimore, MD: Paul H. Brookes Publishing Co.

Mirenda, P. (2009b). Promising innovations in AAC for individuals with autism spectrum disorders. *Perspectives on Augmentative and Alternative Communication, 20*(4), 112–113.

Mirenda, P., & Brown, K. (2009). A picture is worth a thousand words: Using visual supports for augmented input with individuals with autism spectrum disorders. In P. Mirenda & T. Iacono (Eds.), *Autism spectrum disorders and AAC* (pp. 303–332). Baltimore, MD: Paul H. Brookes Publishing Co.

Mirenda, P., & Erickson, K. (2000). Augmentative communication and literacy. In M. Wetherby & B. Prizant (Eds.), *Autism spectrum disorders: A transactional developmental perspective* (pp. 333–369). Baltimore, MD: Paul H. Brookes Publishing Co.

Mirenda, P., & Iacono, T. (Eds.). (2009). *Autism spectrum disorders and AAC.* Baltimore, MD: Paul H. Brookes Publishing Co.

Montgomery, J.K. (2007). *The bridge of vocabulary: Evidence-based activities for academic success.* Minneapolis, MN: NCS Pearson.

National Autism Center (2009). *National Standards Project.* Randolph, MA: Author.

National Joint Committee for the Communication Needs of Persons with Severe Disabilities. (1992). *Guidelines for meeting the communication needs of persons with severe disabilities.* Available from http://www.asha.org/policy or http://www.asha.org/njc

National Research Council, Committee on Education Interventions for Children with Autism, Division of Behavioral and Social Sciences and Education. (2001). *Educating children with autism.* Washington, DC: National Academy Press.

Nunes, D. (2008). AAC interventions for autism: A research summary. *International Journal of Special Education, 23*(2), pp. 17–26.

Ogletree, B., & Harn, W. (2001). Augmentative and alternative communication for persons with autism: History, issues, and unanswered questions. *Focus on Autism and Other Developmental Disabilities, 16*(3), pp. 138–140.

Porter, G., & Cafiero, J. (2009). Pragmatic organization dynamic display (PODD) communication books: A promising practice for individuals with autism spectrum disorders. *Perspectives on Augmentative and Alternative Communication, 18,* 121–129.

Pretti-Frontczak, K., & Bricker, D. (2004). *An activity-based approach to early intervention* (3rd ed.). Baltimore, MD: Paul H. Brookes Publishing Co.

Prizant, B., & Wetherby, A. (1998). Understanding the continuum of discrete-trial traditional behavioral to social-pragmatic, developmental approaches in communication enhancement for young children with ASD. *Seminars in Speech and Language, 19,* 329–353.

Prizant, B., Wetherby, A., Rubin, E., & Laurent, A. (2003). The SCERTS® model: A transactional, family-centered approach to enhancing communication and socioemotional abilities of children with autism spectrum disorder. *Infants and Young Children, 16,* 296–316.

Prizant, B., Wetherby, A., Rubin, E., Laurent, A., & Rydell, P. (2006a). *The SCERTS® model: A comprehensive educational approach for children with autism spectrum disorders. Vol. I: Assessment.* Baltimore, MD: Paul H. Brookes Publishing Co.

Prizant, B., Wetherby, A., Rubin, E., Laurent, A., & Rydell, P. (2006b). *The SCERTS® model: A comprehensive educational approach for children with autism spectrum disorders. Vol. II: Program planning and intervention.* Baltimore, MD: Paul H. Brookes Publishing Co.

Prizant, B.M., Wetherby, A.M., & Rydell, P.J. (2000). Communication intervention issues for children with autism spectrum disorders. In A.M. Wetherby & B.M. Prizant (Eds.), *Autism spectrum disorders: A transactional developmental perspective* (pp. 193–224). Baltimore, MD: Paul H. Brookes Publishing Co.

Robinson, N.B., & Solomon-Rice, P.L. (2009). Supporting collaborative teams and families in AAC. In G. Soto & C. Zangari (Eds.), *Practically speaking: Language, literacy, and academic development for students with AAC needs* (pp. 289–312). Baltimore, MD: Paul H. Brookes Publishing Co.

Romski, R.A., & Sevcik, R.A. (1992). Developing augmented language in children with severe mental retardation. In S.F. Warren & J. Reichle (Eds.), *Communication and Language Intervention Series: Vol. 1. Causes and effects in communication and language intervention* (pp. 113–130). Baltimore, MD: Paul H. Brookes Publishing Co.

Romski, R.A., & Sevcik, R.A. (1996). *Breaking the speech barrier: Language development through augmented means.* Baltimore, MD: Paul H. Brookes Publishing Co.

Romski, M.A., & Sevcik, R.A. (2003). Augmented input: Enhancing communication development. In J.C. Light, D.R. Beukelman, & J. Reichle (Eds.), *Augmentative and Alternative Communication Series: Communicative competence for individuals who use AAC: From research to effective practice* (pp. 147–162). Baltimore, MD: Paul H. Brookes Publishing Co.

Romski, M.A., Sevcik, R.A., Cheslock, M., & Barton, A. (2006). The system for augmenting language: AAC and emerging language intervention. In R.J. McCauley & M. Fey (Eds.), *Treatment of language disorders in children* (pp. 123–147). Baltimore, MD: Paul H. Brookes Publishing Co.

Romski, M., Sevcik, R., Smith, A., Barker, M., Folan, S., & Barton-Hulsey, A. (2009). The system for augmenting language: Implications for young children with autism spectrum disorders. In P. Mirenda & T. Iacono (Eds.), *Autism spectrum disorders and AAC* (pp. 219–245). Baltimore, MD: Paul H. Brookes Publishing Co.

Roseberry-McKibbin, C. (2008). *Multicultural students with special language needs: Practical strategies for assessment and intervention.* Oceanside, CA: Academic Communication Associates.

Rubin, E., Laurent, A., Prizant, B., & Wetherby, A. (2009). AAC and the SCERTS® model: Incorporating AAC within a comprehensive, multidisciplinary educational program. In P. Mirenda & T. Iacono (Eds.), *Autism spectrum disorders and AAC* (pp. 195–217). Baltimore, MD: Paul H. Brookes Publishing Co.

Schlosser, R., & Wendt, O. (2008a). Augmentative and alternative communication intervention for children with autism. In J. Luiselli, D. Russo, W. Christian, & S. Wilczynski (Eds.), *Effective practices for children with autism: Educational and behavioral support interventions that work* (pp. 325–389). Oxford, England: Oxford University Press.

Schlosser, R., & Wendt, O. (2008b). Effects of augmentative and alternative communication intervention on speech production in children with autism: A systematic review. *American Journal of Speech-Language Pathology, 17*(3), 212–230.

Schlosser, R.W., Sigafoos, J., & Koul, R.K. (2009). Speech output and speech-generating devices in autism spectrum disorders. In P. Mirenda & T. Iacono (Eds.), *Autism spectrum disorders and ACC* (pp. 141–169). Baltimore, MD: Paul H. Brookes Publishing Co.

Sennott, S., & Bowker, A. (2009). Autism, AAC, and Proloquo2Go. *Perspectives on Augmentative and Alternative Communication, 18,* 137–145.

Shane, H.C., O'Brien, M., & Sorce, J. (2009). Use of a visual graphic language system to support communication for persons on the autism spectrum. *Perspectives on Augmentative and Alternative Communication, 18,* 130–136.

Sigafoos, J., O'Reilly, M., & Lancioni, G. (2009). Functional communication training and choice-making interventions for the treatment of problem behavior in individuals with autism spectrum disorders. In P. Mirenda & T. Iacono (Eds.), *Autism spectrum disorders and AAC* (pp. 333–353). Baltimore, MD: Paul H. Brookes Publishing Co.

Soto, G. (2000). "We Have Come a Long Way..." AAC and Multiculturalism: From Cultural Awareness to Cultural Responsibility, *Perspectives on Communication Disorders and Sciences in Culturally and Linguistically Diverse Populations, 6,* 1–3.

Soto, G., Huer, M., & Taylor, O. (1997). Multicultural issues. In L. Lloyd, D. Fuller, & H. Arvidson (Eds.), *Augmentative and alternative communication: A handbook of principles and practices* (pp. 407–413). Needham Heights, MA: Allyn & Bacon.

Sulzer-Azaroff, B., Hoffman, A.O., Horton, C.B., Bondy, A., & Frost, L. (2009). The picture exchange communication system (PECS): What do the data say? *Focus on Autism and Other Developmental Disabilities, 24*(2), 89–103.

Swartz, J., & Nye, C. (2006). Improving communication for children with autism: Does sign language work? *EBP Briefs, 1*(2), 1–17.

Van Acker, R., Loncola, J., & Van Acker, E. (2005). Rett syndrome: A pervasive developmental disorder. In F. Volkmar, R. Paul, A. Klin, & D. Cohen (Eds.), *Handbook of autism and pervasive developmental disorders: Diagnosis, development and neurobiology and behavior* (Vol. 1, pp. 148–150). Hoboken, NJ: Wiley.

Volkmar, F., Koenig, K., & State, M. (2005). Childhood disintegrative disorder. In F. Volkmar, R. Paul, A. Klin, & D. Cohen (Eds.), *Handbook of autism and pervasive developmental disorders: Diagnosis, development and neurobiology and behavior* (Vol. 1, pp. 70–87). Hoboken, NJ: Wiley.

Wegner, J.R. (1995). *A guide to augmented input and language intervention* (Unpublished paper). Department of Speech-Language-Hearing, University of Kansas, Lawrence.

Wendt, O. (2009). Research on the use of manual signs and graphic symbols in autism spectrum disorder: A systematic review. In P. Mirenda & T. Iacono (Eds.), *Autism spectrum disorders and AAC* (pp. 83–139). Baltimore, MD: Paul H. Brookes Publishing Co.

Wendt, O., & Schlosser, R. (2007, August). *The effectiveness of speech-generating devices for children with autism: Results from a systematic research review.* Paper presented at the 27th World Congress of the Association of Logopedics and Phoniatrics, Copenhagen, Denmark.

Wendt, O., Schlosser, R., & Lloyd, L. (2004, November). *AAC for children with autism: A meta-analysis of intervention outcomes—Preliminary results.* Paper presented at the 2004 Annual Convention of the American Speech-Language-Hearing Association, Philadelphia, PA.

Wetherby, A.M., & Prizant, B.M. (2000). Introduction to autism spectrum disorders. In A.M. Wetherby & B.M. Prizant (Eds.), *Autism spectrum disorders: A transactional developmental perspective* (pp. 2–7). Baltimore, MD: Paul H. Brookes Publishing Co.

Wood, L., Lasker, J., Siegel-Causey, E., Beukelman, D., & Ball, L. (1998). Input framework for augmentative and alternative communication. *Augmentative and Communication, 14,* 261–267.

Woods, J.J., & Wetherby, A.M. (2003). Early identification and intervention for infants and toddlers who are at risk for autism spectrum disorder. *Language, Speech, and Hearing Services in Schools, 34,* 180–193.

Zangari, C., & Van Tatenhove, G. (2009). Supporting more advanced linguistic communicators in the classroom. In G. Soto & C. Zangari (Eds.), *Practically speaking: Language, literacy, and academic development for students with AAC needs* (pp. 173–193). Baltimore, MD: Paul H. Brookes Publishing Co.

4

Elementary Behavioral Intervention Strategies: Discrete Trial Instruction, Differential Reinforcement, and Shaping

Susan M. Wilczynski, Hanna C. Rue, Melissa Hunter, and Lauren Christian

Given that **discrete trial instruction (DTI)** is such a simple teaching technique, it is surprising how often it is misunderstood and misrepresented, even among specialists in autism spectrum disorders (ASDs). A discrete trial involves four components: a **discriminative stimulus** (e.g., instruction), a **response,** a consequence, and an intertrial interval (i.e., extremely brief break). When you ask individuals who have ever worked with people on the autism spectrum if they have 1) delivered an instruction, 2) waited briefly for a response, 3) provided some form of feedback as a means of helping the individual learn from this experience, then 4) taken a quick break before beginning to teach again, they have to admit they have. Yet these same professionals may vilify the use of DTI. In this chapter, we seek to diminish stereotypes and clarify how this simple teaching technique can be used to effectively target a broad range of skills for anyone, but especially those with ASD.

DTI, also known as discrete trial training and discrete trial teaching, can be applied in diverse ways. Interventionists using DTI make decisions about how to best arrange each trial. For example, questions such as these must be asked: Should a **prompt** be used? What form should the instruction take? How appropriate is the consequence? Does the consequence actually serve as a reinforcer? Another set of decisions must be made about how multiple discrete trials should be delivered over the span of the day. For example, the following questions must be considered: Should a series of discrete trials involving the same target appear sequentially (i.e., in massed trials)? Should they be interspersed with mastered skills (i.e., mastery interspersal) or with other novel targets (i.e., varied trials)? Interventionists must also consider the location of the discrete trials: Should they occur in highly structured environments, or should they occur in natural environments across a range of settings (e.g., community, school, home)? This series of questions alone should help to dispel the myth of a single approach to DTI.

Although DTI often serves as the starting point in the behavioral treatment of ASDs, other important behavioral strategies are frequently used in conjunction with discrete trials (e.g., prompts) or are used at other times as part of a comprehensive treatment approach (e.g., modeling, shaping, antecedent strategies). For example, shaping involves differentially reinforcing behaviors that are increasingly close to the ideal performance of the behavior. To illustrate, if a girl already has the skill of putting her hands together, the behavioral interventionist might shape it into clapping (e.g., to applaud her classmates' accomplishments) or into signing to request preferred items (e.g., cheese or a cookie). A large number of additional behavioral techniques are often used to supplement DTI, but given page limitations, we focus this chapter only on DTI, differential **reinforcement** (i.e., contingent reinforcement), and **shaping.**

DTI, differential reinforcement, and shaping have been successfully used to teach a broad range of skills to a wide variety of populations (Downs, Downs, Johansen, & Fossum, 2007; LeGray, Dufrene, Sterling-Turner, Olmi, & Bellone, 2010; Summers & Szatmari, 2009; Watanabe, Yamamoto, & Kobayashi, 1990). These techniques can be used to teach individuals at many age, developmental, and language levels, and they have been used in classrooms, home-based programs, and community-based programs to improve the communication, social, and adaptive skills of individuals with ASDs (Karsten & Carr, 2009; Newman, Reinecke, & Ramos, 2009). Thus, DTI and other behavioral strategies are robust techniques that can be applied to any number of skills.

TARGET POPULATIONS AND ASSESSMENTS FOR DETERMINING TREATMENT RELEVANCE AND GOALS

A vast literature base exists supporting the use of DTI in teaching individuals with autism and pervasive developmental disorders-not otherwise specified (PDD-NOS; Coe, Matson, Fee, Manikam, & Lanarello, 1990; Howlin, 1981; Lafasakis & Sturmey, 2007). This research base includes evidence of treatment effectiveness for young children with severe cognitive impairments and an extremely limited verbal repertoire (Smith, Groen, & Wynn, 2000). It should be noted that this research support has not been extended to the less frequently occurring ASDs, such as Rett syndrome and childhood disintegrative disorder. The limited outcomes reported on Rett syndrome suggest behavioral treatment may not be an effective intervention with this population (Smith, Klevstrand, & Lovaas, 1995). Although behavioral treatments have been implemented with individuals with Asperger syndrome, DTI has not served as a cornerstone for such treatments. However, given the utility of DTI with most populations, this treatment should not be entirely discounted should a more structured teaching arrangement be required for an individual with Asperger syndrome.

There is no test to determine how appropriate DTI is for an individual on the autism spectrum. However, before communication or social skills are targeted for improvement, behavioral interventionists typically identify the child's preparedness to learn. Assessment of learning readiness skills involves observation of the child's ability to accept objects, respond when others have control over reinforcers, scan an array of items, imitate others, follow simple instructions, and sit down without engaging in self-stimulatory behaviors. If a child lacks these skills, other behavioral interventions (e.g., shaping, modeling, antecedent strategies such as offering choice of preferred stimuli or providing effective instructions) are put in place to help develop these critical skills.

Two popular behavioral tools for identifying which communication and/or social skills should be the target of treatment are the Assessment of Basic Language and Learning Skills-Revised (ABLLS-R; Partington, 2006) and the Verbal Behavior Milestones Assessment and Placement Program (VB-MAPP; Sundberg, 2008). Both are based on Skinner's (1957) *Verbal Behavior*. The ABLLS-R was developed to identify specific skill impairments in the areas of communication, learning readiness, play and leisure, social interaction, group instruction, classroom routines, adaptive skills, and basic academic skills. The assessment is tied to curricular goals so that progress associated with individualized education program (IEP) goals can be regularly monitored. There are no psychometric data available for the ABLLS-R. The ABLLS-R has been used with individuals representing a broad age range (e.g., toddlers through adults); the decision is largely made on the basis of the skill set of the individual on the spectrum as opposed to his or her age.

In addition to Skinner's (1957) work, the VB-MAPP is tied to typical language development milestones. The VB-MAPP (Sundberg, 2008) is based on the assumption that the identification of both existing skill levels and barriers to communication development is needed to avoid developing an inappropriate curriculum. It is designed for children with skill levels at the infant to preschool ages (i.e., up to 48 months). The VB-MAPP has 1) a transition scale that can be used to identify a child's ability to learn in a less restrictive educational environment, 2) a task analysis and tracking system that helps break skills down for progress monitoring, and 3) a section on placement and IEP goals that provides recommendations for program development. Like the ABLLS-R (Partington, 2006), the VB-MAPP has no psychometric support at this time.

THEORETICAL BASIS

Behavior Analysis

To understand the behavioral techniques described in this chapter, it is best to begin with a basic understanding of behavior analysis. From a behavior-analytic perspective, behavior is determined by an individual's environment, learning history, and physiological makeup (Epstein & Skinner, 1981). It is a common and unfortunate misunderstanding that behavior analysts view the actions people take only within the context of the immediate moment, but it is not quite that Zen (i.e., in the moment)! B.F. Skinner, the founder of behavior analysis, proposed that behavior is lawful (i.e., is clearly regulated by environmental factors) and that learning occurs through two distinct processes, respondent (also called classical) conditioning and operant conditioning (Skinner, 1938). Because the behavioral techniques discussed in this chapter largely come from the process of operant conditioning, we will restrict our review to that domain.

Operant conditioning is a type of learning that occurs as a result of an interaction between behavior and its consequences (Cooper, Heron, & Heward, 2007). That is, when we take action in the world, events that occur afterward strongly influence the likelihood we will take the same action again under similar conditions. A trip to the local grocery store provides an illustration. A child repeatedly requests a candy bar in a loud and whiney voice. The parent eventually purchases the candy bar for the child. This event has two effects: 1) the child is more likely to repeatedly request a candy bar in a loud and whiney voice in the future because this resulted in a desirable consequence and 2) the parent is more likely to buy the candy bar in the future because doing so led to the end of an aversive condition when the child quieted and embarrassment was reduced.

The importance of planned and unplanned consequences on human behavior cannot be emphasized strongly enough from the behavior-analytic perspective. Table 4.1 reviews different consequences that may increase appropriate communicative acts, such as speech or sign, or decrease inappropriate communication skills, such as throwing a tantrum or aggression. How does this relate to the behavioral strategies we have discussed? DTI involves structuring a teaching opportunity so that when the child responds, a consequence is delivered with the goal of increasing correct responding. Similarly, the child takes action when shaping techniques are used and consequences are delivered as a result of this action. The probability of positive outcomes in the form of access to reinforcers increases if the behavior more closely approximates the ideal behavior than when the child made attempts in the past.

Operant conditioning also takes into account the influence of antecedents, events that precede a behavior. Antecedents may include events such as an instruction given by a person—for example, "Come here"—or the denial of access to a preferred activity. Antecedents may result in a variety of actions; in response to the instruction "Come here," for example, a child can follow the instruction, not follow it, throw a tantrum, or find something else to do. Antecedents such as instruction are an essential component of DTI. Although antecedents may occur immediately before the behavior of interest, an immediate temporal relationship between all antecedents and behaviors is not always present.

Motivational operations (MOs) are antecedents that result in a reinforcer becoming more valuable (Michael, 2007). Such antecedents may have been experienced at a time other than the time at which they affected behavior. For example, thirst (MO) will cause water to become a more powerful reinforcer when you have not had anything to drink in a while than when you have just consumed an entire bottle of water. When patterns of behavior are hard to predict, behavior analysts seek answers in MOs. For example, an interventionist might notice that when denied access to preferred activities, a boy throws a tantrum on some days and finds something else to do on other days. Tantrums might be more likely to occur on days following poor sleep, and finding something else to do might occur after a full night's rest. Given that both DTI and shaping require the use of potent reinforcers to increase accurate responding, an awareness of MOs may be central to appropriate programming.

Behavioral techniques are used to decrease excesses such as self-injury and aggression (Iwata, Dorsey, Slifer, Bauman, & Richman, 1982) or to ameliorate impairments such as communication and academic skills (Birnbrauer & Leach, 1993; Lovaas, 1987) or social skills (Matson, Matson, & Rivet, 2007). To address these behavioral impairments or excesses, behavioral interventionists sometimes rely on

Table 4.1. Reinforcement and punishment

	Item or activity is *presented*	Item or activity is *removed*
Behavior increases	Positive reinforcement • High-five • Tickles	Negative reinforcement • Break from work
Behavior decreases	Positive punishment • Firm "no"	Negative punishment • Time out • Response cost

DTI, differential reinforcement, and shaping. Not surprisingly, when improvements in communication, social, or other adaptive skills result from the application of these strategies, the frequency of problem behaviors is often reduced. The importance of differential reinforcement in increasing appropriate behavior and decreasing inappropriate behavior cannot be underscored strongly enough. Differential reinforcement involves providing contingent access to reinforcers—that is, reinforcers are available when the individual engages in predefined appropriate behaviors but not when he or she engages in predefined inappropriate behaviors. Differential reinforcement can be used as a technique in isolation, but it is also used in the context of DTI when the consequence that follows a response involves access to reinforcers for correct responding but a lack of access for incorrect responding.

Discrete Trial Instruction

Many individuals erroneously use the term **applied behavior analysis (ABA)** in place of DTI. However, DTI is a technique within the larger field of behavior analysis, whereas ABA is a field of study that involves the collection of data to assess the systematic modification of environmental conditions (Cooper et al., 2007). These modifications are designed to produce socially significant improvements in the lives of children and adults (Cooper et al., 2007). Furthermore, DTI typically involves teaching a child to attend to specific environmental cues to improve responding in a very circumscribed set of conditions (e.g., to be able to say "John" when asked "What is your name?"). In contrast, ABA typically involves a very broad range of environmental conditions that may produce the highest level of success on a broad range of domains. Despite these differences, DTI remains an important component of ABA when serving children who can learn best in highly structured situations. By accumulating highly specialized skills over time and being taught to generalize those skills to relevant situations, the goal of ABA to produce large-scale success can be realized. This will be the case particularly when additional strategies associated with ABA (e.g., shaping, modeling, peer training) are used as part of the teaching repertoire.

The instructor considers each component of DTI (discriminative stimulus, response, consequence, and intertrial interval) as a means by which a child's learning can be enhanced. Thus, DTI is theoretically based on the idea that positive learning outcomes can be obtained by increasing the immediacy between desired behavior and reinforcement, by increasing the value of the reinforcer to the child, and by making certain that the discriminative stimulus is salient. In this section, rationales for specific components of DTI may help readers understand its empirically derived assumptions.

Several important points need to be considered before beginning DTI. First, the instructor needs to have control over the teaching environment. If the child can access a reinforcer whether or not a correct response is delivered, why would learning occur? Given the importance of reinforcers in increasing correct responding, the goal is to arrange the environment so that contingent access to reinforcers (i.e., differential reinforcement) occurs.

Second, the instructor needs to sufficiently understand the child's skill level in order to structure discrete trials so that the child is likely to gain access to reinforcers. For example, when a child first learns a new skill, a series of prompts might be necessary to increase the chances the child will respond correctly. Therefore, to increase a child's identification of an apple in response to use of the word *apple,* we might provide a position prompt or a modeling prompt to increase the likelihood that the child will select the apple from an array of possibilities. It is important to use prompts when necessary. However, it is equally important to fade the use of prompts as quickly as possible so that the child does not become prompt dependent. Prompt dependence can occur when the child fails to use a particular response *until* it is modeled or physically guided by the instructor's using the child's hand and arm to create a pointing gesture. See Table 4.2 for a list of frequently used prompts and suggestions for prompt fading.

Third, maintaining child motivation is critical when teaching, but doing so represents a major challenge for the instructor because many children on the spectrum have restricted interests. Behavioral interventionists often utilize a number of strategies to maintain motivation. **Maintenance interspersal** involves the intermingling of novel tasks with mastered tasks (Winterling, Dunlap, & O'Neill, 1987). To understand the importance of maintenance interspersal, consider how motivated you might be if you had to face only challenging tasks all day long. A second motivational technique often used by behavioral interventionists is choice. Although providing a choice of tasks or reinforcers may not always make a difference in terms of rate of correct responding, offering these choices has been linked to reductions in problem behaviors (Dyer, Dunlap, & Winterling, 1990).

Verbal Behavior

Many skills can be taught using DTI. Our discussion here is restricted to communication skills and a small number of elementary social skills essential for functionally interacting with others. Knowing *how* to teach using DTI is essential. Knowing *what* to teach is every bit as important. Skinner (1957) proposed a theory of language and communication based on operant conditioning, a theory that centers on the function or purpose of language. The term *verbal behavior* is often used to describe a specific approach to teaching language programs using behavior-analytic techniques. Some controversy exists about the relationship between verbal behavior and the field of applied behavior analysis. Some scholars argue that verbal behavior is a novel treatment approach that identifies the function of specific communicative acts and applies a unique set of teaching tools to increase production and understanding of communication. Others argue that the treatment that is often referred to as **verbal behavior** relies on techniques that have emerged from the broader field of applied behavior analysis. We do not expect to resolve this controversy in this chapter, but we believe that it is important for the reader to understand the context in which we interpret verbal behavior. We concur with the second group of scholars that 1) verbal behavior involves strategies for teaching individuals to improve communication, 2) these strategies emanate from the field of applied behavior analysis, and 3) the child's mastery of the treatment targets (i.e., production and comprehension) requires that the communication strategy (e.g., sign, speech) be used in appropriate contexts and that it serves a specific purpose (e.g., requesting, labeling) so that meaningful communication can occur.

A full explication of Skinner's verbal behavior is beyond the scope of this chapter, so we will restrict our brief review to six elementary verbal behaviors: mand,

Table 4.2. Definitions and examples of prompts and prompt fading

Type of prompt	Definition	Example
Physical	The teacher moves a part of the student's body.	A teacher gives the instruction, "Touch the bird," and moves a student's hand to touch a picture of the bird. *Prompt fading:* Gradually reduce the pressure used to move the student's hand. Proceed from a light touch to a brief gesture and no prompt.
Gestural	The teacher uses a nonverbal cue such as nodding, pointing, or smiling.	A teacher gives the instruction, "Touch the bird," and points to the picture of the bird. *Prompt fading:* Move from pointing within an inch of the picture to pointing from several inches away, to a subtle point from a distance, to no prompt.
Verbal	The teacher uses a vocal cue that may include words, sentences, or syllables.	A picture of a bird is placed on the table. The teacher gives the instruction, "What animal?" and follows with the word *bird*. *Prompt fading:* Say "bir," then say "b," then give no prompt.
Visual	The teacher presents a picture or text.	A picture of a bird is placed on the table. The teacher gives the instruction, "What animal?" and holds up a card with the word *bird* printed on it. *Prompt fading:* Delete letters of the word—"bir," "bi," "b"—and then do not present the card.
Modeled	The teacher demonstrates the correct behavior or response.	The teacher gives the instruction, "Touch the bird," and touches the correct picture. *Prompt fading:* See gestural prompt fading.
Positional	The teacher places an item in front of the student in such a manner that the placement increases the likelihood the student will demonstrate the desired behavior.	Three pictures are placed in front of the student. The picture of the bird is placed several inches closer to the student than the other pictures. The teacher gives the instruction, "Touch the bird." *Prompt fading:* Gradually move the target picture closer to the other pictures until the pictures are aligned.

tact, echoic, intraverbal, textual, and transcription. These behaviors are defined as follows:

- A *mand* occurs when an individual emits a communicative act that functions to obtain a desired item or activity.
- A *tact* refers to any instance an individual names or labels an item or activity.
- An *echoic* is any occurrence of an individual echoing the verbalization of another individual.
- An *intraverbal* is a type of vocalization that occurs in response to another individual's question or comment.
- A *textual* is a verbal operant that occurs when an individual reads a written word aloud.
- *Transcription* occurs when an individual writes or spells a word verbalized by another individual.

In the view of interventionists who favor verbal behavior, each of these elementary verbal operants is acquired and maintained by reinforcers that occur as a result of the verbal behavior. For example, a child may say "juice" in order to obtain access to juice. In this example, "juice" is a mand because the vocalization functions to obtain a desired item. The mand is the only verbal operant in which the item or activity identified by the communicative act serves as the reinforcer and in which the likelihood that the communicative act will occur is directly tied to MO. Although Skinner's theory centers primarily on the behavior of the speaker, he acknowledged that interaction of the speaker and listener is critical in the development of language and communication (Sundberg & Michael, 2001).

Language programs typically begin with mand training because it helps the child develop functionally necessary skills to gain access to desired items or activities. Training mands may also result in an added benefit—reducing the frequency of challenging behaviors (e.g., tantrums; Lovaas & Smith, 1989). Some individuals with ASDs scream, cry, or engage in self-injurious behavior that functions to obtain a tangible item. Through mand training, the challenging behavior is often replaced with functional communication. Echoic training and tact training are also basic components of a behavioral program that lay the foundation for more complex communication training.

A language program may begin with the shaping of vocal behavior (often, a mand). For example, the target behavior may be for the child to mand "cookie." If the child begins the language program with the ability to emit the sound "koo," the behavioral interventionist can provide reinforcement for the "koo" sound and slowly attempt to elicit the "kie" sound. Initially, the child is reinforced for emitting an approximation of the "cookie" sound, and later, for the entire word, "cookie."

Echoic training occurs when the behavioral interventionist presents a verbal stimulus and delivers reinforcers when the sound is imitated. Once an echoic response occurs reliably, the procedure can be used to teach other verbal responses (e.g., answering a question). When an instructor provides echoic training, he or she must consider expected developmental issues in the emergence of correctly produced sounds. For example, expecting the correct pronunciation of the word *three* from a 3-year-old may be unreasonable.

Tact training occurs when behavioral interventionists provide reinforcement for correctly labeling items, activities, emotions, places, people, and so forth. When training mands, tacts, and echoics, teaching may occur in both structured and natural environments (Sundberg & Partington, 1998, 1999). Behavioral interventionists may initially establish verbal responses using DTI in a highly structured environment, but they may be just as likely to apply the basic teaching interaction of DTI in a natural environment.

Teaching verbal behavior in the natural environment is a necessity so that naturally occurring cues in the environment begin to signal to the child with an ASD when he or she should appropriately engage in specific verbal behavior. For example, a child may learn to tact the word *bird* when presented with a picture of a bird in a highly structured environment. The child receives social praise or a stuffed toy of a bird that serves as a reinforcer. At this point, training might move to the natural environment outside, where the child may see a bird fly overhead and tact "bird." The child would again receive reinforcement for the verbal behavior. An effective and well-rounded behavioral program for individuals with ASDs promotes generalization of all acquired skills to the natural environment. Rather than moving from a highly structured to a natural environment over time, behavioral interventionists might begin in the natural environment and complete trials when birds become naturally available. There are a variety of reasons the behavioral interventionist might choose one of these approaches over the other. In one case, the child may be very distractible outdoors and therefore may not benefit from the teaching experience. In this event, teaching the child to tact "bird" in a more structured environment would be best, as long as there is an aggressive goal of planning for generalization. Pragmatic reasons may also influence the decision to teach in one environment over another. Teaching a child to tact "bird" during the winter in one of the northern states may prove quite challenging!

Communication is more complicated than simply delivering rote responses to highly structured questions and can involve the use of speech, signs, or pictures. Communication involves both understanding the most basic elements of language and understanding the social purpose of doing so. The social aspect of communication is also targeted in effective behavioral programs for individuals with ASDs. Once the basic elements of language are acquired (e.g., mands, tacts), training to produce sentences, respond to questions, and participate in simple conversations is initiated. The developmental appropriateness of the content of these complex communicative acts and the context and social purpose of the acts are always critical concerns during intervention planning and execution.

Prelinguistic Aspects of Communication

In addition to the use of formal communication systems, prelinguistic components of communication may need to be taught. For example, eye contact, orienting to a speaker, and developing joint attention skills can all be addressed using behavioral techniques. Eye contact and orienting to a speaker are often collateral side effects of mand training. Orientation and eye contact are more likely to occur if the interventionist uses shaping to gradually teach the child that both the production of a mand (e.g., "Spin me") and eye contact are necessary before the preferred event occurs. Similarly, when DTI is combined with other behavioral techniques (e.g., prompting, maintenance interspersal, choice, modeling), joint attention skills, which serve as the foundation of social-communicative interactions, improve (Whalen & Schreibman, 2003).

In conclusion, effective and well-rounded behavioral interventions for individuals with ASDs are based on operant principles of learning. The objective of behavioral interventions is to teach the individual to function independently in the natural environment. This objective is reached by breaking down complex behaviors into simple teachable units of behavior. However, effective behavioral interventions require an understanding of complex issues of child development, motivation, and the function of communication.

EMPIRICAL BASIS

Beginning in the 1960s (Ferster & DeMyer, 1961; Wolf, Risley, & Mees, 1964) and spanning nearly five decades (Gena, Krantz, McClannahan, & Poulson, 1996; Iwata et al., 1982; Rocha, Schreibman, & Stahmer, 2007), researchers have built an impressive body of literature supporting the use of behavioral strategies for the treatment and education of people with ASDs. DTI in particular has been demonstrated to be an effective tool for teaching children with autism a wide variety of skills, such as expressive language (Howlin, 1981), verbal and motor imitation (Coe et al., 1990;

Lafasakis & Sturmey, 2007), play skills (Coe et al., 1990; Nuzzolo-Gomez, Leonard, Ortiz, Rivera, & Greer, 2002), joint attention (Jones, Carr, & Feeley, 2006), and social skills (Downs & Smith, 2004).

Discrete Trial Instruction within Early Intensive Behavioral Intervention Programs

The evidence regarding DTI comes from several sources. We examine DTI in the context of Early Intensive Behavioral Intervention (EIBI). Our examination begins with a review of Lovaas's (1987) seminal work on EIBI and includes review of partial or full replications of his comprehensive treatment approach, which is now known as the UCLA model. In our review, we consider parent-directed intensive behavioral interventions, EIBI for children with severe intellectual disabilities, and the level of intensity required to produce substantial gains.

The best-known source of data supporting the use of DTI is found in EIBI programs such as Alpine Learning Group, Lovaas Institute, May Institute, and Princeton Child Development Institute. Although these comprehensive programs rely on a range of behavior-analytic techniques, DTI plays a central role, particularly in early phases of treatment. EIBI programs have shown positive outcomes for children with ASDs (Bibby, Eikeseth, Martin, Mudford, & Reeves, 2002; Lovaas, 1987; Meyer, Taylor, Levin, & Fisher, 2001; Smith & Lovaas, 1997). The most recognized example is Lovaas's Young Autism Project at UCLA (Lovaas, 1987), which began in the early 1970s as a treatment program for children with ASDs under the age of 4. That program utilized DTI as a primary treatment component and stressed teaching skills in home settings. Early outcome data were exceptionally positive, with 47% of children (9 of 19) who received 40 hr a week of intervention for at least 2 years achieving full inclusion in a general education environment, compared with only 2% of children (1 of 40) in a control group. Significant gains in cognitive skills were also maintained at follow-up (Lovaas, 1987; McEachin, Smith, & Lovaas, 1993).

Lovaas's (1987) work, however, has been criticized on methodological grounds. For instance, critics have noted that different IQ tests were used preintervention and postintervention, thus reducing the reliability with which results can be interpreted (Magiati & Howlin, 2001), and participants were not randomly assigned to treatment groups (Mesibov, 1993). Threats to external validity have also been noted (e.g., reliance on IQ as the primary standardized outcome measure). Furthermore, children who participated in Lovaas's original study were verbal and began the study with relatively high cognitive scores (IQ above 35; Reed, Osborne, & Corness, 2007), which may limit the generalization of these results to children with ASDs who are nonverbal or have even lower cognitive scores. Scholars have provided compelling arguments against the validity of several of these criticisms (Eikeseth, 2001) to get the most balanced perspective. Of course, no single study can ever fully answer any research question, but even with its limitations, Lovaas's (1987) study should be acknowledged as having moved the field forward by providing an early demonstration of the effectiveness of EIBI and having prompted additional research to examine the benefits of structured behavioral techniques for children with ASDs.

Several researchers have attempted to partially or fully replicate the UCLA model. The level of gains made by children varied across these studies, but progress was universally noted. For example, Smith, Groen, and Wynn (2000) followed the

UCLA model of participant selection (e.g., under the age of 42 months and ratio IQ between 35 and 75) and utilized DTI as a primary treatment component. Twenty-eight participants were matched and assigned to either an intensive-treatment group or a parent-training group. The intensive-treatment group received, for 2–3 years, an average of 25 hr per week of DTI and other behavioral interventions. In the comparison group, parents were taught over the course of 3–9 months, for 5 hr per week, how to use behavioral treatment programs in the home and community. On postassessment measures, the intensive-treatment group showed a significant difference from the parent-training group regarding increases in IQ (an average increase of 16 points), visual-spatial skills, academic achievement, and language development. Furthermore, students in the EIBI group were more likely to be placed in less restrictive school settings.

Smith and colleagues (2000) raised the question of whether or not parent-directed intensive behavioral intervention programs could be effective. This question was answered when Sallows and Graupner (2005) examined a community-based program using the UCLA treatment model. Children recruited for this study were between the ages of 24 and 42 months, had a ratio IQ of 35 or higher, and were matched before being divided into a clinic-directed group (UCLA model) and a parent-directed group. Children in the clinic-directed group received intensive services averaging more than 37 hr per week, along with in-home supervision; children in the parent-directed group averaged 31–32 hr of treatment, with parents being responsible for coordination of services. The average IQ for all 24 children increased from 51 to 76, a 25-point increase. Furthermore, 8 of the children had IQs of 85 or higher after 1 year of treatment, and 3 more reached this level of success after 3–4 years of treatment. Children with higher pretreatment IQs were more likely to reach this level. Increases in language and adaptive skills were also reported for both groups. This study demonstrates that parents can effectively implement intensive behavioral treatment for their children.

Other researchers have also attempted to replicate the UCLA model in community settings. In a study conducted by Cohen, Amerine-Dickens, and Smith (2006), participants included 21 children in both the experimental (EIBI) group and the control group. These children had been diagnosed with autism or PDD-NOS, had an IQ of 35 or above, and were under 48 months of age. Students in the EIBI group received intervention based on the Lovaas UCLA model, whereas the comparison group received community services such as Early Head Start, home-based developmental intervention, and public school services. Significantly greater IQ gains were identified in the EIBI group (i.e., a 25-point gain, from 62 to 87 preintervention to postintervention) than in the comparison group, but important gains were also noted for the comparison group (i.e., a 14-point gain, from 59 to 73). Significant greater differences were found in group gains in adaptive skills, with the EIBI group demonstrating a mean increase of 9 points, and the comparison group demonstrating a mean decrease of 4 points. Furthermore, 17 of the 21 EIBI children were included in general education classrooms at the end of the study, whereas only 1 of the comparison children was included. Similar improvements in IQ, symptoms of ASD, and placement have been noted in other community-based EIBI programs as well (Sheinkopf & Siegel, 1998).

As previously noted, the Lovaas (1987) study has been criticized for including only students with a ratio IQ above 35. Given the high comorbidity of ASD and intellectual disabilities, Smith, Eikeseth, Klevstrand, and Lovaas (1997) conducted a study applying the UCLA model to children with the most severe intellectual disabilities (i.e., those who had a pretreatment ratio IQ less than 35). For up to 2 years, the experimental group received more intensive programming (i.e., 30 or more hours of one-to-one behavioral treatment), and the control group received less intensive services (i.e., 10 or fewer hours of one-to-one treatment) in the home or community. Following treatment, the experimental group showed IQ gains (from an average of 28 to 36 points) and improvements in speech (with 10 of 11 demonstrating increased verbal behavior). In contrast, the control group showed decreases in full-scale IQ (27 to 24), and only 2 of 10 students engaged in verbal behavior. Although an improvement of 8 IQ points is not as large as that noted in previous studies, the effect size was .48 (a moderately large effect) among these children with severe cognitive impairments.

An additional question raised by some of these studies is, What intensity of services is necessary for positive treatment gains to occur? One way of measuring intensity involves examining the staff-to-student ratio. It is more cost effective to have lower staff-to-student ratios. Unfortunately, the literature shows that higher staff-to-student ratios (i.e., more staff members to number of students) produces better outcomes. Using a single-subject research design, Graff, Green, and Libby (1998) were able to show that with a 1:1 ratio the student made substantial gains (e.g., reductions in problem behavior and increased functional skills), although the gains were not maintained when the ratio was lowered to one staff member to two students (1:2).

Taubman and colleagues (2001) examined the use of DTI as a group instructional procedure for children with developmental disabilities. This investigation was conducted in a preschool classroom of eight children, only two of whom were diagnosed with autism. Researchers examined DTI under several conditions: sequential (i.e., DTI randomly rotated across students), choral (i.e., all students were presented with the same discriminative stimulus), and overlapping (i.e., trials began for some students while ending for other students). Instructional tasks consisted of premathematics skills, language skills, and a group song. Treatment gains were noted in all three areas. Although Taubman and colleagues concluded that DTI can be applied in a group format within a preschool setting, it should be noted that individual data were not provided for the students with autism, limiting conclusions that can be drawn about the application of the methodology to this specific population. However, the use of a group format in this study suggests that slightly lower staff-to-student ratios may be effective in some contexts and therefore require more investigation.

The role of intensity on the efficacy of DTI has also been explored in terms of number of hours of services. Obviously, a treatment delivery model requiring fewer hours of service delivery seems more cost effective than one requiring more. Unfortunately, as noted in the studies already reviewed, the need for higher levels of treatment intensity has been demonstrated empirically. For example, the literature shows improvements in placement (Meyer et al., 2001) and IQ (Bibby et al., 2002; Harris, Handleman, Gordon, Kristoff, & Fuentes, 1991) following intensive EIBI services of approximately 40 hr per week. However, a few studies (Anderson, Avery, DiPietro, Edwards, & Christian, 1987; Luiselli, Cannon, Ellis, & Sisson, 2000) have found improvements with fewer than 25 hr per week over the course of several years.

Eldevik, Eikeseth, Jahr, and Smith (2006) also investigated the impact of treatment intensity on outcomes. Students in the experimental group received an average of 12 hr per week of EIBI programming, whereas students in the comparison group received an average of 12.5 hr per week of eclectic programming, with only a portion of treatment based on behavioral strategies. The behavioral treatment began with DTI to teach new skills and later shifted to small-group teaching to facilitate generalization of skills. After 20–21 months, the EIBI group showed better gains than the eclectic group on intellectual functioning, language comprehension, expressive communication, and adaptive skills. In addition, the EIBI group gained an average of 8 points on IQ scores, nearly 7 points on language comprehension, and 11 points on expressive language. However, the comparison group lost 2.9 points on measures of IQ, nearly 8 points on language comprehension, and more than 6 points on expressive language. Interestingly, even when levels of intensity were equal between EIBI and eclectic programs, EIBI programs produced more favorable outcomes (Howard, Sparkman, Cohen, Green, & Stanislaw, 2005).

Discrete Trial Instruction Used in Contexts
Other than Early Intensive Behavioral Intervention

Although DTI plays a central role in EIBI programs, it cannot be considered the sole cause of improvement, because additional behavioral techniques are employed in such programs. Let us turn our attention to DTI studies that are not part of EIBI programs. For instance, Wolf and colleagues (1964) provided an early example of DTI to improve vocal imitation of children with autism. Since this early investigation, a number of researchers have found support for the DTI approach to education and treatment of children with ASDs.

Lafasakis and Sturmey (2007) conducted an exploratory study of the effects of behavioral skills training on parents' ability to use DTI with their children with ASDs. Participants in the study were three 4-year-old males with developmental disabilities (including autism) and their parents. Researchers trained and assessed parents' ability to utilize DTI in a university lab setting to teach gross motor imitation skills (such as clapping hands). To assess generalization, data were collected on the parents' ability to teach vocal imitation skills (such as "ah") using DTI, but parents were not directly taught how to teach vocal imitation. Correct parent implementation of DTI components increased substantially following training, and children increased their correct responding by an average of 63% from baseline to treatment.

Additional support for the DTI methodology was provided by Naoi, Yokoyama, and Yamamoto (2007). In that study, the experimenters used DTI techniques (including echoic prompts when an appropriate response was not emitted) to teach children with ASDs to report on animated movies or pictures of preferred items. All three children learned the target response within four sessions, and all three generalized these skills. These changes were described as socially valid by independent raters.

DTI has also been shown to improve joint attention skills. Specifically, Jones, Carr, and Feeley (2006) used DTI and Pivotal Response Treatment (PRT; Chapter 12) to teach five young boys with ASDs the joint attention skills of responding (the child independently alternated his gaze between an object and an adult) and initiating (the child independently directed the adult's attention by alternating his gaze and point-ing to the object). All five participants in the study responded within 19–78 sessions and initiated within 26–157 sessions. All children generalized and maintained skills up to 10 months after treatment concluded. The participants were rated as more similar to a typically developing peer following the intervention than before the intervention (Jones et al., 2006). Jones, Feeley, and Takacs (2007) continued this line of research in their investigation of the use of DTI in teaching spontaneous communicative responses to two 3-year-old children with PDD-NOS within a center-based preschool program. The researchers used a single-participant experimental design involving multiple probes across three communicative responses, and they reported that both students mastered and used three spontaneous responses (e.g., "Bless you" when someone sneezed). In addition, both students generalized these responses across new settings and interlocutors. Because joint attention is such a foundational skill for communication and social interaction, these data suggest that DTI can be an important teaching technique.

Although most studies reported to this point have involved young children (i.e., under the age of 8), DTI has also been shown to be effective with older individuals. For example, Koegel, Dunlap, and Dyer (1980) varied the length of intertrial inter-vals for three elementary- or middle-school-age children. A broad range of skills was targeted (e.g., sequencing, object discrimination, preposition). These older children benefited from DTI most when short intertrial intervals (e.g., 1 s in length) were used. DTI has also been effectively used as a means of helping to develop self-management skills in three school-age children (ages 7, 12, and 13) who demon-strated inappropriate play behaviors with toys (Stahmer & Schreibman, 1992). DTI was used to teach them to discriminate between appropriate and inappropriate toy play behaviors. Once this skill was mastered, a self-management system was put in place so that the children independently engaged in more appropriate toy play.

PRACTICAL REQUIREMENTS

All interventions require not only a working knowledge of strategies to ensure treatment integrity but also an understanding of essential considerations regarding personnel, training, materials, and time. Behavioral programs incorporating DTI for individuals with ASDs are provided in home-, school-, or clinic-based settings. In each of these settings, there is typically a hierarchy of service providers ranging in educational levels and clinical experience. This team of individuals often includes one supervising clinician and a number of assistants who provide direct care to the individual with an ASD (i.e., direct care therapists). Clinicians supervising the behavioral program also work in a coordinated multidisciplinary manner with other professionals to identify target behaviors. For example, a clinician overseeing a home-based behavioral program for a school-age child with an ASD may work with teachers to identify target behaviors necessary for success in the school setting (e.g., sitting in a chair for several minutes) or with speech-language pathologists to identify overlapping interests (e.g., the level of articulation expected given the de-velopmental level, the extent to which skills are being demonstrated in naturalistic environments). Clinicians overseeing behavioral programs also work closely with parents and other caregivers to ensure generalization of skills.

Behavioral services provided in home- or clinic-based settings are often super-vised by a clinician with a master's or doctoral degree. The supervising clinician has experience and formal training in the field of behavior analysis (Maurice, Green, & Luce, 1996) and frequently is a board-certified behavior analyst (BCBA). The Behavior Analyst Certification Board (http://www.bacb.com) ensures a minimal level of educational attainment in specialized coursework, fulfillment of specified fieldwork, and sufficient supervision. Like many certifications, a BCBA does not ensure that the professional has adequate experience with ASDs to meet the needs of an individual client, so caregivers should inquire about the clinician's actual experience with individuals on the autism spectrum.

The supervising clinician oversees individuals implementing the teaching programs. Direct care therapists typically work several sessions per week, with each session typically lasting 2–4 hr. A senior direct-care therapist often works directly with clients but also assists in training direct care therapists, ensures that necessary materials are available, and oversees data collection and graphing of behavioral data.

The hierarchy of service providers may differ slightly for school settings versus home- or clinic-based settings. In a public school setting, there may be a resource room staffed with teachers trained to implement behavioral programs for students. In some public school districts, an outside consultant is contracted to supervise the school-based program. In all settings, behavioral programs for individuals with ASDs require close oversight by experienced clinicians.

As previously noted, home-, school-, and clinic-based behavioral programs require a team of well-trained individuals to implement the teaching programs. However, regardless of which setting is used to teach initial skills, family participation is strongly encouraged. The role of family members varies from family to family. A number of factors determine the extent to which a family participates in behavioral programming. For some families, parents and siblings act as therapists, implementing selected teaching programs. Parents and siblings may help generalize the individual's skills to the home environment. Some parents are limited in the time available because of work outside the home and other family commitments. Others find it emotionally challenging to work in a structured teaching session with their child and opt for working on generalization of skills. Clinicians often recommend that parents participate in some type of parent training to learn basic principles of operant conditioning. This training typically includes information regarding principles of reinforcement and punishment (see Table 4.1), implementation of DTI and shaping, and the importance of maintenance and generalization of skills.

The materials necessary for an effective behavioral program can vary depending on target behaviors and the developmental level of the client. Many behavioral programs have a central location for individualized behavioral data collection. Along with data, instructions for implementing teaching programs are often stored in a three-ring binder. There should be a dedicated area in which to store reinforcers, materials for leisure and play activities, and materials for teaching. Reinforcers may change from day to day or hour to hour. Therefore, it is important to maintain a wide variety of items and activities that may function as reinforcers. There is sometimes a dedicated space in which highly structured teaching occurs.

KEY COMPONENTS

To be certain that children with ASDs make meaningful progress, professionals implementing DTI and other behavioral strategies must first identify appropriate treatment goals. Also, behavior interventionists must be familiar with the four essential components of DTI— discriminative stimulus, response, consequence, and intertrial interval—if they seek to implement DTI with a high degree of treatment fidelity. However, knowing these four essential components is not enough. Good decisions must be made about a range of variants in teaching strategies. For example, should errorless learning strategies be used, or should a trial-and-error approach be adopted? How should the materials be presented to the child? How should the trials be presented? Producing the ideal improvement means the behavior interventionist will also need to plan for generalization and be familiar with other critical behavioral strategies (e.g., shaping). We explore these key components and critical decisions in this section.

Identification of Treatment Goals

Individuals with an ASDs typically present with impairments in language, communication, and social skills and with repetitive patterns of behavior. They often

---

How Many Hours of Treatment Are Required?

The length of time required for a behaviorally based intensive treatment program is a source of controversy. The best outcomes have been produced in treatment programs that provided approximately 40 hr per week for 2 or more years. However, the most common recommendation is a minimum number of 25 hr per week (National Research Council [NRC], 2001). Our recommendations are as follows:

1. Consider how great the discrepancy is between the target child's skills and those of typically developing peers.
2. Identify urgent areas where treatment can decrease the discrepancy and/or avoid a growing discrepancy. To establish urgency, consider
   a. Developmental issues (e.g., mastery of some skills is necessary before subsequent skills can be addressed, skills outside the child's developmental level should generally not be targeted)
   b. A broad range of skill domains (e.g., communication, social interaction, learning readiness, play skills, preacademic/academic skills)
3. Given the large number of domains in which multiple skills must be addressed, identify the amount of time necessary to ensure reasonable progress toward reducing the existing discrepancy. This process is likely to lead to differences in the number of hours required for individual children. However, given the large number of domains in which discrepancies typically exist, it seems that reasonable progress is not likely to occur for most children on the autism spectrum with fewer than the 25 hr recommended by the NRC. Indeed, many children will require considerably more hours per week to avoid a growing discrepancy between expected and actual developmental skills.

experience comorbid conditions (e.g., behavior problems, anxiety, depression) that must be targeted as well (American Psychiatric Association, 2000). Suggested skill domains that should be targeted can be found in Wilczynski, Menousek, Hunter, and Mudgal (2007) or in the curricular guides identified at the end of this chapter. Well-rounded behavioral programs tackle these areas of behavioral excess or impairment simultaneously, sequentially, and cyclically. As noted in the Practical Requirements section, discrepancies between expected and actual developmental skills often exist in a large number of domains for individuals with ASDs. This means that multiple domains must be addressed simultaneously.

In any given domain, however, many of the skills can be arranged in a roughly developmental trajectory and should be addressed sequentially. Skills are also addressed cyclically for several reasons. First, it is important to ensure that a skill is maintained over time, so it is often reintroduced at several later points in time. Second, to maintain sufficient motivation, mastered tasks are often introduced between unmastered tasks to maintain motivation (i.e., mastery interspersal). Third, a skill is often reintroduced when it serves as the foundation for a related but more complicated skill. For example, once a child has learned to label a cookie, the task of labeling "cookie" may serve as a prompt prior to teaching the simple conversational skill of responding to the instruction "Tell me something you like to eat."

The supervising clinician, often in conjunction with a multidisciplinary team, completes a skill assessment and considers developmental trajectories in order to make determinations about what skills should be taught simultaneously, sequentially, and cyclically. This clinician designs the teaching programs, identifies the targets within each program, and determines the frequency with which a program is implemented. The amount of time dedicated to structured programming, naturalistic teaching, and generalization is also determined by the supervising clinician.

Four Key Components of Discrete Trial Instruction

The four key components of DTI—discriminative stimulus, response, consequence, and intertrial interval—are outlined in Figure 4.1.

Although treatment targets are taught in a systematic manner through DTI, the methodology may vary considerably. When a new target is introduced, the discriminative stimulus is often presented repeatedly in the same manner until the client masters the response (e.g., 80% or 90% correct responding). Once the initial discriminative stimulus is mastered, however, variations are introduced to promote generalization. For example, a client may learn to respond to the discriminative stimulus "What is your mother's name?" Generalization may be promoted by using discriminative stimuli such as "Who is your mom?" or "What's your mom's name?" Supervising clinicians often make decisions about when to introduce variation in the discriminative stimulus (e.g., after mastery is demonstrated, as in the preceding example, or initially, to determine how structured the teaching must be to lead to mastery). Prior to each trial, the direct care therapist should know whether or not to include prompts along with the discriminative stimulus.

The therapist must often prompt the client to make the correct response. Prompting procedures are defined as any type of assistance or cueing provided to the client that results in the client's responding correctly (Leaf & McEachin, 1999;

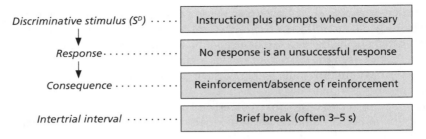

Figure 4.1. Four key components of discrete trial instruction (DTI).

Lovaas, 2002). A broad range of prompts might be used by the therapist. See Table 4.2 for a listing of types of prompts, definitions, and examples of providing and fading prompts.

For learning to occur, a DTI program, like all treatments, must be implemented with integrity. The response or target behavior to be acquired must be clearly defined by the clinician. For example, if a client is learning his or her mother's name, the response may be "Mary" or "Her name is Mary." It is important to clearly define the response so that each therapist can provide consistent feedback and teach the same behavior across trials. Defining the response can also reduce confusion and frustration for the client. The consequences of the client's response are defined in terms of how and when the therapist responds. Consequences for independent and correct responses may include positive reinforcement, whereas consequences for incorrect responses may include ignoring them, responding with a prompt, or following the behavior with a neutral "no." The intertrial interval is the time between the providing of the consequence in one trial and the initiation of the discriminative stimulus in the next trial. The intertrial interval is typically 3–5 s in duration (Ghezzi, 2007), although shorter intertrial intervals have been used very effectively (Koegel et al., 1980). Discrete trials for each teaching program are repeated multiple times over the course of a day. The number and order of presentation of the trials depends on the child's rate of skill acquisition and developmental level, the type of teaching program, and the frequency of challenging behaviors.

Teaching Variants

Errorless Learning versus Trial and Error   Although DTI is a structured teaching methodology, there are different ways to implement the trials. *Errorless learning* occurs when a therapist does not allow the client to make an error or attempts to prevent an error during the trial (e.g., Mueller, Palkovic, & Maynard, 2007). When a new response is introduced using errorless learning, the therapist provides an immediate prompt following the delivery of the discriminative stimulus to ensure that the client makes a correct response. Efforts are made to quickly fade prompts. The therapist attempts to block the incorrect response and quickly prompts for a correct response.

Errorless learning is in contrast to a number of procedures that are referred to as trial-and-error procedures. When using a trial-and-error procedure, a client's incorrect response may be followed by a neutral "no" (e.g., Ferraioli, Hughes, &

Smith, 2005; Lovaas, 2002) or by the therapist's ignoring the response, removing the materials, and presenting the trial again (e.g., Ghezzi, 2007; Smith, 2001). There is discussion in the behavioral literature as to which type of procedure, errorless learning or trial and error, may be most effective for skill acquisition programs (Smith, Mruzek, Wheat, & Hughes, 2006). It is important for clinicians to take into account the client's abilities, his or her history of responding favorably to prompt-fading procedures, and the skills targeted when considering how to implement DTI programs. No specific profile has been identified that predicts which training procedure is preferable. However, given the value of maintaining a child's motivation, errorless learning may be preferred unless a child is challenged by prompt dependency.

Presentation of Teaching Materials Another critical element in DTI programs is the manner in which targets are introduced, generalized, and maintained. The target item may be introduced in isolation (Lovaas, 1981). For example, when teaching a response to the instruction "Show me one that is *not* a fruit," a clinician might begin by repeatedly showing a picture of a truck (which is clearly not a fruit). Conversely, a target may also be introduced with "distractors" or target items for other curricular goals. In this case, the clinician might show a picture of a truck and a picture of an orange. The decision to introduce the target in isolation or with distracters is made on the basis of the initial skill assessment and ongoing evaluation of the child's ability to respond with similar tasks in the presence of distracters.

Interspersal and Varied *Trials* A decision must also be made for the timing of interspersed or *varied* trials. (When unmastered tasks are interspersed, the term *varied trials* may be used.) Interspersing trials means that the therapist presents multiple skills in a teaching session. For example, if a client has just acquired an independent response to "What is your name?" and the target response is "Bill," the therapist may intersperse targets such as "What color is my chair?" or "Where do you live?" Interspersing or intermixing trials may aide in teaching discrimination (i.e., help the client learn when to provide the target response) and ensure mastery of the targeted skill. For some clients, interspersing trials can occur from the onset of teaching, whereas for other clients, an independent response must be made before the target trials can be interspersed or varied. Once again, the child's response in the initial skills assessment is used to guide these decisions (Heflin & Alberto, 2001). For examples of massed and varied trials, see the DVD that accompanies this book.

Generalization

The strategy for planning generalization may also vary across clients. For some clients, generalization is addressed from the onset of instruction for a specific skill. For example, when addressing issues of number identification, the therapist may have the child identify the number of pencils on the desk, potato chips on his or her plate, crayons in the box, and so forth. For other clients, generalizing the response can occur only once the client is able to master the skill in isolation (massed discrete trial format). In either case, generalization may include having the client respond to different forms of the discriminative stimulus, to different interventionists, to related but different materials, and in different environments. If a response is not appropriately generalized, then it does not become a fully functional skill. Data should be used not only to ensure generalization but also to select the plan for generalization.

A skill typically enters the maintenance phase after it has been generalized. Clinicians ensure that maintenance programs are implemented on a regular schedule. That is, the targets in the program will be reviewed periodically during therapy sessions, often through mastery interspersal. The frequency of the maintenance review varies and will change over time. For example, a program may go into the maintenance phase in which the targets are reviewed first once a week, then once a month, and so forth, until the skill no longer requires systematic review.

Shaping

Each of the key elements considered so far relate to DTI, but DTI is not the only essential technique to consider in behavioral programming. As noted in the Theoretical Basis section, shaping is another operant technique used to teach clients with ASDs. Shaping occurs when an interventionist delivers reinforcers for behaviors that more closely resemble the ideal behavior than previous behaviors had. The concepts of shaping and prompting are often confused; because each is central to behavioral programming, we review the differences here.

Prompting is used when the response is already fully formed but the individual with an ASD does not know when to provide the response. For example, prompting is used when the child knows how to point to a picture but does not know which picture to point to when told to identify a specific fruit in an array of pictures of fruit. In contrast, shaping is used when the individual with an ASD has not yet learned to form the desired response correctly. For example, when teaching a child with an ASD to sign "cookie," the initial response might be to put two hands together. This response would be reinforced initially, but gradually the child would need to have a partially open hand with fingers separated and rotations occurring, as is required in the mature production of the sign, before the cookie would be provided. Shaping can be used to teach a variety of behaviors, including gross motor skills (e.g., walking with hands at one's side), fine motor skills (e.g., drawing a circle), self-care skills (e.g., wiping your mouth at mealtime), and some language behaviors. Clinicians outline the target behavior, the mastery criteria for each approximation of the target behavior, and the guidelines for implementing the program. Although these are not the only behavioral strategies used in the treatment of ASD, they are almost always included in behavioral programming.

DATA COLLECTION TO SUPPORT DECISION MAKING

Data collection is an essential component of any behavioral program for individuals with ASDs. Data are collected to monitor the frequency and/or intensity of challenging behaviors (e.g., tantrums, aggressive behavior). Behavioral interventionists regularly review data to determine whether a student is making progress and whether program changes are necessary.

Data are often, but not necessarily, collected for each discrete trial. The interventionist may record each response (trial-by-trial recording) during a teaching program or may record the first and last response. Trial-by-trial recording during a teaching program allows the clinician to monitor all aspects of skill acquisition within each session, but it may mean disrupting the natural social interactions that occur in the context of teaching. In contrast, recording the first and last response during each teaching program is an efficient way to monitor skill acquisition. For example, recording the first response allows the therapist to determine whether additional prompting is necessary. Recording the last response indicates the level of prompting the client requires for the current target and communicates to the interventionist the level of prompting necessary for the next session.

A client's responses are often recorded as correct, incorrect, or prompted. Data should be entered into an electronic spreadsheet to generate a line graph to assist in decision making. If interventionists do not look at a line graph, they are likely to ignore for too long a child's lack of success or ability to retain a mastered skill. A line graph is analyzed by evaluating trends, variability, and ranges within which the data points fall. If the overseeing clinician determines that the client is not making sufficient progress, adjustments may be made to the teaching program. For example, the clinician may change the materials being used, review the prerequisite skills necessary to produce the response, or change the type of prompting provided to the client. The process of recording, graphing, and analyzing behavioral data may seem a daunting task, but the benefits of data collection outweigh the costs.

The clinician identifies the goal or level of correct responding necessary to consider the skill or response mastered. Mastery criteria are often set at 80% or 90% (Anderson, Taras, & Cannon, 1996) correct responding over a specified number of sessions and generalized to different environments. However, reason should be applied—a goal of crossing the street successfully 80% of the time is simply inadequate.

Data collection is likely to be transformed dramatically in the next few years. A number of data collection applications have already been developed that allow a clinician to collect data electronically. These electronic data can be automatically graphed to allow for efficient decision making. However, the clinician will remain responsible for determining whether progress has been made and what treatment modifications will be necessary when sufficient progress is not being made.

CONSIDERATIONS FOR CHILDREN FROM CULTURALLY AND LINGUISTICALLY DIVERSE BACKGROUNDS

Specific information related to the treatment of ASDs in culturally diverse populations is limited, as noted by Wilder and colleagues in their 2004 review of multicultural issues related to teaching students with ASDs (Wilder, Dyches, Obiakor, & Algozzine, 2004). Not surprisingly, therefore, there is little information available about the specific use of DTI for culturally diverse populations. Nonetheless, behavioral treatments including DTI have been utilized internationally (Bernard-Opitz, Ing, & Kong, 2004; Naoi et al., 2007; Yamamoto & Mochizuki, 1988) and have resulted in consistent positive results for students with ASDs.

Several steps can be taken to increase the likelihood that DTI will be successful for learners from diverse backgrounds. One such step is to consider treatment targets within the context of the person's cultural values. For instance, communication goals should always be a part of a treatment plan for children with ASDs. However, many cultures may value communication patterns that differ from those that are common in the dominant culture (Wilder et al., 2004). Consider eye contact as an example. Eye contact is described as a prerequisite skill for the development of other communication behaviors in many DTI programs (Leaf & McEachin, 1999; Lovaas, 2002). However, in some Native American and Asian American cultures, children's avoidance of eye contact with adults is considered a sign of respect (Wilder et al., 2004). As another example, many providers would consider reduction of self-stimulation to be an appropriate target for treatment, but that behavior is largely ignored by Navajo parents of children with disabilities (Connors & Donnellan, 1998) and may very well be ignored by other cultural groups as well.

Teaching strategies may need to be modified to meet the needs of students with cultural values and experiences different from those of the dominant culture. Providers may find it helpful to supplement DTI with strategies such as instruction in English as a second language in the child's school district (Winzer & Mazurek, 1998), use of alternative communication systems such as pictures (Snell & Brown, 2006), and teaching materials in relevant languages (Baca & Cervantes, 1998). Furthermore, if visual or picture symbols are utilized as stimuli for DTI, steps should be taken to ensure that the symbols are culturally meaningful for the child as well as for individuals with whom the child interacts in the home and school settings (Trembath, Balandin, & Rossi, 2005). When addressing social skills impairments, including peer models from cultural backgrounds similar to that of the child with an ASD may help to provide appropriate role models for social skills (Wilder et al., 2004). Finally, perhaps the most important step in addressing cultural diversity concerns is to include families in planning and implementation of treatments.

ISSUES FOR APPLICATION

Researchers investigating long-term outcomes for individuals with ASDs support the conceptualization of ASDs as a lifelong condition that requires treatment and support throughout the life span (Piven, Harper, Palmer, & Arndt, 1996; Venter, Lord, & Schopler, 1992). Although the majority of research on DTI focuses on its use with young children, it is a method that can be used with all individuals with ASDs, regardless of their age or developmental level (Ghezzi, 2007). When planning DTI programming for adolescents and adults with ASDs, consideration of age and developmental level is critical. As individuals with ASDs age, treatment goals often shift away from academic concerns toward independent living skills (Marcus, Kunce, & Schopler, 2007). Because of the potential value of DTI and shaping to individuals with ASDs across the life span, we present two case studies, one involving a child named Carl and one involving a teenager named David.

Application to a Child

The following case discussion is intended to provide the reader with an example of how behavioral strategies described in this chapter may benefit Carl, a hypothetical 3-year-old male diagnosed with PDD-NOS. Despite the potential value of this very specific example, it is important to remember that behavioral intervention should be tailored to meet the unique needs and strengths of each child.

Carl experiences language impairments, limited play repertoire, repetitive movements, restricted interests, food selectivity, and self-injurious behavior. In terms of vocal communication, Carl is able to verbalize several two-word utterances, including "go car," "blue Thomas," and "nuggets please." He plays with Thomas the Tank Engine toys but typically turns the trains upside down to watch the wheels spin. Carl flaps his hands and wiggles his fingers in most environments. In addition to his interest in Thomas toys, Carl enjoys stacking and lining up various objects. His most preferred food is chicken nuggets. Carl engages in self-injurious behavior that includes hitting his head with his fist and biting his arm. An interview with Carl's mother suggests he displays self-injury to gain her attention.

Carl's parents hired a behavior analyst to develop a home-based comprehensive behavioral program. The home program consists of 30 hr a week of one-to-one teaching with graduate students trained as behavioral interventionists. The behavior analyst conducted a functional analysis (an assessment that identifies the purpose of problem behaviors), and she learned that Carl's self-injurious behavior occurred when no attention was available (e.g., when his mom was getting dinner ready). She asked the family to provide praise, pats on the back, and high-fives once every 5 min as long as Carl was not hurting himself.

In the first few weeks of treatment, Carl's parents reported an increase in Carl's eye contact and a decrease in self-injury. Behavioral data indicate that Carl is acquiring targeted skills in most specific treatment domains. Therapists have identified Thomas toys and picture books as effective reinforcers. Although family members are not teaching the specific treatment skills, Carl's parents have been trained on basic learning principles and strategies to increase generalization of skills. Carl's parents have identified similar-age relatives for play dates to target generalization of skills. Initially, Carl's parents reported an increased level of stress in their lives when interventionists started working in the home. They reported difficulty with having people in their home and were uncertain if the treatment was appropriate for their family.

At this point, Carl's parents reviewed the behavioral data with the clinician. The primary skills they have targeted to this point are 1) requesting preferred food, toys, and activities; 2) developing new play skills (e.g., using Legos to build on his interests in stacking); 3) putting hands to his sides when asked to do so; and 4) playing near other children without taking their toys. Carl's skills have increased in each of these domains. Specifically, he has reached the criterion for specific treatment targets (e.g., 90% successful performance in three out of four consecutive sessions). In addition, his self-injurious behavior has decreased to near zero levels.

After reviewing behavioral data and witnessing a change in their son, Carl's parents are more confident in their decision to pursue behavioral treatment. But this does not mean that the clinician should avoid identifying possible changes that could make the program more palatable to the family (e.g., teaching them how to embed these same tasks into everyday life, ensuring that the scheduling of staff is at times that are most convenient for the family). Furthermore, the schedule of reinforcement for not engaging in self-injury should be thinned so that Carl can learn to engage in alternate behaviors for longer periods of time without attention and so that his parent's life can become more manageable.

Application to an Adolescent or Adult

Consider the following case presentation of David. David is a 14-year-old boy who has been diagnosed with Asperger syndrome. He receives support services at school, but he is mainstreamed for all of his classes, has developed a few friendships at school, attends social events with his church group, and overall functions quite well. Currently, David is becoming more aware of the social norms for his age group and would like to "grow his hair out" to keep up with the trend for students his age. However, David's parents report that he does not routinely wash his hair, does not know how to comb his hair or apply hair care products, and becomes verbally aggressive with his parents when they attempt to help him with his hair. In addition, concern was expressed that David does not understand the sequencing of events related to caring for his hair.

A psychologist worked with David's parents to develop an intervention package that uses DTI as a treatment component. Specifically, DTI was used for the initial step of teaching David the sequence of behaviors involved in caring for his hair. David was prompted by his parents to demonstrate each step while his picture was taken. During weekly DTI sessions in the psychologist's office, a massed discrete trial procedure was used to teach David the correct sequence of behaviors, using the following steps: 1) David was presented with the five pictures that represented the sequence of steps involved in caring for his hair and was given the instruction "Put these in order." 2) The therapist utilized a most-to-least prompting strategy to ensure that David made minimal errors in sequencing. 3) David was provided with descriptive praise and encouragement for prompted correct responses. For independent correct responses, David earned tokens that he later exchanged for "time" on his MP3 player. 4) Each DTI teaching session lasted 10 min, and David was given the opportunity, after each session, to listen to his iPod for the amount of time he had earned. Using this procedure, David learned the correct sequence of behaviors within only five 10-min DTI sessions. His parents were then asked to conduct similar sessions in the home environment, and he required only two sessions with his parents to correctly sequence the steps involved in caring for his hair. Once David mastered the sequencing of steps involved in caring for his hair, treatment proceeded to teaching him how to perform each step using modeling and shaping procedures.

FUTURE DIRECTIONS

Although the research on behavioral strategies such as DTI, differential reinforcement, and shaping is impressive, the need to expand the literature continues. For instance, there are often large individual differences reported in the outcomes for children who participate in DTI. Thus, it is important to gather information regarding mediating variables. For example, individuals with different profiles (e.g., age, communication level) may require differing levels of treatment intensity, delivery of services in more structured or more naturalistic environments, or differences in how the interventionist plans for generalization. Furthermore, the extent to which these strategies are effective with individuals diagnosed with Asperger syndrome has not yet been sufficiently demonstrated.

Research on DTI and other behavioral strategies described in this chapter has generally focused on a restricted range of targets. Although improvements have been noted in social domains, these improvements have predominantly been demonstrated using paper-and-pencil adaptive or behavioral instruments. Evidence of meaningful improvements in social relationships with adults and peers would nicely supplement the existing data. Furthermore, indicators of social pragmatics have been largely absent in this literature and require further investigation.

SUGGESTED READINGS

Eikeseth, S. (2001). Recent critiques of the UCLA autism project. *Behavioral Interventions, 16,* 249–264.

Eikeseth provides a nice review of both the criticisms and the counterarguments associated with Lovaas's UCLA Young Autism Project. Because studies coming from this project hardly represent all of the studies on EIBI and DTI, it would be helpful to consider other studies in light of the prevailing arguments.

Leaf, R., & McEachin, J. (Eds.). (1999). *A work in progress: Behavior management strategies and a curriculum for intensive behavioral treatment of autism.* New York, NY: Different Roads to Learning.

This manual provides an overview of the many components required to develop comprehensive programming for young children on the autism spectrum. It addresses topics ranging from behavioral principles that apply to increasing appropriate behavior or decreasing disruptive behavior to strategies for addressing self-stimulatory, sleep, toileting, and eating problems that often interfere with acquiring new skills and participating fully in the environment. It also provides a series of procedural guidelines for teaching basic skills children need to acquire to become more independent learners.

Lovaas, O.I. (2002). *Teaching individuals with developmental delays: Basic intervention techniques.* Austin, TX: PRO-ED.

This manual provides the foundational knowledge required to begin a DTI program. It includes the basic concepts of behavior change; strategies for developing readiness, early learning, and basic expressive language skills; and the variables to consider when running a treatment program.

Sundberg, M.L. (2008). *VB-MAPP: Verbal behavior milestones assessment and placement program guide: A language and social skills assessment program for children with autism or other developmental disabilities.* Concord, CA: AVB Press.

VB-MAPP is an assessment tool that is tied to typical language development milestones. It is based on the assumption that the identification of both existing skill levels and barriers to communication development is needed to avoid developing an inappropriate curriculum.

Learning Activities

To better understand the simplicity and complexity of DTI, develop a treatment program for a hypothetical child. Consider the following questions, posed in the introduction of this chapter, as you develop your treatment program:

* How will you arrange each trial?
* Will you use prompts, and if so, what kinds of prompts will you use and how will you fade them?
* How will you structure the instructions?

- How will you identify an appropriate reinforcer for correct performance?
- Will the discrete trials involving the same skill appear sequentially (i.e., massed trials)?
- Will the trials be interspersed with mastered skills (i.e., mastery interspersal)?
- Will the trials be interspersed with other novel targets (i.e., varied trials)?
- Will you conduct discrete trials in highly structured environments, or should they occur in natural environments across a range of settings (e.g., community, school, home)?
- How will you plan for generalization?
- What kind of data will you collect?
- When will you know the intervention is not working?
- Would an errorless teaching approach be appropriate?

REFERENCES

American Psychiatric Association. (2000). *Diagnostic and statistical manual of mental disorders* (4th ed.). Washington, DC: Author.

Anderson, S.R., Avery, D.L., DiPietro, E.K., Edwards, G.L., & Christian, W.P. (1987). Intensive home-based intervention with autistic children. *Education and Treatment of Children, 10*, 352–366.

Anderson, S.R., Taras, M., & Cannon, B.D. (1996). Teaching new skills to young children with autism. In C. Maurice, G. Green, & S. Luce (Eds.), *Behavioral intervention for young children with autism: A manual for parents and professionals* (pp. 181–194). Austin, TX: PRO-ED.

Baca, L.M., & Cervantes, H.T. (1998). *The bilingual special education interface* (3rd ed.). Upper Saddle River, NJ: Prentice Hall.

Bernard-Opitz, V., Ing, S., & Kong, T.Y. (2004). Comparison of behavioural and natural play interventions for young children with autism. *Autism, 8*, 319–333.

Bibby, P., Eikeseth, S., Martin, N.T., Mudford, O.C., & Reeves, D. (2002). Progress and outcomes for children with autism receiving parent-managed intensive interventions. *Research in Developmental Disabilities, 23*, 81–104.

Birnbrauer, J.S., & Leach, D.J. (1993). The Murdoch Early Intervention Program after 2 years. *Behavior Change, 10*, 63–74.

Coe, D., Matson, J., Fee, V., Manikam, R., & Lanarello, C. (1990). Training nonverbal and verbal play skills to mentally retarded and autistic children. *Journal of Autism and Developmental Disabilities, 20*, 177–187.

Cohen, H., Amerine-Dickens, M., & Smith, T. (2006). Early intensive behavioral intervention: Replication of the UCLA model in a community setting. *Developmental and Behavioral Pediatrics, 27*, 145–155.

Connors, J.L., & Donnellan, A.M. (1998). Walk in beauty: Western perspectives on disability and Navajo family/cultural resilience. In H.I. McCubbin, E.A. Thompson, A.I. Thompson, & J.E. Fromer (Eds.), *Resiliency in Native American and immigrant families* (pp. 159–183). Thousand Oaks, CA: Sage.

Cooper, J.O., Heron, T.E., & Heward, W.L. (2007). *Applied behavior analysis* (2nd ed). Upper Saddle River, NJ: Pearson Merrill Prentice Hall.

Downs, A., Downs, R.C., Johansen, M., & Fossum, M. (2007). Using discrete trial teaching within a public preschool program to facilitate skill development in students with developmental disabilities. *Education and Treatment of Children, 30*(3), 1–27.

Downs, A., & Smith, T. (2004). Emotional understanding, cooperation, and social behavior in high-functioning children with autism. *Journal of Autism and Developmental Disorders, 14*, 625–635.

Dyer, K., Dunlap, G., & Winterling, V. (1990). Effects of choice making on the serious problem behaviors of students with severe handicaps. *Journal of Applied Behavior Analysis, 23*(4), 515–524.

Eikeseth, S. (2001). Recent critiques of the UCLA autism project. *Behavioral Interventions, 16,* 249–264.

Eldevik, S., Eikeseth, S., Jahr, E., & Smith, T. (2006). Effects of low-intensity behavioral treatment for children with autism and mental retardation. *Journal of Autism and Developmental Disabilities, 36,* 211–224.

Epstein, R., & Skinner, B. (1981). The spontaneous use of memoranda by pigeons. *Behaviour Analysis Letters, 1*(5), 241–246.

Ferster, C.B., & DeMyer, M.K. (1961). The development of performance in autistic children in an automatically controlled environment. *Journal of Chronic Diseases, 13,* 312–345.

Ferraioli, S., Hughes, C., & Smith, T. (2005). A model for problem solving in discrete trial training for children with autism. *Journal of Early Intensive Behavioral Intervention, 2,* 224–246.

Gena, A. Krantz, P.J., McClannahan, L.E., & Poulson, C.L. (1996). Training and generalization of affective behavior displayed by youth with autism. *Journal of Applied Behavior Analysis, 29*(3), 291–304.

Ghezzi, P.M. (2007). Discrete trial teaching. *Psychology in the Schools, 44,* 667–679.

Graff, R.B., Green, G., & Libby, M.E. (1998). Effects of two levels of treatment intensity on a young child with severe disabilities. *Behavioral Interventions, 13,* 21–41.

Harris, S.L., Handleman, J.S., Gordon, R., Kristoff, B., & Fuentes, F. (1991). Changes in cognitive and language functioning of preschool children with autism. *Journal of Autism and Developmental Disorders, 21,* 281–290.

Heflin, L.J., & Alberto, P.A. (2001). Establishing a behavioral context for learning for students with autism. *Focus on Autism and Other Developmental Disabilities, 16,* 93–101.

Howard, J.S., Sparkman, C.R., Cohen, H.G., Green, G., & Stanislaw, H. (2005). A comparison of intensive behavior analytic and eclectic treatments for young children with autism. *Research in Developmental Disabilities, 26,* 359–383.

Howlin, P.A. (1981). The effectiveness of operant language training with autistic children. *Journal of Autism and Developmental Disabilities, 21,* 281–290.

Iwata, B., Dorsey, M., Slifer, K., Bauman, K., & Richman, G. (1982). Toward a functional analysis of self-injury. *Journal of Applied Behavior Analysis, 27*(2), 197–209.

Jones, E.A., Carr, E.G., & Feeley, K.M. (2006). Multiple effects of joint attention interventions for children with autism. *Behavior Modification, 30,* 782–834.

Jones, E.A., Feeley, K.M., & Takacs, J. (2007). Teaching spontaneous responses to young children with autism. *Journal of Applied Behavior Analysis, 40,* 565–570.

Karsten, A.M., & Carr, J.E. (2009). The effects of differential reinforcement of unprompted responding on the skill acquisition of children with autism. *Journal of Applied Behavior Analysis, 42,* 327–334.

Koegel, R.L., Dunlap, G., & Dyer, K. (1980). Inter-trial interval duration and learning in autistic children. *Journal of Applied Behavior Analysis, 13*(1), 91–99.

Lafasakis, M., & Sturmey, P. (2007). Training parent implementation of discrete-trial teaching: Effects on generalization of parent teaching and child correct responding. *Journal of Applied Behavior Analysis, 40,* 685–689.

Leaf, R., & McEachin, J. (Eds.). (1999). A work in progress: *Behavior management strategies and a curriculum for intensive behavioral treatment of autism.* New York, NY: Different Roads to Learning.

LeGray, M.W., Dufrene, B.A., Sterling-Turner, H., Olmi, J.D., & Bellone, K. (2010). A comparison of function-based differential reinforcement interventions for children engaging in disruptive classroom behavior. *Journal of Behavioral Education, 19,* 185–204.

Lovaas, O.I. (1981). *Teaching developmentally disabled children: The ME book.* Baltimore, MD: University Park Press.

Lovaas, O.I. (1987). Behavioral treatment and normal educational and intellectual functioning in young autistic children. *Journal of Consulting and Clinical Psychology, 55,* 3–9.

Lovaas, O.I. (2002). *Teaching individuals with developmental delays: Basic intervention techniques.* Austin, TX: PRO-ED.

Lovaas O.I., & Smith, T. (1989). A comprehensive behavioral theory of autistic children. *Journal of Behavioral Therapy and Experimental Psychiatry, 20,* 17–29.

Luiselli, J.K., Cannon, B.O., Ellis, J.T., & Sisson, R.W. (2000). Home-based behavioral intervention for young children with autism/pervasive developmental disorder. *Autism, 4,* 426–438.

76 Wilczynski et al.

Magiati, I., & Howlin, P. (2001). Monitoring the progress of preschool children with autism enrolled in early intervention programmes: Problems of cognitive assessment. *Autism, 5,* 399–406.

Marcus, L.M., Kunce, L.J., & Schopler, E. (2007). Working with families. In F.R. Volkmar, R. Paul, A. Klin, & D. Cohen (Eds.), *Autism and pervasive developmental disorder* (Vol. 2, pp. 1055–1079). Hoboken, NJ: Wiley.

Matson, J.L., Matson, M.L., & Rivet, T.T. (2007). Social-skills treatments for children with autism spectrum disorders: An overview. *Behavior Modification, 31*(5), 682–707.

Maurice, C., Green, G., & Luce, S. (1996). *Behavioral intervention for young children with autism.* Austin, TX: PRO-ED.

McEachin, J.J., Smith, T., & Lovaas, O. (1993). Long-term outcome for children with autism who received early intensive behavioral treatment. *American Journal on Mental Retardation, 97*(4), 359–372.

Mesibov, G.B. (1993). Treatment is encouraging. *American Journal on Mental Retardation, 97,* 359–372.

Meyer, L.S., Taylor, B.A., Levin, L., & Fisher, J.R. (2001). Alpine Learning Group. In J.S. Handleman & S.L. Harris (Eds.), *Preschool education programs for children with autism* (2nd ed., pp. 135–155). Austin, TX: PRO-ED.

Michael, J. (2007). Editorial. *Analysis of Verbal Behavior, 23,* 1–2.

Mueller, M., Palkovic, C.M., & Maynard, C.S. (2007). Errorless learning: Review and practical application for teaching children with pervasive developmental disorders. *Psychology in the Schools, 44*(7), 691–700.

Naoi, N., Yokoyama, K., & Yamamoto, J. (2007). Intervention for tact as reporting in children with autism. *Research in Autism Spectrum Disorders, 1,* 174–184.

National Research Council (2001). *Educating children with autism.* Washington, DC: National Academy Press.

Newman, B., Reinecke, D., & Ramos, M. (2009). Is a reasonable attempt reasonable? Shaping versus reinforcing verbal attempts of preschoolers with autism. *Analysis of Verbal Behavior, 25,* 67–72.

Nuzzolo-Gomez, R., Leonard, M.A., Ortiz, E., Rivera, C.M., & Greer, R.D. (2002). Teaching children with autism to prefer books or toys over stereotypy or passivity. *Journal of Positive Behavior Interventions, 6,* 60–67.

Partington, J.W. (2006). *The assessment of basic language and learning skills: An assessment, curriculum guide, and skills tracking system for children with autism or other developmental disabilities. ABLLS-R protocol.* Pleasant Hill, CA: Behavior Analysts.

Piven, J., Harper, J., Palmer, P., & Arndt, S. (1996). Course of behavioral change in autism: A retrospective study of high IQ adolescents and adults. *Journal of the American Academy of Child and Adolescent Psychiatry, 35,* 523–529.

Reed, P., Osborne, L.A., & Corness, M. (2007). The real-world effectiveness of early teaching interventions for children with autism spectrum disorders. *Exceptional Children, 73,* 417–433.

Rocha, M.L., Schreibman, L., & Stahmer, A.C. (2007). Effectiveness of training parents to teach joint attention to children with autism. *Journal of Early Intervention 29*(2), 154–172.

Sallows, G.O, & Graupner, T. (2005). Intensive behavioral treatment for children with autism: Four-year outcome and predictors. *American Journal on Mental Retardation, 110,* 417–438.

Sheinkopf, S.J., & Siegel, B. (1998). Home-based behavioral treatment of young children with autism. *Journal of Autism and Developmental Disorders, 28,* 15–23.

Skinner, B.F. (1938). *The behavior of organisms: An experimental analysis.* New York, NY: Appleton-Century.

Skinner, B.F. (1957). *Verbal behavior.* New York, NY: Free Press.

Smith, T. (2001). Discrete trial training in the treatment of autism. *Focus on Autism and Other Developmental Disabilities, 16,* 86–92.

Smith, T., Eikeseth, S., Klevstrand, M., & Lovaas, O. I. (1997). Intensive behavioral treatment for preschoolers with severe mental retardation and pervasive developmental disorder. *American Journal on Mental Retardation, 102,* 238–249.

Smith, T., Groen, A.D., & Wynn, J.W. (2000). Randomized trial of intensive early intervention for children with pervasive developmental disorder. *American Journal of Mental Retardation, 105,* 269–285.

Smith, T., Klevstrand, M., & Lovaas, O.I. (1995). Behavioral treatment of Rett's disorder: Ineffectiveness in three cases. *American Journal of Mental Deficiency, 100*(3), 317–322.

Smith, T., & Lovaas, O.I. (1997). The UCLA Young Autism Project: A reply to Gresham and McMillan. *Behavioral Disorders, 22,* 202–218.

Smith, T., Mruzek, D.W., Wheat, L.A., & Hughes, C. (2006). Error correction in discrimination training for children with autism. *Behavioral Interventions, 21,* 245–264.

Snell, M.E., & Brown, F. (2006). *Instruction of students with severe disabilities* (6th ed.). Upper Saddle River, NJ: Prentice-Hall.

Stahmer, A.C., & Schreibman, L. (1992). Teaching children with autism appropriate play in unsupervised environments using a self-management treatment package. *Journal of Applied Behavior Analysis, 25*(2), 447–459.

Summers, J., & Szatmari, P. (2009). Using discrete trial teaching to teach children with Angelman syndrome. *Focus on Autism and Other Developmental Disabilities, 24*(4), 216–226.

Sundberg, M.L. (2008). *VB-MAPP: Verbal behavior milestones assessment and placement program guide. A language and social skills assessment program for children with autism or other developmental disabilities.* Concord, CA: AVB Press.

Sundberg, M.L., & Michael, J.L. (2001). The benefits of Skinner's analysis of verbal behavior for children with autism. *Behavior Modification, 25,* 698–724.

Sundberg, M.L., & Partington, J.W. (1998). *Teaching language to children with autism or other developmental disabilities.* Danville, CA: Behavior Analysts.

Sundberg, M.L., & Partington, J.W. (1999). The need for both discrete trial and natural environment language training for children with autism. In P.M. Ghezzi, W.L. Williams, & J.E. Carr (Eds.), *Autism: Behavior analytic perspectives* (pp. 139–156). Reno, NV: Context Press.

Taubman, M., Brierley, S., Wishner, J., Baker, D., McEachin, J., & Leaf, R.B. (2001). The effectiveness of a group discrete trial instructional approach for preschoolers with developmental disabilities. *Research in Developmental Disabilities, 22,* 205–219.

Trembath, D., Balandin, S., & Rossi, C. (2005). Cross-cultural practice and autism. *Journal of Intellectual and Developmental Disabilities, 30,* 240–242.

Venter, A., Lord, C., & Schopler, E. (1992). A follow-up study of high-functioning autistic children. *Journal of Child Psychology and Psychiatry, 33,* 489–507.

Watanabe, M., Yamamoto, J., & Kobayashi, S. (1990). Teaching survival skills (shopping) to children with developmental disabilities: Task analysis and shaping techniques. *Japanese Journal of Special Education, 28,* 21–31.

Whalen, C., & Schreibman, L. (2003). Joint attention training for children with autism using behavior modification procedures. *Journal of Child Psychology and Psychiatry and Allied Disciplines, 44*(3), 456–468.

Wilczynski, S.M., Menousek, K., Hunter, M., & Mudgal, D. (2007). Individualized education programs for youth with autism spectrum disorders. *Psychology in the Schools, 44*(7), 653–666.

Wilder, L.K., Dyches, T.T., Obiakor, F.E., & Algozzine, B. (2004). Multicultural perspectives on teaching students with autism. *Focus on Autism and Other Developmental Disabilities, 19,* 105–113.

Winterling, V.M., Dunlap, G., & O'Neill, R.E. (1987). The influence of task variation on the aberrant behaviors of autistic students. *Education and Treatment of Children, 10*(2), 105–119.

Winzer, M.A., & Mazurek, K. (1998). *Special education in multicultural contexts.* Upper Saddle River, NJ: Prentice Hall.

Wolf, M.M., Risley, T., & Mees, H. (1964). Application of operant conditioning procedures to the behavior problems of an autistic child. *Behavior Research and Therapy, 1,* 305–312.

Yamamoto, J., & Mochizuki, A. (1988). Acquisition and functional analysis of manding with autistic students. *Journal of Applied Behavior Analysis, (21),* 57–64.

5

An Introduction to the Developmental, Individual-Difference, Relationship-Based (DIR) Model and Its Application to Children with Autism Spectrum Disorder

Sima Gerber

In their book *The Child with Special Needs,* Stanley Greenspan, a child psychiatrist, and Serena Wieder, a child psychologist, introduced the **Developmental, Individual-Difference, Relationship-Based (DIR®) Model** to the world of child development (Greenspan & Wieder, 1998). This model presents a unique comprehensive developmental approach to assessment and intervention for children with developmental disorders, particularly those with autism spectrum disorders (ASDs). This approach is rooted in theoretical foundations and empirical research from child development, neuroscience, ASDs, and early intervention. The DIR Model is distinguished from many other contemporary approaches by its scope and its integration of developmental, interpersonal, biological, and contextual components into the assessment and intervention process.

Three components are addressed in the DIR paradigm: the child's functional emotional developmental level, the child's **individual processing profile,** and the relationship between the child and his or her caregivers. The model reflects the breadth of child and interpersonal development and the complexity of addressing the challenges faced by children and their families when development is derailed.

Educators and clinicians who embrace the DIR Model adopt the view that a number of areas of development are often affected in children with challenges and that developmental problems in one domain (e.g., sensory processing) can significantly impact others (e.g., social interaction), all of which affect the family's life and dynamics.

COMPONENTS OF THE MODEL

A primary goal of the DIR practitioner is to develop a profile of the child and his or her family based on the three major components of the model: the "D," the functional emotional *developmental* levels, which encompass the child's social-emotional-symbolic development (see Table 5.1); the "I," the profile of *individual* differences in sensory, motor, and language abilities (see Table 5.2); and the "R," the caregiver–child *relationships*.

The central innovation and foundation of the DIR approach is its attention to the **functional emotional developmental levels (FEDLs)** that characterize typical development in the early years of life (described later in the chapter).

> The functional emotional developmental approach provides a way of characterizing emotional *functioning* and, at the same time, a way of looking at how all the components of development (cognition, language, and motor skills) work together (as a mental team) organized by the designated emotional goals. In this model, therefore, emotional capacities serve as the orchestra leader that enables all the developmental components to work together in a *functional* manner. (Greenspan, De Gangi, & Wieder, 2001, p. xiii)

The FEDLs are shared attention and **regulation,** engagement and relating, two-way intentional communication, complex problem solving, creative representations and elaboration, and representational differentiation and emotional thinking (see Table 5.1). An understanding of the child's FEDLs anchors the DIR assessment and intervention for the clinician, educator, and parents. The goal of the interven-

Table 5.1. Functional emotional developmental levels and ages at which these levels are achieved in children with typical development

Level	Age	Emotional abilities
1. Shared attention and regulation	Birth–3 months	The child can attend to multisensory affective experience and at the same time organize a calm, regulated state (e.g., looking at, listening to, and following the movement of a caregiver).
2. Engagement and relating	2–6 months	The child can engage with and evidence affective preference and pleasure for a caregiver or caregivers (e.g., showing joyful smiles and affection with a caregiver).
3. Two-way intentional communication	4–9 months	The child can initiate and respond to two-way presymbolic gestural communication (e.g., engaging in the back-and-forth use of smiles and vocalizations).
4. Complex problem solving	9–18 months	The child can organize chains of two-way social problem-solving communications (opening and closing many circles of communication), maintain communication across space, integrate affective polarities, and synthesize an emerging prerepresentational organization of self and others (e.g., taking Dad by the hand to get a toy on the shelf).
5. Creative representations (ideas) and elaboration	18–30 months	The child can create and functionally use ideas as a basis for creative or imaginative thinking and for giving meaning to symbols (e.g., engaging in pretend play, using words).
6. Representational differentiation and emotional thinking	30–48 months	The child can build bridges between ideas as a basis for logic, reality testing, thinking, and judgment. The child can elaborate in both make-believe and dialogues and can plan "how, what, and why," elaborations that give depth to the make-believe dramas or reality-based dialogues (e.g., engaging in opinion-oriented conversations and elaborate planned pretend dramas).

Sources: Greenspan (2004); Greenspan and Wieder (1998).

tion is to facilitate development at and above the child's FEDLs within the context of the child's individual processing profile (sensory modulation, sensory processing, sensory-affective processing, motor planning and sequencing; see Table 5.2). For example, some children will be able to achieve their highest level of social-emotional engagement while they are moving on a swing, whereas others will be most interactive when motor-planning demands are minimal. In addition, parent–child interaction patterns are central to the DIR Model, theoretically and clinically. In fact, guiding the parents' understanding of how best to help the child move to higher FEDLs in light of his or her individual processing patterns becomes a primary goal of the DIR clinician or educator.

CHILDREN SERVED BY THE MODEL

Although DIR is often identified with the assessment of and intervention for children on the autism spectrum, a range of children with developmental disabilities can benefit from the integrated perspective on development inherent in the model, including children with sensory-processing and regulatory disorders, language delays and disorders, cognitive delays, and attachment disorders. Because of the broad age span across which emotional development occurs, and because children with developmental delays are often functioning at earlier developmental levels, the approach is appropriate for infants, toddlers, young children, school-age children, and adolescents. Similarly, children at all stages of language and communication can be treated using this paradigm. The choice of this approach over others has more to do with the practitioner's view of human development and developmental difficulties than with the relevance of the approach for particular etiological categories or developmental language levels.

SERVICE DELIVERY MODEL AND METHODS

The service delivery model is as broad as the theoretical-clinical framework. Therefore, a home program that incorporates the goals and strategies developed by the DIR team, a school program, specific therapies, biomedical intervention, and family support via counseling are all incorporated into the intervention plan. The team working with the child will include professionals from many disciplines who are asked to collaborate closely to ensure that the child's program is an integrated one.

The term *DIR* is often mistakenly used interchangeably with the term *Floortime*. Whereas DIR is the comprehensive model of assessment and interven-

Table 5.2. Elements of the individual processing profile

Sensory modulation, including hypoactivity and hyperactivity in each sensory modality (e.g., touch, sound, smell, vision, movement in space)

Sensory processing, including the capacity to register, decode, and comprehend sequences and abstract patterns in each sensory modality (e.g., auditory processing, visual-spatial processing)

Sensory-affective processing, including the ability to process and react to affect in each modality and the capacity to connect intent or affect to motor planning and sequencing, language, and symbols

Motor planning and sequencing, including the capacity to sequence actions, behaviors, and symbols, such as thoughts, words, visual images, and spatial concepts

Source: Interdisciplinary Council on Developmental and Learning Disorders (2005).

tion just described, **Floortime** is a therapeutic strategy that is specific to the DIR approach. Floortime describes the spontaneous, developmentally appropriate, often one-to-one interactions during which the six FEDLs are mobilized.

Although spontaneous interactions are the hallmark of the DIR approach, semistructured and structured learning activities are also included in each child's program. The use of these alternatives depends on the child's developmental capacities, the priorities for intervention, the contexts of learning in which the child is engaged, and the child's processing profile.

The intervention strategies of DIR can be adapted to the various learning environments that the child experiences throughout his or her day, such as dyadic, small-group, and large-group interactions. In the child's school program, individual spontaneous interactions will be supplemented with semistructured problem-solving interactions. However, even within these more structured interactions, Floortime principles, such as prioritizing the child's intentions and ideas, using supportive rather than directive teaching, and addressing the child's individual sensory processing needs, must be central to the educational approach.

TARGET POPULATIONS AND ASSESSMENTS FOR DETERMINING TREATMENT RELEVANCE AND GOALS

The populations of children most frequently treated with this approach are children with ASDs, pervasive developmental disorder-not otherwise specified (PDD-NOS), and Asperger syndrome. Nonetheless, as previously mentioned, the DIR approach can be used as a model of assessment for any child experiencing developmental delays and disorders, regardless of the child's diagnosis, chronological age, or functioning level.

Based on a DIR assessment (described below), children are described as functioning within one of four types of **neurodevelopmental disorders of relating and communicating** that are set forth in the Interdisciplinary Council on Developmental and Learning Disorders' *Diagnostic Manual for Infancy and Early Childhood (ICDL-DMIC;* ICDL, 2005). The four types (see Table 5.3) refer to levels of functioning within and across developmental domains and individual differences. The range includes the less challenged child, who shows intermittent capacities for relating, reciprocity, and shared problem solving, as well as the more challenged child, who shows fleeting capacities for engagement and reciprocity and may experience multiple regressions.

Because of its comprehensive nature, the DIR functional developmental evaluation involves an interdisciplinary team of professionals, including a physician, a mental health professional, a speech-language pathologist (SLP), an occupational therapist, and an educator. The DIR assessment paradigm consists of the three key components previously mentioned: the FEDLs, the individual differences profile, and the caregiver–child relationships. Each of these is described in the remainder of this section.

Determining where the child is relative to the FEDLs is the hallmark of the assessment. Assessment tools such as the Functional Emotional Assessment Scales (Greenspan et al., 2001) and Social-Emotional Growth Charts (Greenspan, 2004) can be used to determine the child's FEDL. Although, as in all developmental assessments, chronological ages are associated with each level, in DIR a composite of

Table 5.3. Neurodevelopmental disorders of relating and communicating

Type I—Early symbolic with constrictions
Children in this group show intermittent capacities for attending, relating, reciprocal interactions, shared social problem-solving (with support), and the beginning use of meaningful ideas. Children in this group typically show rapid progress.
Type II—Purposeful problem-solving with constrictions
Children in this group show intermittent capacities for attention, relating, and a few back-and-forth reciprocal interactions, with only fleeting capacities for shared social problem-solving and imitation of words. Children in this group tend to make steady progress.
Type III—Intermittently engaged and purposeful
Children in this group show fleeting capacities for attention and engagement and can engage in a few back-and-forth reciprocal interactions (with considerable support). Often, the children in this group have no capacity for using words and ideas, although they may be able to repeat a few words in a memory-based manner. Children with this pattern often make slow but steady progress.
Type IV—Aimless and not purposeful
Children in this group are similar to children in Type III but with a pattern of multiple regressions. These children may also evidence a greater number of neurological challenges, such as seizures. Children with this pattern often make very slow progress.

Source: Interdisciplinary Council on Developmental and Learning Disorders (2005).

the child's strengths and challenges rather than age is used to determine functioning level and intervention targets. The levels are as follows (see Table 5.1 for a more detailed description of each level):

1. Shared attention and regulation (birth through 3 months)
2. Engagement and relating (2–6 months)
3. Two-way intentional communication (4–9 months)
4. Complex problem solving (9–18 months)
5. Creative representations (ideas) and elaboration (18–30 months)
6. Representational differentiation and emotional thinking (30–48 months)

For many children on the autism spectrum, intervention will focus on the early levels of development, because those levels build the foundations for greater emotional, social, cognitive, and language abilities.

The second component of the DIR Model, assessment of the child's individual processing, is critical to determining the goals for intervention as well as the optimal learning contexts for the child. For example, if the child needs to be moving to know where he or she is in space, the SLP would not expect the child to sit at a table when engaging in activities. Greater understanding of such individual differences underscores how the interdisciplinary orientation of the DIR Model impacts all aspects of the child's therapeutic and educational experience. The four areas of individual processing assessed in the DIR Model are sensory modulation, sensory processing, sensory-affective processing, and motor planning and sequencing (see Table 5.2).

The third component of the DIR Model, a description of caregiver–child interactions and family patterns, also is integral to the assessment paradigm and to the intervention. The child is observed while interacting with his or her parent in order to help the clinician understand what patterns are typical of the dyad—for example, whether the parent is more or less directive in his or her interactions with the child, how well the parent is doing reading the child's cues and signals, and whether the parent is finding the appropriate level of stimulation to support engagement. Once these patterns are identified, the parent is guided in understanding the child's developmental stage; how the child's individual differences are impacting his or her ability to learn, engage, and function in the world; and how best to modify their interactive styles to enhance development.

The following outline delineates the steps of a DIR assessment, some of which will be specific to the individual child's and family's needs (ICDL, 2005):

1. Prenatal and developmental history
2. Two or more observational sessions of child–caregiver interactions to develop hypotheses about
   - The child's functional emotional developmental levels
   - The individual processing profile
   - Caregiver interactions and family patterns
3. Evaluation of motor and regulatory-sensory processing, including
   - Sensory modulation
   - Sensory processing
   - Sensory-affective processing
   - Motor planning and sequencing
4. Biomedical evaluations (e.g., nutritional needs, pharmacological interventions, environmental interventions to reduce exposure to allergens in the home)
5. Speech and language evaluation
6. Evaluation of cognitive functions, including neuropsychological and educational assessments
7. Mental health evaluations of family members, family patterns, and family needs

The **Functional Emotional Assessment Scale** (FEAS; Greenspan et al., 2001) is considered the primary assessment tool in the DIR process. The FEAS is used to determine the child's FEDLs as well as the nature of the interactions between the child and his or her caregivers. This determination leads, in turn, to creating a treatment plan based on the child's individual profile and provides a baseline for measuring his or her progress.

Professionals working within a DIR approach will use, in addition to the FEAS, the *ICDL-DMIC* (ICDL, 2005) as a guide for assessing functioning in a range of developmental areas. Each section of the diagnostic manual is intended for several audiences. For example, SLPs will base their assessment in part on the manual's section on language acquisition and language disorders, whereas non-SLPs will read that section to get an overview of typical preschool speech and language development. The DIR professional is obliged to understand many areas of development, and the *ICDL-DMIC* provides an orientation to all disciplines.

THEORETICAL BASIS

The DIR Model is based on an interdisciplinary developmental model that integrates information from cognitive, language, social, emotional, sensory, motor, and interpersonal paradigms of development. Like cognitive and social interaction models of language acquisition (Bates, 1975; Bloom & Lahey, 1978; Bloom & Tinker, 2001; Piaget, 1955), the DIR Model prioritizes the role of the child's stage of development and recognizes the parent–child interaction as key to understanding the developmental process. Unlike these models, DIR considers the child's emotional experiences as foundational, with emotional exchanges leading to symbol formation and intelligence.

In addressing the question of how we learn to think and use symbols, Greenspan and Shanker (2004) proposed that the capacity of humans to exchange emotional signals with each other, which begins early in life, leads to symbols, abstract thinking, language, and a variety of complex emotional and social skills that enable social groups to function. Research (Seigel, 1999; Tronick, 2007) has suggested that the development of specific areas of the brain may be significantly affected by these exchanges of emotional signals. The areas most likely affected include the higher cortical centers dealing with language and thinking, the prefrontal cortex dealing with planning and problem solving, and the integrating pathways that connect subsymbolic systems, which process basic emotions such as fear and anxiety, with cortical symbolic capacities.

> Through their progressive transformations, emotions[,] which can be experienced in an almost infinite number of subtle variations, can organize and give meaning to experience. They can therefore serve as the architect or orchestra leader for the mind's many functions. At each stage in the pathway to intelligence, emotions orchestrate cognitive, language, motor, sensory, and social experience. (Greenspan & Shanker, 2004, p. 51)

Greenspan and Shanker (2004) further suggested that through the interactive experiences between the child and his or her caregivers, emotions, which are first experienced in the baby's physiologic-sensory system, become the vehicles of interpersonal and intrapersonal development.

Underlying Assumptions

The assumptions of the DIR Model address the nature of typical and atypical development; the role of affect in the development of relating, thinking, and communicating; the role of the parent–child interaction; and the nature of assessment and intervention. More specifically, the assumptions are as follows:

1. Early typical development can be described in terms of six levels of functional emotional development and the child's individual processing profile.
2. The emotional signaling and interaction that occurs between the baby and his or her caregiver paves the way for functional developmental capacities.
3. Impairments in the child's functional emotional development may be related to the child's individual processing profile.
4. Disruptions in the development of the functional emotional levels lead to the increased occurrence of developmental disorders.
5. Affect (emotion) is the anchor in the development of thinking, relating, and communicating.
6. Assessment involves a broad range of observations by professionals from different disciplines who can assess the child's capacities in functional emotional development, individual processing patterns, and caregiver–child interactions.

7.   Intervention involves an interdisciplinary program that serves to move the child through the functional emotional levels, address the child's individual processing needs therapeutically and biomedically, coach parent interactions, and develop home and school programs.

Functional Outcomes

Because the DIR Model is interdisciplinary, the target areas encompass all of the developmental domains of early childhood, such as affective, social, cognitive, language, sensory, and motor domains. The priority of intervention is to facilitate the child's capacity to move from shared attention to engagement, to two-way communication, to complex problem solving, to the use of symbols and ideas, and finally, to building logical connections between symbols and ideas. Intervention outcomes are measured by assessing the child's stage of development throughout the treatment process.

Professionals from different disciplines working within a DIR Model will have, in addition to the FEDLs and individual processing targets, functional outcomes based on models from their own disciplines. For example, the language paradigm of the *ICDL-DMIC* (ICDL, 2005) includes an assessment that leads to determining intervention targets in speech, language, and communication. The *Affect-Based Language Curriculum* (Lewis & Greenspan, 2005), based on a somewhat different conceptualization of language development and intervention than that presented here, was developed to serve as a more structured adjunct to DIR intervention, providing parents with a detailed list of speech and language goals to be addressed using a combination of Floortime and semistructured interactions.

Language Focus and Conceptualization

Development of the Language Paradigm of the DIR Model

Speech, language, and communication constitute one of the many developmental areas that are considered in the DIR Model. In an effort to more fully describe the language acquisition process and to provide an assessment and intervention protocol consistent with the most contemporary thinking about typical language acquisition and with the interdisciplinary broad thinking of the DIR Model, a task force of clinicians (Cawn et al., 2005) developed a paradigm that provides a perspective on typical and atypical development (ICDL, 2005). This paradigm reflects a reexamination of the developmental areas that are frequently impaired in children on the autism spectrum and offers a complementary approach to existing protocols and language assessments. The framework is distinguished from other similar conceptualizations by its connection to the DIR Model and its emphasis on particular developmental **modalities,** such as shared attention and affective engagement, that are typically not addressed in more traditional speech and language assessments.

The Developmental Language Levels   Subsequent to the review and organization of information from the research literature on typical language acquisition, six levels of speech, language, and communication development were outlined by the task force. Chronological ages corresponding to each language level were noted, but in practice, the description of any particular child depends on the composite of his or her developmental profile across the modalities, regardless of the child's age. The descriptors of the early language levels are similar to those of the FEDLs, although the language paradigm was developed independently. The similarity in perspectives on the fundamental capacities typical of early development accounts for the overlap in terminology. The six developmental language levels described in the *ICDL-DMIC* (2005) are as follows:

1.   Self-regulation and interest in the world (birth though 3 months)
2.   Forming relationships and affective vocal synchrony (2–7 months)
3.   Intentional two-way communication (8–12 months)
4.   First words: sharing meaning in gestures and words (12–18 months)
5.   Word combinations: sharing experiences symbolically (18–24 months)
6.   Early discourse: reciprocal symbolic interactions with others (24–36 months)

The Modalities   At each language level, development that is typical of selected modalities is considered. Each of these modalities represents an aspect of development that is considered central to the process of acquiring language and to being a successful communicator. The behaviors noted at each of the language levels provide the basis for what will be addressed during assessment and intervention. The modalities are as follows:

Shared attention

Affective engagement

Reciprocity

Shared intentions

Shared forms and meanings

Emerging discourse

Sensory processing and audition

Motor planning

An example of the format of the language paradigm for Language Level 2, Forming relationships and affective vocal synchrony, can be found in Table 5.4. Selected behaviors for each of the modalities are listed. By observing the child during natural interactions with a caregiver, the clinician determines whether the child is demonstrating each behavior (e.g., uses eye gaze with gestures and sounds to coordinate attention; tunes into the affective state of others using smiles, frowns, etc.; vocalizations become part of two-way affective exchanges). Those behaviors that have not yet been achieved would become goals for language intervention.

Use of the Language Paradigm

The use of this paradigm involves determining the level at which the child is functioning in each of the modalities. The primary context for assessment is observation of the child during interactions with his or her caregiver and/or clinician. The analysis is clearly a qualitative rather than a quantitative one. The goal is to generate a dynamic description of the child's capacities at each level in each modality, which will then allow the clinician to identify intervention goals for the comprehension and production of language. When using this paradigm, the clinician must be flexible in determining goals, because observation may show the child to be at different levels depending on the modality. For children who are at the higher levels of the

Table 5.4.   Language Level 2: Forming relationships and affective vocal synchrony (2–7 months)

Shared attention
Uses eye gaze with gestures and sounds to coordinate attention
Shifts gaze between people and objects

Affective engagement
Tunes into the affect state of others using affect cues (smiles, frowns, etc.)
Participates in affective exchanges with caregiver

Reciprocity
Includes vocalizations as components of two-way affective exchanges
Initiates interaction with others using early gestures (reaching), babbling, or cooing

Shared intentions
Responds to other's intentions to regulate behavior and turns to caregiver for comfort
Begins to respond to other's intentions to draw attention to objects

Shared forms and meanings
Discriminates affect state of caregiver
Vocalizes pleasure and displeasure
Varies volume and pitch of vocalizations

Sensory processing and audition
Localizes sounds from farther away
Engages caregiver across space
Is comforted by some sounds, distressed by others

Motor planning
Participates with caregiver in rhythmic movement through touch, looking, listening
Initiates gestures, such as beginning to reach, grab, lift arms up, to indicate communicative intentions

Source: Interdisciplinary Council on Developmental and Learning Disorders (2005).

paradigm, additional assessment through language sampling (Lahey, 1988) and formal testing would be necessary to complete the child's profile of strengths and impairments in speech, language, and communication.

It should be noted that several existing speech-language-communication assessments and interventions target similar areas of language and communication development. These include the Communication and Symbolic Behavior Scales™ (CSBS™; Wetherby & Prizant, 2002), the SCERTS® (Social Communication, Emotional Regulation, and Transactional Supports) Model (Prizant, Wetherby, Rubin, Laurent, & Rydell, 2006), and parent training programs such as *More Than Words* (Sussman, 1999), *Communicating Partners* (MacDonald, 2004), and *Responsivity Teaching* (Mahoney & Perales, 2005). Clearly, the programs mentioned here are more fully developed and comprehensive than the *ICDL-DMIC* (ICDL, 2005), which is not a standardized clinical tool. Nonetheless, the consideration of modalities such as shared attention, affective engagement, and reciprocity not only bridges the language paradigm to the DIR early functional emotional levels but also provides the practitioner with a way to operationalize the origins of language development. Further, the language paradigm of the *ICDL-DMIC* points out that even when a child is verbal, he or she may still be working to achieve the basic foundations of language.

EMPIRICAL BASIS

Several studies and reviews support the DIR approach to working with children with developmental impairments. The first study that provided evidence for the DIR/Floortime model was a retrospective chart review of 200 children (Greenspan

& Wieder, 1997). The children, who ranged in age from 22 months to 4 years at the time of diagnosis, 1) met the criteria for autism or PDD-NOS as described in the American Psychiatric Association's *Diagnostic and Statistical Manual of Mental Disorders* (3rd ed., rev., and 4th ed., American Psychiatric Association, 1987, 1994); 2) scored in the autistic range on the Childhood Autism Rating Scale (CARS; Schopler, Reichler, & Rochen-Renner, 1988), with scores ranging from 30 to 52; and 3) participated in evaluations and interventions for 2 or more years. The children had received at least 2 years of a DIR approach to intervention and were followed over a period of 8 years. The results suggested that after 2 years of intervention using the DIR approach, 58% of the children were described as being in the "good to outstanding" outcome group based on their ability to relate, affectively engage with others, participate in circles of spontaneous verbal communication, and so forth. The children in this outcome group shifted into the non-autistic range on the CARS.

In 2005, Wieder and Greenspan published a 10- to 15-year follow-up study of 16 boys with ASDs who had shown significant improvements in the original group. Their mean age at follow-up was 13.9 years. Between the ages of 2 and 8.5 years, these children received a comprehensive intervention program for a minimum of 2 years and a maximum of 5 years, which included Floortime and DIR consultation. The authors described these adolescent boys as empathetic, creative, and reflective and noted that they were experiencing good peer relationships and academic achievement.

In 2007, Solomon, Necheles, Ferch, and Bruckman reported on the results of the PLAY (Play and Language for Autistic Youngsters) Project Home Consultation, a program that trained parents of children with ASDs in the DIR/Floortime model. Sixty-eight children participated in this study, completing an 8- to 12-month program in which parents were encouraged to do 15 hr per week of one-to-one interaction. The results of ratings on the FEAS (Greenspan et al., 2001) pretraining and posttraining revealed that 45.5% of the children made good to very good functional developmental progress. The parents' overall satisfaction with the program was 90%.

The first randomized controlled trial study on the DIR/Floortime-based treatment approach was conducted at the Milton and Ethel Harris Research Initiative (MEHRI) at York University in Canada. Preliminary results from this study were reported at the International Meeting for Autism Research (Casenhiser, Shanker, & Stieben, 2010). The study includes two groups of 51 children who were stratified by age and language functioning and randomly assigned to one of two groups. One group received DIR-based treatment, and the other group received "community treatment," which was primarily behaviorally based. The DIR treatment involved 2 hr per week with the clinicians; in addition, as is typical in the DIR paradigm, parents were asked to spend 20 hr per week with their children in Floortime intervention. The community treatment group received an average of 4 hr per week of other behavioral interventions, chiefly speech therapy, applied behavior analysis, and occupational therapy.

A modified version of Mahoney's Child Behavior Rating Scale (Kim & Mahoney, 2004) was used to code the following five variables from a videotaped parent–child play interaction: Initiation of Joint Attention, Attention to Activity, Involvement, Enjoyment in Interaction, and Compliance. The children in the MEHRI group did significantly better than the children in the community treatment group on all the scales except Compliance. A regression analysis was performed to see if improvements in the social-interaction behaviors predicted language improvements. This relationship was found for the scale overall, with the strongest predictors being Involvement and Initiation of Joint Attention. Effect sizes (Cohen's d) ranged from 0.51 to 1.02. As might be expected, intervention directed toward improving various aspects of social interaction clearly has an impact on language development (see Kasari, Paparella, Freeman, & Jahromi, 2008).

Two recent studies have reported results that further support the positive effects of using a DIR approach. Pajareya and Nopmaneejumruslers (2011) conducted a pilot study with children with mild to severe ASDs. The parents of these children received home-based training in the overarching themes of DIR, including observing the child's cues, following the child's lead, and implementing the Floortime techniques that were appropriate for their child's particular FEDL. The parents added an average of 15.2 hr per week of DIR/Floortime intervention to their typical schedules for 3 months. Results indicated that the intervention group improved significantly in engagement, relating, and communicating as measured by the FEAS (Greenspan et al., 2001).

A single-case design was used in a study reported by Dionne and Martini (2011). A DIR-trained occupational therapist taught the mother of a 3½-year-old child with autism typical Floortime strategies, including extending circles of communication using playful obstruction; joining the child's play, such as pretending to sleep; and identifying sensory overload. A significant increase in the number of circles of communication was noted in the intervention phase of the study as compared with the observation phase. In addition, the mother reported that she was enjoying the experience of interacting with her child in more typical play situations.

These results are in accord with a growing number of intervention studies that address the feasibility and impact of teaching parents to use responsive social interaction strategies in playful exchanges with their children. McConachie, Randle, and Le Couteur (2005) and Girolametto, Sussman, and Weitzman (2007) found that the children whose parents improved in their responsiveness made gains in vocabulary, frequency of communication, and/or participation in turn-taking routines. Other studies have reported increases in joint attention, initiation of communication, periods of engagement, and expressive language in children whose parents were taught how to change their interaction styles to facilitate relationships and responsiveness with their children (Aldred, Green, & Adams, 2004; Mahoney & Perales, 2005; Siller & Sigman, 2002).

Finally, in 2009, the National Standards Project (National Autism Center [NAC], 2009) disseminated the results of a review of the existing educational and behavioral research in autism interventions published between 1957 and the Fall of 2007. Four categories of treatments were defined—established treatments, **emerging treatments,** unestablished treatments, and ineffective/harmful treatments. DIR was categorized as emerging, that is, among treatments that "have some evidence of effectiveness, but not enough to be confident that they are truly effective" (p. 9). The National Standards Report encourages parents, educators, and service providers to consider factors in addition to treatment effectiveness when making decisions about intervention options; parents and service providers should consider the judgment and data-based clinical recommendations of professionals as well as the values and preferences of the person with an ASD and his or her family and caregivers (NAC, 2009).

PRACTICAL REQUIREMENTS

The practical demands of the DIR Model can be thought of in terms of the personnel needs, that is, the number of different professionals working with the family; the number of hours of intervention provided by these professionals; and the parents' commitment of time and energy.

Each child involved in a DIR program receives individual therapy sessions many times—optimally, six to eight 20-min sessions—throughout the day. If the child is very young, spending most of the day at home, the Floortime interactions are facilitated by the parent who is being coached by a DIR professional (psychologist, SLP, occupational therapist, educator). Similar to other comprehensive programs, the child's individual processing needs (e.g., occupational therapy, visual-spatial training) are a key component of a DIR program and often become a priority in the treatment. Older children involved in a school program participate in individual, small-group, and large-group interactions throughout the day, led by professionals from a variety of disciplines who share a DIR perspective. In the best-case scenario, the team of professionals working with the child coordinates its efforts by meeting and discussing roadblocks and progress on a regular basis.

Optimally, the primary DIR professionals working with the child are certified in DIR or are in the process of being certified. The certification process requires attending specific training, participating in a summer institute where the practitioner presents his or her work to an interdisciplinary team of professionals and DIR faculty members, and ongoing clinical supervision from a DIR faculty member. Currently, this process is under review with the aim of making it more accessible and tailored to different levels of professional training (see http://www.ICDL.org and http://www.Profectum.org).

KEY COMPONENTS

Goals and Activities

Goals

DIR goals address skills in several domains—including social-emotional, affective, language, sensory, regulatory, motor planning, and visual-spatial—as well as patterns of family interaction. The philosophical perspectives discussed throughout this chapter lead to this kind of big-picture thinking relative to DIR intervention. Furthermore, although DIR is often thought of as individually based treatment, a number of schools have adopted the principles of DIR/Floortime and translated them into group contexts within academic programs.

In a DIR program, interdisciplinary goals are targeted simultaneously, although at any point in time, priorities will be set relative to the child's needs and the family's resources. With the number of DIR-certified clinicians within and across the disciplines somewhat limited, families choosing this approach may have to take an active role in enlisting DIR-trained clinicians and educators for their child's program or, in some cases, support the training of the educators and clinicians working with their child.

Each of the six functional emotional levels can be thought of in terms of the specific behaviors targeted by that level (see Table 5.1). In fact, goals, similar to individualized education programs (IEPs), can be operationalized to ensure that the levels are easily translatable into educational or clinical paradigms (Wieder & Kalmanson, 2000). For example, at Level 1 of the FEDLs for shared attention and regulation, a typical goal might be, "The child will sustain shared attention with a special adult in sensorimotor interactive play using the child's preferred and pleasurable sensory and motor modalities" (Wieder & Kalmanson, 2000, p. 299); at a later stage, a goal might be, "The child will sustain shared attention with a peer in interaction" (p. 299). At Level 3, two-way intentional communication, a typical goal might be, "The child will initiate purposeful interactions around desires (open circles) and will close circles following an adult's response to her initiative" (p. 299); and at a later stage, the goal might be, "The child will sustain engagement with a peer with adult mediation (p. 299)." At Level 6, representational differentiation and emotional thinking, a typical goal might be, "The child will close all symbolic circles in both pretend play and reality-based dialogues" (p. 300); at a later stage, the goal might be, "The child will identify motives of other people or characters' actions and understand different points of view and feelings" (p. 300).

The notion of opening and closing circles of communication is a central construct in the model. In this approach, where the child's ideas and interests are used as the basis of the adult's interaction, the child opens a circle by initiating or showing interest in something or someone. The caregiver follows this initiation by joining and expanding the interaction. The child then closes the circle if he or she responds to the adult or, perhaps, begins a new circle with a new initiation or interest. In this exchange, the child becomes more aware of his or her actions, and the caregiver can become more aware of the child's sense of self and interests. By respecting these interests and following the child's lead, the adult can then set the stage for expanding the child's ideas and challenging him or her to move up the developmental ladder (Breinbauer, 2010).

> When a child reaches out—with a look, for example—he opens the circle. When the parent responds—by looking back—he builds on the child's action. When the child in turn responds to the parent—by smiling, vocalizing, reaching, or even turning away— he is closing the circle. When the parent responds to the child's response—by holding out a toy, by saying, "Don't you want to play?", by echoing the child's vocalization—and the child responds with another gesture (a look, smile, or hand movement) they have opened and closed another circle. (Greenspan & Wieder, 1998, pp. 76–77)

Activities

In educational settings, three types of DIR activities are used to support the child's development (ICDL, 2005): 1) Floortime, or spontaneous interactions during which the adult or peer follows the child's lead and facilitates the child's expansion of his or her ideas and intentions; 2) semistructured problem-solving interactions during which specific learning objectives are addressed through dynamic interactions in which the child is encouraged to problem-solve and think creatively; and 3) motor, sensory, perceptual-motor, and visual-spatial activities to address processing challenges.

Because the DIR goals cross developmental disciplines, activities may be specific to particular disciplines. For example, the occupational therapist will see the child in a sensory gym with activities geared toward addressing the child's sensory profile. For speech and language goals, the clinician may engage in spontaneous play-based interactions with the child and parent as well as more semistructured activities to address the child's language comprehension issues. For the educator, goals will be incorporated into group learning activities in the classroom. The mental health professional on the team may meet weekly with the parents to discuss their reactions and responses to their child's challenges, the impact on the child's siblings, and the issues in the couple's marriage.

Finally, the goal of moving the child up through the developmental levels is addressed by embracing Floortime strategies. These strategies include working within the context of play and/or other natural interactions; using a vivid range of affective states to "woo" the child into interpersonal interactions; following the child's lead and ideas, no matter how primitive or perseverative; scaffolding expansion of ideas and/or interaction; facilitating responsiveness by pursuing the child in a playful way; facilitating initiation by responding to all of the child's nonintentional as well as intentional behaviors; coaching the parent to develop interactive strategies; and considering the child's sensory and regulatory needs when planning activities (Wieder, 2004). For examples, see the DVD that accompanies this book.

Parent Coaching

Programs that prioritize the parent–child relationship in the therapeutic process do so because they believe that the parent–child relationship is the key to healthy development and that parents are the most emotionally invested agents of their child's growth. Not only are parents seen as the best facilitators of development, but they also are recognized as the ones who can offer the intensity of intervention recommended by the National Research Council (Lord & McGee, 2001). As such, parents are seen as indispensable to their child's progress in learning to interact and communicate. The DIR approach seeks to empower parents to become their child's primary language and social-emotional facilitator through natural interactions that take place during everyday events, such as mealtime, bath time, or when looking at books. The role of the clinician is seen as providing a collaborative, respectful partnership with the parents, who clearly know their child best (Longtin & Gerber, 2008) but who may need specific instruction in how to help their child climb the social-emotional-symbolic ladder.

In a typical DIR session, the parent is asked to play with the child while the therapist provides suggestions as to how to use the DIR principles. The parent is encouraged to promote circles of communication, or continuous back-and-forth exchanges between the child and the parent, by following the child's lead, joining the focus of the child's interest, using high affect and playfulness, and enjoying the interaction. The clinician reflects with the parent, addressing questions and concerns relative to the roadblocks to achieving interactive flow and higher symbolic capacity. The clinician also guides the parent's understanding of the child's sensory and regulatory challenges and models how the parent might work around and with them. For example, the parent might help the child stay regulated (i.e., calm, alert, attentive) and thereby increase affective interactions, opportunities for face-to-face interactions, and vocalizations by bouncing the child on a large therapy ball.

Although parent involvement in programs for children on the autistic spectrum is often pro forma, dynamic parent coaching that has an interdisciplinary base may be a less familiar part of the intervention process for many SLPs. Those SLPs practicing within the DIR framework will most likely need to be trained in the coaching process. That the parent–child relationship is the preferred intervention context obligates the DIR clinician to embrace his or her own learning about parent counseling, perhaps through reflective supervision, in order to assume the role of coach during the treatment.

DATA COLLECTION TO SUPPORT DECISION MAKING

Initial and ongoing assessments of the child's strengths and challenges that take place within the DIR Model are based on various paradigms of typical development, such as the FEAS (Greenspan et al., 2001), the *ICDL-DMIC* (ICDL, 2005) language model, and the individual processing profile. The evaluation of progress will be discipline-specific relative to the frequency of assessment and the identification of measures to be used for assessing change. For example, SLPs may use language sampling (Lahey, 1988; Systematic Analysis of Language Transcripts [SALT], Miller, 2010) as a measure of the child's progress in language development. In DIR school programs, as in all school programs, data must be collected to chart the child's progress over time and to determine the efficacy of the strategies being used. The familiar procedures noted in Table 5.5 are some of those used in DIR educational settings.

Because the DIR Model is such a comprehensive one, clinicians working in this way will be looking at all developmental domains if the child is not progressing so that they can determine where roadblocks to further progress may lie. One could say that the beauty of the DIR approach is its developmental breadth, which expands the range of interdisciplinary thinking and in that way undoubtedly comes closer to a true integrated understanding of the child's capacities. However, this breadth also obligates the clinician and educator to be versed in a range of possibilities when changes are needed in the child's individual intervention program. Simply put, the DIR professional has to be informed enough in all areas of development to know when and with whom to consult in order to gain a deeper understanding of the child's developmental delays.

The possibility that any particular child will benefit from alternative treatments—for example, nutritional supplements—is considered by a DIR physician (Robinson, 2011). The changing needs of the child and family and the realities of the highs and lows of atypical development suggest that the educator and clinician working with the child should keep an open mind about the possible pathways to development. In this sense, the fact that the DIR professional is encouraged to receive reflective supervision increases the chances that the therapist will remain sensitive to how his or her own perspectives, prejudices, and emotional reactions may influence treatment decisions.

CONSIDERATIONS FOR CHILDREN FROM CULTURALLY AND LINGUISTICALLY DIVERSE BACKGROUNDS

Given the individualized nature of the DIR approach, practitioners working with children from all cultural and linguistic backgrounds can feel comfortable using the model. In fact, DIR-certified clinicians are now practicing in many countries,

Table 5.5. Developmental, Individual-Difference, Relationship-Based (DIR®) Model data collection procedures and options

Indicate change in the percentage of response. For example, for a child who may be closing circles of communication 30% of the time, the specific goal would be to close circles 50% of the time at the next time interval.
Indicate change in the number of responses. For example, if a child is opening and closing 20 circles, the next goal would be 50 circles or that the child will respond three out of five times.
Indicate the time interval designated for the goal—for example, over a 1-week time period or during the next 3 months.
Indicate the amount of time to be spent on the goal, such as 10-min periods 8 times a day.
Consider the use of the Functional Emotional Assessment Scale (FEAS), which has established reliability and provides specific examples for each level. The FEAS could be scored at preintervention and postintervention intervals.
Indicate the context in which the child will demonstrate each developmental capacity, such as at school, on the playground, or at home.
Indicate whether the child will demonstrate the developmental capacity spontaneously or with natural prompts, such as questions during interactions.
Indicate whether the child will demonstrate the developmental capacity independently.

Source: Wieder and Kalmanson (2000).

including Australia, China, Colombia, Ireland, Israel, Italy, Spain, Turkey, and the United Kingdom. DIR faculty from the United States are frequently invited to do training in countries where a core of professionals, including psychiatrists, SLPs, occupational therapists, educators, and/or mental health practitioners, are making inroads in their communities and bringing DIR thinking to the work they do with children and families.

Application to a Child

To illustrate how the DIR Model can be integrated with developmental language goals, a child whom I saw for speech and language therapy at the Queens College Speech-Language-Hearing Center over a 4-year period will be discussed at two points in the DIR intervention he received—at 5 years of age, when he first began the intervention, and at 9 years.

"Mark" had been diagnosed with an ASD at the age of 3 years and had received intensive applied behavior analysis intervention between the ages of 3 and 5, before beginning DIR intervention. The shift to the DIR intervention occurred because Mark's mother, Ms. Z., was concerned about the nature of his treatment under applied behavior analysis and the lack of skill generalization to everyday life. In addition, she noted the lack of improvement in Mark's engagement and his limited capacity for shared emotion. The system of reinforcement being used was also worrisome to Ms. Z., because Mark's "preoccupations" were used as rewards—for example, watching a video. Finally, she questioned why certain behaviors, such as attention, were tied to receiving rewards. Ms. Z. was referred to the author because she was interested in speech and language intervention that was more deeply rooted in DIR and in coaching in DIR principles.

DIR and Language Assessment: Mark at Age 5

To introduce Mark from a DIR perspective, let us begin with Mark's FEDLs and individual sensory profile. At 5, Mark had "islands of capacity" at the first four FEDLs when given persistent and predictable support (see Figure 5.1). He had not yet reached the higher levels, including creating representations and ideas, and representational differentiation and emotional thinking. In reference to his individual sensory-processing profile, specifically, sensory modulation and regulation, Mark was hyperreactive to auditory, tactile, and taste sensations. In terms of sensory processing, Mark could observe and focus on desired objects and differentiate salient visual stimuli; however, he demonstrated challenges in initiating and responding to joint attention through gaze. In the area of sensory-affective processing, Mark demonstrated challenges in the ability to connect intent or affect to the use of symbols, including language. Finally, in reference to motor planning and sequencing, Mark could initiate ideas in play with clear goals and purposes with a few preferred toys but had difficulties developing a play plan and enacting steps of a play sequence across a range of play themes.

When caregiver patterns were analyzed, six areas of interaction were addressed and rated on a scale from 1 (low) to 5 (high) (FEAS; Greenspan et al., 2001). The purpose of this assessment is to help parents discover those areas of interaction where they need support to further enhance their child's availability for deepening relationships and learning. In each of the areas, comforting, finding an appropriate level of stimulation, engaging in the relationship, reading cues and signals, maintaining affective flow for coregulation, and encouraging development, Mark's mother received high ratings. Although this is obviously not typical of all parents or professionals, Ms. Z. was simply a natural in DIR. In fact, Ms. Z and the clinician collaborated in determining intervention goals and strategies, and the therapy process was enhanced by her interpretations of her son's behaviors, such as the origins of Mark's **scripted language.** The term *scripted language* (or *scripts*) refers to the use of phrases, sentences, and longer strings of language that are repeated, often verbatim, from movies, books, television shows, and so forth.

When Mark was 5 years old, his language was assessed based on the language paradigm of the *ICDL-DMIC* (ICDL, 2005). At age 5, Mark's shared attention, affective engagement, and reciprocity did not meet the expectations of typically developing 24-month-olds (see Figure 5.2). These capacities were seen only intermittently in interactions with his mother. Mark's language comprehension and production were compromised, with some strengths in production, including self-generated language, delayed echolalia, and scripts. Mark used scripts frequently to communicate his ideas and feelings. Mark's symbolic play skills were below those for a 24-month-old level, with the majority of his play at the level of exploratory and cause-and-effect play. He did not engage in peer interactions.

Language Intervention Goals and Strategies

The intervention goals developed for Mark were rooted in the DIR paradigm and developmental language models. The focus of Mark's intervention at 5 years was to increase his shared attention, affective engagement, reciprocity, and shared intentions with adults, primarily his mother; to expand his expression of affective states, including frustration,

Draw a line through to the highest level (1–6) the child has reached. Functional capacities	1 Not reached	2 Observed intermittently, with support	3 Observed more consistently, with structure and scaffolding, given high affect, gestural, language, sensorimotor support	4 Not at age-expected level; observed intermittently, without support	5 Age-appropriate level in certain contexts	6 Age-appropriate level, with full range of affect states and emotional themes. Consider robustness and thematic level to give this rating.
1. Shared attention and regulation						
2. Engagement and relating						
3. Two-way intentional communication						
4. Complex problem-solving *Simple two- to three-step actions and presymbolic functional use of toys*						
5. Creative representations and elaboration *Connects three- to four-step sequences to represent realistic ideas; elaborates emotional themes*						
6. Representational differentiation and emotional thinking *Builds bridges between ideas; elaborates abstract themes; has reflective capacities*						

Figure 5.1 Assessment of functional emotional developmental levels for Mark at ages 5 (——▶) and 9 (·····▶). (*Source:* Greenspan and Wieder, 1998.)

Draw a line through to the highest level (1–6) the child has reached.

Modality	1 Not reached	2 Observed intermittently, with support	3 Observed more consistently, with structure and scaffolding, given high affect, gestural, language, sensorimotor support	4 Not at age-expected level; observed intermittently, without support	5 Age-appropriate level in certain contexts	6 Age-appropriate level, with full range of affect states and emotional themes. Consider robustness and thematic level to give this rating.
1. Shared attention						
2. Affective engagement						
3. Reciprocity						
4. Shared intentions						
5. Shared forms and meanings						
6. Emerging discourse						

Figure 5.2. Assessment of speech-language-communication for Mark at age 5 (———▶) and age 9 (·····▶). (*Source:* Interdisciplinary Council on Developmental and Learning Disorders, 2005.)

anger, and delight; to facilitate emotional regulation to help him deal with extreme upset and aggression when his wishes could not be met; to facilitate the development of contingent schemas in play related to favorite activities, such as playing with trains, playing circus, and watering plants; and to coach Ms. Z in Floortime techniques that could be used to address the goals at home.

During early stages of Mark's language intervention, comprehension and production of language were considered secondary goals. His capacities for shared attention, engagement, reciprocity, shared intentions, regulation, expression of affect, and play were prioritized as these foundations for language were significantly compromised. Given the primary goals and the fact that these capacities typically develop in a child's interactions with his or her caregivers, Ms. Z. was often the primary interactant during therapy sessions.

Intervention strategies included following Mark's lead and joining his play contingently, regardless of the focus of the play or the frequency with which the play theme was introduced (e.g., train play); following preferred play scenarios and taking a role in them, including scripted ideas (e.g., circus themes); modeling early form–content relations to code his ideas; and coaching facilitation of goals in mother–child interactions.

Process and Progress

Mark's relatedness with the therapist and the graduate clinicians who were working with him developed well over the course of the first year. Many of the play interactions used during intervention centered around scripted schemas that Mark introduced in the play, such as watering plants or playing circus. The clinicians expanded these scripts by gradually adding to the scenarios (e.g., having dolls perform in the circus; adding an audience, including adult turns in the performance) and then returning to Mark's interest in the scheme. Although the clinicians introduced many different play schemas, Mark had his favorites, and the play often returned to these scenarios.

Mark's persistent interests, such as playing with a train, were not discouraged. Rather, these interests were used to encourage interactions, such as finding the train together, locating the missing pieces, adding people to the play theme, and taking the train to Mark's favorite places (e.g., McDonald's restaurants). Consistent with DIR thinking, joining the child in his or her strongest interests generally leads to greater engagement, affective expression, and continuity of the story line. In fact, over time, Mark stopped requesting the train and went on to explore other play possibilities. Mark's exploration of what he could do with his body was also encouraged, to address his sensory-processing and regulatory needs.

By the end of the first year of DIR-based language intervention, Mark's level of engagement ranged from many circles of affective interactions around simple pretend games (e.g., playing monster) to shorter, more fragmented interactions. Mark's widest range of affect was seen in his interactions with his mother, where high positive affect, humor, frustration, and anger were expressed.

Although not addressed directly, Mark's language production increased both quantitatively and qualitatively. Greater diversity was seen in his vocabulary, word combinations, and early semantic-syntactic relations. Mark began to code a range of ideas (Lahey, 1988) using the basic constituent structure (subject plus verb plus complement) and also demonstrated the beginnings of semantic-syntactic complexity ("I want to go on the bolster"). Despite this progress, Mark's formulation difficulties were apparent, as can be seen in the following utterances: "Can I make a plant some seeds?"; "Put in the more"; "Can I water pour?" More important, Mark's comprehension of decontextualized language continued to be limited.

As previously mentioned, Mark's use of repetitive language and play was considered an opportunity to facilitate both of these domains of development. For example, in the monster game, Mark turned off the lights, went out of the room, waited until we were sleeping and snoring, and then scared us when he came back in. Soon, Mark was one of the sleepers, joining the others in the room and trying to catch the monster when he returned. These shifts in the play schemas allowed for facilitation and expansion of the language and affect associated with this script.

DIR and Language Assessment: Mark at Age 9

To illustrate how a child's intervention program might change over time using the DIR paradigm, selected components of Mark's profile at 9 years will be discussed. In terms of the FEDLs (see Figure 5.1), Mark had achieved the first four levels in certain contexts, although his emotional range continued to be somewhat restricted. His capacity for creating representations and elaboration had expanded, with continuing constriction in his symbolic play abilities. Finally, with persistent and predictable support, Mark demonstrated islands of capacity in representational differentiation and emotional thinking.

In terms of the *ICDL-DMIC* (ICDL, 2005), at 9 years, Mark was a spontaneous and frequent communicator. In certain contexts, he had achieved the shared attention, affective engagement, and reciprocity that are seen in 36-month-old typically developing children (see Figure 5.2). Mark's language comprehension and production were similar to a 36-month-old's level in some ways, below this level in other ways (e.g., difficulty understanding and responding to "why" questions), and above typical developments of 36-month-olds in certain skills (e.g., ability to read). Mark continued to use scripts frequently to communicate his ideas and feelings, and his symbolic play skills were beginning to reach the 36-month-old level. Mark was interested in peer interactions but had difficulty joining and sustaining them.

Language Intervention Goals and Strategies

Intervention goals continued to focus on facilitating shared attention, affective engagement, reciprocity, shared intentions, and emotional regulation. Newer goals included expanding understanding of others' emotional states; facilitating the expansion of new schemas and stories within play scenarios; improving the comprehension of language, specifically, the response to "why" questions; expanding the capacity for symbolic play—decontextualization, themes, organization, and roles (Westby, 2000); supporting problem solving and flexibility; and enhancing "theory of mind" perspectives (Howlin, Baron-Cohen, Hadwin, & Swettenham, 1999).

In terms of intervention strategies, the integration of DIR thinking and developmental language models dictated the procedures that were used. At this point in the therapy, the clinician used Mark's interest in books to address the expression and understanding of emotional themes, the expansion of symbolic play, and the comprehension of language. Mark's scripts continued to be used as a context for the intervention as the clinician joined in the meaning and affective tone of the script, developed an interaction within the context of the script by taking a role in the play, and changed or added to the characters, problems, outcomes, and roles while staying within the story line. Scripts were played out many times, and nonscripted language was modeled to accompany the action.

Process and Progress

One of the most significant signs of progress noted when Mark was 9 was the depth of the relationship that he developed with the graduate clinicians who were working with him. Mark's connection to the students represented a qualitative change in his capacity for relating to people and his capacity for engagement.

Mark's use of spontaneous language and social language with the adults ("Hi guys...what are you doing?") continued to increase and become a more natural part of his repertoire. Mark's interest in reading books led to acting out a story—for example, Mercer Mayer's *Hansel and Gretel*—at first in a prescribed way, and then with changes within the roles and, eventually, in the story's ending. Mark was quite clever about using different props for the reenactment and easily accepted the clinician's suggestions—for example, a basket for the dungeon. The day that Mark announced that he was going to be Gretel after many times of being Hansel, pride in his accomplishment was obvious. We saw Mark's spontaneous, self-initiated role change from Hansel to Gretel as an example of the benefits of replaying the story many times rather than prematurely moving him on or directing the play.

Although we have been delighted with the role Mark's scripts have played in his language development, we are aware that they continue to reflect Mark's challenges in the comprehension and production of language. For example, based on an assessment of Mark's comprehension at 9 years of age, it is apparent that he has mastered the earlier occurring "wh" forms, such as "what, who, where," but not the later developing ones, such as "why" and "how." In his responses, Mark displayed comprehension patterns characteristic of earlier typical development, such as answering later occurring question forms with earlier occurring interpretations (e.g., answering "why" questions as if they were "who" questions).

In terms of production, although Mark continues to expand his use of spontaneous self-generated language, he continues to use scripts to communicate ideas and feelings. In fact, because the author had the opportunity to study Mark's language development over time, she has come to a deeper appreciation of the ongoing role scripts may play in a child's expression of intention and meaning. Although not always apparent to a more naïve listener, a connection can be made between Mark's use of a script and the affect or idea he is trying to communicate. For example, when Mark was feeling nervous during one of his therapy sessions, he borrowed a script used by a character in the movie *Cars* to refer to anxiety.

Before ending this section, it is important to mention how a DIR–developmental language approach to scripting differs from more familiar intervention approaches to this form of communication. In fact, in more traditional approaches, clinicians and educators often address a child's scripting by ignoring it and redirecting the child to activities proposed by the adult, by modeling language that relates to the adult-determined activity, and by telling the child, "We're not talking about that now" when he or she returns to the scripts. These strategies are obviously generated from very different thinking about the origins of language, the reasons that a child might be using scripts, and the interpersonal and intrapersonal functions of the scripts. The principles of intervention shared by a

DIR approach and a developmental language approach speak to the theoretical foundations for generating the intervention goals and strategies, which were used to address Mark's scripting. These include prioritizing affective engagement and reciprocal interaction, following the contents of the child's mind, treating all behaviors as intentional and meaningful, acknowledging that the child's idea is always better than yours, and joining first and then gently expanding the child's affect, ideas, and/or language.

Application to an Adolescent or Adult

Although the topic is not specifically discussed in this chapter, the DIR Model does address higher levels of functional emotional development that would be appropriate to consider for older children, adolescents, and adults (Greenspan & Mann, 2001).

FUTURE DIRECTIONS

Needless to say, all of us working with children with ASDs and with their families understand the importance of improving the quantity and quality of intervention research with this population. Not only is the quality of service dependent on more and better research, but many families are in need of such data to access a greater range of treatment options. Because insurance reimbursement and school districts look to the research findings to support and develop programs, moving forward in this regard needs to be one of our highest priorities.

Having said this, it is clear that research findings for groups of children will always have to be viewed through the lens of the reality of individual differences. The individual complexity of the challenges faced by children with ASDs and their parents necessitates a clear conviction regarding individually designed intervention programs. This, in turn, leads to the recommendation that various types of research, including individual case studies, must be considered seriously for this population of children and no doubt for all children who have atypical developmental trajectories.

SUGGESTED READINGS

Gerber, S. (2003). A developmental perspective on language assessment and intervention for children on the autistic spectrum. *Topics in Language Disorders*, *23*(2), 74–95.

This article addresses how social-pragmatic and developmental models of language, such as Bloom and Tinker's Intentionality Model (2001) and Lahey's (1988) Language Model, can be used as the cornerstones for determining the priorities for language assessment and intervention for young children with ASDs. Profiles of five children with ASDs are used to illustrate developmental goals and contexts of language intervention.

Greenspan, S., & Wieder, S. (1998). *The child with special needs: Encouraging intellectual and emotional growth.* Reading MA: Perseus Books.

In this book, Greenspan and Wieder introduce their unique paradigm of the six key developmental milestones in early childhood and the groundbreaking intervention approach known as Floortime.

Interdisciplinary Council on Developmental and Learning Disorders. (2005). *Diagnostic manual for infancy and early childhood.* Bethesda, MD: ICDL Press.

The *ICDL-DMIC* presents a developmentally based classification system for infants and young children with developmental disorders. The comprehensive classification system can be used to describe challenges in emotional, speech-language, cognitive, regulatory-sensory, and motor capacities.

Interdisciplinary Council on Developmental and Learning Disorders. (2000). *Clinical practice guidelines: Redefining the standards of care for infants, children, and families with special needs.* Bethesda, MD: ICDL Press.

The clinical practice guidelines, which are based on research and clinical experience, address the identification, assessment, and treatment of all relevant areas of developmental functioning in childhood. These include child–caregiver relationships, speech and language, motor functioning, visual-spatial processing, sensory modulation, the functional emotional developmental capacities, cognitive functioning, social skills, family patterns, and peer relationships. The guidelines embrace a functional developmental approach and can serve as the basis for recommendations for changes in screening, assessment, and intervention services and local, state, and federal policies.

Learning Activities

Topics for Further Discussion

- Discuss the similarities and differences in the role of the parent between the DIR Model and other intervention approaches that focus on incorporating the parent into the intervention process (e.g., the Hanen program *More Than Words* [Sussman, 1999]).
- Discuss the areas of developmental functioning embraced in the DIR Model that will be familiar to SLPs and those that will require further exposure and learning.

Ideas for Projects

- Interview the parent of a child with autism who has had experience with both adult-directed approaches to intervention, such as ABA, and child-directed approaches, such as DIR. Ask the parent to discuss the pros and cons of each treatment approach for the child and family.
- Interview an SLP who uses more behavioral interactions in intervention, such as ABA, and one who uses more spontaneous interactions, such as DIR/Floortime. Ask the clinicians to explain what theories and clinical findings have motivated their decisions.
- Interview an occupational therapist and ask him or her to give examples of sensory and regulatory problems that children on the autistic spectrum might experience that would impact their ability to develop nonverbal forms of communication.

Questions

1. Describe the major components of the DIR Model, and give examples of the specific behaviors that would be assessed in each of these areas.
2. Describe how Mark's language intervention program reflects elements of the DIR Model and what the most significant divergences are from more traditional language assessment and intervention approaches.

3.   How would you address the question of what evidence is available to support the DIR approach to intervention?

Writing Assignments

1.   Using the information discussed in this chapter on the FEDLs, the individual sensory profile, and caregiver patterns, write an assessment of a child with whom you are working.

2.   Based on your assessment described in the preceding assignment, generate goals relative to the FEDLs, sensory profile, and caregiver-child interactions.

REFERENCES

Aldred, C., Green, J., & Adams, C. (2004). A new social communication intervention for children with autism: Pilot randomized controlled treatment study suggesting effectiveness. *Journal of Child Psychology and Psychiatry, 45,* 1420–1430.

American Psychiatric Association. (1987). *Diagnostic and statistical manual of mental disorders* (3rd ed., rev.). Washington, DC: Author.

American Psychiatric Association (1994). *Diagnostic and statistical manual of mental disorders* (4th ed.). Washington, DC: American Psychiatric Association Press.

Bates, E. (1975). *Language and context: The acquisition of pragmatics.* New York, NY: Academic Press.

Bloom, L., & Lahey, M. (1978). *Language development and language disorders.* New York, NY: John Wiley & Sons.

Bloom, L., & Tinker, E. (2001). The intentionality model and language acquisition. *Monographs of the Society for Research in Child Development. 66*(4, Serial No. 267).

Breinbauer, C. (2010). Circles of Communication. Lecture presented at the ICDL Graduate School, Functional Emotional Assessment Scale Reliability Training (IMH 401), Interdisciplinary Council on Developmental and Learning Disorders, Bethesda, MD.

Casenhiser, D., Shanker, S., & Stieben, J. (2010, May). *Learning through interaction in children with autism.* Paper presented at the International Meeting for Autism Research, Philadelphia, PA.

Cawn, S., Gerber, S., Greenspan, S., Harrison, C., Lewis, D., Madell, J., & Wetherby, A. (2005). Language disorders. In *ICDL-Diagnostic manual for infancy and early childhood* (pp. 129–166). Bethesda, MD: ICDL Press.

Dionne, M., & Martini, R. (2011). Floortime play with a child with autism: A single-subject study. *Canadian Journal of Occupational Therapy, 78,* 196-203.

Gerber, S. (2003). A developmental perspective on language assessment and intervention for children on the autistic spectrum. *Topics in Language Disorders, 23*(2), 74–95.

Girolametto, L., Sussman, F., & Weitzman, E. (2007). Using case study methods to investigate the effects of interactive intervention for children with Autism Spectrum Disorders. *Journal of Communication Disorders, 40,* 470–492.

Greenspan, S. (2004). *The social-emotional growth charts.* San Antonio, TX: Pearson.

Greenspan, S.I., De Gangi, G.A., & Wieder, S. (2001). *The Functional Emotional Assessment Scale (FEAS) for infancy and early childhood: Clinical and research applications.* Bethesda, MD: ICDL Press.

Greenspan, S., & Mann, H. (2001). Adolescents and adults with special needs: the Developmental Individual differences, Relationship-based (DIR) approach to intervention. In Interdisciplinary Council on Developmental and Learning Disorders, *ICDL clinical practice guidelines: Redefining the standards of care for infants, children, and families with special needs* (pp. 639-656). Bethesda, MD: ICDL Press.

Greenspan, S.I., & Shanker, S.G. (2004). *The first idea: How symbols, language, and intelligence evolved from our primate ancestors to modern humans.* New York, NY: Da Capo Press.

Greenspan, S.I., & Wieder, S. (1997). Developmental patterns and outcomes in infants and children with disorders in relating and communicating: A chart review of 200 cases of children with autistic spectrum disorder. *Journal of Developmental and Learning Disorders, 1,* 87–141.

Greenspan, S.I., & Wieder, S. (1998). *The child with special needs: Encouraging intellectual and emotional growth.* Reading, MA: Perseus Books.

Greenspan, S.I., & Wieder, S. (2001). Developmentally appropriate interactions and practices. In Interdisciplinary Council on Developmental and Learning Disorders, *ICDL clinical practice guidelines: Redefining the standards of care for infants, children, and families with special needs* (pp. 261–281). Bethesda, MD: ICDL Press.

Howlin, P., Baron-Cohen, S., Hadwin, J., & Swettenham, J. (1999). *Teaching children with autism to mind-read.* New York, NY: Wiley.

Interdisciplinary Council on Developmental and Learning Disorders. (2000). *ICDL clinical practice guidelines: Redefining the standards of care for infants, children, and families with special needs.* Bethesda, MD: ICDL Press.

Interdisciplinary Council on Developmental and Learning Disorders. (2005). *Diagnostic manual for infancy and early childhood.* Bethesda, MD: ICDL Press.

Kasari, C., Paparella, T., Freeman, S.N., & Jahromi, L. (2008). Language outcome in autism: Randomized comparison of joint attention and play interventions. *Journal of Consulting and Clinical Psychology, 76,* 125–137.

Kim, J.M., & Mahoney, G. (2004). The effects of mother's style of interaction on children's engagement: Implications for using responsive interventions with parents. *Topics in Early Childhood Special Education, 24*(1), 31–38.

Lahey, M. (1988). *Language disorders and language development.* New York, NY: Wiley.

Lewis, D., & Greenspan, S.I. (2005). *The affect-based language curriculum (ABLC): An intensive program for families, therapists, and teachers* (2nd ed.). Bethesda, MD: ICDL Press.

Longtin, S., & Gerber, S. (2008). Contemporary perspectives on facilitating language acquisition for children on the autistic spectrum: Engaging the parent and the child. *Journal of Developmental and Learning Disorders, 3,* 38–51.

Lord, C., & McGee, J.P. (Eds.). (2001). *Educating children with autism* [National Research Council, Committee on Educational Interventions for Children with Autism, Commission on Behavioral and Social Sciences and Education]. Washington, DC: National Academy Press.

MacDonald, J. (2004). *Communicating partners.* London: Jessica Kingsley Publishers.

Mahoney, G., & Perales, F. (2005). Relationship-focused early intervention with children with pervasive developmental disorders and other disabilities: A comparative study. *Journal of Developmental and Behavioral Pediatrics, 26,* 77–85.

McConachie, H., Randle V., & Le Couteur, A. (2005). A controlled trial of a training course for parents of children with suspected autism spectrum disorder. *Journal of Pediatrics, 147,* 335–340.

National Autism Center. (2009). *National Standards Project—findings and conclusions: Addressing the needs for evidence-based practice guidelines for autism spectrum disorders.* Randolph, MA: Author.

Pajareya, K., & Nopmaneejumruslers, K. (2011). A pilot randomized controlled trial of DIR/Floortime™ parent training intervention for pre-school children with autistic spectrum disorders. *Autism, 15*(5), 563–577.

Piaget, J. (1955). *The language and thought of the child.* Cleveland, OH: Meridian.

Prizant, B., Wetherby, A., Rubin, E., Laurent, A., & Rydell, P. (2006). *The SCERTS® Model: A comprehensive educational approach for children with autism spectrum disorders.* Baltimore, MD: Paul H. Brookes Publishing Co.

Robinson, R. (2011). *Autism solutions: How to create a meaningful life for your child.* Ontario, Canada: Harlequin.

Schopler, E., Reichler, R., & Rochen-Renner, B. (1988). Childhood Autism Rating Scale (CARS). Los Angeles, CA: Western Psychological Services.

Seigel, D. (1999). *The developing mind: How relationships and the brain interact to shape who we are.* New York, NY: Guilford Press.

Shonkoff, J.P., & Phillips, D.A. (Eds.). (2000). *From neurons to neighborhoods: The science of early childhood development.* Washington, DC: National Academy Press.

Siller, M., & Sigman, M. (2002). The behaviors of parents of children with autism predict the subsequent development of their children's communication. *Journal of Autism and Developmental Disorders, 32,* 77–89.

Solomon, R., Necheles, J., Ferch, C., & Bruckman, D. (2007). Pilot study of a parent training program for young children with autism: The PLAY Project Home Consultation model. *Autism: The International Journal of Research and Practice, 11,* 205–224.

Sussman, F. (1999). *More Than Words: Helping parents promote communication and social skills in children with autism spectrum disorders.* Toronto: The Hanen Centre.

Miller, J. (2010). Systematic analysis of language transcripts (SALT; English version 2010) [Computer software]. Middleton, WI: SALT Software, LLC.

Tronick, E. (2007). *The neurobehavioral and social-emotional development of infants and children.* New York, NY: W.W. Norton.

Westby, C. (2000). A scale for assessing development of children's play. In K. Gitlin-Weiner, A. Sandgrund, & C. Schaefer (Eds.), *Play diagnosis and assessment* (2nd ed., pp. 15–58). New York, NY: Wiley.

Wetherby, A., & Prizant, B. (2002). *Communication and Symbolic Behavior Scales™ (CSBS™).* Baltimore, MD: Paul H. Brookes Publishing Co.

Wieder, S. (2004, June). *Building foundations for children and families.* Seminar presented in Tarrytown, NY.

Wieder, S., & Greenspan, S.I. (2005). Can children with autism master core deficits and become empathetic, creative, and reflective? *Journal of Developmental and Learning Disorders, 9,* 39–61.

Wieder, S., & Kalmanson, B. (2000). Educational guidelines for preschool children with difficulties in relating and communicating. In S.I. Greenspan & S. Wieder (Eds.), *ICDL clinical practice guidelines: Redefining the standards of care for infants, children and families with special needs* (pp. 283–333). Bethesda, MD: ICDL Press.

6

Functional Communication Training: Treating Challenging Behavior

V. Mark Durand

C hallenging or **problem behaviors** such as **aggression, self-injury,** stereotyped behaviors, and **tantrums** are highly prevalent among children and adults with autism spectrum disorders (ASDs). Research suggests that problem behavior is three to four times more frequent in this population than in those without disabilities, with between 10% and 40% of children with disabilities displaying frequent and severe challenging behaviors (Einfeld & Tonge, 1996; Lowe et al., 2007). Along with frequency, the stability of these behaviors is also of serious concern (Totsika, Toogood, Hastings, & Lewis, 2008). Several studies document that even with treatment, these behaviors may still be problematic a decade later (Einfeld & Tonge, 1996; Einfeld, Tonge, & Rees, 2001; Emerson et al., 2001; Green, O'Reilly, Itchon, & Sigafoos, 2005; Jones, 1999).

It is difficult to estimate the impact of challenging behaviors on the lives of people with ASDs and their families. These behaviors are among the most frequently cited obstacles to placing students in community settings (Eyman & Call, 1977; Jacobson, 1982). Furthermore, their presence is associated with significantly increased recidivism among those individuals referred to crisis intervention programs from community placements (Shoham-Vardi et al., 1996). Challenging behavior interferes with such essential activities as family life (Cole & Meyer, 1989), educational activities (Koegel & Covert, 1972), and employment (Hayes, 1987). Parental stress is shown to significantly increase when caring for a child with problem behavior. (Floyd & Gallagher, 1997; Hastings, 2002; Saloviita, Itälinna, & Leinonen, 2003). Mothers of children with disabilities tend to have higher rates of depression, and depressed parents are more likely to have a child with behavior problems (Feldman et al., 2007). And, in one of the largest studies of its kind, researchers examining almost 10,000 children found that the single best predictor of early school failure was the presence of behavior problems (Byrd & Weitzman, 1994). In fact, the presence

---

Throughout the chapter, I use the terms *challenging behavior* and *problem behavior* and other variations to indicate those difficulties presented by students that interfere with educational, vocational, and family activities.

of behavior problems was a better predictor of school difficulties than factors such as poverty, speech and hearing impairments, and low birth weight. One study found that almost 40% of preschool teachers reported expelling a child each year because of behavior problems (Gilliam & Shahar, 2006). In addition, such behaviors can pose a physical threat to these individuals and those who work with them.

One of the most frequently used approaches to reducing these challenging behaviors in people with ASDs involves replacing the problem behavior with an alternative behavior—a technique known as **functional communication training (FCT)** (Durand, 1990; Durand & Merges, 2008, 2009). FCT entails a multistep process to 1) assess the function of the challenging behavior to be targeted, 2) select an appropriate alternative behavior, and 3) teach the alternative and fade out prompts to fit the current environment. The types of challenging behaviors that appear to be appropriate targets for FCT run the behavioral gamut, from aggression and self-injury to elopement (Lang et al., 2009) and inappropriate sexual behavior (Fyffe, Kahng, Fittro, & Russell, 2004). Family members and a range of professionals use FCT in homes, schools, and the community (Dunlap, Ester, Langhans, & Fox, 2006; Durand, 1999; Kemp & Carr, 1995). Research on FCT targets individuals across all ages (from infants/toddlers to older adults), developmental levels (from those with pervasive needs for support to those with average or above-average cognitive abilities), and language abilities (Mancil, 2006; Petscher, Rey, & Bailey, 2009; Snell, Chen, & Hoover, 2006). FCT is one of the few skill-focused behavioral interventions cited as having extensive support from initial efficacy studies (Smith et al., 2007).

TARGET POPULATIONS AND ASSESSMENTS FOR DETERMINING TREATMENT RELEVANCE AND GOALS

The FCT approach is designed for use with anyone who displays challenging behavior. Theoretically, therefore, the approach should be effective across a wide spectrum of individuals who receive diagnoses in the autism spectrum. Research on a broad range of individuals with ASDs as well as individuals with a variety of other disorders (e.g., attention-deficit/hyperactivity disorder, schizophrenia, traumatic brain injury) supports the wide-ranging applicability of this approach (Durand & Merges, 2009). In addition, research demonstrates that this approach to reducing challenging behavior can be adapted to individuals with a range of abilities, from those needing the most intensive levels of support (Bird, Dores, Moniz, & Robinson, 1989) to individuals who have no educational or clinical diagnosis and who have typical verbal and cognitive abilities (Petscher et al., 2009).

Functional behavioral assessment is at the core of the process used in FCT (Durand, 1990). The function or functions of challenging behavior are determined, and this information is used to select the alternative communicative behavior that is taught to replace the problem behavior. The primary goal is to identify an appropriate behavior that serves the same function as the problem behavior and that therefore can serve as a replacement for the challenging behavior. To assess the function of a problem behavior, the antecedents and consequences of that behavior need to be identified. The identification can be accomplished in a number of ways (Matson & Minshawi, 2007; Matson & Nebel-Schwalm, 2007). To improve the accuracy of assessment results, it is typically recommended that multiple forms of assessment be used.

A number of functional assessment strategies can be useful for determining the function of behavior—including the use of informal observations, antecedent-behavior-consequence (ABC) charts, functional analyses, and a variety of rating scales. A functional analysis—manipulating aspects of the environment to assess behavior change—is frequently cited as the best method of determining the function of a behavior problem (Hanley, Iwata, & McCord, 2003). However, there are a number of issues to consider prior to conducting this type of assessment (Durand, 1997; Sturmey, 1994). One issue is accessibility to manipulation. There are certain influences that you cannot or would not manipulate or change in order to perform a functional analysis. Factors such as some illnesses, disrupted family life, and chromosomal aberrations can certainly affect behavior problems, but changing these influences to assess their impact is obviously problematic or impossible.

Another concern involves the ethics of conducting a functional analysis. There are other influences that you could manipulate but that you may not want to change if they will result in an increase in challenging behavior. For example, you may want to know why a child runs out into the road, but it would be inappropriate to set up this situation given the potential danger. In many instances, deliberately increasing a severe behavior problem in order to assess it (e.g., by reinforcing challenging behavior) can be questioned on ethical grounds. Also, other problem behaviors can be so severe (e.g., hitting one's head on the floor) that allowing even one instance would be too dangerous. In these cases, assessment that does not involve manipulation (and subsequent increases in challenging behavior) would be recommended.

Typically, the assessment process begins with informal observations and interviews of significant others. Once a broad range of information is collected and hypotheses about the function(s) of the behaviors are developed, more formal assessments are used to validate these hypotheses. A number of assessment instruments are available to provide additional information about the functions of behavior, including the **Motivation Assessment Scale** (Durand & Crimmins, 1992), the Motivation Analysis Rating Scale (Weiseler, Hanson, Chamberlain, & Thompson, 1985), the Functional Analysis Interview Form (O'Neill, Horner, Albin, Storey, & Sprague, 1990), the Functional Assessment Checklist (McIntosh et al., 2008), the Functional Analysis Checklist (Van Houten & Rolider, 1991), and the Questions About Behavioral Function (Paclawskyj, Matson, Rush, Smalls, & Vollmer, 2000). These types of instruments can be used to provide additional and convergent information about behavioral functions. This information is then used to help select the alternative communication to be taught.

THEORETICAL BASIS

It is valuable to understand the theoretical foundation of several aspects of FCT in order to adapt this procedure to diverse individuals and settings. Described next are the concepts behind why challenging behavior is reduced with FCT, why the effects of FCT generalize to new people and settings, and how these concepts lead to understanding the conditions under which FCT is most effective (features of the alternative response).

Functional Equivalence

The mechanism of behavior change that underlies the reduction of problem behavior using FCT is the concept of **functional equivalence** (Carr, 1988; Durand, 1987). The assumption is that problem behaviors are maintained by a particular reinforcer or reinforcers (e.g., attention from others, escape from work). Theoretically, then, these behaviors can be replaced by other behaviors if the new behaviors serve the same function and are more efficient at gaining the desired reinforcers. (See Table 6.1 for examples of common functions of challenging behavior and Figure 6.1 for an illustration of how FCT replaces problem behavior.) For example, if a girl hits herself to get attention from her parent, then teaching her another, more effective way to get this attention (e.g., saying, "Come here, please") should serve the same function for the girl. This, then, would result in a decrease in the frequency of her self-injury as she becomes successful gaining attention in the new way. The presumption is that FCT reduces problem behavior because it involves teaching and reinforcing a replacement behavior that serves the same function.

Natural Communities of Reinforcement

In the special case of FCT as an intervention strategy, using communication as the replacement behavior provides an added benefit because of its unique ability to recruit **natural communities of reinforcement** (Durand, 1990). In other words, if a child learns to ask or otherwise solicit the reinforcers from others, then the child is able to recruit these reinforcers without an interventionist having to specifically train other people how to respond. For example, in one study we examined whether nonverbal children would be able to recruit reinforcers from community members, thereby resulting in a reduction of their challenging behaviors (Durand, 1999). Five students were identified who 1) exhibited severe and frequent behavior problems and 2) were unable to communicate verbally with others. The teachers of these students were shown how to assess the functions of the students' behaviors and select more appropriate alternatives for them to use. The teachers were then

Table 6.1.   Common behavioral functions

Behavioral function	Description
Attention	Behaviors that occur to obtain social attention from others. The attention can be interactions such as praising, spending time together, and comforting, but for some children it can also include yelling or providing explanations. Being left alone can trigger these behaviors.
Tangible	Behaviors that occur to obtain desired things (e.g., toys, foods) or activities. These behaviors can be triggered by a request to end an activity (e.g., stop watching a movie) or to give up a desired item (e.g., a toy picked up at a store).
Escape	Behaviors that occur to remove undesired requests or activities. These behaviors can include actions that may appear to be punitive (sending a child to his or her room) that may instead be desired (leaving the dinner table). These behaviors can be triggered by requests to perform some undesired activity.
Sensory	Behaviors that occur to obtain the sensory feedback provided by the behavior itself. These behaviors can include those that may feel good (face rubbing, twirling in circles), look good (waving hands in front of eyes), taste good (eating things off the floor), or sound good (making unusual noises). Being left alone or overstimulation can trigger these behaviors.

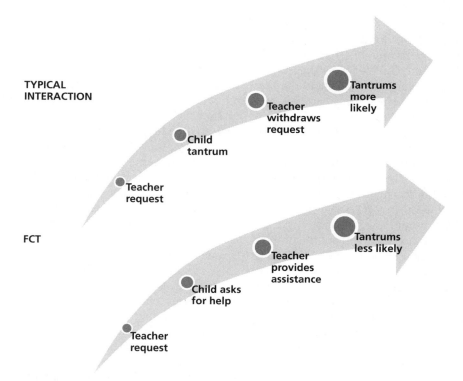

TYPICAL INTERACTION

Tantrums more likely

Teacher withdraws request

Child tantrum

Teacher request

FCT

Tantrums less likely

Teacher provides assistance

Child asks for help

Teacher request

Figure 6.1.   How functional communication training (FCT) replaces problem behavior.

instructed in how to assist their students to use voice output communication aids (VOCAs) to request things, such as assistance or attention, from others. The teachers were successful in teaching the students to use their devices to gain access to the stimuli previously maintaining their challenging behaviors, and they observed significant reductions in problem behavior in the classroom. Next, the teachers took their students out into typical community settings and observed that the students used their devices to appropriately solicit attention and help from untrained people in settings such as the library and stores at the local shopping mall. Again, challenging behavior was significantly reduced in the community settings once the students were able to recruit reinforcers from others. This success was achieved without specifically instructing community members how to respond to the students. The librarians or store clerks responded naturally to the requests made by the students through their devices, and this, in turn, resulted in reduced challenging behavior in the community (Durand, 1999).

The concept of recruiting natural communities of reinforcement (Stokes, Fowler, & Baer, 1978) is central to the success of FCT outside of structured environments staffed with highly trained individuals (Durand, 1990). This is a particularly important aspect of FCT when comparing its outcomes with the outcomes of other intervention strategies. Typically, once a behavioral plan is developed, training ensues for all individuals who come in contact with the person who exhibits the challenging behavior. In fact, if people do not follow the behavioral procedures, it is expected that regression will occur and behavior problems will increase. In contrast, rather than trying to train each person a child encounters on a daily basis to implement a formal behavioral program, FCT essentially allows the child to actively solicit from others the reinforcers that have previously maintained the challenging behavior. In effect, the child becomes the intervention agent.

We conducted an experimental analysis of this bootstrapping aspect of FCT in a study comparing this treatment approach with another, common approach to reacting to challenging behavior—time-out from positive reinforcement (TO) (Durand & Carr, 1992). In this study, we selected 12 school-age students, all of whom engaged in a variety of challenging behaviors (e.g., tantrums, self-injury, aggression). In addition, we screened for students whose challenging behaviors were being maintained by attention from others. The rationale for selecting students who had only attention-maintained problem behavior was to ensure that they would be appropriate for using TO. Selecting TO as an intervention for challenging behavior involves the assumption that the targeted behavior is reinforced by attention and that removing attention will put the problem behavior under extinction. Six students were randomly assigned to one of the two treatment conditions—FCT or TO. The students were then individually placed with teachers who had no knowledge of the study and who were instructed to work with the student on a task. No instructions were given about how to react to behavior problems. Treatment was then introduced by other teachers and was successful in reducing challenging behaviors for each child. Thus, the first finding was that both FCT and TO could successfully reduce challenging behavior. The students were then placed back with the teachers who were naïve to the treatment program. The behavior problems of the students who had received TO as a treatment resumed almost immediately. The students quickly realized that TO would not occur as a consequence in this setting, and they resumed their behavior problems. In contrast, the students who received FCT as a treatment used their communicative responses to request attention, and the naïve teachers responded appropriately, maintaining the reduction of the challenging behavior. In short, the advantage of FCT was not solely in the initial reduction in challenging behavior—which both treatments could produce—but also in its ability to recruit natural communities of reinforcement (in this case, teacher attention; Durand & Carr, 1992). This aspect of FCT is examined more fully in subsequent discussions of the effectiveness of this approach.

One consequence of viewing behavior problems as functionally equivalent to other forms of communication is the idea that these behaviors are not just responses that need to be reduced or eliminated. In the past, the de facto view of problem behaviors was that they were excesses to be reduced. However, a functional view of challenging behaviors suggests that they are just less acceptable (and sometimes much less acceptable) forms of reasonable requests for reinforcers (e.g., attention from others, help on difficult tasks). This perspective reminds us that attempting to eliminate these behaviors through some reductive technique would leave these individuals with no way of accessing their desired reinforcers and that therefore you could anticipate that other maladaptive behaviors would take their place (a result that is sometimes called "symptom substitution" or "response covariation").

Features of the Alternative Response

Although functional equivalence and recruiting natural communities of reinforcement are the major conceptual underpinnings for the effectiveness of FCT, other components of FCT become important for the ultimate success of the intervention in typical settings (Durand & Merges, 2009). These components offer an alternative response that is a functional equivalent and include response match, response success, response efficiency, response acceptability, response recognizability, and response milieu.

Response Match

Response match refers to matching the communicative behavior to the function of the challenging behavior; thus, it is closely related to functional equivalence. In our first study on FCT, we taught students with challenging behavior two different communicative responses—one phrase designed to elicit adult attention and another phrase designed to request assistance (Carr & Durand, 1985). The rationale behind the design of this study was to determine whether just teaching a form of communication that elicited a response from others would be sufficient to reduce challenging behavior. It is sometimes speculated that challenging behavior is used to control one's environment generically. If this were the case, then simply teaching a response that changed the behaviors of others should replace the problem behavior. However, this was not the case: We found that if students had attention-maintained problem behavior, teaching and reinforcing requests for assistance had no impact on their behavior. Similarly, for students with escape-maintained problem behavior, teaching and reinforcing responses for attention produced no behavior change. It was only when we taught responses that matched the function of challenging behavior did the behavior problems reduce in frequency (Carr & Durand, 1985).

Response Success

Using a conventional behavior that functions to elicit a reinforcer that maintains behavior (e.g., attention or escape) alone will not reduce a challenging behavior. For example, simply saying "Help me" without having someone respond with assistance is not likely to result in a reduction in escape-maintained behaviors. Other people must take action in response to these communicative efforts—a concept we refer to as response success. In one of our studies, we used FCT to reduce the chronic and severe challenging behaviors exhibited by three students with ASDs (Durand & Carr, 1991). When we subsequently followed these students across several years, we found that two of the three students continued to use the new communicative responses we taught them, and their challenging behaviors remained at low levels. However, the behaviors of one of the students had returned to prior high levels a year after our initial intervention. Observing him in his classroom, we saw that although he was attempting to request assistance from his new teacher by saying "I don't understand" when he was asked a question (the strategy we had previously taught him), his teacher was not responding. It seemed that the teacher did not know what he was saying because of his articulation and therefore did not respond by prompting him or clarifying the questions she directed to him. As a result, he returned to hitting himself and screaming, which usually resulted in the termination of the teaching session—the same pattern that had occurred prior to our intervening with FCT.

We reintervened with this student by teaching him to more clearly articulate his request for assistance (saying "I don't understand"). Typically, in these cases the teacher would be informed of his articulation difficulties, and she would adapt her teaching style to accommodate his unclear speech. However, we wanted the student to be able to solicit assistance not only from this teacher but also from a variety of other people, so we conducted articulation training with him. Once he was able to more clearly make his request known, his teacher responded as expected—by providing him with prompts when he said he did not understand the question—and his challenging behaviors again were reduced. This study and others highlight the importance of the communicative response in eliciting an appropriate reaction from others in the environment (e.g., Durand & Carr, 1991; Volkert, Lerman, Call, & Trosclair-Lasserre, 2009).

Response Efficiency

Research on FCT suggests that the approach is most effective when the new communicative response is more efficient at eliciting the desired reinforcers than the problem behavior. In other words, if it is easier to say "Help me" to get assistance than it is to scream or hit, FCT will be successful. A number of studies directly examine this aspect of FCT (Fisher, Thompson, Hagopian, Bowman, & Krug, 2000; Horner & Day, 1991; Horner, Sprague, Obrien, & Heathfield, 1990; Richman, Wacker, & Winborn, 2001; Schindler & Horner, 2005). For example, in a series of studies, Horner and his colleagues examined this aspect of functional communication training (Horner & Day, 1991; Horner et al., 1990). In one study, for example, the researchers examined the aggression of one 12-year-old boy (Horner & Day, 1991). They found that his aggressive behavior was maintained by escape from demands and decided to use FCT to teach him how to appropriately request a break from work. The researchers systematically examined the effects of teaching him to sign "I want to go, please" on his aggression. They observed no significant reduction in aggression with this strategy. They then taught him to sign "Break"—a much easier way to communicate for escape—and this resulted in significant reductions in his problem behavior. They hypothesized that effort impacts the outcome of FCT such that if the new communicative response requires more effort than the problem behavior, individuals will choose to continue using their problem behavior. Similarly, they examined the impact of delay in gaining reinforcement and schedule of reinforcement (how often they were reinforced) and saw that individuals choose the most efficient means of gaining their preferred reinforcers, whether it be through communication or problem behavior. These types of studies demonstrate that response efficiency is an important consideration in predicting the success of FCT (Fisher et al., 2000; Horner & Day, 1991; Horner et al., 1990; Richman et al., 2001; Schindler & Horner, 2005).

Response Acceptability

Our clinical experience with FCT suggests that another important consideration in the success of FCT involves whether or not the response is acceptable to significant others (Durand & Merges, 2009). If the new communicative response is seen as unacceptable in community settings, then others will not respond appropriately and the desired consequences will not be obtained.

Response acceptability can be viewed as a cultural consideration—making sure that the relevant local culture will respond appropriately to the communicative requests. For example, in one case, a young woman who was living in a group home would scream and remove her clothing, both extremely disruptive to the other residents (Durand, 1990). We assessed her challenging behavior as being maintained by the attention she subsequently received by staff when she was disruptive. Given her limited communicative repertoire (she had no conventional communication skills), we taught her to raise her hand to signal to the group home staff that she was requesting some of their attention. Although this strategy was initially successful in reducing her disruptive behavior, over the course of several weeks her behavior problems returned to pretreatment levels. We revisited her in the group home and conducted a series of observations to see why FCT was no longer successful. It quickly became clear that the staff was only occasionally responding to her hand raising and that she was gradually shifting from raising her hand to gain attention back to using her disruptive behavior. Staff interviews revealed that although they initially agreed to respond to her request for attention through hand raising, they were too busy with their other tasks and found her constant requests for attention annoying. Subsequently, our efforts involved trying to change their local culture, namely, to educate the staff on the basic need of all people to get attention from others and on how this was part of their role as staff working in a group home. Unfortunately, this strategy was not successful, and they continued to view her requests for attention as problematic.

At this point, we could have abandoned our efforts and assigned blame to the staff. Instead, we decided to switch strategies. Now, rather than having hand raising signifying her request for them to stop their other tasks and come over to her to spend time with her, we instead told the staff that her hand raising was to signal her request to help them with their work. Now, for example, if they were emptying the dishwasher and she raised her hand, they were to go get her and have her help them empty the dishwasher. This minor change was extremely successful in changing whether or not they responded to her and, in turn, resulted in a significant reduction in her challenging behavior. Hand raising still resulted in attention from staff, but now it was in a form that was more acceptable to them. They could continue with their tasks, she could get attention from them, and the bonus was that she was now engaged in more functional activities during the day.

Obviously, this case highlights a dilemma we face when trying to intervene with individuals who engage in challenging behavior. There are times when the response we select to teach them may not be perceived as acceptable to others in the person's immediate community. For example, a clinician once relayed how he had used FCT to reduce problem behavior of an adult in the community. This person's challenging behavior appeared to be maintained by attention, and the clinician taught the man how to request attention from others. The clinician reported that although this strategy (requesting a hug) was successful in his prevocational work environment, it was not successful out in the general community. Although you could argue that this would be a better world if strangers were more open to hugs, realistically, requesting hugs will not be acceptable in most cases. This cultural consideration—making sure that the forms of communication we teach are acceptable to others—is an essential concern for the ultimate success of FCT in reducing challenging behavior (Durand, 1990; Durand & Merges, 2009).

Response Recognizability

An important consideration for individuals with significant communication needs is teaching them a response that can be recognized, especially by others who may not be highly trained, so that it can effectively replace the problem behavior. To date, much of the research on FCT has used verbal and signed speech as the means of communication. Unfortunately, spoken speech can often be misunderstood, and signed speech can be so idiosyncratic that few can understand the message being relayed. Several studies have addressed the issue of the recognizability of the communicative response as it relates to FCT—for example, in the case involving the young boy returning to serious self-injury because poorly intelligible speech did not provide a realistic functional alternative (Durand & Carr, 1991). In this study, we found that by improving the boy's articulation skills, the teacher responded appropriately. Following the improvement in the student–teacher interaction, the boy's challenging behavior was again reduced, which generalized to a new teacher and was maintained one year later (Durand & Carr, 1991).

Response recognizability is of particular importance for students with the most severe disabilities. This issue has lead to a growing number of studies that demonstrate success for students having severe communicative disabilities when they use augmentative and alternative communication (AAC) strategies as the means of communication with FCT (Bingham, Spooner, & Browder, 2007; Durand, 1993, 1999; Durand & Berotti, 1991; Franco et al., 2009; Mirenda, 1997, 2003; Olive, Lang, & Davis, 2008; Schepis, Reid, & Behrman, 1996; Wacker et al., 1990). The rationale is to presumably improve the recognizability of the communicative requests being made by these individuals.

Use of AAC devices improves recognizability of responses not only for students with severe disabilities and their trained communication partners but also for untrained communication partners in the community who understand the requests and respond appropriately (Durand, 1999; Durand & Berotti, 1991). In addition, the devices have at times been programmed to speak in both English and another language when a student's family does not speak English at home and the teacher speaks only English at school. We have, in essence, taught students with severe and multiple disabilities to be bilingual. These devices have permitted us to teach students to make relatively simple responses (pressing a pad on the machine) that can result in successful interchanges. Again, because the output can be recognized by anyone, the success of the communication training has been extended into the community. Chapter 3 discusses more ways to use AAC to reduce challenging behavior and enhance the communication needs of people with disabilities.

Response Milieu

What are the characteristics of the optimal environment in which FCT should take place? Can we describe, and therefore design, settings that will facilitate the success, generalization, and maintenance of reductions in challenging behavior using FCT? Unfortunately, research has not specifically focused on environmental/contextual influences as they relate to this intervention approach. To our knowledge, no research has yet systematically explored the types of environmental variables that would positively or negatively impact on these outcomes. However, based on our extensive experience using FCT in a wide variety of environments, we offer some of our observations on the role of the environment in the success of FCT.

One factor that appears to influence the outcome of efforts to implement FTC is the participant's degree of control or choice. The availability of choice-making opportunities has received considerable attention and has been implicated in the success of various educational activities (Carlson, Luiselli, Slyman, & Markowski, 2008; Dyer, Dunlap, & Winterling, 1990; Watanabe & Sturmey, 2003). Special attention has been paid to communication training that allows individuals to make choices in their day-to-day activities (e.g., choosing when to take a break, when to have a drink, when to get social attention). We have observed that in settings in which choice making is encouraged, FCT is more likely to succeed. Conversely, in settings in which choice making is discouraged, FCT has often had limited success; in these settings, FCT has sometimes been described as "giving in" and has been received with some reticence. Again, this aspect of the intervention environment seems to offer a fruitful avenue for further empirical attention.

A second environmental factor that seems to be implicated in outcomes of FCT involves the ways in which participants are grouped. Despite initiatives to include all students in regular classrooms and community settings, environments still exist in which students are grouped together because of their challenging behavior. Historically, the logic behind such groupings has been that they facilitate students' access to staff who are specially trained to deal with challenging behavior. In addition, such groupings would allow for group-wide programs and contingencies and would minimize disruptions of other students.

Space does not permit a full discussion of the anticipated, as opposed to the actual, results of such homogeneous groupings. However, we have had the opportunity to compare and contrast the ability of these different settings to support efforts at FCT. Our observation has been that staff who work in such "behavior classes" are at particular risk of being overtaxed by the demands of the classroom and may find it especially difficult to be responsive to all of their students. On the other hand, staff members in more heterogeneous groupings appear to have more flexibility. They are able to shift priorities toward activities that may require more intensive, yet temporary, effort (e.g., FCT). This flexibility may be attributable to the other students in these classrooms when FCT is pursued in classrooms containing some students who can benefit from periods of independent work. In such a setting, the teacher is more available to be responsive to the children receiving communication training than a teacher in a "behavior class."

EMPIRICAL BASIS

There is an extensive literature on the outcomes of using FCT to treat and reduce challenging behavior. This section will selectively review the substantial body of research in this area. To date, close to 200 published studies document the successful use of FCT with a range of individuals and their challenging behaviors. Fortunately, several published reviews have documented the depth and breadth of research studies on the outcomes of FCT across populations, on behavior topographies (e.g., aggression, tantrums, noncompliance), and on variations in the methods for using this approach (e.g., Bambara, Mitchellkvacky, & Iacobelli, 1994; Durand & Merges, 2008, 2009; Halle, Ostrosky, & Hemmeter, 2006; Mancil, 2006; Matson, Dixon, & Matson, 2005; Mirenda, 1997; Petscher et al., 2009). For example, Mirenda (1997) reviewed research that used AAC strategies (e.g., manual signing, communication books, VOCAs) as the method for communicating with FCT. A review by Matson and colleagues (2005) evaluated the literature on a number of techniques used to treat aggression and found that FCT was one of the most heavily researched approaches.

Petscher and colleagues (2009) broadly reviewed research using differential reinforcement of alternative behavior, which includes variations of FCT. In fact, FCT is
frequently cited as one of the few behavioral interventions having extensive support
from initial efficacy studies (Smith et al., 2007).

In their review of research on differential reinforcement of alternative behavior, Petscher and colleagues (2009) identified more than 80 studies that used
FCT to treat challenging behavior; met specific criteria, such as being published in
peer-reviewed outlets; and reported behavioral data. They used the standards set
by the American Psychological Association's (APA) Division 12 Task Force on the
Promotion and Dissemination of Psychological Procedures to determine if FCT or its
variations met the task force's criteria for interventions that are "well established,"
"probably efficacious," or "experimental" (Chambless et al., 1996; APA, 1995). The
task force provides criteria for judging the quality of single-subject-design research
(Chambless et al., 1996; APA, 1995; see Table 6.2).

Petscher and colleagues reviewed the studies meeting the task force's criteria
as they pertain to the demonstrated efficacy of FCT. Given the diverse nature of
the behavior topographies examined, the authors decided to combine aggression,
self-injury, property destruction, and other disruptive behaviors into a category they
labeled "destructive behavior." Overall, they found that differential reinforcement of
alternative behavior in general and FCT specifically met the criteria for being well-
established treatments for destructive behavior. This level of evidence was present
whether or not extinction for challenging behavior was added as a component of
the treatment (Petscher et al., 2009). They also noted that these results were obtained with few unwanted side effects across children and adults with a range of
disorders. The results of this review and others attest to the robust nature of FCT
as a treatment for a range of challenging behaviors across a number of different
populations (Bambara et al., 1994; Durand & Merges, 2008, 2009; Halle et al., 2006;
Mancil, 2006; Matson et al., 2005; Mirenda, 1997; Petscher et al., 2009). Occasional
reports of unwanted effects—including using the new communicative response too
often—have been the focus of component analyses of FCT, and we review some of
this research next.

Table 6.2.   Criteria for empirically validated treatments using single-subject designs

Well-established treatments

I.   A large series of single-case-design experiments ($n > 9$) demonstrating efficacy. Such an experiment must have
     A.   Used a good experimental design
     B.   Compared the intervention to another treatment and was found to be superior to a placebo or to the other treatment

II. Experiments must be conducted with treatment manuals.

III. Characteristics of the client samples must be clearly specified.

IV. Effects must have been demonstrated by at least two different investigators or investigating teams.

Probably efficacious treatments

I.   A small series of single-case-design experiments ($n > 3$) otherwise meeting criteria of well-established treatment.

Source: Chambless et al. (1996).

Schedule Thinning

An important issue to address when using FCT is the reinforcement for the alternative communication being used to replace challenging behavior. Initially, a rich schedule of reinforcement is typically recommended to ensure that acquisition occurs quickly (Durand, 1990). As we have seen, if reinforcement is delayed too long or is otherwise not sufficient, the individual will return to using challenging behavior to gain access to preferred reinforcers at an acceptable rate (e.g., escape from demands, attention from others; Horner & Day, 1991). However, continued reinforcement of the new communicative response at high rates (e.g., every time someone makes a request) can itself be viewed as problematic. Constant requests for attention, for example, can be annoying to teachers or family members, regardless of the form they take. Requesting escape from work on a continual basis can seriously interfere with educational and vocational goals. To address this issue, a number of studies examined if and how the schedule of reinforcement for the appropriate communicative behavior could be reduced, or "thinned," from a continuous schedule to a more intermittent one that might be more acceptable in typical settings (e.g., Hagopian, Kuhn, Long, & Rush, 2005; Hagopian, Toole, Long, Bowman, & Lieving, 2004; Hanley, Iwata, & Thompson, 2001; Lerman, Kelley, Van Camp, & Roane, 1999; Lerman, Kelley, Vorndran, Kuhn, & LaRue, 2002; Shirley, Iwata, Kahng, Mazaleski, & Lerman, 1997; Volkert et al., 2009; Worsdell, Iwata, Hanley, Thompson, & Kahng, 2000).

In one study, for example, researchers gradually increased the time between the appropriate request and the reinforcement (Hagopian, Fisher, Sullivan, Acquisto, & LeBlanc, 1998). They found that although this attempt at schedule thinning was successful in reducing the amount of effort to respond to appropriate requests for some individuals, it was not successful for all. Similar problems in using delayed schedules have been noted in other studies as well (Fisher et al., 2000). One difficulty with using delayed schedules of reinforcement with the alternative response is that the individual may not be able to discriminate when and if the request will be satisfied, resulting in increased requesting—a pattern typically observed with fixed-interval reinforcement schedules. Some researchers have found more success using signals (e.g., a red card signaling no response forthcoming, a green card signaling that a request will receive a response) to indicate the temporal nature of the responses (e.g., Hanley et al., 2001).

It is unlikely that one approach to schedule thinning will be appropriate for all cases when using FCT. For example, the ability of the individual to discriminate reinforcement schedules and the person's history of reinforcement will likely influence efforts to reduce the level of reinforcement for appropriate requests. At the same time, it is important to consider what the prevailing environment can support. As we discussed in the section Response Milieu, some environments can support relatively high rates of requests, whereas others cannot. Research on contextual fit with regard to requests for reinforcement and the environment's ability to maintain responses should be an important next step in researching the nature of responses to appropriate requests for reinforcement in FCT.

Consequences of Challenging Behavior

A somewhat controversial concern related to FCT use involves the issue of how to respond to the challenging behavior itself. As previously noted, evidence suggests that

FCT is effective with or without extinction for the challenging behavior (Petscher et al., 2009). In our work with FCT, we have used response-independent consequences as the primary reactive strategy (Durand, 1990). In other words, we try (as much as possible) to continue to behave with the person as if the challenging behavior did not occur. The goal here is to make the challenging behavior "nonfunctional" in the environment. For example, if we are working with the person, and he or she screams, we try to continue working. If the person is alone and starts to tantrum, we will try not to intervene. We will also attempt to avoid what might be perceived as negative consequences, such as reprimands or withdrawing attention, because these may also serve as reinforcers for some individuals. At the same time at which we are teaching an alternative behavior that serves the same function, we try to make the challenging behavior a less efficient (nonfunctional) strategy for obtaining reinforcers.

A caveat is in order when using response-independent consequences. The protection of the student and those around him or her remains the most important priority. In other words, we try not to change the way we behave as a function of the student's challenging behavior. However, when students are engaging in behaviors that are dangerous to themselves or others, we intervene to protect all involved. However, such intervention is always conducted in as neutral a manner as possible, to limit the changes in the environment.

Several studies have examined directly the issue of continuing reinforcement for the challenging behavior. One study looked at whether FCT would be an effective approach if the challenging behavior continued to be reinforced while an alternative response was being taught (Shirley et al., 1997). For three individuals who engaged in self-injurious behavior, manual signing was used as the alternative communicative response. The researchers found that self-injury was not initially reduced if it continued to be reinforced concurrently with the new alternative. However, once extinction was initiated for the challenging behavior, it was reduced and signing increased. Even when extinction was suspended for self-injury, the behavior problems remained at low levels for two of the three individuals (Shirley et al., 1997).

Wacker and colleagues (1990) described the use of FCT with three individuals and the use of specific consequences with two of these people. It was observed that hand biting and aggression in the two people were significantly reduced with a package of procedures including FCT and negative consequences (TO for one person and graduated guidance for the other). The authors observed that when they attempted to remove the negative consequences as part of the package, the challenging behaviors increased. It was concluded that some individuals may require mild forms of negative consequences, at least initially.

It is difficult to interpret why participants in the previous research and the third participant in the study by Wacker et al. (1990) did not require negative consequences to reduce their challenging behavior. One interpretation mentioned by the authors is that because these negative consequences were introduced from the beginning of their treatment, this may have affected their later behavior. It is possible that if the negative consequences had never been introduced concurrent with FCT, these consequences may not have been required to reduce the challenging behavior. These data suggest that behavioral contrast (the tendency to evaluate situations compared with how these situations have been presented previously) may have been at work in this study—with the effectiveness of FCT alone influenced by the removal of the contingencies for challenging behavior (i.e., TO, graduated guidance). For example, if a student is used to getting reinforced frequently and this is abruptly ended when starting FCT, the success of this approach might initially be limited, because the reinforcers expected might be reduced *when compared with the pre-FCT state*. This issue points to the need to be cautious in implementing and interpreting such intervention packages.

One goal in FCT is to make the new communicative response more efficient at receiving reinforcers than the challenging behavior. As we previously discussed, one way to accomplish this goal is to teach a response that is, right from the start, *more* efficient than the challenging behavior. However, as this last section suggests, another avenue to pursue is to make the challenging behavior *less* efficient than the communicative response. Our work has been aimed at accomplishing this by removing the contingency between the challenging behavior and our behavior using response-independent consequences (Durand, 1990).

Outcome Research

Although there is an extensive body of published research assessing the effectiveness of FCT, the vast majority of these studies employ single-case designs with a small number of participants in each study. Although several larger studies exist (e.g., Durand & Carr, 1992; Hagopian et al., 1998; Kurtz et al., 2003; Wacker et al., 1998), there are to date no randomized clinical trials comparing outcomes with no treatment, treatment as usual, or other traditional techniques. This reliance on a single category of research design may limit our understanding of FCT as an intervention.

Several potential limitations on the generalizability of single-subject-design results relate to descriptive information about methods that is routinely described in randomized clinical trials but is rarely included in single-subject-design studies. For instance, how individuals are selected for participation in treatment studies can potentially have a major impact on the interpretation of the results. For example, selecting for parent training only those families who will pay clinical fees out of pocket and who will faithfully attend numerous and long training sessions may limit the extent to which the results can be generalized to low socioeconomic status and less-involved families. Similarly, including only those individuals referred to a clinic known for working with young children with mild behavior problems may limit the study's usefulness with older individuals with more severe challenges. Selection bias—systematically including certain participants in research (and therefore excluding others)—can artificially influence the results in a positive or negative way. One method for reducing selection bias that is used in group experimental research studies involves random assignment to treatment groups. Randomization helps improve internal validity by reducing systematic bias in assignment, although it does not necessarily eliminate all bias in the groups, especially if they are small (Barlow & Hersen, 1984). How do researchers using single-subject designs select the participants for their research studies?

To attempt to answer this question, we conducted a review of the behavioral intervention literature to more accurately gauge how participants are chosen (Durand & Rost, 2005). In reviewing 149 research articles published in the *Journal of Applied Behavior Analysis* from 1968 to 2001, we found that only 26.04% (44 out of 149) indicated any selection criteria, and the percentage of experiments addressing selection bias was 8.28% (14 out of 149). The percentage of experiments that noted attrition was 2.37% (4 out of 149), and the percentage of experiments that addressed attrition bias was 0%. There were no trends suggesting a significant increase in reporting this information in more contemporary research studies.

Overall, we found that a relatively low number of these single-subject-design studies mentioned how they had selected those included in their research (26%), and fewer still mentioned whether they had used procedures to reduce selection bias. Almost none of the studies published over the past three decades indicated whether participants had dropped out of treatment prematurely (3%), and of those few studies that did, none assessed for any potential participant characteristics that would predict differential attrition. In addition, none of the articles reported whether potential participants and/or guardians had refused to be included in their treatment studies. This relative lack of information on potential selection bias and attrition calls into question the generalizability of otherwise positive outcome data on the treatment of challenging behavior.

As we see, the culture in single-subject-design research rarely addresses population issues, an essential concern for issues of clinical efficacy and utility. For example, one handbook on single-subject research methods recommends that researchers select only those participants who will reliably show up for sessions (Bailey & Burch, 2002). Although this is a practical suggestion, its consequences—studying only highly motivated and reliable people—limit conclusions about the larger population of people who request our help. The report from a meeting sponsored by the National Institutes of Health (NIH) on methodological challenges in psychosocial interventions in ASDs (Lord et al., 2005) addresses this issue and lists the need for additional randomized clinical trials in this area as the highest priority.

An important caveat involves representativeness of the treatment literature. The lack of information in these areas cannot be interpreted to suggest that there are significant biases in selection and attrition. We do not know, for example, if the intervention research systematically excludes certain individuals, which in turn improperly influences the results and leaves the research literature open to substantial criticism. To address these serious concerns, research on behavioral interventions for challenging behavior must be subjected to scrutiny that examines these population-related questions (Durand & Rost, 2005).

PRACTICAL REQUIREMENTS

There are a number of reasons why the act of teaching communication to individuals with severe challenging behavior is difficult—the most obvious of which is the challenging behavior itself. Trying to teach someone who is hitting you, is hitting himself or herself, or is generally disruptive in the teaching situation is at best very frustrating and provides a rationale for using extremely restrictive procedures. First, it is assumed that no teaching can go on while the person continues to engage in disruptive behavior. Next, a "temporary" program is recommended, one that uses some form of aversive consequence to reduce the frequency of the problem behavior. The reasoning continues that once the rate of problem behavior is reduced, teaching can finally be carried out.

Our efforts at teaching communication strategies to individuals exhibiting challenging behavior begin prior to reductions in the behavior problems, using teaching efforts adapted so they can continue despite the behavior problems. Often, we have set up the teaching situation so that behavior problems are minimized. However, this has not always been possible, and on rare occasions, we have even taught communication strategies to individuals while they were in mechanical restraints. Challenging behavior should not be viewed as a major barrier to teaching communication.

A second obstacle to teaching communication lies in the training of those who work daily with individuals with ASDs, many of whom do not have extensive training in how to teach communication skills. It is common, for example, that relatively few training resources are available to teach how to properly fade a prompt or to set up the environment to encourage communicative interactions (Durand, 1987). Extraordinary effort is required to successfully intervene when severe behavior problems exist. This is true whether the intervention involves training and safeguards in the use of restrictive procedures—which will be an ongoing, disheartening task—or training and monitoring of programs involving teaching alternative skills—which can often yield more satisfying interactions for all of those involved.

Scheduling Teaching Opportunities

Once the function of the challenging behavior and an appropriate replacement communication skill are determined, one person typically takes responsibility for initial communication training. Time commitments can be as short as 30–60 min per day several days per week. However, an ideal teaching strategy creates numerous teaching opportunities throughout the day in typical settings. For example, if a student in a classroom screams in response to frustrating situations, one strategy is to program minor frustrating situations throughout the student's day. Specifically, we might plan to have the student's typical routines interrupted in order to create teaching opportunities. He would be prompted to open a desk drawer to take out his favorite toy. However, we would tape the drawer closed, making it difficult to open. As soon as he found he could not open the drawer, we would prompt him to request assistance ("Say 'Help me'"). Similar scenarios would be repeated in multiple situations and settings (e.g., putting on his coat, opening the door to go outside, tying his shoes), and all of the adults who came in contact with him would be taught how to prompt him. Just as important, however, they would also be taught how to *fade* their prompts.

Training throughout the day is referred to as "distributed practice" (McDonnell & Hardman, 1988, p. 330). In other words, students are allowed to engage in other activities between teaching trials. This is in contrast to "massed practice," which involves presenting teaching trials one after another, with limited interruptions. Most teaching occurs somewhere along a continuum from highly massed practice (very little time between teaching trials) to highly distributed practice (long delays between trials). Because opportunities to make requests occur at varying times throughout the day, distributed practice more closely resembles these interactions and is therefore preferred when possible.

Despite the advantages of distributed practice, initial use of highly distributed practice with some students may be problematic. Because distributed practice may involve fewer trials (although it does not have to), the opportunities to learn the skill may be sporadic. Acquisition may be slow, creating problems for students who may become disruptive to avoid such training situations. In addition, training for staff in how to identify and use intermittent teaching opportunities may be unavailable in many settings.

Because of these limitations, we have often begun training by using more frequent teaching trials in a concentrated period of time. We do this to ensure rapid acquisition and because we are often faced with situations in which skilled trainers are available only for a limited time during the day. For example, there may be one work supervisor who knows the individual best and who is most capable of carrying out training. However, this person may be available for only 30 min each day to conduct teaching sessions. In these situations, we would set up training so that the supervisor could conduct a number of trials during that 30-min period. Trials typically would be interspersed with breaks, opportunities to manipulate requested objects, or time for access to social interactions. The environment is arranged to create opportunities for communication (e.g., putting an obstacle in the path of a student's wheelchair and prompting the student to ask for assistance). However, distributing sessions across the day would not occur until there was some initial communication success for the student. At that point, the training arrangements might lie somewhere in the middle of the massed practice–distributed practice continuum. As soon as possible, however, training trials are interspersed throughout the student's day (Durand, 1990).

Choosing Contexts for Teaching

The settings or contexts in which such teaching takes place can also be viewed on a continuum, from highly artificial contexts (e.g., teaching social interactions with peers in a speech therapist's office) to more natural contexts (e.g., teaching social interactions with peers at a party). The naturalness of the setting depends largely on where you want the student to use the new communicative response. Using the criterion environment—that is, the environment in which you want the student to communicate—as the training environment may facilitate generalization and maintenance of intervention effects. With the typical model that involves teaching skills in a separate setting (e.g., in the speech therapist's office), once the response is learned, you need to encourage the performance of that behavior in settings where you want it to occur (e.g., in the cafeteria). By beginning training in the natural or criterion setting, extensive programming for generalization is not necessary because it will be occurring where you want it to occur. In addition, obstacles to maintenance can be immediately identified when teaching in the criterion environment (e.g., are the consequences being provided in that setting going to maintain the new response?).

KEY COMPONENTS

Table 6.3 outlines the key steps used to assess behavior and to conduct FCT. These steps can often be complicated, and readers are referred to the section Suggested Readings for more detailed instructions.

Step 1. Assess the Function of the Behavior

To assess the function of a problem behavior, antecedents and consequences of that behavior must be identified. Once the purpose of a targeted behavior is understood, individuals can be taught to request the variables previously obtained by the challenging behavior. The previous section on assessment provides recommendations for conducting this important aspect of FCT.

Step 2. Select the Communication Modality

Once the function of the challenging behavior is identified, the type of response to encourage from the individual needs to be determined. If the individual already has some facility in a mode of communication (e.g., verbal, signing), that mode should be considered for FCT. Usually, if an individual has been unsuccessful in learning to communicate effectively after extensive verbal language training, an alternative signing or symbolic mode should be used. If the person has also been unsuccessful with sign language training (e.g., has not learned to sign or uses poorly demonstrated or incomprehensible signs), we recommend graphic symbolic communication training, at least initially. Symbolic communication training can involve the use of picture books, tokens with messages written on them, or other assistive devices in which symbol selection occurs visually (e.g., VOCAs). This form of communication training has the advantage of being relatively easy to teach, and it is universally recognizable to potential communication partners.

Step 3. Create Teaching Situations

As a next step, the environment is arranged to create opportunities for communication (e.g., putting an obstacle in the way of a person trying to open a door and prompting him or her to ask for assistance). This use of "incidental teaching" (McGee, Morrier, & Daly, 1999)—that is, arranging the environment to establish

Table 6.3. Step-by-step instructions for functional communication training

Step	Description
1. Assess the function of the behavior.	Use two or more functional assessment techniques to determine what variables are maintaining the problem behavior.
2. Select the communication modality.	Identify how you want the individual to communicate with others (e.g., verbally, through alternative communication strategies).
3. Create teaching situations.	Identify situations in the environment that are triggers for problem behavior (e.g., difficult tasks), and use these as the settings for teaching the alternative responses.
4. Prompt communication.	Prompt the alternative communication in the setting in which you want it to occur. Use the least intrusive prompt necessary.
5. Fade prompts.	Quickly fade the prompts, ensuring that no problem behaviors occur during training.
6. Teach new communicative responses.	When possible, teach a variety of alternative communicative responses that can serve the same function (e.g., saying "Help me" or "I don't understand").
7. Modify the environment.	When appropriate, changes in the environment—such as improving student–task match in school—should be implemented.

From Durand, V.M., & Merges, E. (2008). Functional communication training to treat challenging behavior. In W. O'Donohue & J.E. Fisher (Eds.), *Cognitive behavior therapy: Applying empirically supported techniques in your practice* (2nd ed., pp. 222–229). New York, NY: Wiley; reprinted by permission.

situations that elicit interest and that are used as teaching opportunities—is an important part of successful communication training. Using the person's interest in some interaction, whether it be a desire to stop working on a difficult task or to elicit the attention of an adult, is a very powerful tool in teaching generalized communication.

As soon as possible and where appropriate, training trials are interspersed throughout the individual's day. Using the criterion environment (i.e., where you want the person to communicate) as the training environment facilitates generalization and maintenance of intervention effects. In addition, obstacles to maintenance can be immediately identified when teaching in the criterion environment (e.g., the interventionist can determine whether the consequences being provided in that setting are going to maintain the new response).

Step 4. Prompt Communication

Teaching individuals to communicate as a replacement for their challenging behavior requires a range of sophisticated language training techniques (Durand, Mapstone, & Youngblade, 1999). A multiphase prompting and prompt-fading procedure is used to teach the new communicative response. Prompts are introduced as necessary, then faded as quickly as possible. Some individuals negatively resist attempts to be taught important skills (e.g., the individual screams and kicks), others positively resist (e.g., the individual laughs and giggles instead of working), and still others passively resist (e.g., the individual does not look at materials, makes no response). When individuals kick, scream, and rip up work materials whenever they are presented or passively ignore efforts to get them to attend to a task, teaching becomes a major challenge and learning becomes highly unlikely.

One procedure we have used for these types of problems is to teach the individual to request assistance (e.g., "Help me") or a brief "break" from work. Often, the problem behaviors appear to be attempts to avoid or escape from unpleasant situations. It makes sense, then, that if the individual is taught to appropriately request assistance *and then receives it,* the task will seem easier and problem behaviors should be reduced. Similarly, if an individual has been working for some time on a task and is allowed to ask for a break *and receives it,* this individual's problem behavior should be reduced.

Step 5. Fade Prompts

We begin pulling back our prompts by fading them as soon as possible. When necessary, fading can involve going from a full physical prompt to partial prompts (e.g., just touching the hand), to gestural prompts (e.g., motioning to encourage use of the hands), to, finally, only the verbal prompt (e.g., "Say 'break'"; see Figure 6.2). Throughout training, we rely heavily on delayed prompting as another method of fading (Halle, Baer, & Spradlin, 1981; Schwartz, Anderson, & Halle, 1989). After several trials, we intersperse a trial with a delayed prompt (e.g., we wait approximately 5 s), to see if the person will respond without the next level of prompt. For example, if a boy had been responding to just a touch of his hand to prompt the use of a sign, we would make a gesture as if we were going to prompt him, then wait 5 s. If he made the sign for *break,* then we would let him go on the break.

We do not wait until responding is extremely stable to move on to the next level of prompting. In other words, someone does not have to be correctly responding to, say, 9 out of 10 prompts for 2 weeks for us to move to the next step. We would attempt to move to the next step if a person is successful at a step for 3 to 5 consecutive response opportunities. We do this in order to prevent individuals from becoming prompt dependent (i.e., too reliant on prompts to respond). Typically, we find that challenging behavior improves most dramatically as soon as the person begins to make requests without prompts.

Step 6. Teach New Communicative Responses

Once successful, intervention continues by introducing new forms of communication (e.g., requests for food, music, work) while at the same time reintroducing work demands or expanding the settings in which requests are made and introducing new staff into the training program.

Step 7. Modify the Environment

Recommendations are often made concerning environmental and curricular changes. Several authors have described scenarios in which an individual was found to engage in challenging behavior in the presence of certain stimuli (e.g., certain instructional programs, certain staff) but reduced the severity or frequency of the behavior when steps were taken to modify or remove those stimuli from the individual's environment (e.g., Dunlap, Kern-Dunlap, Clarke, & Robbins, 1991; Kennedy & Itkonen, 1993). Therefore, if we observe students engaging in problem behavior when directed to participate in nonfunctional or age-inappropriate activities (e.g., stringing beads), we recommend that they no longer be required to work on those activities. Instead, we suggest alternatives that might be more useful and engaging.

(Steps 1–7 on pp. 125–127 from Durand, V.M., & Merges, E. [2008]. Functional communication training to treat challenging behavior. In W. O'Donohue & J.E. Fisher [Eds.], *Cognitive behavior therapy: Applying empirically supported techniques in your practice* [2nd ed., p. 225]. New York, NY: Wiley; adapted by permission.)

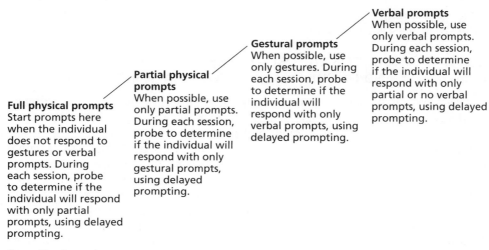

Figure 6.2.   Prompting sequence.

DATA COLLECTION TO SUPPORT DECISION MAKING

Data collection within FCT is conducted to serve four phases associated with successful intervention (Durand & Hieneman, 2008a, 2008b): establishing goals, analyzing patterns of behavior, assessing obstacles in the environment, and monitoring results.

Establishing Goals

This phase involves collecting sufficient information to define the problems, including the person's behaviors of concern and specific changes that are desired at home, at school, or in the community. During the beginning stages of program planning, we typically use interviews and formal checklists (e.g., the Scales of Independent Behavior–Revised; Bruininks, Woodcock, Weatherman, & Hill, 1996) to determine the nature and extent of the problems.

Analyzing Patterns

This phase involves using various forms of functional assessments to understand why the person is behaving in this manner (see the section Target Populations and Assessments for Determining Treatment Relevance and Goals).

Assessing Obstacles

Concurrent with assessing the behavior of the targeted person, we informally assess the learning environment to determine whether it will support the new communicative responses (see the section Response Milieu). In addition, we assess attitudinal obstacles that may be present in family members or educators that can interfere with successful intervention (Durand & Hieneman, 2008a, 2008b; see the section Future Directions).

Monitoring Results

Responsible individuals (e.g., instructional aides, interventionists) are trained to collect data on challenging behavior, communication, and educational progress to ensure that the strategies are working. Data collection continues in order to assess whether changes in the plan are needed (see Durand & Hieneman, 2008a, for an extensive discussion and sample data forms; Durand & Hieneman, 2008b).

CONSIDERATIONS FOR CHILDREN FROM CULTURALLY AND LINGUISTICALLY DIVERSE BACKGROUNDS

Children from culturally and linguistically diverse backgrounds can pose unique challenges in the successful use of FCT to treat challenging behavior. If, for example, a child's teacher speaks only English at school and the family speaks only Spanish at home, not only is home–school communication affected but teaching the student a communication strategy that will be successful in both environments can be difficult, if not impossible. One strategy we have used in cases of a mismatch between home and school languages is to rely on AAC strategies, such as picture books or VOCAs. In one study, we used VOCAs programmed in both languages to teach students functionally equivalent responses (e.g., "Help me" and "Ayuda me") (Durand, 1999; Durand & Berotti, 1991). We have, in essence, taught students having severe and multiple disabilities to be bilingual—making a single selection that is realized in the language appropriate to the language context. These devices have permitted us to teach students to make relatively simple responses (pressing a pad on the machine) that can result in sophisticated output (full sentences) in clear, spoken English and Spanish. Again, because the output can be recognized by anyone within a particular language community, the success of the communication training has been extended more broadly into the community.

Application to a Child

In the section Response Success, we briefly described one of our studies in which we used FCT to reduce the chronic and severe challenging behaviors exhibited by three students with ASDs (Durand & Carr, 1991). One of those boys, Hal, was 9 years old and attending a school for students with developmental disabilities. Teachers reported that Hal frequently became upset at varying times during the day, typically in response to requests he found difficult to respond to and when he could not answer a question presented to him. He would violently slap his face and scream, ultimately falling to the floor. He had some verbal ability, although he would frequently talk rapidly and unclearly.

As a first step, we decided to teach Hal to say "I don't understand" in response to questions for which he did not have an answer. After several weeks of this training, he would reliably and spontaneously use this communication strategy, and the frequency of face slapping and screaming was substantially reduced. A follow-up observation of Hal several months later in a new classroom and with a different teacher, however, revealed that he was again slapping his face and screaming and rarely using the trained phrase.

When we observed Hal with his new teacher, it was clear what was wrong. His teacher would ask a question, such as, "Hal, what's your address?" At times Hal would say, "I don't understand," but very quickly and unintelligibly. Because the teacher did not understand what he was saying, she did not provide him with sufficient prompts. After several interactions like this, Hal would eventually get upset, hit himself, and begin screaming. His teacher would respond by leaving him, saying she would return when he calmed down. In short, not only did the teacher not respond to his statement, but she also appeared to be reinforcing his disruption by ending the task (negative reinforcement).

Our intervention involved working to help Hal slow down and better articulate the phrase "I don't understand." We did this without informing his teacher to see whether she would respond appropriately to his phrase when it was intelligible. After our training, we again observed him in the classroom. We found that he was more understandable and that the teacher would now provide prompts for him (e.g., "Say, 'I live at 25 Smith Street'") when he said he did not understand. In addition, his self-injury and screaming were again reduced. An additional follow-up observation 12 months later found Hal to be using the phrase and remaining well behaved in the classroom.

Application to an Adolescent or Adult

One gentleman, Bill, was brought to our attention because he was engaging in severe aggression (punching and grabbing others), self-injurious behavior (hand and arm biting), and other disruptive behaviors (throwing work materials, knocking over tables and chairs). Bill was 32 years old at the time of the referral and had lived most of his life in a large institution. He had recently moved from the institution to a group home and was attending a vocational education program through a local agency.

The vocational program was concerned because Bill was making minimal progress and on occasion would seriously hurt staff members. An analysis of ABC charts, along with administrations of the Motivation Assessment Scale, indicated that his aggression and self-injury may have been maintained by both escape from demands and access to tangibles (e.g., favorite foods). We decided to begin by teaching him the sign for "Break" and allowing him to take time away from work if he asked. A request to leave work was selected instead of a request for tangibles because the work demands appeared to elicit the most frequent and severe outbursts. A request for a break was chosen instead of a request for assistance because he had no difficulty completing the work (i.e., it wasn't difficult) and because at a job site it was more appropriate to request a period of time away from work than to request help.

Bill's response to our initial training efforts was characteristic of many individuals with whom we have worked. He was fine during the prompting and while he was go- ing on the break. However, when we attempted to bring him back to work, he resisted. Occasionally, he would hit the trainer or passively resist efforts to get back to the work table. During these times, Bill was firmly led back to work in a neutral manner, with no reprimands or lengthy explanations. His resistance quickly abated over several sessions. It appeared as if Bill learned that if he went right back to work, he could escape it within a short amount of time.

We did not wait until responding was extremely stable to move on to the next level of prompting (see Figure 6.2). In other words, he did not have to be correctly respond- ing to, say, 9 out of 10 prompts for 2 weeks for us to move to the next step. We would attempt to move to the next step if he was successful at a step for 3 to 5 consecutive responses. We did this to prevent him from becoming prompt dependent (i.e., too reliant on prompts to respond).

Training progressed quickly over several weeks to the point at which Bill would sign for a break with only the pulling back of the work as a prompt. This too was faded, and within 3 months he was requesting a break without any cues by the trainer. As is typi- cal in our experience, his behavior improved dramatically as soon as he began to make requests without prompts.

Once successful, intervention continued by introducing new signs (e.g., food, music, work), reintroducing work demands, encouraging signs throughout his day, and introduc- ing new staff into the training program. These latter steps were introduced systematically, to avoid having him become disruptive. Nine months after initial intervention, the number of episodes of aggression and self-injury was significantly decreased, he was using a large number of signs spontaneously throughout the day, and he was working at a level that exceeded his preintervention performance.

FUTURE DIRECTIONS

The extensive body of evidence accumulated since we first introduced FCT as an intervention in 1985 (Carr & Durand, 1985) points to its success in reducing challenging behavior. However, we are finding that up to 50% of the families or teachers with whom we work are not able to fully carry out this (or any other) intervention. Evidence is growing that parents differ in their perceptions of themselves (e.g., feeling out of control or inadequate as a parent) and of their child with a disability (e.g., whether or not their child is capable of making behavioral improvements) and in their degree of optimism about future prospects for change. This, in turn, impacts their ability to implement the interventions professionals design for them. And professionals know this. Almost all clinicians struggle with families who actively resist their suggestions (e.g., "That won't work with my child," "We've tried that already") or passively resist participating (e.g., not completing assessments, missing multiple training sessions). Yet, rather than view the unsuccessful families as needing a different approach, we often eventually write them off as being "uncooperative" or "noncompliant" (or worse, as "bad parents").

Typically, the fallback assumption for families who struggle with intervention plans is that they need more support. There is a long history of recommending support for families in the form of financial assistance, respite services, and parent support groups to help reduce some of the obstacles to successful intervention. Although these are important considerations, our experience is that these efforts are less effective with families who are highly pessimistic—perhaps 50% of the families with whom we work (Durand, 2007). Respite, for example, is used as a temporary reprieve for these families rather than an opportunity to learn new skills or prepare them to become reinvolved with their children. Parent support groups are often viewed as negative experiences. For family members who already feel guilty about their performance as parents, being in the company of parents perceived as more successful—for example, those who seem unmoved by people in the supermarket who comment on their misbehaving child—results in even more negative self-talk and pessimism. Families with pessimistic views need very specific intervention to assist them to become engaged in behavioral parent training.

Our recent work addresses the needs of these families by integrating cognitive behavioral interventions (optimism training) with behavioral parent training (positive behavioral support)—a new treatment approach referred to as positive family intervention (Durand, 2011; Durand & Hieneman, 2008a). We not only teach them the skills to better understand and treat their child's challenging behavior but also help them become aware of their thoughts and feelings about themselves and their child and how these might interfere with success. We are finding that tailoring behavioral parent training to meet the particular needs of the family as well as the child leads to highly successful child behavior outcomes (Durand, Hieneman, Clarke, & Zona, 2009). Continuing research in this area promises to broaden the benefits associated with FCT to a larger group of individuals and families affected by FCT and over a longer period of time.

In addition to research on those who implement FCT, continuing research is needed in other aspects of FCT itself. For example, the issue of response acceptability (how individuals in the student's environment respond to new communication forms) is a potentially fruitful and important research topic. A related topic is the aspect of FCT referred to as response milieu (the nature of the environment in which the student is communicating). Both of these areas lack any systematic study, yet they are essential to the success of this treatment approach. To guide intervention efforts in this area, more research is needed to assess environments (e.g., how will others respond to a request for assistance) and if and when to change the communication form or the environment itself (e.g., switching classrooms to one that is more accepting of requests for choices). Answers to these types of questions will likely result in even more successful outcomes for individuals with challenging behavior.

SUGGESTED READINGS

Crimmins, D.B., Farrell, A.F., Smith, P.W., & Bailey, A. (2007). *Positive strategies for students with behavior problems.* Baltimore, MD: Paul H. Brookes Publishing Co.

This book provides a comprehensive approach to using positive strategies (including FCT) in the classroom. Geared especially to teachers, it provides complete, step-by-step instructions on how to conduct functional assessments and how to develop behavior intervention plans.

Durand, V.M. (1990). *Severe behavior problems: A functional communication training approach.* New York, NY: Guilford Press.

This is the first book to describe FCT. It includes extensive case examples that illustrate how to assess significant challenging behaviors in persons with a broad range of abilities (from those who are very verbal to individuals with no functional communication skills) and how to intervene. Step-by-step instructions are included for all assessment and intervention activities.

Durand, V.M., & Hieneman, M. (2008). *Helping parents with challenging children: Positive family intervention: Facilitator guide.* New York, NY: Oxford University Press.

Durand, V.M., & Hieneman, M. (2008). *Helping parents with challenging children: Positive family intervention: Workbook.* New York: Oxford University Press.

These two books are the treatment protocols used to help families with their challenging child. Behavioral interventions (including FCT) are outlined, along with how to change attitudes to assist with implementing these procedures (optimism training). A separate protocol is available for therapists, and a workbook is available for parents.

Learning Activities

1. Topics for Further Discussion

- When would you not recommend using FCT for the treatment of challenging behaviors?
- What would you say to a teacher or family member who declared, "This will not work for my student/child"?
- What does the information about functional equivalence suggest about programs that rely primarily on punishment to reduce the frequency of challenging behaviors?

2. Ideas for Projects

- Select an individual who is engaging in problem behavior and try to determine why the behavior is occurring, including identifying the situations that seem to trigger it.

- Make a list of how family members and/or friends deal with frustrating situations (both the positive strategies, such as asking for help, and the unproductive strategies, such as yelling or blaming others), and describe how their positive strategies could be modified for persons with ASDs.

3. Questions About the Reading Material

- What is the Motivation Assessment Scale?

- Regarding challenging behavior, the emphasis in intervention has changed. What was the earlier emphasis? What is the emphasis now?

- Julie continues to scream at home because her parents spend time with her during her outbursts (i.e., they sit beside her and try to calm her). What appears to be a factor in maintaining Julie's screaming behavior?

- Angela's teacher keeps Angela close by her side throughout the day as Angela participates in her school tasks and activities. She finds that Angela seldom engages in problem behavior. Given this information, what would be your best guess of the function of Angela's behavior?

- What are the steps used in FCT?

4. Writing Assignments

- Write a paper on the controversy over the use of punishment, especially for those individuals with ASDs. Be sure to include issues of ethics as well as evidence for effectiveness.

- FCT was categorized as a "well-established" treatment. Write a paper on the issue of using only evidence-based treatments for individuals with ASDs. Include a discussion about when it might be appropriate to use techniques that currently lack empirical support but that may be useful for an individual with an ASD.

REFERENCES

American Psychological Association, Task Force Promoting Dissemination of Psychological Procedures. (1995). Training in and dissemination of empirically validated psychological treatments: Report and recommendations. *Clinical Psychology: Science and Practice, 48,* 3–23.

Bailey, J.S., & Burch, M.R. (2002). *Research methods in applied behavior analysis.* Thousand Oaks, CA: Sage.

Bambara, L.M., Mitchellkvacky, N.A., & Iacobelli, S. (1994). Positive behavioral support for students with severe disabilities: An emerging multicomponent approach for addressing challenging behaviors. *School Psychology Review, 23*(2), 263–278.

Barlow, D.H., & Hersen, M. (1984). *Single case experimental design: Strategies for studying behavior change* (2nd ed.). Elmsford, NY: Pergamon Press.

Bingham, M.A., Spooner, F., & Browder, D. (2007). Training paraeducators to promote the use of augmentative and alternative communication by students with significant disabilities. *Education and Training in Developmental Disabilities, 42*(3), 339–352.

Bird, F., Dores, P.A., Moniz, D., & Robinson, J. (1989). Reducing severe aggressive and self-injurious behaviors with functional communication training. *American Journal on Mental Retardation, 94*(1), 37–48.

Bruininks, R.H., Woodcock, R.W., Weatherman, R.F., & Hill, B.K. (1996). *Scales of Independent Behavior–Revised.* Chicago, IL: Riverside.

Byrd, R.S., & Weitzman, M.L. (1994). Predictors of early grade retention among children in the United States. *Pediatrics, 93,* 481–487.

Carlson, J.I., Luiselli, J.K., Slyman, A., & Markowski, A. (2008). Choice-making as intervention for public disrobing in children with developmental disabilities. *Journal of Positive Behavior Interventions, 10*(2), 86–90.

Carr, E.G. (1988). Functional equivalence as a mechanism of response generalization. In R.H. Horner, G. Dunlap, & R.L. Koegel (Eds.), *Generalization and maintenance: Lifestyle changes in applied settings* (pp. 194–219). Baltimore, MD: Paul H. Brookes Publishing Co.

Carr, E.G., & Durand, V.M. (1985). Reducing behavior problems through functional communication training. *Journal of Applied Behavior Analysis, 18*(2), 111–126.

Chambless, D.L., Sanderson, W.C., Shoham, V., Bennett Johnson, S., Pope, K.S., Crits-Christoph, P.,...McCurry, S. (1996). An update on empirically validated therapies. *The Clinical Psychologist, 49,* 5–18.

Cole, D.A., & Meyer, L.H. (1989). Impact of needs and resources on family plans to seek out-of-home placement. *American Journal on Mental Retardation, 93,* 380–387.

Crimmins, D.B., Farrell, A.F., Smith, P.W., & Bailey, A. (2007). *Positive strategies for students with behavior problems.* Baltimore, MD: Paul H. Brookes Publishing Co.

Dunlap, G., Ester, T., Langhans, S., & Fox, L. (2006). Functional communication training with toddlers in home environments. *Journal of Early Intervention, 28*(2), 81–96.

Dunlap, G., Kern-Dunlap, L., Clarke, S., & Robbins, F.R. (1991). Functional assessment, curricular revision, and severe behavior problems. *Journal of Applied Behavior Analysis, 24,* 387–397.

Durand, V.M. (1987). "Look homeward angel": A call to return to our (functional) roots. *The Behavior Analyst, 10,* 299–302.

Durand, V.M. (1990). *Severe behavior problems: A functional communication training approach.* New York, NY: Guilford Press.

Durand, V.M. (1993). Functional communication training using assistive devices: Effects on challenging behavior and affect. *AAC: Augmentative and Alternative Communication, 9,* 168–176.

Durand, V.M. (1997). Functional analysis: Should we? *Journal of Special Education, 31,* 105–106.

Durand, V.M. (1999). Functional communication training using assistive devices: Recruiting natural communities of reinforcement. *Journal of Applied Behavior Analysis, 32*(3), 247–267.

Durand, V.M. (2007). Positive family intervention: Hope and help for parents with challenging children. *Psychology in Mental Retardation and Developmental Disabilities, 32*(3), 9–13.

Durand, V.M. (2011). *Optimistic parenting: Hope and help for you and your challenging child.* Baltimore, MD: Paul H. Brookes Publishing Co.

Durand, V.M., & Berotti, D. (1991). Treating behavior problems with communication. *Journal of the American Speech Language Association, 33,* 37–39.

Durand, V.M., & Carr, E.G. (1991). Functional communication training to reduce challenging behavior: Maintenance and application in new settings. *Journal of Applied Behavior Analysis, 24*(2), 251–264.

Durand, V.M., & Carr, E.G. (1992). An analysis of maintenance following functional communication training. *Journal of Applied Behavior Analysis, 25*(4), 777–794.

Durand, V.M., & Crimmins, D.B. (1992). *The Motivation Assessment Scale (MAS) administration guide.* Topeka, KS: Monaco and Associates.

Durand, V.M., & Hieneman, M. (2008a). *Helping parents with challenging children: Positive family intervention: Facilitator guide.* New York, NY: Oxford University Press.

Durand, V.M., & Hieneman, M. (2008b). *Helping parents with challenging children: Positive family intervention, workbook.* New York, NY: Oxford University Press.

Durand, V.M., Hieneman, M., Clarke, S., & Zona, M. (2009). Optimistic parenting: Hope and help for parents with challenging children. In G.D.W. Sailor, G. Sugai, & R. Horner (Eds.), *Handbook of positive behavior support* (pp. 233–256). New York, NY: Springer.

Durand, V.M., Mapstone, E., & Youngblade, L. (1999). The role of communicative partners. In J. Downing (Ed.), *Teaching communication skills to students with severe disabilities within general education classrooms* (pp. 139–155). Baltimore, MD: Paul H. Brookes Publishing Co.

Durand, V.M., & Merges, E. (2008). Functional communication training to treat challenging behavior. In W. O'Donohue & J.E. Fisher (Eds.), *Cognitive behavior therapy: Applying empirically supported techniques in your practice* (2nd ed., pp. 222–229). New York, NY: Wiley.

Durand, V.M., & Merges, E. (2009). Functional communication training to treat challenging behavior. In W. O'Donohue & J.E. Fisher (Eds.), *General principles and empirically supported techniques of cognitive behavior therapy* (pp. 320–327). New York, NY: Wiley.

Durand, V.M., & Rost, N. (2005). Does it matter who participates in our studies? A caution when interpreting the research on positive behavioral support. *Journal of Positive Behavior Interventions, 7,* 186–188.

Dyer, K., Dunlap, G., & Winterling, V. (1990). Effects of choice making on the serious problem behaviors of students with severe handicaps. *Journal of Applied Behavior Analysis, 23*(4), 515–524.

Einfeld, S.E., & Tonge, B.J. (1996). Population prevalence of psychopathology in children and adolescents with mental retardation. II. Epidemiological findings. *Journal of Intellectual Disability Research, 40,* 99–109.

Einfeld, S.E., Tonge, B.J., & Rees, V.W. (2001). Longitudinal course of behavioral and emotional problems in Williams syndrome. *American Journal on Mental Retardation, 106,* 73–81.

Emerson, E., Kiernan, C., Alborz, A., Reeves, D., Mason, H., Swarbrick, R.,…Hatton, C. (2001). Predicting the persistence of severe self-injurious behavior. *Research in Developmental Disabilities, 22,* 67–75.

Eyman, R.K., & Call, T. (1977). Maladaptive behavior and community placement of mentally retarded persons. *American Journal of Mental Deficiency, 82,* 137–144.

Feldman, M., McDonald, L., Serbin, L., Stack, D., Secco, M.L., & Yu, C.T. (2007). Predictors of depressive symptoms in primary caregivers of young children with or at risk for developmental delay. *Journal of Intellectual Disability Research, 51*(8), 606–619.

Fisher, W.W., Thompson, R.H., Hagopian, L.P., Bowman, L.G., & Krug, A. (2000). Facilitating tolerance of delayed reinforcement during functional communication training. *Behavior Modification, 24*(1), 3–29.

Floyd, F.J., & Gallagher, E.M. (1997). Parental stress, care demands and use of support services for school age children with disabilities and behavior problems. *Family Relations, 46*(4), 359–371.

Franco, J.H., Lang, R.L., O'Reilly, M.F., Chan, J.M., Sigafoos, J., & Rispoli, M. (2009). Functional analysis and treatment of inappropriate vocalizations using a speech-generating device for a child with autism. *Focus on Autism and Other Developmental Disabilities, 24*(3), 146–155.

Fyffe, C.E., Kahng, S., Fittro, E., & Russell, D. (2004). Functional analysis and treatment of inappropriate sexual behavior. *Journal of Applied Behavior Analysis, 37*(3), 401–404.

Gilliam, W.S., & Shahar, G. (2006). Preschool and child care expulsion and suspension: Rates and predictors in one state. *Infants and Young Children, 19*(3), 228–245.

Green, V.A., O'Reilly, M., Itchon, J., & Sigafoos, J. (2005). Persistence of early emerging aberrant behavior in children with developmental disabilities. *Research in Developmental Disabilities, 26*(1), 47–55.

Hagopian, L.P., Fisher, W.W., Sullivan, M.T., Acquisto, J., & LeBlanc, L.A. (1998). Effectiveness of functional communication training with and without extinction and punishment: A summary of 21 inpatient cases. *Journal of Applied Behavior Analysis, 31*(2), 211–235.

Hagopian, L.P., Kuhn, S.A.C., Long, E.S., & Rush, K.S. (2005). Schedule thinning following communication training using competing stimuli to enhance tolerance to decrements in reinforcer density. *Journal of Applied Behavior Analysis, 38*(2), 177–193.

Hagopian, L.P., Toole, L.M., Long, E.S., Bowman, L.G., & Lieving, G.A. (2004). A comparison of dense-to-lean and fixed lean schedules of alternative reinforcement and extinction. *Journal of Applied Behavior Analysis, 37*(3), 323–338.

Halle, J.W., Baer, D., & Spradlin, J. (1981). Teachers' generalized use of delay as a stimulus control procedure to increase language use in handicapped children. *Journal of Applied Behavior Analysis, 14,* 389–409.

Halle, J.W., Ostrosky, M.M., & Hemmeter, M.L. (2006). Functional communication training: A strategy for ameliorating challenging behavior. In R.J. McCauley & M.E. Fey (Eds.), *Treatment of language disorders in children* (pp. 509–548). Baltimore, MD: Paul H. Brookes Publishing Co.

Hanley, G.P., Iwata, B.A., & McCord, B.E. (2003). Functional analysis of problem behavior: A review. *Journal of Applied Behavior Analysis, 36,* 147–185.

Hanley, G.P., Iwata, B.A., & Thompson, R.H. (2001). Reinforcement schedule thinning following treatment with functional communication training. *Journal of Applied Behavior Analysis, 34*(1), 17–38.

Hastings, R.P. (2002). Parental stress and behavior problems of children with developmental disability. *Journal of Intellectual and Developmental Disability, 27*(3), 149–160.

Hayes, R.P. (1987). Training for work. In D.C. Cohen & A.M. Donellan (Eds.), *Handbook of autism and pervasive developmental disorders* (pp. 360–370). New York, NY: Wiley.

Horner, R.H., & Day, H.M. (1991). The effects of response efficiency on functionally equivalent competing behaviors. *Journal of Applied Behavior Analysis, 24*(4), 719–732.

Horner, R.H., Sprague, J.R., Obrien, M., & Heathfield, L.T. (1990). The role of response efficiency in the reduction of problem behaviors through functional equivalence training: A case-study. *Journal of the Association for Persons with Severe Handicaps, 15*(2), 91–97.

Jacobson, J.W. (1982). Problem behavior and psychiatric impairment within a developmentally disabled population. I: Behavior frequency. *Applied Research in Mental Retardation, 3,* 121–139.

Jones, R.S.P. (1999). A 10-year follow-up of stereotypic behavior with eight participants. *Behavioral Intervention, 14,* 45–54.

Kemp, D.C., & Carr, E.G. (1995). Reduction of severe problem behavior in community employment using an hypothesis-driven multicomponent intervention approach. *Journal of the Association for Persons with Severe Handicaps, 20*(4), 229–247.

Kennedy, C.H., & Itkonen, T. (1993). Effects of setting events on the problem behavior of students with severe disabilities. *Journal of Applied Behavior Analysis, 26,* 321–328.

Koegel, R.L., & Covert, A. (1972). The relationship of self-stimulation to learning in autistic children. *Journal of Applied Behavior Analysis, 5,* 381–387.

Kurtz, P.F., Chin, M.D., Huete, J.M., Tarbox, R.S.F., O'Connor, J.T., Paclawskyj, T.R., & Rush, K.S. (2003). Functional analysis and treatment of self-injurious behavior in young children: A summary of 30 cases. *Journal of Applied Behavior Analysis, 36*(2), 205–219.

Lang, R., Rispoli, M., Machalicek, W., White, P.J., Kang, S., Pierce, N.,...Lancioni, G. (2009). Treatment of elopement in individuals with developmental disabilities: A systematic review. *Research in Developmental Disabilities, 30*(4), 670–681.

Lerman, D.C., Kelley, M.E., Van Camp, C.M., & Roane, H.S. (1999). Effects of reinforcement magnitude on spontaneous recovery. *Journal of Applied Behavior Analysis, 32*(2), 197–200.

Lerman, D.C., Kelley, M.E., Vorndran, C.M., Kuhn, S.A.C., & LaRue, R.H. (2002). Reinforcement magnitude and responding during treatment with differential reinforcement. *Journal of Applied Behavior Analysis, 35*(1), 29–48.

Lord, C., Wagner, A., Rogers, S., Szatmari, P., Aman, M., Charman, T.,...Yoder, P. (2005). Challenges in evaluating psychosocial interventions for autistic spectrum disorders. *Journal of Autism and Developmental Disorders, 35*(6), 695–708.

Lowe, K., Allen, D., Jones, E., Brophy, S., Moore, K., & James, W. (2007). Challenging behaviours: Prevalence and topographies. *Journal of Intellectual Disability Research, 51*(8), 625–636.

Mancil, G.R. (2006). Functional communication training: A review of the literature related to children with autism. *Education and Training in Developmental Disabilities, 41*(3), 213–224.

Matson, J.L., Dixon, D.R., & Matson, M.L. (2005). Assessing and treating aggression in children and adolescents with developmental disabilities: A 20-year overview. *Educational Psychology, 25*(2), 151–181.

Matson, J.L., & Minshawi, N.F. (2007). Functional assessment of challenging behavior: Toward a strategy for applied settings. *Research in Developmental Disabilities, 28*(4), 353–361.

Matson, J.L., & Nebel-Schwalm, M. (2007). Assessing challenging behaviors in children with autism spectrum disorders: A review. *Research in Developmental Disabilities, 28*(6), 567–579.

McDonnell, A., & Hardman, M. (1988). A synthesis of "best practice" guidelines for early childhood services. *Journal of Early Intervention, 12*(4), 328–341.

McGee, G.G., Morrier, M.J., & Daly, T. (1999). An incidental teaching approach to early intervention for toddlers with autism. *Journal of the Association for Persons with Severe Handicaps, 24,* 133–146.

McIntosh, K., Borgmeier, C., Anderson, C.M., Horner, R.H., Rodriguez, B.J., & Tobin, T.J. (2008). Technical adequacy of the functional assessment checklist: Teachers and staff (FACTS) FBA interview measure. *Journal of Positive Behavior Interventions, 10*(1), 33–45.

Mirenda, P. (1997). Supporting individuals with challenging behavior through functional communication training and AAC: Research review. *AAC: Augmentative and Alternative Communication, 13,* 207–225.

Mirenda, P. (2003). Toward functional augmentative and alternative communication for students with autism: Manual signs, graphic symbols, and voice output communication aids. *Language Speech and Hearing Services in Schools, 34*(3), 203–216.

Olive, M.L., Lang, R.B., & Davis, T.N. (2008). An analysis of the effects of functional communication and a voice output communication aid for a child with autism spectrum disorder. *Research in Autism Spectrum Disorders, 2*(2), 223–236.

O'Neill, R.E., Horner, R.H., Albin, R.W., Storey, K., & Sprague, J.R. (1990). *Functional analysis of problem behavior. A practical assessment guide.* Sycamore, IL: Sycamore.

Paclawskyj, T.R., Matson, J.L., Rush, K.S., Smalls, Y., & Vollmer, T.R. (2000). Questions about behavioral function (QABF): A behavioral checklist for functional assessment of aberrant behavior. *Research in Developmental Disabilities, 21*(3), 223–229.

Petscher, E.S., Rey, C., & Bailey, J.S. (2009). A review of empirical support for differential reinforcement of alternative behavior. *Research in Developmental Disabilities, 30*(3), 409–425.

Richman, D.M., Wacker, D.P., & Winborn, L. (2001). Response efficiency during functional communication training: Effects of effort on response allocation. *Journal of Applied Behavior Analysis, 34*(1), 73–76.

Saloviita, T., Itälinna, M., & Leinonen, E. (2003). Explaining the parental stress of fathers and mothers caring for a child with intellectual disability: A double ABCX model. *Journal of Intellectual Disability Research, 47*(4/5), 300–312.

Schepis, M.M., Reid, D.H., & Behrman, M.M. (1996). Acquisition and functional use of voice output communication by persons with profound multiple disabilities. *Behavior Modification, 20*(4), 451–468.

Schindler, H.R., & Horner, R.H. (2005). Generalized reduction of problem behavior of young children with autism: Building trans-situational interventions. *American Journal on Mental Retardation, 110*(1), 36–47.

Schwartz, I.S., Anderson, S.R., & Halle, J.W. (1989). Training teachers to use naturalistic time delay: Effects on teacher behavior and on the language use of students. *Journal of the Association for Persons with Severe Handicaps, 14*(1), 48–57.

Shirley, M.J., Iwata, B.A., Kahng, S.W., Mazaleski, J.L., & Lerman, D.C. (1997). Does functional communication training compete with ongoing contingencies of reinforcement? An analysis during response acquisition and maintenance. *Journal of Applied Behavior Analysis, 30*(1), 93–104.

Shoham-Vardi, I., Davidson, P.W., Cain, N.N., Sloane-Reeves, J.E., Giesow, V.E., Quijano, L.E., & Houser, K.D. (1996). Factors predicting re-referral following crisis intervention for community-based persons with developmental disabilities and behavioral and psychiatric disorders. *American Journal on Mental Retardation, 101,* 109–117.

Smith, T., Scahill, L., Dawson, G., Guthrie, D., Lord, C., Odom, S.,...Wagner, A.. (2007). Designing research studies on psychosocial interventions in autism. *Journal of Autism and Developmental Disorders, 37*(2), 354–366.

Snell, M.E., Chen, L.Y., & Hoover, K. (2006). Teaching augmentative and alternative communication to students with severe disabilities: A review of intervention research 1997–2003. *Research and Practice for Persons with Severe Disabilities, 31*(3), 203–214.

Stokes, T.F., Fowler, S.A., & Baer, D M. (1978). Training preschool children to recruit natural communities of reinforcement. *Journal of Applied Behavior Analysis, 11,* 285–303.

Sturmey, P. (1994). Assessing the functions of aberrant behaviors: A review of psychometric instruments. *Journal of Autism and Developmental Disorders, 24*(3), 293–304.

Totsika, V., Toogood, S., Hastings, R.P., & Lewis, S. (2008). Persistence of challenging behaviours in adults with intellectual disability over a period of 11 years. *Journal of Intellectual Disability Research, 52*(5), 446–457.

Van Houten, R., & Rolider, A. (1991). Applied behavior analysis. In J.L. Matson & J.A. Mulick (Eds.), *Handbook of mental retardation* (2nd ed., pp. 569–585). New York, NY: Pergamon.

Volkert, V.M., Lerman, D.C., Call, N.A., & Trosclair-Lasserre, N. (2009). An evaluation of resurgence during treatment with functional communication training. *Journal of Applied Behavior Analysis, 42*(1), 145–160.

Wacker, D.P., Berg, W.K., Harding, J.W., Derby, K.M., Asmus, J.M., & Healy, A. (1998). Evaluation and long-term treatment of aberrant behavior displayed by young children with disabilities. *Journal of Developmental and Behavioral Pediatrics, 19*(4), 260–266.

Wacker, D.P., Steege, M.W., Northup, J., Sasso, G., Berg, W., Reimers, T.,...Donn, L. (1990). A component analysis of functional communication training across 3 topographies of severe behavior problems. *Journal of Applied Behavior Analysis, 23*(4), 417–429.

Watanabe, M., & Sturmey, P. (2003). The effect of choice-making opportunities during activity schedules on task engagement of adults with autism. *Journal of Autism and Developmental Disorders, 33*(5), 535–538.

Weiseler, N.A., Hanson, R.H., Chamberlain, T.P., & Thompson, T. (1985). Functional taxonomy of stereotypic and self-injurious behavior. *Mental Retardation, 23,* 230–234.

Worsdell, A.S., Iwata, B.A., Hanley, G.P., Thompson, R.H., & Kahng, S.W. (2000). Effects of continuous and intermittent reinforcement for problem behavior during functional communication training. *Journal of Applied Behavior Analysis, 33*(2), 167–179.

7

Joint Attention Intervention for Children with Autism

Connie Kasari, Danai Kasambira Fannin, and Kelly Stickles Goods

Joint action routines are an important activity that facilitates communication through engaging play and activities. Typically developing children develop language and social skills during these interactive games. This chapter explains what makes these routines important and how to use them as a treatment for atypically developing populations, specifically, children on the autism spectrum.

TARGET POPULATIONS AND ASSESSMENTS FOR DETERMINING TREATMENT OF RELEVANCE AND GOALS

A joint action or joint attention routine is an intervention strategy appropriate for young children with **autism spectrum disorders (ASDs),** because joint attention is a core deficit of autism. Joint attention intervention is also appropriate for children with related neurodevelopmental disabilities who present with language and joint attention impairments. In fact, it can be applied to any preschooler with impairments in joint attention skills. The primary treatment goal, then, is to establish joint attention.

THEORETICAL BASIS

The theoretical basis of this intervention derives from observations that certain early interaction patterns seen in typical development are often missing or later developing in children with ASDs. Thus, establishing these patterns is viewed as helping form the foundation for the emergence of more advanced communication and language skills.

Typical Development

A joint action routine, or joint attentional routine, is a routinized, interactive game, such as Peekaboo and Pat-a-cake, in which mothers and their young children are often engaged (Ratner & Bruner, 1978; Rollins, Wambacq, Dowell, Matthews, & Reese, 1998). In an early study, Ratner and Bruner (1978) analyzed mother–infant interactions during free play. They found that such games include turn taking and involve a restricted set of semantic language, repetitive structure, and opportunities for vocalizations. These types of **play routines** have been linked to language

139

development in typically developing children (Ratner & Bruner, 1978; Tomasello & Farrar, 1986; Tomasello & Todd, 1983).

One of the underlying components of these interactive activities is joint engagement (Bakeman & Adamson, 1984). When two people are actively interacting in toy play (such as a parent and child playing together), they are said to be jointly engaged. This interaction occurs between two people and an object or activity of interest. Joint engagement differs from joint attention. **Joint attention** is used to refer to a specific set of gestures used for sharing. **Joint engagement** refers to the overarching quality and connectedness of the interaction. An individual's joint engagement state indicates the varying quality of the interaction. The states range from "unengaged," in which the child is wandering and not attending to any one person or activity, to "coordinated joint engagement," in which the child is initiating steps of the activity (see Table 7.1). It is important to be able to evaluate the routine not only in terms of the type of communication used (i.e., joint attention) but also in terms of the quality of the connectedness (joint engagement).

A key component of these routines is their focus on communication. For the purposes of this chapter, we distinguish between two main types of communication intents: protoimperatives (requesting communicative actions) and protodeclaratives (joint attention communicative actions). Behaviors related to joint attention are for the sole purpose of sharing something with another person or drawing someone else's attention to an event one is witnessing. An example of a joint attention act is a young child pointing to an airplane flying overhead. In this situation, we assume that the child does not want the airplane but is sharing that event with another person. Behaviors related to requesting are not an attempt to engage the other person in an interesting activity but merely to get that person to provide a desired object, activity, or outcome. An example of a requesting behavior is a child pointing to cookies on a shelf beyond the child's reach during snack time. Both of the examples use the same gestures (pointing), but the *function* of the behavior differs. The first example is of a child pointing to share an interesting event (joint attention), whereas the second example is of a child pointing to get a desired snack item (requesting).

The development of communication is a detailed process that we expect children to develop and to display in measurable ways late in their first year (Adamson, Bakeman, Smith, & Walters, 1987; Bates, Benigni, Bretherton, Camaioni, & Volterra,

Table 7.1. Definitions of joint engagement states

Unengaged	The child is not actively attending to any one object or person.
Object engaged	The child is actively playing with a toy or an object in a functional way; no other person is involved in the activity.
Person engaged	The child is actively interacting with another person without toys or objects (singing songs, playing Pat-a-cake).
Supported joint engagement	The child and adult are interacting with a toy or an object, but the child may not be initiating or overtly aware of the adult's interaction and effect on the interaction. The adult is "supporting" the interaction.
Coordinated joint engagement	The child and adult are both actively interacting. The child is clearly aware of the adult's presence; both parties are initiating during the interaction.

Sources: Adamson, Bakeman, Deckner, and Romski (2008); Adamson, Bakeman, Smith, and Walters (1987); Bakeman and Adamson (1984).

1979; Wetherby, 1986). These early communication skills tend to satisfy the following functions: making requests of others, attracting attention to oneself, directing another's attention to some item or activity, reacting to stimuli, focusing one's own attention to an item or activity, or regulating one's own behavior (Wetherby, 1986). Within mutually sustained interactions between parent and child, specific joint attention skills develop. These joint attention skills "are used to direct attention to objects, but not necessarily to obtain objects or events" (Mundy, Kasari, & Sigman, 1992, p. 378). Specific examples of nonverbal joint attention skills, or gestures, are coordinated joint looks, showing an object, giving to share, and pointing to share an interesting sight (Kasari, Freeman, & Paparella, 2006; see Table 7.2).

Children with Autism Spectrum Disorder

By definition, individuals with autism display marked differences in communication skills. Many of these skills involve joint attention skills—for example, impaired eye gaze; lack of spontaneous sharing of enjoyment, interests, or achievements with others; and weak integration of social, emotional, and communicative behaviors (American Psychiatric Association, 2000; Lord, Cook, Leventhal, & Amaral, 2000; Tager-Flusberg, 1999). In terms of communication development, children with autism may develop the functional (e.g., requesting) and social aspects of communication separately, whereas typically developing children tend to learn both of these types of communicative functions and methods concurrently. Studies have found that children with autism may learn the requesting function first, then develop the social aspects of communication later (Wetherby, 1986).

Studies have found that many children with autism use gestures to communicate requests (a behavioral regulation function) but that socially interactive gestures tend to be delayed. Research has indicated that children with autism are delayed in their development of joint attention behaviors, such as pointing or showing as an act

Table 7.2.   Definitions of joint attention skills

Initiates joint attention	
Coordinated joint look	The child looks between an adult, an object, and back to the adult to share attention. (This can also be done in reverse, from the object, to the adult, then back to the object.) The gesture is used to communicate "Look at that; it's interesting to me!"
Showing	The child has a toy in hand and holds it up toward the adult to share attention. The child does not give the toy to the adult. This gesture is used to communicate "Look what I have!"
Give to share	The child makes a clear attempt to give a toy to the adult purely to share and not to communicate a need for assistance with the item. This gesture communicates "Here's a toy so you can play too!" or "It's your turn!"
Point	The child points to an object purely to direct the adult's attention to something of interest. The child does not want the adult to act on the toy. The gesture communicates "Look at that over there! I think it's interesting."
Responds to joint attention	
Following point	After the adult points to an object, the child responds by following the point and looking at the same object.
Following gaze	The child follows the adult's gaze to what the adult is looking at.

Source: Mundy, Sigman, Ungerer, and Sherman (1986).

of sharing (Curcio, 1978; Wetherby, 1986; Wetherby & Prutting, 1984). Children who do develop these skills often use them less frequently than their typically developing peers. Mundy and colleagues found that initiating joint attention reliably discriminated children with autism from matched children with other developmental delays or typically developing children, providing some evidence of initiating joint attention as a core impairment in autism (Mundy, Sigman, Ungerer, & Sherman, 1986; Wetherby et al., 2004).

The ability to demonstrate joint attention skills correlates with later verbal outcomes for young children with autism (Anderson et al., 2007; Mundy, Sigman, & Kasari, 1990; Thurm, Lord, Lee, & Newschaffer, 2007). Research suggests that the development of joint attention skills is a critical milestone for language development and may mark the beginning of the social-cognitive development necessary for language acquisition (Mundy et al., 1990). It is this delay in joint attention skills, together with its relationship to language outcomes, that makes joint attention skills an important area of intervention to target in young children with autism. In one study, greater impairments in joint attention skills at the age of 2 years, in addition to decreased vocal and motor imitation skills, predicted lack of language development by 5 years of age (Thurm et al., 2007). Another study found that language abilities at age 7 for children with autism predict school placements, social opportunities, academic achievement, and communication skills at age 16 (Venter, Lord, & Schopler, 1992). Clearly, delays and deficits in language development will impact a child's ability to display effective and functional communication skills. Delays in communication skills have a wide variety of negative outcomes: impaired social functioning, decreased academic achievement, and impaired quality of life (Anderson et al., 2007). The focus on preventing negative outcomes associated with poor communication abilities makes joint attention intervention an important direction for children with autism.

EMPIRICAL BASIS

In this section, a summary of the research on joint attention intervention for children with autism is presented. In addition, a group study (Kasari et al., 2006) is presented in detail in order to further support the importance of and potential for intervention in this area.

Interventions specifically targeting joint attention have been created because of the delayed and atypical development of these skills in children with autism. Early research on both typically developing children and children with autism suggests that social communication, or joint attention acts, are developed through routinized social games. These routines, games, and interactions in turn facilitate and predict later language development (Bruner, 1974/1975; Rollins et al., 1998; Wetherby, 1986). Some research has indicated that the types of interventions typically afforded young children with autism (e.g., behavioral programs) may actually be detrimental to teaching the functions of communication. Such programs may be detrimental because they focus on repetition of verbal skills without context and discourage the child's communicative acts because of the strong focus on adult-directed sessions. These aspects are often combined with reinforcers that do not correspond with the behavior elicited—for example, giving food for the child's talking rather than giving food because the child indicated he or she was hungry (Goldstein, 2002; Koegel,

Koegel, & McNerney, 2001; Wetherby, 1986). In addition, many of these programs focus on responding to others' efforts to initiate joint attention rather than the child's initiating joint attention (Hwang & Hughes, 2000; Whalen & Schreibman, 2003; Whalen, Schreibman, & Ingersoll, 2006).

Kasari and colleagues (2006) conducted a study in which they focused on initiations of, rather than responses to bids for, joint attention in young children with autism (see Figure 7.1). All 58 children in this study met criteria for autism on the Autism Diagnostic Observation Schedule (ADOS; Lord et al., 2000; Lord, Rutter, DiLavore, & Risi, 1999) and the Autism Diagnostic Interview-Revised (ADI-R; Lord, Rutter, & LeCouteur, 1994; Lord, Storoschuk, Rutter, & Pickles, 1993) and were between the ages of 3 and 5 years. Several assessment measures were administered for cognitive (Mullen Scales of Early Learning; Mullen, 1995), language (Reynell Developmental Language Scales; Reynell, 1977), joint attention (Early Social Communication Scales [ESCS]; Mundy, Hogan, & Doehring, 1996), and play (Structured Play Assessment [SPA]; Ungerer & Sigman, 1981). In addition, a generalized measure was administered, with the child and his or her caregiver playing with a standard set of toys for 15 min.

Each child was randomly assigned to one of three treatment conditions: joint attention skills training (JA), symbolic play skills training (SP), or a control condition in which an applied behavior analysis (ABA) model of early intervention was implemented (Kasari et al., 2006). Intervention (JA and SP conditions) was conducted individually five times a week for 30 min over 5 to 6 weeks. All participants, including the control group, received one-to-one therapy within the Early Intervention program (EIP). The EIP provided 6 hr of therapy 5 days a week. The therapy included ABA, as well as speech, occupational, and recreational therapies. The EIP represented optimal standard care that would be provided in the community (through school districts and regional centers) in a controlled setting where the services provided were consistent for all participants. That is, all children received the same number of hours of ABA, speech, and other therapies or interventions. The children in the control condition received only these EIP services.

For children in the JA group, joint attention skills were targeted (see Table 7.2). For some children, it was developmentally appropriate to begin with communicative skills that had a requesting function rather than a joint attention function. These skills included "points to request items that are out of reach" and "gives to request."

Skills were targeted for the JA group following a structured protocol called priming, which consisted of directed instruction at a table (table activity), **generalization** to floor play (similar to milieu teaching or naturalistic communication interventions), strict criteria for mastery of a skill, and execution within a developmental framework. Clinician-directed intervention, such as the table activity, is the least natural, whereas client-directed intervention is most natural. No other skills, such as play skills, were targeted within these sessions; however, social play with objects was used as the natural context in which to develop joint attention skills.

The SP group served as a comparison treatment group to the JA group and followed a developmental model of play (Lifter, 2000; Ungerer & Sigman, 1981). Children in this group also met with a therapist daily in a one-to-one setting to target play skills—first primed at the table and then generalized during floor play. The method and the amount of treatment were identical in both the SP and the JA treatments; only the treatment targets differed.

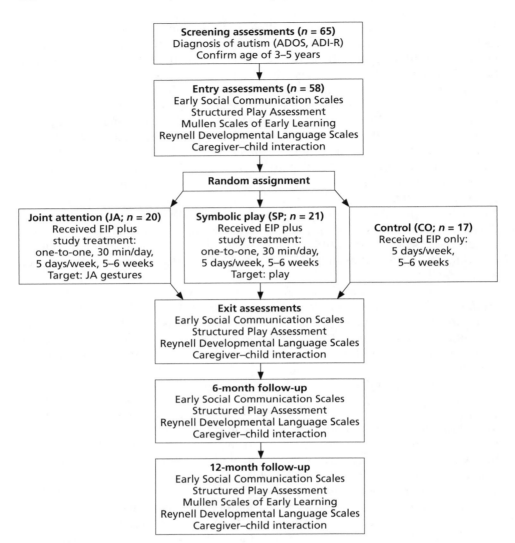

Figure 7.1. Design of study on joint attention intervention conducted by Kasari, Freeman, and Paparella (2006). (*Key:* ADOS, Autism Diagnostic Observation Schedule; ADI-R, Autism Diagnostic Interview–Revised; EIP, Early Intervention program. *Source:* Kasari, Freeman, & Paparella, 2006.)

Following treatment, several exit assessments were completed as outcome measures. All assessments were conducted by independent examiners who were not associated with research staff and were blind to both the study's purpose and hypotheses and to the child's assigned treatment group. Two structured assessments were used: the ESCS (a structured joint attention assessment) and the SPA (Ungerer & Sigman, 1981). There was also a task for generalization of joint attention gestures that was scored from a 10-min videotaped free-play interaction between the primary caregiver and the child. The toys for this interaction were standard across all participants but included items to represent a range of play levels and types of interactions.

At program exit, the JA group displayed more responding to joint attention on the structured joint attention measure (ESCS) as compared with the SP group (Cohen's d = 0.72) and the control group (Cohen's d = 1.13). Both the JA and SP groups demonstrated more "shows toys to adult" when compared to the control group (Cohen's d = 0.57; Cohen's d = 0.59, respectively). In the generalization assessment examining the child and caregiver, the JA group had more child-initiated joint engagement than the control group, as well as more giving and showing than the SP group. In child-initiated joint engagement, the child initiates the play engagement, which is measured for how long it lasts between the adult and the child. The results from this initial phase of the study indicated that joint attention skills not only were taught but also were generalized to other settings and people.

A follow-up to the 2006 publication of the results of the study investigated language outcomes at 6 months and 12 months postintervention (Kasari, Paparella, Freeman, & Jahromi, 2008). Both of the treatment groups (JA and SP) demonstrated gains in expressive language and joint attention initiations as compared with the control group. However, there was a different pattern for children with lower language skills at program entry. Children with lower language abilities initially (i.e., an expressive language age of less than 20 months on the Reynell Developmental Language Scales; produced less than five spontaneous words) made significantly more expressive language gains by the 12-month follow-up as compared with the control and play conditions. Although both of the experimental groups (JA and SP) demonstrated gains in joint attention and language, it was the children with the greatest delays in language who benefited the *most* from an intervention specifically targeting joint attention. These children made, on average, 13 months of language gain in 12 months compared with 3 months and 7 months for the control and SP groups, respectively.

PRACTICAL REQUIREMENTS

This section of the chapter focuses on the practical requirements of our intervention for developing joint attention skills in toddlers. The original intervention model (Kasari et al., 2006) taught joint attention skills in two different contexts, table activity and floor-play teaching. The initial table activity portion of an intervention session consisted of **discrete trial instruction (DTI)** to prime the child to learn the targeted skill in the subsequent, more naturalistic play format. Based on results of additional research, the intervention has transformed into a primarily naturalistic play-based model, phasing out the systematic table portion. Our revised intervention approach is based on two pieces of data from the original study. First, we examined children's learning in the table and floor portions of the intervention and found that joint attention skills were mastered at the same time, regardless of approach (Wong, Kasari, Freeman, & Paparella, 2007). Although the table and floor approaches were not randomly implemented (the table always preceded the floor play), there is little evidence that we needed to teach in a very structured and limited way using DTI for all children. Some children may have benefited more from the table instruction than the floor instruction (in which many more stimuli were available), but we have little evidence of that from this initial study. Second, both of the experimental groups achieved some similar outcomes (improved lower levels of joint attention, such as alternating eye contact, functional play skills, and greater joint engagement with mothers). The underlying commonality of our treatments was likely a focus on obtaining joint engagement with the child through the development of play routines. Thus, in our current intervention studies, we use the play level of the child to achieve longer periods of joint engagement with the child.

Next, we describe how recently published joint attention interventions (Kasari et al., 2006, 2008; Kasari, Gulsrud, Wong, Kwon, & Locke, 2010) were implemented. The following components of the intervention are discussed: 1) time, personnel, and materials demands; 2) key components of the intervention; and 3) data collection and analysis methods.

Time Demands

Our research studies indicate that 30-min sessions daily for 6 weeks can result in significant improvements in play and joint attention skills for children with ASDs. More recent work on parent-mediated models suggests that 24 half-hour sessions (with approximately three sessions per week) can also result in significant benefit in joint attention and joint engagement (Kasari et al., 2010). Given that social communication and language skills are core impairment areas for children with ASDs, continued attention to these areas of development is important. Although positive outcomes in short periods of time occur following the focused treatment described here, ongoing interventions are necessary to keep children moving toward more sophisticated and age-appropriate communication and language abilities.

Personnel Qualifications and Training

The clinician using this approach should have experience working with children with ASDs and be trained in educational psychology, education, speech-language pathology, psychology, special education, or other related disciplines. Caregivers also play a critical role in the intervention by giving input on how the child functions in other settings, such as school and throughout the day at home.

During the randomized controlled trial, personnel were trained by the principal investigator, then were under constant supervision by the investigator as they practiced the intervention with two to three pilot children. Fidelity (accuracy of treatment implementation) was assessed using a checklist representing the treatment protocol. The study coordinator checked the fidelity of treatment implementation during random sessions. Clinicians reached high levels of fidelity, ranging from 79% to 100%, with an average of 92% fidelity prior to working with research participants (Kasari et al., 2006). Ongoing supervision and consultation is beneficial in carrying out this intervention, particularly for children who may be making slow progress.

Setting and Materials

Intervention can be conducted in a lab, home, or school setting. Sessions are best conducted in a room that is free from distractions such as other students, elaborate wall hangings, or too many toys.

Materials for the intervention consist primarily of toys and a treatment manual. Toys should be developmentally appropriate and facilitate a variety of play types within the child's developmental level of play (e.g., toy telephone, picture book, puzzles, stuffed animals, nesting cups, dolls, kitchen utensils and plates, string beads, cars, blocks, pop-up toys). The toys can be selected on the basis of an assessment of the child's play levels, such as the SPA (Ungerer & Sigman, 1981). The clinician uses the treatment manual to outline the treatment strategies to be implemented during the sessions (see Table 7.3).

KEY COMPONENTS

Key components of this intervention are 1) evaluating and planning objectives based on a child's joint attention skills, 2) implementing strategies to increase spontaneous use of joint attention, 3) collecting data and monitoring progress, and 4) terminating treatment.

Evaluating and Planning Objectives

The ultimate goal of joint attention intervention is to improve language skills in children by increasing the frequency of their spontaneous initiations of joint attention. Treatment objectives are individualized for each family and can be determined through observation of interactions and joint attention skills demonstrated by the child. Evaluation to assess joint attention skills might include the following tools:

- Language Use Inventory for Young Children (LUI; O'Neill, 2007), a parent report of pragmatic language development for children aged 18–47 months
- Modified Checklist for Autism in Toddlers (M-CHAT; Robins, Fein, Barton, & Green, 2001), a checklist consisting of yes/no questions about the children's (16–30 months) development, including joint attention skills targeted in the intervention
- ESCS (Mundy et al., 1996; Mundy et al., 2003), a semistructured assessment of the nonverbal communication behaviors (e.g., taking turns, sharing excitement, requesting help) expected of children between 8 months and 30 months

In the research setting, baseline data indicating the child's joint attention skills are collected using the ESCS. Play skills and play level are determined by an SPA (Ungerer & Sigman, 1981). In addition, a 15-min observation of the caregiver and child interacting with toys is recorded to illustrate the joint attention skills being used by the child. In the clinical setting, the interventionist can use the joint attention evaluations and/or Table 7.2 as a guide to what joint attention skills are expected of a typical child and determine goals based on the target child's strengths and weaknesses in those skills. If any of the joint attention skills are not observed (per clinician observation and caregiver report), it can be determined that there may be an impairment or a delay in acquisition of those skills.

From the joint attention assessment data, developmentally appropriate treatment goals are chosen, and the first objective would be to teach an emerging ability, which is a skill the child cannot demonstrate independently but can perform with an adult (Kasari et al., 2006). An emerging ability becomes an independent (mastered) ability if the child can spontaneously demonstrate the skill across three different types of play routines. Further discussion of topics related to assessment of ongoing progress is addressed in a later section of the chapter.

Procedural Description of Activities for Addressing Goals

This intervention consists of hands-on sessions between the clinician and the child. Following is a procedural description of the intervention and how the goals are addressed.

Context

The aim for each session is for the child to spontaneously demonstrate joint attention skills while engaging in play with another person. The intervention sessions are conducted within the context of play, allowing for a more naturalistic, playful setting that is ideal for learning and generalization of skills to other settings. Play is achieved by responding to the child's interests, following the child's lead, and developing play routines that are within the child's developmental level of play. Playing at too low a level is boring for the child, and playing at too high a level is difficult for the child. Both may lead to unengagement. By playing with the child in this context, the clinician can model and scaffold the social and communication goals for the child by capitalizing on the spontaneous opportunities that arise during play.

Procedures

The clinician's primary emphasis is to provide opportunities for the child to initiate interest in a toy and then model joint attention skills. Children with lower skills may not demonstrate any joint attention skills. Thus, the clinician's goal should be to apply strategies such as following the child's lead once the child shows any kind of interest in a toy. Table 7.3 presents suggested strategies and examples of how to carry them out.

The clinician can enable the teaching of joint attention skills by setting up the environment. First, for example, the clinician uses this strategy within a play context by adjusting physical orientation (e.g., the clinician faces the child and is within close proximity to the child—no more than 3 feet away). The clinician considers the environment and how it affects the play interaction and sets up the environment with developmentally appropriate toys that can facilitate the establishment of a play routine. If the toys are not desirable, interesting, or feasible for the child to use, there is a low likelihood that the child will initiate play with those toys. Next, the clinician sets up the environment to reduce distractions by removing from the area extra toys or items that may cause challenging behavior (e.g., any gadget, such as a cell phone or laptop, that the child likes to touch).

The strategy of expanding language is instrumental in **scaffolding** the child's joint attention skills. This can be done through acknowledging and labeling the child's interest (e.g., "It's an infant!") or repeating what the child says. All the while, the clinician is modeling joint attention skills via nonverbal communication (e.g., pointing to the infant) and eye contact. The clinician does not need to use all of the strategies at once in order to effectively set up the environment or expand on language, but this example illustrates how various strategies are helpful in meeting individual objectives.

Using multiple strategies is crucial for scaffolding the child's joint attention skills. These strategies can include imitating the child's actions (e.g., the clinician brings another doll and feeds it the same way the child is feeding his or her doll),

Table 7.3. Suggested strategies

Strategy	Examples
Set up the environment	Sit close to the child to make eye contact. Arrange toys within reach. Remove distractions. Use the environment to facilitate the child's social and communicative attempts.
Follow the child's lead	Wait before acting. Allow the child to explore the room. Show high interest in the child's toy choice.
Scaffold skills	Identify the joint attention skill to scaffold. Provide ample positive reinforcement of the child's skills. Use the prompt hierarchy to facilitate skill learning.
Expand language	Talk about what the child is doing. Repeat what the child says. Expand on the child's communication. Give corrective feedback.
Imitate	Imitate the child's actions on toys. Mirror back language.

Sources: Kasari et al. (2006); Kasari et al. (2010).

repeating what the child says (e.g., if the child says an approximation of the word "train," the clinician says "train"), and expanding on what the child says (e.g., if the child says "train," the clinician says "Thomas the train!" or "red train"). Drawing on several of the suggested strategies within the play context, the clinician can prompt the child to increase joint attention skills, model the skills, and recognize and create opportunities for the child to independently demonstrate the skills.

Prompts

As previously mentioned, it may be difficult to engage children with lower skills in a play interaction in which joint attention skills can readily be elicited. Thus, if the child does not choose a toy or initiate an activity, the clinician can lead the child into a shared interaction by using a hierarchy of prompts, starting with the least directive prompt (see Table 7.4).

Potential Difficulties

In the case of a child who has difficulty engaging with objects, the clinician can intersperse the toy play with short periods of playing with the child without toys in what might be called person-engaged play (or primary intersubjectivity). In this type of interaction, the clinician omits objects, and the dyad is involved in face-to-face interactions (e.g., playing Pat-a-cake, singing a song). Some children with lower skills naturally use more of these types of interactions with adults than object-based play. They may therefore need to initially use person-engaged play as a reprieve from the more novel, difficult object-based play. In order for clinicians to make well-informed decisions about individualized goals for each child and how to interact with him or her, they must consider factors such as the child's temperament or preference for objects versus people-based play.

Table 7.4. Prompt hierarchy

Level	Prompt	Example
1	General verbal prompt	"What toy should we pick?"
2	Specific verbal suggestion	"Let's play with the Dora doll."
3	Verbal command	"Get the Dora doll."
4	Verbal command with gesture	Saying, "Get Dora," while pointing to Dora.
5	Partial physical prompt	Nudging the child's arm toward Dora.
6	Full physical prompt	Fully helping the child get Dora.

DATA COLLECTION TO SUPPORT DECISION MAKING

Assessment of Goals over Time and Evaluation of Progress

The criterion for mastery is met when the child demonstrates a joint attention skill without prompting for a minimum of three times across two sessions. Skills that are demonstrated less frequently or with prompting are considered to be emerging. For this reason, goals should be assessed frequently and simultaneously to accurately establish the development of the skills. In addition, once a skill is mastered in the intervention period, the clinician should continue to elicit that skill throughout the intervention (see Figure 7.2). The continued elicitation of mastered skills will help a child maintain those skills and generalize them to other situations.

Thus, a simultaneous approach to data collection and evaluation is most conducive to teaching multiple skills because it is *not* imperative that the child master each skill sequentially before the clinician responds appropriately to other emerging skills. Even though the clinician may respond to another emerging skill that is demonstrated before it is targeted, however, getting the child to independent mastery of the targeted skill before officially moving to another skill is still the clinician's priority. For instance, the child may demonstrate the targeted skill of "distal point" (a point to an object more than 4 inches away; Kasari et al., 2006) when modeled and verbally prompted by the clinician in a session during the third week. In the same session, the child may "give to share" for the first time. The child may have learned this behavior from another adult who modeled it at home or school, or the child may be responding to the clinician who modeled the skill even though it was not the specific target. Hence, the clinician may capitalize on this moment to optimize learning by 1) reinforcing the child's "give to share," 2) modeling another "give to share," or 3) prompting the child to demonstrate a "give to share" if a naturally occurring opportunity arises later in the session. Meanwhile, the targeted "distal point" has not yet met the definition of independent mastery in this session because it was prompted, so the clinician would continue to teach the "distal point" until it is mastered. Essentially, the clinician must be keenly observant of all of the child's emerging abilities and vigilantly collect data to properly evaluate progress. If the clinician finds this simultaneous data collection and evaluation difficult in the beginning (especially with children who have more skills), the session can be videotaped for later review. This allows the clinician to conduct a more meticulous evaluation of the child's behaviors.

Data can be collected at each session through observation of the frequency of joint attention skills and of whether the child demonstrates the skills prompted, unprompted, or independently. The clinician should be sure to differentiate between the specific nonverbal and verbal joint attention behaviors demonstrated by the child.

Strategies to Determine How Adjustments Should Be Made

The intervention allows flexibility when adjustments need to be made to enable children to master skills they may find difficult. If the child does not seem to be maintaining a previously mastered skill, the clinician can always address the skill again. For example, a child may not be demonstrating an independent and mastered "distal point" at all or as frequently as desired once the clinician begins to target a new skill. In that case, even though the clinician has moved on to the next target—for example, "showing"—he or she can continue to scaffold the "distal point" throughout the rest of the treatment period until the child begins to spontaneously demonstrate the skill.

Generalization

For collection of generalization information, an independent observer, that is, someone other than the clinician, can check for the child's carryover of skills into other settings. For example, a caregiver or teacher can report to the clinician whether the child is demonstrating the joint attention skills outside of treatment sessions. If an independent observer who did not provide the intervention (i.e., teacher, other interventionist, caregiver) is unavailable, the clinician can visit the learning environment the child attends to observe the child's interactions with teachers and peers. In the clinical trial for the Kasari et al. (2006) intervention, children generalized

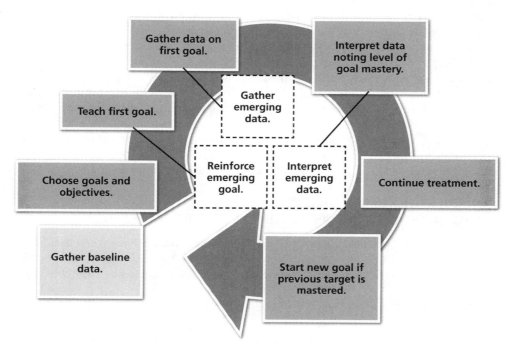

Figure 7.2. Model of goal assessment and data collection in joint attention intervention.

joint attention skills learned in interactions with the clinicians to play interactions with their caregivers. The clinician should expect generalization to occur but should collect data in different settings and across people to document this.

Termination of Intervention

Children in the Kasari et al. (2006) study received the intervention for only 5–6 weeks on average. This limited amount of intervention was used because of the constraints of the EIP that the children attended as outpatient clients before transitioning to community settings after about 6 weeks. In practice, clinicians will need to continue the treatment past 6 weeks, particularly if progress is not made. Clinicians will also probably see more progress if they bring other members of the child's network into the treatment. Thus, teaching caregivers how to carry out the strategies and having them use the strategies across daily activities in the home will increase the density of the intervention and promote generalization of skills across settings.

As always, interventionists should use their clinical judgment to determine whether the child is experiencing a negative physical or psychological reaction to the intervention that requires termination of treatment. The child and clinician may require a few sessions to develop joint play routines. Because this intervention is conducted within a developmentally appropriate play context, there is little risk to the child, and the benefits of the intervention outweigh the risk.

Additional Evaluation

Once intervention ends, clinicians can evaluate the child's progress in language and cognitive development using their usual assessment tools. For example, Kasari and colleagues (2006) measured language skills using the Reynell Developmental Language Scales (Reynell, 1977), a standardized scale used to assess receptive and expressive language of children ages 1–7 years. Cognitive development was measured using the Mullen Scales of Early Learning (Mullen, 1995), a standardized test of overall cognitive and language abilities for children from infancy to 68 months. Follow-up assessments were conducted 6 months after intervention and then again 12 months after intervention. In a school or center-based setting in which the clinician may have ongoing contact with the child after treatment, however, the clinician can make informal observations of the child's language in different contexts to see if the child is maintaining learned joint attention skills. If informal observation indicates that ongoing services might be needed, formal assessments of language and cognition can then be conducted, provided that school policy permits and caregivers consent to additional evaluation to guide additional or ongoing treatments and goals.

CONSIDERATIONS FOR CHILDREN FROM CULTURALLY AND LINGUISTICALLY DIVERSE BACKGROUNDS

Considerations for cultural[1] and linguistic differences must be made when designing and implementing any intervention. In addition, however, the clinician must refrain from the assumption that every family in a certain cultural group will demonstrate

---

[1]The United Nations Educational, Scientific and Cultural Organization (2002) described culture as the "set of distinctive spiritual, material, intellectual and emotional features of society or a social group,… encompass[ing], in addition to art and literature, lifestyles, ways of living together, value systems, traditions and beliefs." Within large societies, religion, race, ethnicity, gender, class, political persuasion, sexual orientation, or a combination of these subcultural factors can define membership in subcultures. For the purposes of this chapter, the term *culture* will be used broadly unless a specific subcultural factor (e.g., race/ethnicity, socioeconomic status, gender) is specified explicitly.

the typical characteristics. Among other things, an interventionist who belongs to the mainstream culture should understand that although certain joint attention skills seem intuitive, the U.S. population is increasingly diverse, and the approach to teaching skills may need to be adjusted to account for the different cultural norms. Although the nonverbal behaviors targeted in the intervention (e.g. pointing, eye contact, showing) sometimes differ across cultures, similar joint attention skills have indeed been observed in various cultures. Individuals from culturally and linguistically diverse groups can be successfully taught to implement these skills with their children.

For example, in a study of the joint attention behaviors of typically developing Japanese and Euro-American (EA) children in mother–child dyads, the Japanese mothers demonstrated fewer joint attention skills, but there was no significant difference in the amount of joint attention initiated by the Japanese and EA children (Dennis, Cole, Zahn-Waxler, & Mizuta, 2002). Thus, although the mothers differed in the frequency of their use of joint attention gestures, the Japanese children still displayed joint attention skills at a rate similar to that for EA children.

In another study of joint attention, no difference was found between Latino and EA mothers in their joint attention efforts, although the EA mothers used more nonverbal joint attention bids then their Latina counterparts (DeLaOssa, 2002). Once mothers' educational levels were controlled, however, the trend of EA mothers using more nonverbal joint attention bids disappeared. Thus, other factors, such as educational level or socioeconomic status (SES), may be responsible for group differences in joint attention bids.

Low SES families have long been characterized as being less verbal than higher SES families (Hart & Risley, 1995). In their study of joint attention skills and dyadic reciprocity, Hustedt and Raver (2002) found some of the low-SES mothers to be verbal, attentive, and more variable in their joint attention skills than others in the same low-SES group. Furthermore, no SES or ethnicity differences were found in joint attention bids in a study on race, gender, and SES characteristics of mother–toddler dyads (Terrill & Reilly, 1999). Hence, we would conclude that one should expect mother–child dyads from non-EA, low-SES families to demonstrate joint attention skills at varying degrees and that mothers of all cultures can be taught to enhance these skills to facilitate the development of joint attention and communication skills in a child with an ASD.

Besides SES, ethnicity, or educational status, biculturalism may be another cultural factor to consider when determining the appropriateness of joint attention intervention. In fact, Gutierrez and Sameroff (1990) posited that biculturalism was a stronger predictor of parents' perceptions of their child's development than ethnicity. Consequently, the way parents interpret their child's behavior might influence how they coordinate attention with their child. For instance, DeLaOssa (2002) found that the degree to which mothers are bicultural, more so than belonging to a nonmainstream ethnic group alone, better predicted the frequency of joint attention bids demonstrated by the Latina mothers.

A limited amount of research conducted on cross-cultural joint attention behaviors suggests that many cultures (e.g., Laos, Queensland aborigines) demonstrate joint attention behaviors such as pointing (Enfield, Kita, & Ruiter, 2007; Haviland, 1993) or eye contact (Gullberg & Holmqvist, 2006). Nonetheless, these behaviors are still thought to emerge under culturally and socially defined norms, explaining any variance across and within cultures in the frequency or style in which the joint attention skills are displayed (Gullberg & Holmqvist, 2006; Roseberry-McKibbin, 2007).

Because research shows that similar joint attention behaviors occur in various cultures, the goals of a joint attention intervention (Kasari et al., 2006) may be universally appropriate and attainable. However, the intervention would benefit from careful consideration of the subtle cultural differences that may be evident. For example, African Americans do not necessarily adhere to the turn-taking conventions found in the mainstream culture, and the African American conversational style is characterized by highly competitive conversations in which interruptions are allowed and turn taking is very rapid, leaving little room for pauses and waiting between each turn (Kochman, 1981; Roseberry-McKibbin, 2007; Schieffelin & Eisenberg, 1984; van Kleeck, 1994). Although this is *not* a disordered way of interacting and may be typical in African American culture, the clinician should simply be aware that when advising a mother to practice the joint attention strategies of turn-taking routines or waiting for a response from the child, she may be asking the mother to do something outside her cultural norms.

Facial expressions and the amount of smiling have also been known to differ across cultures (Battle, 1997), and some Native Americans do not typically want to perform tasks that seem silly or seemingly have no meaning to them, especially when the interaction partner is younger (Wallace, Inglebret, & Friedlander, 1997). Therefore, when implementing joint attention intervention, the clinician may encounter some reluctance when advising caregivers to be animated and silly while playing with their child.

Hispanic bilingual fathers and Muslim males may also demonstrate differences in eye contact behavior in which they do not tend to make continuous eye contact with female interventionists (Ali, 1993; Pena, 1998). Although we have described primarily an interventionist–child model of joint attention, other models may include caregiver-mediated approaches (Kasari et al., 2010). Therefore, it would be helpful for the interventionist to realize that a father's diverted eye gaze may not necessarily indicate disinterest or lack of buy-in to the intervention but rather a cultural difference in eye gaze behavior. This information raises the question as to whether the adult eye contact behavior influences how the child demonstrates eye contact. Indeed, sustained eye contact can be considered a sign of disrespect in Latino and African American cultures, and a child's diverted eye gaze actually indicates respect and attention (Wyatt, 2002). Furthermore, many Asian children are taught to not make eye contact with adults (Roseberry-McKibbin, 2007; Wyatt, 2002). Accordingly, the clinician should know that, again, they may be asking the caregiver and child to do something uncomfortable when asking them to elicit/make eye contact and facilitate coordinated joint gazes in their children.

Although joint attention intervention is promising for families of culturally and linguistically diverse populations, there remains a dearth of minority participants in samples of studies on autism intervention efficacy (Miranda et al., 2005). Thus, more data are needed to confirm whether our joint attention interventions are equally effective with diverse families.

Application to a Child

The following case study provides a description of a child for whom this joint attention treatment is considered appropriate and effective. Of course, this case is only one example of the many ways in which an ASD might manifest itself in a child who would benefit. Thus, an important factor in determining if a child is a good candidate for this intervention would be to remember that the ultimate goal is to remediate an impairment in joint attention skills so that other areas of communication and language development can subsequently be facilitated.

Because of the parents' concerns about their son's communication and social development, James, a 2-year- and 3-month-old boy was evaluated to determine eligibility for joint attention intervention. He was assessed by the ADOS, the Reynell Developmental Language Skills, the Structured Play Assessment, the ESCS, observation of caregiver–child interaction, and a classroom observation. James had no other medical diagnoses or concerns at the time of evaluation and presented with certain traits consistent with autistic disorder.

James's vocal quality was slightly inappropriate, characterized by an exaggerated, overly excited, and enthusiastic prosody. Language concerns included stereotypical utterances, such as repetition of "zoo-zee." James also labeled a hyena as a "dog-tiger." In the area of nonverbal communication, James failed to coordinate his gaze when he pointed to distant objects and did not use any other gestures except for a point. During interaction with adults, James did not maintain a consistent gaze with vocalizations but did demonstrate gaze coordination with adults' eyes or objects, independent of other strategies, such as vocalizing. He displayed shared enjoyment but did not smile when a smile was purposefully elicited by the examiner and his mother; neither did he consistently respond to his name being called. James directed facial expressions to adults in a communicative manner, but this behavior was most often utilized to show emotional extremes, such as distress or happiness. James's joint attention skills included giving items for the purpose of sharing, orienting to the examiner's eyes, and showing his mother toys, although this showing skill lacked a coordinated gaze. He also occasionally initiated joint attention without including a coordinated gaze.

James's play skills were mostly functional, with some higher level functional play skills, such as hugging a doll and feeding a pop-up toy. During play, other concerns included crying when being separated from toys, and stereotypical behaviors such as hand flapping, walking on his toes, hoarding toys, and counting repetitively. James had low compliance during the cognitive testing and also repetitively mislabeled test items. For example, when an examiner asked "What is this?" while pointing to a chair, James would label the chair "dog." Redirecting James from the purposeful giving of incorrect labels was difficult, even when he was given the correct labels for the items.

James met the criteria for a diagnosis of autistic disorder per the ADOS and the ADI-R. His most prominent impairments were in the areas of reciprocal social interaction (especially with peers), socioemotional reciprocity, and verbal and nonverbal communication (viz., language delay and low amount of gestural use). Finally, he demonstrated repetitive, stereotypical, restricted patterns of interests and behaviors. Because of his diagnosis and these findings, joint attention intervention was implemented to improve James's language via cultivation of joint attention skills.

Over the course of the 10-week, 20-session intervention, James made gains in the area of play, with his higher level functional play skills moving to an emerging symbolic play level. In the domain of social communication and joint attention, James added to his repertoire the skills of showing with a coordinated gaze, pointing, commenting, and giving for joint attention purposes. James and his mother also increased the duration of time spent in sustained, engaged play with a toy. Furthermore, James began to initiate more ideas during those sustained play interactions, and during the caregiver–child interaction, his mother implemented turn-taking episodes, prompted for joint attention skills, and modeled positive affect.

James's language skills improved significantly as a result of the intervention. Three months postintervention, James's age-equivalent scores on word production had increased by 7 months; on receptive language, by 13 months; and on expressive language, by 12 months. For preacademic skills, James improved his visual reception age-equivalent scores by 4 months, fine motor skills increased by 3 months, receptive language increased by 11 months, and expressive language increased by 9 months. James clearly made gains in the targeted area of joint attention and subsequent language and developmental skills.

Application to an Adolescent or Adult ||||||||||||||||||||||||||||||||||||||||||||||||||||||||||||||||||

Joint attention intervention is designed specifically for young children who are in the early stages of social relatedness and communication and thus is not used with older individuals.

||||||||||||||||||||||||||||||||||||||||||||||||||||||||||||||||||||||||||||||||||||||||||||||||||||||||||||||||||||||||||||||||||||||||||||||||||||||||||||

FUTURE DIRECTIONS

Several ideas for future directions in joint attention research have emerged from the research to date, and funding agencies have offered suggestions about targeting certain populations. In particular, future research on joint attention will include validation of a caregiver-mediated model of intervention in which establishing and increasing the duration of joint engagement states (Bakeman & Adamson, 1984) between the caregiver and child will be targeted. Caregiver-mediated treatment differs from traditional treatment models in that the caregiver is taught to administer the same treatment as the interventionist. In addition, we will explore the effects of this intervention on a wider variety of children, including samples of children who are nonverbal and those from underrepresented and multilingual populations.

We currently have several ongoing research trials employing this intervention. One intervention study is a randomized clinical trial comparing a caregiver-mediated model with a caregiver education model of joint attention. Both interventions are manualized. The caregiver-mediated model features hands-on sessions among the clinician, caregiver, and child in which the goal is for the caregiver–child dyad to be in a joint engaged state (Bakeman & Adamson, 1984). Within this overarching goal, the child is also expected to demonstrate joint attention skills independently. The clinician discusses strategies with the caregiver and works with the child and caregiver over several weeks, with a primary emphasis on showing the caregiver how to provide opportunities for the child to initiate interest in a toy, establish joint engagement, and independently demonstrate joint attention skills.

In addition, a multisite, randomized clinical trial on joint attention/engagement intervention is under way with a focus on recruiting participants from underserved and underrepresented populations. Evidence from these groups of participants will better reflect the U.S. population and therefore aid in the development of guidelines on how to better reach and serve these populations. Bilingual children with ASDs might also be included in these samples, and this is an important factor to consider when designing future studies. Cross-linguistic research has shown that language skills are affected differently across languages. Because of the lack of research on ASDs in bilingual populations, however, best practices for intervention with bilingual children have yet to be established. Therefore, knowledge on this matter could inform guidelines for best practices when implementing joint attention intervention with children from culturally and linguistically diverse backgrounds. Another consideration for future directions in joint attention intervention is the language ability of the children at baseline. Kasari and colleagues (2008) found that baseline language ability was an important moderator in treatment outcomes, with nonverbal children making the most language gains when they received a treatment focused on joint attention. The sample included only a small portion of nonverbal children; future samples should include more nonverbal children to determine the effects of treatments on children with the least amount of language.

Finally, it is conceivable that children with additional diagnoses of other neuro-developmental disabilities may display an impairment in joint attention skills when they are examined using tools such as the M-CHAT or ESCS. Therefore, research on the efficacy of joint attention intervention with children with autism who have other comorbid neurodevelopmental disabilities, such as Down syndrome or fragile X syndrome, would be in order.

These future lines of inquiry have the potential to guide clinicians who provide treatment for children with ASDs. The inclusion of caregivers as interventionists, children with other neurodevelopmental disabilities, those from culturally and linguistically diverse populations, and more nonverbal children in studies is integral to the concerted effort to advance understanding of how ASD treatment works, moving the field closer to providing evidence-based treatment for all children with ASDs.

SUGGESTED READINGS

Adamson, L.B., Bakeman, R., Deckner, D.F., & Romski, M.A. (2008). Joint engagement and the emergence of language in children with autism and Down syndrome. *Journal of Autism and Developmental Disorders, 39* (1), 84–96.

This article presents a longitudinal study demonstrating that joint engagement experiences predict language outcomes in children with ASDs and Down syndrome. A detailed description of joint engagement states in child–adult dyads is provided.

Kasari, C., Freeman, S., & Paparella, T. (2006). Joint attention and symbolic play in young children with autism: A randomized controlled intervention study. *Journal of Child Psychology and Psychiatry, 46* (6), 611–620.

This article summarizes the findings of a randomized controlled intervention study comparing joint attention and symbolic play interventions to standard ABA treatment. Outcomes are examined in the areas of joint attention and play skills.

Kasari, C., Paparella, T., Freeman, S., & Jahromi, L.B. (2008). Language outcome in autism: Randomized comparison of joint attention and play interventions. *Journal of Consulting and Clinical Psychology, 76*(1), 125–137.

A 12-month follow-up to an earlier efficacy study (Kasari et al., 2006) of symbolic play and joint attention intervention is outlined, and language outcomes are presented.

Learning Activities

Review Questions

1. How do joint attention skills facilitate language development?
2. Describe the overall goal of joint attention intervention to a person who is not familiar with the terminology of health care or education, such as a parent.
3. For what populations of children is joint attention intervention appropriate? Why?

Topics for Further Discussion

1. Discuss the difference between joint engagement and joint attention skills. How might a focus on joint engagement foster the growth of joint attention skills?
2. Discuss any other cultural considerations to be made when implementing joint attention intervention. How might intervention be adjusted for families of different cultures?

Ideas for Projects

1. Based on the case study in the section Application to a Child, identify potential emerging skills you might target with James. Once these skills have been determined, describe a hypothetical session, including 1) which toy you would use depending on his play level, 2) which strategies you would implement during the session, 3) any reinforcement and prompts that would be helpful, and 4) how you would teach the skills. Next, videotape yourself practicing this session with a classmate or child (typically developing is fine) whose parent has given you permission to do so. Once recorded, review the videotape primarily to observe your comfort level in implementing the strategies, highlighting any successes or any incidences needing improvement in implementation.
2. To facilitate generalization of skills and involve parents in the treatment, write a one-page handout for parents, outlining a particular strategy you would use in intervention. For example, the handout could include topics such as why setting up the environment is important, how you use the strategy in the session when playing with toys, and examples of how a parent can use it in other settings, such as playing at home in the backyard.

Writing Assignment

Conduct a literature review to present the pros and cons of milieu and DTI. Using the resources you have explored, argue why one, the other, or both styles of teaching would be the most appropriate method to use in joint attention intervention.

REFERENCES

Adamson, L.B., Bakeman, R., Deckner, D.F., & Romski, M.A. (2008). Joint engagement and the emergence of language in children with autism and Down syndrome. *Journal of Autism and Developmental Disorders, 39*(1), 84–96.

Adamson, L.B., Bakeman, R., Smith, C.B., & Walters, A.S. (1987). Adults' interpretation of infants' acts. *Developmental Psychology, 23*(3), 383–387.

Ali, A.Y. (1993). *The meaning of the holy Qur'an* (5th ed.). Brentwood, MD: Amana Corporation.

American Psychiatric Association. (2000). *Diagnostic and statistical manual of mental disorders* (4th ed., text rev.). Washington, DC: Author.

Anderson, D., Lord, C., Risi, S., DiLavore, P., Shulman, C., Thurm, A.,...Pickles, A. (2007). Patterns of growth in verbal abilities among children with autism spectrum disorder. *Journal of Consulting and Clinical Psychology, 75,* 594–604.

Bakeman, R., & Adamson, L. (1984). Coordinating attention to people and objects in mother–infant and peer–infant interaction. *Child Development, 55,* 1278–1289.

Bates, E., Benigni, L., Bretherton, I., Camaioni, L., & Volterra, V. (1979). *The emergence of symbols: Cognition and communication in infancy.* New York, NY: Academic Press.

Battle, D. (1997). Multicultural considerations in counseling communicatively disordered persons and their families. In T. Crowe (Ed.), *Applications of counseling in speech-language pathology and audiology* (pp. 118–144). Baltimore, MD: Williams & Wilkins.

Bruner, J.S. (1974/1975). From communication to language: A psychological perspective. *Cognition, 3,* 255–287.

Curcio, F. (1978). Sensorimotor functioning and communication in mute autistic children. *Journal of Autism and Developmental Disorders, 8,* 281–292.

DeLaOssa, J.L. (2002). Joint attention in middle childhood: Problem solving in caregiver–child interactions. *Dissertation Abstracts International: Section B. Sciences and Engineering, 60*(9-B), 4926.

Dennis, T.A., Cole, P.M., Zahn-Waxler, C., & Mizuta, I. (2002). Self in context: Autonomy and relatedness in Japanese and U.S. mother–preschool dyads. *Child Development, 73*(6), 1803–1817.

Enfield, N.J., Kita, S., & de Ruiter, J.P. (2007). Primary and secondary pragmatic functions of pointing gestures. *Journal of Pragmatics, 39,* 1722–1741.

Goldstein, H. (2002). Communication intervention for children with autism: A review of treatment efficacy. *Journal of Autism and Developmental Disorders, 32*(5), 373–396.

Gullberg, M., & Holmqvist, K. (2006). What speakers do and what addressees look at: Visual attention to gestures in human interaction live and on video. *Pragmatics and Cognition, 14*(1), 53–82.

Gutierrez, J., & Sameroff, A.J. (1990). Determinants of complexity in Mexican-American and Anglo-American mothers' conceptions of child development. *Child Development, 61*(2), 384–394.

Hart, B., & Risley, T.R. (1995). *Meaningful differences in the everyday experience of young American children.* Baltimore, MD: Paul H. Brookes Publishing Co.

Haviland, J.B. (1993). Anchoring, iconicity, and orientation in Guugu Yimithirr pointing gestures. *Journal of Linguistic Anthropology, 31*(1), 3–45.

Hustedt, J.T., & Cybele Raver, C. (2002). Scaffolding in low-income mother-child dyads: Relations with joint attention and dyadic reciprocity. *International Journal of Behavioral Development, 26*(2), 113–119.

Hwang, B., & Hughes, C. (2000). The effects of social interactive training on early social communicative skills of children with autism. *Journal of Autism and Developmental Disorders, 30,* 331–343.

Kasari, C., Freeman, S., & Paparella, T. (2006). Joint attention and symbolic play in young children with autism: A randomized controlled intervention study. *Journal of Child Psychology and Psychiatry, 46*(6), 611–620.

Kasari, C., Gulsrud, A., Wong, C., Kwon, S., & Locke, J. (2010). Randomized controlled caregiver mediated joint engagement intervention for toddlers with autism. *Journal of Autism and Developmental Disorders, 40,* 1045–1056.

Kasari, C., Paparella, T., Freeman, S., & Jahromi, L.B. (2008). Language outcome in autism: Randomized comparison of joint attention and play interventions. *Journal of Consulting and Clinical Psychology, 76*(1), 125–137.

Kochman, T. (1981). *Black and white styles in conflict.* Chicago, IL: University of Chicago Press.

Koegel, R.L., Koegel, L.K., & McNerney, E.K. (2001). Pivotal areas in intervention for autism. *Journal of Clinical Child Psychology, 30,* 19–32.

Lewy, A.L., & Dawson, G. (1992). Social stimulation and joint attention in young autistic children. *Journal of Abnormal Child Psychology, 20,* 555–566.

Lifter, K. (2000). Linking assessment to intervention for children with developmental disabilities or at-risk for developmental delay: The developmental play assessment (DPA) instrument. In K. Gitlin-Weiner, A. Sandgrund, & C. Schafer (Eds.), *Play diagnosis and assessment* (2nd ed., pp. 228–261). New York, NY: Wiley.

Lord, C., Cook, E.H., Leventhal, B.L., & Amaral, D.G. (2000). Autism spectrum disorders. *Neuron, 28,* 355–363.

Lord, C., Risi, S., Lambrecht, L., Cook, E.H., Jr., Leventhal, B.L., DiLavore, P.C.,...Rutter, M. (2000). The Autism Diagnostic Observation Schedule–Generic: A standard measure of social and communication deficits associated with the spectrum of autism. *Journal of Autism and Developmental Disorders, 30,* 205–223.

Lord, C., Rutter, M., DiLavore, P.C., & Risi, S. (1999). *Autism diagnostic observation schedule–WPS edition (ADOS-WPS).* Los Angeles, CA: Western Psychological Services.

Lord, C., Rutter, M., & LeCouteur, A. (1994). Autism Diagnostic Interview–Revised: A revised version of a diagnostic interview for caregivers of individuals with possible developmental disorders. *Journal of Autism and Developmental Disorders, 24,* 659–685.

Lord, C., Storoschuk, S., Rutter, M., & Pickles, A. (1993). Using the ADI-R to diagnose autism in preschool children. *Infant Mental Health Journal, 14,* 234-252.

Miranda, J., Bernal, G., Lau, A., Kohn, L., Hwang, W., & LaFromboise, T. (2005). State of the science on psychosocial interventions for ethnic minorities. *Annual Review of Clinical Psychology, 1*(1), 113–142.

Mullen, E.M. (1995). *Mullen Scales of Early Learning* (AGS ed.). Circle Pines, MN: American Guidance Service.

Mundy, P., Delgado, C., Block, J., Venezia, M., Hogan, A., & Seibert, J. (2003). *A manual for the abridged Early Social Communication Scales.* Coral Gables, FL: University of Miami.

Mundy, P., Hogan, A., & Doehring, P. (1996). *A preliminary manual for the abridged Early Social Communication Scales.* Coral Gables, FL: University of Miami.

Mundy, P., Kasari, C., & Sigman, M. (1992). Nonverbal communication, affective sharing and intersubjectivity. *Infant Behavior and Development, 15,* 377–381.

Mundy, P., Sigman, M., & Kasari, C. (1990). A longitudinal study of nonverbal joint attention and language development in young autistic children. *Journal of Autism and Developmental Disabilities, 20,* 115–128.

Mundy, P., Sigman, M.D., Ungerer, J., & Sherman, T. (1986). Defining the social deficits of autism: The contribution of non-verbal communication measures. *Journal of Child Psychology and Psychiatry and Allied Disciplines, 27,* 657–669.

Ninio, A., & Bruner, J. (1978). The achievement and antecedents of labeling. *Journal of Child Language, 5,* 1–15.

O'Neill, D. (2007). The Language Use Inventory for young children: A parent-report measure of pragmatic language development for 18- to 47-month-old children. *Journal of Speech, Language and Hearing Research, 50,* 214–228.

Paul, R., & Cascella, P. (2006). *Introduction to Clinical Methods in Communication Disorders* (2nd ed.). Baltimore, MD: Paul H. Brookes Publishing Co.

Pena, B. (1998). Tips for working with Hispanic bilingual patients. *Communication Disorders and Sciences in Culturally and Linguistically Diverse Populations, 4,* 7.

Ratner, N., & Bruner, J. (1978). Games, social exchange, and the acquisition of language. *Journal of Child Language, 5,* 391–401.

Reynell, J.K. (1977). *Reynell Developmental Language Scales.* Windsor, UK: NFER Publishing Co.

Robins, D.L., Fein, D., Barton, M.L., & Green, J.A. (2001). The Modified Checklist for Autism in Toddlers: An initial study investigating the early detection of autism and pervasive developmental disorders. *Journal of Autism and Developmental Disorders, 31,* 131–144.

Rollins, P.R., Wambacq, I., Dowell, D., Matthews, L., & Reese, P.B. (1998). An intervention technique for children with autistic spectrum disorder: Joint attentional routines. *Journal of Communication Disorders, 31*(2), 181–193.

Roseberry-McKibbin, C. (2007). *Language disorders in children: A multicultural and case perspective.* Boston, MA: Allyn & Bacon.

Schieffelin, B.B., & Eisenberg, A.R. (1984). Cultural variations in children's conversations. In R. Schiefelbusch & J. Pickar (Eds.), *The acquisition of communicative competence* (pp. 377–420). Baltimore, MD: University Park Press.

Tager-Flusberg, H. (1999). A psychological approach to understanding the social and language impairments in autism. *International Review of Psychiatry, 11* (4), 325–334.

Terrill, F.S., & Reilly, J.T. (1999). Joint attention and toddler characteristics: Race, sex and socioeconomic status. *Early Childhood Development and Care, 149,* 59–69.

Thurm, A., Lord, C., Lee, L., & Newschaffer, C. (2007). Predictors of language acquisition in preschool children with autism spectrum disorders. *Journal of Autism and Developmental Disorders, 37*(9), 1721–1734.

Tomasello, M., & Farrar, M.J. (1986). Joint attention and early language. *Child Development, 57,* 1454–1463.

Tomasello, M., & Todd, J. (1983). Joint attention and lexical acquisition style. *First Language, 4*(12), 197–211.

Ungerer, J.A., & Sigman, M. (1981). Symbolic play and language comprehension in autistic children. *American Academy of Child Psychiatry, 20,* 318–337.

United Nations Educational, Scientific and Cultural Organization. (2002). *Universal Declaration on Cultural Diversity.* Retrieved March 13, 2012, from http://www.unesco.org/education/imld_2002/unversal_decla.shtml#1.

van Kleeck, A. (1994). Potential cultural bias in training parents as conversational partners with their children who have delays in language development. *American Journal of Speech-Language Pathology, 3*(1), 67–78.

Venter, A., Lord, C., & Schopler, E. (1992). A follow-up study of high-functioning autistic children. *Journal of Child Psychology and Psychiatry and Allied Disciplines, 33*(3), 489–507.

Wallace, G.L., Inglebret, E., & Friedlander, R. (1997). American Indians: Culture, communication and clinical management. In G.L. Wallace (Ed.), *Multicultural neurogenics: A resource for speech-language pathologists providing services to neurologically impaired adults from culturally and linguistically diverse backgrounds* (pp. 193–226). San Antonio, TX: Communication Skill Builders.

Wetherby, A. (1986). Ontogeny of communicative functions in autism. *Journal of Autism and Developmental Disorders, 16,* 295–315.

Wetherby, A., & Prutting, C. (1984). Profiles of communicative and cognitive-social abilities in autistic children. *Journal of Speech and Hearing Research, 27*(3), 364–377.

Wetherby, A., Woods, J., Allen, L., Cleary, J., Dickinson, H., & Lord, C. (2004). Early indicators of autism spectrum disorders in the second year of life. *Journal of Autism and Developmental Disorders, 34*(5), 473–493.

Whalen, C., & Schreibman, L. (2003). Joint attention training for children with autism using behavior modification procedures. *Journal of Child Psychology and Psychiatry, 44*(3), 456–468.

Whalen, C., Schreibman, L., & Ingersoll, B. (2006). The collateral effects of joint attention training on social initiations, positive affect, imitation, and spontaneous speech for young children with autism. *Journal of Autism and Developmental Disorders, 36*(5), 655–664.

Wong, C., Kasari, C., Freeman, S., & Paparella, T. (2007). The acquisition and generalization of joint attention and symbolic play skills in young children with autism. *Research and Practice for Persons with Severe Disabilities, 32*(2), 101–109.

Wyatt, T.A. (2002). Assessing the communicative abilities of clients from diverse cultural and language backgrounds. In D.E. Battle (Ed.), *Communication disorders in multicultural populations* (3rd ed., pp. 415–450). Boston, MA: Butterworth-Heinemann.

8

Implementing Enhanced Milieu Teaching with Children Who Have Autism Spectrum Disorders

Terry B. Hancock and Ann P. Kaiser

There is empirical support for the effectiveness of **enhanced milieu teaching (EMT)** for children who have a diagnosis of autistic disorder (Hancock & Kaiser, 2002; Hancock, Ton, & Crowe, 2008; Kaiser, Hancock, & Nietfeld, 2000; Kaiser, MacFarland, & Hancock, 2008; Olive et al., 2007), Asperger syndrome (Kaiser et al., 2000), and pervasive developmental disorder-not otherwise specified (PDD-NOS; Hancock & Kaiser, 2002; Kaiser et al., 2000; Kaiser et al., 2008; Olive et al., 2007). Although EMT has been used effectively with children who have varying spectrum diagnoses, it is not necessarily the diagnosis that predicts how rapidly children will acquire language skills when adults implement EMT strategies. Most children who participated in research on EMT had foundational language and learning strategies that increased the likelihood they would respond to this intervention. Typically, these children 1) were verbally imitative when prompted, 2) demonstrated a productive vocabulary of at least 10 words, and 3) had mean lengths of utterances (MLU) between 1.0 and 3.5 units. Variations of EMT have also been demonstrated to be effective with children diagnosed with an autism spectrum disorder (ASD) who are not yet communicating verbally (see Warren et al. [2006] and Yoder and Stone [2006a, 2006b] for more information on responsive education/ milieu teaching with children who are prelinguistic; see Olive et al. [2007] for the effects of EMT and voice output communication aids [VOCAs]).

The focus of this chapter is EMT with children with ASDs who have foundational verbal skills. When children can verbally imitate, they are able to respond to adult models, who are the core of milieu prompting procedures. This, in turn, enables the children to practice new communication forms in functional contexts. When children have some spontaneous production of language, the adult implementing EMT has more opportunities to provide expanded models in response to the child, and the child is more likely to practice the functional use of his or her existing language within the supportive context of the EMT session. The EMT approach appears to be highly effective with children who are in the early stages of language

Preparation of this manuscript was supported in part by NIH grants (R01 HD45745-01A1 and P50DC03282).

learning, particularly children who do not verbalize frequently and who are learning vocabulary or early semantic relationships.

EMT includes four components: 1) **environmental arrangement,** 2) **responsive interaction,** 3) specific **language modeling,** and 4) **milieu teaching** (see Table 8.1). When implementing EMT according to these components, the adult arranges the environment to set the stage for adult–child interactions and to increase the likelihood that the child will initiate to the adult (environmental arrangement). The adult also models specific language targets appropriate to the child's skill level in response to the child's communication and connected to the child's play and focus of interest (modeling, responsive interaction). In addition, the adult responds to the child's requests with prompts for elaborated language consistent with the child's targeted skills (milieu teaching) and functionally reinforces the child's production of prompted target forms in a variety of ways. Functional reinforcement can be provided by allowing access to requested objects (milieu teaching), continuing adult interaction (responsive interaction), offering feedback in the form of expansions (modeling), and confirming the meaning and pragmatic functions of the child's utterances (responsive interaction).

TARGET POPULATIONS AND ASSESSMENTS FOR DETERMINING TREATMENT RELEVANCE AND GOALS

Children with ASDs who have been included in our intervention research are screened for eligibility using a global language measure, such as the Preschool Language Scale–4 (PLS-4; Zimmerman, Steiner, & Pond, 2002), a verbal imitation task, and a 30-min language sample using a standard protocol and set of toys. Children who are able to imitate at least 80% of words presented on the imitation task, who spontaneously produce a minimum of 10 words during the language sample, and whose MLU is not more than 3.0 are eligible for inclusion. Research suggests that when children's MLU is greater than 3.0, they can often learn efficiently with responsive interaction strategies alone (Kaiser, Hancock, & Lambert, 1997; Kaiser et al., 1996; Kaiser, Lambert, Hancock, & Hester, 1998). For children who pass the screening criteria, additional standardized assessments, parent report measures, and observations are completed to provide a more comprehensive picture of their entry language skills. Providing broader information about children's vocabulary knowledge are a receptive vocabulary assessment, such as the Peabody Picture Vocabulary Test–4 (PPVT-4; Dunn & Dunn, 2007); a productive vocabulary assessment, such as the Expressive Vocabulary Test–2 (EVT-2; Williams, 2007); and a parent-reported vocabulary measure, such as the MacArthur-Bates Communication Development Inventory–2 (MCDI-2; Fenson et al., 2007). Natural observations of children's language are obtained with one or two unfamiliar therapists and the parent, across different settings (clinic and home), and across various activities (play, snack, book reading, and cleanup). Children's utterances are transcribed and analyzed using Systematic Analysis of Language Transcripts (SALT; Miller, 2008). Information from all assessments is summarized and used to determine appropriate vocabulary and syntactic language targets.

For children with an ASD diagnosis, it is also important to determine their functional use of language and other communication skills by observing them with their parent(s) and unfamiliar adults. Vocabulary knowledge and MLU are not

Table 8.1.   Rationales for the components of enhanced milieu teaching (EMT), with examples

EMT component	Rationale	Examples
Environmental arrangement	Promote child's requesting	Present choices of snacks or give the child a little bit of the snack at a time to promote verbal requests.
	Promote child's engagement to maintain and extend child's play and interaction with adult	Provide additional materials to extend play—such as water when playing with the farm, so the child can give the animals a bath or a drink.
	Prevent and manage child's behavior problems by arranging physical surroundings	Designate a play space with a physical cue, such as a carpet square; limit the number of toys/materials that are within the child's reach.
Responsive interaction	Engage child in positive interactions	Follow the child's play or conversational lead so there is no pressure for the child to "perform."
	Prime child for responding	Mirror the child's actions and verbally "map" corresponding language, both of which support the child in orienting to adult communication.
	Maintain space for child to engage in conversations	Pace the interaction so there is plenty of time (at least 5 s) for the child to participate as an equal conversational partner.
	Reinforce child for any and all communication attempts	Respond contingently to any verbal, vocal, or nonverbal child turn.
Modeling of child's targets and target-level language	Provide child with salient, specific models of target language	Model all of the child's selected language targets in the context of the child's interests.
	Prime child to imitate targets spontaneously	Expand the child's responses by embedding the selected targets before prompting these targets with EMT procedures.
Milieu teaching prompts	Support child in acquiring new forms	Provide a model prompt to teach the child unknown labels for fruit the child enjoys for a snack.
	Support child in making verbal choices	Provide a visual choice of apples and melon, using the labels for each in the choice question.
	Support child in answering questions	Ask the child what fruit he or she wants for a snack.
	Cue child to initiate a more elaborated request	Hold up the melon and wait for the child to request it using his or her selected language targets.

always the best indicators of children's functional communication skills. Children with ASDs may have an inflated MLU if they frequently use rote phrases that are longer than their more functional, spontaneous speech. We ask parents to list their children's rote phrases, and we exclude these phrases when estimating the number of different words produced and MLU based on transcripts of interactions analyzed with SALT. This approach provides a more accurate estimate of the complexity and variety of children's functional language as a basis for selecting targets for teaching.

THEORETICAL BASIS

Several reviews of communication interventions for children with ASDs have characterized the components of EMT as representing a contemporary applied behavior analysis (ABA) model (Corsello, 2005; Ogletree, Oren, & Fischer, 2007; Prizant, Wetherby, & Rydell, 2000) and a developmental pragmatic communication approach (Rogers, 2006). Because EMT is a "blended" intervention with distinct components (environmental arrangement, responsive interaction, modeling, and milieu teaching), both of these theoretical perspectives are represented in the intervention.

Contemporary Applied Behavior Analysis

Contemporary ABA is rooted in a behavioral perspective on language learning and instruction (Hart & Rogers-Warren [Kaiser], 1978) but is more naturalistic than traditional ABA instructional strategies and more consistent with a transactional approach to language learning (Ogletree et al., 2007). According to Prizant and his colleagues (2000), contemporary ABA interventions include

1. incidental language teaching (Hart, 1985)
2. a natural-language paradigm (Koegel & Johnson, 1989)
3. milieu teaching (Kaiser, Yoder, & Keetz, 1992)

At the core of contemporary ABA interventions are the "instructional value of natural routines, the caregiver–child dyad, and the creation of typical communication opportunities as the primary instructional context" (Ogletree et al., 2007, p. 238). Our current version of EMT with children who are on the autism spectrum (Hancock et al., 2008; Kaiser et al., 2008) is primarily parent-implemented and occurs in typical home routines, including play, book reading, and snacking. In a behavioral approach to language instruction, methods such as modeling, imitation, and prompted practice of expressive language skills are key. Adults prompt children to use language by presenting antecedent stimuli (models, time delays, mands [e.g., questions or instructions to talk]) that signal when to talk and what to say. When children respond to these prompts, they are reinforced by the consequences adults provide that are contingent on their communication. Contingent adult responding plays an important role in this behavioral paradigm because it presumably functions as a reinforcer that increases the frequency with which children communicate. In addition, it provides differential feedback for children's more complex language. Imitation and production practice, with contingent adult feedback, are essential child behaviors for learning language in this framework. Embedded within milieu teaching, prompting procedures (elicitive model, mand model, time delay, incidental teaching) are strategies for facilitating more frequent child initiations. First, children learn to imitate when given adult models. Next, they learn to respond to questions of increasing complexity (mand model). Finally, children initiate requests and comments (time delay, incidental teaching), thus becoming more independent language users.

Contemporary ABA interventions address some of the criticisms of traditional ABA therapies, including limited generalization of treatment outcomes and the lack of flexibility in communication skills that children often have when they complete ABA therapy. A contemporary ABA perspective includes a strong interest in both the acquisition of language and communication skills and the generalization and maintenance of newly learned forms. Studies of milieu teaching and EMT with children with and without ASDs have demonstrated systematic generalization across 1) settings (Alpert & Kaiser, 1992; Hancock & Kaiser, 1996; Kaiser et al., 2000), 2) partners (Hancock & Kaiser, 2002), 3) specific classes of language structures (Warren, Gazdag,

Bambara, & Jones, 1994), and 4) global indicators of language development (Hancock & Kaiser, 2002; Kaiser et al., 2000). Adult prompts are faded within EMT from most supportive (models) to least supportive (time delays) as new language forms are being acquired. This encourages children to use their newly learned language skills more flexibly and independently than may occur when children participate in more traditional ABA instruction. Children with ASDs have particular difficulty in generalizing social communication skills across settings and people (Goldstein, 2002). Thus, teaching in everyday communicative contexts, teaching parents to provide support for communication across contexts, and including practice across different people and settings may be especially important for these children.

Developmental Pragmatic Communication Approach

The developmental pragmatic communication approach is built on research related to 1) descriptions of the development of language in typical children, 2) comparative descriptions of the development of language in atypical children, and 3) studies of parental and environmental influences on language development in typical and atypical children. This model is characterized by a facilitative adult approach that promotes child initiations by following the child's communication lead and responding to all of the child's communicative attempts as if they were purposeful (Ingersoll & Dvortcsak, 2006; Ogletree et al., 2007). Some of the defining features of the developmental pragmatic communication model include adult–child interactions that are characterized by shared affect and verbal turn taking, adult scaffolding of child communication attempts to make these attempts more meaningful, and teaching communication in activities specifically of interest to children so that they are motivated to communicate with adults (Rogers, 2006).

Both children and parents are influenced by the context in which they interact and by the supports provided as part of this context. For typically developing children, parents' linguistic input matches children's needs for systematic examples of the language system. Parents adjust their input and feedback based on their children's responses, and there is a smooth bidirectional or transactional flow between adult and child partners. This degree of fit between children and parents is reflected in the adequacy of ongoing communication as well as in the children's acquisition of new communicative forms and strategies.

This developmental pragmatic communication model of language provides a framework within which children with ASDs can be viewed as bringing a set of early social, cognitive, and communicative skills to the interactions in which more complex forms of social communication will be taught. The specific characteristics of children interface with the skills and abilities of their parents and other conversational partners to provide and constrain opportunities for language learning.

Children with ASDs generally speak less often, are less likely to seek out a communication partner, use fewer words, and have greater difficulty understanding the meaning of parent talk (Landa, 2007). Parents can have difficulty matching their linguistic input to their child's existing knowledge. A mismatch can occur between the language input needed for learning and the input parents provide. This mismatch may decrease the frequency as well as the usefulness of these interactions from a communication and language-learning transactional perspective. From an intervention perspective, the developmental pragmatic communication model serves as a means for tailoring parent responses to children's utterances by using the children's current language level to inform the appropriateness of new input provided to them (Camarata & Yoder, 2002). Parent responsivity to child communication attempts must be increased to scaffold or directly reinforce the child's attempts to communicate. Following children's leads in interactions and conversations, modeling language that describes the children's actions, and expanding their utterances will increase input that more closely matches the children's focus and conceptual understanding. Parents are ideal communication partners because they often understand children's communicative intent more easily than other adults and thus have more opportunities to model functional language for children to use to convey their meaning. These responsive interaction strategies (following the child's lead, equal turn taking, language modeling, and expansions) are associated with better language development outcomes when children have significantly delayed language, including children who are on the autism spectrum (Kaiser, Hester, & McDuffie, 2001; Yoder & Warren, 2004).

EMPIRICAL BASIS

Across the last two decades, milieu teaching strategies have been expanded to include environmental arrangement and responsive interaction strategies, as well as elicitive modeling, mand modeling, time delay, and incidental teaching. Since 1990, this expanded model of milieu teaching has been referred to as enhanced milieu teaching (Kaiser, 1993). Initial studies of milieu teaching extended and specified the incidental teaching model of Hart and Risley (1968, 1975). Since then, more than 50 studies incorporating variants of milieu teaching have been conducted (Kaiser & Trent, 2007). The EMT model blends four main components: 1) environmental arrangement to set the physical and interactional stage for promoting children's engagement with activities and communication partners (Ostrosky & Kaiser, 1991), 2) responsive interaction strategies to build a social, conversational interaction (Weiss, 1981), 3) the modeling of new language forms to expose children to a variety of words, and 4) limited milieu teaching episodes in response to children's requests. See Hancock and Kaiser (2006) for more detailed information about the empirical basis of EMT.

The empirical literature reports on several variants of EMT that are being implemented with children with ASDs. The research on EMT with children with ASDs included in this section met the following minimum intervention criteria: 1) occurred in typical routines across a day (play, snacking, reading books), 2) included prompts that were embedded to support children's use of more complex language skills, 3) balanced prompting procedures of milieu teaching with responsive interaction strategies, and 4) incorporated environmental arrangement strategies to support the communication connection between the adult and the child and to increase opportunities for the child to use language. In addition, for the purposes of this chapter, we included research on EMT only with children who were verbal communicators. Additional information about the empirical basis for variants of EMT with children who are prelinguistic can be found by reading about responsivity education/prelinguistic milieu teaching (RPMT; Warren et al., 2006; Yoder & Stone, 2006a, 2006b) or EMT when used in combination with a voice output communication aid (VOCA; Olive et al., 2007).

The studies included in this section represent the range of EMT studies conducted between 1995 and 2010 that have included children with ASDs (Hancock &

Kaiser, 2002; Hancock et al., 2008; Kaiser et al., 2000; Kaiser et al., 2008). Specifically, we have completed intervention research on EMT when implemented 1) primarily by EMT therapists (Hancock & Kaiser, 2002), 2) by parents who were trained in EMT (Kaiser et al., 2000), and 3) by teams of EMT therapists and parents who were trained in EMT strategies and worked collaboratively with children (Hancock et al. 2008; Kaiser et al., 2008).

Data for the therapist-implemented EMT study (Hancock & Kaiser, 2002) and the parent-implemented EMT study (Kaiser et al., 2000) were selected from a longitudinal study comparing the effects of three different naturalistic intervention models with children who had significant language delays (Kaiser et al., 1998). In the larger study (Kaiser et al., 1998), 76 children were assigned randomly to one of three intervention groups: 1) parent-implemented EMT, 2) therapist-implemented EMT, and 3) parent-implemented responsive interaction. Data for both of the selected studies included those children with an ASD diagnosis who were randomly assigned to the specific EMT condition (therapist-implemented EMT or parent-implemented EMT) and who had complete data through the follow-up phase. Both of these selected studies examined the effects of EMT on the social communication skills of preschool children with autism when delivered by trained interventionists (Hancock & Kaiser, 2002) or by parents trained in EMT (Kaiser et al., 2000) in a modified single-subject design across children. They also investigated the indirect effects of the EMT intervention on children's interactions with the family at home.

Therapist-Implemented Enhanced Milieu Teaching

Four preschool children with autism and their mothers participated in the study (Hancock & Kaiser, 2002). Three of the four children were boys. Two of the boys were diagnosed with autistic disorder, and the third boy was diagnosed with PDD-NOS. The girl had a diagnosis of PDD-NOS. The children ranged in age from 35 to 54 months, and their measured IQ scores ranged from <50 to 95. Expressive and receptive skills were in the 20- to 28-month range as measured by the Sequenced Inventory of Communication Development (SICD; Hedrick, Prather, & Tobin, 1975), and average MLU at entry was 1.29 (range 1.03–2.00).

Children in this study completed either 5 or 7 baseline sessions, 24 intervention sessions, and 6 follow-up sessions (one each month for the 6 months after the intervention ended), with each session lasting 15–20 min. Therapists did not use EMT strategies during baseline play sessions but did use EMT strategies with a high level of precision and well above established levels of fidelity during intervention and follow-up sessions. Generalization of the children's use of social communication with their untrained parents was assessed in the families' homes in 9 sessions: 3 each at baseline, intervention, and 6-month follow-up.

The children were assessed on a battery of standardized language tests during baseline, at the end of intervention, and again at the end of the follow-up phase, which included the SICD (Hedrick et al., 1975), the Peabody Picture Vocabulary Test–Revised (PPVT-R; Dunn & Dunn, 1981), the Expressive One-Word Picture Vocabulary Test–Revised (EOWPVT-R; Gardner, 1990), and two 30-min language samples. On the basis of these standardized assessments and observations, early semantic language targets were selected for each child, including two-word forms (viz., agent–action, action–object, attribute–object, two-word request) or three-word forms (viz., agent–action–object, three-word request).

Observational time series data indicated that all four children showed positive increases for specific target language use (prompted and unprompted) across the 24 intervention sessions, and these results were maintained through the 6-month follow-up observations (Hancock & Kaiser, 2002). There was also evidence of positive changes in the children's complexity (MLU increases for three children) and diversity of language (all four children) used during the intervention sessions. Three of the four children generalized these positive language effects to interactions with their mothers at home, with the greatest change seen immediately after the intervention ended.

Therapist-delivered EMT (Hancock & Kaiser, 2002) resulted in positive changes for children's social communication assessed across settings and measures. In addition, these changes generalized to interactions with their parents who had not been trained in the EMT intervention. The results of this study indicate that shorter amounts of a powerful, focused intervention positively impact the language skills of children with ASDs. Younger children whose language development was less delayed relative to their age showed the greatest increases in the acquisition, maintenance, and generalization of language skills. The child who did not show the same level of changes as the other three children may have needed more than 24 intervention sessions or more intense sessions for longer than 15–20 min to show positive language changes.

Parent-Implemented Enhanced Milieu Teaching

Kaiser, Hancock, and Nietfeld (2000) examined the effects of training parents to implement EMT with their preschoolers with ASDs. A modified single-subject design across six families was used to assess the parent's acquisition and generalized use of EMT strategies. The six male children in this study ranged in age from 32 to 54 months and included three children who had a diagnosis of autistic disorder, two who had a diagnosis of PDD-NOS, and one child who had a diagnosis of Asperger syndrome. At entry, the children scored, on average, 24 months on the expressive section of the SICD and 25 months on the receptive section of the SICD. The children's average MLU at the beginning of the intervention was 1.48 (range 1.00–2.37). Their IQ scores ranged from <50 to 85; however, low scores were associated with nonresponsiveness during the testing. The participating parents were mothers who ranged in age from 30 to 37 and averaged 3 years of college. All parent training sessions and parent–child play sessions (baseline, intervention, follow-up) were conducted in a clinic setting. Generalization sessions were conducted and videotaped in the families' homes (baseline, end of intervention, follow-up).

Before intervention began, children were pretested using a battery of standardized language assessments, including the SICD, the PPVT-R, and the EOWPVT-R; parent report measures of children's language on the MCDI; and two 30-min language samples taken from play interactions between the children and a trained research assistant. Based on these standardized assessments, observations, and parent input, early semantic language targets were selected for all children. Individual targets ranged from single nouns and action verbs to three-word requests or three-word forms, such as agent–action–object. The assessments were repeated at the end of intervention and again at the end of the follow-up phase.

Following the completion of the baseline phase, 24 intervention sessions were conducted with the parent and child. Intervention sessions lasted about 45 min and included providing the parent with information about EMT strategies, allowing the parent to practice EMT strategies in a play session with the child while the EMT therapist provided live coaching, and providing the parent with suggestions for using the procedures at home. After the end of intervention, follow-up sessions were completed once a month for 6 months to assess parents' maintenance of EMT strategies and children's use of communication skills. No coaching or feedback was provided during these follow-up sessions.

Five of the six parents learned all of the EMT procedures to criterion levels within the 24 intervention sessions. Parents maintained their use of these EMT strategies during the follow-up, sometimes at higher levels than had been observed at the end of intervention, but always well above baseline levels. Five of the six parents showed consistent generalization across most EMT procedures at the post-intervention observation and sustained their performance during the follow-up observations.

All six children showed increases in their spontaneous use of language targets, which were maintained during the clinic follow-up sessions. Four of the six children showed increases in MLU or diversity of words used at the end of intervention, and all six children showed changes in these measures during the follow-up period. Children showed similar increases in targets, MLU, and diversity of words in the home generalization sessions with their parents. Evidence of developmental changes was indicated on standardized assessments for all six children on the SICD (average increase of 10 months on receptive communication from baseline to follow-up; average increase of 9 months on expressive communication from baseline to follow-up) and for all six children on the EOWPVT-R (average increase of 18 months from baseline to follow-up). In this first study of parent-implemented EMT with children with ASDs, results indicated that parents could implement these strategies effectively and efficiently and that their children showed positive effects in their observed and assessed social communication skills as a result of their parents' use of EMT.

Enhanced Milieu Teaching Implemented Jointly by Parent and Therapist

Our previous research examining variants of EMT has demonstrated that children may show more rapid growth in language targets, MLU, and vocabulary diversity during intervention sessions when skilled therapists, rather than parents, implement EMT (Kaiser et al., 2002). However, when parents deliver EMT, children show better generalization to home and greater improvement on standardized measures of language development and clinic observations of language complexity at the 6- and 12-month follow-ups than children who receive EMT from therapists only (Kaiser & Hancock, 2000). The next generation of EMT intervention includes a collaborative model, employing skilled therapists, who can accelerate children's use of more complex language skills, and parents trained in EMT, who can support children's generalized use of social communication skills over time and settings.

Kaiser, Hancock, and colleagues investigated the effects of an EMT intervention implemented jointly by parents and therapists on the communication skills of three children with autism (Hancock et al., 2008; Kaiser et al., 2008). These children and their parents were part of a larger ongoing study (Kaiser, 2012) investigating the effects of two models of EMT on the language performance of children with cognitive impairments and significant language delays. The larger study of EMT randomly assigned children to two different delivery conditions: 1) when delivered by two skilled therapists in the clinic and at home or 2) when implemented by the children's trained parent and a skilled therapist (parent plus therapist) in the clinic and at home. The children who participated in the single-subject-design study were the first three children with autism who were randomly assigned to the parent-plus-therapist condition in the larger study.

The three children—two boys and one girl ranging in age from 36 to 48 months—all had an autistic disorder diagnosis. The children's average standard score on receptive language was 50, and their average standard score on expressive language was 58 as assessed by the PLS-4 (Zimmerman et al., 2002). The children's average MLU before beginning the intervention was 1.13 (range 1.04–1.22), and their nonverbal IQ scores ranged from 62 to 76 on the Leiter International Performance Scale–Revised (Leiter-R; Roid & Miller, 1997).

A multiple baseline design across participants was used to evaluate the effects of the parent-plus-therapist EMT intervention on the children's language. Following the procedures for multiple baseline designs (Tawney & Gast, 1984), baseline observations occurred for 5 to 7 sessions or until stable levels and trends were observed in child and adult data. The intervention was introduced sequentially across three parent–child dyads. When the effects of the intervention were observed for the first child (6 to 10 sessions), the intervention was introduced for the next child. The same procedure was followed for the third child. The intervention continued until 36 sessions were completed. Follow-up intervention observations in the clinic occurred at 6 months and 12 months after the intervention ended.

All three children had the same two-word target forms (agent–action, action–object, modifier–noun, two-word request) that were selected based on their pretest assessments. Intervention sessions were conducted in the clinic (24 sessions) and in the children's homes (12 sessions interspersed with clinic sessions). Each clinic-based intervention session lasted about an hour and included four parts: 1) training on a specific EMT strategy, 2) the therapist-implemented EMT session, 3) the parent-implemented EMT session, and 4) a review of the day's session and a plan for the next session. During home intervention sessions, the parent coach supported the parent's use of the targeted strategy during four activities in the home: playing with the child's toys, snacking, book reading, and a cleanup task.

By the end of intervention, parents implemented EMT at levels consistent with those of the skilled therapists who worked with their children. Two of the three children showed increases in their use of targets, MLU, and diversity of vocabulary during the intervention and at both the 6- and 12-month follow-up assessments. On average, the children showed an increase of 23 points on their PPVT standard scores from baseline to the 12-month follow-up and a 28-point increase on their EVT standard scores from baseline to the 12-month follow-up.

The results of this study (Kaiser et al., 2008) suggest that the EMT intervention implemented jointly by parent and therapist may be an efficient and effective protocol for teaching new language skills to young children with ASDs. Immediately upon entry into the intervention condition, children received systematic intervention to learn their targeted forms and more elaborated language with skilled therapists while their parents were learning each component of EMT to criterion. Children's increased communication initiations and responses primed by skilled therapists potentially provided parents with more opportunities to practice their newly learned EMT skills. As parents became proficient in their use of EMT strategies, they facilitated their children's use of new language skills on a daily basis at home and continued the intervention when the clinic intervention with the skilled therapist was completed.

Summary of the Evidence to Date

These three initial studies (Hancock et al., 2008; Kaiser, 2012; Kaiser et al., 2008) provide empirical evidence of the effectiveness of EMT when implemented by parents or therapists with children with ASDs. Together, they represent systematic replication of EMT, progressive development of this model, and consistent evidence of generalization by children and parents trained in EMT. Future studies of EMT with children who have ASDs need to address limitations of these studies, which include 1) lack of published group studies to date; 2) all of these studies were completed in the same lab; 3) variability in child outcomes; and 4) heterogeneity of the samples.

PRACTICAL REQUIREMENTS

Implementing EMT at high levels of fidelity requires a significant time commitment, but most parents who participated in EMT training reported that the positive outcomes for their children far outweighed the time devoted to training and practice. Many parents in our research program brought their children to a university clinic twice each week for EMT sessions. About one third of participating parents drove more than 50 miles to participate in the training. Over time, we modified aspects of the protocol to reduce parents' time commitments and to promote better generalization to the home setting. One third (12) of the intervention sessions in our last study were conducted at home (Hancock et al., 2008). When needed, a second staff member accompanied the parent coach and provided care for siblings so the parent and the parent coach could focus on practicing the intervention with the target child. Home intervention sessions were conducted using routine activities (e.g., snacking, cleanup, reading a book, play) and materials and settings within the home that had been identified by the family.

Although interventionists do not need to meet any specific professional requirements to receive training in EMT, most have an educational background in speech and language sciences, psychology, or special education and have previous experience with young children who have special needs, including children with ASDs. Interventionists receive training in EMT through observing and coding the discrete behaviors of EMT; attending an intensive, interactive workshop on the principles and components of EMT; and implementing EMT strategies with "practice children" while receiving systematic coaching and feedback from experienced staff.

After successful completion of the EMT training program, interventionists are paired with experienced staff, who provide ongoing feedback on their implementation of EMT strategies with children. Interventionists also receive systematic feedback through coded and summarized session data and support through weekly research meetings.

For those child interventionists who want to become a parent coach, additional training is provided (Kaiser & Hancock, 2003; Kaiser, Hancock, & Windsor, 2007). Even when an interventionist is skilled in implementing EMT with several children, giving feedback to another adult about the intervention requires an entirely different skill set. Information about effective parent training and coaching strategies are provided in readings, handouts, and video examples. Interventionists then learn to apply this information in an apprentice model with an experienced parent coach who provides ongoing feedback and support (see Kaiser & Hancock, 2003, and Kaiser et al., 2007, for more detailed information about training parent coaches). The entire training process for an EMT interventionist who also trains parents in the intervention from learning to code to functioning as a primary parent coach takes from 6 months to 1 year to complete. This apprentice approach ensures that children and parents receive the most effective intervention while trainees are fully supported in becoming skilled and independent.

KEY COMPONENTS

The four components of EMT are 1) environmental arrangement, 2) responsive interaction, 3) specific language modeling, and 4) milieu teaching prompts (see Table 8.1 for specific examples of each of these components). There can be special challenges when implementing each of these EMT components with children with ASDs. Children with ASDs frequently exhibit behaviors that make implementation of EMT procedures more difficult. These behaviors include restricted interests in activities and toys, limited joint attention skills, limited social engagement with adults during activities, perseverative behavior, verbal echolalia, and other challenging behaviors (e.g., throwing materials, physical aggression). Specific adaptations of EMT strategies to accommodate children with ASDs and make the intervention more effective and functional for them have been developed. These adaptations are included in the discussion of the four components of EMT that follows. For an example of an EMT session, see the DVD that accompanies this book.

Environmental Arrangement

The purpose of environmental arrangement is to create a context for teaching and learning language. Selecting and arranging materials and activities of interest supports child engagement and increases interactions with adults. Generally, when children are interested in activities, they are motivated to engage with adults in communication interactions for longer periods of time. Selecting interesting materials and activities for children with ASDs, however, can be challenging because these children often have restricted interests. In addition, sometimes children with ASDs find a particular toy or material so interesting that they exclude the adult from the interaction, either by focusing exclusively on the toy or by refusing to allow the adult to enter into the play. Inviting the child to choose a toy from a set of moderately preferred toys (and not offering toys that set the occasion for exclusionary play) provides an immediate assessment of child interest. For children with limited attention or few play skills, toy choices may be offered at the beginning of a play session and at several intervals during the session when the child loses interest. Selecting sets of materials that are presented sequentially can extend the time spent in shared play (e.g., introducing a toy garage and cars, followed by people who fit into the cars, sponges and buckets for washing cars, brushes and pretend paint for painting cars).

Environmental arrangement serves two other important purposes: 1) building and extending play routines as context for modeling new vocabulary and other target forms (see the Language Modeling section) and 2) providing a foundation for using milieu teaching prompts to promote language production (see the Milieu Teaching section). First, including a variety of toys, activities, and play schemes allows adults to model a range of vocabulary and syntax forms. Novel materials and actions introduced into an established play routine can be used to draw attention to the verbal model of the label and the action. Routines provide repeated opportunities to model sequences of utterances that describe cohesive action schemes ("The boy feeds the cows, then they go into the barn, and then they go to sleep"). Second, the purposeful arrangement of materials promotes child requesting and offers opportunities to prompt production of new forms when the child requests. For example, an adult might 1) provide the material of interest to the child in a container that only the adult can open so that the child will have to engage the adult by requesting assistance in opening it, 2) block the next logical action in an established play routine so that the child will request an action to continue the routine (e.g., "Move your hand"), or 3) display (in sight but out of reach) interesting supplemental pieces to a toy of interest so that the child will request these supplements from the adult.

Children with ASDs often have restricted interests in toys and play routines, which can limit opportunities for modeling and prompting diverse language forms. There is often a delicate balance between providing a toy with which the child will play for an extended time and exposing the child to different toys so that the adult can model a variety of vocabulary. Some balance can be achieved by allowing the child to play with a favorite toy while the adult slowly introduces novel, attractive materials to the child. Then the adult may require the child to play with these newly introduced materials for increasingly longer periods of time before accessing the favorite toy. For example, if a child perseverates on trains, the adult may begin the play session with a train and add other materials or expand play to build an extended play scheme. The adult might have the train go down the track to the train washing station, where the child can spray soap and water to wash the train. The train may transport animals or people. Each train car may carry a piece of Mr. Potato Head that is assembled when the train reaches the station. Expanding play by modeling and prompting new actions helps children with ASDs extend their time playing and increases the diversity of play actions.

Responsive Interaction

Following the child's lead in play and conversation, verbal and nonverbal turning taking, and mirroring actions while providing verbal descriptions or mapping child actions are core strategies included in the responsive interaction component of EMT. The purpose of these strategies is to engage the child in nonverbal and verbal interactions that provide the opportunities for modeling new language forms and make it more likely that the child will interact with the adult as a conversational partner. Play with toys and nonverbal engagement between the child and adult set the context for language modeling; however, implementing these responsive interaction strategies is challenging when children with ASDs have limited functional play skills, engage in repetitive or inappropriate actions with toys, or have low rates of engagement with adults.

Following the child's lead and nonverbal mirroring are intended to promote connection between the child and adult and extend nonverbal engagement; however, these strategies also reinforce existing behavior when the adult responds contingently. To use these strategies effectively, the adult must wait until the child performs an appropriate action or play behavior. In addition, following the child's lead or mirroring the child's actions is often enough to promote a nonverbal connection between the child and the responsive adult. However, these strategies must also be balanced with moving the child to a more complex play schema or routine by expanding the child's play actions with new materials or by modeling new actions.

Language Modeling

Language modeling provides children with salient, specific models of targeted language forms in ongoing interactions with adults. Language modeling can also prime children to imitate targets spontaneously. Modeling targets at the child's selected language level, however, can be problematic for some children with ASDs. Adults may need to pay particular attention to modeling diverse vocabulary, which can be difficult when children have restricted interests. Supplementing children's restricted toy interest with additional materials may provide adults with opportunities to model more diverse vocabulary. Adults may need to pay particular attention to modeling when interacting with children who are imitative and initiate language with a pronoun reversal, saying "you" when they mean "I." Prompting the child to use "I" is one way for the child to practice using pronouns correctly, especially when the child is requesting, but it doesn't necessarily support the child's ability to comment appropriately. Having the adult model "I" when he or she is mirroring a child's actions and mapping language that corresponds to the actions can be an important strategy for supporting children who are learning to comment about their own actions. For instance, when the adult and child are scooping and pouring beans, the adult can map the action by saying "I scoop the beans." When the child imitates this statement in the ongoing play activity, the child is commenting about his or her play using "I" correctly. This practice may make it easier for the child to spontaneously comment about what he or she is doing in future activities.

Milieu Teaching

The prompting procedures of milieu teaching are designed to facilitate children's productive use of new communication forms. In milieu teaching, the sequence of prompts follows a most-to-least support strategy so that children are progressing from imitating to independently initiating target forms. Three characteristics of the verbal behavior of children with ASDs may interfere with effective use of the prompts: 1) indiscriminate imitation, 2) verbal echolalia, and 3) resistance to verbal prompting. Based on individual children's specific verbal response, the prompting procedures may require modifications to be effective for children with ASDs. When children imitate the controlling prompt in modeling episodes, the controlling prompt can be eliminated or given minimal emphasis. The model procedure begins with the controlling prompt "Say," signaling the child to imitate the adult model. When children with ASDs repeat the complete adult utterance, including the prompt "Say," the adult may drop the cue "say" and state emphatically what she wants the child to say so it is clear that the intent is for the child to imitate. For example, when the adult prompts the child "Say, want juice" as the child reaches for juice and the child says "Say want juice," the adult may prompt by saying only "Want juice." Children with verbal echolalia may repeat a choice mand rather than making the choice. For example, if the adult says "Play with bubbles or the ball?" and the child responds by imitating the question "Bubbles or ball?" the adult may provide more support by offering a visual referent concurrent with the verbal choice. The adult shows the child bubbles and the ball while saying "Play with bubbles or the ball?" With the concurrent visual and verbal prompts, the child may be able to process the choices visually while having the labels embedded in the question. Even if the child imitates the adult's prompt again, he or she will usually signal a choice by reaching for the preferred object or looking at it. At that point, the adult can provide a model so that the child is fully supported in responding with an accurate request, "I want the ball." When implementing any prompting procedure in milieu teaching (model, mand model, time delay, incidental teaching), the adult should also always allow sufficient time for the child to indicate a preference or social intention—via physical orientation to the adult and/or the object or by reaching for or looking at the object.

Some children who have participated in therapies that involve repeated prompts for verbal behavior in a drill-and-practice format may refuse to respond to prompts as embedded in the EMT procedures. Alternatively, these children may *only* respond when prompted and not independently initiate language use. For children with these behaviors, it may be useful to initially limit prompting. Increasing child verbal and nonverbal engagement using environmental arrangement and responsive interaction strategies should be the first phase of intervention. Even without prompting, modeling in context and expanding child nonverbal and verbal communication by modeling new forms of language can be a powerful intervention. To increase responding to EMT prompts with prompt-resistant children, adults should choose very high probability occasions to prompt (i.e., the child has requested a preferred object and is highly motivated to respond). Reducing the frequency of prompting when intervening with children who are prompt-dependent may initially decrease the frequency of child verbalizations; however, responding, expanding, and commenting contingent on child spontaneous communication attempts should increase child frequency over the course of two to six sessions. Because the goal of EMT is productive, spontaneous, and meaningful communication using new language forms, it is important to address the challenges posed by children who are either prompt-resistant or prompt-dependent early in the intervention process.

DATA COLLECTION TO SUPPORT DECISION MAKING

Effective intervention requires ongoing monitoring of both the adult's use of the EMT strategies and the child's communication progress. When conducting research on applications of EMT, we employ a comprehensive data collection process that includes videotaping adult–child interactions, transcribing adult and child utterances, coding adult and child behavior, and summarizing and graphing the data. A SALT analysis is completed on each transcribed session to provide data on child and adult MLU, diversity, and number of utterances. This level of data collection allows us to monitor whether the adult is implementing the EMT strategies with high levels of fidelity and whether the child is progressing in the use of targeted language forms. Because this level of data collection is time and cost intensive, we have developed other data collection strategies for professionals in the field who are implementing EMT.

To track a child's progress across EMT sessions, an adult can complete a data sheet based on an audio or video recording of the session or by having another adult observe the session and record the child's behaviors as they occur. Data can be collected on whether a child's target was spontaneously produced, imitated, or prompted by the adult. Each of the child's targets can be listed, and the adult can record examples of each target or can tally the occurrence of each form. When determining how to "code" a child's utterance, a "spontaneous" production is a child utterance that is different from the preceding adult utterance. Determining whether a child utterance is spontaneous can sometimes be difficult when a child with an ASD has delayed echolalia and imitations do not occur directly after the imitated adult utterance. In general, we code an "imitation" when a child utterance is stated within 5 s of the adult utterance and repeats all or part of that preceding utterance. A "prompted" utterance is recorded when the child uses the target form response within 5 s of an EMT prompt, such as a model ("Say dog") or choice question ("Want dog or cat?"). A child response after a time delay is also recorded as a "prompted" target. The adult can also record specific models or expansions if this information is important to implementation of the overall EMT package. Tracking whether children use targeted language forms spontaneously or prompted provides the adult with information about whether the child has mastered those forms or needs more adult support to learn them.

Depending on the child's social communication targets, it may also be important to track the child's communication functions during a session. For many children with ASDs, increasing child commenting can be key to the child's becoming a conversational partner. Therapists or parents can also track language behaviors that are specific and important to monitor for each child. For example, if a child uses mostly scripted talk (e.g., talk that is repeated from a video or a book or memorized utterances that are used as whole units rather than individual words) when interacting with an adult, it might be important to track the number or percentage of utterances that include scripted talk in order to determine whether the child is beginning to communicate in more spontaneous and flexible ways. Summarizing each session and graphically displaying the child's use of targets and the adult's implementation of EMT is essential for the data-based evaluation of progress. Such data can be used to report progress to parents and track progress toward individualized education program (IEP) goals.

CONSIDERATIONS FOR CHILDREN FROM
CULTURALLY AND LINGUISTICALLY DIVERSE BACKGROUNDS

Although our research with children who have ASDs has included families from culturally diverse backgrounds (African American, African, Indian), participants in the intervention research to date have been limited to children who are from homes in which English is the primary language spoken (Hancock & Kaiser, 2007; Kaiser & Hancock, 2000). Parent coaches work closely with all families when choosing toys and materials for the intervention to ensure that the activities are consistent with family values, regardless of cultural background. In addition, at least a third of the intervention sessions occur in the family's home with familiar toys, books, and food, which the parent chooses. Because the intervention is based in naturally occurring interactions, each family can adapt EMT to make it consistent with their family's interaction style and daily activities by choosing routines in which parents and children typically interact. It is important to note that parents who participate in intervention research self-select by contacting us; thus our findings and experiences may not apply to the full range of cultural and linguistic diversity found in families of children with ASDs. Although we do have experience in using EMT with children from African American families of low socioeconomic status, these children did not have ASDs (see Hancock, Kaiser, & Delaney, 2002).

Other studies completed by colleagues trained in EMT have included linguistically and culturally diverse parents and children with ASDs. In China, Wang (2008) investigated the effects of a parent-training program on the parents' interactions with their children with ASDs. Parents who were interested in participating were randomly assigned to the training group (n = 15) or the control group (n = 12). Participating children were, on average, about 5 years old (range 3–9 years), and all children had an ASD diagnosis. Parents in the training group received 20 hr of training, 16 hr of group training, and 4 hr of individualized coaching with the parent and child in their home. Parents learned naturalistic teaching strategies, such as following the child's lead to engage children in play interactions and supporting children's communication skills using EMT prompting procedures. Parents in both groups were observed during play interactions with their children at home before and after the training. Videotaped interactions were coded for parent responsiveness, affect, achievement orientation, and directedness using the Maternal Behavior Rating Scale (Mahoney, 1999). After the completion of training, parents in the training group were observed to be more sensitive to their children's interests, showed more enjoyment of their children in play interactions, expressed more warmth to their children, and responded more appropriately to their children's behavior than parents in the control group. Although this study did not investigate the effects of changes in parent behavior on the behavior or communication skills of the children with ASDs, it provides a first step in understanding the feasibility and acceptability of a naturalistic intervention, such as EMT, implemented by parents of children with ASDs in China. Wang presented a strong case for the importance of further developing effective naturalistic intervention programs for parents in China with children who have an ASD. She stated that parent-implemented interventions for children with ASDs in the United States are typically supplemental to primary interventions that children receive in schools or from therapists, whereas in China, parents are the primary intervention agent for their children with ASDs because of limited educational/therapeutic resources. Wang also stated that even though the intervention was based on the "values and customs of western middle class Caucasian culture" (2008, p. 102), parents in this study eagerly applied these strategies to interactions with their children. She concluded that these naturalistic interventions "appear to address the needs of these Chinese families" (p. 102).

In another study of EMT with parents who were from linguistically diverse backgrounds, Olive and her colleagues (Olive et al., 2010) investigated the effects of teaching four Korean mothers to use EMT strategies with their children. The children were between the ages of 21 and 54 months. Two of the four children included in the study had an ASD diagnosis. The children's language targets were single nouns and verbs, and the mothers modeled these targets in Korean. A multiple-probe design across the four mother–child dyads was used. The four mothers demonstrated varying ability to implement the EMT procedures, and the children showed modest changes in communication skills. In addition, each child generalized communication skills to a second communication partner. The investigator used a rating scale to measure parent perceptions of the intervention's effectiveness and acceptability. The mothers reported that they believed the EMT intervention was

effective in increasing their children's language skills and that they found the intervention to be consistent and acceptable with their values.

These two studies (Olive et al., 2010; Wang, 2008) provide preliminary evidence
suggesting that naturalistic language interventions such as EMT may be effective
with children who have ASDs and whose primary language is not English as well
as being acceptable to their parents as a language intervention. Certainly, further
research is needed to validate the effectiveness and appropriateness of EMT with
culturally and linguistically diverse families of children with ASDs.

Application to a Child

Carly was 34 months old and recently diagnosed with PDD-NOS. Carly's mom, Becky,
was concerned that little of Carly's spoken language was self-initiated. Instead, she frequently imitated what she heard adults saying. When Carly met new people, she would
greet them with "Hi Carly," and when she was excited about completing her puzzles,
she would say "Yay Carly." Carly was screened, and her results qualified her for inclusion
in our EMT intervention research project (see Table 8.2 for preintervention assessment
results). She and her mother were randomly selected to participate in the parent-plus-
therapist condition.

During the baseline phase, Carly participated in three 10-min play sessions with
an assigned child therapist who was affectively positive during the play but did not use
the EMT procedures at criteria. Carly also participated in three 10-min play sessions with
her mother, who was instructed to play with Carly as she typically would. Additional
language assessments were completed during this phase, including the PPVT-4 (Dunn &
Dunn, 2007), the EVT-2 (Williams, 2007), two 20-min language samples in the clinic, and
one 20-min language sample in Carly's home.

Before we began the intervention with Carly, we completed a workshop with Becky
that included individualized information about language development, behavior, play,
environmental arrangement, and routines that are all foundational to the EMT intervention. During this workshop, the parent coach and Becky discussed and agreed upon a
list of specific language forms that would be targeted for Carly during the intervention
sessions. When asked about her language goals for Carly, Becky told the parent coach
that she wanted Carly to 1) use "Momma"; 2) label some healthy foods she enjoyed,
such as "apple" and "raisins"; and 3) use "me" or "I" instead of incorrectly substituting
"you." The parent coach provided Becky with a list of words Carly had used during the
baseline sessions and language samples. Becky's language goals for Carly were combined
with words Carly was observed using during the baseline, making it more likely that Carly
would successfully use targeted two-word utterances including "Help me," "Momma
help," "Eat apple," "Give apple," and "I eat." Combining a known and a novel word
could potentially help Carly use words more flexibly.

Carly and Becky started the intervention phase the next day. Intervention sessions
occurred three times a week—two times per week in the clinic and one time at their
home. During the clinic sessions, the parent coach and Becky talked about the strategy
Becky would practice in the play session. The parent coach always gave Becky a handout
of the information on the strategy but also used other teaching strategies, such as role
playing and watching video examples of the strategy. Next, Becky observed from an

Table 8.2. Summary of enhanced milieu teaching (EMT) results for Becky and Carly

Becky's EMT intervention results				
	Clinic		Home	
EMT strategy (criterion)	Baseline	Intervention	Baseline	Intervention
No. pause errors (< 2)	81	0	68	1
Turn-taking ratio (adult:child; 1.00)	5.76	1.06	4.88	.98
% responsiveness (>80%)	59	98	63	97
% expansions (>50%)	4	74	2	69
No. targets (>40)	7	88	5	73
Correct milieu (5–10)	0	9	0	6
% correct milieu (>80%)	0	92	0	89

Carly's EMT intervention results				
	Clinic		Home	
Language outcomes	Baseline	Intervention	Baseline	Intervention
No. spontaneous utterances	12	52	15	61
No. total targets	2	27	1	22
No. spontaneous targets	0	15	0	12
% utterances of two or more words	2	34	3	37
MLU	1.07	1.65	1.11	1.59
Diversity	21	78	12	54

Carly's assessment results		
Assessment	Baseline results	Intervention results
PLS–Auditory	50	58
PLS–Expressive	61	69
PPVT-4	40	55
EVT-2	45	68
Clinic language sample MLU	1.04	1.56
Clinic language sample–diversity	17	58
Home language sample–MLU	1.10	1.41
Home language sample–diversity	24	50

Key: MLU, mean lengths of utterances; PLS, Preschool Language Scale (Zimmerman, Steiner, & Pond, 2002); PPVT-4, Peabody Picture Vocabulary Test (Dunn & Dunn, 2007); EVT-2, Expressive Vocabulary Test (Williams, 2007).

observation room as the child therapist used the EMT strategies in a 10-min play session with Carly. The parent coach watched with Becky and pointed out examples when the child therapist used the "strategy of the day." When the child therapist completed her session, Becky and the parent coach went into the same playroom, and Becky practiced the strategy with live coaching and modeling by the parent coach. At the end of the session, the parent coach and Becky made a plan for the home intervention session, including what toys Becky wanted to use and how the EMT strategy she was learning could be integrated in her home routines with Carly. In the home intervention sessions, Becky practiced the EMT strategies while reading a book to Carly for 5 min, eating a snack with her for 5 min, playing with her for 10 min, and then engaging in a brief cleanup activity with the toys. The intervention phase included 36 sessions of intervention—24 at the clinic and 12 at home—with the EMT strategies taught in a stepwise fashion. As Becky met the criterion set for one strategy, the parent coach began teaching the next strategy in the sequence.

At the end of 36 sessions, Carly was reassessed using the battery first used during the screening and baseline period. After the assessment data were processed, the parent coach met with Becky to discuss the intervention results (see Table 8.2 for a summary). Becky's use of EMT strategies in the clinic included the average of the last three baseline sessions and the last three intervention sessions, whereas home data included the average of two home play sessions during baseline and two home play sessions at the end of intervention. As seen in Table 8.2, by the end of the intervention, Becky had implemented all of the EMT strategies at or above the set criteria in the clinic and at home. Carly made consistent changes in her communication in play sessions with her mother in the clinic and at home, showing increases in the number of total and spontaneous targets she used, her MLU, and diversity of vocabulary. In addition, her scores on the standardized assessments all increased from preintervention to postintervention. At the exit meeting, Becky told the parent coach that she felt she had the skills to continue supporting Carly's language across the day using the EMT strategies she had learned. At the end of the meeting, she said, "It's funny that after completing this EMT language intervention, I find myself at a loss for words to tell you what a difference this has made in our family's life with Carly."

Application to an Adolescent or Adult

The EMT approach is designed specifically for young children in the beginning stages of communication and typically is not used with older individuals.

FUTURE DIRECTIONS

The EMT approach has been implemented effectively with children who have ASDs and are between the ages of 2½ and 5 years (Hancock & Kaiser, 2002; Hancock et al., 2008; Kaiser et al., 2000; Kaiser et al., 2008). The next steps for EMT appear to be determining whether the procedures are effective in addressing the language needs of related groups of children, including 1) children who have ASDs and are not yet verbal, 2) children with ASDs who are younger than 2½ or older than 5 years, and 3) children who at risk for ASDs and/or language delays because they are younger siblings of children diagnosed with an ASD.

There is a great need in the field for developing interventions that are effective with children with ASDs who are not yet verbal. Anderson and Lord and their colleagues (2007) followed a sample of 84 children with autism beginning at age 2 and found that 29% were nonverbal at age 9. In that study, the investigators found that nonverbal IQ and joint attention were the strongest predictors of children's verbal skills. We have been working on a collaborative cross-site study (Center for

Cognition in Nonverbal Individuals with Autism [CCNIA][2]) investigating the effects of combining EMT with a joint attention (JA) and symbolic play (SP) intervention for children with ASDs who are 5–8 years of age and who are nonverbal despite having been involved in at least 2 years of intervention (see Chapter 7 for more discussion of joint attention). Both EMT (Hancock & Kaiser, 2002; Kaiser et al., 2000) and JA–SP intervention (Kasari, Paparella, Freeman, & Jahromi, 2008) have been found to be effective with preschool children with ASDs who have at least entry-level verbal skills (a minimum of 10 words). In the ongoing study, participating investigators (viz., Kasari, Kaiser, Landa, and Mathey) will determine whether these two interventions can be combined and adapted for older, nonverbal children with autism.

We have also extended EMT to younger children in a pilot study investigating the effects of EMT with toddlers who have a sibling with an ASD (Kaiser et al., 2008; MacFarland, 2008). In this study, a single-subject multiple baseline across three EMT procedures was completed with two parents and their children. The target children were 18 months of age and considered at risk for ASDs and/or language delay because each had a sibling who had been diagnosed with an ASD (Constantino, Zhang, Frazier, Abbacchi, & Law, 2010). Parents were trained to use EMT in 24 intervention play sessions at home. In addition, generalization data were collected in probes to book reading and snacking. At the end of intervention, parents demonstrated more balanced conversational turns with their children and increased their use of expansions and correct milieu-teaching procedures. Children increased their total communication attempts during the intervention sessions and showed significant increases from preintervention to postintervention on the Mullen Scales of Early Learning (Mullen, 1984), with an average standard score preintervention of 76 and an average standard score postintervention of 103; an increase in the number of words used expressively as reported by parents on the MCDI (mean number of words preintervention was 38; mean number of words postintervention was 193); and increases in MLU, diversity of vocabulary, and frequency of intelligible words in a 20-min language sample. These preliminary data suggest that EMT may be effective in preventing communication impairments in children who are at high risk for being diagnosed with an ASD and/or developing related social communication impairments.

SUGGESTED READINGS

Hancock, T.B., & Kaiser, A.P. (2002). The effects of trainer-implemented enhanced milieu teaching on the social communication of children who have autism. *Topics in Early Childhood Special Education, 22*(1), 39–54.

This study examines the effects of EMT on the social communication skills of preschool children with ASDs when delivered by trained interventionists. Observational data indicated that all of the children showed positive increases for specific target language use at the end of 24 intervention sessions, and these results were maintained through the 6-month follow-up.

---

[2]CCNIA Developmental and Augmented Intervention for Facilitating Expressive Language (Autism Speaks), 2009–2011. University of California, Los Angeles, principal investigator Connie Kasari; Vanderbilt University, principal investigator Ann Kaiser; Kennedy Krieger/Johns Hopkins University, principal investigator Rebecca Landa; Kennedy Krieger/Johns Hopkins University, investigator Pam Mathey.

Hancock, T.B., & Kaiser, A.P. (2006). Enhanced milieu teaching. In R.J. McCauley & M.E. Fey (Eds.), *Treatment of language disorders in children* (pp. 203–236). Baltimore, MD: Paul H. Brookes Publishing Co.

This chapter provides an overview of EMT procedures and their theoretical and empirical bases, with a specific emphasis on parent-implemented applications. It includes detailed information about the three components of EMT and illustrates the application of EMT through case histories of two children.

Kaiser, A.P., Hancock, T.B., & Trent, J.A. (2007). Teaching parents communication strategies. *Early Childhood Services: An Interdisciplinary Journal of Effectiveness, 1*(2), 107–136.

This paper provides recommendations for teaching parent-implemented EMT to families of toddlers and preschoolers with significant language delays. The recommendations are based on a series of studies conducted with approximately 150 families.

Learning Activities

1. List the ways EMT can be adapted when implementing it with children who have an ASD.

2. This chapter listed several common behavior challenges to address when implementing EMT with a child who has an ASD—restricted interests, issues in joint attention, limited engagement with others in activities, perseveration, and echolalia. Choose another behavior challenge you have encountered when working with a child who has an ASD, and list how you would adapt the components of EMT (environmental arrangement, responsive interaction, language modeling, and milieu teaching) so that it can be used most effectively with that child.

3. Write a script of what you would say when talking with parents about why EMT may be an effective language intervention for their child with an ASD.

REFERENCES

Alpert, C.L., & Kaiser, A. (1992). Training parents as milieu language teachers. *Journal of Early Intervention, 16*(1), 31–52.

Anderson, D.K., Lord, C., Risi, S., Shulman, C., Welch, K., DiLavore, P.S.,...Pickles, A. (2007). Patterns of growth in verbal abilities among children with autism spectrum disorder. *Journal of Consulting and Clinical Psychology, 75*(4), 594–604.

Camarata, S., & Yoder, P. (2002). Language transactions during development and intervention: Theoretical implications for developmental neuroscience. *International Journal of Developmental Neuroscience, 20,* 459–467.

Constantino, J.N., Zhang, Y., Frazier, T., Abbacchi, A.M., & Law, P. (2010). Sibling recurrence and the genetic epidemiology of autism. *American Journal of Psychiatry, 167,* 1349–1356.

Corsello, C.M. (2005). Early intervention in autism. *Infants and Young Children, 18*(2), 74–85.

Dunn, L.M., & Dunn, D.M. (1981). *Peabody Picture Vocabulary Test–Revised.* Circle Pines, MN: American Guidance Service.

Dunn, L.M., & Dunn, D.M. (2007). *Peabody Picture Vocabulary Test–Fourth Edition.* Bloomington, MN: NCS Pearson.

Fenson, L. Marchman, V.A., Thal, D.J., Dale, P.S., Reznick, J.S., & Bates, E. (2007). *MacArthur-Bates Communicative Development Inventories (CDIs)* (2nd ed.). Baltimore, MD: Paul H. Brookes Publishing Co.

Gardner, M.F. (1990). *Expressive One-Word Picture Vocabulary Test–Revised.* Novato, CA: Academic Therapy Publications.

Goldstein, H. (2002). Communication intervention for children with autism: A review of treatment efficacy. *Journal of Autism and Developmental Disorders, 32*(5), 373–396.

Hancock, T.B., & Kaiser, A.P. (1996). Siblings' use of milieu teaching at home. *Topics in Early Childhood Special Education, 16*(2), 168–190.

Hancock, T.B., & Kaiser, A.P. (2002). The effects of trainer-implemented enhanced milieu teaching on the social communication of children who have autism. *Topics in Early Childhood Special Education, 22*(1), 39–54.

Hancock, T.B., & Kaiser, A.P. (2006). Enhanced milieu teaching. In R.J. McCauley & M.E. Fey (Eds.), *Treatment of language disorders in children* (pp. 203–236). Baltimore, MD: Paul H. Brookes Publishing Co.

Hancock, T.B., & Kaiser, A.P. (2007, March). *An ecological model for facilitating parent-generalization of newly learned naturalistic teaching strategies.* Paper presented at the biennial meeting of the Society for Research in Child Development, Boston, MA.

Hancock, T.B., Kaiser, A.P., & Delaney, E.M. (2002). Teaching parents of high-risk preschoolers strategies to support language and positive behavior. *Topics in Early Childhood Special Education, 22*(4), 191–212.

Hancock, T.B., Ton, J., & Crowe, C. (2008, February). *The effects of parent and therapist implemented enhanced milieu teaching on the language production of children with autism.* Poster presented at the Sixth Biennial Conference on Research Innovations in Early Intervention, San Diego, CA.

Hart, B. (1985). Naturalistic training techniques. In S. Warren & A.K. Rogers-Warren (Eds.), *Teaching functional language: Generalization and maintenance of language skills* (pp. 63–88). Baltimore, MD: University Park Press.

Hart, B.M., & Risley, T.R. (1968). Establishing the use of descriptive adjectives in the spontaneous speech of disadvantaged preschool children. *Journal of Applied Behavior Analysis, 1,* 109–120.

Hart, B.M., & Risley, T.R. (1975). Incidental teaching of language in the preschool. *Journal of Applied Behavior Analysis, 8,* 411–420.

Hart, B.M., & Rogers-Warren, A.K. (1978). Milieu teaching approaches. In R.L. Schiefelbusch (Ed.), *Bases of language intervention* (Vol. 2, pp. 193–225). Baltimore, MD: University Park Press.

Hedrick, D.L., Prather, E.M., & Tobin, A.R. (1975). *Sequenced Inventory of Communication Development.* Seattle, WA: University of Washington Press.

Ingersoll, B., & Dvortcsak, A. (2006). Including parent training in the early childhood special education curriculum for children with autism spectrum disorders. *Journal of Positive Behavior Interventions, 8,* 79–87.

Kaiser, A.P. (1993). Teaching functional language. In M.E. Snell (Ed.), *Enhancing children's communication: Research foundations for intervention* (pp. 347–379). Baltimore, MD: Paul H. Brookes Publishing Co.

Kaiser, A.P., & Hancock, T.B. (2000, April). *Supporting children's communication development through parent-implemented naturalistic interventions.* Paper presented at the Second Annual Conference on Research Innovations in Early Intervention, San Diego, CA.

Kaiser, A.P., & Hancock, T.B. (2003). Teaching parents new skills to support their young children's development. *Infants and Young Children, 16,* 9–21.

Kaiser, A.P., Hancock, T.B., & Lambert, W. (1997, March). *The effects of teaching parents two naturalistic language-teaching strategies.* Paper presented at the 30th Annual Gatlinburg Conference on Research and Theory in Mental Retardation and Developmental Disabilities, Riverside, CA.

Kaiser, A.P., Hancock, T.B., & Nietfeld, J.P. (2000). The effects of parent-implemented enhanced milieu teaching on the social communication of children who have autism. *Journal of Early Education and Development, 11*(4), 423–446.

Kaiser, A.P., Hancock, T.B., & Trent, J.A. (2007). Teaching parents communication strategies. *Early Childhood Services: An Interdisciplinary Journal of Effectiveness, 1*(2), 107–136.

Kaiser, A.P., Hemmeter, M.L., Ostrosky, M.M., Fischer, R., Yoder, P., & Keefer, M. (1996). The effects of teaching parents to use responsive interaction strategies. *Topics in Early Childhood Special Education, 16*(3), 375–406.

Kaiser, A.P., Hester, P.P., & McDuffie, A.S. (2001). Supporting communication in young children with developmental disabilities. *Mental Retardation and Developmental Disabilities Research Reviews, 7*(2), 143–150.

Kaiser, A.P., Lambert, W., Hancock, T.B., & Hester, P.P. (1998, March). *Differential outcomes of naturalistic intervention on vocabulary growth.* Paper presented at the 32nd Annual Gatlinburg Conference on Research and Theory in Mental Retardation and Developmental Disabilities, Charleston, SC.

Kaiser, A.P., MacFarland, T., & Hancock, T.B. (2008, March). *Individual differences in parent-implemented enhanced milieu teaching: Effects on children with ASD.* Paper presented at the 41st Annual Gatlinburg Conference on Research and Theory in Intellectual and Developmental Disabilities, San Diego, CA.

Kaiser, A.P., & Roberts, M.Y. (in press). Parent-implemented enhanced milieu teaching with preschool children with intellectual disabilities. *Journal of Speech, Language, and Hearing Research.*

Kaiser, A.P., & Trent, J.A. (2007). Communication intervention for young children with disabilities: Naturalistic approaches to promoting development. In S.L. Odom, R.H. Horner, M.E. Snell, & J. Blacher (Eds.), *Handbook of developmental disabilities* (pp. 224–245). New York, NY: Guilford Press.

Kaiser, A.P., Yoder, P.J., & Keetz, A. (1992). Evaluating milieu teaching. In S.F. Warren & J. Reichle (Eds.), *Causes and effects in communication and language intervention* (Vol. 1, pp. 9–47). Baltimore, MD: Paul H. Brookes Publishing Co.

Kasari, C., Paparella, T., Freeman, S.F., & Jahromi, L. (2008). Language outcomes in autism: randomized comparison of joint attention and play intervention. *Journal of Consulting and Clinical Psychology, 76*(1), 125–137.

Koegel, R., & Johnson, J. (1989). Motivating language use in autistic children. In G. Dawson (Ed.), *Autism: New perspectives on diagnosis, nature and treatment* (pp. 310–325), New York, NY: Guilford Press.

Landa, R. (2007). Early communication development and intervention for children with autism. *Mental Retardation and Developmental Disabilities Research Reviews, 13,* 16–25.

MacFarland, T.L. (2008). *Naturalistic language intervention for at-risk siblings of children with ASD.* (Unpublished master's thesis.) Peabody College at Vanderbilt University, Nashville, TN.

Mahoney, G. (1999). *The Maternal Behavior Rating Scale-Revised.* [Available from the author, Mandel School of Applied Social Sciences, 11235 Bellflower Rd., Cleveland, OH 44106-7164.]

Miller, J. (2008). Systematic analysis of language transcripts (SALT; English version 2008) [Computer software]. Middleton, WI: SALT Software, LLC.

Mullen, E.M. (1984). *Mullen Scales of Early Learning (MSEL).* Circle Pines, MN: American Guidance Service.

Ogletree, B.T., Oren, T., & Fischer, M.A. (2007). Examining effective intervention practices for communication impairment in autism spectrum disorder. *Exceptionality, 15*(4), 233–247.

Olive, M.L., de la Cruz, B., Davis, T.N., Chan, J.M., Lang, R.B., O'Reilly, M.F., & Dickson, S.M. (2007). The effects of enhanced milieu teaching and a voice output communication aid on the requesting of three children with autism. *Journal of Autism and Developmental Disorders, 37*(8), 1505–1513.

Olive, M.L., Kim, H.M., Kong, N., Kang, S., Choi, H., & O'Reilly, M.F. (2010). *Examining the use of enhanced milieu teaching with Korean families.* Unpublished manuscript. Minneapolis, MN: College of Education & Leadership, Walden University.

Ostrosky, M.M., & Kaiser, A.P. (1991). Preschool classroom environments that promote communication. *Teaching Exceptional Children, 23*(4), 6–10.

Prizant, B.M., Wetherby, A.M., & Rydell, P.J. (2000). Communication intervention issues for young children with autism spectrum disorders. In A.M. Wetherby & B.M. Prizant (Eds.), *Autism spectrum disorders: A transactional developmental perspective* (pp. 193–224). Baltimore, MD: Paul H. Brookes Publishing Co.

Rogers, S.J. (2006). Evidenced-based interventions for language development in young children with autism. In T. Charman & W. Stone (Eds.), *Social and communication development in autism spectrum disorders: Early identification, diagnosis, and intervention* (pp. 143–179). New York, NY: Guilford Press.

Roid, G., & Miller, L. (1997). *Leiter-R.* Wood Dale, IL: Stoelting.

Tawney, J.D., & Gast, D. (1984). *Single-subject research in special education.* Columbus, OH: Merrill.

Wang, P. (2008). Effects of a parent training program on the interactive skills of parents of children with autism in China. *Journal of Policy and Practice in Intellectual Disabilities, 5*(2), 96–104.

Warren, S.F., Bredein-Oja, S.L., Fairchild Escalante, M., Finestack, L.H., Fey, M.E., & Brady, N.C. (2006). Responsivity education/prelinguistic milieu teaching. In R.J. McCauley & M.E. Fey (Eds.), *Treatment of language disorders in children* (pp. 47–76). Baltimore, MD: Paul H. Brookes Publishing Co.

Warren, S.F., Gazdag, G.E., Bambara, L.M., & Jones, H.A. (1994). Changes in the generativity and use of semantic relationships concurrent with milieu language intervention. *Journal of Speech and Hearing Research, 51,* 924–934.

Weiss, R.S. (1981). INREAL intervention for language handicapped and bilingual children. *Journal of the Division for Early Childhood, 4,* 40–52.

Williams, K.T. (2007). *Expressive Vocabulary Test, 2nd Edition.* Minneapolis, MN: Pearson Assessments.

Yoder, P., & Stone, W.L. (2006a). A randomized comparison of the effect of two prelinguistic communication interventions of the acquisition of spoken communication in preschoolers with ASD. *Journal of Speech, Language and Hearing Research, 49*(4), 698–711.

Yoder, P., & Stone, W.L. (2006b). Randomized comparison of two communication interventions for preschoolers with autism spectrum disorders. *Journal of Consulting and Clinical Psychology, 74*(3), 426–435.

Yoder, P.J., & Warren, S.F. (2004). Early predictors of language in children with and without Down syndrome. *American Journal on Mental Retardation, 109,* 285–300.

Zimmerman, I.L., Steiner, V.G., & Pond, R.E. (2002). *Preschool Language Scale* (4th ed.). San Antonio, TX: The Psychological Corporation.

9

Early Social Interaction Project

Juliann J. Woods, Amy M. Wetherby, Shubha Kashinath, and Renee Daly Holland

E arly social interaction (ESI) is an approach for toddlers who are at risk for or have a diagnosis of autism spectrum disorder (ASD) and their families. It was originally developed as a model demonstration project funded by the Office of Special Education Programs of the U.S. Department of Education (2002–2006). A preliminary preintervention–postintervention study provided support for the model and the feasibility of implementation (Wetherby & Woods, 2006). Research funding from Autism Speaks and the National Institute of Mental Health is supporting an ongoing randomized clinical trial of ESI with about 80 toddlers with ASDs beginning at 18 months of age and their families in a collaborative study at Florida State University and the University of Michigan. This chapter describes the essential features of ESI and the rationale for its implementation with young children and their caregivers.

The ESI Project was designed to incorporate the recommendations of the National Research Council (National Research Council [NRC], 2001) within the context of a family-guided, natural-environments approach, consistent with the delivery of the Individuals with Disabilities Education Improvement Act of 2004 (PL 108-446) Part C services and supports (American Speech-Language-Hearing Association [ASHA], 2008; National Early Childhood Technical Assistance Center [NECTAC], 2008; Sandall, Hemmeter, Smith, & McLean, 2005). Situating the NRC recommendations within the Part C guidelines for delivery of early intervention services facilitated the development of an approach that would be replicable within statewide service delivery systems by early intervention teams while promoting evidence-based practices.

The NRC (2001) conducted a systematic, rigorous review of research on educational interventions for children with ASDs from birth through 8 years that revealed significant progress in response to intervention for a substantial proportion of children with ASDs. However, the vast majority of studies reviewed included preschool-age children with ASDs and had only limited representation of studies including toddlers. Although the NRC review reflected a range of intervention techniques, the committee concluded that there was a convergence of evidence identifying the following characteristics as essential active ingredients of effective interventions for children with ASDs (2001, p. 219):

- Entry into intervention programs as soon as an autism spectrum diagnosis is seriously considered
- Active engagement in intensive instructional programming for a minimum of the equivalent of a full school day, 5 days (at least 25 hours) a week, with full year programming varied according to the child's chronological age and developmental level
- Sufficient amounts of adult attention
- Inclusion of a family component, including parent training
- Mechanisms for ongoing program evaluation and assessments of individual children's progress, with results translated into adjustments in programming

In addition, the NRC identified the following as essential: priority for instruction on functional, spontaneous communication; social instruction across settings; play skills with a focus on peer interaction; new skill acquisition, maintenance, and generalization, in natural contexts; functional assessment and positive behavior support to address problem behaviors; and functional academic skills, when appropriate.

The ESI approach is more than a specific intervention strategy for social communication disorders associated with ASDs. It is a comprehensive developmental approach that includes process and procedures for initial and ongoing programmatic assessment for program planning, Individualized Family Service Plan development and monitoring, intervention, and transition that is congruent with Part C legislation and adaptable to meet state standards and guidelines. The specific components of the approach are described within this chapter.

TARGET POPULATIONS AND ASSESSMENTS FOR DETERMINING TREATMENT RELEVANCE AND GOALS

Young children, generally under 3 years of age, identified as at risk for social communication impairments or with early red flags for ASDs (e.g., lack of response to name, limited sharing of warm, joyful expressions) participate in an assessment process that mirrors the basic tenets of the approach for intervention. Families participate with their children throughout the evaluation and assessment. They describe their priorities and concerns and identify their child's and family's preferred activities and routines, as well as those that are challenging for them. Observations of the child and parent within typical play and caregiving routines are combined with standardized assessment measures.

Child Measures of Social Communication

We use standard sampling procedures (Wetherby & Prizant, 2002) to derive measures of the child's use of social communication from the Communication and Symbolic Behavior Scales Developmental Profile™ (CSBS DP™) sample. A parent joins the early interventionist and is present during an introductory caregiving routine and play interaction and a complete communication evaluation. Parents are instructed to respond naturally and to encourage spontaneous communication and play but not to direct the child's behavior. The evaluation begins with a warm-up of about 10 min and continues for 30–40 min. The interventionist first presents the child with a series of communicative temptations (i.e., a wind-up toy, a balloon, bubbles, a jar containing food, a bag with toys, books designed for young children from the test kit) to entice spontaneous communication. Next, the interventionist offers the child a feeding toy set and stuffed animal for symbolic play and blocks for constructive play to assess knowledge of play behaviors. The sample consists of six activities during which the child's skills are rated. Also included are probes of gaze and point to follow (the examiner looks and points to something interesting and waits to see if the child follows the gaze and point) and comprehension of object names, person names, and body parts that are interspersed between activities. Information about the reliability and validity of the CSBS DP is distributed across several publications (see Wetherby, Allen, Cleary, Kublin, & Goldstein, 2002; Wetherby, Goldstein, Cleary, Allen, & Kublin, 2003; Wetherby & Prizant, 2002). For a child being considered for ESI, the CSBS DP may be administered in a clinical setting or the child's home in cooperation with the local early intervention (EI) program or upon referral from the EI program, the family, the child's physician, or other community agencies.

Child Measure of Language Stage

During the collection of each behavior sample, we describe the child's language stage using criteria based on expressive language use that were established by Wetherby and Prizant (2002). Those criteria are as follows: preverbal—fewer than two words; early one-word stage—two to five different words; late one-word stage—six to nine different words; multiword stage—ten or more different words and two or more different word combinations.

Curriculum-Based Assessment

The **SCERTS®** Model is a curricular-based assessment and intervention approach that targets the most significant challenges faced by children with ASDs (Prizant, Wetherby, Rubin, Rydell, & Laurent, 2006). The curriculum provides a plan for implementing a comprehensive and evidence-based program by targeting individualized intervention goals and objectives for children in the domains of social communication (SC) and emotional regulation (ER). In addition, goals and objectives in the domain of transactional supports (TS) are targeted for the communication partners (i.e., parents, siblings, peers) to support learning in the natural environment. SCERTS is child centered, activity based, developmentally grounded, and family centered.

The initial phase of developing a SCERTS program involves completion of the SCERTS Assessment Process (SAP). This process involves gathering information from multiple sources, including the parents, teachers or childcare providers, and other familiar caregivers, and observation of the child across multiple settings and communicative partners. The purposes of the process are 1) to establish a profile of developmental strengths and needs, 2) to determine meaningful and motivating goals, and 3) to select learning contexts and appropriate intervention strategies and supports. Additional considerations for selecting child goals include identification of those targets that are likely to have the greatest positive impact and those that are priorities for the family. Tracking of progress occurs regularly throughout the implementation of a SCERTS program, including weekly tracking logs and quarterly updates of the SAP.

The second step in developing a SCERTS educational program involves SCERTS Activity Planning. This process involves development of a daily schedule to embed within everyday activities SC and ER objectives and partner TS objectives. Educational activities are structured in a manner that includes the following: 1) clear beginning, middle, and end; 2) joint focus of attention and joint interaction; 3) clear roles for child and partner, with a balance of turns; 4) opportunities for language learning; and 5) predictability across activities and routines.

THEORETICAL BASIS

Blending Developmental and Behavioral Approaches

ESI utilizes a developmental framework for goal setting and intervention planning. However, it shares many key features with contemporary naturalistic behavioral approaches and is compatible with these along many, if not most, dimensions (Prizant & Wetherby, 1998; Wetherby & Woods, 2008) of both developmental and contemporary behavioral approaches. The following section describes the key features of both developmental and contemporary behavioral approaches that are incorporated into ESI.

Developmental Framework for Targeting Goals

Developmental intervention approaches for ASDs described in the literature (e.g., Greenspan & Wieder, 1997; Klinger & Dawson, 1992; Prizant, Wetherby, & Rydell, 2000; Rogers & Lewis, 1989) are child directed. The environment is arranged to provide opportunities for communication, the child initiates the interaction or teaching episode, and the adult follows the child's lead by being responsive to the child's intentions and imitating or expanding on the child's behavior. Environmental arrangements and responsive interactions are also found in approaches, such as enhanced milieu teaching (EMT; see Chapter 8), that blend developmental and behavioral approaches.

Another key feature of developmental models is the use of development to prioritize individualized child goals and objectives. The developmental pragmatics framework of Bates and her colleagues (Bates, 1976; Bates, Camaioni, & Volterra, 1975) was monumental in going beyond the models of Piaget and Vygotsky to influence our understanding of how children proceed from intentional to symbolic to linguistic communication in typical development and to offer a road map to guide interventionists (Bates, O'Connell, & Shore, 1987). Developmental theories view language learning as an active process in which children "construct" or build knowledge and shared meanings based on emotions and interactions with people and experiences in their environment (Bates, 1979; Bloom, 1993; Tronick, 1989). Stern (1985) described three developmental achievements that contribute to a child's sense of self and capacity to use language to share experiences about events and things, thus providing the foundation for social communication development. These include sharing the focus of attention ("interattentionality"), sharing of intentions ("interintentionality"), and sharing of affective states ("interaffectivity"). These three achievements lead to the capacity of "intersubjective relatedness" as the infant discovers that he or she has a mind, that other people have minds, and that inner subjective experiences can be shared. From a developmental perspective, the language impairments of children with ASDs reflect core impairments in these social underpinnings—shared attention, shared intentions, and shared affect—leading to difficulties in sharing experiences (i.e., intersubjective relatedness). The SCERTS assessment and curriculum incorporate this expansive literature on typical development both for understanding core social communication impairments in ASDs and for guiding developmentally appropriate interventions.

Pragmatic-social interactive theories have placed great emphasis on the context of social interaction in language development (Bates, 1976; Bloom & Lahey, 1978; McLean & Snyder-McLean, 1978; Sameroff, 1987). Children are viewed as active participants who learn to affect the behavior and attitudes of others through active signaling and gradually learn to use more sophisticated and conventional means to communicate through caregivers' contingent social responsiveness (Dunst, Lowe, & Bartholomew, 1990; Sameroff, 1987). Proponents of developmental pragmatic theory believe that because successful communication involves reciprocity and mutual negotiation, child development can be understood only by analysis of the interactive context, not by focusing solely on the child or the caregivers (Bates, 1976; Bruner, 1978, 1981). Rooted in the theory of Vygotsky (1986) that the acquisition of communicative symbols is a social enterprise, Tomasello, Kruger, and Ratner (1993) suggested that two components are essential for a child to develop language: a cultural context that structures events for the child, and the child's special capacity to learn from this cultural structuring. Cultural structuring for language acquisition entails routines, culturally prescribed activities that employ coordinated attention and delineated roles. The child's capacity requires the social-cognitive skills of being able to attribute intentions to others and to see events from the other's perspective.

Wetherby, Schuler, and Prizant (1997) identified three significant principles drawn from the developmental literature that are critical for children with ASDs and should be incorporated into a developmental intervention. First, social communication development involves continuity from preverbal to verbal communication. That is, the development of preverbal communication is a necessary precursor to the development of the intentional use of language to communicate. For children with ASDs who are not yet talking, emphasis should be placed on developing preverbal social communication skills, and words should be mapped onto preverbal communication skills. Second, being a competent communicator is the outcome of a developmental interaction of the child's cognitive, social-emotional, and language capacities and the language learning environment. A child's developmental profile across these domains should provide the basis for decision making about communication enhancement. Third, in a developmental framework, all behavior should be viewed in reference to the child's relative level of functioning across developmental domains. For example, many of the challenging behaviors used by children with ASDs can be understood as attempts to communicate if such behaviors are interpreted relative to developmental discrepancies and as coping strategies in the face of significant communicative limitations. These three principles are incorporated into the SCERTS Model and tailored to toddlers and their families in ESI.

These rich developmental theories and the research that they have generated also offer a framework for understanding a child's developing competencies in relationship to the social context and how these patterns change over developmental transitions. Many patterns and sequences of development in children with ASDs are similar to those of typical development, although the timing of acquisition may be different. Consequently, the combination of skills (i.e., discrepancies across social, cognitive, and linguistic domains) that a child with an ASD has at any point in time is unlikely to be seen in typical development. Too rigid an interpretation of a developmental model has resulted in "readiness models," which require that a certain level of ability must be reached before working on subsequent skills (Wetherby et al., 1997). Working within a developmental model, however, should not imply teaching to a developmental checklist. Rather than merely offering a guideline for sequencing communication objectives, a developmental framework provides a reference for understanding a child's behavioral competencies and for individualizing appropriate, developmentally sensible goals and objectives. Furthermore, a developmental framework offers strategies used by caregivers to support communication and language development in typically developing children as reasonable strategies to support communication and language development in children with ASDs.

Developmental approaches, including ESI, focus on addressing the core impairments of children with ASDs, because improvement or lack thereof predicts later cognitive, social, and language outcomes in children with ASDs. Skills emphasized in these core impairment areas include expanding the use of gestures, initiating verbal and nonverbal communication, understanding and using words with referential meaning, initiating and responding to joint attention, and demonstrating reciprocity in interaction. Because of the importance of skill building in the core impairment areas, ESI interventionists advocate for the use of nonspeech communication systems (e.g., sign language or picture communication) to jump-start the speech system and boost cognitive and social underpinnings. Nonspeech communication systems can provide an important bridge between parents and their children to reduce challenges that frequently occur because of the child's communication impairments. Therefore, developmental interventions focus not only on targeting goals directly on the ASD core impairments of the child but also on targeting strategies for the parent to use that support social communication development.

Family-Centered Practices

In a developmental intervention, the child is recognized as part of a larger family system, which is the focus of assessment and intervention efforts and which benefits from **family-centered services and supports.** Cultural and family values are considered throughout the process. Families tend to be more involved in the achievement of goals if they have been stakeholders in selecting them. Research has shown that parents recognize that working together toward a common goal has a positive impact on their child (Sperry, Whaley, Shaw, & Brame, 1999). In fact, the NRC (2001) identified family involvement as a key component of effective interventions with the strongest research evidence for children with ASDs.

Families are maximally involved in the services for infants and toddlers with ASDs because of the child's age and reliance on parents for nurturance. Despite variations in the amount and type of parent participation in the intervention process, which can range from the role of primary teacher to that of an observer and informant, two results are clear. First, for more than 20 years, **parent-implemented interventions** have been shown to be effective for children with varying types of developmental delays and specifically for children with ASDs across a wide range of adaptive, behavioral, social, and communication child outcomes (Koegel, Bimbela, & Schreibman, 1996; McClannahan, Krantz, & McGee, 1982; Meadan, Ostrosky, Zaghlawan, & Yu, 2009; Schreibman, Kaneko, & Koegel, 1991; Seifer, Clark, & Sameroff, 1991). Second, parents can indeed learn a variety of broad and specific intervention strategies to teach their children functional and meaningful outcomes (Kaiser, Hancock, & Nietfeld, 2000). Guiding parents to help them implement intervention strategies during everyday activities is a logical method to achieve the intensity of active engagement needed for young children with ASDs (Wetherby & Woods, 2006).

Research conducted on the effectiveness of parent-implemented interventions far exceeds research on methods of teaching parents to implement interventions (Meadan et al., 2009). Developmental approaches to parent-implemented interventions are sensitive to the learning strengths of both the child and the communication partner and incorporate the use of **adult learning** strategies within the intervention approach. Adult learning strategies supported by research included in the ESI approach emphasize building on the adult's experiences and interests with the child, using their preferred routines and activities as the context for intervention, and incorporating demonstration and specific feedback on the parent-child interaction and implementation of the intervention. Parent-implemented interventions that result in optimal learning require planning and problem solving with the parents to ensure a sufficient number of instructional opportunities are embedded within specific routines and activities (Strain, McGee, & Kohler, 2001). For example, when introducing interactive toys, visual supports, or social games that might be used in a clinician-directed session, the ESI interventionist must provide adequate demonstration and guided practice to the parent on what, how, when, and how often to use the specific strategies with the child. Simply providing or arranging an environment that supports communication, play, and social interaction is not sufficient for independent parent implementation. Adult learning research supports the use of problem-solving strategies between the interventionist and the parent to increase independent decision making and generalized use of information when the interventionist is not present. Furthermore, value is added to these teaching and problem-solving interactions because research shows that time spent by parents working with their child can enhance their confidence and competence in interacting with their child, increase the child's independence in family activities, and improve the quality of the family's life (Turnbull & Ruef, 1997). For examples of parent involvement, please see the video for this chapter on the DVD that accompanies this book.

In developmental approaches, it is recognized that most learning in childhood occurs in the social context of daily activities and experiences. The ecological context of everyday routines, activities, and settings (Bronfenbrenner, 1979; Dunst, Hamby, Trivette, Raab, & Bruder, 2000) serves as an anchor for the transactional interplay between caregivers and the child in which learning occurs (Sameroff, 1987; Seifer et al., 1991). Efforts to support a child's development need to occur primarily with caregivers and familiar partners in everyday activities in a variety of social situations rather than with interventionists working with the child in isolation. **Natural environments** are the everyday routines, activities, and places that are typical or natural for the family; they usually include locations such as the home, the child care center, family and friends' homes, and other community locations such as the park or place of worship. Daily routines such as dressing, mealtime, and play provide excellent opportunities to embed teaching of objectives that are functional and meaningful and therefore naturally support acquisition and generalization of learning (Woods & Wetherby, 2003). Most young children spend the majority of their waking hours engaged in frequently occurring play and caregiving routines.

When carefully analyzed for maximal teaching opportunities and supportive instructional strategies, these routines can have a joint focus of attention, a logical and predictable sequence, turn taking, and repetition. It is well documented that generalization of child and family outcomes is enhanced by embedding intervention in family-preferred routines and contexts (Dunst et al., 2000; Woods, Kashinath, & Goldstein, 2004). Further, incorporating intervention into existing family routines provides a context for the family and interventionist to develop an active, mutually respectful partnership.

Naturalistic Teaching Strategies

Both developmental and contemporary behavioral approaches have emphasized the importance of teaching strategies that encourage children with communication impairments to initiate communication and language use. In the developmental literature, the pragmatics movement has led to strategies that follow the child's lead to develop communication and conversational abilities (MacDonald & Carroll, 1992; Yoder, Warren, McCathren, & Leew, 1998). The developmental literature emphasizes the importance of caregiver responsivity to enhance communication and language and shift the balance of power, or control, to the child (see MacDonald, 1989; Prizant & Wetherby, 1998). If there is not a balance of power or shared control in interactions with a child, the child may become a passive partner or use challenging behavior to claim power (MacDonald, 1989).

The contemporary behavioral literature has described "incidental language teaching" as a method of achieving a more naturalistic approach to language training. In contrast to a discrete trial format in which the trainer controls the interaction, an incidental teaching episode is initiated by the child. The adult waits for a child to initiate a communicative behavior (i.e., gesture, vocalization), focuses attention on the child and the child's topic, asks for a language elaboration or models a verbal response for the child to imitate, then indicates the correctness of the child's language or gives the child what is asked for. Incidental teaching has been found to enhance generalization in teaching language to children with severe disabilities, including ASDs (Hancock & Kaiser, 2002; McGee, Morrier, & Daly, 1999).

The literature describes numerous strategies for designing the environment to encourage the initiation of communication in **naturalistic language intervention** (Prizant & Wetherby, 1998). The developmental literature has emphasized the importance of "engineering," or arranging, the environment to provide opportunities and reasons for the child to initiate communication. The contemporary behavioral literature has described specific strategies to occasion language use, such as introducing delays at critical moments in natural routines and interrupting chains of behavior by removing an object needed to complete the child's apparent goal-directed action (Kaiser, 1993; Rowland & Schweigert, 1993). By making the initiation of communication a priority, natural opportunities for communicating can be capitalized upon in all settings.

Collaborative Consultation Approach

As mentioned previously, although we have significant evidence to support the effectiveness of parent-implemented developmental interventions on child outcomes, we have less evidence on the adult teaching and learning methods that are effective to promote adoption and use of the intervention practices by the parents. Recently published research syntheses on adult learning provide evidence for the implementation of effective consulting and coaching strategies within parent-implemented interventions—strategies that have not been widely available previously (Bransford, Brown, & Cocking, 2000; Donovan, Bransford, & Pellegrino, 1999; Dunst & Trivette, 2009; Fixsen, Naoom, Blasé, Friedman, & Wallace, 2005). Findings that are essential to the implementation of ESI include, first, the importance of establishing what the learner—in our approach, the parent—knows and believes when entering a learning environment. Parents have beliefs and values about how children learn, what is important for them to learn, and the ways they should be taught. Learning what the parent understands about early intervention guides the interventionist in building consensus. For example, parents may be expecting the intervention to be conducted by the interventionist and believe that the interventionist as expert can offer intervention of a superior quality than what they as parents can provide. They may also be expecting "therapy" in the sense of that offered in a medical or educational model and may be suspicious of the use of routines and play activities.

Findings reported in *How People Learn: Brain, Mind, Experience, and School* (Bransford et al., 2000; Donovan et al., 1999), a review of research on the science of adult learning, point to the importance of having a strong understanding of the content. Understanding the content supports the adult's organization, application, and generalization of learning. For families, who are often new to ideas and terminology associated with early intervention systems, child development, a diagnosis of an ASD, and the constructs of teaching and learning, there is much to learn. Expecting parents to grasp all of the facts and details of this information immediately is unrealistic. It requires a consistent continuum of supports with frequent review and rechecks to ensure knowledge and skills are developing.

Adults also benefit from active participation in the learning process. They are the best judge of what is important for them to learn and how they want to learn it (Bransford et al., 2000; Donovan et al., 1999). Including family members in the decision-making process is important for effective adult learning as well as an essential family-centered practice. Coaching practices in early intervention are built on the premise that the adults involved collaborate in the planning, implementing. and evaluation of the process (Rush, Shelden, & Hanft, 2003). Adults, similar to children, learn best in context. That is, parents participating in intervention with their child, rather than observing or talking about it, are more likely to understand what to do and to link it to why it is important (Dunst & Trivette, 2009). This finding is the premise of the system for identification of routines and play activities that is used within ESI; however, it has not been systematically addressed in research on parent-implemented interventions.

Within the ESI consultation process, a systematic coaching plan is developed for the parent congruent with the child's intervention plan (Buysee & Wesley, 2005). Goals for the child and the parent are identified, discussed, and implemented to build the capacity of the parent within an adult learning framework. This means that each parent is recognized as a unique learner with varying preferences and motivations for learning. Specific teaching or coaching practices are identified and matched to the caregiver to improve existing abilities, develop new skills, and gain a deeper understanding of his or her practices for use in current and future situations. Although early intervention providers report that more traditional child-focused interventions are both more comfortable and easier for them to provide

(Campbell & Halbert, 2002), ESI is built upon a **consultative coaching approach** and relationship with caregivers that facilitates their capacity to provide the child's intervention.

Interventionists implementing ESI learn specific consultation strategies matched to the caregiver's learning preferences and their competence with embedding intervention in a variety of child and family routines. Interventionists are coached on their implementation of the continuum of strategies, on the match to the caregiver's performance, and on their feedback to the caregivers. The use of video collected during home and playgroup sessions allows interventionists or more senior providers to observe, problem solve, and provide feedback to the newer team members.

EMPIRICAL BASIS

ESI was designed to extend the recommendations of the NRC (2001) to toddlers with ASDs using a parent-implemented intervention embedding naturalistic teaching strategies in everyday routines compatible with Part C of the Individuals with Disabilities Education Improvement Act of 2004 (PL 108-446). The NRC recommendations were developed using the strongest available evidence at that time. Many newer studies have been conducted that support those recommendations. ESI is a new model, and therefore the evidence base is emerging. But the model was developed based on two primary sources of evidence. First, research on the core impairments of ASDs in young children is the foundation for what is targeted in ESI. Second, research on parent-implemented intervention strategies has been incorporated into ESI.

Core Impairments of Autism Spectrum Disorders in Young Children

There is a growing body of research supporting earlier identification of young children with ASDs and the importance of intervention addressing the core impairments. This research has defined core social communication impairments of toddlers and preschool children with ASDs. An impairment is considered to be *core* if it distinguishes children with ASDs from other children with developmental delays (DD) and children with typical development (TD; Sigman, Dijamco, Gratier, & Rozga, 2004). Two core social communication impairments are 1) an impairment in joint attention, which is reflected in difficulty coordinating attention between people and objects; and 2) an impairment in symbol use, which is evident in difficulty learning conventional meanings through gestures, words, and actions in play (Charman et al., 1997; Dawson et al., 2004; Loveland & Landry, 1986; Mundy, Sigman, & Kasari, 1990; Sigman, Mundy, Sherman, & Ungerer, 1986; Stone, Ousley, Yoder, Hogan, & Hepburn, 1997; Wetherby, Prizant, & Hutchinson, 1998).

A number of longitudinal studies provide evidence of a relationship between early social communication skills and language outcomes. Mundy and colleagues (1990) found that responding to and initiating gestural joint attention at a mean age of 3 years 9 months were significant predictors of language development 13 months later for children with ASDs, whereas none of the other nonverbal measures, initial language scores, mental age, chronological age, or IQ were significant predictors. These findings were further substantiated in a long-term follow-up study demonstrating that initial joint attention skills of 51 children with ASDs at a mean age of about 4 years predicted gains in expressive language at a mean age of about 13 years (Sigman & Ruskin, 1999).

The majority of parents of children identified as having ASDs notice symptoms or delays in development within the first two years of life, with concerns about language development being the most frequent (Chawarska et al., 2007). Furthermore, most families initially express concern to their pediatrician by the time their child is 18 months old (Howlin & Moore, 1997). Observational studies of social communication skills in children under 2 years of age with ASDs are emerging from two different sources of information—retrospective analyses of home videotapes and prospective longitudinal designs. The largest cohort of retrospective analyses is based on home videotapes from first birthday parties of children later diagnosed with ASDs. Osterling and colleagues (Osterling & Dawson, 1994; Osterling, Dawson, & Munson, 2002) found that children with ASDs could be distinguished at their first birthday party with four features—lack of pointing, lack of showing, lack of looking at faces, and lack of orienting to name, although children with DD also showed the first two features. Although these findings are interesting, they have limitations both in the representativeness of the samples and in the context in which behaviors were studied, and these limitations highlight the need for prospective studies.

One line of research employing prospective longitudinal designs has been to screen general pediatric samples in order to identify very young children at risk for ASDs, then study differences between these children and matched groups of children with DD and TD. A series of studies involving two prospective cohorts identified before 2 years of age from a general pediatric screen have been published. The first cohort consists of children identified using the Checklist for Autism in Toddlers (CHAT; Baron-Cohen et al., 1996; Charman et al., 1997; Swettenham et al., 1998). The second cohort consists of children identified using the CSBS DP (Pierce et al., 2012; Wetherby et al., 2004; Wetherby, Watt, Morgan, & Shumway, 2007; Wetherby, Brosnan-Maddox, Peace, & Newton, 2008). Findings from these studies indicate that core impairments in shifting gaze between people and objects, responding to and initiating joint attention, using conventional gestures, and rate of communicating (i.e., number of communicative behaviors per unit of time) distinguish children with ASDs from those with DD and TD by 18 months of age. Charman and colleagues (2003) found that measures of joint attention late in the second year predicted language at 3 years of age. Wetherby and colleagues (2007) examined a larger set of predictive measures and found that many measures, including joint attention, predicted language outcome at 3 but that understanding of language in the second year was the strongest predictor. In addition to social communication impairments, Wetherby and colleagues (2004) found red flags in repetitive movements with objects and body that distinguished children with ASDs in the second year. In a follow-up study of red flags in a larger sample, McCoy, Wetherby, and Woods (2009) found that 20 behaviors significantly differentiated 60 children with ASDs from 30 with DD and 60 with TD at 18–24 months of age. They found that a cutoff of 8 of these 20 red flags resulted in a sensitivity of 87% and specificity of 84%. Large significant correlations were observed between the total number of red flags and standardized measures of social communication and autism symptoms. These findings indicate the importance of using a combination of red flags, rather than any single one, to improve early detection of ASDs.

Collectively, the growing body of research on early red flags indicates that children with ASDs can be distinguished from those with DD and TD in the second year based on a combination of lack of typical behaviors and presence of atypical behaviors. Thus, they underscore the importance of social communication along with repetitive behaviors in earlier identification of ASDs and as targets for early intervention. Further, because these findings increase the viability of identifying children with ASDs when they are toddlers, they emphasize the pressing need for interventions that are appropriate and effective for very young children with ASDs and their families.

Parent-Implemented Intervention with Young Children with Autism Spectrum Disorders

There are several well-designed randomized controlled trials documenting the effectiveness of clinician-implemented treatments blending developmental and behavioral approaches with young children with ASDs (Dawson et al., 2010; Kasari, Paparella, Freeman, & Jahromi, 2008; Yoder & Stone, 2006). Although it is broadly accepted that parent-implemented interventions can have positive effects on child communication, there is limited research on parents implementing intervention outside of a clinical setting, and even less that supports generalization of implementation across multiple contexts. Kashinath, Woods, and Goldstein (2006) examined the effects of facilitating generalized use of naturalistic teaching strategies by parents of five preschool children with ASDs. Using a multiple-baseline design across teaching strategies, they taught each parent three of the following six strategies: environmental arrangement, natural reinforcement, time delay, contingent imitation, modeling, and gestural/visual cues. Programming of generalization occurred by systematic selection of routines and by embedding intervention in multiple routines. Parents learned to use two teaching strategies in target routines to help them synchronize with their child's attentional focus and address individualized communication objectives. Routines were categorized into one of six classes: play routines, outdoor or recreation, caregiving routines, household chores, community activities, and other health or comfort routines. For example, playing with puzzles, blocks, ball, bubbles, and music toys were different exemplars of indoor play routines. Diapering, hand washing, bath, and mealtime were caregiving routines. Results were that all five parents demonstrated proficient use of teaching strategies and generalized their use across routines both in the same class and across classes of routines. No consistent differences were noted in the frequency of strategy use across routines from the same class and from a different class. To illustrate distributed use throughout the child's and family's day, generalization data were collected by measuring strategy use in untrained routines both within the same routine class and across classes of routines. The intervention had positive effects on communication outcomes for four of the five children. All five parents perceived the intervention to be useful in facilitating their child's communication.

Wetherby and Woods (2006) reported on a pretest–posttest quasi-experimental study as a preliminary effort to evaluate the effects of ESI on social communication outcomes in a group of 17 children with ASDs who entered ESI in the second year of life. Parents were taught naturalistic teaching strategies in two weekly sessions in natural environments over the course of a year. Intervention goals were individualized and selected from a developmental framework targeting social interaction, joint attention, communication, imitation, play, and emotional regulation (Prizant, Wetherby, & Rydell, 2000). Results indicated significant improvement, with large effect sizes on 11 of 13 social communication outcomes measured with the CSBS DP (Wetherby & Prizant, 2002). It is particularly noteworthy that significant changes were demonstrated in initiating and responding to joint attention, because few studies have demonstrated significant changes on these measures.

In an effort to strengthen this design, the ESI group was compared with a no-treatment contrast group of 18 children with ASDs who entered early intervention during the third year of life. Social communication measures were collected from the contrast group at the same age as the ESI group at posttest and compared with the ESI group. Thus, the contrast group provides some information about the possible effects of maturation without treatment. However, pretest measures are not available for the contrast group, because these children were not identified at a younger age, and therefore it cannot be determined whether the groups were comparable at pretest. The contrast group was comparable to the ESI postintervention group on communicative means and play but had significantly poorer performance, with moderate to large effect size on all other measures of social communication. At a mean age of 31 months, 77% of the ESI group was using words compared with 56% of the contrast group. A weakness of the study was that it was not possible to determine that the groups were comparable in the second year of life because children in the contrast group had not been identified and tested at a younger age. These findings offer promise for the use of parent-implemented intervention to impact social communication in toddlers with ASDs.

PRACTICAL REQUIREMENTS

Providing intervention of adequate intensity for very young children with ASDs is challenging for the health care and education systems. Services delivered by professionals within Part C of the Individuals with Disabilities Education Improvement Act of 2004 (PL 108-446) average 2–3 hr per week (Scarborough et al., 2004). In only a few states that have developed guidelines for intensive services for children with ASDs will services be as high as 20-plus hr per week. Although the intensity of intervention for optimal outcomes is not yet determined for infants and toddlers with ASDs, it has been shown that the amount of time spent in active and productive engagement impacts outcomes for preschoolers, with a critical minimum threshold of at least 5 hr per day, 5 days per week (NRC, 2001). Children with ASDs participating in activities with other children would not be expected to learn simply by being there. Inclusive opportunities must have adequate support for the child with an ASD to learn from engagement with the materials, activities, and other children (Strain et al., 2001). Providing intervention in the natural environment, as ESI proposes, is a way to maximize learning throughout the day and thus achieve the intensity of active engagement that is critical for children with ASDs. However, it presents some additional programmatic considerations.

Personnel Preparation

The ESI approach, although congruent with Part C recommended practice, goes beyond the generalized knowledge and skills necessary to serve most children with other types of delays and disabilities and their families; it requires personnel to receive specialized training for working with children with ASDs and their families. As a result, there are several areas of specialized training that have been identified within this chapter. Providers of ESI first must be knowledgeable of the core impairments of ASDs as well as the typical and atypical behaviors toddlers with ASDs are likely to exhibit. When personnel use ESI with very young children, they also need knowledge of early red flags—changes that may occur during the second and third years as the child's social communication behaviors improve or regress—and the possible sequence or point in time when behaviors become red flags (e.g., less interest in people than objects or repetitive movements with objects). Interventionists in ESI must also be fluent in the use of positive behavior support (PBS) to teach communication as replacements for challenging behaviors if they develop.

Providers of ESI must be fluent in child assessment and intervention planning using the SCERTS. SCERTS is used as a curriculum for routines-based individualized interventions in the home as well as for parent–child playgroups and child care–based or community-based programs. Learning to use the SCERTS requires time in both training and feedback for proper implementation. However, it becomes more of a "routine" over time and provides a comprehensive approach for team members and a coordinated plan for implementation.

Learning to consult with families using a systematic process of interventionist–caregiver supports to promote caregiver competence and independence may also be a new knowledge and skill set for the interventionist. Providers of ESI must be both skilled interventionists working with children and competent consultants supporting adult learners to implement interventions within their daily routines and activities. The ability to apply coaching strategies that facilitate the caregiver's capacity to promote child learning with diverse caregivers also takes experience and performance feedback from other skilled interventionists or team members.

Caregiver and Team Participation

ESI may not be for all families. Although few families have discontinued the project to date, some have questioned the time commitment of the family members, and others have preferred an interventionist-directed approach. For those questioning how they could possibly engage their child for 25 hr a week with only 2–4 hr of support from the EI team, the ESI handout "Do the Math! Who Receives More Intervention—James or Jamaal?" has been helpful in illustrating what family members do and the amount of time spent without setting aside special times for therapy when the intervention is embedded in routines (see Figure 9.1).

It is essential to have a primary caregiver who will provide the majority of the embedded intervention with the child. However, most of the participating families have included other communication and social interaction partners throughout the day. For example, Larry's grandpa has brought Larry's big brother home after school to provide a consistent outdoor play partner for Larry for 60–90 min most days. Jose's mom and dad divided up types of routines and times of day to maximize opportunities, increase controlled variations, and enhance generalization. In other families, paid sitters or nannies were trained to complete portions of the intervention. The use of multiple caregivers can enhance outcomes for children and their families but does create an important consideration for the interventionist, who must ensure that all partners are competent and coordinated in their efforts.

DO THE MATH!

Who receives more intervention?

James

Day / Activity	MON	TUES	WED	THURS	FRI	Total Time
Activity	*Occupational Therapy* • Moves with music and swings	*Speech Therapy* • Names picture cards and takes turns activitating toys		*Occupational Therapy* • Moves with music and swings	*Speech Therapy* • Names picture cards and takes turns activitating toys	
Professional Time	45 Minutes	45 Minutes		45 Minutes	45 Minutes	3 Hours
Child Time	45 Minutes	45 Minutes		45 Minutes	45 Minutes	3 Hours

Jamaal

MON	TUES	WED	THURS	FRI	Total Time
Morning – 45 minutes: • Requests food and drink items at breakfast • Plays social games (peek, twinkle) during diaper change • Fills turn in songs during dressing **Playtime – 30 minutes:** • Takes turns in simple action games (rolls ball, stacks block, activates toy) • Chooses book and points to pictures • Requests more (bubbles, swing, music) **Chores – 15 minutes:** • Gives toys to mom during pick up • Reaches up to mom to request pick up or comfort when chores are done • Puts laundry in baskets and puts stuffed toys on bed during room pick up **Lunch – 45 minutes:** • Requests food and drink items at breakfast • Plays social games (peek, twinkle) during diaper change • Fills turn in songs during hand washing	**Getting Ready for Nap – 15 minutes:** • Reaches up to mom to request pick up • Plays a social game with music while rocking to sleep **Playtime – 30 minutes:** • Takes turns in simple action games (rolls ball, stacks block, activates toy) • Chooses book and points to pictures • Requests more (bubbles, swing, music) **Car Travel – 15 minutes:** • Sing songs with mom on school pick up **Outside Play – 30 minutes:** • Swings and plays ball with his big brother **Dinner– 45 minutes:** • Requests food and drink items at dinner • Carries cups and plates to dad for clean up, takes turn labeling **Bath/Bedtime–30 minutes:** • Requests toys for tub • Takes turns with dad in dump and fill play • "Finds" body parts in songs			**Morning – 30 minutes:** • Requests food and drink items at breakfast • Plays social games (peek, twinkle) during diaper change • Fills turn in songs during dressing **Playgroup – 90 minutes:** • Plays with parent and peers **Lunch – 45 minutes:** • Requests food and drink items at lunch • Plays social games (peek, twinkle) during diaper change • Fills turn in songs during hand washing **Getting Ready for Nap – 15 minutes:** • Reaches up to mom to request pick up • Plays a social game with music while rocking to sleep **Mother's Play Date – 1 Hour:** • Games, songs, play, snack with friends **Dinner – 30 minutes:** • Requests food and drink items at dinner • Carries cups and plates to dad for clean up, takes turn labeling **Bath/Bedtime – 30 minutes:** • Requests toys for tub • Takes turns with dad in dump and fill play • "Finds" body parts in songs	
Professional Time	Two 1 Hour Home Visits Per Week			90 Minutes	3:30 Hours
Child Time	5 Hours Daily			5 Hours	25 Hours

Figure 9.1   Do the math: Who receives more intervention—James or Jamaal? Copyright 2008, Florida State University. All rights reserved.

203

Teaming in ESI necessitates time, attention, and ongoing communication. It also improves outcomes and family satisfaction. As with any team, multiple providers must coordinate child outcomes, routine plans, and caregiver supports to ensure consistency. When multiple providers are not coordinated and family guided, we have seen "ownership" transferred to professionals so that, for example, snack time belongs to the occupational therapist for working on sensory concerns and feeding, whereas stories and play are the domain of the speech-language pathologist working to increase communication. In ESI, routines or activities do not belong to different disciplines but rather to the child and family. Our view is that families should not be asked to become three or four different types of interventionists and divide their day between specialized procedures; they are parents. The use of SCERTS increases the individualization of the plans for each child and family and the identification of the most appropriate targets for identified routines regardless of the domain or discipline.

The ESI interventionist may be identified by the team to serve as the family service coordinator. Service coordinators take on multiple roles around quality assurance, family satisfaction, and accomplishment of program goals and services. They also assist the family in accessing resources, completing referrals for other services and supports, and providing information. All team members, and especially the ESI interventionist, share information with caregivers. Along with giving the "how-to" coaching that caregivers are anxious to learn, the interventionist provides information to explain the "what" and "why" of ASDs and to address family concerns, such as family acceptance of the diagnosis of autism, feeding problems, or the prevention of the development of challenging behaviors. Addressing the information and resource needs of families enhances their capacity to use the information for problem solving, decision making, and generalization to other settings and routines. Bringing families together within the parent–child playgroups facilitates the sharing of information and resources between parents and fosters support and socialization for the parents.

KEY COMPONENTS

The key components of the ESI approach are family-guided routines, individualized child and family curriculum, parent-implemented embedded intervention, collaborative consultation, positive behavior supports, and team-based community coordination.

Family-Guided Routines

Intervention practices in Part C of the Disabilities Education Improvement Act (2004) emphasize the delivery of supports and services within the context of the child and family's everyday routines, activities, and places (NECTAC, 2008). Embedding the intervention into the family's daily routines and activities supports the caregiver's role as the child's communication partner, playmate, and parent. ESI occurs in the home, in a community-based parent–child playgroup, and within community early care and education programs. Although the routines, activities, and opportunities afforded parents and children are different in the settings, the goals are similar. In all settings, the role of the interventionist is to coach parents and caregivers how to interact positively with the child, to support the child's engagement in the interactions, to increase the frequency of interactions between caregiver and child, and to guide the caregiver's use of evidence-based intervention strategies to practice social communication and emotional regulation goals that are functional, predictable, and meaningful for the child and likely to occur throughout the day.

Intervention sessions are scheduled to accommodate the child's attention, the family's preferences, work/school schedules, and the specific routines (e.g., dressing, snacks and meals, bath time, play with siblings) that are identified for intervention. We recommend two home visits per week initially, to facilitate parent implementation and to monitor child progress. The number of home visits that actually take place each week varies, primarily because of family circumstances (e.g., work schedules, birth of new siblings, vacations, illnesses) and the capacity of the family to embed intervention within their daily routines successfully. It takes time for most families to learn how to embed interventions in routines with their child throughout the day at a level sufficient to provide adequate intensity for learning. The interventionists offer make-up sessions to maintain intensity when possible and maintain contact via e-mail and phone calls to ensure that families are supported.

Although daily routines appropriate for intervention may seem obvious, they are individual to the family based on their interests, beliefs, and unique characteristics. To ensure that an individualized contextual match is provided for each child and family (Bernheimer & Weismer, 2007), families are encouraged to go beyond describing the schedule of their days, evenings, and weekends in order to also consider their interests, hobbies, favorite times with their child, challenging routines or activities, community participation, regular appointments, and so forth. The conversation seeks to identify the child's current interests and motivators as well as his or her level of engagement, independence, and participation within the activities and routines (Campbell, Milbourne, & Wilcox, 2008; McWilliam, 2005; Woods & Lindeman, 2008). Observing the parent and the child in routines promotes an understanding of the strategies the caregiver is already using that are supporting or preempting the child's participation and communication.

ESI advances the practice of routines-based intervention for young children with ASDs through the careful selection of routines and activities that support the teaching and learning priorities for both the child and the parent. The family and interventionist choose, from the list that was generated in the interview, routines and play activities that 1) either do or could occur at high frequency, 2) are motivating to the child and parent, and 3) include multiple opportunities for joint interaction, communication, and other core intervention targets (Kashinath et al., 2006). After an initial set of routines are implemented, other routines are added to the plan to expand practice opportunities (e.g., hand washing expands to tooth brushing and combing hair), include additional play or communication partners (e.g., grandpa after school, trips to the playground), increase types of routines and activities to support generalization (e.g., snacks at a friend's house, a trip to McDonald's), and promote development of new skills (e.g., initiating play with peers at the park, taking care of the family pet). The total number of routines and play activities, as well as the rate of implementation, is individualized for each family and child. Although the numbers will vary, a variety of routines and play activities for each family is always used to encourage the dispersing of learning opportunities throughout the day, participation within functional and meaningful events in the family life, and promotion of the child's growth and development.

Another feature of ESI that is compatible with the Part C practices is the use of objects, toys, and materials that belong to the family and are used within their routines and settings. For example, indoor play routines include the child's favorite toys, music, or constructive materials, and outdoor play materials consist of the child's ball, swing set, or scooter. No special equipment or materials are brought into the home setting. However, parents may select toys and materials to borrow from the parent–child playgroups to use at home if they are motivating to the child and relevant to the child's current targets. It is also important to point out that within each routine, the interventionist supports the parent's use of controlled variations to decrease the likelihood the routine will become a ritual and to increase opportunities for additional practice through the introduction of moderate novelty.

Individualized Child and Family Curriculum

SCERTS is used as a curriculum for home visitation, within playgroups, and community settings as a mechanism that links assessment with goals and objectives, and as a tool to monitor progress. The SC and ER are the primary developmental dimensions targeted to support the development of children with ASDs, and the TS dimension is the target for their families. In SCERTS, it is recognized that most learning in childhood occurs in the social context of daily activities and experiences (Prizant, Wetherby, Rubin, & Laurent, 2003; Prizant et al, 2006). Interventionists teach families how to target SC and ER goals and objectives by implementing transactional supports within daily activities. These are taught across home and community settings and in both individual and group sessions in order to help communicative partners who will be interacting with the child with ASDs in everyday learning contexts.

In addition to the home-based sessions, each child participates in a parent–child playgroup guided by two interventionists through the FIRST WORDS Project (2007), a longitudinal research investigation in the Autism Institute of the College of Medicine at Florida State University. Up to 10 parent–child dyads (a blend of children with TD and DD) meet as part of the parent–child playgroups. The children in the infant groups range in age from 6 to 13 months, and the children in the toddler groups range in age from 14 to 24 months. Each parent–child dyad attends a playgroup for at least 9 weeks during participation in ESI. The playgroups are held in a 600-square-foot room organized into play centers: music circle, books, dress up, doctor's office, infant washing, infant beds, blocks, trucks, toys, kitchen and feeding area, and fluid play activities. The routine of each playgroup includes predictable opening and closing songs, book times, and new play centers each week.

The interventionists provide information and a handout about specific weekly topics. The topics include how and why young children communicate, how to respond to your child's communication, daily routines and play, games for young children, learning through the senses, sharing books with your child, communication and behavior in toddlers, and social interaction and play with peers. In addition to learning about the weekly topics, the families have opportunities to focus on interacting with their child, to support peer interaction with other participants, and to receive feedback on their strategy use. The interventionists provide information to families through discussion and handouts, responses to questions, modeling, and individual coaching by setting up opportunities and making suggestions. Further, the playgroups offer the families opportunities to observe their children in a group with same-age peers and to network with other parents of children with and without ASDs, which may be helpful to parents in adjusting to the realization that their child has an ASD.

Parent-Implemented Embedded Intervention

ESI is a parent-implemented intervention approach. Following the identification of the child's priority goals and initial routines and play, the interventionist and parent begin the process of embedding goals within routines, using a variety of general and specific intervention strategies and parent supports. Within the SCERTS curriculum, multiple evidence-based strategies are identified for each child target and parent support. The interventionist systematically consults with each parent on the strategies or cluster of strategies that are appropriate for the child's identified priority goals and are the best fit for the child and parent's current knowledge and skills. Building upon the developmental model for children and adult learning for parents, the ESI interventionist selects the supports that are most immediately relevant to improve the parent's ability to encourage the child to initiate social communication and follow the child's attentional focus. Strategies are individualized based on the parent's observed skill level, on evidence that use of the strategies would influence their child's communication goals, and on the parent's indication that the strategies could be implemented multiple times within routines.

Collaborative Consultation in Adult Learning Framework

ESI interventionists individualize the methods for teaching parents to embed interventions within their routines so that they accommodate the interventionists' and parents' preferred teaching and learning styles, respectively. Parents can choose from easy-to-read handouts, videos, or demonstrations of specific strategies and examples of their use in family-identified routines. Interventionists follow the continuum of teaching, model the strategies within the routines, and provide opportunities for parents to ask clarifying questions or receive guided practice in which the parent implements the intervention and the interventionist observes and supports the parent as needed (Figure 9.2).

Parents and interventionists discuss strategy use and possible barriers to implementation and identify additional instances of potential strategy use across routines. Parent input is solicited regarding types of teaching methods used to increase their satisfaction and ownership of the intervention. Parents are encouraged to evaluate what works best during the summary and planning time with the interventionist. Each week, the interventionist observes the parent implementing the intervention within the routines selected. If the parent does not embed the goal or use the intervention strategy as coached, the interventionist demonstrates and reviews the training to facilitate problem solving about what is working and what is challenging for the parent. They practice together to increase caregiver's competence and develop another plan. If the caregiver is implementing as planned, then they discuss what the next steps are for the child to further enhance the quality of the interaction or expand the level of the child's independence or sophistication in communication.

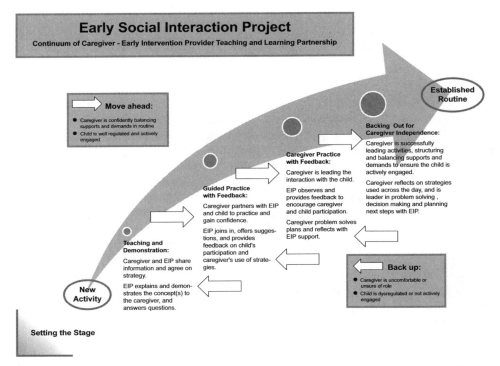

Figure 9.2. Early social interaction continuum of caregiver—early intervention provider teaching and learning partnership. Copyright 2008–2012, Florida State University. All rights reserved.

ESI is implemented systematically to achieve both child and caregiver outcomes. For example, the interventionist introduces a specific intervention strategy, such as contingent imitation, for the caregivers to use with the child to expand turn taking and increase initiations during bath and play with cars. Each strategy is chosen specifically with the caregiver to address the child's outcomes and is relevant to the identified routines on each visit. This is in contrast to other approaches that teach a general principle or strategy, such as imitation without consideration for the child's current targets or the context in which to practice it functionally. Attention is also given to the caregiver's learning curve. In this example, the strategy is new for the caregiver and is embedded in two familiar and preferred child routines, bath and play. The interventionist supports the caregiver by demonstrating contingent imitation and guiding practice in the routines, observing the caregiver and child and offering feedback. As the caregiver's confidence increases, the interventionist will provide less hands-on support and more indirect feedback. The strategy will be embedded in additional appropriate routines to continue to expand the child's use and to facilitate generalization. Problem solving is used throughout by the interventionist as a learning check for caregiver understanding, to increase caregiver confidence through verbal rehearsal, and to use the problem-solving power provided by multiple perspectives.

Caregivers have opportunities to determine the easiest-to-use methods of collecting data on the child's goals and the implementation of the strategies within routines. For example, one parent may identify the use of a daily diary or log sheet as the easiest method for noting the child's participation, whereas another uses wipe-off boards in the bathroom and on the refrigerator to take notes immediately after the routine. Treatment fidelity is monitored through the completion of a self-assessment checklist to ensure that each home visit includes the following components (Wetherby & Woods, 2006):

- Initial review of child and family outcomes and intervention intensity since the previous visit
- Observation of and participation by the parent in multiple routines
- Guided practice in implementing the intervention for specific goals within the routines
- Discussion about when, how often, and where the intervention would occur between visits
- Development of a plan for the next visit

Positive Behavior Support

ESI interventionists are trained in functional assessment and implementation of positive behavior support (PBS), which entails methods designed to limit the occurrence of problem behaviors. Children enrolled in ESI may or may not need PBS within their intervention plan. Initial energies are focused on development of early communication and social interaction skills, and if that development is successful, the need for PBS can be prevented; however, if children are not identified early enough or do not develop early communication that is easily understood, the likelihood that challenging behaviors will develop increases (Fox, Dunlap, Hemmeter, Joseph, & Strain, 2003). PBS is incorporated in the ESI approach on a child-by-child basis. However, features of PBS, such as environmental arrangements to prevent challenging behavior, the use of visual supports, and the importance of responding to the child's communication, are also common features of ESI and therefore provide common foundations for learning appropriate communication and social interaction.

Team-Based Community Coordination

In many situations, the ESI interventionist serves as the child's primary service provider. As such, the ESI interventionist may coach the caregiver to integrate outcomes across multiple areas or developmental domains of child skills. The primary service provider approach promotes coordination (rather than potential conflict) on outcomes or intervention methods. It also provides opportunities for exchange of more traditional discipline content and strategies to promote a unified approach for the caregiver's implementation within meaningful daily routines and activities. The ESI interventionist coordinates with the team to meet the needs of the child and family, ensures that the team communication with the family provides a consistent message, and collaborates with community resources as appropriate. Community supports are encouraged and recommended.

Social interaction with peers is encouraged. As children increase their social communication skills, opportunities to join peers in community activities are facilitated. Combination home, early care, and education programs are a natural progression in ESI. Family preferences and access to group settings are highly variable, based on resources, family values, and geographic availability. Some ESI families have identified child care or mother's morning out options for a morning or two a week initially, whereas others have sought a more formal nursery or preschool program. Still others have developed community cooperative programs and play dates to support social interaction as a less formal or inexpensive option. Whatever the family choice, ESI providers offer initial training to child care or preschool teachers; help to arrange the environment to support communication, interaction, and positive behavior; develop visual supports as needed; and practice with the child to facilitate transition to the setting. Just as with the parent, the continuum of consultation supports are provided for the teacher. As the child is successful and the teacher gains confidence, the ESI interventionist decreases time with the child in the program and establishes regular consultation visits to review the program, add new or revise existing outcome targets, and solve problems with the teacher, thereby increasing his or her capacity to generate additional social communication and play opportunities between peers.

DATA COLLECTION TO SUPPORT DECISION MAKING

Based on the belief that the earlier the intervention, the better the outcomes for the child, ESI collects data at multiple levels. First, it is important to know that the intervention is taking place. Data on the amount of time spent in intervention are collected by the interventionist and include the time provided by ESI, other team members, and the parents. Families share information during each session with the interventionist on the routines they completed between visits, on time spent in community activities, and on new routines or activities initiated. When intensity drops or is consistently low, problem solving between the parent and interventionist is initiated. Solutions may include identifying other potential partners (e.g., grandpa, older sibling, high school volunteer) or activities (e.g., mother's morning out, Early Head Start) to promote the child's practice or reorganizing the current routines and activities to provide more time for the parent at the end of the day when their other children return home from school. Support to any additional partners becomes a part of the child's program to ensure consistency of implementation. Although intensity is crucial, it is not essential that only one parent deliver the intervention, and over time, additional partners can support generalization.

Child data are collected throughout sessions on the specific intervention targets observed and are updated quarterly during reassessment using the SCERTS. Child targets need to be monitored closely to ensure that progress is occurring, and if it is not, then revisions in the plan need to occur immediately. Again, time is of the essence. Finally, on a less formal basis, parents' use of supports and strategies is monitored and shared with them as feedback during home visits.

To be efficient and usable within early intervention programs, data collection must be manageable. ESI interventionists use a home visit note to record samples of child outcomes, routines and activities implemented, and caregiver utilization. Planning for what is to occur between visits by the parent is an important component of the home visit that sets the stage for the next round of data collection on what actually occurred. Families report data on specific targets and routines throughout the week using a variety of methods, including refrigerator logs or tally sheets, wipe-off boards, e-mails, or video clips. Increased access to technology by families makes data collection a very dynamic process. Videos sent via cell phones are becoming more frequent.

CONSIDERATIONS FOR CHILDREN FROM CULTURALLY AND LINGUISTICALLY DIVERSE BACKGROUNDS

Family-guided services are by definition culturally responsive and respectful (Woods & Wetherby, 2003). ESI builds on this principle by joining in the families' daily routines and activities rather than assigning specific lessons or therapeutic activities. The provider works with the family as a partner through the intervention process, establishing a relationship that honors the family's beliefs as well as their priorities and concerns for their child's social communication needs. The individualized curriculum for the child and family allows the ESI provider to build upon the child and family's strengths and interests and choose from the menu of evidence-based instructional strategies that are most comfortable and compatible with the family's culture and their learning style. For some children and families, this may mean starting with play or familiar social interaction games and songs that promote joint attention and turn taking before evolving into more typical caregiving routines or household chores. Other families want to make the most of what they do and find that embedding outcomes during bath time or while folding laundry makes sense, increases opportunities for interaction, and keeps family life moving forward. ESI is often the entry point to early intervention for the child and family. We believe the family education component of the individualized curriculum is key to successful child and family outcomes. Families are not just new to ESI and early intervention but new to a diagnosis and to the recognition that their child is at risk for or has autism. At this time, families are often concerned about the impact of the diagnosis and are in a particularly vulnerable state. They may be experiencing a range and intensity of emotions, including remorse, blame, anger, frustration, or denial or questioning of the diagnosis. Education of the family in the ESI approach is an integral part of each home visit and is integrated throughout the session by conversations, information sharing, and problem solving to answer questions, clarify family understanding, apply content to the family's contexts, and address immediate family concerns. The family and the relationship established with the provider guide the specific consultation strategies used. Strategies are jointly identified to be compatible with the family's preferences, culture, and learning style.

The provider addresses with families the content that is core to their children's progress but that may be affected by culture in order to increase their understanding and implementation. For example, sometimes families are comfortable with a "quiet" child, who only responds and does not initiate, or with a child who "entertains" himself or herself. Through ongoing parent education, the interventionist will demonstrate the value of joint attention and engagement to enhance communication and interaction. Whether it is family culture, history, education, or expediency, some families preempt opportunities for the child to gain independence and would prefer to complete the routine *for* their child to show their love for their child and their competence as a parent. Again, the ESI interventionist would support family members along the continuum of consultation to gain understanding of the importance of child opportunities for practice and independence.

To date, the ESI model has been supported by studies using a limited sample size and therefore providing few examples of cultural and linguistic diversity. However, a large randomized control study across multiple geographic regions is now under way, and its results will serve to inform the intervention procedures and process. The sample reported in this chapter has included families representing the demographic distribution of Tallahassee, Florida, including white, African American, Hispanic, and Asian families. Only one bilingual family has been served, and in this case, the family was fluent in English and translated for their child. However, other studies using developmental and naturalistic interventions within parent-implemented approaches for preschool children have had more a diverse cultural sample (e.g., Wang, 2008). We anxiously await learning more about the ESI components and their acceptability to diverse cultural and linguistic populations.

Application to a Child

Jay was referred at 18 months and began intervention with the completion of the SAP. He was at the SCERTS social partner stage because he did not yet have recognizable words or symbols. The profile summary from the SAP report by his family and the SAP observation of him at home in a variety of everyday activities indicated relative strengths and weaknesses in SC and ER. Jay was just beginning to use intentional communication. He directed his gaze to others occasionally but was not yet coordinating his gaze, gestures, and vocalizations. He smiled and laughed occasionally but did not share positive affect with others or respond with laughter differentially. His rate of communication was low, and he used communication primarily to request comfort or continuation of a social game. If not redirected, Jay spent much of his time rolling objects, which seemed to be a self-regulation strategy. Jay's family identified favorite play routines as listening to music in the family room and in the car, swinging, and collecting and rolling small objects. Although Jay did not participate in many family or caregiving routines without considerable adult support, he did request favorite foods and drinks with vocalizations and was comforted by rocking in his rocking chair.

Using the SAP, the initial goals for Jay were to have him shift his gaze between people and objects, request comfort when distressed, combine a vocalization and gesture to gain attention, imitate familiar actions in a turn-taking sequence, use familiar objects functionally, and make choices with gestures. The ESI interventionist and the family members discussed how Jay's specific goals would be practiced within the routines as they occurred throughout the day. Goals for his parents included increasing their consistency in responding immediately to any communication initiation by Jay by imitating him back; using environmental arrangements, such as limiting access to preferred materials until he communicated a request or choice; and marking clear beginnings and endings to the routines so that Jay knew what was expected of him. Within the first few weeks, he began to imitate actions with his dad in favorite games. His parents reported an increase in distress when objects were removed or when they required him to transition to another activity without advance warning.

Jay's parents learned how to use positioning to support Jay's participation; make activities predictable with balanced turns; respond to his gestural, vocal, and facial signals to request and to stop interaction; and wait for Jay to take a turn or communicate a choice. Intervention strategies were embedded in cereal and drink routines, in which he was given a choice of juice or water or of a type of cereal at breakfast but was given smaller portions so that he could vocalize to request more. Jay's father is usually responsible for breakfast while his mother drives older siblings to school. The father pulled up his chair to face Jay in his highchair, watched for him to make his initial drink request, and offered him the choices and then modeled the label of the choice that he had made (i.e., apple juice). He took a turn drinking his coffee after Jay took a drink and then watched for Jay again and responded. The process of embedding the goals would occur within each routine as appropriate and would be jointly planned by the family members and service provider(s). Routines would be added over time, as illustrated in Figure 9.3, to help his family learn how to embed intervention strategies in routines 25 hr per week to promote Jay's active engagement. In addition to expanding routines at home and in the community, Jay's family with support from his ESI interventionist would begin seeking opportunities to interact with peers in group settings and to plan his transition from early intervention to appropriate community- or school-based services at 3 years of age.

Jay's family routine categories			
Play routines		**Caregiver routines**	
Play with objects/ constructive play	**Pretend play**	**Comfort-/disability- related routines**	**Dressing-related routines**
Ball playing Bowling games Hammer/ball toy Cars and planes	Feeding Batman Cooking dinner with Mom	Rocking with Dad Playing with beanbag/ listening to music in living room	Getting dressed/ undressed Putting on shoes
Physical play	**Social games (roles)**	**Hygiene-related routines**	**Food-related routines**
Backyard run Basketball Walk in neighborhood Run and catch with sisters Slide/swing at park	Rough-and-tumble play with Dad	Hand washing Diapering Having a bath	Snack Breakfast Lunch Dinner Juice/getting a drink
Preacademic routines		**Community and family routines**	
Reading books	**Songs and rhymes**	**Community and family errands**	**Family chores**
Ladybug book *Finding Nemo* Old MacDonald book	Listening to music on the computer	Grocery shopping Laundromat Sibling gymnastic classes	Folding laundry Cooking and setting the table
Computer, TV, video	**Fluid play**	**Socialization activities**	**Recreation**
Any Disney movie Music CDs on the computer	Coloring with crayons	Library hour Church, park, and playground	Eating out Visiting family in a different town Long car rides

Figure 9.3 Categories and examples of Jay's family routines.

Application to an Adolescent or Adult ︴︴︴︴︴︴︴︴︴︴︴︴︴︴︴︴︴︴︴︴︴︴︴︴︴︴︴︴︴︴︴︴︴︴︴︴

ESI is an intervention designed for toddlers and is not used with older individuals.

FUTURE DIRECTIONS

Ongoing research is investigating the active ingredients of ESI, with emphasis on the impact of parent's support on the child's active engagement within a variety of everyday activities. Earlier identification of red flags for ASDs provides a unique opportunity for prevention of significant social and communication delays and an interruption of the progression of the disorder. Families served by ESI voiced concerns about their child's development and identified multiple red flags by 12–18 months. With increased public and physician awareness, earlier identification of red flags is occurring. Consequently, a future direction for ESI is to develop a streamlined family education program to help families "get ahead" of ASDs when red flags are identified. Educating parents through individual sessions or parent–child playgroups may serve as a prevention tool. Appropriate education goals in such contexts would support responsive interaction, increased engagement in family-identified meaningful activities, and focus with the parents on the development of joint attention skills.

For ESI to be effective in the local early intervention arena, it is essential to identify competencies for personnel training and for developing user-friendly and easily accessible continuing education and mentoring opportunities. ESI has a web site (http://esi.fsu.edu) with training materials, a manual, and video illustrations. However, without support to learn the consultation or coaching strategies described as essential for families to become skilled at engaging their children in embedded intervention, it is unlikely that providers will gain the confidence and competence to implement the procedures with a high degree of fidelity (Landry, Anthony, Swank, & Monseque-Bailey, 2009). Consultation and coaching intervention approaches are believed to be effective but still not used widely in the field (Campbell & Halbert, 2002). Fixsen and colleagues (2005) identify complexity, distance from familiar and comfortable practice, and the need for additional training as reasons why providers are unlikely or unwilling to utilize procedures. Although ESI was designed for and implemented collaboratively within a Part C early intervention program, that ideal situation is the exception rather than the rule and was implemented by highly qualified providers with ongoing training and mentoring. Each of the components of the approach (i.e., family-guided routines, individualized child and family curriculum, parent-implemented embedded intervention, collaborative consultation, team-based community coordination, and positive behavior support) necessitates competence by the providers in a bundle of practices, which, although recommended, are not currently implemented with consistency and may be considered controversial (Dunst & Trivette, 2009). Therefore, an important future direction for ESI is to disseminate training and mentoring opportunities more widely.

SUGGESTED READINGS

Early Social Interaction web site (http://esi.fsu.edu).

This site is a repository for materials developed for the original model demonstration project, as well as ongoing research. New materials will be posted as developed. This site also has links to FIRST WORDS (http://firstwords.fsu.edu/), which provides information on early communication identification and intervention resources, and to Tactics (http://tactics.fsu.edu), which as information on family-guided, routines-based intervention.

Wetherby, A., & Woods, J. (2006). Effectiveness of early intervention for children with autism spectrum disorders beginning in the second year of life. *Topics in Early Childhood Special Education, 26*, 67–82.

This article describes the original quasi-experimental study for ESI.

Autism Speaks web site (http://autismspeaks.com).

This interactive web site includes up-to-date information on early identification and intervention for ASDs across the age span. Of particular interest is the video library that illustrates early red flags helpful to early identification.

Positive Behavioral Interventions and Supports (PBIS) Technical Assistance Center web site (http://www.pbis.org/).

This site, sponsored by the U.S. Department of Education's Office of Special Education Programs (OSEP), offers extensive information for families, team members, and administrators on evidence-based practice and tool kits to support implementation.

Learning Activities

1. Identify how the processes and procedures of ESI reflect a family-guided and developmental theoretical perspective.

2. It can be challenging to identify and build routines that are meaningful to the family and provide multiple opportunities for the child's communication and engagement. There isn't a list of best options, and no two families are alike. Develop a checklist of important considerations to ensure you are jointly identifying the most facilitative contexts that also facilitate adequate intervention intensity.

3. Cara's mom and dad agree that she has social communication delays and would benefit from early intervention, but they can't see why you just don't do it. They are sure you have more expertise than they do, and they fear they will just be in your way. What would you tell them?

4. Joey says several single words and sometimes uses them appropriately to make requests for favorite foods and toys. His dad is convinced he is verbal and wants you to work on two- and three-word combinations so he sounds more like the other kids at his child care center. You are more worried about his limited joint attention and turn taking. How would you proceed to work closely with Joey's dad to choose appropriate early communication and social interaction goals?

5. The team, including the family members, has been pleased with Tyler's progress. He is initiating interactions; coordinating gaze, gestures, and a few words in familiar routines; playing with his toys functionally; and beginning to combine actions. In addition, he has decreased his repetitive spinning behaviors. Everyone agrees the next step is to integrate him into a small group or classroom setting, but the teacher at the program the family chose is not sure she can continue a program of the kind he has had up to this point. How can the team use the continuum of caregiver supports in an early care and education program?

REFERENCES

American Speech-Language-Hearing Association. (2008). *Roles and responsibilities of speech-language pathologists in early intervention: Guidelines.* Available from http://www.asha.org/policy

Baron-Cohen, S., Cox, A., Baird, G., Swettenham, J., Nightingale, N., Morgan, K.,...Charman, T. (1996). Psychological markers in the detection of autism in infancy in a large population. *British Journal of Psychiatry, 168,* 158–163.

Bates, E. (1976). *Language and context: The acquisition of pragmatics.* New York, NY: Academic Press.

Bates, E. (1979). *The emergence of symbols: Cognition and communication in infancy.* New York, NY: Academic Press.

Bates, E., Camaioni, L., & Volterra, V. (1975). The acquisition of performatives prior to speech. *Merrill-Palmer Quarterly, 21,* 205–226.

Bates, E., O'Connell, B., & Shore, C. (1987). Language and communication in infancy. In J. Osofsky (Ed.), *Handbook of infant development* (pp. 149–203). New York, NY: Wiley.

Bernheimer, L., & Weisner, T. (2007). "Let me tell you what I do all day...": The family story at the center of intervention research and practice. *Infants and Young Children, 20*(3), 192–201.

Bloom, L. (1993). *The transition from infancy to language.* New York, N.Y: Cambridge University Press.

Bloom, L., & Lahey, M. (1978). *Language development and language disorders.* New York, NY: Wiley.

Bransford, J., Brown, A., & Cocking, R.R. (Eds.). (2000). *How people learn: Brain, mind, experience, and school.* Washington, DC: National Academy Press.

Bronfenbrenner, U. (1979). *The ecology of human development: Experiments by nature and design.* Cambridge, MA: Harvard University Press.

Bruner, J. (1978). From communication to language: A psychological perspective. In I. Markova (Ed.), *The social context of language* (pp. 17–48). Chichester, UK: Wiley.

Bruner, J. (1981). The social context of language acquisition. *Language and Communication, 1,* 155–178.

Buysee, V., & Wesley, P. (2005). *Consultation in early childhood settings.* Baltimore, MD: Paul H. Brookes Publishing Co.

Campbell, P.H., & Halbert, J. (2002). Between research and practice: Provider perspectives on early intervention. *Topics in Early Childhood Special Education, 22*(4), 213–226.

Campbell, P., Milbourne, S., & Wilcox, M. (2008). Adaptation interventions to promote participation in natural settings. *Infants and Young Children, 21*(2), 94–106.

Charman, T., Swettenham, J., Baron-Cohen, S., Cox, A., Baird, G., & Drew, A. (1997). Infants with autism: An investigation of empathy, pretend play, joint attention, and imitation. *Developmental Psychology, 33,* 781–789.

Chawarska, K., Paul, R., Klin, A., Hannigen, S., Dichtel, L., & Volkmar, F. (2007). Parent recognition of developmental problems in toddlers with autism spectrum disorders. *Journal of Autism and Developmental Disorders, 37,* 62–72.

Dawson, G., Rogers, S., Munson, J., Smith, M., Winter, J., Greenson, J.,...Varley, J. (2010). Randomized, controlled trial of an intervention for toddlers with autism: The Early Start Denver model. *Pediatrics, 125,* e17–e23.

Dawson, G., Toth, K., Abbott, R., Osterling, J., Munson, J., Estes, A., & Liaw, J. (2004). Early social attention impairments in autism: Social orienting, joint attention, and attention to distress. *Developmental Psychology, 40,* 271–283.

Disabilities Education Improvement Act of 2004, 20 U.S.C. § 1400 *et seq.*

Donovan, M.S., Bransford, J.D., & Pellegrino, J.W. (1999). *How people learn: Bridging research and practice.* Washington, DC: National Academy Press.

Dunst, C.J., Hamby, D., Trivette, C.M., Raab, M., & Bruder, M.B. (2000). Everyday family and community life and children's naturally occurring learning opportunities. *Journal of Early Intervention, 23*(3), 151–164.

Dunst, C., Lowe, L.W., & Bartholomew, P.C. (1990). Contingent social responsiveness, family ecology, and infant communicative competence. *National Student Speech Language Hearing Association Journal, 17,* 39–49.

Dunst, C.J., & Trivette, C.M. (2009). Using research evidence to inform and evaluate early childhood intervention practices. *Topics in Early Childhood Special Education, 29,* 40–52.

FIRST WORDS Project (2007). The Florida State University Research Foundation. Retrieved from http://firstwords.fsu.edu/

Fixsen, D. L., Naoom, S. F., Blasé, K. A., Friedman, R. M., & Wallace, F. (2005). *Implementation research: A synthesis of the literature.* Tampa: Florida Mental Health Institute, University of South Florida.

Florida State University, Early Social Interaction Project (n.d.). Continuum of partnership. Retrieved from http://esi.fsu.edu/index.php/early-esi.

Florida State University, Early Social Interaction Project (n.d.). Who receives more intervention—James or Jamaal? Retrieved from http://esi.fsu.edu/index.php/early-esi.

Fox, L., Dunlap, G., Hemmeter, M.L., Joseph, G., & Strain, P. (2003). The Teaching Pyramid: A model for supporting social competence and preventing challenging behavior in young children. *Young Children, 58*(4), 48–53.

Greenspan, S.I., & Wieder, S. (1997). Developmental patterns and outcomes in infants and children with disorders in relating and communicating: A chart review of 200 cases of children with autistic spectrum diagnoses. *Journal of Developmental and Learning Disorders, 1,* 87–141.

Hancock, T.B., & Kaiser, A.P. (2002). The effects of trainer-implemented enhanced milieu teaching on the social communication of children who have autism. *Topics in Early Childhood Special Education, 22*(1), 39–54.

Howlin, P., & Moore, A. (1997). Diagnosis of autism: A survey of over 1200 patients in the UK. *Autism, 1,* 135–162.

Individuals with Disabilities Education Improvement Act (IDEA) of 2004, PL 108-446, 20 U.S.C. §§ 1400 *et seq.*

Kaiser, A. (1993). Functional language. In M. Snell (Ed.), *Instruction of students with severe disabilities* (pp. 347–379). New York, NY: Macmillan.

Kaiser, A., Hancock, T., & Nietfeld, J. (2000). The effects of parent-implemented enhanced milieu teaching on the social communication of children who have autism. *Early Education and Development, 11,* 423–446.

Kasari, C., Paparella, T., Freeman, S., & Jahromi, L. (2008). Language outcome in autism: Randomized comparison of joint attention and play interventions. *Journal of Consulting and Clinical Psychology, 76,* 125–137.

Kashinath, S., Woods, J., & Goldstein, H. (2006). Enhancing generalized teaching strategy use in daily routines by parents of children with autism. *Journal of Speech, Language, and Hearing Research, 49,* 466–485.

Klinger, L., & Dawson, G. (1992). Facilitating early social and communicative development in children with autism. In S. Warren & J. Reichle (Eds.), *Causes and effects in communication and language intervention* (pp. 157–186). Baltimore, MD: Paul H. Brookes Publishing Co.

Koegel, R., Bimbela, A., & Schreibman, L. (1996). Collateral effects of parent training on family interactions. *Journal of Autism and Developmental Disorders, 26,* 347–359.

Landry, S.H., Anthony, J.L., Swank, P.R., & Monseque-Bailey, P. (2009). Effectiveness of comprehensive professional development for teachers of at-risk preschoolers. *Journal of Educational Psychology, 101*(2), 448–465.

Loveland, K., & Landry, S. (1986). Joint attention and language in autism and developmental language delay. *Journal of Autism and Developmental Disorders, 16,* 335–349.

MacDonald, J. (1989). *Becoming partners with children.* San Antonio, TX: Special Press.

MacDonald, J., & Carroll, J. (1992). A social partnership model for assessing early communication development: An intervention model for preconversational children. *Language, Speech, and Hearing Services in Schools, 23,* 113–124.

McClannahan, L.E, Krantz, P.J., & McGee, G.G. (1982). Parents as therapists for autistic children: A model for effective training. *Analysis and Intervention in Development Disabilities, 2,* 223–252.

McCoy, D., Wetherby, A., & Woods, J. (2009, May). *Screening children between 18 and 24 months using the systematic observation of red flags (SORF) for autism spectrum disorders: A follow-up study.* Oral presentation at the International Meeting for Autism Research, Chicago, Illinois.

McGee, G., Morrier, M., & Daly, T. (1999). An incidental teaching approach to early intervention for toddlers with autism. *Journal of the Association for Persons with Severe Handicaps, 24,* 133–146.

McLean, J., & Snyder-McLean, L. (1978). *A transactional approach to early language training.* Columbus, OH: Charles E. Merrill.

McWilliam, R.A. (2005). Assessing the resource needs of families in the context of early intervention. In M.J. Guralnick (Ed.), *A developmental systems approach to early intervention* (pp. 215–234). Baltimore, MD: Paul H. Brookes Publishing Co.

Meadan, H., Ostrosky, M., Zaghlawan, H., & Yu, S. (2009). Promoting the social and communicative behavior of young children with autism spectrum disorders: A review of parent-implemented intervention studies. *Topics in Early Childhood Special Education, 29*(2), 90–104.

Mundy, P., Sigman, M., & Kasari, C. (1990). A longitudinal study of joint attention and language development in autistic children. *Journal of Autism and Developmental Disorders, 20,* 115–128.

National Early Childhood Technical Assistance Center, Workgroup on Principles and Practices in Natural Environments. (2008). *Agreed-upon practices for providing early intervention services in natural environments.* OSEP TA Community of Practice—Part C Settings. Retrieved from http://www.nectac.org

National Research Council. (2001). *Educating children with autism.* Washington, DC: National Academy Press.

Osterling, J., & Dawson, G. (1994). Early recognition of children with autism: A study of first birthday home videotapes. *Journal of Autism and Developmental Disorders, 24,* 247–257.

Osterling, J., Dawson, G., & Munson, J. (2002). Early recognition of one year old infants with autism spectrum disorder versus mental retardation: A study of first birthday party home videotapes. *Development and Psychopathology, 14,* 239–252.

Pierce, K., Carter, C., Weinfeld, M., Desmond, J., Hazin, R., Bjork, R., & Gallagher, N. (2011). Detecting, studying, and treating autism early: The one-year well-baby check-up approach. *Journal of Pediatrics, 159*(3), 458–465.

Prizant, B.M., & Wetherby, A.M. (1998). Understanding the continuum of discrete-trial traditional behavioral to social-pragmatic developmental approaches in communication enhancement for young children with autism/PDD. *Seminars in Speech and Language, 19,* 329–353.

Prizant, B., Wetherby, A., & Rydell, P. (2000). Issues in enhancing communication and related abilities for young children with autism spectrum disorders: A developmental transactional perspective. In A. Wetherby & B. Prizant (Eds.), *Autism spectrum disorders: A transactional developmental perspective* (pp. 193–234). Baltimore, MD: Paul H. Brookes Publishing Co.

Prizant, B.M., Wetherby, A.M., Rubin, E., & Laurent, A. (2003). The SCERTS® Model: A transactional, family-centered approach to enhancing communication and socioemotional abilities of children with autism spectrum disorder. *Infants and Young Children, 16,* 296–316.

Prizant, B.M., Wetherby, A.M., Rubin, E., Laurent, A., & Rydell, P. (2006). *The SCERTS® Model: A comprehensive educational approach for children with autism spectrum disorders.* Baltimore, MD: Paul H. Brookes Publishing Co.

Rogers, S.J., & Lewis, H. (1989). An effective day treatment model for young children with pervasive developmental disorders. *Journal of the American Academy of Child and Adolescent Psychiatry, 28,* 207–214.

Rowland, C., & Schweigert, P. (1993). Analyzing the communication environment to increase functional communication. *Journal of the Association for Persons with Severe Handicaps, 18,* 161–176.

Rush, D.D., Shelden, M.L., & Hanft, B.E. (2003). Coaching families and colleagues: A process for collaboration in natural settings. *Infants and Young Children, 16,* 33–47.

Sameroff, A. (1987). The social context of development. In N. Eisenburg (Ed.), *Contemporary topics in development* (pp. 273–291). New York, NY: Wiley.

Sandall, S., Hemmeter, M.L., Smith, B.J., & McLean, M.E., (2005). *DEC recommended practices: A comprehensive guide for practical application in early intervention/early childhood special education.* Longmont, CO: Sopris West.

Scarborough, A.A., Spiker, D., Mallik, S., Hebbeler, K.M., Bailey, D.B., Jr., & Simeonsson, R.J. (2004). A national look at children and families entering early intervention. *Exceptional Children, 70,* 469–483.

Schreibman, L., Kaneko, W., & Koegel, R. (1991). Positive affect of parents of autistic children: A comparison across two teaching techniques. *Behavior Therapy, 22,* 479–490.

Seifer, R., Clark, G.N., & Sameroff, A. (1991). Positive effects of interaction coaching on infants with developmental disabilities and their mothers. *American Journal of Mental Retardation, 96,* 1–11.

Sigman, M., Dijamco, A., Gratier, M., & Rozga, A. (2004). Early detection of core deficits in autism. *Mental Retardation and Developmental Disabilities Research Reviews, 10,* 221–233.

Sigman, M., Mundy, P., Sherman, T., & Ungerer, J. (1986). Social interactions of autistic, mentally retarded and normal children and their caregivers. *Journal of Child Psychology and Psychiatry and Allied Disciplines, 27*(5), 647–656.

Sigman, M., Arbeile, S., Corona, R., Dissanayake, C., Espinosa, M., Kim, N.,...Ruskin, E. (1999). Continuity and change in the social competence of children with autism, Down syndrome, and developmental delays. *Monographs of the Society for Research in Child Development, 64,* 1–114.

Sperry, L.A., Whaley, K.T., Shaw, E., & Brame, K. (1999). Services for young children with autism spectrum disorder: Voices of parents and providers. *Infants and Young Children, 11,* 17–33.

Stern, D. (1985). *The interpersonal world of the infant.* New York, NY: Basic Books.

Stone, W., Ousley, O., Yoder, P., Hogan, K., & Hepburn, S. (1997). Nonverbal communication in 2- and 3-year old children with autism. *Journal of Autism and Developmental Disorders, 27,* 677–696.

Strain, P., McGee, G., & Kohler, F. (2001). Inclusion of children with autism in early intervention environments. In M. Guralnick (Ed.), *Early childhood inclusion: Focus on change* (pp. 337–363). Baltimore, MD: Paul H. Brookes Publishing Co.

Swettenham, J., Baron-Cohen, S., Charman, T., Cox, A., Baird, G., Drew, A.,...Wheelwright, S. (1998). The frequency and distribution of spontaneous attention shifts between social and nonsocial stimuli in autistic, typically developing, and nonautistic developmentally delayed infants. *Journal of Child Psychology and Psychiatry, 39,* 747–753.

Tomasello, M., Kruger, A.C., & Ratner, H.H. (1993). Cultural learning. *Behavioral and Brain Sciences, 16,* 495–552.

Tronick, E. (1989). Emotions and emotional communication in infancy. *American Psychologist, 44,* 112–119.

Turnbull, A.P., & Ruef, M. (1997). Family perspectives on inclusive lifestyle for people with problem behavior. *Exceptional Children, 63,* 211–227.

Vygotsky, L. (1986). *Thought and language* (A. Kozulin, Ed. & Trans.). Cambridge, MA: MIT Press.

Wang, P. (2008). Effects of a parent training program on the interactive skills of parents of children with autism in China. *Journal of Policy and Practice in Intellectual Disabilities, 5* (2), 96–104.

Wetherby, A., Allen, L., Cleary, J., Kublin, K., & Goldstein, H. (2002). Validity and reliability of the Communication and Symbolic Behavior Scales Developmental Profile with very young children. *Journal of Speech, Language, and Hearing Research, 45,* 1202–1218.

Wetherby, A., Brosnan-Maddox, S., Peace, V., & Newton, L. (2008). Validation of the Infant-Toddler Checklist as a broadband screener for autism spectrum disorders from 9 to 24 months of age. *Autism, 12,* 487–512.

Wetherby, A., Goldstein, H., Cleary, J., Allen, L., & Kublin, K. (2003). Early identification of children with communication disorders: Concurrent and predictive validity of the CSBS Developmental Profile. *Infants and Young Children, 16*(2), 161–174.

Wetherby, A., & Prizant, B. (2002). *Communication and Symbolic Behavior Scales Developmental Profile™–First Normed Edition.* Baltimore, MD: Paul H. Brookes Publishing Co.

Wetherby, A.M., Prizant, B.M., & Hutchinson, T. (1998). Communicative, social-affective, and symbolic profiles of young children with autism and pervasive developmental disorder. *American Journal of Speech-Language Pathology, 7,* 79–91.

Wetherby, A., Schuler, A., & Prizant, B. (1997). Enhancing language and communication development: Theoretical foundations. In D. Cohen & F. Volkmar (Eds.), *Handbook of autism and pervasive developmental disorders* (2nd ed., pp. 513–538). New York, NY: Wiley.

Wetherby, A., Watt, N., Morgan, L., & Shumway, S. (2007). Social communication profiles of children with autism spectrum disorders in the second year of life. *Journal of Autism and Developmental Disorders, 37,* 960–975.

Wetherby, A., & Woods, J. (2006). Effectiveness of early intervention for children with autism spectrum disorders beginning in the second year of life. *Topics in Early Childhood Special Education, 26,* 67–82.

Wetherby, A., & Woods, J. (2008). Developmental approaches to treatment of infants and toddlers with autism spectrum disorders. In F. Volkmar, A. Klin, & K. Chawarska (Eds.), *Autism spectrum disorders in infancy and early childhood* (pp. 170–206). NY: Guilford Press.

Wetherby, A., Woods, J., Allen, L., Cleary, J., Dickinson, H., & Lord, C. (2004). Early indicators of autism spectrum disorders in the second year of life. *Journal of Autism and Developmental Disorders, 34,* 473–493.

Woods, J., Kashinath, S., & Goldstein, H. (2004). Effects of embedding caregiver-implemented teaching strategies in daily routines on children's communication outcomes. *Journal of Early Intervention, 26,* 175–193.

Woods, J., & Lindeman, D. (2008). Gathering and giving assessment information with families. *Infants and Young Children, 21*(4), 272–284.

Woods, J., & Wetherby, A. (2003). Early identification and intervention for infants and toddlers at risk for autism spectrum disorders. *Language, Speech, and Hearing Services in Schools, 34,* 180–193.

Yoder, P., & Stone, W. (2006). Randomized comparison of two communication interventions for preschoolers with autism spectrum disorders. *Journal of Consulting and Clinical Psychology, 74,* 426–435.

Yoder, P., Warren, S., McCathren, R., & Leew, S. (1998). Does adult responsivity to child behavior facilitate communication development? In A.M. Wetherby, S.F. Warren, & J. Reichle (Eds.), *Transitions in prelinguistic communication* (pp. 39–58). Baltimore, MD: Paul H. Brookes Publishing Co.

10

Peer-Mediated Support Interventions

Erik W. Carter, Lynn G. Sisco, and Yun-Ching Chung

Promoting social interactions and friendships among students with and without disabilities—including autism spectrum disorders (ASDs)—has long been considered a central tenet of **inclusive education** (Ryndak & Fisher, 2003). Through interactions with their peers, children and youth with ASDs can develop important social-communication and language skills, learn academic and functional life skills, access emotional and instrumental supports, establish friendships, and participate more actively in the life of their school (Bellini, Peters, Brianner, & Hopf, 2007; Carter & Hughes, 2007; Kennedy, 2001). The relationships students experience can also contribute to their sense of belonging, encourage independence, increase school engagement, and promote overall well-being and quality of life (Rubin, Bukowski, & Laursen, 2009; Schnorr, 1997). Recognizing these and other benefits, researchers and practitioners have focused sustained efforts on identifying effective strategies for promoting peer interactions within inclusive schools.

Although educators, parents, and other adults can be instrumental in enhancing socially related outcomes for children and youth with ASDs, emphasis increasingly is turning to the promising role peers can play in promoting social, communication, and other educational outcomes for students with ASDs. **Peer-mediated support interventions** involve equipping one or more peers without disabilities to provide ongoing social or academic support, or both, to peers of similar age with disabilities under the guidance of educators, paraprofessionals, or other school staff (Carter & Kennedy, 2006). These interventions typically involve identifying students with ASDs and their peers who would benefit from involvement in these interventions, orienting peers to their new roles, providing regular opportunities for students to interact within instructional or noninstructional school settings or both, and offering needed guidance and support to ensure all participating students are benefiting as anticipated. As students gain experience working together, adults incrementally fade their proximity and their direct support to promote independence. For school-age children with ASDs, these support arrangements have emerged as an effective alternative to schools' widespread use of individually assigned, one-to-one adult supports (e.g., paraprofessionals, special educators) to support students' access to the general curriculum and involvement in extracurricular activities (Giangreco, 2010).

A broad array of peer-mediated instruction and intervention strategies have been described and evaluated in the professional literature (see Bellini et al., 2007; Carter, Sisco, Chung, & Stanton-Chapman, 2010; Goldstein, Kaczmarek, & English, 2001; Harper & Maheady, 2007; Janney & Snell, 2006; McConnell, 2002). This chapter focuses on the subset of peer-mediated approaches that 1) involve peers in providing ongoing and direct support (vs. occasional or incidental support) to their classmates with ASDs; 2) enhance social interactions among similar-age students with ASDs and their peers without disabilities (vs. an exclusive focus on acquisition of social skills, interactions with adults, or interactions with other classmates with disabilities); and 3) are implemented in inclusive elementary, middle, or high school settings (i.e., grades 1–12).

TARGET POPULATIONS AND ASSESSMENTS FOR DETERMINING TREATMENT RELEVANCE AND GOALS

Peer-mediated support interventions were developed primarily for students with severe disabilities who require extensive or pervasive supports to participate fully within inclusive classes, extracurricular activities, and other school-sponsored events. These students typically receive special education services under the categories of autism, intellectual disability, multiple disabilities, or deaf-blindness and may be eligible for a state's **alternative assessments.** However, ample evidence exists that students with mild or moderate developmental disabilities (who experience intermittent support needs) may similarly benefit from these intervention approaches.

As with all special education programming, decisions about intervention appropriateness, design, and delivery should be determined individually within collaborative teaming models (Hunt & McDonnell, 2007; Hunt, Soto, Maier, & Doering, 2003). Typically, peer-mediated support interventions are considered appropriate for students with ASDs who exhibit one or more of the following characteristics: 1) have **individualized education program** (IEP) goals addressing the quality or quantity, or both, of their interactions or relationships with peers; 2) experience limited interactions with same-age peers, despite being in close proximity (e.g., enrollment in the same class or club activity); 3) evidence substantial impairments in social or communication skills or both; and 4) require considerable support to participate in classroom or school activities. Students' interest in working with and receiving support from their peers should also be a primary consideration. Unfortunately, the empirical literature offers little guidance on how each of these considerations should be weighed or used to inform specific alterations to intervention packages.

Direct observational assessments are the primary approach used to determine the appropriateness and focus of peer-mediated support interventions for school-age children with ASDs. For example, observations can be conducted by educators, paraprofessionals, or other school staff to identify those settings (e.g., specific classrooms, extracurricular activities, cafeteria, hallways, playground) and instructional contexts (e.g., large-group lecture or discussion, small-group activities, independent seat work) during which peer-mediated supports may be particularly beneficial. These direct observations focus on existing interaction opportunities within particular school settings, the extent to which and ways in which students with ASDs are accessing those opportunities, and potential factors that may influence social participation (Boyd, Conroy, Asmus, McKenney, & Mancil, 2008; Carter, Sisco, Brown, Brickham, & Al-Khabbaz, 2008). At the same time, because these interventions involve peer-delivered academic supports, the analysis should also consider the nature of students' educational goals within the general education curriculum.

As they progress through elementary, middle, and high school, students with ASDs should become more actively involved in determining their own supports within and beyond the classroom (Test et al., 2004). Although the perspectives of students are infrequently sought, person-centered planning and preference assessments offer avenues for giving students a voice in determining how they receive support and from whom. For students with complex communication challenges, alternative avenues for determining these preferences should be explored (Canella, O'Reilly, & Lancioni, 2005). For example, a student might use pictures of his or her classmates to indicate with whom he or she would like to work.

THEORETICAL BASIS

Peer-mediated support interventions have been associated with substantial improvements in social interaction outcomes for school-age children and youth with ASDs. Although these strategies draw upon diverse theoretical foundations, two theories may be particularly relevant to understanding the impact of these interventions. Most of the peer-mediated strategies reviewed in this chapter reflect a behavioral perspective on social interaction and learning. Behavioral theory focuses on the antecedents and consequences of behaviors and their relation to the future occurrence of those behaviors.

Most peer-mediated support interventions involve equipping peers without disabilities to prompt, model, and reinforce the social, academic, and other target behaviors of their partners with disabilities. During initial training sessions led by special educators, researchers, or other school staff, peers may be taught how to elicit and encourage specific social and communicative behaviors by their partners with disabilities, deliver verbal or other reinforcement when those behaviors are appropriately demonstrated, and model their effective use when they are not. Arranging for students with and without disabilities to interact with one another within collaborative activities expands the opportunities students with ASDs have to practice critical social behaviors, receive natural feedback from peers, and connect with new communities of reinforcement. The close proximity of peers expands the number of conversational initiations directed to students with ASDs, while increasing the likelihood that students' communication attempts will be reinforced. In other words, these interventions create structured contexts within which the social and communication efforts of students with ASDs are encouraged, facilitated, and supported by peers. In addition, the involvement of multiple peers within most of these intervention approaches may promote generalized social outcomes by embedding multiple exemplars of prosocial behavior (Stokes & Baer, 1977).

Improvements in the quantity and quality of interactions between students with ASDs and their peers without disabilities may also be partially attributed to observational learning. Social learning theory (Bandura, 1977) posits that people learn through the process of observing behaviors exhibited by others in their environment and witnessing the outcomes—both positive and negative—of those behaviors. This framework emphasizes the considerable influence peers can have on the social and communication development of their schoolmates with disabilities.

Within peer-mediated interventions, participating peers serve as both explicit and incidental models of age-appropriate social, communication, academic, and other related skills for the partner with an ASD. Through participation in shared activities or involvement in interdependent instructional arrangements (e.g., cooperative learning groups, peer support arrangements), students with ASDs gain increased opportunities to observe their peers interacting effectively with other classmates and to observe the positive consequences of those behaviors within the context of social interactions. Thus, explicit reinforcement may not be necessary to promote acquisition of all social and communication skills. When students with ASDs are enrolled in inclusive classrooms and other school activities, these peer models may already be present. However, peer-mediated arrangements increase the proximity and number of peer models accessible to students with ASDs. Moreover, they may strengthen the appropriateness and salience of those models. For example, educators often recruit peers who are competent communicators, evidence strong interpersonal skills, and have high social status (e.g., Garrison-Harrell, Kamps, & Kravits, 1997; Jackson & Campbell, 2009). Moreover, initial orientation and training sessions for these peers often emphasize the importance of peer modeling and teach specific strategies for demonstrating age-appropriate, contextually relevant skills to their partners with ASDs.

Peer-mediated support interventions also appear to address several salient barriers to social interaction existing within many elementary, middle, and high schools. First, despite legislative initiatives and school reform efforts challenging schools to promote greater access to the general education curriculum for students with disabilities, the majority of children and youth with ASDs spend at least 60% of their school day outside the general education classroom, apart from their peers without disabilities (U.S. Department of Education, 2009). Even within inclusive classrooms, students with ASDs may be on the periphery of ongoing activities or may be pulled to other locations for individualized instruction. Peer-mediated interventions establish regular, teacher-sanctioned opportunities for students with and without autism to interact with one another within the context of ongoing, shared activities.

Second, the extensive reliance on individually assigned adults to support general education enrollment may unintentionally limit the opportunities students have to interact socially with their classmates without disabilities (Carter et al., 2008). When students with ASDs always receive one-to-one support from paraprofessionals or special educators, peers may be reluctant to initiate conversations, perceive that their interactions must always be relayed through an adult, or assume that their classmates with disabilities are not capable of communicating effectively on their own. At the same time, students with ASDs may be more likely to turn first to adults rather than to their peers for needed academic, emotional, or instrumental support. Peer-mediated intervention arrangements communicate expectations that students with and without disabilities should learn from and interact with one another, and they provide a supportive context for students to spend time together. Such approaches also more closely reflect the typical avenues through which most students typically participate in classroom activities—alongside their peers and with their support.

Third, some students may initially be hesitant to initiate or maintain interactions with a classmate who engages in stereotypical behavior, communicates in unconventional ways, or participates somewhat differently in typical class activities. The information and training peers receive—along with the ongoing coaching and support provided by educators and paraprofessionals—can enable them to feel confident in their interactions with and capacity to support their classmates with ASDs.

EMPIRICAL BASIS

Our review of the literature yielded 29 empirical studies that 1) involved at least one elementary, middle, or high school student with an ASD; 2) evaluated the efficacy of ongoing peer-mediated support interventions; and 3) targeted social interactions with same-age peers without disabilities as a primary intervention outcome. To facilitate discussion of the efficacy of peer-mediated support interventions, we have organized these studies based upon whether the peer-delivered support primarily focused on involving peers in providing *social supports* (see Table 10.1) or *academic supports* (see Table 10.2), as well as the general approach to that support. We note, however, that most studies report evaluations of multicomponent intervention packages in which peer-mediated supports are combined with other intervention elements, such as social, self-management, or communication skills instruction for students with ASDs; adult facilitation efforts; or additional environmental arrangements. Therefore, isolating the unique contributions of peer-mediated support components to improvements in social and communication outcomes remains particularly difficult.

Participating Students

Although peer-mediated support interventions were designed broadly for students with developmental disabilities, the efficacy of these strategies has been evaluated in more than 29 published empirical studies involving at least 63 school-age children and youth with ASDs (see Tables 10.1 and 10.2). The vast majority (94%) of the students in these studies are described as having autistic disorder, with relatively few studies including students with Asperger syndrome (Hunt, Farron-Davis, Wrenn, Hirose-Hatae, & Goetz, 1997; Owen-DeSchryver, Carr, Cale, & Blakeley-Smith, 2008) or Rett's syndrome (Shukla, Kennedy, & Cushing, 1998, 1999). Rarely did the studies include reports of diagnostic information obtained using standardized assessment tools (i.e., Autism Behavior Checklist, Krug, Arick, & Almond, 1980; Autism Diagnostic Observation Schedule, Lord, Rutter, DiLavore, & Risi, 1999; Childhood Autism Rating Scale, Schopler, Reichler, & Renner, 1988; PsychoEducation Profile Revised, Schopler, Reichler, Dashford, Lansing, & Marcus, 1990). Given that impairments in social interaction are a defining characteristic of students with ASDs, this application of peer-mediated support interventions is not surprising.

Although peer-mediated support interventions appear to hold promise for a wide range of students, the empirical studies included in Tables 10.1 and 10.2, which describe these interventions, offer little consistency regarding the specific communication, language, and behavior profiles of participating students (cf., Carter & Hughes, 2005; Goldstein, 2002). Narrative descriptions or standardized assessments (i.e., Arizona Articulation Proficiency Scale, Fudala & Reynolds, 2000;

Table 10.1. Social-related peer-mediated support studies for children with autism spectrum disorders (ASDs)

Study authors (Year)	Participants with ASDs[a]/setting	Intervention(s)/treatment integrity/experimental design	Primary social-related outcomes
Brady, Shores, McEvoy, Ellis, and Fox (1987)	2 of 2 students 2 male *Elementary school*	Peer trainers taught to use initiation strategies to engage participants in interactions No treatment integrity reported *Multiple baseline across peer trainers*	More frequent social interactions with peer trainers (2/2) and nontraining peers (1/2); increase in participant responses to peer initiations (2/2); increase in duration of interactions with peers (2/2)
Garrison-Harrell, Kamps, and Kravits (1997)	3 of 3 students 1 female, 2 male *Elementary school*	Peer networks plus augmentative communication and social skills training for participants No treatment integrity reported *Multiple probe design across settings, nested within a multiple baseline across participants*	Increased frequency and duration of peer interactions (3/3); increased total duration of using communication boards during interactions for participants and network peers (2/3)
Gonzalez-Lopez and Kamps (1997)	2 of 4 students 1 female, 1 male *Elementary school*	Treatment A: Students participated in playgroups without instructions (baseline) Treatment B: Social skills training for participants and peers in playgroups Treatment C: Reinforcement plus Treatment B High treatment integrity reported *Reversal design (ABCAC)*	Increased total duration time of peer interactions in Treatment B (1/2) and Treatment C (2/2); increased mean frequency of peer interactions in Treatment B (1/2) and Treatment C (2/2)
Haring and Breen (1992)	1 of 2 students 1 male *Middle school*	Peer networks plus self-monitoring training for participant No treatment integrity reported *Multiple baseline across participants*	Increased number of social interactions with network peers (1/1); increased appropriate responding (1/1)
Harper, Symon, and Frea (2008)	2 of 2 students 2 male *Elementary school*	Peer-delivered Pivotal Response Training for participants High treatment integrity reported *Concurrent multiple baseline across participants*	Increased use of gaining peer attention (1/1) and initiations to play (1/1)[b]; increased number of turn-taking exchanges (2/2)
Hunt, Farron-Davis, Wrenn, Hirose-Hatae, and Goetz (1997)	1 of 3 students 1 male *Elementary school*	Individualized intervention packages: peer training and class meetings; augmentative communication training for participants and the use of interactive media; adult facilitation High treatment integrity reported *Multiple baseline across participants*	Increased reciprocal interactions with peers and participant-initiated interactions (1/1); increased interactions with comments to and from peers (1/1)
Hunt, Staub, Alwell, and Goetz (1994)	1 of 3 students 1 male *Elementary school*	Treatment A: Cooperative learning groups (baseline) Treatment B: Peers delivered cues and feedback to facilitate participants' responses in Treatment A High treatment integrity reported *Reversal design (ABAB)*	Increased correct prompted communication responses (1/1); increased independent communication responses (1/1)

Study	Participants	Intervention/Design	Outcomes
Kamps et al. (1992)	3 of 3 students 3 male *Elementary school*	Social skills training for participants and peers in playgroups No treatment integrity reported *Multiple baseline across participants*	More frequent and longer social interactions (3/3); increased duration of social interactions (3/3); increased initiations and responses from participants (3/3) and peers (2/3)
Kamps, Potucek, Lopez, Kravits, and Kemmerer (1997)	2 of 3 students 2 male *Elementary school*	Peer networks established across settings; peers received training to provide academic and social support to participants High treatment integrity reported *Multiple probe design across settings*	Increased total duration of social interactions with peers (2/2)
Loftin, Odom, and Lantz (2008)	3 of 3 students 3 male *Elementary school*	Peer response training plus social initiation and self-monitoring training for students High treatment integrity reported *Multiple baseline across participants*	More social initiations from participants (3/3); increased time engaging in social interactions with peers (3/3)
Owen-DeSchryver, Carr, Cale, and Blakeley-Smith (2008)	3 of 3 students 3 male *Elementary school*	Peers received friendship awareness training and taught strategies to interact with participants No treatment integrity reported *Multiple baseline across participants*	More initiations and responses from peers (3/3); more responses to peers' initiations (3/3); more initiations toward peers (2/3)
Sasso and Rude (1987)	X of 8 students Gender not specified *Elementary school*	Treatment A: Students received no instructions (baseline) Treatment B: Peer initiation training for high-status peers Treatment C: Peer initiation training for low-status peers No treatment integrity reported *Reversal design (ABAC, ACAB)*	More positive social initiations and responses from untrained peers and participants in Treatment B condition[c]
Schleien, Heyne, and Berken (1988)	5 of 6 students 5 male *Elementary school*	Special friends in inclusive physical education program No treatment integrity reported *Group design comparison by age level (i.e., younger vs. older)*	Decreased inappropriate play behaviors for the younger group (2/2)[c]; no changes for the older group (3/3)
Weiner (2005)	1 of 3 students 1 male *Elementary school*	Peers taught to request repair and reinforce participants' responses No treatment integrity reported *Multiple baseline across participants, multiple probes across peers*	Less unintelligible responses and more repair responses to peer's requests (1/1); more conversational turns by participant and peer (1/1)

[a]Number of students with ASDs (when available) out of the total study participants.

[b]Participants had different social outcomes.

[c]Results for participants with autism not disaggregated from group findings.

Table 10.2. Academic peer-mediated support studies for children with autism spectrum disorders (ASDs)

Study authors (Year)	Participants with ASDs[a]/setting	Intervention(s)/treatment integrity/experimental design	Results for primary social-related outcomes
Carter, Cushing, Clark, and Kennedy (2005)	2 of 3 students 1 female, 1 male *Middle school*	Treatment A: Peer supports comprised of 1 peer Treatment B: Peer supports comprised of 2 peers No treatment integrity reported *Reversal design (ABAB, BABA)*	More frequent social interactions with peer supports when working with two peers (2/2); no differences in overall quality of interaction or interaction frequency with other classmates (2/2)
Cole, Vandercook, and Rynders (1987)	2 of 53 students Gender not specified *Elementary school*	Treatment 1: Special friends program Treatment 2: Peer tutors program No treatment integrity reported *Group design comparison by program and age level (i.e., same-age vs. cross-age dyads)*	More balanced positive affect when peers were only 0 to 5 years older than participants[b]; peers who were much older or younger than participants offered toys more than peers who were closer in age to participants[b]
Cole, Vandercook, and Rynders (1988)	2 of 53 students Gender not specified *Elementary school*	Treatment 1: Special friends program Treatment 2: Peer tutors program No treatment integrity reported *Group design comparison by program*	Peers in Treatment 2 exhibited more assisting/teaching than participants and peers in Treatment 1[b]; peers in Treatment 1 exhibited more toy requesting than participants[b]
Dugan et al. (1995)	2 of 2 students 1 female, 1 male *Elementary school*	Treatment A: Teacher lecture (baseline) Treatment B: Cooperative learning groups No treatment integrity reported *Reversal design (ABAB)*	Increased total duration of student interaction for participants and peers (2/2)
Eichinger (1990)	2 of 8 students 2 male *Elementary school*	Treatment A: Participants paired with peers to work on classroom jobs (baseline) Treatment B: Dyads worked individually and received individual feedback during activities Treatment C: Dyads worked cooperatively No treatment integrity reported *Reversal design (ABAB, ACAC)*	Participants in Treatment C had more positive affect and more frequent cooperative plays than participants in Treatment B[b]; peers in Treatment C made more comments to participants than peers in Treatment B[b]; participants in Treatment B had more neutral affect and less vocalizations than participants in Treatment C[b]
Hunt, Soto, Maier, and Doering (2003)	1 of 6 students 1 male *Elementary school*	Unified plans of support with individualized curricular modifications and interaction supports High treatment integrity reported *Multiple baseline across participants*	Increased reciprocal interactions with peers (1/1)
Johnson, Johnson, DeWeerdt, Lyons, and Zaidman (1983)	1 of 9 students Gender not specified *Middle school*	Treatment 1: Cooperative learning condition Treatment 2: Individualistic learning condition High treatment integrity reported but not quantified *Group design comparison by condition*	More task and management social interactions initiated by participants and peers in Treatment 1[b]; peers initiated more task and social interactions toward participants than toward other peers in Treatment 1[b]
Kamps, Barbetta, Leonard, and Delquadri (1994)	3 of 3 students 3 male *Elementary school*	Classwide peer tutoring No treatment integrity reported *Multiple baseline across participants with a reversal*	Increased mean duration of social interactions with peers (3/3)
Kamps, Leonard, Potucek, and Garrison-Harrell (1995; study 1)	1 of 1 student 1 male *Elementary school*	Treatment A: Teacher lecture (baseline) Treatment B: Cooperative learning groups Treatment C: Social skill lessons plus Treatment B No treatment integrity reported *Reversal design (ABAC*	Increased total duration of social interactions with peers in Treatment B and Treatment C (1/1); no differences in frequency of interaction (1/1)

Study	Participants	Design/Treatment	Findings
Kamps, Leonard, Potucek, and Garrison-Harrell (1995; study 2)	2 of 2 students 2 female *Elementary school*	Treatment A: Teacher lecture (baseline) Treatment B: Cooperative learning groups No treatment integrity reported *Reversal design (ABAB)*	Increased total duration of social interactions with peers (2/2)
Kamps et al. (2002; study 1)	4 of 5 students 2 female, 2 male *Elementary school*	Treatment A: Existing practices (baseline) Treatment B: Cooperative learning groups Treatment C: Social skills groups No treatment integrity reported *Reversal design (ABAB, ACAC)*	More frequent social interactions and increased total duration of interactions with peers in Treatment B (2/2) and Treatment C (2/2)
Putnam, Rynders, Johnson, and Johnson (1989)	2 of 16 students Gender not specified *Elementary school*	Treatment 1: Group learning activities with collaborative skill instructions Treatment 2: Group learning activities without collaborative skill instructions No treatment integrity reported *Group design comparison by condition*	Peers in Treatment 1 produced more social behaviors toward participants[c]; no differences in participants' social behaviors[c]
Sasso, Mitchell, and Struthers (1986)	4 of 4 students 4 male *Elementary school*	Treatment A: Free play with no instructions (baseline) Treatment B: Peer tutoring Treatment C: Interaction activities with peer training No treatment integrity reported *Reversal design (ABAC, ACAB)*	Peer initiated more cooperative interactions in Treatment C (3/4) and more instructional interactions in Treatment B (2/4)
Sasso, Mundschenk, Melloy, and Casey (1998; study 2)	3 of 3 students 1 female, 2 male *Elementary school*	Peer initiation training for high-status peers (HH), low-status peers (LL), and high- and low-status peers (HL) in triad arrangement No treatment integrity reported *Multiple baseline across participants with embedded reversal design*	More peer initiations in LL (3/3); more peer responses in HH (3/3); more initiations to nontraining peers in HH (2/3) and to low-status peers in HL (2/3); increased sustained interactions across triad arrangements (3/3)
Shukla, Kennedy, and Cushing (1998)	1 of 3 students 1 female *Middle school*	Treatment A: Adult support arrangements (baseline) Treatment B: Peer support arrangements Treatment C: Peers received adult supervision No treatment integrity reported *Reversal design (ACABACAB)*	More frequent social interactions with peer support in Treatment B (1/1); more social interactions with non-training peers in Treatment C (1/1)
Shukla et al. (1999)	1 of 3 students 1 female *Middle school*	Treatment A: Adult support arrangements (baseline) Treatment B: Peer support arrangements No treatment integrity reported *Reversal design (ABABAB [social studies], BABAB [math])*	More frequent and increased duration of social interactions with peer supports and untrained peers in Treatment B (1/1); more frequent social support behaviors with peers in Treatment B

[a]Number of students with ASDs (when available) out of the total study participants.

[b]Results for participants with autism not disaggregated from group findings.

[c]Participants had different social outcomes.

Topeka Association for Retarded Citizens assessment system, Sailor & Mix, 1975) of communication level were provided for 91% of participants, of whom 39 were verbal, 8 were nonverbal, and 10 were not characterized in terms of verbal abilities. Students who communicated verbally were generally reported to use single words, short phrases, or echolalic words. Many also relied on either unaided (e.g., adapted signs, gestures) or aided (e.g., electronic devices, picture books) communication modes to supplement—or provide alternatives to—speech. Few studies have reported findings from intelligence tests (e.g., Leiter International Performance Scale, Leiter, 1969; PsychoEducational Profile Revised, Schopler et al., 1990; Stanford-Binet Intelligence Scales, Thorndike, Hagen, & Sattler, 1986; Wechsler Intelligence Scale for Children, Wechsler, 1991) and adaptive behavior assessments (e.g., Vineland Adaptive Behavior Scales, Sparrow, Balla, & Cicchetti, 1984). However, many of the participating students were served under the secondary special education category of intellectual disability or were described broadly as having severe disabilities. Finally, 51% of participating students were reported to engage in stereotypical behaviors (e.g., rocking, spinning) and/or challenging behaviors (e.g., aggression, noncompliance, tantrums). Collectively, these studies suggest the appropriateness of peer-mediated support interventions for students with complex communication challenges and a range of support needs.

Peer-Mediated Social Supports

Most peer-mediated support interventions have emphasized the arrangement of peer-delivered social supports through 1) **peer interaction training** or 2) **peer network strategies** (see Figure 10.1).

Peer Interaction Training   Peer-related issues frequently are cited as potential barriers to social interaction and relationships for students with developmental disabilities (Siperstein, Norins, & Mohler, 2007). Such barriers highlight the importance of providing peers with targeted information or strategy instruction to foster interaction with students with disabilities. For example, students may perceive themselves as lacking the knowledge and skills needed to interact socially with their classmates with ASDs. Others may initially feel hesitant or uncertain about initiating and maintaining conversations with their classmates without guidance from educators. Still others may hold negative attitudes or inaccurate stereotypes about students with ASDs (Campbell, Ferguson, Herzinger, Jackson, & Marino, 2005). Peer interaction training is the most common peer-mediated approach to promoting social interaction represented in the empirical literature. Moreover, peer interaction training is often an important element of other multicomponent intervention approaches that are described in this chapter (e.g., Garrison-Harrell, Kamps, & Kravits, 1997; Haring & Breen, 1992; Shukla et al., 1998, 1999).

Hunt, Staub, Alwell, and Goetz (1994) conducted a series of single-case design studies examining the efficacy of intervention packages involving peer interaction training components. Hunt and colleagues taught second graders without disabilities to cue, prompt, and reinforce their partner with an ASD to communicate during cooperative learning groups. Although participating students were members of the inclusive class, the specific criteria used to select peers were not specified. The researchers reminded the peers of their support roles during a brief meeting prior to each math session (meeting duration was not specified) and provided ongoing

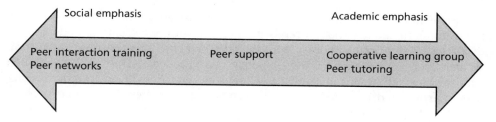

Examples of social-related supports

Prompting student to interact with other classmates

Encouraging other classmates to interact with student

Making introductions to others

Explicitly teaching specific social-related skills

Prompting use of an aided communication device

Reinforcing communication attempts

Providing emotional support or giving advice

Helping student self-manage his or her own behavior

Modeling appropriate social skills

Examples of academic-related supports

Helping check the accuracy of assignments

Sharing or assisting in taking notes

Sharing class materials other than notes

Paraphrasing lectures or class discussions

Prompting to answer a question or idea

Explaining a key concept or how to solve a problem

Writing down answers given orally or using augmentative and alternative communication

Providing instruction on completing tasks

Reviewing class content to ensure understanding

Helping student participate in group activity

Reading aloud a section of a book or assignment

Making simple modifications to tasks

Redirecting student when he or she is off-task

Helping student keep organized

Figure 10.1.   Peer-mediated social supports.

feedback during the class, but gradually faded their involvement over time. Among the children with ASDs, the intervention produced higher rates of prompted and independent communication responses as well as generalized effects within a new cooperative learning group. Hunt and colleagues (1997) evaluated the efficacy of individualized support packages that involved establishing partner systems, arranging interactive activities, developing conversation books, and providing training in peer interaction. All peers were classmates of the student with an ASD, but no other selection criteria were described. The peer interaction training component included weekly classwide diversity awareness activities and explicit instruction to partners without disabilities on using the conversation book and a turn-taking structure with their classmate with Asperger syndrome. The conversation book training provided to the student with Asperger syndrome lasted 8 to 15 sessions, but the duration of other intervention elements were not reported. Increases in initiations, reciprocal interactions, and communication book use—as well as decreases in time spent alone—were documented within a multiple-baseline design.

Some interventions have been shown to increase social interactions by providing training to peers without directly intervening with participating students with
disabilities (e.g., Brady, Shores, McEvoy, Ellis, & Fox, 1987; Sasso & Rude, 1987;
Weiner, 2005). For example, Owen-DeSchryver and colleagues (2008) focused their
training on small groups of elementary-age peers. In three 30- to 45-min sessions,
peers participated in friendship awareness activities, received information about
the strengths and preferences of focus students, and learned strategies to interact with the focus students. Participating peers were selected on the basis of their
satisfactory attendance records and capacity to follow instructions. Participating
students with ASDs evidenced higher rates of social initiations and responses after
peer training was introduced within a multiple-baseline design. The intervention
also demonstrated effects with untrained peers, who subsequently increased their
initiations toward students with ASDs. Harper, Symon, and Frea (2008) provided
seven 20-min training sessions to peers of participants with ASDs during recess
activities. Peers were classmates of the student who had regular attendance, were
proficient in English, had excellent social and communication skills, and had a history of volunteering. The researchers taught third graders without disabilities to
use naturalistic social facilitation strategies (i.e., gaining attention, varying activities, narrating play, reinforcing attempts, turn taking) to promote social interaction
with two schoolmates with ASDs. Both participating students with ASDs substantially increased their contact and social initiations with peers and maintained their
performance after prompts to peers were withdrawn.

In other studies, peer interaction training has been accompanied by the provision of social-related skill instruction to students with ASDs (e.g., Gonzalez-Lopez
& Kamps, 1997; Schleien, Heyne, & Berken, 1988). For example, in one 5- to 10-min
session, Loftin, Odom, and Lantz (2008) taught elementary-age peers to gain the
attention of the classmates with ASDs and to respond positively during lunch to
their social initiations. Peers were selected based on the preference of students with
ASDs as well as their enthusiasm to help other classmates and work with adults.
Three participants with ASDs also received individualized social interaction and
self-monitoring instruction (the length of training was not specified). All of the
three students with ASDs demonstrated increased social initiations toward peers,
and two of them maintained their gains following the intervention. Kamps and colleagues (1992) simultaneously provided training to first-grade students with and
without autism that addressed targeted social skills (e.g., initiating and maintaining
conversations, exchanging compliments, turn taking, helping behaviors) drawn from
published curricula. Criteria used to select peers were not reported. Training for
each social skill spanned eight to twelve 10-min sessions. All of these interventions
produced substantial improvements in social interaction outcomes for participating
students immediately following the intervention and during 1-month follow-ups.

Peer Network Strategies   Peer network interventions are designed to pro-
mote social and communication outcomes within the classroom and across the
school day by establishing structured social groups around a focus student with disabilities. Establishing these interventions typically involves 1) determining the potential focus student's interest in participating and soliciting suggestions regarding
the composition of the network; 2) inviting a small group of four to six peers without disabilities to an initial meeting to organize the network; 3) providing students

with information about the purpose of the peer network and background about the focus student (e.g., interests, hobbies, talents, preferences, involvement in school activities); 4) arranging when and where network members will spend time with and support the focus student; and 5) meeting regularly to share ideas for providing social support, increasing the student's involvement in school activities, and problem-solving any challenges that may arise. Although educators and/or paraprofessionals remain involved in initiating and maintaining the intervention, their roles typically become more facilitative and indirect over time.

Garrison-Harrell and colleagues (1997) examined the effects of peer network strategies within multicomponent intervention strategies for three elementary students with ASDs. Five peers without disabilities were selected to compose each student's network on the basis of their high social status (as evaluated by peer nomination measures) and the teacher's judgment of direction following, school attendance, and age-appropriate social and language skills. These peers received training in the use of **augmentative and alternative communication systems** and relevant social skills (e.g., initiating, responding, turn taking, sharing) during eight 30-min training sessions. Each student with an ASD also received individual training on the use of the communication system within eighteen to twenty-one 20-min sessions. Interaction opportunities among students with disabilities and their network members were arranged across at least three different school activities (e.g., reading, language arts, lunch, computers, recess, library). Introduction of the peer network intervention within a multiple-baseline design was associated with substantial increases in the frequency and duration of social interactions, functional verbal behavior, and augmentative communication system use. No generalization data were measured or reported.

Kamps, Potucek, Lopez, Kravits, and Kemmerer (1997) used a multiple-probe design to evaluate the efficacy of peer network intervention packages for elementary students with ASDs across up to six settings. Peer network members were selected on the basis of their social skills and the absence of a negative history with the participating students with ASDs. In addition to training peers without disabilities and scheduling regular interaction activities (i.e., three to four times per week with a minimum of 10 min per activity), adults provided verbal feedback and visual reinforcement to peers at the end of each interactive activity. Participating students with disabilities demonstrated substantial increases in their duration of peer interaction across all settings, with some generalization noted for two students. In both of these studies, social and communication skills instruction was provided concurrently to participating students with disabilities.

Haring and Breen (1992) employed a multiple-baseline design to examine the efficacy of peer networks at increasing the social interactions of two students with moderate to severe disabilities, one of whom had both an ASD and repetitive and noncompliant behaviors. Unlike studies by Kamps and colleagues, these interventions focused exclusively on noninstructional contexts beyond the classroom (e.g., hallways, cafeteria, before and after school). A peer was selected as a network member if he or she had some prior contact with the student with an ASD (e.g., sharing interests, attending the same classes) or the student with an ASD expressed interest toward the peer. The network consisted of recruitment of four to five peers without disabilities, weekly 30-min planning meetings with adult facilitation and feedback, intentional scheduling of interactions, teacher-delivered social skills training for the student with an ASD (two 15-min sessions per week), and peer-delivered reinforcement of the focus students' social behavior. Baseline observations were conducted prior to establishing peer networks. The introduction of the peer network intervention was associated with substantial increases in the frequency of social interactions, appropriate responding, and contact with peers. The effects were maintained during 1- and 2-month follow-ups. The student with disabilities, however, was also taught to self-manage appropriate social responding using a wrist counter. To date, peer network interventions have not been evaluated at the high school level.

Peer-Mediated Academic Supports

Peer-mediated support interventions have also been designed to enhance academic performance and support access to the general curriculum for students with ASDs (see Figure 10.1). **Peer tutoring, cooperative learning groups,** and **peer support arrangements** represent the most widely known variations of these intervention approaches. Although supporting academic engagement and promoting class participation often comprise the central focus of these interventions, the sustained opportunities students have to work together and the inclusion of social facilitation components appear to be associated with collateral improvements in social interaction outcomes.

Peer Tutoring Peer tutoring is a widely used instructional arrangement designed to improve the academic performance of students with and without disabilities (Maheady, Harper, & Mallette, 2001). Within these interventions, peers serve as instructional agents for their classmates by providing direct academic support to promote skill development in targeted domains. Although primarily implemented to increase time spent engaged with peers and academic skill acquisition, the social interaction outcomes associated with these interventions have also been the focus of several studies.

Kamps, Barbetta, Leonard, and Delquadri (1994) used a multiple-baseline design to evaluate the efficacy of classwide peer tutoring on the academic performance and social interactions of students with ASDs enrolled in inclusive second- and third-grade classrooms. Within this approach, peer tutoring was implemented on a classwide basis and involved 1) assigning tutor-learner pairs each week; 2) alternating tutor-learner roles within each tutoring session; 3) having tutors provide reinforcement and corrective feedback as learners read passages orally; and 4) providing individual students and groups with feedback and reinforcement on their performance. All of the peers were enrolled in the same classes with the students with ASDs who participated in the study; therefore, no specific criteria were used to include or exclude peers. Students received training in these approaches over three 45-min sessions before working together three to four times per week during 25–30 min tutoring sessions. In addition to improving reading fluency, the intervention produced longer and more frequent social interactions among students with and without autism during free-time activities immediately following the peer tutoring sessions. No maintenance or generalization data were reported.

Cole, Vandercook, and Rynders (1987, 1988) compared the interactions among 106 elementary students with and without severe disabilities occurring within peer tutoring or special friends programs. Dyads comprised of students with and without disabilities were randomly assigned to each program by classroom. No criteria were described for selecting peers. A researcher provided training to peers without disabilities during eight meetings (the length of the meetings was not specified). Peer tutoring consisted of teaching peers without disabilities basic instructional strategies (e.g., prompting, contingent reinforcement), communication skills, and problem-solving techniques. Training for peers without disabilities participating in the special friends program addressed disability-specific information, communication and play skills, and discussion of inclusion and friendship. In addition, peers joined their partners with disabilities for two to four 15-min interaction sessions per week for 8 weeks, in which an educator provided reinforcement contingent on either instructional or friendship behaviors, depending on the program. Interactions among students with and without disabilities within peer tutoring programs were less reciprocal and rated as more hierarchical than those occurring within special friends programs. No generalization data were reported. Similarly, Sasso, Mitchell, and Struthers (1986) used a single-case reversal design to document differences in the nature of peer interactions of four students with ASDs. Researchers recruited similar-age peers who had minimal prior contacts with students with disabilities. Depending on whether interaction activities were tutorial or noninstructional, peers without disabilities participated in two 30-min sessions to receive training related to their different roles. Tutorial activities were associated with lower occurrences of interaction among elementary students with and without autism, and any interactions tended to be primarily instructional. No maintenance or generalization data were reported.

Cooperative Learning Groups   Use of cooperative learning groups typically involves dividing classes into small groups of students, establishing common learning goals toward which each group works collaboratively, delineating the specific roles each student will assume within the group (e.g., checker, facilitator, recorder, timekeeper), and promoting group accountability by requiring all students to work together to accomplish their goals. Such arrangements establish interdependent contingencies that reward collaborative work, provide frequent interaction opportunities, and create a socially supportive environment for all students. Although classroom teachers provide instruction for the entire class, peers exchange direct and indirect support to other members of their group when working together.

Johnson and colleagues used group experimental designs to examine the efficacy of cooperative learning groups in elementary (Putnam, Rynders, Johnson, & Johnson, 1989) and middle school (Johnson, Johnson, DeWeerdt, Lyons, & Zaidman, 1983) science classes. Within the cooperative condition (ten 45 to 55-min sessions), students with developmental disabilities were paired with two or three classmates without disabilities and given instruction in collaborative skills (e.g., sharing materials and ideas, encouraging participation, checking understanding); teacher reinforcement was contingent on group performance. In neither study did the authors describe the criteria used to select students with disabilities for membership in the groups. Within the comparison conditions, students worked alone, with reinforcement based on individual performance (Johnson et al., 1983), or in small groups, with reinforcement based on task performance (Putnam et al., 1989). In both studies, students with disabilities working in cooperative learning groups received significantly higher rates of social initiations (i.e., orienting, commenting) from their peers without disabilities. Neither study described generalization effects

of the intervention. Eichinger (1990) used a single-case reversal design to compare
the nature of elementary students' social interactions within cooperative learning
groups and individualistic conditions. Peers were randomly chosen from a group of
volunteering students. Twice a week, each student with disabilities participated in
a 30-min recess session with a peer without disabilities. Overall, during cooperative
learning groups (versus when working alone), students with disabilities evidenced
a significantly higher percentage of intervals of positive affect and cooperative play,
as well as fewer intervals without vocalizations. However, these social interactions
did not generalize to free-play sessions, even though peers without disabilities in the
cooperative condition made more comments toward students with disabilities.

Kamps and colleagues used single-case reversal designs to compare the efficacy of cooperative learning groups versus traditional teacher-led instruction for
students with ASDs enrolled in either an inclusive fourth-grade social studies class
(Dugan et al., 1995; Kamps et al., 2002) or an inclusive third-grade reading class
(Kamps, Leonard, Potucek, & Garrison-Harrell, 1995). No criteria were reported
for selecting group members. Group members were assigned roles within the team,
given training on cooperative learning procedures and group social skills (20 to
25 min), and received reinforcement from educators and paraprofessionals for
implementing these procedures. In addition to demonstrating increased academic
engagement and other performance gains, all students with ASDs evidenced substantial increases in the frequency and duration of initiations and responses to
their peers without disabilities within cooperative learning groups. Kamps and colleagues (2002) further demonstrated that although students' peer interactions generalized to other school settings, these interactions were more likely to occur with
peers without disabilities who had previously participated in structured interaction
programs (e.g., peer tutoring, special friends) involving students with disabilities.
Although not specifically analyzed, prior familiarity may play a key role in these
interventions.

Peer Support Arrangements   Peer support arrangements involve equipping one or two peers from within the same classroom to provide academic *and*
social support to students with severe disabilities in inclusive classrooms (Carter
& Kennedy, 2006). Peer supports are taught by educators or paraprofessionals to
support the individualized goals of students related to academics (e.g., providing
feedback on performance, highlighting key concepts, collaborating on assignments,
reviewing course content), class participation (e.g., encouraging contributions,
sharing class materials, modeling self-management strategies), communication
(e.g., modeling relevant social skills, encouraging use of an augmentative and alternative communication (AAC) system, reinforcing communication attempts),
and/or social interaction (e.g., conversing about shared interests, making introductions to classmates). After being oriented to their roles, students receive needed
information and guidance from paraprofessionals or educators as they support their
classmate with disabilities. This approach is distinguished from peer tutoring by its
comparable emphasis on promoting both academic and social participation and differs from cooperative learning group interventions in the individualized nature of
support provided by peers and the smaller number of participating peers.

Shukla and colleagues (1998, 1999) used single-case withdrawal designs to
compare the efficacy of individually assigned adult support versus adult support that

was augmented by peer support on the social interactions of students with severe disabilities that were enrolled in inclusive middle school classrooms (e.g., English, math, social studies, related arts, vocational). In Shukla and colleagues' 1998 study, peers were recruited if they performed at or below a "C" grade level. No selection criteria for peers were specified by Shukla and colleagues in the 1999 study. During baseline conditions, paraprofessionals or special educators provided one-to-one support (e.g., systematic instruction, adapting activities, implementing behavior supports) while seated directly next to the focus students. Peer support arrangements were systematically introduced and withdrawn for participating students throughout the semester. During the peer support condition, peers without disabilities received one to three class periods of training as well as ongoing feedback from special educators or paraprofessionals following the training. The social interactions of students with ASDs were longer and more frequent when they received direct support from peers rather than exclusively from adults. Moreover, students with disabilities received a greater variety of social support behaviors (i.e., greetings, information, access to others, material aid, emotional support, companionship) when working with their classmates. In Shukla and colleagues' 1999 study, a student with an ASD maintained her performance one month later. Hunt and colleagues (2003) also established peer support arrangements when implementing Unified Plans of Support for elementary students with severe disabilities during reading, writing, and math. The researchers did not describe the criteria used to select participating peers without disabilities. For each student, collaborative planning teams detailed the adult- and peer-delivered supports that would be established throughout the school day. In addition to increasing the engagement of students with disabilities in ongoing classroom activities, this intervention resulted in those students' increased initiations and reciprocal interactions with peers. No generalization data were reported.

Research suggests that the configurations of peer support arrangements may differentially affect the social outcomes experienced by participating students without disabilities. Carter, Cushing, Clark, and Kennedy (2005) used a single-case withdrawal design to examine the effects of varying the number of peers participating in these intervention approaches within inclusive core academic classrooms (e.g., English, science). A peer was selected if he or she was enrolled in the same class and was perceived by the classroom teacher as competent in providing support to a classmate with severe disabilities. Peers without disabilities received initial training for 2 to 4 days, as well as subsequent monitoring and feedback from special educators or paraprofessionals. Substantially higher levels of social interaction among students with and without disabilities were evident when two versus one peer supported middle and high school students with disabilities. Across conditions, differences were not evident in the quality of students' interactions or the percentage of intervals during which students interacted with other classmates not directly involved in the intervention. No maintenance or generalization data were reported. This finding is consistent with a study by Sasso, Mundschenk, Melloy, and Casey (1998) in which elementary students with ASDs tended to engage in higher rates of social interaction within dyadic versus triadic peer group arrangements. Peers with disabilities, who were selected on the basis of their ages and their high or low social status, received a 1-hr initiation training implemented by the special educator. The social interactions among students with ASDs and untrained peers remained unchanged following the intervention.

Design Features

Experimental Designs   Given the low incidence of autism and intellectual disability, as well as the heterogeneity among students served under this disability category, it is not surprising that the majority of studies ($n = 24$, 83%) utilized single-case research designs to evaluate intervention efficacy. Among these, 13 studies employed variants of the multiple-baseline design (e.g., multiple probe) and 11 employed variants of withdrawal/reversal designs. Because most studies included heterogeneous samples comprised of both students with and without autism, individual single-case studies often included fewer than three replications of intervention effects for participants with ASDs, and group designs rarely disaggregated results for students with and without autism. The literature also includes relatively few of the following: 1) comparative studies examining which of these intervention approaches is more effective (e.g., Cole et al., 1987, 1988; Sasso et al., 1986) or 2) parametric and component analyses examining how intervention variations influence outcomes (e.g., Carter et al., 2005; Sasso et al., 1998). At present, practitioners have little guidance upon which to draw when they want to know which intervention approach is likely to prove most effective for particular outcomes and students.

Social-Related Intervention Outcomes   Discrete measures of peer interaction (e.g., initiations, responses, social interactions, reciprocity/reciprocal interactions) represented the primary social and communication outcomes in these studies. Qualitative aspects of conversational exchange—such as affect, conversational topics, appropriateness, interaction quality, and social support behaviors—were explored less often (e.g., Carter, Sisco, Melekoglu, & Kurkowski, 2007; Shukla et al., 1999), and such studies provided few insights into how the nature of students' interactions with their peers might change as a result of these strategies. Moreover, few studies documented the collateral effects on students' language and communication skill acquisition, stereotypical behaviors, or social status.

Intervention Fidelity   Fewer than one third of the studies ($n = 9$) reported that intervention fidelity data were collected, and only six studies provided numerical information about the extent to which the intervention was implemented as intended. Furthermore, none of these studies examined how variations in fidelity may influence intervention efficacy. When fidelity data were reported, high levels of treatment integrity were documented. However, it should be noted that almost all of these studies were implemented directly by researchers, so that the potential for unintended bias is high. The extent to which these strategies retain their effectiveness when researchers are less directly involved in their implementation has rarely been examined (cf., Carter et al., 2007). Nonetheless, the tractability of these strategies and feedback from participating educators suggest they are readily transferable to everyday school settings.

Generalization   The extent to which intervention effects were maintained over time was assessed in less than one quarter of the studies ($n = 7$). Within these studies, intervention effects generally were maintained at or above intervention levels for up to 2 months postintervention, indicating that these interventions have short-term impact. The degree to which improvements in social and communication outcomes generalized to additional settings or peers other than those represented in the intervention condition was assessed in only nine studies. Deliberate efforts to promote generalization (e.g., using multiple exemplars, programming common stimuli across settings and peers) may be essential to obtaining broader outcomes.

Social Validity Explicit evidence of the social validity of these interventions was provided in fewer than one third of the studies ($n = 9$). When some indicator of social validity was offered, the goals of these interventions were considered important and the social outcomes considered desirable. Less attention was given in these studies to the tractability of the intervention procedures. However, surveys of general educators, special educators, paraprofessionals, and other school staff suggest that peer-mediated support intervention approaches are perceived to be effective at increasing interaction among students with and without disabilities and fairly feasible to implement given resources available to educators (Carter & Pesko, 2008; Odom, McConnell, & Chandler, 1994). Similarly, interviews of children and youth without disabilities who might be recruited as peers consistently affirm their willingness to participate and their perception that they have much to gain from their involvement in these interventions (Copeland et al., 2004; Hughes et al., 2001; Kamps et al., 1998).

PRACTICAL REQUIREMENTS

Researchers studying the adoption of educational interventions have cautioned that even effective practices are unlikely to be adopted and implemented with fidelity if they do not align with everyday instructional practices or are simply too difficult to implement (Boardman, Argüelles, Vaughn, Hughes, & Klingner, 2005; Snell, 2003). Fortunately, research addressing the implementation of peer-mediated support interventions with students with developmental disabilities suggests that educators value peer-mediated strategies and consider them feasible. Although the implementation requirements vary somewhat depending on the type and configuration of peer-mediated supports being utilized, several practical requirements typically are associated with implementing these interventions.

Special Educators

Although peers without disabilities play a direct role in providing support to their schoolmates with ASDs, the school staff remains actively involved in initiating, monitoring, and supervising peer-mediated support interventions. Special educators have primarily assumed responsibility for planning and implementing these interventions, particularly for students with extensive support needs. In part, this is because many students with severe disabilities have traditionally received one-to-one support from individually assigned adults within inclusive classrooms and extracurricular activities. Moreover, these are the school staff typically most familiar with students' individualized educational goals, support needs, and instructional history. Special educators typically lead orientation and training activities (see the Key Components section) for peers without disabilities involved in these interventions, particularly when this training requires meeting with students outside of class. For example, a teacher might hold orientation sessions with students without disabilities involved in a peer network or peer support arrangement during one or two lunch periods, before or after school, during recess, or during a free period. The time required to carry out this initial training depends on the nature of the supports peers will be asked to provide, the number of peers involved, the characteristics of the students who will be receiving support, and the school settings in which they will require support. For most interventions described in this chapter, only one or two initial meetings (about 20 to 45 min long) with peers are required. In addition, some peers will benefit from one or more follow-up meetings during which they can discuss their experiences, share any concerns, and address challenges that may have arisen.

Paraprofessionals

Paraprofessionals also have a role in implementing peer support interventions. Many schools rely extensively on individually assigned paraprofessionals to support the general education participation and extracurricular involvement of students with ASDs and other developmental disabilities (Giangreco, 2010). As peers begin supporting their classmates with disabilities socially or academically or both, one-to-one paraprofessionals gradually fade their direct support and assume a more flexible role in which they provide ongoing feedback and assistance to students with and without disabilities participating in these interventions. For example, paraprofessionals may model the use of appropriate support strategies as students work together, facilitate peer interactions and collaborative work, collect data on student outcomes, and/or troubleshoot any challenges that arise. Given their regular presence within the classroom, it is advantageous to involve paraprofessionals in the initial orientation and training of peers. Paraprofessionals also must maintain regular communication with general educators, special educators, club sponsors, or providers of **related services.**

General Educators

Within inclusive classrooms, general educators often assume an active—albeit typically less direct—role in establishing and supporting peer-mediated support interventions. General educators usually assume primary responsibility for determining the curricular content and instructional approaches that characterize a classroom; they often are most familiar with the academic standards and learning objectives that students must meet. Thus, it is essential that they discuss their expectations and recommendations for peer-mediated supports with the special educators and paraprofessionals who support students with ASDs in their classroom. General educators also assist with identifying students without disabilities who might serve effectively in providing support to their classmates with disabilities.

Team-Based Planning

An important element of high-quality, inclusive educational experiences for students with ASDs is collaborative teaming (Hunt & McDonnell, 2007). Supporting the meaningful participation of students with ASDs typically requires special educators, general educators, paraprofessionals, and related service providers to work collaboratively to identify a student's social and educational goals. Peer-mediated support interventions are certainly no exception, particularly when intervention approaches span multiple contexts within a school (e.g., peer network interventions).

Several individualized planning models can be used by educational teams to outline the specific peer-mediated and adult-delivered supports students with ASDs will need to participate in various school contexts, including the Instructional Activities Assessment (Cushing, Clark, Carter, & Kennedy, 2005), Unified Plans of Support (Hunt et al., 2003), and the Beyond Access Model (Sonnenmeier, McSheehan, & Jorgensen, 2005).

KEY COMPONENTS

As evidenced in the previous sections, peer-mediated support strategies represent an approach to social and communication intervention that can be implemented with some flexibility. The core components of these interventions typically involve 1) identifying students with ASDs and their peers who would benefit from involvement in these interventions, 2) equipping peers to provide social and/or academic support, 3) arranging ongoing opportunities for students to interact with and support one another, and 4) monitoring students and their peers and offering needed guidance to students involved in the intervention. The following sections elaborate on each of these steps and highlight variations that may be associated with different intervention approaches.

Recruiting Peers

The specific procedures and criteria employed when recruiting peers without disabilities for these interventions has garnered relatively little attention in the professional literature. The recruitment process typically involves determining 1) the number of participating peers, 2) the attributes peers should possess, and 3) the approaches used to extend invitations. The number of peers typically involved in these interventions depends on the specific approach being implemented. For example, arrangements for peer tutoring and peer support typically involve students working within dyads (one peer) or triads (two peers), primarily because of the academic focus of peer-delivered supports. Research suggests that triadic arrangements may be associated with higher rates of social interaction but comparable rates of academic engagement (Carter et al., 2005). Cooperative learning groups may involve two to five students without disabilities, although these interventions are usually implemented classwide. In the latter case, every student in a given classroom receives guidance on cooperative learning strategies. Peer network interventions involve recruiting a somewhat larger number of peers (i.e., four to six) determined primarily by the size of the participating peers' social circle and the number of different settings in which students with disabilities will receive support (e.g., transitions between classes, lunch, recess, before and after school). Of the commonly used arrangements for peer interventions, peer interaction training has been implemented most flexibly, with the number of peers receiving training ranging from three students to the entire class (e.g., 25 students). This number is based primarily on the number of peers whom the student with an ASD will encounter during targeted classroom or school activities. Within most approaches, peers without disabilities are identified from within the same classroom, club, or other school activities. Exceptions include cross-age peer tutoring (Kamps, Dugan, Potucek, & Collins, 1999) and "reverse mainstreaming" approaches—in which peers without disabilities are brought into special education classrooms (e.g., special friends).

Although the literature includes no established criteria for determining *which* students without disabilities will participate most effectively within peer-mediated support interventions, several qualities and characteristics of peers have been identified as potential considerations during recruitment. For example, peers who already know the focus student with an ASD, have regular school attendance, exhibit age-appropriate social skills, and share some interests with the student with disabilities often are asked to participate in peer-mediated interventions. When a desired intervention outcome involves the development of friendships, the social status, gender, and residential neighborhood of peers may be relevant considerations. Relationships may be more likely to develop when peers themselves have an established network of friends, when students are the same gender, and when students live close enough to see one another outside of school (Carter, Cushing, & Kennedy, 2009). When the primary intervention outcome is academic performance, peers should evidence a willingness and capacity to learn basic instructional strategies. Although academically successful peers are often identified for academic-focused interventions, research suggests that peers who are struggling academically themselves may benefit from assuming these support roles (Shukla et al., 1998). With the exception of some whole-class interventions (e.g., classwide peer tutoring, collaborative learning groups), peers should always express an interest in and willingness to assume these support roles. Indeed, it is important to ensure that these interventions are mutually beneficial for all participating students.

Similarly, a variety of methods have been used to recruit and select peers for participation in these interventions. To the greatest extent possible, the preferences of students with ASDs should be sought when determining which peers to involve in these interventions. However, some students with complex communication challenges or limited existing friendships within a classroom may have difficulty expressing their perspectives. Other often-used approaches include soliciting recommendations from teachers or club sponsors, general class announcements, "circle of friends" procedures, and teacher-determined pairings (Carter et al., 2009; Whitaker, Barratt, Joy, Potter, & Thomas, 1998).

Equipping Peers

After agreeing to participate, peers receive initial training from school staff on their roles and responsibilities within peer-mediated support interventions. The information and strategies addressed during these orientation sessions—as well as the avenues through which training is delivered—varies somewhat depending on the intervention approach being implemented. Moreover, the content addressed is tailored to reflect the individualized social and educational support needs of participating students with ASDs within specific school settings.

Nonetheless, several common topics are typically addressed during initial meetings with peers. When students do not already know one another well, peers may be provided general information about their partner's interests, strengths, hobbies, school activities, and broad educational goals (e.g., to meet more of his or her classmates, to participate more actively in small-group work, to use his or her communication device more frequently). Such information provides a launching point for initial conversations among participating students. The importance of using respectful language and maintaining confidentiality also are emphasized. Because some peers may have had limited knowledge about and experience with disability, training for peers has historically emphasized disability awareness elements.

The primary focus of training typically involves teaching peers targeted strategies for supporting the communication, social participation, and/or academic engagement of their partner with an ASD. When social and communication outcomes are the primary intervention focus, conversation-enhancing skills often receive particular emphasis. For example, peers may be shown specific strategies for eliciting initiations, prompting use of an AAC device, extending conversational turns, interacting with someone who uses a communication device, redirecting inappropriate conversations, reinforcing conversation attempts, and modeling relevant social skills.

Within approaches that also emphasize academic outcomes (e.g., peer tutoring, peer support arrangements), peers may learn systematic instruction techniques, such as prompting, modeling, reinforcement, and corrective feedback. Peers also are shown strategies for promoting academic engagement through working together on assignments, providing feedback effectively, reviewing course content, highlighting key concepts, sharing class materials, or modeling self-management strategies. Other relevant student-specific information might also be shared with peers, such as explanations of the communicative intent of any stereotypical or challenging behaviors their partner might exhibit or guidance on how to respond appropriately to these behaviors. Providing students with relevant information and equipping them with targeted skills is expected to increase their confidence and effectiveness as they undertake their new support roles. In addition, students must know when they should turn to adults (e.g., paraprofessionals, special educators, related service providers) for needed assistance and which support roles they should not assume (e.g., feeding, toileting, responding to behavioral challenges, such as physical aggression).

Special educators and/or paraprofessionals (see Practical Requirements section) typically lead the initial training sessions, although other school staff could also assume this responsibility. Within most research studies, training has been delivered to peers by pulling them aside from ongoing class activities or meeting with them separately in a different location within the school (e.g., another classroom, during recess or lunch). Some exceptions, however, exist to this approach. Collaboration skills typically are taught to all students within a classroom at the same time prior to initiation of cooperative learning groups. Similarly, peer interaction training is sometimes delivered to all students with and without disabilities simultaneously in a classroom (e.g., Brady et al., 1987; Kamps et al., 1992), as a way of increasing every student's capacity to interact effectively with others. As with other elements of these intervention approaches, the number of initial training sessions will vary widely depending on the approach being used, the individualized support needs of participating students with ASDs, and the abilities of participating peers. Overall, most intervention evaluations have required relatively few training sessions (e.g., one to three) of approximately 45–60 min in length to produce substantial improvements in social interaction outcomes.

Arranging Interaction Opportunities

After completing recruitment efforts and initial training, educators next establish regular opportunities for students with and without disabilities to interact with one another during the school day. Although many barriers to peer interaction exist within schools, the limited opportunities students with ASDs have to learn and work alongside their peers without disabilities may be the most prominent. When students with ASDs receive educational services in separate classrooms, eat lunch in other parts of the same cafeteria, travel school hallways at different times, or do not participate in extracurricular or other school-sponsored activities, their opportunities to interact with their peers without disabilities are severely curtailed (Newman, 2007). Even within general education classes, students with ASDs often are observed working one-to-one with paraprofessionals at the periphery of the classroom (Carter et al., 2008). Establishing shared activities during which interaction is both allowed and encouraged is an essential component of peer-mediated support interventions.

In the general education classroom, increasing environmental support for interaction typically involves either relocating students with and without ASDs so they are sitting next to one another or designing interactive activities during which all students can readily converse with one another (e.g., small-group projects, play-based activities). Within peer support arrangements, peer tutoring, and collaborative learning groups, students with ASDs sit next to participating peers throughout the duration of the class or during specified instructional times. As students work together within these interdependent instructional arrangements, the social interactions they have with one another are both praised and encouraged by the classroom teacher, creating interaction opportunities that might not otherwise have existed. In special education classrooms, peers without disabilities are brought in from other classrooms for either specific activities or an entire class period.

When interventions are implemented outside the classroom, designated times are established for students to spend time together during lunch, at recess, in between classes, or within extracurricular activities. Although these represent noninstructional times during which social opportunities naturally exist, many students with ASDs rarely access these opportunities. Coordinating students' schedules and arranging intentional social supports increases the social and communication opportunities that students encounter, as well as the likelihood that their conversational initiations will be reciprocated.

Research suggests that the types of activities arranged for students with and without severe disabilities may influence the nature and extent of their interactions with one another (Hughes, Carter, Hughes, Bradford, & Copeland, 2002; McMahon, Wacker, Sasso, Berg, & Newton, 1996). Specifically, recreational and leisure activities appear to promote social conversations more typical of interactions occurring among friends, whereas academic and instructional activities tend to promote more task-related interactions. These findings suggest that educators should consider carefully the contexts in which they implement peer-mediated interventions, particularly in light of the specific social and communication outcomes they hope to promote.

Feedback and Guidance

As students with and without disabilities participate in shared activities, adults monitor their interactions to ensure that peers are delivering supports effectively. In addition, adults ensure that *all* students are benefiting socially and/or academically from their involvement in the intervention. As students begin working together, the supervision that adults provide is more intensive. For example, a special educator might watch students to determine whether peers are using support strategies correctly and consistently and might check in to make sure they have the information and direction they need. In addition, the teacher might observe whether the student with an ASD has effective avenues for communicating with his or her peers, appears to enjoy spending time with them, and continues to make adequate progress toward his or her individualized goals. As needed, adults might provide additional assistance by sharing ideas for including focus students in ongoing activities, suggesting alternative support strategies, modeling new instructional approaches, redirecting students when they are off-task, brainstorming solutions to unexpected challenges, or introducing adaptations and modifications to promote greater participation of students with disabilities. Moreover, adults initially provide thick schedules of verbal and/or written reinforcement for students and their peers. Often, this feedback can be provided within the flow of ongoing class activities as students work together.

As students with and without disabilities gain experience working together, adults fade their direct involvement and assume more facilitative roles in which they provide feedback and guidance to students only as needed. Within classroom-based interventions (e.g., peer support arrangements, peer tutoring, cooperative learning groups), peers may soon only need to check in with educators or paraprofessionals at the beginning or end of the class period, or as specific needs arise. Within peer network interventions, adult facilitators gradually turn leadership responsibilities for network meetings over to peers as they gain more experience and confidence, remaining available as needed to address unanticipated challenges or to redirect the group. Adults are encouraged to find the appropriate balance between encouraging student independence and providing just enough support to promote meaningful interaction. Because the curriculum and instructional strategies typically change as the school year progresses, it is recommended that adults periodically check with peers and students with disabilities to discuss their experiences, address their concerns, and solicit ideas for refining the intervention.

DATA COLLECTION TO SUPPORT DECISION MAKING

Direct observations represent the primary approach used to determine whether peer-mediated support interventions are working as intended and promoting desired outcomes, as well as whether additional refinements or alternative approaches may be necessary. Observing students as they work together enables school staff to ascertain the extent to which peers are delivering social and instructional supports with sufficient fidelity and whether students with ASDs are benefiting through communication and social interactions outcomes. For example, observations might focus on characteristics of students' social interactions (e.g., reciprocity, appropriateness, conversational topics, overall quality), the social and communication skills used by students (e.g., initiations, responses, extensions, affect, communication mode), the contexts within which these interactions occur (e.g., small groups, large groups, transitions, free time), and the individuals involved in these interactions (e.g., peer supports, other classmates, adults). Recognizing the complexity of peer relationships and the numerous dimensions along which peer interaction might be assessed, teachers should prioritize and operationally define desired social outcomes. Paraprofessionals, special educators, or related services providers can conduct formal classroom or other school-based observations prior to and after initiating peer-mediated interventions. Observational approaches and measures used in the studies described in this chapter (see Tables 10.1 and 10.2) and elsewhere (e.g., Carter & Hughes, 2005; Carter et al., 2010; Kennedy, Shukla, & Fryxell, 1997; Webster & Carter, 2007) can be readily adapted and implemented by school staff.

At the same time, several qualitative studies highlight the value of supplementing direct observations with student and teacher interviews (Broer, Doyle, & Giangreco, 2005; Copeland et al., 2004; Schnorr, 1997). Educators can ask students with ASDs about 1) their experiences receiving support from their peers, 2) whether they enjoy spending time with their classmates, 3) other classmates they would like to work with or get to know better, and 4) whether they would like to continue receiving social and/or academic support from their peers. At the same time, educators should informally interview participating peers about their perspectives regarding 1) their emerging relationships with their partner with disabilities; 2) their perceptions of how they and their partner are benefiting from their ongoing interactions; 3) support strategies that are and are not working well; and 4) additional information, assistance, or supports that they think would enhance their interactions with their partner. As noted elsewhere, peers have a unique perspective into the social culture of the school and often can share insightful ideas and recommendations for enhancing the social participation of their classmates with disabilities. Finally, conversations with other teachers and school staff can reveal whether an intervention is producing noticeable improvements in social and communication outcomes, aligns well with other instructional and intervention approaches being used, is practical to initiate and maintain, and produces broad improvements in students' social participation across multiple school contexts.

CONSIDERATIONS FOR CHILDREN FROM CULTURALLY AND LINGUISTICALLY DIVERSE BACKGROUNDS

Schools across the country are serving an increasingly diverse population of students, including children and youth with ASDs (U.S. Department of Education, 2009). Although the effectiveness of peer-mediated support interventions has been demonstrated with a wide range of students in diverse geographic locales, relatively little information about the cultural and linguistic backgrounds of participating students is reported in the empirical literature. For example, in our review, race/ethnicity was reported for just five of 63 students with ASDs, three of these students were European American, one was Asian American, and one was Hispanic. Similarly, little information is available regarding the socioeconomic status of participating students with and without disabilities. As a result, this literature offers little direct guidance regarding implementation considerations for children from culturally and linguistically diverse backgrounds.

Supporting student and parent involvement in the intervention planning process offers one primary avenue for ensuring that the goals and intervention procedures associated with these strategies reflect the priorities and values of these families. During educational planning meetings, parents should be asked for their input into the design and delivery of peer-mediated supports. Moreover, parents can provide information about whether and how their child talks about his or her relationships with peers at school. Parent involvement becomes especially critical if intervention efforts are intended to facilitate peer interactions and relationships that extend beyond the school day (Laugeson, Frankel, Mogil, & Dillion, 2009; Turnbull, Pereira, & Blue-Banning, 1999).

APPLICATION TO A CHILD

Keagan (age 9) was a third-grade student with an ASD. She was included in general education classes throughout the school day but received speech and language therapy in a separate room several times per week. Keagan had IEP goals focused on increasing the frequency and appropriateness of her conversational initiations, using her voice output communication aid with greater fluency, and improving the quality of her social interactions with her classmates. However, observations within the classroom indicated that Keagan rarely used her communication device, never interacted with her classmates, and received most of her instruction and support from an individually assigned paraprofessional. Conversations with several classmates revealed that they felt unsure of how to interact with someone who used a communication device and did not understand why Keagan engaged in certain stereotypical behaviors (e.g., rocking, hand waving).

During parts of two class periods when Keagan was absent, the special educator and general educator provided peer interaction training to all of Keagan's classmates. They discussed the importance of friendships, provided general disability awareness information, shared ideas for conversational topics that reflected Keagan's interests and strengths, discussed strategies for gaining Keagan's attention and encouraging her to use her communication device, and brainstormed ways the students could help Keagan participate in activities within the classroom, lunchroom, and at recess. In addition, the classroom teacher established cooperative learning groups within the classroom during certain instructional times. During language arts and math, Keagan began working in a small group with three other students, each of whom was assigned a specific role as they completed their group projects. Additional information and guidance was provided to the two peers who sat directly next to Keagan within these groups.

As the students began working together, the paraprofessional modeled ways of communicating with Keagan and introduced additional support strategies as needed. As the students got to know one another and felt more comfortable working together, the paraprofessional gradually faded her direct involvement and began working with a wider range of students within the classroom. However, she continued to monitor Keagan's interactions with her classmates and collected data on her progress toward her social-related IEP goals. Throughout the semester, Keagan was observed interacting more frequently with the students in her cooperative group as well as with other students in the class. She also began initiating more conversations with her communication device and participating more actively in class activities.

Application to an Adolescent or Adult

A similar approach would be taken in using peer-mediated interventions with adolescents or adults.

FUTURE DIRECTIONS

Although a fairly sizable literature evaluating the efficacy of peer-mediated support strategies for school-age children with ASDs has accumulated, additional research is needed to further refine these interventions and increase our understanding of their impact on participating students. First, the steps taken to select and train peers to provide support are salient factors that likely influence the outcomes associated with these intervention approaches. Few studies have examined how the characteristics of peers or the content and delivery of initial training to peers affect subsequent social interactions or skill acquisition. Such considerations warrant closer examination.

Second, although the proximal impact of peer-mediated support interventions are well documented, less is known about the extent to which the social interactions and relationships established within these arrangements 1) extend to other peers not directly involved, 2) spill over to other contexts during or beyond the school day, or 3) maintain over multiple semesters or school years. Future research should explore how best to promote the generalized and longitudinal impact of these interventions.

Third, the intervention approaches described in this chapter involve peers in providing a wide array of social, academic, and other supports to their schoolmates with ASDs. A more fine-grained analysis of the specific supports students exchange within these arrangements is needed (Carter, Moss, Hoffman, Chung, & Sisco, 2011), along with a closer examination of how particular peer-delivered supports contribute to students' social, communication, and skill acquisition. Such information would enrich our understanding of just how these interventions work and could inform the design of orientation and training efforts.

Fourth, although peer-mediated support interventions promote increases in social interaction, less is known about their impact on the communication and language skill acquisition of students with ASDs. Therefore, use of measures designed to examine these outcomes should be undertaken more routinely in research on peer-mediated interventions.

Finally, the increasing involvement of youth and young adults with ASDs in postsecondary education raises questions regarding the implementation and efficacy of peer-mediated support strategies within inclusive college programs (Hendricks & Wehman, 2009). Although the focus of this chapter was on school-age children with ASDs, research examining the extension of these strategies to other contexts and ages is needed.

SUGGESTED READINGS

The following articles, books, and chapters expand on the implementation requirements and empirical evidence for the peer-mediated support interventions introduced in this chapter.

Carter, E.W., Cushing, L.S., & Kennedy, C.H. (2009). *Peer support strategies for improving all students' social lives and learning.* Baltimore, MD: Paul H. Brookes Publishing Co.

This step-by-step planning guide provides information to educators and administrators on how to implement peer support strategies in their schools.

Carter, E.W., & Hughes, C. (2007). Social interaction interventions: Promoting socially supportive environments and teaching new skills. In S.L. Odom, R.H. Horner, M. Snell, & J. Blacher (Eds.), *Handbook on developmental disabilities* (pp. 310–329). New York, NY: Guilford Press.

This chapter reviews the research literature from the prior decade on social interaction interventions for students with developmental disabilities across the grades. The authors focus on intervention strategies that have demonstrated increased social interactions between students with and without developmental disabilities, such as peer support arrangements, establishing cooperative learning groups, and social skills instruction.

Carter, E.W., & Kennedy, C.H. (2006). Promoting access to the general curriculum using peer support strategies. *Research and Practice for Persons with Severe Disabilities, 31*, 284–292.

This article addresses the efficacy and social validity of peer support interventions as an approach for engaging youth with severe disabilities in the general curriculum. The authors discuss the core elements of peer support interventions, as well as the research supporting the academic and social benefits for students participating in these programs.

Goldstein, H., Kaczmarek, L.A., & English, K.M. (Eds.) (2001). *Promoting social communication: Children with developmental disabilities from birth to adolescence.* Baltimore, MD: Paul H. Brookes Publishing Co.

This book reviews research on social and communication development for children with developmental disabilities from birth to adolescence. Empirically supported assessment and intervention approaches are also presented.

Thiemann, K., & Kamps, D. (2007). Promoting social-communicative competence of children with autism in integrated environments. In R.L. Simpson & B.S. Myles (Eds.), *Educating children and youth with autism* (pp. 267–298). Austin, TX: PRO-ED.

This chapter presents recommended goals and intervention approaches to increase the social-communicative function of children with autism in inclusive social environments. These goals and intervention approaches are based on research documenting the positive effects of comprehensive social programming and teaching children functional communication skills with their peers in inclusive social settings.

Learning Activities

1. Students with and without disabilities have unique insight into the barriers to peer interaction existing in their school, as well as the factors that could enhance relationships. Talk with students to learn their perspectives regarding the information, supports, and opportunities that would enable them to work together and encourage them to get to know one another. In addition, ask how they see their roles in promoting friendships within their school.

2. Most peers are quite willing to play a role in supporting their classmates with ASDs when invited by educators. Often, the challenge is determining which

and how many peers to invite. When deciding which peers to involve in these interventions, what qualities and characteristics would you consider to be most important? How might your answer change depending on the primary focus of the peer-mediated support intervention and the specific social and communication outcomes you hope to obtain? What steps could you take to make sure students with ASDs have a meaningful voice in determining which peers will be involved in providing support?

3.   Research findings describing the effectiveness and feasibility of peer-mediated support strategies are very promising. As with all educational interventions, however, questions may arise about the implementation of these strategies. What concerns might teachers, paraprofessionals, administrators, parents, or others raise about implementing peer-mediated support interventions for students with ASDs? Consider how you could address or reduce each of these concerns when establishing and maintaining these interventions.

REFERENCES

(*Asterisks denote articles included in the review.)

Bandura, A. (1977). *Social learning theory.* Morristown, NJ: General Learning Press.

Bellini, S., Peters, J.K., Brianner, L., & Hopf, A. (2007). A meta-analysis of school-based social skills interventions for children with autism spectrum disorders. *Remedial and Special Education, 28,* 153–162.

Boardman, A.G., Argüelles, M.E., Vaughn, S., Hughes, M.T., & Klingner, J. (2005). Special education teachers' views of research-based practices. *Journal of Special Education, 39,* 168–180.

*Brady, M.P., Shores, R.E., McEvoy, M.A., Ellis, D., & Fox, J.J. (1987). Increasing social interactions of severely handicapped autistic children. *Journal of Autism and Developmental Disorders, 17,* 375–390.

Broer, S.M., Doyle, M.B., & Giangreco, M.F. (2005). Perspectives of students with intellectual disabilities about their experiences with paraprofessional support. *Exceptional Children, 71,* 415–430.

Boyd, B.A., Conroy, M.C., Asmus, J.M., McKenney, E.L.W., & Mancil, G.R. (2008). Descriptive analysis of classroom setting events on the social behaviors of children with autism spectrum disorder. *Education and Training in Mental Retardation and Developmental Disabilities, 43,* 186–197.

Campbell, J.M., Ferguson, J.E., Herzinger, C.V., Jackson, J.N., & Marino, C.A. (2005). Peers' attitudes toward autism differ across sociometric groups: An exploratory investigation. *Journal of Developmental and Physical Disabilities, 17,* 283–301.

Canella, H.I., O'Reilly, M.F., & Lancioni, G.E. (2005). Choice and preference assessment research with people with severe to profound developmental disabilities: A review of the literature. *Research in Developmental Disabilities, 26,* 1–15.

*Carter, E.W., Cushing, L.S., Clark, N.M., & Kennedy, C.H. (2005). Effects of peer support interventions on students' access to the general curriculum and social interactions. *Research and Practice for Persons with Severe Disabilities, 30,* 15–25.

Carter, E.W., Cushing, L.S., & Kennedy, C.H. (2009). *Peer support strategies for improving all students' social lives and learning.* Baltimore, MD: Paul H. Brookes Publishing Co.

Carter, E.W., & Hughes, C. (2005). Increasing social interaction among adolescents with intellectual disabilities and their general education peers: Effective interventions. *Research and Practice for Persons with Severe Disabilities, 30,* 179–193.

Carter, E.W., & Hughes, C. (2007). Social interaction interventions: Promoting socially supportive environments and teaching new skills. In S.L. Odom, R.H. Horner, M. Snell, & J.

Blacher (Eds.), *Handbook on developmental disabilities* (pp. 310–329). New York, NY: Guilford Press.

Carter, E.W., & Kennedy, C.H. (2006). Promoting access to the general curriculum using peer support strategies. *Research and Practice for Persons with Severe Disabilities, 31,* 284–292.

Carter, E.W., Moss, C.K., Hoffman, A., Chung, Y., & Sisco, L.G. (2011). Efficacy and social validity of peer support arrangements for adolescents with disabilities. *Exceptional Children, 78,* 107–125.

Carter, E.W., & Pesko, M.J. (2008). Social validity of peer interaction intervention strategies in high school classrooms: Effectiveness, feasibility, and actual use. *Exceptionality, 16,* 156–173.

Carter, E.W., Sisco, L.G., Brown, L., Brickham, D., & Al-Khabbaz, Z.A. (2008). Peer interactions and academic engagement of youth with developmental disabilities in inclusive middle and high school classrooms. *American Journal on Mental Retardation, 113,* 479–494.

Carter, E.W., Sisco, L.G., Chung, Y., & Stanton-Chapman, T. (2010). Peer interactions of students with intellectual disabilities and/or autism: A map of the intervention literature. *Research and Practice for Persons with Severe Disabilities, 35,* 63-79.

Carter, E.W., Sisco, L.G., Melekoglu, M., & Kurkowski, C. (2007). Peer supports as an alternative to individually assigned paraprofessionals in inclusive high school classrooms. *Research and Practice for Persons with Severe Disabilities, 32,* 213–227.

*Cole, D.A., Vandercook, T., & Rynders, J.E. (1987). Dyadic interactions between children with and without mental retardation: Effects of age discrepancy. *American Journal of Mental Deficiency, 92,* 194–202.

*Cole, D.A., Vandercook, T., & Rynders, J.E. (1988). Comparison of two peer interaction programs: Children with and without severe disabilities. *American Educational Research Journal, 25,* 415–439.

Copeland, S.R., Hughes, C., Carter, E.W., Guth, C., Presley, J., Williams, C.R., & Fowler, S. E. (2004). Increasing access to general education: Perspectives of participants in a high school peer support program. *Remedial and Special Education, 26,* 342–352.

Cushing, L.S., Clark, N.M., Carter, E.W., & Kennedy, C.H. (2005). Access to the general education curriculum for students with severe disabilities: What it means and how to accomplish it. *Teaching Exceptional Children, 38,* 6–13.

*Dugan, E., Kamps, D., Leonard, B., Watkins, N., Rheinberger, A., & Stackhaus, J. (1995). Effects of cooperative learning groups during social studies for students with autism and fourth-grade peers. *Journal of Applied Behavior Analysis, 28,* 175–188.

*Eichinger, J. (1990). Goal structure effects on social interaction: Nondisabled and disabled elementary students. *Exceptional Children, 56,* 408–416.

Fudala, J., & Reynolds, W. (2000). *Arizona Articulation Proficiency Scale* (3rd ed.). Los Angeles, CA: Western Psychological Services.

*Garrison-Harrell, L., Kamps, D., & Kravits, T. (1997). The effects of peer networks on social-communicative behaviors for students with autism. *Focus on Autism and Other Developmental Disabilities, 12,* 241–254.

Giangreco, M.F. (2010). One-to-one paraprofessionals for students with disabilities in inclusive classrooms: Is conventional wisdom wrong? *Intellectual and Developmental Disabilities, 48,* 1–13.

Goldstein, H. (2002). Communication intervention for children with autism: A review of treatment efficacy. *Journal of Autism and Developmental Disorders, 32,* 373–396.

Goldstein, H., Kaczmarek, L.A., & English, K.M. (Eds.) (2001). *Promoting social communication: Children with developmental disabilities from birth to adolescence.* Baltimore, MD: Paul H. Brookes Publishing Co.

*Gonzalez-Lopez, A., & Kamps, D.M. (1997). Social skills training to increase social interactions between children with autism and their typical peers. *Focus on Autism and Other Developmental Disabilities, 12,* 2–14.

*Haring, T.G., & Breen, C.G. (1992). A peer-mediated social network intervention to enhance the social integration of persons with moderate and severe disabilities. *Journal of Applied Behavior Analysis, 25,* 319–333.

Harper, G.F., & Maheady, L. (2007). Peer-mediated teaching and students with learning disabilities. *Intervention in School and Clinic, 43,* 101–107.

*Harper, C.B., Symon, J.B.G., & Frea, W.D. (2008). Recess is time-in: Using peers to improve social skills of children with autism. *Journal of Autism and Developmental Disorders, 38,* 815.

Hendricks, D.R., & Wehman, P. (2009). Transition from school to adulthood for youth with autism spectrum disorders. *Focus on Autism and Other Developmental Disabilities, 24,* 77–88.

Hughes, C., Carter, E.W., Hughes, T., Bradford, E., & Copeland, S.R. (2002). Effects of instructional versus non-instructional roles on the social interactions of high school students. *Education and Training in Mental Retardation and Developmental Disabilities, 37,* 146–162.

Hughes, C., Copeland, S.R., Guth, C., Rung, L.L., Hwang, B., Kleeb, G., & Strong, M. (2001). General education students' perspectives on their involvement in a high school peer buddy program. *Education and Training in Mental Retardation and Developmental Disabilities, 36,* 343–356.

*Hunt, P., Farron-Davis, F., Wrenn, M., Hirose-Hatae, A., & Goetz, L. (1997). Promoting interactive partnerships in inclusive educational settings. *Journal of the Association for Persons with Severe Handicaps, 22,* 127–137.

Hunt, P., & McDonnell, J. (2007). Inclusive education. In S.L. Odom, R.H. Horner, M. Snell, & J. Blacher (Eds.), *Handbook on developmental disabilities* (pp. 269–291). New York, NY: Guilford Press.

*Hunt, P., Soto, G., Maier, J., & Doering, K. (2003). Collaborative teaming to support students at risk and students with severe disabilities in general education classrooms. *Exceptional Children, 69,* 315.

*Hunt, P., Staub, D., Alwell, M., & Goetz, L. (1994). Achievement by all students within the context of cooperative learning groups. *Journal of the Association for Persons with Severe Handicaps, 19,* 290–301.

Jackson, J.N., & Campbell, J.M. (2009). Teachers' peer buddy selections for children with autism: Social characteristics and relationships with peer nominations. *Journal of Autism and Developmental Disorders, 39,* 269–277.

Janney, R., & Snell, M.E. (2006). *Social relationships and peer support* (2nd ed.). Baltimore, MD: Paul H. Brookes Publishing Co.

*Johnson, R.T., Johnson, D.W., DeWeerdt, N., Lyons, V., & Zaidman, B. (1983). Integrating severely adaptively handicapped seventh-grade students into constructive relationships with nonhandicapped peers in science class. *American Journal of Mental Deficiency, 87,* 611–618.

*Kamps, D.M., Barbetta, P.M., Leonard, B.R., & Delquadri, J. (1994). Classwide peer tutoring: An integration strategy to improve reading skills and promote peer interactions among students with autism and general education peers. *Journal of Applied Behavior Analysis, 27,* 49–61.

Kamps, D.M., Dugan, E., Potucek, J., & Collins, A. (1999). Effects of cross-age peer tutoring networks among students with autism and general education students. *Journal of Behavioral Education, 9,* 97–115.

Kamps, D.M., Kravits, T., Lopez, A.G., Kemmerer, K., Potucek, J., Harrell, L.G., & Garrison, L. (1998). What do the peers think? Social validity of peer-mediated programs. *Education and Treatment of Children, 21,* 107–134.

*Kamps, D.M., Leonard, B., Potucek, J., & Garrison-Harrell, L. (1995). Cooperative learning groups in reading: An integration strategy for students with autism and general classroom peers. *Behavioral Disorders, 21,* 89–109.

*Kamps, D.M., Leonard, B.R., Vernon, S., Dugan, E.P., Delquadri, J.C., & Gershon, B. (1992). Teaching social skills to students with autism to increase peer interactions in an integrated first-grade classroom. *Journal of Applied Behavior Analysis, 25,* 281–288.

*Kamps, D.M., Potucek, J., Lopez, A.G., Kravits, T., & Kemmerer, K. (1997). The use of peer networks across multiple settings to improve social interaction for students with autism. *Journal of Behavioral Education, 7,* 335–357.

*Kamps, D., Royer, J., Dugan, E., Kravits, T., Gonzalez-Lopez, A., Garcia, J., Carnazzo, K.,... Kane, L.G. (2002). Peer training to facilitate social interaction for elementary students with autism and their peers. *Exceptional Children, 68,* 173–187.

Kennedy, C.H. (2001). Social interaction interventions for youth with severe disabilities should emphasize interdependence. *Mental Retardation and Developmental Disabilities Research Reviews, 7,* 122–127.

Kennedy, C.H., Shukla, S., & Fryxell, D. (1997). Comparing the effects of educational placement on the social relationships of intermediate school students with severe disabilities. *Exceptional Children, 64,* 31–47.

Krug, D., Arick, J., & Almond, P. (1980). *Autism Screening Instrument for Educational Planning.* Austin, TX: PRO-ED.

Laugeson, E., Frankel, F., Mogil, C., & Dillon, D. (2009). Parent-assisted social skills training to improve friendships in teens with autism spectrum disorders. *Journal of Autism and Developmental Disorders, 39,* 596–606.

Leiter, R.G. (1979). *Leiter International Performance Scale.* Wood Dale, IL: C.H. Stoelting.

*Loftin, R., Odom, S., & Lantz, J. (2008). Social interaction and repetitive motor behaviors. *Journal of Autism and Developmental Disorders, 38,* 1124–1135.

Lord, C., Rutter, M., DiLavore, P.C., & Risi, S. (1999). *Autism Diagnostic Observation Schedule.* Los Angles, CA: Western Psychological Services.

Maheady, L., Harper, G.F., & Malette, B. (2001). Peer-mediated instruction and interventions and students with mild disabilities. *Remedial and Special Education, 22,* 4–14.

McConnell, S.R. (2002). Interventions to facilitate social interaction for young children with autism: Review of available research and recommendations for educational intervention and future research. *Journal of Autism and Developmental Disorders, 32,* 351–372.

McMahon, C.M., Wacker, D.P., Sasso, G.M., Berg, W.K., & Newton, S.M. (1996). Analysis of frequency and type of interaction in peer-mediated social skills intervention: Instructional vs. social interactions. *Education and Training in Mental Retardation and Developmental Disabilities, 31,* 339–352.

Newman, L. (2007). *Secondary school experiences of students with autism.* Menlo Park, CA: SRI International.

Odom, S.L., McConnell, S.R., & Chandler, L.K. (1994). Acceptability and feasibility of classroom-based social interaction interventions for young children with disabilities. *Exceptional Children, 60,* 226–236.

*Owen-DeSchryver, J.S., Carr, E.G., Cale, S.I., & Blakeley-Smith, A. (2008). Promoting social interactions between students with autism spectrum disorders and their peers in inclusive school settings. *Focus on Autism and Other Developmental Disabilities, 23,* 15–28.

*Putnam, J.W., Rynders, J.E., Johnson, R.T., & Johnson, D.W. (1989). Collaborative skill instruction for promoting positive interactions between mentally handicapped and non-handicapped children. *Exceptional Children, 55,* 550–557.

Rubin, K.H., Bukowski, W.M., & Laursen, B. (Eds.). (2009). *Handbook of peer interactions, relationships, and groups.* New York, NY: Guilford Press.

Ryndak, D., & Fisher, D. (Eds.). (2003). *The foundations of inclusive education: A compendium of articles on effective strategies to achieve inclusive education* (2nd ed.). Baltimore, MD: TASH.

*Sasso, G., & Rude, H. (1987). Unprogrammed effects of training high-status peers to interact with severely handicapped children. *Journal of Applied Behavior Analysis, 20,* 35–44.

*Sasso, G.M., Mitchell, V.M., & Struthers, E.M. (1986). Peer tutoring versus structured interaction activities: Effects on the frequency and topography of peer initiations. *Behavioral Disorders, 11,* 249–259.

*Sasso, G.M., Mundschenk, N.A., Melloy, K.J., & Casey, S.D. (1998). A comparison of the effects of organismic and setting variables on the social interaction behavior of children with developmental disabilities and autism. *Focus on Autism and Other Developmental Disabilities, 13,* 2–16.

Sailor, W., & Mix, B. (1975). *The Topeka Association for Retarded Citizens assessment system.* Austin, TX: PRO-ED.

*Schleien, S.J., Heyne, L.A., & Berken, S.B. (1988). Integrating physical education to teach appropriate play skills to learners with autism: A pilot study. *Adapted Physical Activity Quarterly, 5,* 162–192.

Schnorr, R.F. (1997). From enrollment to membership: "Belonging" in middle and high school classes. *Journal of the Association for Persons with Severe Handicaps, 22,* 1–15.

Schopler, E., Reichler, R., Dashford, A., Lansing, M., & Marcus, L. (1990). *PsychoEducation Profile Revised.* Austin, TX: PRO-ED.

Schopler, E., Reichler, J., & Renner, B. (1988). *The Childhood Autism Rating Scale.* Los Angeles, CA: Western Psychological Services.

*Shukla, S., Kennedy, C.H., & Cushing, L.S. (1998). Adult influence on the participation of peers without disabilities in peer support programs. *Journal of Behavioral Education, 8,* 397–413.

*Shukla, S., Kennedy, C.H., & Cushing, L.S. (1999). Intermediate school students with severe disabilities: Supporting their social participation in general education classrooms. *Journal of Positive Behavior Interventions, 1,* 130–140.

Siperstein, G.N., Norins, J., & Mohler, A. (2007). Social acceptance and attitude change: Fifty years of research. In J.W. Jacobson, J.A. Mulick, & J. Rojahn (Eds.), *Handbook of intellectual and developmental disabilities* (pp. 133–154). New York, NY: Springer.

Snell, M.E. (2003). Applying research to practice: The more pervasive problem? *Research and Practice for Persons with Severe Disabilities, 28,* 143–147.

Sonnenmeier, R., McSheehan, M., & Jorgensen, C. (2005). A case study of team supports for a student with autism's communication and engagement within the general education curriculum: Preliminary report of the Beyond Access model. *Augmentative and Alternative Communication, 21,* 101–115.

Sparrow, S.S., Balla, D.A., & Cicchetti, D.V. (1984). *Vineland Adaptive Behavior Scale (VABS).* Circle Pines, MN: American Guidance Service.

Stokes, T.F., & Baer, D.M. (1977). An implicit technology of generalization. *Journal of Applied Behavior Analysis, 10,* 349–367.

Test, D.W., Mason, C., Hughes, C., Konrad, M., Neale, M., & Wood, W.M. (2004). Student involvement in individualized education program meetings. *Exceptional Children, 70,* 391–412.

Thorndike, R.L., Hagen, E.P., & Sattler, J.M. (1986). *The Stanford-Binet Intelligence Scale* (4th ed.). Itasca, IL: Riverside.

Turnbull, A.P., Pereira, L., & Blue-Banning, M.J. (1999). Parents' facilitation of friendships between their children with a disability and their friends without a disability. *Journal of the Association for Persons with Severe Handicaps, 24,* 85–99.

U.S. Department of Education. (2009). *28th annual report to Congress on the implementation of the Individuals with Disabilities Education Act, 2006.* Washington, DC: Author.

Webster, A.A., & Carter, M. (2007). Social relationships and friendships of children with developmental disabilities: Implications for inclusive settings. A systematic review. *Journal of Intellectual and Developmental Disability, 32,* 200–213.

Wechsler, D. (1991). *Wechsler Intelligence Scale for Children* (3rd ed.). San Antonio, TX: Harcourt Assessment.

*Weiner, J.S. (2005). Peer-mediated conversational repair in students with moderate and severe disabilities. *Research and Practice for Persons with Severe Disabilities, 30,* 26–37.

Whitaker, P., Barratt, P., Joy, H., Potter, M., & Thomas, G. (1998). Children with autism and peer group support: Using "circle of friends." *British Journal of Special Education, 25,* 60–64.

Picture Exchange Communication System (PECS)

Richard L. Simpson and Jennifer B. Ganz

The Picture Exchange Communication System (PECS) is an aided picture/icon-based augmentative system designed for individuals who are nonverbal or have limited verbal abilities (Charlop-Christy, Carpenter, Le, LeBlanc, & Kellet, 2002; Frost & Bondy, 2002). Although not intended exclusively for learners with autism spectrum disorders (ASDs), PECS is most notably and commonly used with individuals with autism-related diagnoses. Created in 1985 by Bondy and Frost (1994), PECS has been unique among **augmentative and alternative communication** (AAC) programs because of its focus on instructing individuals with **communication** impairments to initiate contact with others to obtain preferred items or activities. Thus, PECS teaches individuals to use functional social communication skills by requiring them to initiate self-motivated requests. These requests—made by giving a teacher, therapist, or trainer a picture or icon of a desired item—result in the individual receiving the item or activity designated by the presented PECS card.

Compared with other AAC programs, PECS is noteworthy for other reasons. First, it does not rely on complex technology or expensive materials and equipment. Indeed, materials associated with using PECS are easily available to most educators. Teachers, speech-language pathologists, parents, and others are able to implement the PECS program in a variety of settings; and the cards, icons, and related apparatus needed for PECS can be made easily using relatively inexpensive and commonly available materials. Second, PECS, by design, provides users with direct reinforcement by delivering desired items or activities when the learner presents a PECS symbol or picture. Hence, the PECS system is not dependent on social or indirect reinforcement. Rather, desired items and activities are used as reinforcement for an individual requesting them via presentation of PECS pictures. It is also significant that PECS is structured such that learners are not required to first undergo instruction in labeling items designated on corresponding pictures or icons or otherwise demonstrating prerequisite skills such as eye contact. PECS is also relatively easy to use in a number of settings with a variety of individuals. Thus, the PECS system is inherently designed to promote skill generalization. Furthermore, PECS has been used with a wide variety of individuals. Although most commonly applied with children, it has been successfully used with adolescents. Finally, PECS has been effectively used with individuals with a range of developmental and **language** levels.

The PECS protocol for teaching learners to trade pictures or icons for desired activities or items involves six basic phases (Frost & Bondy, 2002). As noted in Table 11.1, instruction in both Phase I and Phase II involves teaching individuals to exchange pictures or icons for desired items and activities. In Phase I training, the communicative partner of the learner is in close proximity. In Phase II, the learner is required to travel a short distance to retrieve and exchange pictures and icons. Phase II instruction also involves teaching individuals to increase their repertoire of pictures and icons so that they are able to have access to an increased number and variety of activities and items from which to choose. In Phase III, learners are taught to discriminate among various icons and pictures. Discrimination training involves instructing PECS learners to choose between desired and undesired items and eventually to choose among an array of desired items. Phase IV training involves requiring the learner to expand his or her requests to communicate in complete sentences. In Phase V, learners are taught to answer questions, and Phase VI training focuses on commenting.

TARGET POPULATIONS AND ASSESSMENTS FOR DETERMINING TREATMENT RELEVANCE AND GOALS

Language and social-communication impairments constitute a core component of ASDs (American Psychiatric Association [APA], 2000; Ogletree, 2008). To be sure, the continuum of communication severity ranges from people who lack speaking skills to highly verbal people with high-functioning autism. Furthermore, communication abilities correlate positively with quality-of-life measures and postschool outcomes (Koegel, Koegel, Shoshan, & McNerney, 1999; Prizant, Wetherby, & Rydell, 2000). Accordingly, development of functional, effective communication

Table 11.1. The six basic phases of the Picture Exchange Communication System (PECS) protocol

Instructional phase	Description of instruction
Phase I	Learners are taught to exchange single pictures or icons for desired items and activities. Exchange training is done with two teachers who work in close proximity to learners. Learners are taught to make exchanges without leaving their seats.
Phase II	Learners are taught to exchange pictures or icons for an increased number and variety of desired items and activities. Learners are required to travel short distances to retrieve and exchange pictures and icons and to exchange pictures and icons with a variety of communicative partners who gradually move farther away.
Phase III	Learners are taught to discriminate among various icons and pictures, to choose between desired and undesired items, and to choose among an array of desired items.
Phase IV	Learners are taught to expand their requests to communicate in complete sentences.
Phase V	Learners are taught to answer questions using PECS icons, pictures, and words.
Phase VI	Learners are taught to expand their use of PECS icons, pictures, and words and to use the PECS system to comment.

skills is a common goal for most individuals with ASDs. To achieve this goal, **aided AAC systems** based on pictures have been widely used for decades with individuals with autism-related disabilities and other developmental delays, especially those individuals with severe forms of autism who have limited expressive language and functional communication skills (Fey, 1986; Mirenda, 2001).

The PECS approach appears to be most appropriate for use with, and has demonstrated efficacy for, a variety of learners on the autism continuum, including those diagnosed with autistic disorder, pervasive developmental disorder-not otherwise specified, Rett syndrome, and childhood disintegrative disorder (Bondy & Frost, 2001; Ganz & Simpson, 2004). However, it is not the clinical diagnosis that makes PECS and other AAC systems suitable intervention tools for a particular learner. Rather, the suitability of PECS training for an individual is a function of his or her communication skills. That is, PECS training is most suitable for an individual who lacks a functional communication system and/or has limited expressive language. Accordingly, PECS is less frequently recommended for learners with Asperger syndrome and higher functioning autism because they generally have more typical development of expressive language than individuals with more classic and severe forms of autism. Furthermore, the nature of communication impairments commonly shared by individuals with higher functioning ASDs, such as problems with pragmatic language use (**pragmatics**) and social-language fluency, can be addressed most effectively using other methods (Wetherby & Prizant, 2005).

According to Ogletree and Burns-Daniels (1993), to be of demonstrated utility, an assessment method or protocol must reliably identify typical communicative behaviors and needs across communication settings and provide additional information needed to select maximally effective treatments and interventions. Following this recommendation and logic, socially valid assessment targets include variables related to 1) communicative intent (e.g., **communicative forms** and **communicative functions**), 2) interaction skills (e.g., joint attention, interaction-related initiations and responses), and 3) environmental considerations (e.g, learners' preferences for communicative partners and settings) (Ogletree, Fischer, & Turowski, 1996). Consistent with this theme, the assessment of potential PECS users calls for a variety of methods. Informal interviews with parents, family members, educators, and caregivers can assist in identifying the student's needs, communication styles, and preferred reinforcers, items, and activities, as well as the strategies the student uses to attempt to communicate with others. Direct observations can also assist in identifying whether an individual appears to be a good candidate for an AAC system. Such observations can also suggest specific directions for designing a PECS program that is related to the individual's unique communication forms, functions, social contexts, settings, communication-related material preferences, and communication-effort outcomes.

Formal assessment measures, including standardized and norm-referenced diagnostic assessment tools, adaptive behavior scales, and developmental scales, can assist in identifying communication-related strengths and weaknesses. Examples of some of these include the Test of Early Language Development (Hresko, Reid, & Hammill, 1999) and the Brigance Diagnostic Inventory of Early Development (Brigance, 2004). Similarly, informal assessment methods, such as the Assessment of Social and Communication Skills for Children with Autism (Quill, Bracken, & Fair, 2000) and the Assessment of Basic Language and Learning Skills (Partington

& Sundberg, 1998), can be helpful in obtaining social and communication information, as well as data needed for an overall understanding of students' strengths and impairments.

Relative to identifying individuals for whom PECS instruction may be most appropriate, it is noteworthy that the Pyramid Educational Consultants web site (2012b) states that "currently, we do not have a formal evaluation for people who might be good candidates for PECS." However, Pyramid Educational Consultants offers several basic questions for identifying suitable candidates. These questions address 1) whether a person has a functional communication system for making his or her needs and wants known, 2) the extent to which a person's communication attempts are understood by others, 3) whether a person's communication and language system is sufficient to accommodate his or her needs and wants, and 4) whether the system allows for spontaneous communication and communication in response to an assortment of questions. If the answer to any of these questions is "No," the inference is that the learner is likely a suitable candidate for PECS.

THEORETICAL BASIS

By definition, individuals diagnosed with autism-related disabilities have an array of communication-related problems (APA, 2000). These challenges include expressive communication impairments, ranging from a complete lack of expressive communication skills to difficulty in appropriately using words to communicate with others (Wetherby & Prizant, 2005). Because of these impairments, the role of PECS for individuals with autism-related disabilities is clear: PECS is designed explicitly to address fundamental and pivotal communication problems, namely, the failure to initiate communication. The finding that long-term outcomes are closely aligned with development of functional communication skills underscores the importance of being able to initiate communication (Koegel et al., 1999; National Research Council [NRC], 2001).

Evidence also supports that individuals diagnosed with ASDs commonly lack the motivation and social skills to effectively communicate (Ogletree, Oren, & Fischer, 2007; Sigafoos, Drasgow, & Schlosser, 2003). Social-communication impairments include a failure to orient and attend to others; problems in sharing or displaying appropriate affection and emotions with social cohorts; difficulty in establishing and maintaining proper eye contact; and difficulty using symbolic communication, such as gesturing and pointing (Lord & Paul, 1997; Ogletree, 2008). It is also common for people with ASDs to use aberrant or other negative forms of behavior to attempt to communicate their needs and manipulate their environments (Carr & Durand, 1986; Charlop-Christy et al., 2002).

These pivotal autism-related characteristics and challenges form the foundational and operative role for PECS. That is, PECS addresses the social-communication features of ASDs by offering an instructional system that systematically teaches people to use functional communication skills in a fashion that parallels and incorporates the social rudiments of typical spoken communication. In other words, users of PECS substitute exchangeable icons and pictures for spoken words and are thus able to communicate in a fashion analogous to traditional conversation. For example, an individual with autism who has a limited repertoire of spoken words is able to secure the use of a computer or other desired item by presenting an icon of the item to a teacher or other PECS partner. The social exchange process of PECS parallels the more typical verbal initiations, responses, and exchanges of a typically developing student requesting use of a computer. In addition, it does so using the same conceptual and fundamental features used in traditional word exchanges.

A significant theoretical underpinning of PECS is the principles and techniques of behaviorism (Skinner, 1953; Watson, 1930) and applied behavior analysis (Baer, Wolf, & Risley, 1968; Cooper, Heron, & Heward, 2007). In accordance with the principles of applied behavior analysis, PECS is based on the notion that verbal and nonverbal communication skills are learned behaviors that are controlled by environmental factors. In addition, PECS incorporates elements of applied behavior analysis training, such as prompting, modeling, and shaping (Alberto & Troutman, 2006; Cooper et al., 2007). Finally, PECS encompasses direct-observation assessment, collection of reliable and ongoing data, and systematic data analysis.

Another theoretical basis for PECS involves its reliance on visual learning. Many individuals with ASDs are thought to be visual learners (Schopler, Mesibov, & Hearsey, 1995). In accordance with this thinking, a visual mode is frequently assumed to be the most efficient and effective means of structuring learning for individuals with autism-related diagnoses (Earles-Vollrath, Cook, & Ganz, 2006; Hodgdon, 1995). Visual and graphic symbols, such as photographs and icons, have long been recommended for individuals with ASDs and serve as conventional features of many AAC systems (Mirenda, 2001; NRC, 2001).

Several studies have shown that visually based systems can facilitate learning and skill generalization among individuals with ASDs (Ganz, 2007; Heflin & Alaimo, 2007; Scheurmann & Webber, 2002; Van Bourgondien, Reichle, & Schopler, 2003). For example, Simpson and colleagues (2005) judged visual schedules and visual supports as salient features of structured programs, as well as foundational necessities of programs that serve learners with ASDs. Specific to teaching communication skills, evidence exists that visual presentation of stimuli can enhance the ability of learners to initially learn and functionally use skills (Mirenda, 2001; Ogletree et al., 2007). Visual representation of communication-linked items appears to take advantage of the visual strengths of people with ASDs and the concreteness of visual stimuli (Ogletree, 2008). Furthermore, as noted by Heflin and Alaimo (2007), the consistent and nondynamic nature of visual systems enables people with ASDs to rely on recognition rather than recall memory to engage others in functional communication activities and understand shared context.

A final consideration that deserves mention is the direct reinforcement system that is used to motivate individuals who use PECS. The PECS system teaches individuals with expressive language impairments to initiate nonverbal communication behaviors in pursuit of clearly specified outcomes. Individuals learn that they are able to exchange symbols in the form of icons and pictures for the actual item or activity. Thus, unlike many reinforcement programs that use indirect training methods (e.g., a child learns to point to a "cup" on command in order to receive a preferred toy), learners who use the PECS system are rewarded with the item depicted on the picture or icon they give to a PECS communicative partner.

EMPIRICAL BASIS

A variety of studies have been conducted on the implementation of PECS, including both efficacy and effectiveness studies.

Efficacy Studies

In the last 10 years, PECS has received increased attention in the professional literature. In particular, several efficacy studies have been conducted. Efficacy studies include those that are conducted in controlled environments using precisely defined procedures (Robey & Schultz, 1998). For the purposes of this review, we include here those studies that were conducted primarily in individual sessions or in clinical settings (e.g., university sites other than grade schools or preschools on campus), and those in which PECS training was primarily conducted by the researcher(s) or with direct supervision of each training session by the researcher(s).

Several efficacy studies have demonstrated the use of the PECS protocol to teach children with ASDs who lack functional communication skills to communicate (Angermeier, Schlosser, Luiselli, Harrington, & Carter, 2008; Beck, Stoner, Bock, & Parton, 2008; Ganz & Simpson, 2004; Ganz, Simpson, & Corbin-Newsome, 2008; Tincani, 2004; Yoder & Stone, 2006b). Many of these studies also reported effects in other targeted behaviors, including increased verbalizations (Beck et al., 2008; Carr & Felce, 2007b; Ganz & Simpson, 2004; Tincani, Crozier, & Alazetta, 2006; Yoder & Stone, 2006a), increased social initiations (Carr & Felce, 2007a), decreases in undesirable behaviors (Charlop-Christy et al., 2002), and improvisation with PECS to request items not previously taught (Marckel, Neef, & Ferrari, 2006). Furthermore, some of these studies compared PECS to other interventions (Beck et al., 2008; Tincani, 2004; Yoder & Stone, 2006b) or used two different types of pictures (Angermeier et al., 2008). Table 11.2 summarizes several of these salient studies.

Single-Case Research Design Efficacy Studies

Angermeier and colleagues (2008) implemented a single-case, alternating-treatment design with four children with ASDs to compare the use of more versus fewer iconic symbols for use in Phases I–III of PECS instruction. Four elementary-age participants with a diagnosis of autism or pervasive developmental disorder rapidly mastered PECS Phases I and II, and two of the participants mastered Phase III, making independent exchanges using picture cards for 80% or more of the trials during each session for three consecutive sessions. Observational data collected within a clinical assessment setting revealed that the degree to which an icon resembled the actual item being taught to a learner did not correlate with learning patterns. That is, icons with less resemblance to actual items being taught were no more easily learned than items that had high resemblance. Maintenance data were collected for each participant one week following cessation of intervention, and each participant maintained the level of skill he or she demonstrated during the last phase of intervention. This study did not report collection of data on intervention fidelity, generalization, or social validity.

Beck and colleagues (2008) compared the implementation of PECS with the use of a speech-generating device (SGD) using a single-case, alternating-treatment design with four preschool children, three of whom had an ASD. The fourth child had developmental disabilities, albeit without a clear diagnosis of autism. Probe data were collected during individual sessions with the investigators and classroom personnel. Two of the three participants with an ASD mastered Phase I PECS independent exchanges for 80% or more of the trials during two of three consecutive sessions. In addition, one of the participants with an ASD mastered the first three phases of

Table 11.2. Summary of Picture Exchange Communication System (PECS) efficacy and effectiveness studies

Publication (author/year)	Description of participants	Procedures/ methods	Research design	Summary of outcomes/findings
Efficacy studies				
Angermeier, Schlosser, Luiselli, Harrington, and Carter (2008)	Four children ages 6–10 with a diagnosis of autism or pervasive development disorder.	PECS levels presented per standard PECS protocol in a private assessment setting.	Single-case, alternating-treatment design combined with a multiple baseline across participants.	All students achieved mastery of PECS Phases I and II. Two students mastered Phase III and demonstrated independent exchanges on 80% of trials. No significant difference was observed between picture items with high or low resemblance to actual items.
Beck, Stoner, Bock, and Parton (2008)	Four preschool students; three had a diagnosis of an autism spectrum disorder (ASD). The fourth student had a diagnosis of developmental delay and exhibited many characteristics associated with autism.	PECS levels presented per standard PECS protocol in the student's school classroom. Training involved 3–5 sessions per week, for 15–30 min.	Single-case, alternating-treatment design. PECS was compared with student's communication using a speech-generating device (SGD).	All students mastered Phase I of PECS and one student mastered Phase III.
Carr and Felce (2007a)	Twenty-four students ages 3–7. Each student had an ASD diagnosis.	PECS presented per standard protocol, 3–4 sessions per week for 4–5 weeks. Each student received a total of 15 hr of instruction.	Treatment and control group comparison design.	Child-to-adult initiations increased in the group using PECS. Verbal speech by students in the PECS group also increased.
Carr and Felce (2007b)	Students ages 4 to 7 years old with an ASD diagnosis.	PECS presented per standard protocol, 3–4 sessions per week for 4–5 weeks.	Treatment and control group comparison design.	Students receiving PECS increased spoken words. One student in control group increased spoken words.
Charlop-Christy, Carpenter, Le, LeBlanc, and Kellet (2002)	Three students, ages 3–12, with autism.	Participants each received PECS training for 15 min twice a week.	Multiple-baseline design. Attention was focused on how long students took to master the different phases of PECS.	All students learned PECS through Phase IV. Mean: 170 min; 146 trials.

(continued)

Table 11.2.   *(continued)*

Publication (author/year)	Description of participants	Procedures/ methods	Research design	Summary of outcomes/findings
Ganz and Simpson (2004)	Three students (two preschoolers, and one elementary student) with either an ASD diagnosis or a developmental delay and a score within the autism range on the Childhood Autism Rating Scale (CARS).	PECS sessions took place in each student's home classroom, 2–5 sessions per week for 15 trials per session. Data were collected on PECS proficiency, intelligible words spoken, and the absence of unintelligible utterances.	Single-case, alternating-treatment design, changing criterion.	All students mastered the four phases of PECS. Some spontaneous verbalizations were observed in Phase IV.
Ganz, Simpson, and Corbin-Newsome (2008)	Three preschool students (two had an ASD diagnosis; one had a developmental disability diagnosis). All scored within the autism range on the CARS.	Students received PECS training per standard PECS protocol for 41–110 sessions.	Multiple-baseline, single-case design, across participants.	All students demonstrated an increase in functional communication. No increase in spoken language was observed.
Lund and Troha (2008)	Three 12- to 17-year-old students with ASD diagnoses and visual impairments.	PECS was taught using tactile symbols, per the needs of students with visual impairments.	Multiple-baseline, single-case design.	All students increased percentage of independent exchanges using PECS. One student mastered PECS Phase III.
Marckel, Neef, and Ferreri (2006)	Two students with an ASD diagnosis, ages 4 and 5.	The students received 35–45 PECS training sessions.	Changing-criterion design (across PECS phases).	Both students were able to independently make requesting and labeling sentences with PECS.
Tincani (2004)	Two elementary school students diagnosed with autism. Students were in a self-contained classroom in a large suburban school.	Students were instructed in sign language and PECS. PECS was administered per standard protocol. Signs were taught as approximated English.	Alternating-treatment design was used to compare sign language skill acquisition and PECS exchanges.	One student advanced through PECS Phase III. The other student demonstrated more independent requests using sign language.
Tincani, Crozier, and Alazetta (2006)	Two male students with autism, ages 10 and 11.	PECS presented per standard protocol. Sessions provided 30 response opportunities.	Multiple-baseline design.	Both participants advanced to Phase II of PECS; one advanced through Phase IV. Both students increased independent requests during PECS training.

(continued)

Table 11.2. *(continued)*

Publication (author/year)	Description of participants	Procedures/ methods	Research design	Summary of outcomes/findings
Yoder and Stone (2006b)	Thirty-six preschool students (18–60 months of age). Each had a diagnosis of an ASD or pervasive developmental disorder-not otherwise specified and fewer than 20 functional words.	Responsive Education and Prelinguistic Milieu Teaching (RPMT) and PECS were applied 3 times per week for 20 min for 6 months.	Randomized group design.	PECS group had higher generalized request rates than RPMT group. Students with pretreatment joint attention were superior with RPMT.
Effectiveness studies				
Frea, Arnold, Vittimberga, and Koegel (2001)	Four-year-old with autism.	The participant was taught PECS Phases I–III in a typical preschool setting.	Multiple-baseline, single-case design across settings.	Resulted in increased use of PECS and decreased use of maladaptive behaviors.
Kravits, Kamps, Kemmerer, and Potucek (2002)	Six-year-old girl with autism.	PECS Phases I–III were implemented in home and school settings during natural activities.	Multiple-baseline, single-case design across settings.	Resulted in increased spontaneous use of pictures and some increased use of verbal language to make requests, comments, and expansions.
Magiati and Howlin (2003)	Thirty-four children with ASDs, ages 5–12.	The participants' teachers were taught to use PECS, then they implemented PECS with the participants.	Controlled-group study design.	Statistically signifi-cant improvement in PECS use, num-ber of PECS vocab-ulary words used, number of manual signs, number of spoken words, number of spoken phrases, and level of spontaneous communication, but no significant decrease in chal-lenging behavior.

PECS. In contrast, only one participant with an ASD mastered the first phase of the SGD intervention. Researchers also collected data on use of verbalizations during both conditions, finding variable results. That is, two of the participants with an ASD increased use of verbalizations to some degree; one participant's verbalizations increased more with the SGD, and the other's verbalizations increased slightly with both conditions. The researchers collected data on intervention fidelity, which was calculated as 100% for all phases of intervention. Generalization data probes were conducted with one of the participants with an ASD in his home 1 week after the end of intervention. It is not clear how long the generalization sessions were, but the participant was reported to use PECS three times and the SGD 17 times during the generalization session. These initial generalization data were inferred to bode well for continuation of PECS communication in untrained settings; however, without additional information, it is difficult to judge this interpretation objectively. Social validity was not reported.

Ganz and Simpson (2004) implemented the first four phases of PECS with three young children (two preschool children and one elementary-age student). One child was diagnosed with autism, and the other two were diagnosed with developmental delays; all scored within the autism range on the Childhood Autism Rating Scale (CARS; Schopler, Reichler, & Renner, 1988). Ganz and Simpson implemented a variation of a single-case, changing-criterion design. The researchers investigated the impact of PECS instruction on the participants' independent exchanges, use of intelligible words, and nonword vocalizations; data were collected during individual intervention sessions. All of the participants rapidly mastered the four phases of PECS, and each began to use some intelligible and functional verbalizations by Phase IV. However, the overall and functional use of expressive words was not consistent, and expressive language among the children was not always intelligible and did not independently supplant use of PECS symbols. Data were not collected on intervention fidelity, maintenance and generalization, or social validity.

Ganz, Simpson, and Corbin-Newsome (2008) replicated Ganz and Simpson's (2004) study and implemented PECS with three preschoolers, two of whom had autism and one of whom had global developmental delays and scored within the autism range on the CARS. Two of the participants completed PECS training through Phase IV. A single-case, multiple-baseline design across participants was employed. One of the participants learned PECS through Phase IV during a total of 89 sessions. The second participant also mastered the four phases of PECS, although it took the child 29 sessions to master Phase 1 and even longer for the other phases. The third participant did not master any phases of PECS. Expressive verbal communication was not considerably affected in any of the participants, though one participant did begin to use slightly more word approximations during the final phase of PECS. These data were collected during PECS training sessions in discrete trials. Data were not collected on intervention fidelity, maintenance and generalization, or social validity.

Tincani (2004) implemented an alternating-treatment design to compare PECS with sign language for two early-elementary-age students with ASDs. Tincani found that of the two participants, the one who initially displayed better motor imitation skills more easily learned to use sign language to make independent requests, though at a generally modest rate (i.e., he correctly imitated 43% of hand movements). The other participant more easily learned to make independent requests via PECS; that is, she emitted approximately three times as many independent responses in PECS Phase I training as in sign language training. Both interventions resulted in increased vocalizations. For the child with the better motor imitation skills, vocalizations were approximately twice as common during sign language sessions compared with PECS training. For the child who excelled in using PECS, vocalizations significantly increased during both PECS and sign language training. Participants maintained the ability to use their "best treatment" to make independent requests at rates near those for intervention. As a result, the study author observed that "for learners without hand-motor imitation skills, including many children with autism, PECS training may be more appropriate [than sign language], at least in terms of initial mand acquisition" (p. 159). In addition, social validity was assessed using open-ended written questions given to the participants' parents and teacher, resulting in generally positive feedback regarding both PECS and sign language treatments.

Lund and Troha (2008) investigated the implementation of a modification of PECS (using tactile symbols) with three 12- to 17-year-olds who had both autism and visual impairments. The authors used a single-case, multiple-baseline design. Data were collected during training sessions. Only one participant mastered the first three phases of PECS (80% independent exchanges for two consecutive sessions); however, the other two participants did increase their percentage of independent exchanges from baseline levels. Intervention fidelity, maintenance and generalization, and social validity data were not reported.

Tincani and colleagues (2006) implemented two studies investigating requesting and verbalizations resulting from PECS teaching with three boys with autism, ages 9–11. The researchers first applied a single-case, multiple-baseline design across two participants; next, a reversal design was used with one of the participants from the first study. From the first phase of their study, using a multiple-baseline design, the researchers noted that one of the students increased vocal approximations in Phase IV of PECS. As a result, they conducted a second study with this participant, using a reversal design, to better understand the role that reinforcement was playing in relationship to **speech** development. The participant who was able to learn to use the first four phases of PECS, when compared with the other participant who only mastered PECS through Phase I, showed increased vocal approximations when a short time delay was implemented before being given access to requested items and verbally praised. When the more PECS-advanced participant made an immediate vocal approximation, he received the items and was immediately praised. Data were collected during training sessions. Intervention fidelity data were collected and were reported to be high, although specific data were not provided. Generalization probe data were collected during the last four sessions of the study, with a novel communicative partner. The identity of the participants' teacher varied, as did rates of independent requesting and vocal approximations, but these rates were near the levels reported at the end of intervention. Maintenance and social validity were not reported.

Charlop-Christy and colleagues (2002) implemented a single-case, multiple-baseline design to address a variety of skills in three 3- to 12-year-old boys with autism who rarely spoke spontaneously. Data were collected during PECS training, play, and academic work sessions. Results indicated that the participants rapidly learned to use PECS. All participants also increased use of spontaneous and imitated verbalizations; all increased use of eye contact, joint attention, or play; and for the two participants who initially displayed challenging behaviors, such behaviors decreased during and after PECS training. Gains were maintained in the weeks immediately following PECS training. Furthermore, gains in PECS use and speech were maintained when assessed 10 months following the intervention for the participant who was available for long-term follow-up (data were not reported for challenging behaviors during follow-up). Fidelity of treatment and social validity were not reported.

Marckel and colleagues (2006) implemented a single-case, multiple-baseline design across behaviors with two preschool boys with autism. Probe data were collected in the participants' homes during training sessions. The children were successfully taught to improvise requests that included function, color, and shape to describe desired items for which individual pictures were not sufficient or available. These effects generalized to the use of function, color, and shape to request novel items. Data assessing generalized use with communicative partners other than those who participated in training were not collected, although the authors noted anecdotally that this occurred. Data were not reported for intervention fidelity, maintenance of treatment effects, or social validity.

Group Research Design Efficacy Studies

Yoder and Stone (2006b) compared PECS ($n = 19$) instruction to responsivity education and prelinguistic milieu teaching (RPMT; $n = 17$) using a randomized group design examining joint attention, turn taking, and requesting. Participants were 36 preschool students with diagnoses of autism or pervasive developmental disorder-not otherwise specified. Both treatments were implemented for approximately 6 months, 3 times weekly, for 20-min sessions. Data were collected prior to and following treatment using standardized measures of communication and social skills and observational data during free play with examiners and with parents, as well as within semistructured activities. Results indicated that RPMT resulted in higher rates of initiations of joint attention and turn taking, though joint attention was only found to be higher in children who had initially higher rates of joint attention. Instruction in PECS resulted in higher rates of requests in children who initially had low rates of initiating joint attention. Intervention fidelity data were collected, with high fidelity reported for both interventions. Maintenance and social validity data were not collected; however, data collection consisted of measures of generalization of skills outside of intervention sessions and conditions.

Yoder and Stone (2006a) also conducted a randomized comparison of PECS ($n = 19$) and RPMT ($n = 17$), providing 6 months of training, 3 times per week, with the aim of investigating the occurrence of spontaneous speech. Data were collected using standardized measures, observational data during free play with examiners, and semistructured activities. Results indicated that PECS resulted in higher rates of spontaneous speech than RPMT. Intervention fidelity data were collected and were high for both interventions. Maintenance and social validity data were not collected.

Carr and Felce (2007b) compared the use of spoken words among 10 children between ages 4 and 7 who had a diagnosis of autism. Using nonrandom assignment of participants to either a treatment or control group, children who received PECS instruction through Phase III ($n = 5$) were compared with controls ($n = 5$). Participants were selected from a larger group because they used at least one spoken word during an observation session. Data were collected via 2-hr observations of the participants' interactions with classroom staff. Results indicated that whereas all children in the PECS group demonstrated increases in spoken words, only one child in the control group did so. Intervention fidelity, maintenance, and social validity data were not reported.

Carr and Felce (2007a) conducted a controlled study, implementing the first three phases of PECS with 24 children and comparing them on adaptive behavior and language to a nonrandomly assigned control group of 17 children. Group means were comparable on standardized assessments of adaptive behavior and language and for age. Data were collected during classroom observations of the participants with their teachers and classroom paraprofessionals. Results indicated increased social interactions and communicative initiations for the PECS group but not the control group. Intervention fidelity, maintenance, and social validity data were reported.

Summary of Efficacy Studies

Review of the existing literature examining the efficacy of PECS reveals that children who receive PECS intervention tend to benefit from the experience. These benefits include increased functional communication initiations, increased vocalizations, and improved interactions with others. Yet, as positive as these findings are, a number of salient research questions connected to PECS efficacy remain unanswered. For example, relatively limited information is available on which diagnoses and other characteristics make children good candidates for PECS or an alternate method. It is also clear that the existing efficacy studies vary in quality, with even the best of these studies frequently failing to describe subjects and procedures fully and failing to provide information on treatment fidelity, generalization, and so forth. Accordingly, although there is much room for optimism about the efficacy of PECS, much work remains to be done in this area.

Effectiveness Studies

Studies of effectiveness include those that are conducted in natural settings and conditions (Robey & Schultz, 1998). For the purposes of this review, studies of effectiveness include those in which the participants' teachers and/or parents conducted most of the PECS training or those in which most of the data were collected in natural environments (e.g., classrooms, homes). Few studies of effectiveness of PECS in natural settings and with trainers already present in those settings are reported in the professional literature. Two studies of effectiveness reported that the implementation of PECS resulted in increased independent requesting (Magiati & Howlin, 2003; Kravits, Kamps, Kemmerer, & Potucek, 2002); an additional study reported decreased challenging behaviors (Frea, Arnold, Vittimberga, & Koegel, 2001).

Magiati and Howlin (2003) conducted a controlled study of 34 children with ASDs. The participants' teachers were taught to use PECS, and they then implemented PECS with the participants. Parents and teachers completed study measures, which included standardized checklists and assessments. Data were collected four times, including prior to intervention and three more times over a 6-month period following the teachers' PECS training. Results indicated statistically significant improvement, including improvements in overall PECS use, number of PECS vocabulary words used, frequency of PECS use, number of manual signs used, number of spoken words used, number of spoken phrases used, and level of spontaneous communication used. Scores in measures of challenging behavior were not significantly improved. Magiati and Howlin assessed social validity as reported by the teachers, who generally reported that they valued PECS, though one teacher reported difficulties in implementing PECS.

Kravits and colleagues (2002) implemented a single-case, multiple-baseline design across settings with a 6-year-old girl with autism. In this study, PECS Phases I–III were implemented in home and school settings, and data were collected during natural activities involving interactions with the participant's mother, teachers, and peers. Results indicated increased spontaneous use of pictures and some increased use of verbal language to make requests, comments, and expansions following

PECS training. Generalization of PECS use with peers indicated increases as well. Follow-up sessions conducted weeks or months after the intervention indicated maintenance of use of PECS and verbalizations. Treatment fidelity and social validity data were not reported.

Frea and colleagues (2001) implemented a single-case, multiple-baseline design across settings with a 4-year-old with autism in a preschool setting comprised of children without disabilities. The participant was taught PECS Phases I–III, then data were collected during free play in the home center of the preschool and in the manipulative center. Results indicated increased use of PECS and decreased use of challenging behaviors, including physical aggression. Treatment fidelity, maintenance, and social validity data were not reported. Generalization data were not explicitly reported; however, all of the data were collected in contexts other than those in which PECS training occurred.

PRACTICAL REQUIREMENTS

Following the design of other aided picture/icon-based augmentative programs, PECS requires use of several basic and widely available items. The most basic and essential of the materials needed to implement PECS programs are individualized reinforcers for students and corresponding pictures and/or icons that learners are taught to use to obtain the desired items. By design, these items and activities are selected based on unique student interests, needs, and wants. Because these reinforcers typically are items and activities already available to potential learners, they often do not need to be purchased or obtained expressly for PECS training.

Training in PECS is available through Pyramid Educational Consultants. Training is regularly offered throughout the world. Instructional costs vary, falling generally around $395 for basic training and $295 for the advanced training.

The basic level of approved Pyramid Educational Consultant training is designed for individuals who wish to implement PECS programs. According to requirements published on the Pyramid Educational Consultants web site, individuals seeking implementation certification status must provide proof of attendance at a Basic PECS Workshop conducted by Pyramid Educational Consultants within 2 years of the application date, pass a written exam, and demonstrate the following skills:

- Competency in employing the six phases of PECS
- Competency in following PECS error-correction protocol
- Competency in applying PECS as a part of functional activities
- Competency in developing PECS-related lessons
- Competency in collecting data within all phases of PECS
- Competency in writing PECS implementation summaries
  (Pyramid Educational Consultants, 2012a)

Upon completion of the above requirements, individuals are entitled to receive a "PECS Implementer Certificate" that is renewable every 3 years and a listing on the Pyramid Educational Consultants web site as a certified PECS implementer. Pyramid Educational Consultants gives explicit rules and guidelines related to the rights and privileges of individuals who complete each level of PECS training (Pyramid Educational Consultants, 2012a). This protocol and policy information includes using PECS with appropriate students, coaching and monitoring others in using PECS, and demonstrating use of PECS with colleagues and families.

Pyramid Educational Consultants also provides "PECS Supervisor" training. This more advanced training is designed for individuals who have demonstrated 1) knowledge and skill in applying all phases of PECS in accordance with the Pyramid Educational Consultants protocol and 2) the capacity to provide productive and positive feedback regarding PECS usage. Individuals who complete PECS supervisor training are permitted, contingent upon approval, to provide PECS overview information and training within their employment site and with co-workers who have acquired basic PECS training. However, these individuals are not permitted to offer PECS training workshops or other trainings or use titles such as "PECS expert" to work outside their own place of employment (Pyramid Educational Consulting, 2012a).

KEY COMPONENTS

The key components and phases of PECS instruction are summarized below. The detail provided here, however, does not replace the need for individuals who wish to use PECS to further study the PECS manual (Frost & Bondy, 2002) and attend a PECS basic workshop prior to attempting its implementation.

Frost and Bondy (2002) describe several key elements essential for PECS implementation. The most important component of PECS is functional instructional goals and objectives. That is, skills are taught expressly for the purpose of spontaneously and independently teaching individuals to use pictures and icons to communicate with others and make their needs and ideas understood. Next, the PECS protocol stresses the importance of determining what items, foods, and activities are reinforcing to students and using those reinforcers to promote learning new communication skills, including making requests and social responses, and to reinforce appropriate behaviors via differential reinforcement (Frost & Bondy, 2002; Skinner, 1957). The PECS system also involves addressing behaviors that are inappropriate to particular contexts and replacing them with functionally equivalent, often communicative, behaviors (Frost & Bondy, 2002). The final elements include planning and teaching for generalization by using effective, research-proven instructional methods, such as discrete trial, chaining, naturalistic instruction, prompting, and cueing, and decreasing student mistakes via error-correction techniques.

Instruction in PECS focuses on several key communication skills (Frost & Bondy, 2002). These include the following expressive communication skills: 1) requesting reinforcing items or activities, 2) requesting help, 3) requesting a break from required tasks, 4) rejecting offers for undesired items or activities, and 5) affirming offers for desired items or activities. Receptive communication skills targeted via PECS include the following: 1) following a direction to wait, 2) responding to directions, and 3) following transitional cues and visual schedules. These skills are taught via the six phases of PECS instruction and additional recommendations provided in the PECS manual (Frost & Bondy, 2002). Instructors must determine which of these skills their students are lacking and plan accordingly to address them systematically.

Prior to PECS instruction, instructors—who may include teachers, parents, speech therapists, or other professionals—make preparations (Frost & Bondy, 2002). First, instructors must set the stage for communicative opportunities throughout the day and in numerous settings. That is, they set up the environment so that students do not have easy access to preferred items (e.g., objects are placed out of reach but

in view; students are given a small portion of a preferred food or brief access to preferred items; Frost & Bondy, 2002; Hart & Risley, 1982; Wetherby & Prizant, 1989).
Prior to preparing materials, instructors assess for preferred reinforcers (Frost &
Bondy, 2002). This step involves caregivers determining what items and activities
the child prefers, which is done in two ways: 1) most notably by observing the student
during free time to determine what items or activities he or she chooses frequently
and 2) by formally identifying reinforcers by repeatedly offering several items at a
time and noting which ones the child tends to prefer (Bondy & Frost, 1994).

Once several reinforcers have been identified and communication objectives
have been determined, instructors prepare PECS materials (Frost & Bondy, 2002).
In addition to already identified materials related to reinforcing items and activities, necessary materials include 1) "pictures" for the student to exchange (e.g., line
drawings, photos, clip art, written words), usually laminated and with Velcro on the
back; 2) a communication binder to store the pictures; and 3) a plastic strip for the
student to use to construct more complex ideas with several pictures. Once materials are prepared, PECS instruction may begin, though new pictures will continue to
be made and added to the student's communication binder throughout his or her use
of PECS.

Phase I of PECS involves teaching the student to spontaneously exchange a picture with a "communicative partner" when the student sees an item he or she wants
(Frost & Bondy, 2002). Most other language programs for children with language
delays begin with instruction in labeling items. However, because children with
ASDs are more motivated to communicate to obtain preferred items (i.e., requests)
than for social purposes (i.e., labeling), PECS instruction first focuses on teaching
students to make requests. A key component of this phase is teaching the child to
approach a communicative partner. Many children with ASDs engage in echolalia,
or repetition of speech without a clear communicative purpose. One of the aims of
Phase I is to reinforce communication via exchanging pictures. To teach a student
Phase I skills, two trainers must be present. One should be in front of the student
within arm's reach (the communication partner), and the other should be behind
the student, ready to provide physical prompts (the prompter). The communicative
partner holds a preferred reinforcer and places a picture of the item on a surface
in front of the child. The communicative partner should entice the child by showing the item, such as by eating a small bite of the food or otherwise bringing the
child's attention to the item without naming it or asking the child what he or she
wants. When the child indicates that he or she wants the item by reaching for it, the
prompter helps the child pick up the picture, reach toward the communicative partner, and then place the picture in his or her hand. Next, the communicative partner
accepts the picture with an open hand, then immediately gives the child the desired
item, verbally labels the item, and praises the child. While the child has brief access
to the item, the communicative partner places the picture back in front of the child.
Then, the communicative partner begins the sequence again by offering another
bite of the food or retrieving the item or toy (e.g., by saying, "my turn," while gently
taking the item back) and enticing again. The prompter fades his or her prompts
via backward chaining over several trials. While the student is mastering Phase I,
opportunities to exchange pictures for preferred items should occur throughout the
day, with a variety of communicative partners, in a variety of settings, and with a
variety of items, all of which promotes generalization.

During Phase II, students are taught generalized use of pictures by instructing them to cross distances to acquire pictures, independently take pictures out of their communication binders, and deliver the items to a variety of communicative partners in a variety of settings (Frost & Bondy, 2002). The main objective is the same as in Phase I, with the addition of teaching the student to be more persistent in communicating requests and traveling gradually further distances to his or her pictures and the communicative partner. Phase II also requires two trainers, one to serve as the communicative partner and the other as the physical prompter. There is also continued expansion of the student's picture vocabulary. As before, neither trainer provides verbal prompts to tell the student to get the picture or to walk to the communicative partner. Furthermore, in this phase, both trainers need to eliminate quickly any cues (e.g., eye contact, leaning toward the student, facial expression, shaking the item noisily) that signal to the student that there is an opportunity to communicate. This is done so the student does not become dependent upon such cues and instead makes requests for something desirable. As in Phase I, the role of the communicative partner should rotate so the student learns to approach individuals (possibly including peers) who have access to the desired items. Furthermore, PECS should be implemented across a variety of settings and with an increasing variety of items. This is the last phase of PECS training that requires two trainers; however, if students experience difficulty in Phase III, the use of multiple trainers may be continued.

In Phases I and II, students are taught to use PECS with a variety of items; however, the pictures for each item are presented one at a time. In Phase III, students are taught to discriminate between pictures (Frost & Bondy, 2002). The terminal goal for this phase is that the student will be able to select a picture from a large number of pictures within his or her communication binder with the selected picture corresponding to the item he or she desires. Phase III usually takes place with the communicative partner and the student seated face-to-face with the communication binder between them. Initially, the student is taught to discriminate between two pictures—one a preferred item and one a nonpreferred item (Phase IIIa). In this phase, the communicative partner has two items and places corresponding pictures on the front of the child's binder. When the student reaches for a picture, the communicative partner either gives brief positive vocal reinforcement if the student touches the correct (i.e., desired item) picture, or gives no vocal feedback if the student selects the incorrect (i.e., nondesired item) picture. Once the student exchanges the picture, the communicative partner gives him or her the corresponding item. If the child receives the nondesired item, he or she will probably push it away or otherwise refuse it, and the communicative partner then completes an error-correction technique. This technique involves four steps. First, the instructor taps the correct picture, then he or she verbally (or physically if necessary) prompts the student to give the correct picture to the instructor, then the instructor provides a distraction (e.g., gives the student an easy and brief task), and finally, the instructor begins again by enticing the child with the item.

Phase IIIb involves discriminating between more than one desired item (Frost & Bondy, 2002). Training is similar to Phase IIIa training in that it includes periodic correspondence checks for discrimination and gradual increases in the numbers of pictures displayed on the child's communication binder and number of items that may be requested at a given time. Correspondence checks are conducted by showing the child at least two items to choose from, and then when the child hands a picture to the adult, the items are offered while the adult watches to see which item is chosen. If the child reaches for an item that does not correspond with the picture given to the instructor, the adult blocks access and then completes the error-correction technique described above, teaching to the item and picture the child reached for, on the assumption that it is the more desired item at that moment. Throughout Phase III, the instructor should frequently vary both the desired and nondesired pictures and items and should vary the position of the pictures on the communication binder. Eventually, the child should be able to choose from a variety of items by scanning through the pictures in his or her communication binder and begin requesting items that are out of sight.

Phase IV involves teaching the student to construct sentences (Frost & Bondy, 2002). Ultimately, the student will be able independently to place a picture indicating *I-WANT* on a sentence strip, place a picture of a desired item or activity to the right of the *I-WANT* picture, and take the sentence strip to the communicative partner. This sequence is taught via backward chaining. That is, the student is initially physically prompted to do all of the steps except the final step (i.e., handing the sentence strip to the communicative partner), then the remaining prompts are gradually faded from the end of the sequence to the beginning. As before, during each exchange, the communicative partner reads the words on the exchanged pictures, either holding the sentence strip or pointing to the words as they are spoken, or physically prompting the student to point to the words as the communicative partner says them. Once the student has mastered the physical exchange, the communicative partner may introduce a time delay, usually starting at the end of the sentence. For example, he or she may read, "I…want…," and then pause for 2–3 seconds before finishing the sentence. Some students, though not all, will begin to say the sentences as they are exchanging the sentence strips; however, speech is never required. Communicative attempts with PECS are reinforced whether they are accompanied by speech or not.

Once the student has mastered sentence construction for requesting, he or she is taught to use descriptors or attributes to clarify which item he prefers when different types (e.g., color, shape, size) are available (Frost & Bondy, 2002). For example, the student may be coloring and will need to request markers of different colors, particularly if the student prefers some colors over others. Attribute instruction is not considered an independent phase of PECS; instead, it is taught throughout the remaining phases. Addition of attribute pictures within sentences is taught in a similar manner to Phase III discrimination instruction; thus, it includes the use of backward chaining to teach the student to use the additional picture, as well as the error-correction procedure to ensure discrimination. It is essential to teach a variety of items with each attribute (e.g., *big cookie, big cracker, big ball*) to encourage generalization.

Phase V of PECS involves teaching the student to respond to the question, "What do you want?" (Frost & Bondy, 2002). Prior to this phase, PECS instruction focuses on spontaneous requests. Once Phase V is taught, the student should make both spontaneous requests and respond to opportunities to answer, "What do you want?" Initially, when the communicative partner asks, "What do you want?" he or she prompts by pointing to the *I-WANT* picture on the student's communication binder. This prompt is faded gradually by inserting a time delay following the question and before the point.

In Phase VI, the student is taught to comment spontaneously and in response to questions, such as "What do you see?" and "What do you hear?" (Frost & Bondy, 2002). This phase is taught in a similar manner to Phase V, with the addition of sentence-starter pictures for making comments (e.g., *I-SEE, I-HEAR*). However, unlike previous phases, in this phase, students are not handed the items on which they comment. This change provides a means of contrasting the social function of commenting from that of requesting. Throughout this phase, the communicative partner sets up a variety of opportunities to comment throughout each day. Eventually, the questions asked by the communicative partner are faded until the student spontaneously comments on items he or she sees and hears. Although the formal PECS system ends with the six formal phases of PECS and attribute lessons, Frost and Bondy provide recommendations for providing instruction in a number of additional expressive and receptive communication skills. A video of a child using PECS to obtain desired items is included on the DVD accompanying this book.

DATA COLLECTION TO SUPPORT DECISION MAKING

Consistent with its roots in applied behavior analysis, PECS is a data-based program that is structured to provide ongoing feedback on progress toward acquiring the communication skills that correspond to program Phases I–VI. Specifically, progress is monitored in terms of the number of trials learners require to become proficient in each phase of PECS. Frost and Bondy (1994) recommend continuing training within each phase until the student is able to independently demonstrate a correct response score of 80% or higher for a minimum of 3 days.

Both researchers and practitioners have also shown interest in tracking the broader development of expressive language skills associated with PECS training. Early in the development of PECS, Frost and Bondy (1994) reported that children exposed to it began speaking. More recent reports have confirmed that development of the use of spoken words and utterances may sometimes follow PECS training (Ganz & Simpson, 2004). Data suggest that this response does not follow a predictable pattern and may in fact not occur with some PECS users (Ganz, Davis, Lund, Goodwyn, & Simpson, 2012). However, this phenomenon has obvious social value and thus is a variable that at least some PECS instructors will want to monitor.

Practitioners and researchers have also shown interest in examining the impact of PECS training on challenging behaviors and aberrant responses (Charlop-Christy et al., 2002; Ogletree et al., 2007). Similarly, learners' generalization of PECS skills has been of interest to PECS users (Ganz, Sigafoos, Simpson, & Cook, 2008). These outcome variables carry obvious importance and thus are clearly worthy of attention during evaluation.

CONSIDERATIONS FOR CHILDREN FROM CULTURALLY AND LINGUISTICALLY DIVERSE BACKGROUNDS

Little has been reported in the literature regarding best practices in teaching English language learners (ELLs) with moderate to severe disabilities (Mueller, Singer, & Carranza, 2006). However, recommendations for typically developing ELLs promote instruction in both the student's primary language and in English, focusing first on proficiency in the primary language (Donovan & Cross, 2002). Mueller and colleagues found that teachers of students with moderate to severe disabilities are ill prepared to provide bilingual services in addition to special education services. Nonetheless, they recommend making decisions regarding language of instruction based on discussions with family members and implications regarding long-term living decisions. That is, the language of instruction should reflect future living arrangements, either with family members who speak the primary language or in English-speaking community settings.

The PECS approach may be well suited for use with children from linguistically diverse backgrounds. In particular, the visual nature of the system is well suited for use with a variety of languages. Although such an approach has not been empirically tested, pairing pictures with written words in either English or the child's first language, or both, may logically promote acquisition of language by supporting receptive, and possibly expressive, vocabulary development (Frost & Bondy, 2002). Teachers or caregivers may verbally model either or both languages when their students exchange pictures to make requests or to carry out more complex language functions. However, some additional factors must be considered when moving beyond the first three phases of PECS. Beginning in Phase IV, sentence construction is taught. At this point, the child may be taught using primarily one language, for greater simplicity in dealing with syntactic and morphological structures that will be language specific. Alternatively, both languages may be used, perhaps focusing on English in the school setting and the child's first language at home, similar to the approach many parents take to using language with their bilingual children. Other variations may be implemented, with attention paid to the child's response to each variation. Ultimately, this is a decision to be made through analysis of an individual student's learning data and discussions with stakeholders, especially the student's family members, and with support of the school or school district staff responsible for ELL students.

Application to a Child

Rosario is a 4½-year-old with autism and severe language delay. She received a score of 50.5 on the CARS (Schopler et al., 1988), indicating severe autism. She attends a public preschool class for children with disabilities at her neighborhood school. Rosario also receives 10 hr per week of behavior therapy during school hours, and 1 hr each of speech-language therapy and occupational therapy per week.

Rosario is able to use a few verbal approximations (e.g., "ca" for "car"), though she does so infrequently and rarely speaks spontaneously, and her voice has a rough, seemingly laborious, quality. Instead of conventional means of communicating, Rosario frequently grabs items she wants or cries when they are out of reach. Attempts have been made previously to teach Rosario to use manual sign language; however, she does not consistently use any signs and has fine motor difficulties that impede her use of the few signs she can imitate. Her teacher collected data during several free-play sessions, observing challenging behaviors (e.g., self-stimulatory hand flapping) and a general absence of foundational communication skills, such as eye contact and joint attention.

Rosario's teacher, Mike, met with the school district's assistive technology (AT) specialist, the school's behavior specialist, and Rosario's mother, Anel, during the second month of school to discuss a plan for addressing the above described behavior and communication issues. The AT specialist recommended teaching Rosario to use PECS.

Though Anel initially expressed concern that PECS would inhibit Rosario's budding speech development, the AT specialist shared professional literature indicating that PECS use correlated with increased speech in some children with ASDs. The team agreed to give PECS an initial 2-week trial, followed by further instruction if notable increases in Rosario's use of the functional communication system and notable decreases in problem behaviors were observed.

During the first 2 weeks of PECS instruction, the AT specialist brought Mike the necessary materials and helped Mike perform a reinforcement assessment and teach Rosario the first two phases of PECS. After approximately 4 weeks of instruction, Rosario progressed through the first four phases of PECS and, though she did not speak much during the first three phases, she began using more spontaneous verbal word approximations as she exchanged a sentence strip for a preferred item.

Application to an Adolescent or Adult

Only a few studies have appeared in the professional literature supporting the use of PECS with older children (Charlop-Christy et al., 2002; Tincani et al., 2006) and adolescents (Lund & Troha, 2008), and one included significant modification of the PECS protocol (Ganz, Sigafoos, et al., 2008). Though little research has been conducted in this area, the promise of social validity extended by PECS is clear. It is well known that the lack of effective communication skills frequently leads to behavior difficulties, which make it hard for adults with autism to obtain independent or semi-independent living arrangements and employment (Koegel et al., 1999; Prizant et al., 2000). Thus, if PECS were to reduce problem behaviors effectively and increase functional communication, its use would be socially validated.

Hank is a 16-year-old adolescent with autism. He attends public school in a self-contained class for individuals with autism and moderate disabilities. Hank's challenging behaviors include tantrums that involve screaming, self-abusive behaviors (e.g., head banging, arm biting), and aggression toward others (e.g., head butting, hitting). The behavior specialist at his school conducted a functional analysis, which demonstrated that the function of these behaviors was usually to obtain desired food or recreation items. Hank does not speak, but he does vocalize. He can make requests via pointing, using a few manual sign approximations (e.g., "juice," "cookie"), or leading a communicative partner by the arm to a desired item.

Hank's individualized education program team was beginning to make transition plans, and his parents were particularly concerned about future living arrangements, because they wanted Hank to live as independently as possible, hopefully in a group home. An outside consultant hired by the school stressed the importance of ameliorating Hank's problem behaviors and improving his ability to communicate effectively. The consultant recommended that Hank be taught to use PECS initially, and once that was mastered, that the team consider a voice output communication aid.

Hank had previously been through compliance training during which he was rewarded with food for sitting and waiting with his hands in his lap. Thus, he did not behave as a young child would by reaching for the desired items. During PECS Phase I training, Hank's communicative partner had to interpret more subtle behaviors as requests and began cuing the physical prompter when Hank looked at the item and subtly leaned toward the communicative partner. Phase II training involved adding the step of shaping Hank to leave his chair to retrieve PECS pictures because in previous training he had been reprimanded for leaving his chair without permission. Once he had achieved the criterion for Phase II, however, Hank was able to progress through subsequent phases. This progression was not without setbacks: On more than one occasion Hank became frustrated when pushed to apply his PECS program to communicate his needs to others. His teacher, however, generally noted fewer episodes of challenging behaviors when Hank had access to his communication binder. In summary, PECS was found to be a utilitarian tool for improving Hank's ability to communicate.

FUTURE DIRECTIONS

A number of recommendations can be made regarding future PECS research. Generalization of PECS use should be investigated, especially generalization across settings other than the school and clinical settings that have received the most investigation so far. In addition, generalization under conditions in which students are confronted with communication obstacles warrant particular attention (Ganz, Sigafoos, et al., 2008). Examples of such obstacles include challenges faced by students who have advanced to using aided AAC when their communication devices are out of reach or malfunctioning or by students who desire items for which no corresponding pictures are available.

Furthermore, research is needed to help identify which individuals with autism would most benefit from PECS instruction (Ganz, Simpson, et al., 2008)—this category would include both those individuals who would make particularly significant gains using PECS and those who may require PECS in order to become active initiators of communication. Because PECS is a time-consuming intervention, particularly in its early phases, practitioners are advised to use PECS only with students who require intensive individualized intervention. Furthermore, not all students learn PECS easily, so future studies may investigate potential modifications of PECS that may benefits such students.

Future research is also required on the components of PECS. Although the whole package has been demonstrated to be effective with some individuals with ASDs, it is possible that only some components or steps are keys to successful use. Identification of such key components could help reduce the complexity of the method and potentially make it both more effective and efficient.

Finally, there is a paucity of PECS research related to adolescents and adults. To be sure, there appears to be potential for use of PECS with youth and adults with autism and other severe language delays and impairments. However, without further research it is impossible to efficiently and effectively capitalize on this potential with these older participants.

SUGGESTED READINGS

Bondy, A., & Frost, L. (1998). The Picture Exchange Communication System. *Seminars in Speech and Language, 19,* 373–389.

This overview article discusses the major elements of PECS, including its theoretical and applied behavior analysis roots. The article also discusses guidelines for PECS and its purported advantages when compared with other alternative and augmentative communication systems.

Charlop-Christy, M.H., Carpenter, M., Le, L., LeBlanc, L., & Kellet, K. (2002). Using the Picture Exchange Communication System (PECS) with children with autism: Assessment of PECS acquisition, speech, social-communicative behavior, and problem behaviors. *Journal of Applied Behavior Analysis, 35,* 213–231.

This article presents one of the first attempts to investigate the empirical efficacy of PECS via use of a controlled methodology. Using a multiple-baseline design with three children with autism, the authors report that all participants met the PECS acquisition criteria, as well as achieving concomitant increases in verbal speech.

Frost, L., & Bondy, A. (2002). *The Picture Exchange Communication System training manual* (2nd ed.). Cherry Hill, NJ: Pyramid Educational Consultants.

This manual describes the basic PECS program and the instructional phases of PECS. Other fundamental elements of PECS use are also included in this manual.

Ganz, J., & Simpson, R. (2004). Effects on communicative requesting and speech development of the Picture Exchange Communication System in children with characteristics of autism. *Journal of Autism and Developmental Disabilities, 34,* 395–409.

This study focuses on examining the effects of PECS on the expressive language of three young children with ASDs and related developmental delays. The authors report that the participants not only mastered the PECS protocol but also demonstrated increases in word productions and grammatical complexity.

Mirenda, P., & Iacono, T. (Eds.) (2009). *Autism spectrum disorders and AAC.* Baltimore, MD: Paul H. Brookes Publishing Co.

This book provides an overview of a variety of AAC systems, including **aided AAC systems** and **unaided AAC systems,** used by individuals with ASDs. A variety of systems are summarized and the research support for AAC use with individuals with ASDs is described.

Learning Activities

1. Following the PECS procedures described in this chapter, role-play a PECS training session. The role-play activity should be for PECS Phases I–VI and for various ages and levels of functioning for a child or youth with autism. In conducting the simulation exercises, one individual should assume the part of a child or youth with autism. Another person, taking the part of the teacher or PECS program implementer, should implement the PECS program, in accordance with the outline in this chapter. For Phases I and II, in which a second trainer is involved in implementing the PECS procedures, another individual plays the role of assisting the person role-playing the part of the teacher. Another person connected to the activity should assume the role of an evaluator. Individuals should change roles after completing the exercise such that each team member has an opportunity to participate as the primary teacher/therapist and support implementer.

2. After completing the role-playing activity just described, members of the group should role-play a dissemination activity. This activity will involve individuals playing the role of a teacher/therapist and parent. The person playing the part of the teacher/therapist describes the PECS program to a person playing the part of a parent.

REFERENCES

Alberto, P., & Troutman, A. (2006). *Applied behavior analysis for teachers* (7th ed.). Upper Saddle River, NJ: Merrill/Prentice Hall.

American Psychiatric Association. (2000). *Diagnostic and statistical manual of mental disorders* (4th ed., text revision). Washington, DC: Author.

Angermeier, K., Schlosser, R.W., Luiselli, J.K., Harrington, C., & Carter, B. (2008). Effects of iconicity on requesting with the Picture Exchange Communication System in children with autism spectrum disorder. *Research in Autism Spectrum Disorders, 2,* 430–446.

Baer, D., Wolf, M., & Risley, T. (1968). Some current dimensions of applied behavior analysis. *Journal of Applied Behavior Analysis, 1,* 91–97.

Beck, A.R., Stoner, J.B., Bock, S.J., & Parton, T. (2008). Comparison of PECS and the use of a VOCA: A replication. *Education and Training in Developmental Disabilities, 43,* 198–216.

Bondy, A., & Frost, L. (1994). The Picture Exchange Communication System. *Focus on Autistic Behavior, 9,* 1–19.

Bondy, A., & Frost, L. (2001). The Picture Exchange Communication System. *Behavior Modification, 25*(5), 725–744.

Brigance, A. (2004). *Brigance Diagnostic Inventory of Early Development–II.* North Billerica, MA: Curriculum Associates.

Carr, D., & Felce, J. (2007a). Brief report: The effects of PECS teaching to phase III on the communicative interactions between children with autism and their teachers. *Journal of Autism and Developmental Disorders, 37,* 724–737.

Carr, D., & Felce, J. (2007b). Brief report: Increase in production of spoken words in some children with autism after PECS teaching to phase III. *Journal of Autism and Developmental Disorders, 37,* 780–787.

Carr, E., & Durand, V. (1986). The social-communicative basis of severe behavior problems in children. In S. Reiss & R. Bootzin (Eds.), *Theoretical issues in behavior therapy* (pp. 219–254). New York, NY: Academic Press.

Charlop-Christy, M.H., Carpenter, M., Le, L., LeBlanc, L.A., & Kellet, K. (2002). Using the Picture Exchange Communication System (PECS) with children with autism: Assessment of PECS acquisition, speech, social-communicative behavior, and problem behavior. *Journal of Applied Behavior Analysis, 35,* 213–231.

Cooper, J., Heron, T., & Heward, W. (2007). *Applied behavior analysis.* Upper Saddle River, NJ: Pearson and Merrill/Prentice Hall.

Donovan, S.M., & Cross, C.T. (Eds.) (2002). *Minority students in special and gifted education.* Washington, DC: National Academy Press.

Earles-Vollrath, T., Cook, K., & Ganz, J. (2006). *How to develop and implement visual supports.* Austin, TX: PRO-ED.

Fey, M. (1986). *Language intervention with young children.* Austin, TX: PRO-ED.

Frea, W.D., Arnold, C.L., Vittimberga, G.L., & Koegel, R.L. (2001). A demonstration of the effects of augmentative communication on the extreme aggressive behavior of a child with autism within an integrated preschool setting. *Journal of Positive Behavior Interventions, 3,* 194–198.

Frost, L., & Bondy, A. (1994). *The Picture Exchange Communication System training manual.* Cherry Hill, NJ: Pyramid Educational Consultants.

Frost, L., & Bondy, A. (2002). *The Picture Exchange Communication System training manual* (2nd ed.). Cherry Hill, NJ: Pyramid Educational Consultants.

Ganz, J.B. (2007). Classroom structuring methods and strategies for children and youth with autism spectrum disorders. *Exceptionality, 15*(4), 249–260.

Ganz, J.B., Davis, J., Lund, E., Goodwyn, F., & Simpson, R.L. (2012). Meta-analysis of PECS with individuals with ASD: Investigation of targeted versus non-targeted outcomes, participant characteristics, and implementation phase. *Research in Developmental Disabilities, 33,* 406–418.

Ganz, J.B., Sigafoos, J., Simpson, R.L., & Cook, K.E. (2008). Generalization of a pictorial alternative communication system across trainers and distance. *Augmentative and Alternative Communication, 24*(2), 89–99.

Ganz, J.B., & Simpson, R.L. (2004). Effects on communicative requesting and speech development of the Picture Exchange Communication System in children with characteristics of autism. *Journal of Autism and Developmental Disorders, 34,* 395–408.

Ganz, J.B., Simpson, R.L., & Corbin-Newsome, J. (2008). The impact of the Picture Exchange Communication System on requesting and speech development in preschoolers with autism spectrum disorders and similar characteristics. *Research in Autism Spectrum Disorders, 2,* 157–169.

Hart, B., & Risley, T.R. (1982). *How to use incidental teaching for elaborating language.* Lawrence, KS: H & H Enterprises.

Heflin, J., & Alaimo, D. (2007). *Students with autism spectrum disorders: Effective instructional practices.* Upper Saddle River, NJ: Pearson and Merrill/Prentice Hall.

Hodgdon, L. (1995). Solving social-behavioral problems through the use of visually supported communication. In K. Quill (Ed.), *Teaching children with autism: Strategies to enhance communication and socialization* (pp. 265–286). New York, NY: Delmar.

Hresko, W., Reid, D., & Hammill, D. (1999). *Test of Early Language Development.* Austin, TX: PRO-ED.

Koegel, L., Koegel, R., Shoshan, Y., & McNerney, E. (1999). Pivotal response intervention II: Preliminary long-term outcome data. *Journal of the Association for Persons with Severe Handicaps, 24,* 186–198.

Kravits, T.R., Kamps, D.M., Kemmerer, K., & Potucek, J. (2002). Brief report: Increasing communication skills for an elementary-aged student with autism using the Picture Exchange Communication System. *Journal of Autism and Developmental Disorders, 32,* 225–230.

Lord, C., & Paul, R. (1997). Language and communication in autism. In D. Cohen & F. Volkmar (Eds.), *Handbook of autism and pervasive developmental disorders* (pp. 195–225). New York, NY: Wiley.

Lund, S.K., & Troha, J.M. (2008). Teaching young people who are blind and have autism to make requests using a variation on the Picture Exchange Communication System with tactile symbols: A preliminary investigation. *Journal of Autism and Developmental Disorders, 38,* 719–730.

Magiati, I., & Howlin, P. (2003). A pilot evaluation study of the Picture Exchange Communication System (PECS) for children with autistic spectrum disorders. *Autism, 7,* 297–320.

Marckel, J.M., Neef, N.A., & Ferrari, S.J. (2006). A preliminary analysis of teaching improvisation with the Picture Exchange Communication System with children with autism. *Journal of Applied Behavior Analysis, 39,* 109–115.

Mirenda, P. (2001). Autism, augmentative communication and assistive technology: What do we really know? *Focus on Autism and Other Developmental Disabilities, 16*(3), 141–151.

Mueller, T.G., Singer, G.H.S., & Carranza, F.D. (2006). A national survey of the educational planning and language instruction practices for students with moderate to severe disabilities who are English language learners. *Research and Practice for Persons with Severe Disabilities, 31,* 242–254.

National Research Council (NRC), Committee on Educational Interventions for Children with Autism. (2001). *Educating children with autism.* Washington, DC: National Academy Press.

Ogletree, B. (2008). The communicative context of autism. In R. Simpson & B. Myles (Eds.), *Educating children and youth with autism* (pp. 223–265). Austin, TX: PRO-ED.

Ogletree, B., & Burns-Daniels, D. (1993). Communication-based assessment and intervention for prelinguistic infants and toddlers: Strategies and issues. *Infants and Young Children, 5*(3), 22–30.

Ogletree, B., Fischer, M., & Turowski, M. (1996). Assessment targets and protocols for nonsymbolic communicators with profound disabilities. *Focus on Autism and Other Developmental Disabilities, 11*(1), 53–58.

Ogletree, B., Oren, T., & Fischer, M. (2007). Examining effective intervention practices for communication impairment in autism spectrum disorder. *Exceptionality, 15*(4), 233–247.

Partington, J., & Sundberg, M. (1998). *The assessment of basic language and learning skills: An assessment, curriculum guide, and skills tracking system for children with autism and other developmental disabilities.* Pleasant Hill, CA: Behavior Analysts.

Prizant, B.M., Wetherby, A.M., & Rydell, P.J. (2000). Communication intervention issues for young children with autism spectrum disorders. In A. Wetherby & B. Prizant (Eds.), *Autism spectrum disorders: A transactional developmental perspective* (pp. 193–224). Baltimore, MD: Paul H. Brookes Publishing Co.

Pyramid Educational Consultants. (2012a). Certification for Individuals section. Retrieved February 15, 2012, from http://www.pecsusa.com/individuals.php

Pyramid Educational Consultants. (2012b). What types of children and adults are appropriate candidates for PECS? (Frequently Asked Questions, section Implementing PECS). Retrieved February 15, 2012, from http://pecs.org.uk/general/faq.htm

Quill, K., Bracken, K., & Fair, M. (2000). Assessment of social and communication skills. In K. Quill (Ed.), *Do–watch–listen–say: Social and communication intervention for children with autism* (pp. 54–74). Baltimore, MD: Paul H. Brookes Publishing Co.

Robey, R.R., & Schultz, M.C. (1998). A model for conducting clinical outcome research: An adaptation of the standard protocol for use in aphasiology. *Aphasiology, 12,* 787–810.

Scheurmann, B., & Webber, J. (2002). *Autism: Teaching does make a difference.* Belmont, CA: Wadsworth.

Schopler, E., Mesibov, G., & Hearsey, K. (1995). Structured teaching in the TEACCH system. In E. Schopler & G. Mesibov (Eds.), *Learning and cognition in autism* (pp. 243–267). New York, NY: Plenum.

Schopler, E., Reichler, R.J., & Renner, B.R. (1988). *The Childhood Autism Rating Scale (CARS).* Los Angeles, CA: Western Psychological Services.

Sigafoos, J., Drasgow, E., & Schlosser, R. (2003). Strategies for beginning communicators. In R. Schlosser (Ed.), *The efficacy of augmentative and alternative communication* (pp. 324–341). New York, NY: Academic Press.

Simpson, R., deBoer-Ott, S., Griswold, D., Myles, B., Byrd, S.E., Ganz, J.B., . . . Adams, L.G. (2005). *Autism spectrum disorders: Interventions and treatments for children and youth.* Thousand Oaks, CA: Corwin Press.

Skinner, B.F. (1953). *Science and human behavior.* New York, NY: Macmillan.

Skinner, B.F. (1957). *Verbal behavior.* Englewood Cliffs, NJ: Prentice Hall.

Tincani, M. (2004). Comparing the Picture Exchange Communication System and sign language training for children with autism. *Focus on Autism and Other Developmental Disabilities, 19,* 152–163.

Tincani, M., Crozier, S., & Alazetta, L. (2006). The Picture Exchange Communication System: Effects on manding and speech development for school-aged children with autism. *Education and Training in Developmental Disabilities, 41,* 177–184.

Van Bourgondien, M., Reichle, N., & Schopler, E. (2003). Effects of a model treatment approach on adults with autism. *Journal of Autism and Developmental Disorders, 33,* 131–140.

Watson, J.B. (1930). *Behaviorism.* New York, NY: Norton.

Wetherby, A.M., & Prizant, B.M. (1989). The expression of communicative intent: Assessment guidelines. *Seminars in Speech and Language, 10,* 77–91.

Wetherby, A., & Prizant, B. (2005). Enhancing language and communication development in autism spectrum disorders: Assessment and intervention guidelines. In D. Zager (Ed.), *Autism spectrum disorders: Identification, education, and treatment* (pp. 327–365). Mahwah, NJ: Lawrence Erlbaum.

Yoder, P., & Stone, W.L. (2006a). A randomized comparison of the effect of two prelinguistic communication interventions on the acquisition of spoken communication in preschoolers with ASD. *Journal of Speech, Language, and Hearing, 49,* 698–711.

Yoder, P., & Stone, W.L. (2006b). Randomized comparison of two communication interventions for preschoolers with autism spectrum disorders. *Journal of Consulting and Clinical Psychology, 74,* 426–235.

12

Pivotal Response Treatment

Yvonne Bruinsma and Erin K. McNerney

Pivotal **Response Treatment** (PRT) is an empirically validated, play-based intervention approach that utilizes applied behavior analysis (ABA) techniques and a developmental perspective to target the core impairments of autism. As a comprehensive service-delivery model, PRT focuses on teaching all key stakeholders in the child's life, thus increasing the total number of intervention hours. Ideally, every waking moment is a teaching moment. Because teaching is provided within the natural environment, across typical routines, PRT inherently targets generalization. Family involvement is critical, and parents are seen as primary interventionists.

TARGET POPULATIONS AND ASSESSMENTS FOR DETERMINING TREATMENT RELEVANCE AND GOALS

The PRT approach was initially developed to teach language to children with autism (R.L. Koegel & Koegel, 2006); over the years, it has been shown to be useful for teaching a variety of skills to this group of children. Effectiveness research on PRT has included adolescents and adults with autism, as well as individuals diagnosed with other autism spectrum disorders such as Asperger syndrome, pervasive developmental disorder-not otherwise specified, and language or cognitive delays (Dyer, Dunlap, & Winterling, 1990; L.K. Koegel & Koegel, 1986). Strategies based on PRT can be used to teach first words (R.L. Koegel, O'Dell, & Koegel, 1987) and basic social skills (Stahmer, 1995) and to help highly verbal individuals develop more sophisticated language and social skills (Boettcher, 2004). No standardized assessments are available to determine the applicability of PRT to specific populations or individuals. Developmental, adaptive behavior, and language assessments may be used, however, to gauge the individual's skill level, assist in development of program goals, and monitor progress.

Although no formal assessments exist to determine who will benefit from PRT, Sherer and Schreibman (2005) found two distinct behavior profiles for children who responded positively to PRT, compared with a group of children who did not evince a notable response to treatment. Preliminary results from their study suggest that at intake, children who subsequently responded well to PRT demonstrated a moderate to high interest in toys, were able to tolerate another person nearby, and had low to moderate rates of nonverbal stereotypy and moderate to high rates of verbal self-stimulatory behavior. Following intervention, these children demonstrated increases in raw scores on language assessment, as well as appropriate toy play and language during structured social settings. Those who did not respond to PRT did not demonstrate these gains; however, the authors report that the majority of their participants fell between these two extremes. Research in this area is in its beginning stages, and insufficient data are available to identify either specific assessments for determining eligibility or behavior characteristics that can predict how an individual will respond to PRT.

THEORETICAL BASIS

Pivotal areas (also referred to in the literature as pivotal responses or pivotal behaviors) are areas that, when targeted, lead to large collateral changes in other, often untargeted, areas of functioning and responding. Pivotal responses, once acquired, result in widespread and generalized improvements in children with autism (R.L. Koegel & Koegel, 2006).

The primary goals of PRT are to move the individual toward a typical developmental trajectory by targeting broad areas of functioning and providing an opportunity for the individual to live and function in inclusive environments. This method focuses on increasing the child's motivation by incorporating child choice, turn taking, and direct and natural reinforcement; by reinforcing attempts; and by interspersing maintenance tasks within the teaching sessions. These strategies are particularly important for the generalization of skills across activities, settings, and people. Through creating teaching sessions, as well as integrating PRT into existing routines in the child's natural environment, PRT creates opportunities for children to *practice* target behaviors rather than merely *being exposed* to situations in the hope that their skills will develop. This treatment allows children to rely on both adults and peers to help structure teaching opportunities in a way that motivates and ensures successful learning. The four aspects of PRT that provide a theoretical basis for its use are 1) family involvement in design and delivery of intervention, 2) treatment in natural environments, 3) treatment of key pivotal target behaviors, and 4) implementation in home and school environments.

Family Involvement

For many years, research has shown parent education to be a critical element of effective behavioral interventions for children with disabilities (Baker et al., 2004). As early as 1971, Schopler and Reichler reported the use of parents as "co-therapists" in a developmental therapy program and found that children demonstrated better developmental skills with their parents than with the therapists. In addition, because parents had been taught the same strategies as those used by the therapists, intervention could continue at home and was not limited to a therapy setting. In addition, parents can see themselves as change agents because they not only implement behavioral procedures but also contribute to the design and delivery of therapy in PRT. Given that intervention is delivered within natural contexts and family routines, parents play a large role in determining which routines and skills will be targeted.

The emphasis in PRT on parent involvement and natural routines is related to a transactional model of development (Sameroff, 1975), which describes development as building upon the interplay between child behavior, caregiver response, and the environmental context influencing the behaviors of both child and caregiver (McLean, 1990; Sameroff, 1986; Snyder-McLean & McLean, 1978). In PRT, parents address impairments by implementing strategies that motivate the child to respond to and interact with his or her environment, which, in turn, affects the parents' response. In this manner, parents and caregivers play a critical role in the child's development. For examples of the kinds of PRT interactions in which a parent might engage, see the DVD that accompanies this book.

Treatment in the Natural Environment

Children with autism have great difficulty maintaining and generalizing learned skills. A drawback to intervention in a clinical setting is the risk of the child acquiring skills that are neither maintained across different contexts nor generalized across people, places, and activities. A key feature of natural language approaches such as PRT is the inherent incorporation of generalization and maintenance into the intervention. Thus, PRT is typically implemented in the environments in which the child interacts on a day-to-day basis, including the home, the school setting, and other community settings. For example, McGee, Krantz, Mason, and McClannahan (1983) demonstrated that incidental teaching during lunch preparation activities resulted in much improved receptive labeling skills that generalized to untrained settings.

Key Pivotal Behaviors

Four pivotal behaviors—motivation, responsivity to **multiple cues, self-initiations,** and **self-management**—have been the focus of considerable research. Each is described below.

1. Motivation

Research indicates that children with autism often do not understand the communicative efforts of those around them and have a difficult time understanding the contingency relationship of responses and reinforcers (R.L. Koegel & Egel, 1979; R.L. Koegel, O'Dell, & Dunlap, 1988). This difficulty is then seen as leading to low levels of responding and what is hypothesized to be a form of learned helplessness. The initial goal of PRT is to promote skill development by eliminating learned helplessness using **motivational strategies** that force the child's exposure to the response–reinforcer contingency (R.L. Koegel, Openden, Matos Fredeen, & Koegel, 2006). If a child is unable to understand and interpret the social cues around him or her, the child is likely to lose the motivation to interact and communicate with others and unlikely to learn and retain information taught during a teaching session. In short, motivation is targeted in PRT on the theoretical premise that the more motivated a child is, the more likely he or she will engage in the teaching activity and with the individuals around him or her.

2. Responsivity to Multiple Cues

One difference between children with autism and their peers with typical development is the way in which they perceive and respond to complex environmental stimuli consisting of multiple cues or components (Rosenblatt, Bloom, & Koegel, 1995). Children with autism often demonstrate *overselectivity,* meaning that they attend to only one cue (or part) of the stimulus, even though it may be an irrelevant cue. For example, the child may focus on someone's eyeglasses or the hand gestures someone makes when talking, thus failing to recognize that person when those cues are absent (Lovaas, Koegel, & Schreibman, 1979). Furthermore, the child may focus on visual rather than verbal information (or vice versa), when these are being presented simultaneously—regardless of which source of information is more relevant. Overselectivity in children with autism appears to be stable over time and unlikely to change without intervention. It may lead to a child experiencing difficulties in many areas and may play a role in his or her perceived unresponsiveness (given that the child may be attending to irrelevant cues). Overselectivity may have an impact on the development of social behavior, language acquisition, learning of new behaviors, generalization, and safety (L.K. Koegel & Koegel, 1995).

3. Self-Initiations

Initiations can be defined as verbal or nonverbal behavior that a child directs toward another person that is not preceded by instructions to talk or do something (R.L. Koegel & Koegel, 2006). There are many different types of initiations, including independent requests, initiations via question asking, initiations for play, initiations for social conversation, and initiations of joint attention. Underlying all types of initiation is the independent formulation of social-communicative goals, without scaffolded support from communicative partners (Matos Fredeen & Koegel, 2006). Although children who are developing typically demonstrate initiations in a variety of contexts (e.g., asking questions, seeking attention, showing items), children with autism often do not initiate to the extent necessary to create and sustain social interactions. Strategies that teach children with autism to initiate social and teaching interactions may promote learning in language, social skills, and pragmatics (R.L. Koegel, Koegel, & McNerney, 2001). Advantages to being able to make initiations include increased independence, more control over interactions, and increased frequency of interaction.

4. Self-Management

Self-management, or the ability to independently monitor one's own behavior and respond using a desired or target behavior, is directly related to an individual's motivation to respond, because repeated failures to respond to the environment in the expected manner typically result in an individual's overdependence on others. This situation can result in a cyclical pattern in which the child's dependence on others teaches and reinforces the child's perception that his own behaviors (responses) are unrelated to environmental consequences (reinforcers) (L.K. Koegel & Koegel, 1995). Self-management increases both responsiveness to the environment and the likelihood that the child will experience natural reinforcers for responding. It can be used for extended periods of time in the absence of an interventionist or clinician and can be used across a variety of natural settings (home, school, community, work). As children learn to identify and manage their own behavior, they reduce their dependence on others while simultaneously building their skills.

Implementation in Home and School Environments

Interventions in natural settings naturally lend themselves to better coordination between home and school environments (R.L. Koegel, Koegel, Kellegrew, & Mullen, 1996), thereby promoting a single, comprehensive program (rather than several disjointed programs targeted in specific environments). In an unpublished dissertation using PRT, McNerney (2003) examined how teaching parents in the home setting could potentially be used to coordinate with the school setting. She held a brief in-service training for staff members at two preschools who had a child with autism in their class (one class with one child with autism and one class with two children with autism). Video clips included in that presentation showed parents of those children using PRT techniques to promote expressive verbalizations. Results indicated that teachers rated the videotape communication format as informative, useful, and supportive of their needs as general education teachers. Following the staff training, all three children in the study showed increases in the number of their functional verbalizations at school (approaching the mean range of their typical peers), and the teachers showed some increases in the number of verbalization opportunities they provided to the child with autism and, more notably, increases in their use of PRT procedures. As discussed previously, PRT can address numerous skills during naturally occurring home routines. The method can also be used to target academic areas, such as homework (R.L. Koegel, Tran, Mossman, & Koegel, 2006), and self-management has been shown to increase in class on-task behavior (L.K. Koegel, Harrower, Koegel, 1999). Work by R.L. Koegel, Tran, and colleagues (2006) provides specific examples of how PRT can be implemented in school settings across preschool, elementary, middle, and high school.

EMPIRICAL BASIS

Since the late 1970s, a large body of empirical evidence supporting PRT has accumulated. For many years, PRT was also known as the "Natural Language Paradigm" (NLP) (R.L. Koegel, Koegel, & Surratt, 1992; R.L. Koegel, O'Dell, et al., 1987); however, it is now most often referred to as Pivotal Response Treatment. The available evidence for the PRT model can be organized into the following categories: efficacy studies for PRT pivotal behaviors, efficacy studies for parent education using PRT, and studies of overall effectiveness.

Efficacy Studies Examining Collateral Effects of Changes in Pivotal Behaviors

As described earlier, pivotal behaviors are behaviors that, once changed, affect many other behaviors. The most frequently cited analogy is that of tossing a rock into a pond. The initial splash from the rock is the change in the pivotal behaviors, while the ripples created by the splash are analogous to the collateral effects of the initial splash. The literature suggests evidence for four pivotal behaviors: motivation, responsivity to multiple cues, self-initiations, and self-management. In this section, we report on studies that use a variety of interventions to promote changes in these pivotal behaviors as a way of demonstrating their "pivotal" nature—that is, of demonstrating that changes in *these* variables appear to promote widespread changes in important untreated variables.

Motivation

Typically, motivation as a pivotal behavior is operationally defined in research studies in terms of 1) the number of responses by the child to social and environmental stimuli (often referred to as *child responsivity*), 2) decreases in response latency, and 3) the quality of the child's affect during interactions (e.g., interest, enthusiasm, happiness) (L.K. Koegel, Koegel, Harrower, & Carter, 1999; R.L. Koegel & Koegel,

2006; R.L. Koegel, Koegel, & Carter, 1999). From a clinical perspective, other variables may be observed that also could be used to indicate motivational levels, as pointed out by Ward in his excellent book on teaching social games and motivational variables (Ward, 2009). For example, if a child is highly motivated, a clinician would probably need to use fewer and less intrusive prompts to obtain a response, and there would be less need or no need for extrinsic reinforcers. In addition, a child's high motivation could be observed in terms of low interresponse times and high response magnitudes (Ward, 2009).

Global evidence for motivation as a pivotal behavior that results in widespread collateral effects comes from a number of single-case-design studies. In a particularly seminal study, Koegel, O'Dell, and colleagues (1987) compared two treatment models using a multiple-baseline design across two children with autism spectrum disorders (ASDs). Both participants were nonverbal and were 4 and 5 years of age. During the baseline condition, which lasted 2 months and 19 months, respectively, the participants were taught to verbally imitate a word using traditional teaching methods. This "analogue" treatment used flashcards; social and edible reinforcers; and repeated trials, manual prompts, and shaping procedures. Participants made no or very few correct imitative attempts during the baseline condition and showed no generalization of imitative utterances inside or outside the clinic setting. After the baseline interval, motivational strategies were applied to the teaching situation, including the use of child choice, task variation, less intrusive prompting, reinforcing of attempts, and natural reinforcers (e.g., access to the toy, praise). These strategies resulted in immediate and substantial increases in responding for both children, and, at least as important, imitative utterances generalized to other settings and to other adults, with gains maintained at a 4-month follow-up for one child. In retrospect, the sample size and lack of treatment fidelity for this study were limiting; however, the substantial improvements in learning rate and response generalization spawned a multitude of studies examining other collateral effects and the effectiveness of each motivational strategy. The collateral effects that were specifically related to motivational strategies included improvements in speech intelligibility (R.L. Koegel, Camarata, Koegel, Ben-Tall, & Smith, 1998), decreases in challenging behaviors, such as tantrums and physical aggression (R.L. Koegel, Koegel, et al., 1992; Oke & Schreibman, 1990), increases in appropriate social behaviors and language use (Stahmer, 1999), and increases in eye gaze alternation to share enjoyment (Bruinsma, 2004).

In addition to studies examining the motivational "package," substantial research has also been conducted examining the motivational strategies incorporated in PRT that differentiate it from other treatment models. We discuss four in depth in this chapter. The first two, interspersal of maintenance tasks and incorporating child choice (and following the child's lead), are important when setting up a learning opportunity and are called antecedent-based strategies (i.e., implemented before the child responds). The second two, using natural reinforcers and reinforcing attempts, are consequence-based strategies. The therapist uses these strategies following the child's response. Although the full motivational-strategy package contains three other strategies (child attention, clear prompts, and contingent reinforcement), they are not discussed here because they are analogous to strategies used in other treatment models. In addition, empirical evidence supporting their value abounds in the ABA literature. For a review of the literature supporting components of PRT, see the work of L.K. Koegel, Koegel, Harrower, et al. (1999).

Interspersing of Maintenance Tasks   This antecedent strategy is sometimes referred to as *task variation.* It refers to the alternation of tasks that are already learned, called *maintenance tasks,* and new tasks, called *acquisition tasks.* As discussed in the general ABA literature, interspersing of maintenance tasks can be likened to the building of behavioral momentum (Belfiore, Lee, Scheeler, & Klein, 2002; Kennedy, Itkonen, & Lindquist, 1995) and is often used to increase general compliance (Singer, Singer, & Horner, 1987). In PRT, maintenance tasks are employed to keep the child highly motivated through consistent interspersing of low effort–high success probability trials. Several studies have shown increases in participant response rate and stability and increases in observer ratings of participants' positive affect (enthusiastic, happier, more interested, better behaved) when the experimenters not only varied the acquisition task but also interspersed maintenance tasks randomly between acquisition tasks (Dunlap, 1984; Dunlap & Koegel, 1980; L.K. Koegel & Koegel, 1986).

Incorporating Child Choice and Following the Child's Lead   This motivational strategy allows the child to play an active role in the selection and use of stimulus materials, including activities, toys, topics, and materials. The use of child choice is well understood in the behavioral literature and has been shown to be effective in many programs (for a review, see Kern et al., 1998). Within the PRT paradigm, Carter (2001) convincingly demonstrated with a reversal design that incorporating choice into game play for three children with ASDs resulted in lower levels of disruptive behavior, as well as higher levels of appropriate social play and pragmatic skills. In addition to choice, using child-preferred activities rather than adult-directed activities during teaching trials decreases social avoidance behaviors in children with ASDs and increases the length of conversational interactions (R.L. Koegel, Dyer, & Bell, 1987). Furthermore, research suggests that even when using highly preferred stimulus items, it may be even more beneficial to follow the child's lead and provide learning opportunities only when the child has already intentionally communicated about the target object or is observed to sustain attention to a target object (Yoder, Kaiser, Alpert, & Fischer, 1993). A similar strand of evidence offered by Siller and Sigman (2002) showed that if a parent was able to "synchronize" his or her behavior with the child's behavior (follow the child's lead and provide little redirection), the child was more likely to demonstrate better joint attention and language abilities 1, 10, and even 16 years later.

Despite the importance of child choice and following the child's lead, it is important to note that teaching using PRT is systematic and not completely controlled by the child (L.K. Koegel, Koegel, Harrower, & Carter, 1999). Parents are taught to follow the child's lead, give choices, and *share* control with their child, rather than to either give up or keep all control (L.K. Koegel, Koegel, Bruinsma, Brookman, & Fredeen, 2003; R.L. Koegel et al., 1989).

Natural Reinforcers   Natural reinforcers (as opposed to arbitrary or artificial reinforcers) are reinforcers that are directly related to the child's response. For example, if the child says "ball," he or she is handed a ball (natural reinforcer) and will probably play with the ball. In contrast, an arbitrary reinforcer is not related to the response: For example, the child receives a raisin and praise for saying "ball." R.L. Koegel and Williams (1980) and Williams, Koegel, and Egel (1981) persuasively demonstrated that natural reinforcers lead to much more rapid and stable acquisition of target skills (including receptive and expressive communication and motor imitation tasks) compared with trials when arbitrary reinforcers were used. The use of natural reinforcers in PRT may be one of the reasons for the consistently encouraging data across studies regarding response generalization and stimulus generalization (Schreibman, Stahmer, & Suhrheinrich, 2009). Strengthening a direct response–reinforcer relationship may play an important role in bringing behaviors under general stimulus control in the natural environment. That is, as a child receives a naturally occurring reinforcer for making a response in the natural environment (e.g., the child sees a cup of juice in the kitchen, says "drink," and subsequently receives the juice), the child will quickly learn that he or she will receive a drink by saying "drink." This type of direct response–reinforcer relationship is in contrast to methods in which a clinician might show the child a picture of a cup, have the child label it (e.g., drink, cup), and then provide the child with a token or piece of candy, neither of which will increase the likelihood the child will ask for a drink when he or she sees one at home.

Reinforcing Reasonable Attempts   This motivational strategy refers to the reinforcement of "reasonable" attempts to communicate rather than shaping successive motor approximations of speech sounds. Reasonable attempts are typically defined as those with intent, related to the task, and performed with a body/facial orientation toward the task or the communicative partner (R.L. Koegel et al., 1988; R.L. Koegel et al., 1989). R.L. Koegel and colleagues (1988) demonstrated that a reinforcing attempts condition for four children with severe communication delays resulted in substantially larger gains for all four children than a motor speech shaping condition. In addition, the children were rated as happier and as exhibiting more appropriate behaviors in the reinforcing attempts condition. Four-year follow-up data for three of the children showed that only the two children in the reinforcing attempts treatment continued to make progress and were speaking in one- to four-word phrases. The third child, who had received only motor shaping treatment, remained nonverbal.

Responsivity to Multiple Cues

The incorporation of multiple cues or, more specifically, the teaching of conditional discriminations to children with ASDs, specifically targets underlying stimulus overselectivity (Lovaas, Schreibman, Koegel, & Rehm, 1971; Rosenblatt et al., 1995; Schreibman, 1997). Overselectivity refers to the difficulty children with ASDs often exhibit in attending to all the features of an object, which results in incorrect responses based on a restricted number of cues. For example, some children may favor visual cues (e.g., a colored card held up to indicate "stop"), while others favor auditory cues (e.g., a beep or alarm to let them know time is up).

Several studies have demonstrated that teaching children to attend to multiple characteristics of their environment can reduce stimulus overselectivity (Burke & Cerniglia, 1990; R.L. Koegel, Dunlap, Richman, & Dyer, 1981; R.L. Koegel & Schreibman, 1977; R.L. Koegel, Schreibman, Britten, & Laitinen, 1979; Schreibman, Charlop, & Koegel, 1982). Attention to multiple cues can be taught by using two approaches—each well documented in the literature. The first approach, within-stimulus prompting (Schreibman, 1975), involves exaggerating the relevant features of a stimulus (e.g., elongating the straight lines in the letters "p" and "b" to emphasize how they are different). Once the child is able to discriminate the target stimulus (the "p" or "b"), the exaggerated features are slowly faded back to typical proportions. This approach appears especially successful when teaching academic skills, such as letter recognition and prepositions (Schreibman, 1975; Summers, Rincover, & Feldman, 1993; Wolfe & Cuvo, 1978).

The second approach, extra-stimulus prompting, often uses environmental obstructions and arrangements to provide the child with ongoing conditional discriminations in the natural environment. This means the child must attend to a variety of stimuli in order to respond correctly and receive reinforcement. For example, as part of an ongoing PRT program, the child would be taught to attend to all relevant cues regarding Thomas the Tank Engine trains: color, size, sex, expression, number of smokestacks, side plates, number of cars it is pulling, and so forth. Burke and Cerniglia (1990) showed that children with ASDs indeed had difficulty attending to multiple component discriminations. The authors then taught these children to attend to the multiple component discriminations and showed that this led to a generalized improvement in responding to complex directions. Most important, though, the authors found that the children improved in their correct responding to multicomponent social stimuli after receiving this type of training. Increased attention to multiple cues reduces stimulus overselectivity. An increased ability to attend to relevant multiple cues leads to increases both in academic (L.K. Koegel, Koegel, Harrower, et al., 1999) and social functioning. Attention to multiple cues appears to be a pivotal behavior, as changes in this skill correspond with changes in additional, untargeted skill areas.

Self-Initiations

Self-initiations appear to be a pivotal behavior. Initiations allow an individual to independently access a wide range of social and other reinforcers in the natural environment. The long-term importance of initiations was examined in an exploratory study by L.K. Koegel, Koegel, Shoshan, and McNerney (1999). These authors examined archival data to identify predictors related to later outcomes. They conducted follow-up measures for children who had received similar therapy and found that, 7–12 years postintervention, they fell into two groups: those with favorable outcomes and those with poor outcomes. The children in the favorable outcome group were very close to their typical peers on a number of measures, including pragmatics, standardized adaptive behavior scores, and social and academic functioning. The poor outcome group was placed in more restrictive educational settings, exhibited severe challenging behaviors, and did not engage in extracurricular activities. The researchers found that the children with good long-term outcome differed dramatically from the poor-outcome group in the total number of spontaneous initiations to the parent prior to intervention. As a second phase in the study, the authors selected, from a different pool of children, four children who did not demonstrate any initiations. These children were subsequently taught a variety of initiations, including question asking, attention-seeking phrases, initiation phrases to peers, and mands for assistance. Follow-up measures were collected 6 years later for all four children in the second phase. The authors found that their outcomes were similar to the highly favorable outcome group in Phase 1 of the study: They functioned close to or at the same levels as their typical peers both academically and socially.

Three effectiveness studies have been completed specifically on teaching question asking to children with ASDs, and these studies have demonstrated the immediate success of the intervention, as well as the generalization and maintenance of treatment gains (Esbenshade & Rosalez-Ruiz, 2001; L.K. Koegel, Carter, & Koegel, 2003; L.K. Koegel, Camarata, Valdez-Menchaca, & Koegel, 1998).

In addition to studies that teach initiations through question asking, the literature provides several other studies in which initiation is taught using **naturalistic teaching** strategies, albeit not necessarily strictly PRT. These include initiations for affection (Charlop & Walsh, 1986), initiations of spontaneous mands (Charlop, Schreibman, & Thibodeau, 1985), general initiations (Ryan, Hemmes, Sturmey, Jacobs, & Grummet, 2008), play initiations to peers (Haring & Lovinger, 1989), and social initiations to peers (Oke & Schreibman, 1990; Pierce & Schreibman, 1995).

Beginning in the late 1990s, the field has begun to focus on teaching initiations for joint attention. Studies published in this area have shown promise in terms of skill acquisition but some difficulty with skill maintenance and generalization (Whalen & Schreibman, 2003; Whalen, Schreibman, & Ingersoll, 2006). One study suggests that targeting motivation using PRT may increase the simplest type of joint-attention initiation (eye gaze alternation to share enjoyment) (Bruinsma, 2004).

Newman and Ten Eyck (2005) successfully taught three students with autism to initiate toward peers. Initially, staff reinforced the students for initiations; however, once the skill was acquired, the students were taught to self-manage their behavior. The self-management was faded and the skill was maintained over time.

Self-Management

This pivotal behavior is similar to self-initiations in that it also highlights the individual's need for independence. Self-management requires a student to monitor and adjust a target behavior following short discrimination training that teaches the child to recognize and record the occurrence of the target behavior (R.L. Koegel, Koegel, & Parks, 1992). Self-monitoring decreases the need for constant vigilance by adults and allows the student to determine their reinforcement following self-evaluation. These teaching procedures can increase an individual's autonomy and empower him or her to become an active participant in behavior-change programs (L.K. Koegel, Harrower, & Koegel, 1999; Lee, Simpson, & Shogren, 2007).

Making a student aware and responsible for his or her behavior may also allow for collateral untargeted behavior change. For example, R.L. Koegel and Frea (1993) found that two adolescents with ASDs generalized across nontargeted social behaviors after using self-management for other specific social behaviors. Subjective ratings made by blind raters of the overall appropriateness of their social interactions also improved following self-management. Research has also shown that using self-management to increase responsivity to social questions (e.g., "What did you eat for lunch today?") across community, school, and home settings resulted in concomitant decreases in disruptive behaviors without the need for further intervention (L.K. Koegel, Koegel, Hurley, & Frea, 1992). Stahmer and Schreibman (1992) successfully taught three children with ASDs to engage in appropriate play in unsupervised settings using self-management—a behavior that also generalized to other settings and was accompanied by a decrease in self-stimulatory behavior.

Self-management has been used with a wide range of functioning levels and target behaviors. It has proven effective for reducing challenging or inappropriate behaviors, including stereotypic behavior (R.L. Koegel & Koegel, 1990), inappropriate vocalizations (Mancina, Tankersley, Kamps, Kravits, & Parrett, 2000), and disruptive behaviors (R.L. Koegel, Koegel, & Parks, 1992).

Sometimes decreasing inappropriate behavior and increasing appropriate behaviors are targeted at the same time. For example, L.K. Koegel and colleagues reduced disruptive behavior and simultaneously increased time on task in a classroom
setting for two children with developmental disabilities (L.K. Koegel, Harrower, et
al., 1999). The behavior change was maintained after the self-management program
was faded. Several self-management studies have been published that show the
procedure is successful at increasing the performance of a particular target skill,
such as time on task (Callahan & Rademacher, 1999), schedule following (Newman,
Buffington, O'Grady, & McDonald, 1995), daily living skills (Pierce & Schreibman,
1994), on-topic question asking (Boettcher, 2004), and increasing initiations
(Morrison, Kamps, Garcia, & Parker, 2001). In a meta-analysis of self-management,
Lee and colleagues (2007) found support for self-management efficacy across 11
single-case studies focused on increasing appropriate behaviors.

Self-management is an intervention that is thought to lend itself especially
well to use in inclusive settings. It is not intrusive, and by transferring control
to the individual with the disability, the need for constant staff supervision and
direction is reduced. In short, self-management appears to be an ideal teaching
strategy for children with ASDs, with a broad evidence base across many settings
and target behaviors.

Efficacy Studies for Parent Education Using PRT

Parent education is widely recognized as a necessary and even essential component of
successful intervention programs for children with ASDs (National Research Council,
2001; Schreibman, 2000). Active involvement and follow-through on program components by parents and other caregivers is more likely to produce sustained, long-term
improvements in a child's skills and adaptive behaviors (R.L. Koegel, Schreibman,
Britten, Burke, & O'Neill, 1982; Lovaas, Koegel, Simmons, & Long, 1973). Teaching
parents to successfully apply teaching strategies throughout the day with their child
dramatically increases the total number of intervention hours and provides for a
range of generalization opportunities (R.L. Koegel, Koegel, Frea, & Smith, 1995).

The PRT model of intervention has always included parent education as a
focal element. Several empirical studies have been conducted that successfully
taught parents to implement PRT strategies (Brookman-Frazee, 2004; Bruinsma,
2004; Gillett & LeBlanc, 2007; Ingersoll & Dvortcsak, 2006; R.L. Koegel, Bimbela,
& Schreibman, 1996; R.L. Koegel, Symon, & Koegel, 2002; Laski, Charlop, &
Schreibman, 1988; Rocha, Schreibman, & Stahmer, 2007; Schreibman, Kaneko, &
Koegel, 1991; Stahmer & Gist, 2001; Symon, 2005).

Parent training can also have collateral effects for the parents themselves. Some
studies have reported stress reduction and more positive affect in mothers during
interactions with their child following PRT training (Moes, 1995; Schreibman et
al., 1991). For example, R.L. Koegel, Bimbela, and colleagues (1996) investigated
differences in parent affect when parents were taught one of two teaching models. One group of parents was taught to implement PRT strategies, while the other
group was taught to address individual target behaviors in a discrete trial format.
Following training, parents in the PRT condition were rated by independent observers as showing significantly more positive affect during interactions with their child.
Such results may be especially important in terms of parent follow-through upon
completion of training.

Brookman-Frazee (2004) contributed further to this line of research by demonstrating that collaborating with rather than directing a parent during PRT parent-training sessions resulted in lower levels of parent stress and higher levels of observed parent confidence. In addition, children in the collaboration condition displayed higher levels of responding and more positive affect. Finally, an exploratory study (R.L. Koegel, Schreibman, Johnson, O'Neill, & Dunlap, 1984) provided some insight into more general collateral effects of parent training that pertain to quality-of-life variables. This study showed that after parent training, families reported spending significantly less time in supporting their children in daily living activities, probably because their children had become more independent. In addition, the families that received parent training spent more time in leisure activities. Such quality-of-life changes may well have lasting effects on families' day-to-day lives.

In the last 10 years, parent training has become increasingly more important for pragmatic reasons. Although ASD diagnoses have increased, in many areas resources are limited both financially and in terms of staffing. This discrepancy has highlighted the need for cost-effectiveness and efficiency of intervention models (Symon, Koegel, & Singer, 2006). To address the needs of families that live far away from intervention providers, a weeklong intensive PRT parent-training program was developed (R.L. Koegel et al., 2002). Intervention data from that program suggested that parents improved their use of PRT strategies and maintained these skills up to one year later in follow-up. In a separate follow-up study, Symon (2005) showed that, upon returning home, parents were also able to teach the procedures they had learned to family members and other service providers, thus dramatically expanding the effect of the initial intervention.

Another way to increase cost-effectiveness is to offer PRT parent training in a group format. One study explored the use of intensive workshops to teach parents PRT skills (Openden, 2005). In groups of seven to ten families, participants received five-hour workshops over four consecutive days. The workshops used didactic instruction, video examples, and feedback on self-recorded video examples showing the parent implementing the PRT procedures with their own child. Data were collected from videotaped interactions between the child and parent at pre- and postintervention. A wait-list control group was used for increased experimental control. A total of 37 families participated in the study, and statistical analysis of the data indicated significant positive differences on all dependent variables, including fidelity of implementation of PRT motivational procedures, parent positive affect, child responsivity to language opportunities, and functional verbal utterances by the child. A similar workshop model was used by Bryson and colleagues (2007); this model will be discussed in greater detail in the next section.

A second study (Boettcher-Minjarez, Williams, & Hardan, 2011) provided 10 weeks of group training in PRT to a total of 17 families (mother, father, or both) with about 8 families in each group. The training consisted of 10 weekly group meetings of 90 min each. Most of the training time was spent reviewing videotaped interactions between participating parents and their children. At least once, the clinician met with the parent(s) and child individually in Week 7 and again, if needed, in Week 10. There was a statistically significant pre- to postintervention change in the parent's ability to implement PRT strategies. In addition, the data showed a statistically significant increase in the number of verbal utterances by children during 10-min probes in post- versus preintervention probes. These results are encouraging and warrant more research in this training format.

Another way of providing increasingly cost-effective and efficient services is to involve peers, siblings, and other caregivers of children with ASDs. Peer mediation may be especially valuable in light of the suggested relationship between level of peer social avoidance and overall treatment outcomes for children with ASDs. For example, Ingersoll, Schreibman, and Stahmer (2001) showed that the preintervention level of peer social avoidance predicted outcome for language use 6 months later. Peer-implemented PRT has been shown to be successful in increasing social initiations, turn taking, increasing time in social interaction, play and conversation initiations, increased engagement in language, and joint attention behaviors (Harper, Symon, & Frea, 2008; Pierce & Schreibman, 1995, 1997).

Another approach to peer participation in intervention is to use contextual support during play dates between children with ASDs and typical peers to increase social interaction (R.L. Koegel, Werner, Vismara, & Koegel, 2005; Werner, Vismara, Koegel, & Koegel, 2006). Contextual support consisted of the use of mutually reinforcing activities and adult facilitation of cooperative arrangements (Kennedy & Itkonen, 1996). These studies showed reciprocity and affect improved between the child with an ASD and his or her typical peer when contextual support was in place. Involvement of siblings in intervention was shown to be successful by Schreibman, O'Neill, and Koegel (1983), while the involvement of other caregivers, such as aides in a summer camp setting, also provided promising outcomes (Brookman et al., 2003).

Some preliminary studies of larger scale implementation of PRT have been published, with two notable studies providing some promising data. Each evaluated the effectiveness of PRT in a slightly different context. The first study examined outcomes for a community-based parent-education PRT program (Baker-Ericzén, Stahmer, & Burns, 2007). Parents were enrolled in a 12-week parent-education program and received 1 hr per week of individual training in PRT. Sessions took place in a clinic setting, and the trainer provided feedback on PRT principles to the parent while the parent interacted and played with the child. Parents were given homework, which included practicing at home and in the community. A total of 158 parents participated in the study. Families were of diverse ethnicity and socioeconomic status. The children ranged from 24 months to 113 months of age, with a mean age of 49.36 months. The ability of parents to implement PRT as a result of this training was not reported in the study, because a previous study of a 12-week parent-education program showed most parents improved in their use of PRT techniques (Stahmer & Gist, 2001). Child outcome was measured using the Vineland Adaptive Behavior Scales (Sparrow, Balla, & Cicchetti, 1984). Improvement in standard scores from pre- to postintervention was significant for the Adaptive Behavior Composite as well as the four domains (communication, daily living skills, socialization, motor skills). As the authors appropriately concede, the results may be somewhat limited because this instrument provides a parent report measure, and parents may have been biased as to their reports of change in their child following intervention. Nevertheless, the Vineland Adaptive Behavior Scales have been found to be a reliable and valid instrument for the purpose of measuring adaptive behavior, and the results are encouraging for these types of short-term parent-education programs.

The second study provides an extensive program description and some preliminary data on two participants from a large-scale PRT replication project in Nova Scotia, Canada (Bryson et al., 2007). The project consisted of three phases: 1) direct training of stakeholders, including parents and behavior therapists, using a workshop format; 2) training of trainers in the project; and 3) collection of follow-up data on the intervention teams' skills, program fidelity, and child outcomes. In the first phase, a group of 27 children was selected to participate in the training, along with most of their intervention teams, including their parents and behavior therapists. Teams participated first in a pretraining workshop of 2–3 days, which covered general topics, such as information about ASDs and basic ABA concepts. Subsequently, teams received weeklong training in PRT by staff with extensive PRT experience. The workshops included lectures and daily feedback on videotaped interactions with the child. Following the workshops, social validity was assessed, resulting in highly positive ratings by participants of the workshops. In the second phase, a 5-day train-the-trainer workshop was conducted, with the objective of teaching five trainees how to provide in-person PRT training and how to collect data and design a child's program. This workshop was highly individualized in terms of direct feedback on video-recorded implementation. Trainees also rated these workshops as highly positive.

In the third and last phase of the project, data were collected on the implementation and outcomes of the project, and preliminary data for two participants were reported in the study. These two participants not only improved in the fidelity of their implementation of PRT strategies but also maintained their improvements, while the children's language (number of functional utterances) improved substantially after PRT implementation. Publication of a larger sample of data will elucidate the outcomes of this project further.

A final relevant study is a critical literature review by Delprato (2001), who analyzed eight studies that compared the use of discrete trial instruction and PRT and, in two cases, discrete trial instruction versus incidental teaching (a naturalistic approach that shares similarities with PRT). Delprato (2001) concluded that

> the preponderance of the evidence supports the possible superiority of normalized behavioral training over discrete-trial training for developing a significant range of language responses in young children with autism and that the main factor limiting the contribution of this series of studies was their restricted habilitative review. (p. 323)

The author calls for large-scale and comprehensive outcome studies of PRT that take into account multiple developmental domains as well as comparative studies between discrete trial instruction and more naturalistic treatment models (such as PRT). However, as Sherer and Schreibman (2005) noted, it is at least as imperative that research be conducted to help identify which treatment model is most effective for which child and family, given that a single model will not work for everyone.

PRACTICAL REQUIREMENTS

PRT is designed to be easily integrated into a family's current routines, with minimal modifications. The next section answers practical questions about who can implement PRT, where it can be implemented, how much PRT a child should receive, how one acquires training in PRT, and how to ensure that PRT is being implemented correctly.

Interventionists

No specific requirements exist regarding who can effectively use PRT. Because PRT was initially developed so that parents could act as "co-therapists," it is user-friendly; that is, use of technical jargon is limited, and concepts are explained in terms most can understand. There are some basic personal characteristics, however, that increase the likelihood that someone will be able to effectively implement PRT. An individual is more likely to be a successful co-therapist if he or she is actively involved in the child's intervention program, aware of the skill areas being targeted, willing to participate in training to learn PRT strategies, and receptive to feedback regarding fidelity of implementation of those strategies. In addition, because PRT is a play-based approach occurring in natural settings, the ability to play (and have fun!) without following a rigid curriculum is an essential quality of a successful PRT interventionist.

PRT techniques, especially the motivational strategies, were developed for implementation by parents so that learning for the child with an ASD could occur throughout the child's day. In fact, parents are seen as an "integral part of intervention" (R.L. Koegel, Openden, et al., 2006, p. 9). Furthermore, because intervention intensity increases as more stakeholders are able to follow through on naturally occurring learning opportunities during all daily routines and activities, it is recommended that all care providers, including perhaps a nanny or grandparents, be taught how to use motivational strategies.

Teaching Environment

Developers of the PRT model intend it for use in an individual's typical environment and advocate for inclusive settings (e.g., L.K. Koegel, Koegel, Harrower, et al., 1999). Services are delivered in the home, as well as in schools or other community settings. Teaching environments can easily be adapted to provide additional structure, as well as to create communication temptations. Involvement of peers and siblings early in the program allows greater generalization to multiple communicative partners.

When parents or therapists are working with children in the home, skills are practiced in all areas of the house and a variety of toys and activities is typically present. These toys are matched with the child's interest and developmental as well as chronological age. Some toys, such as those with multiple or interchangeable parts, lend themselves more easily for use in PRT sessions because they provide a natural opportunity for sharing and turn taking. Toys that consist of only one piece are less preferable, especially for parents just learning PRT, as they make it more difficult for the parent to obtain shared control with the child. In addition, daily living activities in the home provide a constant flow of learning opportunities.

Intervention Intensity

The National Research Council (2001) recommended 20–25 hr per week of services for children with ASDs. In the PRT model, the child is learning during all waking hours through intensive, systemwide service delivery. Services are typically most intensive in the beginning and can be faded as the child becomes more responsive and learns to create his or her own learning opportunities through self-management and initiations (L.K. Koegel, Koegel, Harrower, et al., 1999).

Fidelity of Implementation

Correct implementation of PRT motivational strategies is typically measured by expert scoring of videotaped interactions between the service provider or parent and child. Therapist or parent behavior is scored in ten 1-min video clips on each of the seven strategies, which are described in the next section of this chapter. Fidelity is considered acceptable when the parent reaches 80% or higher on all strategies across the ten 1-min intervals.

PRT Training

Training in the fundamental motivational strategies until fidelity of implementation with one child is met usually requires an average of 25–30 hr of training (Bryson et al., 2007; R.L. Koegel et al., 2002), although positive results have been reported following a 12-hr parent-training course (Stahmer & Gist, 2001). Bryson and colleagues (2007), in their description of the PRT program in Nova Scotia, reported in detail how lectures, workshops, and feedback on videotaped interactions for parents and interventionists allowed participants to reach fidelity of implementation after 30 hr of training.

In general, PRT parent training consists of modeling by the clinician as well as direct feedback on each of the strategies to the parent or clinician while he or she is playing with the child or engaged in daily routines (R.L. Koegel et al., 2002). The feedback provided to the parent is very specific, positive, and encouraging. In addition, the parent is empowered and included in the decision-making process throughout training and service delivery.

Although many service providers offer PRT, initially no official training or certification was available. Most providers were trained through conference workshops and by reading the PRT manuals and books available from the PRT clinics at the University of California, Santa Barbara, and the University of California, San Diego. An official certification program is now available through the University of California, Santa Barbara. This program consists of different certification levels, from basic to more advanced. Certification may help safeguard procedural integrity for PRT and produce well-trained therapists, resulting in an increased level of public confidence in correct PRT implementation.

KEY COMPONENTS

PRT is an incredibly flexible therapy, as it can be incorporated by anyone interacting with the child (parent, sibling peer, teacher, etc.) and at any time within a child's day that a teaching moment occurs (or is created). Typical goal areas include receptive, expressive, and spontaneous language; play and social interaction; self-help skills; and preacademic and academic concepts. This list is by no means exhaustive, however. Goals are often targeted simultaneously in PRT because one can create opportunities for language, play, and social interaction during a single activity. Skills within a given area (e.g., language) are generally targeted sequentially; however, sequences can vary by child, and goals and objectives should be individualized to a child's specific needs (R.L. Koegel, Openden, et al., 2006). The PRT methodology does not employ a standardized curriculum; however, certain key areas can be identified as common elements in PRT programs (see Table 1.2 in R.L. Koegel, Openden, et al., 2006, pp. 24–27).

Pivotal Response Treatment Strategies

Seven key techniques are used in the implementation of PRT (Table 12.1). They fall into two types: 1) those related to the presentation of opportunities to provide

Table 12.1. Application and examples of Pivotal Response Treatment (PRT) techniques

Strategy	Explanation	Application and examples
Antecedent-based PRT strategies		
Getting the child's attention and creating a learning opportunity	Obtain the child's attention *before* creating a learning opportunity, thus creating an opportunity for the child to respond to reinforcement. Instructions should be clear and appropriate to the child's age and developmental level. The opportunity presented is based on the child's expected response (e.g., request, initiation, question). Keep in mind your target area (language, social, play).	Get within close proximity. Lean in to gain eye contact. Tap the child's shoulder. Use an attention-gaining cue (e.g., "Look at this!" "Check it out!"). Look expectantly. Wait. Entice. Ask a question. Offer a choice. Present an instruction. Withhold an item. Offer a small portion. Model a target or desired behavior.
Incorporating multiple cues	Use items that have multiple features so that the child will have to attend to all relevant cues (size, shape, color, etc.). Vary your questions/instructions so that the child will not always expect you to ask something in the same way each time.	Have big and small blocks of several colors available; have the child ask for the block using a specified cue (e.g., the *big* block or the *red* block). Expect the child to be able to respond to a variety of different instructions or questions (e.g., "What color block?" "Find a *small* block," "Get *two* blocks").
Interspersing maintenance tasks	Intersperse easier and more established responses with acquisition (harder) tasks. Build behavioral momentum. Maintain a quick pace.	Mix simple concepts/tasks with more complex problems. Build in "fun" tasks. Take some time for play (noncontingent reinforcement).
Sharing control	Use toys and materials that the child prefers or selects. Offer choices. Follow the child's lead. Consider motivation when selecting teaching materials.	Offer choice of location, materials, order of completion, topics, and so forth. Observe toys that the child gravitates toward and use those materials to create an opportunity. Use "motivating" and preferred toys in teaching opportunities. Take turns with materials.
Consequence-based PRT strategies		
Reinforcing contingently and immediately	Attempts are reinforced as quickly as possible to ensure the child learns the response-reinforcer relationship. Reinforcement is provided when the child makes an attempt. It is not provided in the absence of an attempt toward the target behavior.	For example, the child says "car" and is immediately given the car. If the child is prompted to say "car" but *does not* respond, he is *not* given the car. It may be important to reduce the difficulty of the instruction, for example, by prompting the child to make a car-like sound instead of the word.
Reinforcing attempts	*Reasonable* attempts should be reinforced. Closer approximations receive greater reinforcement. Attempts should be clear, unambiguous, and goal directed.	Reinforce the child for beginning a difficult task, saying part of a word as a request, or offering any other indication of effort.
Using natural, direct reinforcers	Reinforcers are functionally and directly related to response. The child should contact the same reinforcement in the natural environment as during training.	Child requests "juice" and receives juice, counts raisins and then receives raisins as reinforcement, or writes his or her name to sign in for a preferred activity.

Source: Openden, Symon, Koegel, and Koegel (2006).

a response and 2) those related to the reinforcement that should be given to the child following his or her response. For example, when working with a child, the clinician must first create the circumstances needed to present a learning opportunity. The clinician presents the discriminative stimulus, or opportunity, and the child responds. That response can either be the target response (or a satisfactory attempt or approximation), no response, an incorrect response, or an inappropriate behavior. In all cases, the child's behavior constitutes a response, and the clinician must provide the appropriate consequence or reinforcement.

Gaining and Maintaining the Child's Attention

Instructions should be clear, concise, appropriate to the task, uninterrupted, and presented when the child is attending to the individual or task at hand. Instructions should not be presented if the child is not attending, having a tantrum, or engaged in stereotypic behavior.

Establishing Shared Control

Shared control, also known as child choice, involves a balance between the clinician or parent maintaining control of the teaching environment and the child having choice about the activity and/or stimulus items. It does *not* consist of allowing the child to "run the show." This balance is obtained by offering choices of stimulus item(s), activities, environments, and/or order of activities and by following the child's lead to determine items or activities of interest. At no time should the child have total control. The child is encouraged to make choices and learns to take turns with stimulus items, which involves give-and-take interactions between the child and the adult or peer. Teaching occurs during the activity, game, or other natural routine. It is ideal to provide at least three opportunities per minute for the child to respond; however, the pace may be quicker or slower, depending on the child and the activity.

Interspersing Maintenance Tasks

Maintenance tasks draw on skills that have been previously learned. They should be interspersed frequently, presented along with acquisition trials, used to keep up behavioral momentum, presented before difficult tasks, and used to enhance overall level of success within teaching sessions. A maintenance task can be anything the child is able to do fluently, such as responding with a single word or nodding his or her head. At times, maintenance may just be allowing the child to play a bit longer with an item in the absence of external demands. In PRT, there is no set ratio or plan for the presentation of maintenance versus acquisition tasks, because the presentation should be based on the child's motivation and behavioral momentum. At some times, a child may do well with interspersal of a maintenance task after every two or three acquisition tasks; at other times, the same child may remain engaged and motivated with far fewer maintenance tasks (e.g., occurring after every seven or so acquisition tasks).

Addressing the Child's Responsivity to Multiple Cues

Addressing the child's responsivity to multiple cues helps to reduce the frequent problem of stimulus overselectivity. This component involves activities that require the individual to attend and respond to two or more elements of an instruction (e.g., the green block; the small cow). This component should be incorporated in a way that is appropriate to the child's developmental level. For example, just as one would not expect a typically developing 3-year-old to attend to more than three different cues (e.g., "big," "blue," "round"), one would want to adopt expectations that are appropriate to the developmental level of the child with an ASD.

Reinforcing Contingently

Reinforcers need to be delivered immediately following the occurrence of the target behavior. They should be contingent upon the occurrence of the target behavior (or an attempt), uninterrupted, and effective and appropriate.

Reinforcing Attempts

It is important to encourage continued responding by reinforcing reasonable attempts to respond even if the response is not exactly what was desired. Any reasonable attempt to respond correctly is reinforced. If a child has previously demonstrated mastery and fluency with a particular skill, his or her attempts need not always be reinforced. What is considered a valid attempt to reinforce will depend on where the child is in terms of development of a skill, as well as on factors in the situation (e.g., whether the child is feeling ill, hungry, or sleep deprived).

Providing a Clear and Direct Response–Reinforcer Relationship

Reinforcers should be natural consequences for the desired behavior (to the greatest extent possible). They should be directly related to the desired behavior (e.g., when the child makes a request for water, he receives water). In PRT, reinforcers are also generally paired with social praise (e.g., "Yay!" "Good job!"), although care must be taken that the child learns the response–reinforcer contingency (e.g., saying "water" results in the child receiving water, not necessarily a "good job!").

DATA COLLECTION TO SUPPORT DECISION MAKING

Because PRT is based on ABA, it is impossible to implement a PRT program without including a comprehensive data collection system. Representative data are collected on both child and interventionist behavior throughout treatment to help the interventionist monitor and evaluate progress as well as to adjust skill and behavior goals. Nevertheless, data collection can be an overwhelming task for parents and challenging for even experienced therapists. Taking data at a table during a structured session is very different from taking data while hanging upside down from the monkey bars with the child and his or her peers! Moreover, data collection needs to be discreet to ensure the child with an ASD does not stand out from his or her peers because of the intervention. The following suggestions for data collection are the result of clinical experience and have not been empirically tested.

Parent Data

The significance of parent data collection is easily underestimated, and it can be difficult to motivate parents to collect data on a regular basis. In our experience, some simple strategies can help ease the burden and simplify the process. First, reviewing the data with the parent during weekly sessions and including them and their data in the decision-making process shows the parent how the data are used and empowers them as an active member of the team. Second, it can be helpful to modify data sheets so they can be used as checklists (for example, a checklist on antecedents of behavior) or to ask parents to sample behavior once a day for a short period. Finally, data on both the child's and the parent's skills can be collected during weekly parent consultation sessions.

Child Data

Because it can be challenging to collect continuous data in the natural environment, videotaped probes can be helpful to ensure accurate data collection. However, scoring data from videotapes is a time-intensive and not necessarily cost-effective process. For some skills, representative probes can be collected in the natural environment. For example, progress in overall language development can be tracked by transcribing a 10-min interaction that can be scored for variables such as prompting levels, mean length of utterance, the child's responsivity, and any specific language goal. A sample language probe datasheet (Figure 12.1) is provided as an example. Such a probe can also support troubleshooting when a child is not progressing: Perhaps the therapist is providing the wrong types of prompts or relying too much on model prompts.

In community programs, each child typically has a variety of datasheets in a data binder. Current datasheets are attached to a clipboard, and the therapist collects data on the child's goals throughout the session. Because therapists are never working on just one goal (because they are interspersing maintenance and varying the task), it can be helpful to select a goal to collect data on for a certain period. Some therapists prefer to carry small index cards or write on their hands while in the community or following the child. For simple frequency counts, golf watches or wristwatches with a repeat chronograph function can also be used.

CONSIDERATIONS FOR CHILDREN FROM CULTURALLY AND LINGUISTICALLY DIVERSE BACKGROUNDS

In all clinical intervention programs, sensitivity to the needs of children and families from culturally and linguistically diverse backgrounds is essential for follow-through and maintenance of program gains. The PRT model lends itself especially well to work with culturally and linguistically diverse families because of its focus on parent education and parent empowerment. This model is congruent with the focus in the literature on collaborative partnerships (Turnbull, Blue-Banning, Turbiville, & Park, 1999), as well as the research that emphasizes the importance of parents feeling that they are respected and their input is valued (Zionts, Zionts, Harrison, & Bellinger, 2003).

In addition, PRT fits well within the ecocultural framework (Gallimore, Weisner, Bernheimer, Guthrie, & Nihira, 1993; Sze & Koegel, 2006), which highlights the importance of recognizing and using a family's daily routines when individualizing intervention. A family's everyday routine is the context in which intervention must be embedded and therefore provides the constraints under which the intervention must succeed (O'Donnell, Tharp, & Wilson, 1993). By employing the family's daily routines as a basis for intervention, cultural background and preferences are relatively easily incorporated. Two studies by Moes and Frea (2000, 2002) suggested more positive outcomes with incorporation of contextual variables during behavior change procedures. Such research provides some additional support for parent education in the embedding of PRT motivational procedures into family routines and daily activities, and it suggests the inclusion of these variables is crucial for the development of meaningful and sustainable interventions.

LANGUAGE PROBE

Date:_____ Therapist:_____

Context:_____

Start time:_____ End time: _____

Key: I, independent/spontaneous; TD, time delay; OE, open ended; MP, model prompt; Echo, echolalic; NR, no response; S, self-stimulatory vocalization; Inc, incorrect; #, length of utterance

TRANSCRIBE 10 MIN and sum totals in gray box at the bottom

I	TD	OE	MP	Echo	NR	S	Inc	#	Exact transcription of utterances
Total number of opportunities:									

Figure 12.1. Sample language probe datasheet.

Two other closely related concepts important in the provision of services to families with culturally and linguistically diverse backgrounds are "goodness of fit" (Bailey et al., 1990) and "contextual fit" (Albin, Lucyshyn, Horner, & Flannery, 1996). The idea of goodness of fit pertains to the match between the characteristics of a family and the interventions services, whereas contextual fit broadens this idea to multiple contexts and variables. In a case description, Santarelli, Koegel, Casas, and Koegel (2001) described how a PRT parent-education program was adapted to meet the needs and provide a better goodness of fit to a Hispanic family of lower socioeconomic status. Adaptations included assigning Spanish-speaking clinicians, providing services in the home and in the evenings when the father would be home, providing simple checklists for data collection to overcome the obstacle of limited literacy skills, and including extended family in the intervention (Santarelli et al., 2001). Such adaptations provide excellent examples of intervention individualization and efforts to improve goodness of fit for PRT services.

In summary, the PRT service delivery model lends itself exceptionally well to the provision of services to families with culturally and linguistically diverse backgrounds. The focus in PRT on parent education, as well as on creating naturally occurring learning opportunities during daily routines, provide for a culturally sensitive model that is easily adapted for each individual family. In addition, as Sze and Koegel (2006) noted, incorporating motivators throughout routines that fit with a family's cultural and ethnic background may both increase a family's motivation to collaborate with professionals and help sustain behavior modification procedures.

Application to a Child

Dylan was 3 years, 4 months old when he started receiving PRT. He lives with his typically developing sister (age 5) and his parents. Dylan knew some letters, the numbers 1–10, and colors. He understood some basic commands such as "Come here" and "Sit down"; however, his compliance was minimal. Dylan would occasionally make an approximation of a word (e.g., "wawa" for water); however, he was basically nonverbal and relied on pulling others, screaming, and having tantrums to communicate his needs. Dylan demonstrated some perseveration (continuing something over and over) and rigidity. Whenever he was exposed to a new activity, he expected it to repeat in the same way. For example, one day he was given a new type of yogurt while he was sitting outside in the backyard. Subsequently, every time he was given the yogurt, he tried to run outside to the backyard to eat it. When Dylan's routines were interrupted, he tantrummed for 30–60 min. Dylan did not play much with toys and did not imitate others' play actions; however, he did enjoy some interaction with his sister and parents. He loved being tickled and chased. He enjoyed completing simple puzzles, looking at books, and watching videos.

For Dylan, PRT began with assessing which activities he found most motivating. Initially, he loved watching the same Thomas the Tank Engine video repeatedly, and, once he started watching it, would resist when his parents tried to pull him away to engage in other activities. A consultant met with Dylan's parents at home 2 hr a week, specifically to teach them basic ABA strategies and PRT techniques. To target Dylan's motivation, his parents were first taught to use his favorite video to increase his verbal requests. They were shown how to periodically pause the video, then prompt him to say "play" for the video to continue. As Dylan became familiar with this routine, his parents were taught to intersperse other preferred activities (tickling, chase games), and then newer (and less familiar) activities with his favorite video. Time with the Thomas video began to decrease.

Dylan began using more and more word approximations (book, puzzle, ball, chase, tickle, etc.) throughout his day. His parents were taught how to incorporate his older sister into routines by having them take turns chasing each other, kicking a ball to each other, and so forth. Dylan's receptive language also increased, as instructions were incorporated into the motivating activities (get the ball, find the animal puzzle, find the red block, sit down, etc.). His play skills improved as he was more motivated to imitate play actions and sequence them together. As his parents continued to practice PRT strategies, Dylan's vocabulary increased dramatically. His affect improved, and his parents reported he enjoyed playing more social games with them and with his sister. He became more flexible with routines, and although he would occasionally protest when a routine changed (the family decided to walk a different route to the park), he no longer had tantrums for extended periods. Dylan's parents also made changes. Instead of following the same routines to prevent tantrums, they began trying new things and going new places.

One year later, Dylan was a "different child," according to his parents. He no longer watched any Thomas videos, preferring to play with toys such as cars and blocks, look at books, or complete puzzles. He enjoys playing Hide and Seek, playing chase, and kicking a soccer ball with his parents. He is combining two words to communicate (and sometimes more). He is able to request what he wants, tell others he does not want something, and ask basic "Wh__" questions ("What is it?" "Where is it?"). He can initiate play with others ("Come play!"). Dylan tolerates changes in his routine with minimal protests. Although he still engages in some perseverative behavior, he can easily be redirected to other activities, especially now that he has a larger repertoire of things he enjoys. Dylan's parents continue to utilize PRT throughout their day. Although they face ongoing challenges as Dylan must learn new skills, they report they are able to do things they did not dream of being able to do just 1 year ago.

Application to an Adolescent or Adult

Sophia is a 13-year-old girl who lives with her parents and two younger siblings (ages 9 and 7). She is in seventh grade in a general education classroom. Sophia communicates using phrases and sentences. She is performing at age level on academic tasks (although she sometimes becomes confused with tasks involving multiple steps or directions); however, when she was referred for consultation, her teachers and parents reported she had no friends and spent recess alone engaging in solitary activity, usually involving one of her specific interests (looking at road maps or auto advertisements, repeating her favorite television shows word for word, etc.). During class she is often off task and requires many verbal prompts to follow along with the lesson. At home, Sophia prefers to spend time in her room, engaging in a perseverative activity (one of her preferred interests). She sometimes has tantrums when asked to do homework. She does not interact much with her siblings. Sophia's parents report they do not often go anywhere as a family, as Sophia often protests, and, when they do go out, she often wanders away from the family when something catches her interest.

Sophia's parents began learning about PRT 6 months ago and receive consultation 4 hr a week in their home. The consultant also makes monthly visits to Sophia's classroom to consult with her teacher.

Sophia's parents were taught PRT strategies. They quickly discovered that Sophia was able to use fuller sentences and respond more quickly when they use the techniques. Sophia and her parents were also taught how to use a self-management system to increase Sophia's on-task behavior during homework, as well as in the classroom. Sophia quickly learned how to recognize when she was "on task" for the designated period. At first she had some difficulty recognizing when she had been "off task" (gazing away from her work or the teacher, fiddling with things in her desk, doodling on her paper instead of doing the work, etc.). With a few role-play sessions, she was able to discriminate between on- and off-task behavior and enjoyed "paying" herself with tokens she was able to "cash in" at home for preferred activities or items. As Sophia demonstrated increased ability to manage this behavior (staying on task), Sophia's parents were taught some simple ways to make homework more motivating by incorporating some of her favorite things into the activity such as following a "road map" with different assignments as places on the map (this also incorporated shared control as Sophia could choose which path she wanted to take, and thus choose the order of her assignments).

As Sophia began to show improvements in the targeted areas, her engagement with peers in the classroom also began to increase. Her teacher began reporting she was talking more to her classmates, although she still spent recesses alone. At home, Sophia's parents were taught ways to facilitate social interaction between Sophia and her siblings, initially using specific games such as Hide and Seek, Twenty Questions, and scavenger hunts. A self-management system was then created to increase Sophia's social interactions with her peers at school. After receiving intervention for 9 months, Sophia was learning how to increase her ability to engage in conversation, to make nice comments to her peers, and to initiate interactions. Her teacher reported that she was starting to use these behaviors in the classroom and at recess. Sophia's parents arranged some structured, time-limited, fun activities at home during which Sophia can invite a peer and practice these skills (e.g., baking cookies, making bead bracelets, etc.). They reported that although she still did not have many "friends," she had had several play dates and had had one girl over twice, with the second visit initiated by the peer. Sophia continued to have some restricted interests; however, as she learned more social competencies, her parents reported that her interests were expanding—so much so, in fact, that they found her looking not at *Auto Trader* but at a teen magazine!

FUTURE DIRECTIONS

Pivotal Response Treatment has emerged in the past decade as a strong, comprehensive treatment model that provides services in inclusive settings and uses a systemwide approach to maximizing treatment access. Evidence abounds for the focus on pivotal areas and for each of the PRT teaching strategies across different populations and treatment providers. In addition, it is anticipated that the PRT certification system will allow greater fidelity of implementation across community providers, thereby ensuring the maintenance of quality standards. Careful research on certification procedures and the maintenance of certified skills will probably be a necessary component of future directions.

To date, limited research has been conducted on the large-scale use of PRT in community-based programs. Although preliminary data are reported for a few studies, final outcomes are pending. To further substantiate the effectiveness of PRT, such outcome studies, as well as more general longitudinal outcome studies using control groups, could be conducted. Furthermore, as Schreibman (2000) suggested, research is necessary to help with the identification of treatment outcome predictors and behavior profiles to match individual learning characteristics. Finally, research on the application of PRT for high-functioning teens and adults with ASDs is relatively limited.

Several additional areas warrant further research and development. First, although some research has been conducted to identify which children could benefit most from PRT intervention (Sherer & Schreibman, 2005), a comprehensive model of child variables could be developed to maximize treatment effects per child characteristic, type of intervention strategy, and type of goal. Such a model would move our field to a more blended approach with high-quality intervention tailored to the child and the specific skills being taught. Thompson (2011) provides an example of a blended intervention model that can serve as an example for researchers in PRT. Research that thoroughly addresses questions about child characteristics, predictive power of these characteristics in terms of outcome, and outcome data will be necessary to address these empirical questions.

A second area in need of continued research is staff training. No studies have been published that show staff performance data after initial or ongoing training in PRT, and no studies exist on staff training or specific staff training methods (e.g., video modeling versus coaching versus classroom teaching). Furthermore, treatment fidelities have been limited to fidelities of teaching expressive communications skills, even though PRT is used to teach a wide variety of skills. As PRT becomes widely available, it is imperative that there be a method to measure and monitor consistent and correct implementation of PRT techniques to ensure the integrity of the model.

SUGGESTED READINGS

Koegel, L.K., & Lazebnik, C. (2009). *Growing up on the spectrum: A guide to life, love, and learning for teens and young adults with autism and Asperger's.* New York, NY: Penguin.

Koegel, R.L., & Koegel, L.K. (1995). *Teaching children with autism: Strategies for initiating positive interactions and improving learning opportunities.* Baltimore, MD: Paul H. Brookes Publishing Co.

Koegel, R.L., & Koegel, L.K. (2006). *Pivotal Response Treatments for autism: Communication, social, and academic development.* Baltimore, MD: Paul H. Brookes Publishing Co.

Ward, S. (2009). *What you need to know about motivation and teaching games: An in-depth analysis.* Raleigh, NC: Lulu Publishing.

Learning Activities

The following are some ideas regarding discussion topics, projects, and writing assignments. The activities can be completed by parents, therapists, or paraprofessionals who can focus on a specific child.

Discussion Topics

Some skills lend themselves easily to natural reinforcement (e.g., verbal requests for preferred items). Others, however, require a little more planning. Think about skills that are not always naturally reinforced from day to day, for example, following instructions such as "come here and sit down" or some preacademic skills such as learning colors and shapes. Discuss ways to incorporate motivational strategies into learning activities and create natural reinforcement. For example, when teaching a child to respond to "Come here," you could initially begin with a game in which the child gets a hug, praise, and a preferred item or toy for a reasonable attempt at coming over when called.

Project Ideas

1. *Planning learning opportunities:* Learning can occur throughout a child's day. To maximize opportunities, go over the child's schedule and list major routines (breakfast, getting ready for school, afternoon free time, running errands, bath time, bedtime, etc.). Do this for weekdays and weekends. Start with one routine (e.g., snack time) and list as many ways you can think of to teach a skill. For example, during snack time, you could provide choices and have the child request specific food items, have the child get requested utensils or items ("get the *big, blue* cup"), etc. The natural reinforcer is getting to eat a snack. Try this with each routine. You may be surprised how many learning opportunities you can fit into a day.

2. *Playing to learn:* Gather up some toys, or make a list of at least 10 toys or activities. Get a partner (another adult or older child who can help) and go play! Think of as many things you can do within an activity. Remember that you do not always have to play with a toy the way it was intended! Write down your ideas and try to come up with at least 10 different ways to play with a toy. Do this for each toy or activity.

Writing Assignments

1. *Shared control:* Think of three activities (e.g., playing with trains, blowing bubbles, etc.) and list ways you could establish shared control within that activity (for example, giving the child a piece of track but not the train, etc.).

2. *Creativity worksheet:* List at least five of the child's favorite activities (playing with blocks, completing puzzles, etc.). Then list at least three acquisition goals the child has (e.g., two-word requests, receptive understanding of colors, following instructions including a preposition, etc.). Now, think about and list how you might target each goal within the first activity while playing. For example, when building with blocks, the child could request "big block" (verbal request), pick the specified color when given a choice of two blocks ("take the red block"), and put the block in a specific location (put the block "in the car"). Do this for each activity. Think about how you can make each activity naturally reinforcing.

REFERENCES

Albin, R.W., Lucyshyn, J.M., Horner, R.H., & Flannery, K.B. (1996). Contextual fit for behavioral support plan: A model for "goodness of fit." In L.K. Koegel & R.L. Koegel (Eds.), *Positive behavioral support: Including people with difficult behavior in the community* (pp. 81–98). Baltimore, MD: Paul H. Brookes Publishing Co.

Bailey, D.B., Simeonson, R.J., Winton, P.J., Huntington, G.S., Comfort, M., Isbell, P...Helm, J.M. (1990). Family focused intervention: A functional model for planning, implementing, and evaluating individualized family services in early intervention. *Journal of the Division for Early Childhood, 10,* 156–171.

Baker, B., Brightman, A., Blacher, J., Heifetz, L., Hinshaw, S., & Murphy, D. (2004). *Steps to independence: A skills training guide for parents and teachers of children with special needs* (4th ed.). Baltimore, MD: Paul H. Brookes Publishing Co.

Baker-Ericzén, M., Stahmer, A., & Burns, A. (2007). Child demographics associated with outcomes in a community-based Pivotal Response Training program. *Journal of Positive Behavior Interventions, 9*(1), 52–60.

Belfiore, P., Lee, D., Scheeler, C., & Klein, D. (2002). Implications of behavioral momentum and academic achievement for students with behavior disorders: Theory, application, and practice. *Psychology in the Schools, 39*(2), 171–179.

Boettcher, M.A. (2004). *Teaching social conversation skills to children with autism through self-management: An analysis of treatment gains and meaningful outcomes* (Unpublished doctoral dissertation). University of California, Santa Barbara.

Boettcher-Minjarez, M., Williams, S.E., & Hardan, A.Y. (2011). Pivotal Response group training program for parents of children with autism. *Journal of Autism and Developmental Disorders, 41*, 92–101.

Brookman-Frazee, L. (2004). Using parent/clinician partnerships in parent education programs for children with autism. *Journal of Positive Behavior Interventions, 6*(4), 195–213.

Brookman, L., Boettcher, M., Klein, E., Koegel, R., Koegel, L., & Openden, D. (2003). Facilitating social interactions in a community summer camp setting for children with autism. *Journal of Positive Behavior Interventions, 5*(4), 249–252.

Bruinsma, Y. (2004). *Increases in the joint attention behavior of eye gaze alternation to share enjoyment as a collateral effect of Pivotal Response Treatment for three children with autism* (Unpublished doctoral dissertation). University of California, Santa Barbara.

Bryson, S.E., Koegel, L.K., Koegel, R.L., Openden, D., Smith, I.M., & Nefdt, N. (2007). Large scale dissemination and community implementation of Pivotal Response Treatment: Program description and preliminary data. *Research and Practice for Persons with Severe Disabilities, 32*(2), 142–153.

Burke, J., & Cerniglia, L. (1990). Stimulus complexity and autistic children's responsivity: Assessing and training a pivotal behavior. *Journal of Autism and Developmental Disorders, 20*(2), 233–253.

Callahan, K., & Rademacher, J. (1999). Using self-management strategies to increase the on-task behavior of a student with autism. *Journal of Positive Behavior Interventions, 1*(2), 117–122.

Carter, C. (2001). Using choice with game play to increase language skills and interactive behaviors in children with autism. *Journal of Positive Behavior Interventions, 3*(3), 131–151.

Charlop, M., Schreibman, L., & Thibodeau, M. (1985). Increasing spontaneous verbal responding in autistic children using a time delay procedure. *Journal of Applied Behavior Analysis, 18*(2), 155–166.

Charlop, M., & Walsh, M. (1986). Increasing autistic children's spontaneous verbalizations of affection: An assessment of time delay and peer modeling procedures. *Journal of Applied Behavior Analysis, 19*(3), 307–314.

Delprato, D. (2001). Comparisons of discrete-trial and normalized behavioral intervention for young children with autism. *Journal of Autism and Developmental Disorders, 31*(3), 315–325.

Dunlap, G. (1984). The influence of task variation and maintenance tasks on the learning and affect of autistic children. *Journal of Experimental Child Psychology, 37*(1), 41–64.

Dunlap, G., & Koegel, R. (1980). Motivating autistic children through stimulus variation. *Journal of Applied Behavior Analysis, 13*(4), 619–627.

Dyer, K., Dunlap, G., & Winterling, V. (1990). Effects of choice making on the serious problem behaviors of students with severe handicaps. *Journal of Applied Behavior Analysis, 23*(4), 515–524.

Esbenshade, P., & Rosales-Ruiz, J. (2001). Programming common stimuli to promote generalized question-asking: A case demonstration in a child with autism. *Journal of Positive Behavior Interventions, 3*(4), 199–210.

Gallimore, R., Weisner, T., Bernheimer, L., Guthrie, D., & Nihira, K. (1993). Family responses to young children with developmental delays: Accommodation activity in ecological and cultural context. *American Journal on Mental Retardation, 98*(2), 185–206.

Gillett, J., & LeBlanc, L. (2007). Parent-implemented natural language paradigm to increase language and play in children with autism. *Research in Autism Spectrum Disorders, 1*(3), 247–255.

Haring, T., & Lovinger, L. (1989). Promoting social interaction through teaching generalized play initiation responses to preschool children with autism. *Journal of the Association for Persons with Severe Handicaps, 14*(1), 58–67.

Harper, C., Symon, J., & Frea, W. (2008). Recess is time-in: Using peers to improve social skills of children with autism. *Journal of Autism and Developmental Disorders, 38*(5), 815–826.

Ingersoll, B., & Dvortcsak, A. (2006). Including parent training in the early childhood special education curriculum for children with autism spectrum disorders. *Journal of Positive Behavior Interventions, 8*(2), 79–87.

Ingersoll, B., Schreibman, L., & Stahmer, A. (2001). Brief report: Differential treatment outcomes for children with autistic spectrum disorder based on level of peer social avoidance. *Journal of Autism and Developmental Disorders, 31*(3), 343–349.

Kennedy, C.H., & Itkonen, T. (1996) Social relationships, influential variables, and change across the lifespan. In L.K. Koegel, R.L. Koegel, & G. Dunlap (Eds.), *Positive Behavior Support: Including people with difficult behavior in the community* (pp. 287–304). Baltimore, MD: Paul H. Brookes Publishing Co.

Kennedy, C., Itkonen, T., & Lindquist, K. (1995). Comparing interspersed requests and social comments as antecedents for increasing student compliance. *Journal of Applied Behavior Analysis, 28*(1), 97–98.

Kern, L., Vorndran, C., Hilt, A., Ringdahl, J., Adelman, B., & Dunlap, G. (1998). Choice as an intervention to improve behavior: A review of the literature. *Journal of Behavioral Education, 8*(2), 151–169.

Koegel, L.K., Camarata, S., Valdez-Menchaca, M., & Koegel, R.L. (1998). Setting generalization of question-asking by children with autism. *American Journal on Mental Retardation, 102*(4), 346–357.

Koegel, L.K., Carter, C., & Koegel, R.L. (2003). Teaching children with autism self-initiations as a pivotal response. *Topics in Language Disorders, 23*(2), 134–145.

Koegel, L.K., Harrower, J., & Koegel, R. (1999). Support for children with developmental disabilities in full inclusion classrooms through self-management. *Journal of Positive Behavior Interventions, 1*(1), 26–34.

Koegel, L.K., & Koegel, R.L. (1986). The effects of interspersed maintenance tasks on academic performance in a severe childhood stroke victim. *Journal of Applied Behavior Analysis, 19*(4), 425–430.

Koegel, L.K., & Koegel, R.L. (1995). Motivating communication in children with autism. In E. Schopler & G.B. Mesibov (Eds.), *Learning and cognition in autism* (pp. 73–87). New York, NY: Plenum.

Koegel, L.K., Koegel, R.L., Bruinsma, Y., Brookman, L., & Fredeen, R. (2003). *Teaching first words to children with autism and communication delays using pivotal response training: A training manual.* Santa Barbara, CA: University of California.

Koegel, L.K., Koegel, R.L., Harrower, J., & Carter, C. (1999). Pivotal response intervention I: Overview of approach. *Journal of the Association for Persons with Severe Handicaps, 24*(3), 174–185.

Koegel, L.K., Koegel, R., Hurley, C., & Frea, W. (1992). Improving social skills and disruptive behavior in children with autism through self-management. *Journal of Applied Behavior Analysis, 25*(2), 341–353.

Koegel, L.K., Koegel, R.L., Shoshan, Y., & McNerney, E. (1999). Pivotal response intervention II: Preliminary long-term outcome data. *Journal of the Association for Persons with Severe Handicaps, 24*(3), 186–198.

Koegel, R.L., Bimbela, A., & Schreibman, L. (1996). Collateral effects of parent training on family interactions. *Journal of Autism and Developmental Disorders, 26*(3), 347–359.

Koegel, R.L., Camarata, S., Koegel, L.K., Ben-Tall, A., & Smith, A. (1998). Increasing speech intelligibility in children with autism. *Journal of Autism and Developmental Disorders, 28*(3), 241–251.

Koegel, R.L., Dunlap, G., Richman, G., & Dyer, K. (1981). The use of specific orienting cues for teaching discrimination tasks. *Analysis and Intervention in Developmental Disabilities, 1*(2), 187–198.

Koegel, R.L., Dyer, K., & Bell, L. (1987). The influence of child-preferred activities on autistic children's social behavior. *Journal of Applied Behavior Analysis, 20*(3), 243–252.

Koegel, R.L., & Egel, A. (1979). Motivating autistic children. *Journal of Abnormal Psychology, 88*(4), 418–426.

Koegel, R.L., & Frea, W. (1993). Treatment of social behavior in autism through the modification of pivotal social skills. *Journal of Applied Behavior Analysis, 26*(3), 369–377.

Koegel, R.L., & Koegel, L.K. (1990). Extended reductions in stereotypic behavior of students with autism through a self-management treatment package. *Journal of Applied Behavior Analysis, 23*(1), 119–127.

Koegel, R.L, & Koegel, L.K. (2006). *Pivotal Response Treatments for autism:Communication, social, and academic development.* Baltimore, MD: Paul H. Brookes Publishing Co.

Koegel, R.L., Koegel, L.K., & Carter, C. (1999). Pivotal teaching interactions for children with autism. *School Psychology Review, 28*(4), 576–594.

Koegel, R.L., Koegel, L.K., Frea, W., & Smith, A. (1995). Emerging interventions for children with autism: Longitudinal and lifestyle implications. In R.L. Koegel & L.K. Koegel (Eds.), *Teaching children with autism: Strategies for initiating positive interactions and improving learning opportunities* (pp. 1–15). Baltimore, MD: Paul H. Brookes Publishing Co.

Koegel, R.L., Koegel, L.K., Kellegrew, D., & Mullen, K. (1996). Parent education for prevention and reduction of severe behavior problems. In L.K. Koegel, R.L. Koegel, & G. Dunlap (Eds.), *Positive behavioral support: Including people with difficult behavior in the community* (pp. 3–30). Baltimore, MD: Paul H. Brookes Publishing Co.

Koegel, R.L., Koegel, L.K., & McNerney, E. (2001). Pivotal areas in intervention for autism. *Journal of Clinical Child Psychology, 30*(1), 19–32.

Koegel, R.L., Koegel, L.K., & Parks, D.R. (1992). *How to teach self-management to people with severe disabilities: A training manual.* Santa Barbara, CA: University of California.

Koegel, R.L., Koegel, L.K., & Surratt, A. (1992). Language intervention and disruptive behavior in preschool children with autism. *Journal of Autism and Developmental Disorders, 22*(2), 141–153.

Koegel, R.L., O'Dell, M., & Dunlap, G. (1988). Producing speech use in nonverbal autistic children by reinforcing attempts. *Journal of Autism and Developmental Disorders, 18*(4), 525–538.

Koegel, R.L., O'Dell, M., & Koegel, L. (1987). A natural language teaching paradigm for nonverbal autistic children. *Journal of Autism and Developmental Disorders, 17*(2), 187–200.

Koegel, R.L., Openden, D., Matos Fredeen, R., & Koegel, L.K. (2006). The basics of Pivotal Response Treatment. In R.L. Koegel & L.K. Koegel (Eds.), *Pivotal Response Treatments for autism: Communication, social, and academic development* (pp. 3–31). Baltimore, MD: Paul H. Brookes Publishing Co.

Koegel, R.L., & Schreibman, L. (1977). Teaching autistic children to respond to simultaneous multiple cues. *Journal of Experimental Child Psychology, 24*(2), 299–311.

Koegel, R.L., Schreibman, L., Britten, K.R., Burke, J.D., & O'Neill, R.E. (1982). A comparison of parent training to direct child treatment. In R.L. Koegel, A. Rincover, & A.L. Egel (Eds.), *Educating and understanding autistic children* (pp. 260–279). San Diego, CA: College-Hill Press.

Koegel, R.L., Schreibman, L., Britten, K., & Laitinen, R. (1979). The effects of schedule of reinforcement on stimulus overselectivity in autistic children. *Journal of Autism and Developmental Disorders, 9*(4), 383–397.

Koegel, R.L., Schreibman, L., Good, A., Cerniglia, L., Murphy, C., & Koegel, L.K. (1989). *How to teach pivotal behaviors to children with autism: A training manual.* Santa Barbara, CA: University of California.

Koegel, R.L., Schreibman, L., Johnson, J., O'Neill, R.E., & Dunlap, G. (1984). Collateral effects of parent training on families with autistic children. In R.F. Dangel & R.A. Polster (Eds.), *Behavioral parent-training: Issues in research and practice* (pp. 358–378). New York, NY: Guild Press.

Koegel, R.L., Symon, J., & Koegel, L.K. (2002). Parent education for families of children with autism living in geographically distant areas. *Journal of Positive Behavior Interventions, 4*(2), 88–103.

Koegel, R.L., Tran, Q.H., Mossman, A., & Koegel, L.K. (2006). Incorporating motivational procedures to improve homework performance. In R.L. Koegel & L.K. Koegel (Eds.), *Pivotal Response Treatments for autism: Communication, social, and academic development* (pp. 81–92). Baltimore, MD: Paul H. Brookes Publishing Co.

Koegel, R.L., Werner, G., Vismara, L., & Koegel, L.K. (2005). The effectiveness of contextually supported play date interactions between children with autism and typically developing peers. *Research and Practice for Persons with Severe Disabilities, 30*(2), 93–102.

Koegel, R.L., & Williams, J. (1980). Direct versus indirect response-reinforcer relationships in teaching autistic children. *Journal of Abnormal Child Psychology, 8*(4), 537–547.

Laski, K., Charlop, M., & Schreibman, L. (1988). Training parents to use the Natural Language Paradigm to increase their autistic children's speech. *Journal of Applied Behavior Analysis, 21*(4), 391–400.

Lee, S., Simpson, R., & Shogren, K. (2007). Effects and implications of self-management for students with autism: A meta-analysis. *Focus on Autism and Other Developmental Disabilities, 22*(1), 2–13.

Lovaas, O., Koegel, R., & Schreibman, L. (1979). Stimulus overselectivity in autism: A review of research. *Psychological Bulletin, 86*(6), 1236–1254.

Lovaas, O., Koegel, R., Simmons, J., & Long, J. (1973). Some generalization and follow-up measures on autistic children in behavior therapy. *Journal of Applied Behavior Analysis, 6*(1), 131–166.

Lovaas, O., Schreibman, L., Koegel, R., & Rehm, R. (1971). Selective responding by autistic children to multiple sensory input. *Journal of Abnormal Psychology, 77*(3), 211–222.

Mancina, C., Tankersley, M., Kamps, D., Kravits, T., & Parrett, J. (2000). Reduction of inappropriate vocalizations for a child with autism using a self-management treatment program. *Journal of Autism and Developmental Disorders, 30*(6), 599–606.

Matos Fredeen, R., & Koegel, R.L. (2006). The pivotal role of initiations in habilitation. In R.L. Koegel & L.K. Koegel (Eds.), *Pivotal Response Treatments for autism: Communication, social, and academic development* (pp. 3–31). Baltimore, MD: Paul H. Brookes Publishing Co.

McGee, G., Krantz, P., Mason, D., & McClannahan, L. (1983). A modified incidental-teaching procedure for autistic youth: Acquisition and generalization of receptive object labels. *Journal of Applied Behavior Analysis, 16*(3), 329–338.

McLean, L.K. (1990). Communication development in the first two years of life: A transactional process. *Zero to Three, 11,* 13–19.

McNerney, E.K. (2003). *Videotape communication between school and clinic and its effects on teacher behavior and generalization of expressive language to classroom settings for children with autism* (Unpublished doctoral dissertation). University of California, Santa Barbara.

Moes, D. (1995). Parent education and parenting stress. In R.L. Koegel, & L.K. Koegel (Eds.), *Teaching children with autism: Strategies for initiating positive interactions and improving learning opportunities* (pp. 79–93). Baltimore, MD: Paul H. Brookes Publishing Co.

Moes, D., & Frea, W. (2000). Using family context to inform intervention planning for the treatment of a child with autism. *Journal of Positive Behavior Interventions, 2*(1), 40–46.

Moes, D., & Frea, W. (2002). Contextualized behavioral support in early intervention for children with autism and their families. *Journal of Autism and Developmental Disorders, 32*(6), 519–533.

Morrison, L., Kamps, D., Garcia, J., & Parker, D. (2001). Peer mediation and monitoring strategies to improve initiations and social skills for students with autism. *Journal of Positive Behavior Interventions, 3*(4), 237–250.

National Research Council. (2001). *Educating children with autism.* Washington, DC: Author.

Newman, B., Buffington, D., O'Grady, M., & McDonald, M. (1995). Self-management of schedule following in three teenagers with autism. *Behavioral Disorders, 20*(3), 190–196.

Newman, B., & Ten Eyck, P. (2005). Self-management of initiations by students diagnosed with autism. *Analysis of Verbal Behavior, 21,* 117–122.

O'Donnell, C., Tharp, R., & Wilson, K. (1993). Activity settings as the unit of analysis: A theoretical basis for community intervention and development. *American Journal of Community Psychology, 21*(4), 501–520.

Oke, N., & Schreibman, L. (1990). Training social initiations to a high-functioning autistic child: Assessment of collateral behavior change and generalization in a case study. *Journal of Autism and Developmental Disorders, 20*(4), 479–497.

Openden, D.A. (2005). *Pivotal Response Treatment for multiple families with children with autism: Probable efficacy and effectiveness of a group parent education workshop* (Unpublished doctoral dissertation). University of California, Santa Barbara.

Openden, D., Symon, J.B., Koegel, L.K., & Koegel, R. L. (2006). Developing a student respite provider system for children with autism. *Journal of Positive Behaviour Interventions,* 8(2), 119–123.

Pierce, K., & Schreibman, L. (1994). Teaching daily living skills to children with autism in unsupervised settings through pictorial self-management. *Journal of Applied Behavior Analysis, 27*(3), 471–481.

Pierce, K., & Schreibman, L. (1995). Increasing complex social behaviors in children with autism: Effects of peer-implemented pivotal response training. *Journal of Applied Behavior Analysis, 28*(3), 285–295.

Pierce, K., & Schreibman, L. (1997). Using peer trainers to promote social behaviors in autism: Are they effective in enhancing multiple social modalities? *Focus on Autism and Other Developmental Disabilities, 12,* 207–218.

Ryan, C., Hemmes, N., Sturmey, P., Jacobs, J., & Grummet, E. (2008). Effects of a brief staff training procedure on instructors' use of incidental teaching and students' frequency of initiation toward instructors. *Research in Autism Spectrum Disorders, 2,* 28–45.

Rocha, M., Schreibman, L., & Stahmer, A. (2007). Effectiveness of training parents to teach joint attention in children with autism. *Journal of Early Intervention, 29*(2), 154–172.

Rosenblatt, J., Bloom, P., & Koegel, R.L. (1995). Overselective responding: Description, implications, and interventions. In R.L. Koegel & L.K. Koegel (Eds.), *Teaching children with autism: Strategies for initiating positive interactions and improving learning opportunities* (pp. 33–42). Baltimore, MD: Paul H. Brookes Publishing Co.

Sameroff, A. (1975). Transactional models in early social relations. *Human Development, 18,* 65–79.

Sameroff, A. (1986). Environmental context of child development. *Journal of Pediatrics, 109,* 192–200.

Santarelli, G., Koegel, R., Casas, J., & Koegel, L. (2001). Culturally diverse families participating in behavior therapy parent education programs for children with developmental disabilities. *Journal of Positive Behavior Interventions, 3*(2), 120–123.

Schopler, E., & Reichler, R. (1971). Parents as co-therapists in the treatment of psychotic children. *Journal of Autism and Childhood Schizophrenia, 1*(1), 87–102.

Schreibman, L. (1975). Effects of within-stimulus and extra-stimulus prompting on discrimination learning in autistic children. *Journal of Applied Behavior Analysis, 8*(1), 91–112.

Schreibman, L. (1997). The study of stimulus control in autism. *Environment and behavior* (pp. 203–209). Boulder, CO: Westview Press.

Schreibman, L. (2000). Intensive behavioral/psychoeducational treatments for autism: Research needs and future directions. *Journal of Autism and Developmental Disorders, 30*(5), 373–378.

Schreibman, L., Charlop, M., & Koegel, R. (1982). Teaching autistic children to use extra-stimulus prompts. *Journal of Experimental Child Psychology, 33*(3), 475–491.

Schreibman, L., Kaneko, W., & Koegel, R. (1991). Positive affect of parents of autistic children: A comparison across two teaching techniques. *Behavior Therapy, 22*(4), 479–490.

Schreibman, L., O'Neill, R., & Koegel, R. (1983). Behavioral training for siblings of autistic children. *Journal of Applied Behavior Analysis, 16*(2), 129–138.

Schreibman, L., Stahmer, A., & Suhrheinrich, J. (2009). Enhancing generalization of treatment effects via Pivotal Response Training and the individualization of treatment protocols. In C. Whalen (Ed.), *Real life, real progress for children with autism spectrum disorders: Strategies for successful generalization in natural environment* (pp. 21–40). Baltimore, MD: Paul H. Brookes Publishing Co.

Sherer, M., & Schreibman, L. (2005). Individual behavioral profiles and predictors of treatment effectiveness for children with autism. *Journal of Consulting and Clinical Psychology, 73*(3), 525–538.

Siller, M., & Sigman, M. (2002). The behaviors of parents of children with autism predict the subsequent development of their children's communication. *Journal of Autism and Developmental Disorders, 32*(2), 77–89.

Singer, G., Singer, J., & Horner, R. (1987). Using pretask requests to increase the probability of compliance for students with severe disabilities. *Journal of the Association for Persons with Severe Handicaps, 12*(4), 287–291.

Snyder-McLean, L., & McLean, J. (1978). Verbal information gathering strategies: The child's use of language to acquire language. *Journal of Speech and Hearing Disorders, 43*(3), 306–325.

Sparrow, S.S., Balla, D.A., & Cicchetti, D.V. (1984). *Vineland adaptive behavior scales.* Circle Pines, MN: American Guidance Service.

Stahmer, A. (1995). Teaching symbolic play skills to children with autism using pivotal response training. *Journal of Autism and Developmental Disorders, 25*(2), 123–141.

Stahmer, A. (1999). Using pivotal response training to facilitate appropriate play in children with autistic spectrum disorders. *Child Language Teaching and Therapy, 15*(1), 29–40.

Stahmer, A., & Gist, K. (2001). The effects of an accelerated parent education program on technique mastery and child outcome. *Journal of Positive Behavior Interventions, 3*(2), 75–82.

Stahmer, A., & Schreibman, L. (1992). Teaching children with autism appropriate play in unsupervised environments using a self-management treatment package. *Journal of Applied Behavior Analysis, 25*(2), 447–459.

Summers, J., Rincover, A., & Feldman, M. (1993). Comparison of extra- and within-stimulus prompting to teach prepositional discriminations to preschool children with developmental disabilities. *Journal of Behavioral Education, 3*(3), 287–298.

Symon, J. (2005). Expanding interventions for children with autism: Parents as trainers. *Journal of Positive Behavior Interventions, 7*(3), 159–173.

Symon, J.B., Koegel, R.L., & Singer, G.H.S. (2006). Parent perspectives of parent education programs. In R.L. Koegel & L.K. Koegel (Eds.), *Pivotal Response Treatments for autism: Communication, social, and academic development* (pp. 93–115). Baltimore, MD: Paul H. Brookes Publishing Co.

Sze, K., & Koegel, R.L. (2006). Ecocultural theory and cultural diversity in intervention programs. In R.L. Koegel & L.K. Koegel (Eds.), *Pivotal Response Treatments for autism: Communication, social, and academic development* (pp. 117–127). Baltimore, MD: Paul H. Brookes Publishing Co.

Thompson, T. (2011). *Individualized autism intervention for young children: Blending discrete trial and naturalistic strategies.* Baltimore, MD: Paul H. Brookes Publishing Co.

Turnbull, A., Blue-Banning, M., Turbiville, V., & Park, J. (1999). From parent education to partnership education: A call for a transformed focus. *Topics in Early Childhood Special Education, 19*(3), 164–172.

Ward, S. (2009). *What you need to know about motivation and teaching games: An in-depth analysis.* Raleigh, NC: Lulu Publishing.

Werner, G.A., Vismara, L.A., Koegel, R.L., & Koegel, L.K. (2006). In R.L. Koegel & L.K. Koegel (Eds.), *Pivotal Response Treatments for autism: Communication, social, and academic development* (pp. 199–216). Baltimore, MD: Paul H. Brookes Publishing Co.

Whalen, C., & Schreibman, L. (2003). Joint attention training for children with autism using behavior modification procedures. *Journal of Child Psychology and Psychiatry, 44*(3), 456–468.

Whalen, C., Schreibman, L., & Ingersoll, B. (2006). The collateral effects of joint attention training on social initiations, positive affect, imitation, and spontaneous speech for young children with autism. *Journal of Autism and Developmental Disorders, 36*(5), 655–664.

Williams, J., Koegel, R., & Egel, A. (1981). Response–reinforcer relationships and improved learning in autistic children. *Journal of Applied Behavior Analysis, 14*(1), 53–60.

Wolfe, V., & Cuvo, A. (1978). Effects of within-stimulus and extra-stimulus prompting on letter discrimination by mentally retarded persons. *American Journal of Mental Deficiency, 83*(3), 297–303.

Yoder, P., Kaiser, A., Alpert, C., & Fischer, R. (1993). Following the child's lead when teaching nouns to preschoolers with mental retardation. *Journal of Speech and Hearing Research, 36*(1), 158–167.

Zionts, L., Zionts, P., Harrison, S., & Bellinger, O. (2003). African American families' perceptions of cultural sensitivity within the special education system. *Focus on Autism and Other Developmental Disabilities, 18*(1), 41–50.

Social Stories

Tiffany L. Hutchins

Autism spectrum disorders (ASDs) are characterized by impairments in social, behavioral, and communicative functioning (American Psychiatric Association, 2001), although tremendous variation in these abilities is evident. Related impairments in **social cognition**—the process by which people make sense of the self and others and acquire, use, and understand social knowledge—is also considered a universal feature of ASDs. As a result, individuals with ASDs often have difficulty identifying relevant and meaningful social information and interpreting this information accurately. These difficulties may, in turn, lead to challenging behaviors that limit the individual's ability to participate in family, school, and community life (Crozier & Tincani, 2005; Dunlap & Fox, 1999). Thus, strategies to enhance social understanding and reduce challenging behaviors have the potential to significantly improve quality of life and facilitate access to educational opportunities among individuals with ASDs (Carr et al., 2002; Crozier & Tincani, 2005).

Social Stories™ represent one of the most popular intervention strategies to remediate the core impairments of ASDs (Hess, Morrier, Heflin, & Ivey, 2008; Reynhout & Carter, 2009). Introduced in 1993 by Carol Gray, an educational consultant and former teacher, Social Stories are carefully written, individualized stories that are designed to facilitate social understanding in individuals with autism by providing "direct access to social information" (Gray & Garand, 1993, p. 2). Social Stories adhere to a "specific format and guidelines to objectively describe a person, skill, event, concept, or social situation" (Gray, 1998, p. 171). They are most often written out, typically in a storybook format, and are composed of simple sentences and a title. Key messages conveyed in text in a Social Story are often, but not always, reinforced using visual supports (e.g., line drawings, icons, photographs, videos) or other media (e.g., audiotapes). A frequent goal of Social Stories is to share relevant information in the context of a challenging situation. This information often includes a description of where and when a situation takes place, who is involved, what is happening, and why (Gray, 1998), as well as suggestions for expected behaviors. Social Story intervention is also intended as a nonthreatening, positive, patient, and nonjudgmental support; preservation of self-esteem is considered a critical component (Gray, 2010).

Social Stories have been used to facilitate a wide range of social, behavioral, and communicative functions in preschool and school-age children and adolescents with ASDs who vary widely in their cognitive and linguistic profiles. Still, the efficacy of Social Stories for those individuals with ASDs involving the most severe challenges remains an open question (Scattone, Tingstrom, & Wilczynski, 2006). Social Stories have been employed in a range of service delivery models (e.g., pull-out, classroom-based, and community-based models; self-contained special education classrooms) and may be particularly useful for facilitating inclusion of students with ASDs in general education classrooms (Chan & O'Reilly, 2008; Gray & Garand, 1993; Greenway, 2000; Swaggart et al., 1995).

TARGET POPULATIONS AND ASSESSMENTS
FOR DETERMINING TREATMENT RELEVANCE AND GOALS

Although originally developed for individuals with ASDs, some studies have found support for the use of Social Stories with individuals with learning disability (Kalyva & Agaliotis, 2009; Moore, 2004), dyslexia (Haggerty, Black, & Smith, 2005), language impairment (Schneider & Goldstein, 2010), fragile X syndrome (Kuttler, Myles, & Carson, 1998), and hyperlexia (Soenksen & Alper, 2006), as well as very young typically developing children (Briody & McGarry, 2005; Burke, Kuhn, & Peterson, 2004). Social Stories have not been evaluated for use with individuals with Rett syndrome or childhood disintegrative disorder, probably because of their relatively low rates of prevalence.

Gray and Garand (1993) proposed early on that Social Stories were most likely to benefit individuals with intellectual disabilities who could be trained to learn and who had basic language skills. In line with this supposition, their early reports focused on how to construct effective Social Stories for individuals with high-functioning autism and Asperger syndrome. Subsequently, Gray (1998) suggested that, with slight modification, Social Stories can be used successfully for individuals with autism, including those with more severe challenges. Several studies have found support for the effectiveness of Social Story intervention not only for individuals with high-functioning autism and Asperger syndrome (e.g., Bledsoe, Smith, & Simpson, 2003; Rogers & Myles, 2001; Sansoti, Powell-Smith, & Kincaid, 2004; Scattone, 2008), but also for those with pervasive developmental disorder-not otherwise specified (PDD-NOS; e.g., Dodd, Stephen, Hupp, Jewell, & Krohn, 2008; Ivey, Heflin, & Alberto, 2004; Kuoch & Mirenda, 2003), and autistic disorder (e.g., Lorimer, Simpson, Myles, & Ganz, 2002; Mancil, Haydon, & Whitby, 2009; Norris & Datillo, 1999). However, investigations of the efficacy of Social Stories for individuals with ASDs who have severe intellectual impairment or very limited language skills are comparatively rare and the evidence for their use with this population is mixed (see Barry & Burlew, 2004; Quirmbach, Lincoln, Feinberg-Gizzo, Ingersoll, & Andrews, 2009; Swaggart et al., 1995).

THEORETICAL BASIS

> *It's hard for me to understand some things...I just don't have that social link in my brain.*
> —Steven (a pseudonym), an 11-year-old boy diagnosed with Asperger syndrome

Steven's lucid description of his challenges involving social understanding underscore what is considered to be a universal feature of ASDs. The premise underlying the use of Social Stories is that they facilitate the development of social understanding through the sharing of accurate and meaningful information (e.g., Gray, 1998, 2010; Gray & Garand, 1993). Gray has emphasized that Social Stories are not intended as a direct tool for behavior change. Instead, "the theory is that the improvement in behavior that is frequently credited to a Social Story is the result of improved understanding of events and expectations" (Gray, 2010, p. xxxi).

Various terms and descriptions are used to refer to and describe the mechanisms believed to be responsible for affecting social understanding through the use of Social Stories. Gray (1998) implicated **theory of mind** as one causal agent underlying the success of Social Stories. In its broadest application, theory of mind is used interchangeably with terms such as *social cognition, mind-reading,* and *perspective-taking* and may be defined for present purposes as the ability to reason about the inner mental worlds of self and others and to understand that others may have perspectives that differ from one's own. As Gray (1998) argued, "theory of mind provides most people with access to a 'secret code': a system of unspoken communication that carries essential information; a system that eludes individuals with [ASDs]" (p. 160).

In addition, Gray (1998) invoked the notion of **weak central coherence** as a factor in the social cognition difficulties of people with ASDs. Weak central coherence is a cognitive style, believed to be present in ASDs, in which the processing of parts takes precedence over the processing of wholes (Frith, 1989; Happe, 1999). For example, making accurate social judgments requires, among other things, the ability to read social cues in context and relate them to the physical and social environment in order to extract meaningful and relevant information. This gestalt understanding of social information is a routine achievement among neurotypical individuals, but it is often elusive to individuals with ASDs and thus "raises awareness of yet another 'secret' that influences the ability to understand and relate meaningfully to daily encounters and activities" (p. 169). In short, Gray (1998) suggested that impairment in theory of mind and the tendency of individuals with ASDs to acquire the cognitive style of weak central coherence together limit these individuals' access to social knowledge. The theory behind Social Stories is that they "translate these 'secrets' surrounding social interaction into practical, tangible social information" (Gray, 1998, p. 169).

Using different terminology, Rowe (1999) invoked the notion of **schemata** (plural of **schema**) to describe the theoretical mechanism underlying the use of Social Stories to enhance social understanding. Borrowing from Davenport (1993), Rowe described schemata as

> mental representations or ideas about what things are and how we deal with them. You have schemas [sic] for eating with a knife and fork, crossing the road and buying things in shops. We don't all have schemas [sic] for eating with chopsticks, swimming, or being a shop assistant. (Rowe, 1999, p. 14)

Rowe (1999) argued that because effective communication relies on shared schemata, Social Stories, which make an implicit schema explicit, scaffold or help to support understanding. Simply put, the idea is that Social Stories help organize experiences into a shared framework (Rowe, 1999).

The terms *theory of mind, weak central coherence,* and *schemata* each have a rich history and considerable currency in the autism and psychology literature. In the current discussion, these terms have been invoked to identify the cognitive impairments or styles characteristic of ASDs that are believed to undergo transformation through the use of Social Stories. This transformation, in turn, may result in more appropriate behaviors.

Underlying Assumptions

One important assumption underlying the use of Social Stories is that the social impairments of ASDs do not lie solely within the affected individual but rather in the social space between people. Gray (1998) argued that people make a variety of assumptions based on a common social understanding that, when applied to someone who perceives the world differently, can be wrong. "The result is a shared social impairment: two parties responding with equally valid but different perceptions of the same event" (p. 168). Thus, we can develop the most meaningful interventions by abandoning the assumptions we make in most social situations. To accomplish this, interventionists need to have a good understanding of social cognition in ASDs (Gray, 1998). Social Stories are written from the perspective of the audience (i.e., the individual for whom the story is written) after thoughtful consideration of how a social situation is experienced and interpreted by that person.

Social Stories may be effective not only because they are individualized and personally relevant but also because the activities, by nature, are in accord with certain practices commonly identified as especially useful for people with ASDs (Hutchins & Prelock, 2006; Smith, 2001). As Smith (2001) recounted, Social Stories capitalize on the strengths of people with ASDs, which often include a preference for visually cued instruction. Because they are permanent, Social Stories can be shared with important others (e.g., parents, teachers, members of the community), who can read or revisit the story across settings. Social Stories are written in simple language that is sensitive to the child's language level and vocabulary. They are situation specific and written in a predictable style using prescribed conventions. They are factual and accurate yet unusual in that they focus directly on how people think and feel, thus "adding to the child's theory of mind" (Smith, 2001, p. 339). Social Stories are also inherently family-centered in that they should be developed through careful observations of the child, discussions with the child, and information gathering from those who know the child best: the parents.

Targets of Treatment

Social Stories are not intended to target *directly* any functional limitation but do address *indirectly* a range of functional outcomes through enhanced social understanding. The range of such outcomes that has been addressed in practice and research has been truly remarkable. Among the outcomes studied is the reduction of disruptive behaviors (e.g., Scattone, Wilczynski, Edwards, & Rabian, 2002), including tantrums (e.g., Hutchins & Prelock, 2008), aggression (e.g., Swaggart et al., 1995), and self-injurious acts (Del Valle, McEachern, & Chambers, 2001). Social Stories have also been used to establish more appropriate behavioral routines (e.g., Del Valle et al., 2001; Toplis & Hadwin, 2006), to introduce changes in routines (Del Valle et al., 2001), and to acquaint the individual with an unfamiliar event (e.g., Gray & Garand, 1993). They have been used to promote social skills, such as getting a peer's attention (Soenksen & Alper, 2006; Thiemann & Goldstein, 2001), making choices and playing independently (Barry & Burlew, 2004), and increasing peer engagement and participation (Delano & Snell, 2006; Ivey et al., 2004). They have also been used to remediate communicative impairments in ASDs, such as reducing echolalia (Brownell, 2002; Kuttler et al., 1998), interrupting (Lorimer et al., 2002), and loud talking (Brownell, 2002).

A meta-analysis by Kokina and Kern (2010) suggested that Social Stories targeting the reduction of challenging behaviors may be more effective than those that teach appropriate social skills; however, researchers have rarely considered whether and which prerequisite skills or social understandings are needed to achieve social interaction goals (Kokina & Kern, 2010)—an important direction for future research that will be described more fully later in the chapter.

Additional targets of Social Stories have been anxiety (O'Conner, 2009), physical inactivity (Zimbelman, Paschal, Hawley, Molgaard, & St. Romain, 2007), sleep disturbances (Burke et al., 2004; Moore, 2004), messy eating (Bledsoe et al., 2003), sensory issues (Marr, Mika, Miraglia, Roerig, & Sinnott, 2007), and sexual education (Tarnai & Wolfe, 2008), to name a few. Other applications suggested by Gray (1998, 2010) include teaching academic skills and acknowledging the individual's achievements; however, these remain largely unexplored in the literature (Kokina & Kern, 2010). Thus, Social Story intervention has been used to address a range of social, communicative, and behavioral outcomes. From a theoretical perspective, any behavior that would benefit from enhanced social cognition may be an appropriate target of Social Stories, so long as the intervention is responsive to the individual's developmental level.

EMPIRICAL BASIS

One approach to characterize the findings of a body of research is to make a distinction between studies of efficacy and studies of effectiveness. Efficacy studies, which illustrate the usefulness of an intervention under conditions that allow for rigorous experimental control, are typically performed prior to studies of effectiveness, which illustrate the usefulness of an intervention under the conditions of everyday practice (Robey & Schultz, 1998). Because Social Stories are intended as a personalized instructional strategy, they are well-suited to the needs of scientist-practitioners working with individuals with ASDs across a range of settings and service delivery models. As a result, Social Stories research has not conformed to the standard model of clinical outcome research; studies of effectiveness are plentiful, but studies of efficacy are lacking. Table 13.1 summarizes the peer-reviewed single-subject studies conducted to date (dissertations and case studies using anecdotal data are not included).

Single-Subject Designs

The history of Social Story research has been relatively short, increasingly active, and dominated by the use of single-subject designs. As inspection of Table 13.1 reveals, a handful of studies have used a preexperimental AB (A, baseline; B, treatment phase) design. The remainder used more rigorous designs (e.g., ABA, ABAB, multiple-baseline designs), although some of these involved a single participant, which limits the ability to draw causal conclusions and evaluate the generalizability of results. The majority of studies (21 of 33) yielded positive results, an additional 11 studies yielded mixed results (i.e., treatment was associated with positive outcomes for some individuals or behaviors but not for others), and one study (Hanley-Hochdorfer, Bray, Kehl, & Elinoff, 2010) yielded null results only. Thus, a cursory review of the single-subject literature suggests that intervention using Social Stories is a promising approach; however, considerable variation in outcome exists.

Table 13.1. Summary of peer-reviewed, single-subject studies (dissertations and case studies using anecdotal data are not included)

Study	Sample size	Age (years)	Diagnosis	Design[a]	Targets of intervention	Outcome data	Other instructional strategies	Results
Adams, Gouvousis, VanLue, and Waldon (2004)	1	7	ASD	ABAB	Crying, falling, hitting, and screaming	Tallies of target behaviors during homework sessions, parental and teacher subjective survey	Verbal cueing	+
Barry and Burlew (2004)	2	7, 8	Autism	Multiple baseline across participants	Choice-making, appropriate play in classroom, how to play with a peer	Level of prompting for choices, duration of appropriate play, anecdotal teacher report	Photographs, corrective feedback, prompting, peer modeling, teacher-led instructional phase	+
Bernad-Ripoll (2007)	1	9	Asperger syndrome	AB	Recognizing and understanding emotions in self, identifying appropriate response	Percent accuracy of 1) identifying emotion, 2) explaining emotion and giving appropriate response	Photographs, videotapes, reinforcers	+
Bledsoe, Smith, and Simpson (2003)	1	13	Asperger syndrome and ADHD	ABAB	Decreasing food spilling and increasing mouth wiping	Frequency of behaviors during lunchtime	None	+
Brownell (2002)	4	6–9	Autism	ABAB	"TV talk," following directions, using a quiet voice	Tallies of target behaviors during 60-min observation sessions	Mayer-Johnson picture symbols, verbal prompting, musical (song) format	+
Chan and O'Reilly (2008)	2	5, 6	Autism	Multiple probe across behaviors	Inappropriate social interactions, appropriate hand raising, inappropriate vocalizations, appropriate social initiations	Frequency and percent of opportunities for target behaviors during 60-min observation sessions	Verbal prompts, comprehension questions, role play	+
Chan et al. (2011)	3	8	Autism	Multiple baseline across participants	Appropriate sitting, attending to the teacher during group lessons, working independently	Percent of 10-s intervals during 30-min session with performance of target behavior	Comprehension questions	+

318

Study	Sample size	Age (years)	Diagnosis	Design[a]	Targets of intervention	Outcome data	Other instructional strategies	Results
Crozier and Tincani (2005)	1	8	Autism	ABAC	Talking disruptively during classroom activities	Number of "talk-outs" during 30-min observation	Comparison between Social Story with and without prompting	+
Crozier and Tincani (2007)	3	3, 3, 5	Autism	ABAB	Appropriate sitting, talking with peers, appropriate play with peers	Total duration of target behavior during 10-min session; tally of events of target behavior during 10-min session	Comprehension questions, verbal prompting, color icons	+
Delano and Snell (2006)	3	6, 6, 9	Autism Typical peers	Multiple probe across participants	Appropriate social engagement with peer, inappropriate social engagement, absence of engagement	Duration of behavior, frequency of behavior during 10-min sessions	Comprehension questions, play with peer, verbal prompting	+
Dodd, Stephen, Hupp, Jewell, and Krohn (2008)	2	9, 12	PDD-NOS	Multiple baseline across behaviors/participants	Decreasing excessive "directions" to others; increasing compliments	Frequency of target behaviors during play session	Comprehension questions, photographs, clip art	+/–
Graetz, Mastropieri, and Scruggs (2009)	3	12, 12, 13	Autism	Multiple baseline across participants	Standing independently during gym class, appropriate voice pitch, hands down and materials away from lips	Percent of time doing inappropriate behavior during either 45-min observations or 15-s intervals during 20-min observations	Photographs with "call outs" (speech bubbles), comprehension questions, and/or comments	+
Hagiwara and Myles (1999)	3	7, 7, 9	Autism	Multiple baseline across settings	Washing hands, on-task behavior	Percent completion of hand-washing steps; average duration per occurrence of on-task behavior during 20-min observation	Video self-modeling presented on computer, verbal prompting	+/–
Hanley-Hochdorfer, Bray, Kehl, and Elinoff (2010)	4	6, 9, 11, 12	Asperger syndrome (3) Autism (1)	AB	Verbal initiations, contingent responses to peers	Frequency of target behaviors during 15-min lunch observation	Comprehension questions	–

(continued)

319

Table 13.1. *(continued)*

Study	Sample size	Age (years)	Diagnosis	Design[a]	Targets of intervention	Outcome data	Other instructional strategies	Results
Hutchins and Prelock (2006)	2	6, 12	ASD	AB	Reducing negative behavior toward sister, increasing ability to stop doing a preferred activity when others had had enough	Maternal subjective daily diary data	Comic strip conversations	+/−
Hutchins and Prelock (2008)	1	5	ASD	ABA	Increasing ability to stay calm, use words to talk about situation, take others' perspectives	Maternal subjective daily diary data	Comic strip conversations	+
Ivey, Hefflin, and Alberto (2004)	3	5, 7, 7	PDD-NOS	ABAB	Remaining on task, following directions/rules, using provided materials, using target vocabulary word, requesting (measured during four types of novel events)	Tally of target behaviors during 10-min observations	Photographs, illustrations, verbal and gestural prompting, behavior modeling	+
Kuoch and Mirenda (2003)	3	3, 5, 6	Autism (2) PDD-NOS (1)	ABA (2) ACABA (1)	Aggression, tantrums, eating problems, touching self inappropriately, game-playing skills	Tally of responses per minute (varying lengths of observation)	Cartoon pictures, verbal prompting, verbal corrective feedback	+
Kuttler, Myles, and Carlson (1998)	1	12	Autism, fragile X, and intermittent explosive disorder	ABAB	Reducing precursors to tantrum behavior (inappropriate vocalizations and dropping to the floor)	Tally of precursors to tantrum behavior in classroom and at lunch	Mayer-Johnson pictures, token economy	+
Lorimer, Simpson, Myles, and Gantz (2002)	1	5	Autism	ABAB	Reducing precursor to tantrum behavior	Tally of interrupting vocalizations and frequency of tantrums/day	Mayer-Johnson line drawings	+
Mancil, Haydon, and Whitby (2009)	3	6, 7, 8	Autism	ABABCBC	Pushing (grabbing, touching, shoving) peers	Mean frequency of pushing per 5-min session	Verbal prompts, pictures of peers, interactive text in PowerPoint version	+

Study	Sample size	Age (years)	Diagnosis	Design[a]	Targets of intervention	Outcome data	Other instructional strategies	Results
Marr, Mika, Miraglia, Roerig, and Sinnott (2007)	4	4, 4, 4, 5	Autism	ABA	Remaining in assigned seat, reducing stereotypical behaviors	Percent of observation sessions with targeted behavior	"Sensory story," illustrations, verbal and physical cues	+/–
Norris and Dattilo (1999)	1	8	Autism	AB	Reducing inappropriate social behaviors (talking or singing to herself) and increasing appropriate alternative behaviors	Percent of 10-s intervals during 8-min observation with inappropriate, appropriate, or no social interactions with peers during lunch	Picture symbols, behavior management systems, comprehension questions	+/–
Ozdemir (2008)	3	7, 8, 9	Autism	Multiple baseline across participants	Disruptive behaviors (using a loud voice, chair tipping, cutting in line at lunch)	Percent of 15-s partial intervals of disruptive behavior during 20-min observations	Illustrations of stick figures with "call outs," photo of aide	+
Pasiali (2004)	3	7, 8, 9	Autism	ABAB	Aberrant vocalizations during meals, increasing appropriate use of video player, decreasing "rummaging" in the kitchen	Daily tallies of target behaviors	Listening to music, playing rhythmic instruments, singing, picture schedule	+/–
Sansoti and Powell-Smith (2006)	3	9, 10, 11	Asperger syndrome	Multiple baseline across participants	Sportsmanship, maintaining conversations with peers, joining in peer play	Percent of 15-s partial intervals with target behavior during 15-min observation	Social Story journal	+/–
Scattone (2008)	1	9	Asperger syndrome	Multiple baseline across behaviors	Eye contact, smiling, initiations	Percent of 10-s intervals with target behavior during 5-min observations	Video modeling (by two adults), comprehension questions	+/–
Scattone, Wilczynski, Edwards, and Rabian (2002)	3	7, 7, 15	Autism	Multiple baseline across participants	Chair tipping, staring at girls, shouting	Percent of 10-s partial intervals with target behavior during 20-min observation	Comprehension questions, verbal prompting	+

(continued)

Table 13.1. (continued)

Study	Sample size	Age (years)	Diagnosis	Design[a]	Targets of intervention	Outcome data	Other instructional strategies	Results
Scattone, Tingstrom, and Wilczynski (2006)	3	8, 8, 13	Autism (2) Asperger syndrome (1)	Multiple baseline across participants	Increasing appropriate social interactions	Percent of 10-s partial intervals of appropriate social interactions during 10-min observation	Comprehension questions, verbal prompting	+/−
Schneider and Goldstein (2010)	3	6, 6, 9	Language impairment and social impairment	Multiple baseline across participants	Following directions, completing work, making eye contact, raising hand	Percent of 10-s intervals with on-task behavior with varying observation length; percent of 15-s intervals during 5-min observation	Mayer-Johnson pictures, comprehension questions	+
Swaggart et al. (1995)	3	11, 7, 7	Autism (2) PDD-NOS (1)	AB	Greeting, reducing aggression, sharing toys	Number of aggressions/ day, mean percent of sessions with target behaviors	Illustrations, response cost, prompting	+
Thiemann and Goldstein (2001)	5	6, 7, 8, 11, 12	Autism (4) Language and social impairment (1)	Multiple baseline across skills and participants	Contingent responses, securing attention, initiating comments, initiating requests	Number of behaviors recorded during 15-s intervals of a 10-min session, teacher and graduate-student subjective ratings of social behaviors	Comprehension checks, role play, pictorial and written cues, verbal cues, video feedback, token economy	+/−
Toplis and Hadwin (2006)	5	Mean age = 7.5	Behavioral difficulties	ABAB	Decreasing disruptive behavior during lunch at school	Tally of appropriate/ inappropriate behaviors during lunch	Illustrations, picture icons, verbal/physical prompting	+/−

Key: +, effect associated with treatment; −, null results; +/−, mixed results; ASD, autism spectrum disorder; PDD-NOS, pervasive developmental disorder–not otherwise specified.
[a] Experimental design phases: A, baseline; B, treatment; C, second treatment.

322

Crucially, the literature is replete with examinations of the use of Social Stories combined with other instructional methods, so it is difficult to determine their effects when used in isolation. As Table 13.1 indicates, the parallel methods have included video modeling, visual schedules, comic-strip conversations, token economies, prompting, role playing, and music therapy. Interestingly, Reynhout and Carter (2006) found little difference in effect sizes across studies using Social Stories alone and those using Social Stories in combination with other instructional strategies. Schneider and Goldstein (2010) found a large effect associated with Social Stories alone; however, the effect size increased when a visual schedule was introduced. Thus, they conclude, "additional components…may be useful for optimizing performance" (p. 149).

The Social Story literature is commonly criticized for a lack of data on generalizability, maintenance, and social validity (e.g., Nichols, Hupp, Jewell, & Zeigler, 2006; Reynhout & Carter, 2006). Nonetheless, newer studies (e.g., Chan & O'Reilly, 2008; Crozier & Tincani, 2005, 2007; Graetz, Mastropieri, & Scruggs, 2009) tend to include two or more of these issues in analyses, a development that will be discussed briefly here. Although examinations of the *generalizability of treatment effects* are relatively infrequent, some researchers have reported generalization to untrained settings (e.g., Hagiwara & Myles, 1999; Hutchins & Prelock, 2008; Kuttler et al., 1998; Mancil et al., 2009) and behaviors (e.g., Hutchins & Prelock, 2006; Theimann & Goldstein, 2001).

Studies examining the *maintenance of skills* following Social Story intervention have yielded mixed results. For example, Theimann and Goldstein (2001) implemented Social Story intervention with additional instructional strategies to target social communication skills (e.g., contingent responding, initiating requests) in five children diagnosed with autism. They characterized maintenance data as "not compelling" (p. 443), although a return to baseline performance did provide a strong argument for the causal effects of intervention. They targeted social skills and noted that skill difficulty, length of training, adult prompting, and visual cue fading may have accounted for the lack of maintenance. Conversely, other research has found convincing evidence for maintenance. For example, Chan and O'Reilly (2008) used Social Stories paired with comprehension checks (i.e., questions to test comprehension) and role playing to teach appropriate social behaviors to two students. Appropriate social behaviors increased, inappropriate behaviors decreased, and the effects were maintained at a 10-month follow-up. Given the paucity of data and the mixed results from existing data, future examinations of the factors that predict maintenance and generalizability of effects are warranted.

Social validity data for Social Stories have been collected in the form of interviews, questionnaires, and formal and informal rating scales to assess the feasibility and perceived effects of treatment among parents and professionals. Another strategy to assess social validity has involved comparisons between the behaviors of individuals with disability and those of their typically developing peers (Chan et al., 2011). When data for social validity are available, the results have been quite positive. In a study of social validity, Reynhout and Carter (2009) surveyed 45 teachers working with children with ASDs. Teachers agreed that

Social Stories are an acceptable (100%) and effective intervention (93%), appropriate for a wide variety of children (78%), behaviors and skills (93%), that can be easily implemented in a wide variety of settings (93%), and that are complementary to other interventions (100%). In contrast a minority of teachers (45%) agreed that Social Stories result in generalized behavior change and only 53% agreed that Social Stories maintain well. (p. 241)

Group Designs

Very few peer-reviewed group studies have been conducted to examine the efficacy of Social Stories. Smith (2001) described the first group study, which involved the training of several teachers to implement Social Story intervention. Subjective teacher evaluation of intervention efficacy (using a 0–10 scale anchored by "not at all" and "completely") revealed that 16 of 19 stories received a rating above the midpoint. Although this has been taken as evidence for the usefulness of Social Stories, Smith (2001) and others (Ali & Fredrickson, 2006) have identified a number of methodological weaknesses in this study (e.g., use of additional interventions, operation of a social desirability bias) and the results must be interpreted with extreme caution.

To address the need for a large, experimentally controlled group study, Quirmbach and colleagues (2009) examined the efficacy of Social Stories as the sole method of intervention for 45 children with ASDs who varied widely in cognitive and language skills. They used a standard Social Story (i.e., it was the same for all children) to address communication in the context of game play. The Social Story explained how to greet and initiate appropriate interactions (e.g., "Hello," "Do you want to play with me?" "What game do you want to play next?"). The stories did not include photographs or icons.

Results from pre- and posttest assessments indicated that 30 of the 45 student participants improved game-play skills that generalized to a similar game-play context and were maintained at 1 week postintervention. Interestingly, Quirmbach and colleagues (2009) found that verbal comprehension skills contributed the greatest amount of variance in predicting success with Social Stories. Authors concluded that individuals with extremely low verbal comprehension (i.e., less than a standard score of 69 on the Verbal Comprehension Index of the Wechsler Intelligence Scale for Children, 4th edition [Weschler, 2003]) may not benefit from Social Stories that do not include pictures. On the other hand, Quirmbach and colleagues recognized that the targets of intervention may have been too advanced and therefore inappropriate for children with very low comprehension. Moreover, the Social Stories used in the study were lengthy and contained many complex sentences (e.g., "When I am finished playing my game, it makes other people happy if I ask, 'What game do you want to play?'"). Thus, the findings of Quirmbach and colleagues (2009) cannot be taken as indisputable evidence for a lack of efficacy of Social Stories when used with children with the most limited receptive language. Rather, the findings may actually underscore the importance of tailoring interventions to the child's developmental level.

Descriptive and Quantitative Reviews

Several common themes have emerged from descriptive (Ali & Frederickson, 2006; Karkhaneh et al., 2010; Nichols et al., 2006; Rust & Smith, 2006; Sansoti et al., 2004) and quantitative reviews (Kokina & Kern, 2010; Reynhout & Carter, 2006, 2011; Test, Richter, Knight, & Spooner, 2010) of the Social Story literature. Most authors agree that the preponderance of evidence suggests that Social Stories are a promising intervention. Nevertheless, authors almost universally acknowledge a number of serious methodological limitations in the research base. These include confounding treatment variables and lack of experimental control, weak designs, small treatment effects, and a general lack of studies establishing treatment fidelity, reliability of measurement, and maintenance and generalizability of outcomes. This range of issues has led some to conclude that it would be premature to recognize Social Stories as an evidence-based practice (Kokina & Kern, 2010; Test et al., 2010).

The conclusions of other reviewers have been more positive. For example, Ali and Frederickson (2006) noted that although single-subject designs, such as those used in support of Social Stories, have traditionally been considered to occupy a lower tier of evidence, there are ways in which internal and external validity can be established within and across studies. "As the number and diversity of acceptable studies using single-case designs accumulate, so the confidence in consistent findings can increase" (Ali & Frederickson, 2006, p. 372). This approach to the evidence is consistent with the conclusions of the National Standards Project (National Autism Center, 2009), which has identified Social Story intervention as one of 11 established treatments. The National Standards Project concluded that there is sufficient quality, quantity, and consistency in the evidence base to confidently conclude that the treatment produces beneficial effects for some individuals with autism. Of course, several research questions continue to warrant further investigation, as described in a later section.

PRACTICAL REQUIREMENTS

Carol Gray has created a web site (http://thegraycenter.org) that offers information regarding resources and training opportunities to support effective strategies for developing Social Stories that adhere to Gray's stated guidelines. One option for learning how to write Social Stories as developed and defined by Gray entails participating in a DVD workshop (Writing Social Stories with Carol Gray) that is accompanied by a workbook. *The New Social Story Book: 10th Anniversary Edition* (Gray, 2011) describes Gray's most recent guidelines for writing Social Stories. This book includes a series of tutorials to gain practice writing Social Stories and more than 150 standard Social Stories that may be borrowed or adapted. The web site also lists a schedule of presentations offered by Carol Gray and other highly trained individuals.

Generally speaking, the materials required to construct a Social Story are portable and inexpensive. Social Stories were traditionally composed of words on paper; however, a variety of innovative additions can be used appropriately (Test et al., 2010), including the use of video and audio recordings, photographs, and illustrations. The most widely used visual supports are photographs and illustrations such as Picture Communication Symbols (PCS), also referred to as Mayer-Johnson or Boardmaker pictures. Using these pictures requires a computer, word processing software, custom photographic software, and/or Boardmaker, depending on what is desired. Authors of Social Stories might also consider using computer-assisted Social Stories (Mancil et al., 2009) or other technological enhancements (Doyle & Arnedillo-Sanchez, 2011) that can enhance flexibility and interest for some individuals.

KEY COMPONENTS

Gray has described the characteristics of Social Stories and processes for developing and implementing them. Gray's most recent criteria (2010) represent adjustments of previous versions (e.g., Gray, 1995, 1998; Gray & Garand, 1993). Moreover, researchers and practitioners (e.g., Nichols et al., 2006; Scott, Clark, & Brady, 2000;

Swaggert et al., 1995; Tarnai & Wolfe, 2008) have offered their own recommendations for implementing a Social Story intervention. As a result, Social Stories have
been developed in accordance with guidelines that have been continuously evolving for nearly 20 years. A synthesis of the most common and salient elements and
recommendations for practice is offered in this section. However, the collection of
baseline and intervention data critical for evaluation of the intervention is discussed
more fully in the following section.

Determine a Topic

The first step in conducting a Social Story intervention is to determine a topic. Gray
(2010) stresses the importance of adequate data collection to enable the clinician
to discover, rather than invent, a potential story topic. The following example illustrates the value of thorough data collection when working with a verbal individual
with an ASD:

> Andrew, a student in Mrs. Clark's first-grade class, struggled in math. Only once
> had he raised his hand for help...I decided to try drawing a picture with Andrew to
> learn more...While doing so, Andrew said, "I'm never going to raise my hand again.
> My teacher doesn't know anything about math." I asked why he felt that way. "Well, I
> raised my hand. Mrs. Clark came over and said, 'Okay Andrew, what's the first num-
> ber?' Mrs. Gray, she doesn't even know her numbers!" The story topics became clear.
> I wrote two of them. One described what his teacher knows...The second story ex-
> plained why teachers ask questions when they already know the answers. Immediately
> after reading both stories, Andrew began raising his hand once again. (Gray, 2010,
> pp. xxxiv–xxxv)

Review of the literature and practical experience suggest that Social Story topics are most often identified by looking at situations that result in challenging behaviors. Salient topics may also be identified through an examination of situations that
continue to present difficulty after implementation of a social skills curriculum or
other positive interventions to address the problem have been deemed unsuccessful
(Gray, 1995). Authors may also anticipate how novel situations or changes in routine
might be experienced in order to support the individual with accurate information in
advance of when it is needed (Gray, 1998). Although often overlooked, Social Stories
should acknowledge success, which is an excellent topic for a "first story" (Gray,
1998, p. 174), to establish a positive introduction to this instructional strategy. In a
related vein, when improvement in challenging behaviors is demonstrated through
the use of Social Stories, the stories may be adapted to acknowledge success and
foster confidence. In fact, Gray (2010) recommends that no less than 50% of Social
Stories applaud what the individual is doing well. "The rationale is simple. Given that
Social Stories are helpful in teaching new concepts and skills, they may also be just
as powerful in adding meaning and detail to praise" (Gray, 2010, p. xxxv).

Gather Individualized Information

"Social Stories are documents that are worthy of the trust of their audience. To
accomplish this, authors need to...gather accurate information" (Gray, 2010, p.
xxxiii). In fact, the steps of topic identification and information gathering should
be viewed as a dynamic process in which one may inform the other. Once a topic is
identified, it is necessary to gather detailed, relevant, and individualized information—an important process that is often overlooked (Gray, 2010). Several examples

in the literature can be turned to as illustrations of appropriately rich data collection practices (Crozier & Tincani, 2005, 2007; Delano & Snell, 2006; Hutchins & Prelock, 2008; Lorimer et al., 2002). For example, Hutchins and Prelock (2008) used a collaborative, family-centered approach to gather information from parents and teachers and conducted interviews, observations of child behavior, record review, and formal assessments of language and social cognition to determine appropriate intervention targets and content. Cozier and Tincani (2005) completed teacher interviews, child observation, and the Motivation Assessment Scale (MAS; Durand & Crimmins, 1992) to understand behaviors (their frequency, context, precursors, antecedents, consequences, causes, and underlying motivations) and ensure that their Social Story would accurately address the target behavior.

These examples illustrate that information gathering done to aid in Social Story composition can make creative use of formal, informal, direct, and indirect methods. Going forward, parents, researchers, and other professionals are encouraged to look beyond the behaviors themselves by using a variety of techniques to better understand the cause and purpose of behaviors. Ideally, a team may conduct observations, interviews with relevant others, and, when resources allow, a **functional behavioral assessment** (FBA), a problem-solving process designed to identify the purpose of a behavior and strategies to address it. In support of this recommendation, a meta-analysis concluded that studies that used some form of FBA yielded higher effect sizes than those that did not (Kokina & Kern, 2010).

Authors of Social Stories may also find Gray's recommendations for process helpful. Gray (2010) describes a two-step process for gathering accurate and relevant information. The first step involves a third-person "fly on the wall" (p. xxxiv) perspective to determine the relevant cues that define a situation. In the second step, the observer assumes the perspective of the individual in context, so that the experience is considered in light of the individual's perceptions. The information-gathering process should focus on the "relevant cues, the typical sequence of events, ideas from those involved in the situation and the perspective of the [individual with an ASD]" (Gray, 1998, p. 174). The importance of the information-gathering process cannot be overstated. This process directly informs the content of the Social Story by providing a clear link between contextual variables and the individual's behavior (Sansoti et al., 2004).

Develop the Social Story

Careful consideration of the gathered information guides the writing of the Social Story. Social Stories are typically written in the first person to reflect the perspective of the individual, but third-person narratives, called Social Articles (Gray, 2010), are recommended for an older or more advanced audience. They often incorporate a newspaper format (e.g., columns, Times New Roman font) to minimize "any 'babyish' or insulting quality in the text" (Gray, 2010, p. xlvii). By contrast, younger individuals or those who are at a less advanced developmental level are believed to benefit from shorter narratives with a larger font, in which each page contains only one or two simple sentences (e.g., Swaggart et al., 1995). "Irrelevant information has usually been eliminated, with the story highlighting the most pertinent events, words, and gestures involved in the targeted situation" (Nichols et al., 2006, p. 91). The length and complexity of Social Stories (and font and formatting choices) should be guided by individual factors such as age, verbal comprehension, reading level, and attention span (Attwood, 1998).

As a positive behavioral intervention, the content of Social Stories should be stated in positive terms. Thus, a sentence such as "I will try to remember to stay calm" is appropriate, whereas the sentence "I will not hit and scream" is not. The Social Story should be written using vocabulary that is meaningful to the individual and language that is developmentally appropriate. In addition, the use of flexible language (e.g., "sometimes," "usually") is preferred to inflexible language (e.g., "always," "never") because the former is more likely to be literally accurate.

Gray (2010) recommends that Social Stories be composed of a title and three basic parts: an introduction that clearly identifies the topic, a body that adds relevant detail, and a conclusion that summarizes the story and reinforces key messages. Gray has proposed that Social Stories be comprised of specific types of sentences, although the number and kind of sentences has changed over the years. People familiar with the evolution of Social Story guidelines will be familiar with descriptive, perspective, directive, affirmative, control, and cooperative sentences. A description of each of Gray's (2010) most recent sentence types, which are conceptually similar to their predecessors, is presented in Table 13.2.

Gray (2010) states that the sentences in a Social Story must adhere to a ratio such that the total number of descriptive, perspective, affirmative, and partial sentences divided by the total number of sentences that coach the audience, team, or the individual is equal to or greater than two. This ratio (which has also changed over the years) is driven by the notion that Social Stories should *describe more than direct* (italics in original, Gray, 1998, p. 179). Although this statement reflects the goal and theoretical bases of Social Stories as an instructional strategy that aims to enhance social understanding, the ratio lacks empirical support and many have questioned its utility and appropriateness. Specifically, the literature offers several examples of Social Stories that were deemed effective when they deviated from Gray's ratio (see Reynhout & Carter, 2006, 2011).

Table 13.2.   Social Story sentence types

Sentence type	Description
Descriptive sentences	Factual, objective, assumption-and-debate free statements that describe context and/or the relevant but often unspoken aspects of a situation, person, activity, skill, or concept.
Perspective sentences	Statements that accurately refer to or describe a person's internal state, or their knowledge, thoughts, feelings, beliefs, opinions, motivation, or physical condition, or health.
Sentences that coach the audience	Statements that gently guide the behavior or the audience by describing a suggested response or a choice of responses.
Sentences that coach the team	Statements that guide the behavior of the audience or members of his or her team. They describe a suggested response, a choice of responses, or self-coaching strategies.
Self-coaching sentences	Statements written by the audience to identify a personal strategy to recall and apply its content in practice.
Affirmative sentences	Statements that enhance the meaning of surrounding statements and often express a commonly shared value or opinion within a given culture.
Partial sentences	Fill-in-the-blank statements that check for comprehension, encourage the audience to make guesses regarding the next step in a situation, the response of another individual, or his or her own response.

Source: Gray (2010).

In fact, Quirmbach and colleagues (2009) systematically isolated sentence type by comparing "standard" stories (i.e., those that conformed to Gray's ratio) to "directive stories" (i.e., those that used only directive sentences). Contrary to Gray's recommendations, the authors concluded that "the 'active ingredient' in Social Stories seems to come from the directive sentences" (p. 315). In an investigation of perspective sentences, Okada, Ohtake, and Yanagihara (2008) found that, although Social Stories without perspective sentences can have a positive impact, the addition of perspective sentences may boost improvement of the target behaviors. At present, the influence of different sentence types is unclear, and the recommendation that Social Story authors adhere to a prespecified ratio is controversial. For the time being, one defensible proposal is that authors avoid preoccupation with the Social Story ratio. A primary focus on content that is "responsive to the specific contexts and targets of intervention may be more appropriate" (Hutchins & Prelock, 2006, p. 49).

Gray's ideas about the value of visual supports that may accompany a Social Story have also undergone revision over the years. The use of graphics in a Social Story was initially discouraged on the grounds that they may distract or lead to inaccurate interpretation (Gray & Garand, 1993). This consideration is especially important given the tendency of individuals with ASDs to interpret information (including images) literally. "For example, if an illustration depicts a child tying his shoe, seated next to a cat on a blue carpet, the student may interpret this to mean that shoes should be tied only when seated, next to a cat, on a blue carpet" (Gray & Garand, 1993, p. 4).

Gray (1998) later reconsidered this position in light of further clinical experience and research that demonstrated a strong rationale for the use of visual supports in the development of understanding in ASDs. Indeed, research has shown that inclusion of images in Social Stories is associated with more success (Kokina & Kern, 2010). Gray now emphasizes the importance of the appropriateness of visual stimuli, which can take many different forms. Whatever the choice, the goal of visual supports should be to highlight or summarize information, captivate interest, and improve comprehension (Gray, 2010). Gray offers several questions to consider when making decisions about whether and which visual supports will be effective, including the following:

- Does the audience have the prerequisite skills to use this form of illustration?
- Has the audience previously demonstrated interest in this type of illustration?
- Would a combination of two or more forms of illustration work best? (2010, p. xliii)

Authors of Social Stories need to be as thoughtful about the use of visual supports as they are about the content of a story's text and must consider any potential negative influence of images. Crucially, Social Stories must be developed in a way that is emotionally and physically safe for the audience. Consider the following example offered by Gray:

A mom writes a story for her son, Harrison, about swimming at the beach. She includes a photo of Harrison in the water. There is no one else in the photo. Dad was right next to the child when the photo was taken, although he was out of the range of the viewfinder. Interpreted at face value—through the eyes and mind of Harrison—the photo may seem to give him permission to swim alone. (2010, p. xxxi)

A number of books containing ready-made stories (e.g., "Standing in Line at School") are available for purchase (e.g., Gray, 2000, 2010; Gray & White, 2002).

Although using such books may seem to violate the recommendation that Social Stories use individualized information (Ali & Fredrickson, 2006); their use seems reasonable if they are selected after careful review and are subsequently adapted to meet the needs of the individual (Ali & Fredrickson, 2006; Gray, 2010).

Consider Additional Supports

The use of additional supports is widely advised in the Social Story literature as a means to promote good outcomes (Gray, 2010; Nichols et al., 2006; Tarnai & Wolfe, 2008). In considering additional supports, Social Story authors should consider strategies that have been successful with an individual in the past or otherwise have the potential to improve comprehension, participation, or interest (e.g., picture-schedules, prompting, modeling, role playing, token economies, multimedia presentations, video modeling). The identification of prerequisite skills or understanding and appropriate environmental supports is important in practice and is essential when Social Stories are developed to teach social skills, which are particularly challenging for individuals with ASDs (Kokina & Kern, 2010).

Review and Share the Social Story

Before the Social Story is introduced, a draft is shared with parents, teachers, or others who have direct contact with the individual and knowledge of the topic. Ideally, these people will have participated in the information-gathering process and are situated to provide critical review of content. The goal is to catch inaccuracies or missing details that should trigger revision (Gray, 1998).

The Social Story may then be distributed to relevant others, along with an implementation plan that outlines review schedules (who, when) and any additional instructional strategies to be used (Gray, 1998). This process has the potential to foster shared responsibility and the involvement of a team (Gray, 1998). Moreover, it may help reinforce key messages across contexts by demonstrating to the individual that multiple people have the same social information (Gray, 1995).

Introduce the Social Story

Social Stories should be introduced to the individual in a relaxed and nonthreatening manner (Gray, 1998, 2010). Often a simple statement, such as "Here is a story that I wrote for you," is sufficient, but the complexity and content of the introduction will vary with circumstance. The individual can be encouraged to turn pages or read independently if appropriate, and there is some evidence that Social Story intervention is more effective when the individual is responsible for reading the story independently (Kokina & Kern, 2010). A priming procedure is often employed in which the Social Story is read immediately prior to a novel or challenging situation (Scattone, 2007).

Social Stories may be introduced to address single or multiple targets of intervention. When multiple targets are identified, they can be introduced simultaneously (Kokina & Kern, 2010) or sequentially (e.g., Gray, 2010). It is possible that new skills and understandings may be taught in a single exposure (e.g., Gray, 2010) or after several repetitions (e.g., Hutchins & Prelock, 2006, 2008; Norris & Datillo, 1999). Thus, the number of presentations required to effect change (if change occurs) is expected to vary considerably. Because Social Stories are a personalized intervention, the recommendation regarding the reading schedule is that it be "read frequently enough to provide review without needless repetition" (Gray, 1995, p. 229).

Provide Comprehension Checks and Revision

Closely monitoring the individual's response to the Social Story (Gray, 1995, 1998, 2010; Tarnai & Wolfe, 2008) will promote modifications when aspects of the story lack meaning or are misconstrued. Comprehension checks can be conducted in a variety of ways, including the use of comprehension checklists (Gray, 1998) and written or spoken question-answer or fill-in-the-blank activities (Tarnai & Wolfe, 2008). Meta-analyses (Kokina & Kern, 2010; Reynhout & Carter, 2006) have concluded that Social Stories procedures that incorporate comprehension checks yield better outcomes than those that do not. "Therefore, it is recommended that professionals and parents conduct at least brief comprehension checks when using Social Stories" (Kokina & Kern, 2010, p. 24).

Generalization Training, Maintenance, and Fading

When gains are demonstrated, a common recommendation is to implement procedures designed to promote the generalization of skills (Nichols et al., 2006; Swaggart et al., 1995; Tarnai & Wolfe, 2008). Although research in this area is lacking (Sansoti et al., 2004), recommendations have focused on including peers in the intervention, reading of the Social Story by other people in a wider variety of settings, and expanding Social Story content to include other situations in which newly acquired skills are relevant. As Gray (2010) argued, "there may be no such thing as a 'retired' Social Story!" (p. xxi) because previously used stories can be updated to share new and related information.

Another common recommendation for practice is that successful Social Stories be maintained following gains but systematically faded by extending the time periods between readings or by shifting more responsibility to the individual for independent reading when appropriate (Swaggart et al., 1995). At this phase, new topics for Social Story intervention are often considered.

DATA COLLECTION TO SUPPORT DECISION MAKING

Clinicians and educators have experienced increasing pressure from consumers, professional organizations, legislatures, and courts to be accountable for their practices and have been asked to provide objective data to support and guide their decision making for intervention (Gast, 2010). Because Social Stories are tailored interventions that have been administered by a variety of professionals across a range of settings, many different ways to evaluate their effectiveness have been employed. Table 13.1 reveals the variability evident in the research methods used to assess outcomes. These include simple frequency tallies of behaviors during an activity (e.g., recess, circle time) or fixed period of time, the percentage of time engaged in an activity, the percentage of accurate responses given in semistructured tasks, the number of steps in a behavioral routine completed, subjective daily ratings of behavior, the number of prompts needed to facilitate a desired behavior, time/event sampling (e.g., the percentage of 10-s intervals in which a behavior occurs), and various methods to assess social validity (e.g., interviews, questionnaires). There has also been some discussion in the Social Story literature surrounding whether the most appropriate outcomes focus on decreasing undesirable behaviors, increasing desirable behaviors, or both (Nichols et al., 2006; Rust & Smith, 2006). In short, the nature of the data and its appropriateness as evidence to guide decision making may follow from the intervention target and goals, the individuals and setting, and practical considerations related to resources. In any event, what is taken as the index of success should be clearly operationalized and personalized to reflect what is functional and meaningful in the life of the individual (Ali & Fredrickson, 2006).

In research and practice, baseline and intervention-phase data are often gathered to evaluate the treatment, frequently in the form of an AB or simple time-series design. Only correlational conclusions are possible given this design (Gast, 2010). However, in educational and clinical settings, simple AB designs may be preferable to more extensive experimental designs (e.g., ABA, ABAB, multiple-baseline designs), which are difficult or impossible to implement in such settings. Practitioners might also consider the use of simple probes across baseline, intervention, and withdrawal phases to monitor the effectiveness of intervention.

Gray and Garand (1993) noted that when Social Story treatment is effective, results are often dramatic and apparent within 1 week. Swaggart and colleagues (1995) recommended that if desired behavior changes fail to occur after 2 weeks, the program should be altered. However, given the dynamic nature of Social Story intervention, there is no single criterion or time interval that can be offered to facilitate decisions regarding treatment. This caveat is particularly important in light of the fact that the number of times a Social Story must be read to reach a desired level of functioning (if this indeed occurs) is expected to vary significantly across individuals and behaviors and, for many individuals, any effect of treatment will emerge gradually (Gray, 1998).

If Social Story intervention is not deemed effective, authors should consider the possibility that the lack of change may be due to several factors (Gray & Garand, 1993), including the reading schedule, the accuracy and content (words and images) of the Social Story, the complexity of the language used, the motivation of the individual, and the appropriateness of the intervention target. For this reason, it is advisable to monitor, rethink, and revise a Social Story or its plan for implementation prior to abandoning it, as adjustments or additional supports may be needed to secure desirable outcomes (Gray, 1995).

CONSIDERATIONS FOR CHILDREN FROM CULTURALLY AND LINGUISTICALLY DIVERSE BACKGROUNDS

Macro- and microlevel cultural and linguistic differences underscore the importance that Social Stories be developed in close collaboration with families, who know the child best. The goal of Social Stories is to share relevant social information, the content of which can be expected to vary among individuals from culturally and linguistically diverse backgrounds. Indeed, members of different cultures often differ with regard to the importance they place on self-reliance and social conformity and how they construe appropriate social interaction. For instance, reduced eye contact is considered to be part of the impaired nonverbal behavior in ASDs; however, direct eye contact with authorities may be considered a sign of disrespect in Asian culture (Bernier, Mao, & Yen, 2010), as well as in other cultures. In this situation, the development of a Social Story to increase eye contact is probably not appropriate because it likely violates the social norms of the individual's culture. Thus, it is essential to consider differences in how families prioritize various developmental skills to ensure that the goals of treatment are consistent with the culturally relevant goals of the family. In fact, professionals may find it useful to focus on improving the specific impairments about which the family is most concerned (Mandell & Novak, 2005).

The involvement of families in developing Social Story content is also important to ensure that appropriate language is used. Families can provide input regarding whether the language is developmentally appropriate and incorporates vocabulary choices that have currency in the individual's life. In summary, collaboration with families should be viewed as a basic component of Social Story intervention that may be particularly important for individuals from culturally and linguistically diverse communities. Not only does consultation with families ensure that treatment goals are integrated in a culturally appropriate way, but it also has the potential to keep families engaged and potentially improve outcomes (Bernier et al., 2010).

Of course, the structure and explicit nature of Social Stories (e.g., "My mom likes it when I brush my teeth") may seem strange to some people of culturally and linguistically diverse backgrounds as well as to families who are not familiar with this intervention. For this reason, the rationale behind Social Stories should be made clear and adjustments in literary style should be considered with the proviso that the accuracy of all statements is preserved. Appropriate visual supports should also be used that draw on the relevant people and objects in the individual's life. When using Boardmaker, a variety of symbols is available that can be appropriate for people from a wide range of racial and ethnic backgrounds.

APPLICATION TO A CHILD

The stories help him think through problems. They really work for him. I've been telling everyone at his school to just "go wild with Social Stories!"

—A mother of a 5-year-old boy diagnosed with autistic disorder

We met Zach (pseudonym) and his mother when they participated in a study examining the effectiveness of Social Stories for facilitating social cognition and remediating challenging behaviors (Hutchins & Prelock, 2008). At the time, Zach was 5 years old and he had recently been diagnosed with autistic disorder. He was enrolled in a general education classroom and was receiving services from a school-based speech-language pathologist and special educator. As a first step in developing the intervention, we engaged in an information-gathering process that included child observation, joint interviews with Zach's mother and teacher, the administration of standardized measures to assess social, communicative, and "theory of mind" functioning, and a record review (i.e., individualized education program and diagnostic evaluations). Our goals were to understand Zach's strengths and challenges and to identify an intervention target that would be both responsive to parental priorities and sensitive to Zach's linguistic and social cognitive developmental level.

We learned that Zach was a sensitive and affectionate child who strived to please his parents. He demonstrated good receptive language skills and emerging "theory of mind" capacities, including the ability to engage in sustained episodes of joint attention, recognize facial expressions, and understand desire-based emotion (e.g., that people are happy when they get what they want). We planned to capitalize on these strengths to support his development toward enhanced social understanding and more appropriate behaviors. In particular, the sources of information that we consulted converged to identify "willful," "oppositional," and "explosive" aggressive acts that usually occurred in situations requiring adjustment and transitioning.

On the basis of the information gathered, a small research team developed the Social Story. Care was taken to ensure that the language level was appropriate, that the words chosen would be meaningful to Zach, and that all statements were accurate. We then asked Zach's mother to review and edit the Social Story for language level and accuracy of content.

The study that Zach participated in employed an ABA design. Subjective data in the form of behavior ratings and daily diaries were collected over baseline, intervention, and withdrawal phases of study. Zach's mother was asked to rate Zach's ability to "stay calm" and "use words to talk" in the context of the challenging situation. During the intervention phase, we read the Social Story to Zach 15 times over the course of 5 weeks (about three times per week) in his home. Each Social Story was preceded by a Comic Strip Conversation (a related story-based intervention procedure that uses visual supports during conversation; see Gray, 1994) during which Zach drew, and talked about, a recent challenging event that required adjustment or transitioning. The subjective maternal ratings of Zach's behaviors across ABA phases of study are presented in Figure 13.1. Zach's mother also provided a number of comments describing Zach's behavior at home and school (see Hutchins & Prelock, 2008, for more detail). A few of the comments that she offered during the intervention phase were "Better at remaining calm in most situations in general" and "He comes to me now when he gets upset and says 'I'm angry' and asks for help."

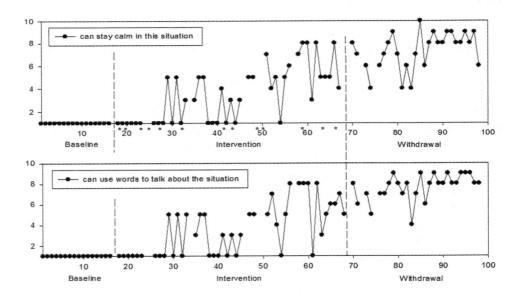

Figure 13.1. Maternal subjective ratings of Zach's ability to "stay calm" and "use words to talk" during a challenging situation (asterisks denote the days on which the Social Story was read). (From Hutchins, T.L., & Prelock, P.A. [2008]. Supporting theory of mind development: Considerations and recommendations for professionals providing services to individuals with autism spectrum disorder. *Topics in Language Disorders, 28*(4), 340–364; adapted by permission.)

This example illustrates several important features of Social Story intervention. First, as review of the literature reveals, Social Stories are often combined with other instructional strategies. In this case, Social Stories were combined with Comic Strip Conversations, which can be an effective companion strategy to enhance social cognition (Gray, 1998). The example also underscores the importance of the information-gathering process and describes one way in which researchers, families, and educators can collaborate to develop appropriate and effective intervention strategies for use in the home or other settings. This example also highlights the variety of data collection techniques that have been used to evaluate Social Story intervention. Several methods for evaluating Zach's response to treatment were available, but the use of subjective maternal daily diaries (both quantitative and qualitative data) was desirable for the purposes of the study for a few reasons: It allowed collection of relevant and personalized information, it was feasible, and it was socially valid. As has been reported by others (e.g., Norris & Datillo, 1999), several repetitions of the story were needed before change was detected, and a positive effect of treatment was maintained following treatment withdrawal. Zach's mother indicated her newfound enthusiasm for Social Stories and promptly instructed his school team to "go wild with Social Stories!"

APPLICATION TO AN ADOLESCENT OR ADULT

Jacob needs a specific visual cognitive prosthesis to understand the who, what, where, when, how, and why of our culture and how he fits and belongs.

—Mother of a 17-year-old boy diagnosed with PDD-NOS

Jacob, a 17-year-old diagnosed with PDD-NOS, was enrolled in a general education classroom and was receiving services from a speech-language pathologist, special educator, case manager, and paraeducator at his local high school. Jacob was a sensitive young man who had an especially deep connection with his mother. He loved wind chimes and music, and he could play a variety of instruments in a truly gifted manner. Previous assessments indicated that oral language comprehension was an area of impairment for Jacob, that productive language was limited to two- to five-word sentences, and that reading and writing were areas of great strength. To enhance Jacob's communication, one important goal involved his voice, which was often soft and whispery and tended to trail into silence. Following an examination that revealed normal structure and function of the larynx, Jacob began voice therapy with a university-based speech-language pathologist. Jacob worked hard over the course of several weeks to find what he called his "excellent voice," which was louder and easier to understand. Unfortunately, gains made in the clinic failed to generalize to other settings.

Because Jacob could produce an "excellent voice," a Social Story was developed with some specific objectives in mind. One objective was to enhance Jacob's understanding of the social importance of using his "excellent voice." Another objective was to recruit the participation of those who had frequent and direct contact with Jacob. We collaborated with Jacob, Jacob's mother, and his university-based speech-language pathologist to learn about the "who, what, when, where, and why" that surrounded the production of his different voices. The use of the Motivation Assessment Scale (MAS; Durand & Crimmins, 1992) and our previous observations of Jacob facilitated this effort.

TITLE

Using My Excellent Voice

INTRODUCTION

2 descriptive sentences	Descriptive sentence
My name is Jacob. I am 17 years old and in high school.	I have many different voices.

BODY

Descriptive sentence	Descriptive sentence	Perspective sentence	1 perspective and 1 descriptive sentence
Sometimes my voice is a low **basso profundo** voice.	Other times my voice is very soft and whispering.	When I use my soft whispering voice, it's hard for people to hear what I am saying.	My mom likes what she calls my natural or real voice. I call it my excellent voice.

Descriptive sentence	Perspective sentence	2 sentences that coach the team	Sentences that coaches the team
I have worked hard with [Name] and [Name] and have found my excellent voice.	When I use my excellent voice, it is easier for people to hear what I am saying.	[Name] and [Name] will try to help me use my excellent voice. They can remind me to use my excellent voice.	They can also speak clearly to me, use short sentences, and give me more time to talk.

CONCLUSION

Partial sentence	Affirmative sentence
When I talk, I will try to remember to	My excellent voice is EXCELLENT!

Figure 13.2. Jacob's Social Story. (The Picture Communication Symbols © 1981–2010 by Mayer-Johnson LLC. All Rights Reserved Worldwide. Used with permission. Boardmaker™ is a trademark of Mayer-Johnson LLC.)

A Social Story entitled "Using My Excellent Voice" was drafted and revised with input from Jacob's mother to ensure accuracy of content. The Social Story adhered to Gray's (2010) recommendations. When asked about pictures, Jacob noted that he would like Boardmaker pictures in his story, so Picture Communication Symbols were added. Particular font and formatting choices were incorporated to highlight key messages. We then introduced the story to Jacob and followed this with brief comprehension checks of the text and images. Jacob's Social Story is presented in Figure 13.2, and a brief video showing Jacob's introduction to the Social Story is provided on the DVD that accompanies this book.

Hard and electronic copies of the Social Story were shared with Jacob, Jacob's mother, and Jacob's school-based speech-language pathologist, paraeducator, special educator, and case manager, who agreed to read the Social Story across contexts with the hope that this would facilitate acquisition and generalization of skills. The electronic version of the Social Story was deemed particularly important for Jacob, who often used an iPod Touch; the use of this media was expected to enhance Jacob's interest in and access to the story. All participants (including Jacob) agreed to read the Social Story once or twice a week for several weeks to ensure that the story was read frequently. A plan for data collection was developed by the school team to track Jacob's use of an "excellent voice" over several weeks using an ABA design.

This example of the development of a Social Story underscores the nature of Social Story intervention as a collaborative process. Our team identified a topic that seemed critical to Jacob's success as a communicative partner. Through testing, discussion, and observation, we determined that the target represented an area in which Jacob had demonstrated some competency, which increased the likelihood that it was a developmentally appropriate target. Through this collaborative process our team began to identify some things we could do to support Jacob. In particular, we learned that Jacob was more likely to use his "excellent voice" when others spoke to him using short sentences and gave him more time to respond. Working as a team helped us to develop a schedule for reading the Social Story and data collection procedures to evaluate treatment. In summary, the collaborative process helped us refine our thinking, coordinate workable plans, and develop shared responsibility for supporting Jacob's success. Indeed, the increasing popularity of Social Stories may be explained not only by effects they can have on the audience but also by the effects they can have on the authors (Ali & Fredrickson, 2006).

FUTURE DIRECTIONS

The Social Story literature has raised a number of questions representing important directions for future research (see also Ali & Fredrickson, 2006; Nichols et al., 2006; Sansoti et al., 2004). Based on scant or mixed evidence, some of the more salient research directions address the following questions:

- What variables predict maintenance of skills?
- Do intervention procedures that involve multiple readers across contexts result in better outcomes or outcomes that are more likely to generalize to untrained settings or people?
- Is the Social Story intervention effective and appropriate for adults and what modifications, if any, could be made to best serve this population?

- Which individual characteristics (e.g., age, verbal ability, reading level) predict success with Social Stories?
- What is the effect of stories that praise or applaud what the individual has achieved or is already doing well?
- What are good procedures for determining whether visual supports should be used and if used, what procedures can inform choices about the number and kind of images?
- Do particular schedules of review (including the number of presentations, the intensity and duration of treatment, and fading procedures) predict success and how might these vary with individual characteristics?

In addition, there is a need to determine whether certain targets of intervention are more amenable or resistant to change. Kokina and Kern (2010) suggested that Social Stories targeting the reduction of challenging behaviors may be more effective than those teaching social skills. Yet the success of a particular target is likely contingent on the individual's motivation, strengths, and challenges (Kokina & Kern, 2010). Although researchers and professionals have acknowledged the importance of developmentally appropriate language within Social Stories, very few have considered whether a particular social-cognitive understanding is a developmentally appropriate goal (Hutchins & Prelock, 2008). Examining the importance of developmental appropriateness in the selection of social-cognitive goals seems crucial given that the theoretical basis of Social Stories is to enhance social understanding.

This direction of inquiry raises a related question regarding the need to test the theoretical assumptions of Social Stories. When Social Stories are deemed effective, good outcomes may result from more advanced social understanding or from the use of a nonepistemic strategy in which solutions are derived from logic or rote learning. Differentiating between these alternative explanations has important implications for maintenance and generalizability. If Social Stories have the potential to remediate a core impairment in social understanding as opposed to a behavioral symptom, then shifts in understanding should lead to sustained and positive changes across the range of behaviors and situations for which that understanding is relevant. In contrast, if behavioral learning is all that is occurring, evidence should show reduced generalizability and, perhaps, reduced maintenance. Thus, a need exists to develop sensitive ways of assessing whether Social Stories lead to meaningful changes in affect and social cognition, as much of the research has focused on behavior (Ali & Fredrickson, 2006).

Whether Social Stories result in epistemic or nonepistemic changes seems to be at the heart of the debate surrounding the utility of different sentence types (directive and perspective sentences in particular) and Gray's (2010) proposed ratio by extension. However, a couple of issues complicate this discussion. First, sentences often serve multiple functions within Gray's typology. For example, the sentence "My mom likes what she calls my real or natural voice" has both a descriptive component (it provides information about how mom refers to a voice) and a perspective component (it provides information about mom's internal state). Second, a need exists to examine other sentence or story dimensions that may influence effectiveness, and some researchers have begun to explore a few candidates (i.e., Okada, Ohtake, & Yanagihara [2008] argued that the generality vs. specificity of sentences may make a difference). Certainly, there are several dimensions that might be evaluated to determine recommendations for Social Story construction. Pursuing this line of questioning may reveal new and relevant features of Social Story content beyond Gray's traditional sentence types.

SUGGESTED READINGS

Ali, S., & Fredrickson, N. (2006). Investigating the evidence base of Social Stories™. *Educational Psychology in Practice, 22*(4), 355–377.

This article offers a descriptive review of Social Stories research and describes the strengths and weaknesses of selected studies. Conclusions about ways to develop the evidence base of Social Stories are offered that remain relevant today.

Gray, C. (2010). *The new Social Story book.* Arlington, TX: Future Horizons.

This book describes Gray's most recent criteria that define Social Stories. A series of tutorials and exercises to develop competency with writing Social Stories is offered. The book also includes more than 150 standard Social Stories that may be adapted for use.

Hutchins, T.L., & Prelock, P.A. (2008). Supporting theory of mind development: Considerations and recommendations for professionals providing services to individuals with autism spectrum disorder. *Topics in Language Disorders, 28*(4), 340–364.

This article describes a developmental perspective on "theory of mind" that may assist in the education planning of individuals with ASDs. A case vignette is offered that illustrates a collaborative approach to effective Social Story intervention.

Rust, J., & Smith, A. (2006). How should the effectiveness of Social Stories™ to modify the behavior of children on the autistic spectrum be tested? *Autism, 10*(2), 125–138.

This article recounts the variability evident in the Social Stories literature and focuses on several factors that should be considered when evaluating the effectiveness of Social Stories.

Learning Activities

1. Read *The New Social Story™ Book* (Gray, 2010). A series of tutorials and exercises to develop competency with writing Social Stories is offered. Complete the activities in the book.

2. Consider what approach to take in Vincent's case. Vincent is a verbal 6-year-old African American boy diagnosed with autistic disorder who is enrolled in a general education classroom. Vincent's speech-language pathologist is concerned about behaviors that appear to limit Vincent's ability to engage in appropriate, reciprocal social interaction. Chief among these are loud talking and a tendency to interrupt others to gain the conversational floor. What kinds of information would you collect to determine whether these are appropriate targets for intervention? What sources of information could help you understand the behaviors better?

3. Consider what approach to take in Stuart's case. Stuart is a 6-year-old boy of European descent diagnosed with PDD-NOS. Formal testing revealed that Stuart has significant impairments in cognition and in receptive and expres-

sive language. Stuart's level of reading comprehension is unclear but writing is a relative strength, and he seems to enjoy writing, doodling, and looking at books. In the opinion of his special educator, Stuart engages in behaviors that will stigmatize him among peers and others. He constantly picks his nose and ears, possibly because of sensory issues. Would Stuart be a good candidate for Social Story intervention given his cognitive and linguistic profile? If you decide to pursue Social Story intervention, what strategies could you use to ensure that the Social Story is presented in a way that preserves Stuart's self-esteem and is a positive behavioral intervention? Identify one way to evaluate the effect of intervention, making sure that the outcome is clearly operationalized and personally relevant and meaningful in the child's life.

4.   Examine the Social Story presented below. Identify each sentence according to Gray's (2010) seven types (i.e., descriptive, perspective, affirmative, sentence that coaches the team, sentence that coaches the audience, self-coaching sentence, and partial sentence).

Waiting in the Lunch Line

My name is Patty.
I go to school at Catamount Elementary.
When I am at school, I usually eat lunch with the other children.
Most days, we all wait in the lunch line to get our food.
Sometimes, I don't want to wait in the lunch line.
I might walk to the front of the line without waiting my turn.
This is called "cutting the line."
The other children might be unhappy or upset when I cut the line.
Cutting the line isn't fair to the other children because they have already waited.
If I cut the line in front of them, they have to wait even longer.
This is just how waiting in line works.
I will try to remember to wait my turn in the lunch line.
I can think of a line that gets longer for everyone else when I cut to the front.
My teacher and the school staff can also help me wait by reminding me about fairness.
When I have to wait in the lunch line, that is okay and I am okay.
Waiting my turn in the lunch line is simply the _____ thing to do.

Were some sentence types more difficult to identify than others? Did you ever get the sense that a sentence type did not really fit or that a sentence could reasonably fit more than one type? What implications might this have for Gray's (2010) assertion that Social Stories should conform to a specific sentence type ratio?

REFERENCES

Adams, L., Gouvousis, A., VanLue, M., & Waldon, C. (2004). Social story intervention: Improving communication skills in a child with autism spectrum disorder. *Focus on Autism and Other Developmental Disabilities, 19*(2), 87–94.

Ali, S., & Fredrickson, N. (2006). Investigating the evidence base of Social Stories™. *Educational Psychology in Practice, 22*(4), 355–377.

American Psychiatric Association (2001). *Diagnostic and statistical manual of mental disorders* (4th ed.). Washington, DC: American Psychiatric Association.

Attwood, T. (1998). *Asperger's Syndrome: A guide for parents and professionals.* Philadelphia, PA: Jessica Kingsley Publishers.

Barry, L.M., & Burlew, S.B. (2004). Using Social Stories™ to teach choice and play skills to children with autism. *Focus on Autism and Other Developmental Disabilities, 19*(1), 45–51.

Bernad-Ripoll, S. (2007). Using a self-as-model video combined with Social Stories™ to help a child with Asperger syndrome understand emotions. *Focus on Autism and Other Developmental Disabilities, 22*(2), 100–108.

Bernier, R., Mao, A., & Yen, D. (2010). Psychopathology, families, and culture: Autism. *Child and Adolescent Psychiatric Clinics of North America, 19,* 855–867.

Bledsoe, R., Smith, B.S., & Simpson, R. (2003). Use of social story intervention to improve mealtime skills of an adolescent with Asperger syndrome. *Autism: The International Journal of Research and Practice, 7,* 289–295.

Briody, J., & McGarry, K. (2005). Using Social Stories™ to ease children's transitions. *Young Children, 60,* 38–43.

Brownell, M.D. (2002). Musically adapted Social Stories™ to modify behaviors in students with autism: Four case studies. *Journal of Music Therapy, 39*(2), 117–144.

Burke, R.V., Kuhn, B.R., & Peterson, J.L. (2004). Brief report: A "storybook" ending to children's bedtime problems: The use of a rewarding social story to reduce bedtime resistance and frequent night waking. *Journal of Pediatric Psychology, 29,* 389–396.

Carr, E.G., Dunlap, G., Horner, R.H., Koegel, R.L., Turnbull, A.P., Sailor, W.,...Fox, L. (2002). Positive behavior support: Evolution of an applied science. *Journal of Positive Behavior Interventions, 4*(1), 4–6.

Chan, J.M., & O'Reilly, M.F. (2008). A Social Stories™ intervention package for students with autism in inclusive classroom settings. *Journal of Applied Behavior Analysis, 41,* 405–409.

Chan, J.M., O'Reilly, M.F., Lang, R.B., Boutot, E.A., White, P.J., Pierce, N., & Baker, S. (2011). Evaluation of Social Stories™ intervention implemented by pre-service teachers for students with autism in general education settings. *Research in Autism Spectrum Disorders, 5,* 715–721.

Crozier, S., & Tincani, M.J. (2005). Using a modified social story to decrease disruptive behavior of a child with autism. *Focus on Autism and Other Developmental Disabilities, 20*(3), 150–157.

Crozier, S., & Tincani, M.J. (2007). Effects of Social Stories™ on prosocial behavior of preschool children with autism spectrum disorders. *Journal of Autism and Developmental Disorders, 37,* 1803–1814.

Davenport, G.C. (1993). *An introduction to child development.* London, UK: Collins Educational.

Delano, M., & Snell, M.E. (2006). The effects of Social Stories™ on the social engagement of children with autism. *Journal of Positive Behavior Interventions, 8*(1), 29–42.

Del Valle, P.R., McEachern, A.G., & Chambers, H.D. (2001). Using Social Stories™ with autistic children. *Journal of Poetry Therapy, 14*(4), 187–197.

Dodd, S., Stephen, D., Hupp, A., Jewell, J.D., & Krohn, E. (2008). Using parents and siblings during a social story intervention for two children diagnosed with PDD-NOS. *Journal of Developmental and Physical Disabilities, 20,* 217–229.

Doyle, T., & Arnedillo-Sanchez, I. (2011). Using multimedia to reveal the hidden code of everyday behavior to children with autism spectrum disorders (ASDs). *Computers and Education, 56,* 357–369.

Dunlap, G., & Fox, L. (1999). A demonstration of behavioral supports for young children with autism. *Journal of Positive Behavioral Interventions, 1*(2), 77–87.

Durand, V.M., & Crimmins, D.B. (1992). *The motivation assessment scale.* Topeka, KS: Monaco & Associates.

Frith, U. (1989). *Autism: Explaining the enigma.* Oxford, UK: Blackwell.

Gast, D.L. (2010). *Single subject research methodology in behavioral sciences.* New York, NY: Taylor & Francis.

Graetz, J.E., Mastropieri, M.A., & Scruggs, T.E. (2009). Decreasing inappropriate behaviors for adolescents with autism spectrum disorders using modified Social Stories™. *Education and Training in Developmental Disabilities, 44*(1), 91–104.

Gray, C. (1994). *Comic Strip Conversations.* Arlington, TX: Future Horizons.

Gray, C. (1995). Teaching children with autism to "read" social situations. In K.A. Quill (Ed.), *Teaching children with autism: Strategies to enhance communication and socialization* (pp. 219–241). New York, NY: Delmar Publishers.

Gray, C. (1998). Social Stories™ and comic strip conversations with students with Asperger syndrome and high-functioning autism. In E. Schopler (Ed.), *Asperger syndrome or high functioning autism?* (pp. 167–194). New York, NY: Plenum Press.

Gray, C. (2000). *The new Social Story book: Illustrated edition.* Arlington, TX: Future Horizons.

Gray, C. (2010). *The new Social Story book.* Arlington, TX: Future Horizons.

Gray, C. (2011). *The new Social Story™ book: 10th anniversary edition.* Arlington, TX: Future Horizons.

Gray, C., & Garand, J.D. (1993). Social Stories™: Improving responses of students with autism with accurate social information. *Focus on Autistic Behavior, 8*(1), 1–10.

Gray, C., & White, A.L. (2002). *My Social Stories™ book.* London, UK: Jessica Kingsley Publishers.

Greenway, C. (2000). Autism and Asperger syndrome: Strategies to promote prosocial behaviors. *Educational Psychology in Practice, 16*(3), 469–486.

Haggerty, N.K., Black, R.S., & Smith, G.J. (2005). Increasing self-managed coping skills through Social Stories™ and apron story-telling. *Teaching Exceptional Children, 37,* 40–47.

Hagiwara, T., & Myles, S.B. (1999). A multimedia social story intervention: Teaching skills to children with autism. *Focus on Autism and Other Developmental Disabilities, 14,* 82–95.

Hanley-Hochdorfer, K., Bray, M.A., Kehl, T.J., & Elinoff, M.J. (2010). Social Stories™ to increase verbal initiation in children with autism and Asperger's disorder. *School Psychology Review, 39*(3), 484–492.

Happe, F. (1999). Autism: Cognitive deficit or cognitive style? *Metaphor and Symbolic Activity, 10,* 275–295.

Hess, K.L., Morrier, M.J., Heflin, L.J., & Ivey, M.L. (2008). Autism treatment survey: Services received by children with autism spectrum disorders in public school classrooms. *Journal of Autism and Developmental Disorders, 38,* 961–971.

Hutchins, T.L., & Prelock, P.A. (2006). Using Social Stories™ and comic strip conversations to promote socially valid outcomes for children with autism. *Seminars in Speech and Language, 27*(1), 47–59.

Hutchins, T.L., & Prelock, P.A. (2008). Supporting theory of mind development: Considerations and recommendations for professionals providing services to individuals with autism spectrum disorder. *Topics in Language Disorders, 28*(4), 340–364.

Ivey, M.L., Heflin, J., & Alberto, P. (2004). The use of Social Stories™ to promote independent behaviors in novel events for children with PDD-NOS. *Focus on Autism and Other Developmental Disabilities, 19,* 164–176.

Kalyva, E., & Agaliotis, I. (2009). Can Social Stories™ enhance the interpersonal conflict resolution skills of children with LD? *Research in Developmental Disabilities, 30,* 192–202.

Karkhaneh, M., Clark, B., Ospina, B.M., Seida, J.C., Smith, V., & Hartling, L. (2010). Social Stories™ to improve social skills in children with autism spectrum disorder: A systematic review. *Autism, 14*(6), 641–662.

Kokina, A., & Kern, L. (2010). Social Story™ interventions for students with autism spectrum disorders. *Journal of Autism and Developmental Disabilities, 40,* 812–826.

Kuoch, H., & Mirenda, P. (2003). Social story interventions for young children with autism spectrum disorders. *Focus on Autism and Other Developmental Disabilities, 18,* 219–227.

Kuttler, S., Myles, B.S., & Carlson, J.K. (1998). The use of Social Stories™ to reduce precursors to tantrum behavior in a student with autism. *Focus on Autism and Other Developmental Disabilities, 13,* 176–182.

Lorimer, P.A., Simpson, R.L,. Myles, B.S., & Ganz, J.B. (2002). The use of Social Stories™ as a preventative behavioral intervention in a home setting with a child with autism. *Journal of Positive Behavioral Interventions, 4,* 53–60.

Mancil, R.G., Haydon, E., & Whitby, P. (2009). Differentiated effects of paper and computer-assisted Social Stories™ on inappropriate behavior in children with autism. *Focus on Autism and Other Developmental Disabilities, 24*(4), 205–215.

Mandell, D.S., & Novak, M. (2005). The role of culture in families' treatment decisions for children with autism spectrum disorders. *Mental Retardation and Developmental Disabilities, 11,* 10–115.

Marr, D., Mika, H., Miraglia, J., Roerig, M., & Sinnott, R. (2007). The effects of sensory stories on targeted behaviors in preschool children with autism. *Physical and Occupational Therapy in Pediatrics, 27*(1), 63–79.

Moore, P.S. (2004). The use of Social Stories™ in a psychology service for children with learning disabilities: A case study of a sleep problem. *British Journal of Learning Disabilities, 32,* 133–138.

National Autism Center. (2009). *National Standards Project—findings and conclusions: Addressing the needs for evidence-based practice guidelines for autism spectrum disorders.* Randolph, MA: Author. Retrieved from http://www.nationalautismcenter.org

Nichols, S.L., Hupp, S.D., Jewell, J.D., & Zeigler, C.S. (2006). Review of Social Story interventions for children diagnosed with autism spectrum disorders. *Journal of Evidence-Based Practices for Schools, 6*(1), 90–120.

Norris, C., & Dattilo, J. (1999). Evaluating effects of a social story intervention on a young girl with autism. *Focus on Autism and Other Developmental Disabilities, 14,* 180–186.

O'Conner, E. (2009). The use of social story DVDs to reduce anxiety levels: A case study of a child with autism and learning disabilities. *Support for Learning, 24*(3), 133–136.

Okada, S., Ohtake, Y., & Yanagihara, M. (2008). Effects of perspective sentences in Social Stories™ on improving the adaptive behaviors of students with autism and related disabilities. *Education and Training in Developmental Disabilities, 43*(1), 46–60.

Ozdemir, S. (2008). The effectiveness of Social Stories™ on decreasing disruptive behaviors of children with autism: Three case studies. *Journal of Autism and Developmental Disorders, 38,* 1689–1696.

Pasiali, V. (2004). The use of prescriptive therapeutic songs in a home-based environment to promote social skills acquisition by children with autism: Three case studies. *Music Therapy Perspectives, 22*(1), 11–20.

Quirmbach, L.M., Lincoln, A.J., Feinberg-Gizzo, M.J., Ingersoll, B.R., & Andrews, S.M. (2009). Social Stories™: Mechanisms of effectiveness in increasing game play skills in children diagnosed with autism spectrum disorders using a pretest posttest repeated measures randomized control group design. *Journal of Autism and Developmental Disorders, 39*(2), 299–321.

Reynhout, G., & Carter, M. (2006). Social Stories™ for children with disabilities. *Journal of Autism and Developmental Disorders, 36,* 445–469.

Reynhout, G., & Carter, M. (2009). The use of Social Stories™ by teachers and their perceived efficacy. *Research in Autism Spectrum Disorders, 3,* 232–251.

Reynhout, G., & Carter, M. (2011). Evaluation of the efficacy of Social Stories™ using three single subject metrics. *Research in Autism Spectrum Disorders, 5,* 885–900.

Robey, R.R., & Schultz, M.C. (1998). A model for conducting clinical-outcomes research: An adaptation of the standard protocol for use in aphasiology. *Aphasiology, 12*(9), 787–810.

Rogers, M.G., & Myles, B.S. (2001). Using Social Stories™ and comic strip conversations to interpret social situations for an adolescent with Asperger syndrome. *Intervention in School and Clinic, 38,* 310–313.

Rowe, C. (1999). Do Social Stories™ benefit children diagnosed with autism in mainstream primary schools? *British Journal of Special Education, 26,* 12–14.

Rust, J., & Smith, A. (2006). How should the effectiveness of Social Stories™ to modify the behavior of children on the autistic spectrum be tested? *Autism, 10*(2), 125–138.

Sansoti, F.J., Powell-Smith, K.A., & Kincaid, D. (2004). A research synthesis of social story interventions for children diagnosed with autism spectrum disorders. *Focus on Autism and Other Developmental Disabilities, 19,* 194–204.

Sansoti, F.J., & Powell-Smith, K.A. (2006). Using Social Stories™ to improve the social behavior of children with Asperger syndrome. *Journal of Positive Behavior Interventions, 8*(1), 43–57.

Scattone, D. (2007). Social skills interventions for children with autism. *Psychology in the Schools, 44*(7), 717–726.

Scattone, D. (2008). Enhancing the conversation skills of a boy with Asperger's disorder through Social Stories™ and video modeling. *Journal of Autism and Developmental Disorders, 38*, 395–400.

Scattone, D., Tingstrom, D.H., & Wilczynski, S.M. (2006). Increasing appropriate social interactions of children with autism spectrum disorders using Social Stories™. *Focus on Autism and Other Developmental Disabilities, 21*(4), 211–222.

Scattone, D., Wilczynski, S.M., Edwards, R.P., & Rabian, B. (2002). Decreasing disruptive behaviors of children with autism using Social Stories™. *Journal of Autism and Developmental Disorders, 32*(6), 535–543.

Schneider, N., & Goldstein, H. (2010). Social Stories™ improve the on-task behavior of children with language impairment. *Journal of Early Intervention, 31*(3), 250–264.

Scott, J., Clark, C., & Brady, M. (2000). *Students with autism: Characteristics and instructional programming for special educators.* San Diego, CA: Singular.

Smith, C. (2001). Using Social Stories™ to enhance behavior in children with autistic spectrum difficulties. *Educational Psychology in Practice, 17*(4), 337–345.

Soenksen, D., & Alper, S. (2006). Teaching a young child to appropriately gain attention of peers using a social story intervention. *Focus on Autism and Other Developmental Disabilities, 21*(1), 36–44

Swaggart, B.L., Gagnon, E., Bock, S.J., Earlies, E.L., Quinn, C., Myles, B.S., & Simpson, R.L. (1995). Using Social Stories™ to teach social and behavioral skills to children with autism. *Focus on Autistic Behavior, 10*, 1–15.

Tarnai, B., & Wolfe, P.S. (2008). Social Stories™ for sexuality education for persons with autism/pervasive developmental disorder. *Sexual Disability, 26*, 29–36.

Test, D.W., Richter, S., Knight, V., & Spooner, F. (2010). A comprehensive review and meta-analysis of the Social Stories™ literature. *Focus on Autism and Other Developmental Disabilities.* Advance online publication. doi:10.1177/1088357609351573

Theimann, K.S., & Goldstein, H. (2001). Social Stories™, written text cues, and video feedback: Effects on social communication of children with autism. *Journal of Applied Behavior Analysis, 34*(4), 425–446.

Toplis, R., & Hadwin, J.A. (2006). Using Social Stories™ to change problematic lunchtime behavior in school. *Educational Psychology in Practice, 22*(1), 53–67.

Weschler, D. (2003). *Weschler intelligence scales for children* (4th ed.). San Antonio, TX: The Psychological Corporation.

Zimbelman, M., Paschal, S., Hawley, S.R., Molgaard, C.A., & St. Romain, T. (2007). Addressing physical inactivity among developmentally disabled students through visual schedules and Social Stories™. *Research in Developmental Disabilities, 28*, 386–396.

14

Video Modeling Applications for Persons with Autism

Tom Buggey

Students with autism present parents and educators with a great challenge. How do you educate children who have difficulty attending to a task and who sometimes set up a range of defenses that appear to be specifically designed to avoid attending to the people instructing them? A large proportion of instructional time with these children is spent providing them with models of appropriate behaviors and progressively more complex academic skills. Unless adults can penetrate the social barriers presented by people with autism, the effects of instruction will be muted. One way around this dilemma may be to use video models as a medium of instruction.

Television and computer screens act as magnets to many children and youth. The medium alone is a powerful attractor, yet aside from this widespread appeal, there may be reasons why video-based instruction holds special promise for people with autism. Video modeling has been developed with this possibility in mind. Video modeling can be defined as an instructional method in which an individual develops a skill or behavior by viewing images of someone demonstrating that skill or behavior. The model may be a peer, an adult, an animation, or, in the case of video self-modeling, the viewer him- or herself. Video modeling can be used to teach new skills or behaviors, to improve a skill or behavior, or to replace or extinguish challenging behavior. A salient feature of all video-modeling formats is that demonstrated behavior is always positive. These methods do not address what *not* to do. There is another form of video instruction, typically referred to as **self-observation** (Piersel & Kratochwill, 1979), in which raw video is analyzed so that observers can learn from mistakes as well as from successes. Sports teams often watch videos of past games to analyze performance by using self-observation. In contrast, in video-modeling movies, all evidence of inappropriate behavior and any errors made while recording are typically removed (Dowrick, 1983), thus making this method a good fit as a positive behavioral support.

Video-modeling seems to be effective across all age ranges, with the possible exception of very young children from birth to 2½ years old. There is simply no research available on which to base claims about this age group. In addition, some evidence suggests that people with severe autism who also have severe cognitive disabilities may not benefit from video modeling (Buggey, 2009); however, ample evidence suggests that video modeling can be effective with children who are classified in the moderate to severe range of the spectrum (e.g., Bellini, Akullian, & Hopf, 2007; Buggey, Toombs, Gardner, & Cervetti, 1999; LeBlanc et al., 2003).

Video modeling can be used to supplement other methods, such as applied behavior analysis (ABA), or can be used as the main intervention. Anyone with knowledge of developmental sequences who has some basic skills with a video camera and video editing software can produce videos appropriate for use in video modeling. Production of the videos varies in complexity across the three main types of **video modeling: adult/peer modeling, point-of-view modeling,** and **self-modeling.** The actual editing of video footage is the same across the various methods, but the strategy for arranging and composing the scenes to be shot is very different. Adult and peer modeling videos are relatively simple to create because the movies' "stars" will be totally cooperative and easily coached. Point-of-view modeling is also fairly simple to carry out. One needs to task-analyze a behavior and walk through the sequence of steps with the camera held at a child's eye level. The view from the camera, simulating the child's viewpoint, becomes the central instructional component. Self-modeling is more complicated because one must manipulate the recording and editing of the video footage to make it appear that learners are more advanced than they typically are. This task can be challenging if the model tends to shy away from social interaction or has difficulty following directions.

Because video modeling is a relatively new methodology, there is little written about its delivery. Video modeling has relevance in occupational, physical, and speech and language therapies, as well as in psychological and even vocational counseling. It has also been used effectively for academic instruction. The critical factor in determining which form of video modeling is used, where it is used, and who will be responsible for creating videos seems to be available time for the providers involved. A video using point-of-view modeling can probably be produced in less than an hour. Adult and peer modeling videos will take somewhat longer and will require more coordination and participants. Self-modeling videos can be produced in the same amount of time as the other methods under ideal conditions and with a cooperative "star," but they usually take longer.

The time commitment necessary for producing modeling videos puts some constraints on who is likely to create them. Classroom teachers may not have the available time or the flexibility in scheduling to devote to video modeling. Counselors, therapists, and parents are more likely to have the time and resources to devote to creating videos.

TARGET POPULATIONS AND ASSESSMENTS
FOR DETERMINING TREATMENT RELEVANCE AND GOALS

Video modeling has been successfully applied to people with autism across the full range of the spectrum from mild autism or Asperger syndrome (Delano, 2007; Sansosti & Powell-Smith, 2008; Scattone, 2008) to severe autism (Buggey et al., 2005). Research has not been carried out with people with rarer forms of autism spectrum disorder (ASD) such as Rett syndrome and childhood disintegrative disorder, probably because of the paucity of children with these disorders.

Little has been written about who could most benefit from video modeling. Nor is there any research concerning client attributes that would preclude the use of video-modeling intervention. It is logical to assume there is a bottom age limit or a threshold of cognitive ability needed for success with video modeling. The few instances in the literature in which video modeling has been unsuccessful have tended to involve preschool children for whom age or developmental levels may have been a deciding factor (Buggey, Hoomes, Sherberger, & Williams, 2011; Clark, Beck, Sloane, Jenson, & Bowen, 1993). A prerequisite skill often ascribed to self-modeling is self-recognition (Dowrick, 1983). This claim becomes dubious when one considers the success of other forms of modeling. It may be that self-recognition, which typically develops between 18 and 24 months (Lewis & Brooks-Gunn, 1979), occurs at the same time as many other developmental milestones, and it is these other areas of development that are the critical factors. Certainly, much more research is needed in this area to settle this issue.

There are no standardized or criterion-referenced tests that can be used to determine whether video modeling might be effective with any given person. Much of the evaluation prior to implementation of video modeling takes the form of direct observation. A key observation is whether television attracts an individual's attention. Although video seems to attract most people and some people with autism can even exhibit selective attention to video, this is not always the case. Other observation tools used in video modeling are related to functional behavioral assessment and curriculum-based measurement, which will be addressed later in this chapter.

THEORETICAL BASIS

Video modeling is supported by several lines of research (e.g., Dowrick, 1983; Wright & Smith, 2009) and theory (Bandura, 1969, 1997). Some researchers (e.g., Buggey, 2005; Hine & Wolery, 2006; Nikopoulos & Keenan, 2007) have focused on the use of video modeling with people with autism. Additional support has come from anecdotal evidence for the method provided by families who are using similar approaches to teach their children (Neumann, 1999; J. Benkert, personal communication, March 3, 2009) and from testimonials provided by people with autism. For example, the testimonial offered by Temple Grandin has had great influence. Dr. Grandin is a professor at Colorado State University in the field of animal husbandry who has autism. In her book *Thinking in Pictures,* Grandin (2010) offers at least two reasons why video modeling may be particularly effective with people with autism. The first is that video images are not socially threatening. Emotional barriers often seen in people with autism during human interactions are not necessarily present when two-dimensional video images are involved: There are no social obligations (or penalties) in the context of video characters. A second reason why video modeling might be effective involves the tendency for people with autism to be visual- rather than language-based thinkers (Bauman, 1999; Bryan & Gast, 2000). Grandin described her thinking process as follows:

> I think in pictures. Words are like a second language to me. I translate both spoken and written words into full-color movies, complete with sound, which run like a VCR tape in my head. When somebody speaks to me, his words are instantly translated into pictures. (p. 1)

If this is the case with more than a handful of individuals with autism, then video modeling may present a particularly potent method of instruction.

There are several additional reasons why self-modeling might be particularly effective and appropriate for use with people with autism. The fact that the child serves as his or her own model has important implications. Bandura (1969, 1997) carried out extensive studies on the influence of models. He found that the most effective models were those who had attributes that were most similar to the viewer's. This included such traits as gender, age, race, and—interestingly—ability. The best models were not the paragons of success but those who were only slightly more advanced than the observer. These findings indicate two advantages that video self-modeling may have over other forms of modeling. First, it would be impossible to find anyone more similar to the observer than the observer him- or herself. Second, and related to the first, the model will be only slightly more advanced than the observer. Even though the model and observer are the same person, the model will be pictured as more advanced in the targeted skill. In Bandura's later writings, he addressed self-modeling as possibly the purest form of modeling. Following Bandura's line of logic here, it would seem that adults would serve as the weakest of the model types when children are the observers, peers would be better, and self would be the best. However, the research comparing peers and self as models tends to present more comparable results (McCurdy & Shapiro, 1988; Schunk & Hanson, 1989). The video medium may account for making results across model types more equivalent, but clearly this is another area in which more research is needed.

Another aspect of Bandura's research dealt with **self-efficacy** or the confidence felt by people regarding their ability to successfully carry out a task (Bandura, 1997). A person's feeling of self-efficacy is often directly related to his or her success. Providing direct evidence of the potential for success by showing the child succeeding may have a strong impact on the person's feeling of self-efficacy.

Some research in sports physiology indicates that visually imaging performance may do much more than raise feelings of self-efficacy or provide information: It may change physiology. Wright and Smith (2009) conducted a study in which they compared five different strength-training regimens on bicep development. One group did a set of two exercises on a curl machine, one group used conventional mental imagery of arm curls, while another group worked on the curl machine for one exercise set and watched videos of themselves doing curls for a time equivalent to doing another set. The other two groups consisted of a control group and one that used self-modeling only. After 6 weeks it was found that the only groups that gained strength were the physical exercise only and the self-modeling/exercise groups. This seems logical and validates the "no pain, no gain" theory of workouts. What was surprising was that there was no significant difference between these two groups although the combined group (video self-modeling and exercise) gained 28% in strength and the exercise group gained 25%. More validation needs to be done with this research, and it is ongoing; however, if the findings are replicated, it would suggest that self-modeling can facilitate changes in physiology. The fact that self-modeling alone caused no changes in strength indicates that a functional component is probably needed to promote improvement, at least when it comes to motor learning.

One last factor that should be considered is how self-modeling affects memory and how this in turn can affect habits. Kehle and his colleagues addressed this possibility after working with children with emotional disturbance (Kehle, Bray, Margiano, Theodore, & Zhou, 2002). They hypothesized that having children view themselves performing positive, adaptive behaviors would not only add a new visual memory but also cause memories of the older challenging behavior to be supplanted. If this turns out to be true, it would go a long way in explaining why behavior change is so rapid in some cases and why self-modeling has been shown to be effective in changing habitual behaviors that have been resistant to other forms of intervention. This is another area in need of further research.

We tend to view the forms of modeling, be it of the self, adult, or peer variety, as being roughly equivalent, with the primary difference being the person featured as the model. However, there is strong evidence that indicates that the brain processes images of self and images of others in different areas and that our physiological reactions to these images are different (Kircher et al., 2000). Viewing images of oneself produces stronger galvanic skin responses and heart rates than viewing peers or strangers. This heightened physical sense may translate to higher and more sustained interest, yet there is no evidence to support this, nor do we know whether the stronger physiological reaction holds true for children with autism.

There are few limitations on what can be addressed with video modeling. If it is observable and measurable, it can be depicted in video format. Much of the research on the use of video modeling with people with autism has focused on social-skill training, including recognition of emotions on faces (Golan & Baron-Cohen, 2006), expanding time engaged in play (Bellini et al., 2007), and training social language skills (Buggey, 2005; Maione & Mirenda, 2006; Scattone, 2008; Wert & Neisworth, 2003). Some work has focused on attempts to train academic skills using video modeling (Delano, 2007).

EMPIRICAL BASIS

The research base for the use of video modeling with people with autism is growing rapidly. Most studies use a multiple-baseline, single-subject design across participants or behaviors and are aimed at measuring effectiveness of video-modeling methods. Results indicate almost unanimous positive outcomes across a range of behaviors and ages. One of the difficulties in evaluating the efficacy of video modeling in some of these studies is that it is often paired with another teaching strategy, such as ABA, prompting and cueing, or live modeling (Charlop-Christy, Le, & Freeman, 2000; Dauphin, Kinney, Stromer, & Koegel, 2004; Gena, Couloura, & Kymissis, 2005). Consequently, it is difficult to determine what contributed to the changes reported in these studies.

Another shortcoming of the research on all forms of video modeling is that most studies rely on single-subject designs that typically have between one and three participants. Therefore, despite the value of such research, relatively few children have been involved in the research; thus, information about the generalizability of these findings is limited. In spite of such shortcomings, the results are encouraging. Bellini and Akullian (2007) confirmed the overall positive results achieved using video modeling. They conducted a meta-analysis of studies involving children with autism that addressed both video modeling using adults and peers and video self-modeling in which editing is used to make it appear children are performing slightly beyond their present ability. Twenty-three such studies were analyzed—fifteen of which dealt with video modeling with peers and adults and eight of which involved self-modeling. Moderate treatment effects were found for both techniques. Overall, the percentage of nonoverlapping data, or PND (one method of looking at treatment effects in single-subject designs) was 81% for peer and adult modeling and 77% for self-modeling. The difference was not statistically significant. Likewise the results for maintenance and generalization effects in these studies were positive, yet there were no significant differences between the two methods. Bellini and Akullian (2007) suggested that video modeling using self or others was successful in training social, language, and functional skills in children with autism. These authors also stated that both forms of video modeling met the Council for Exceptional Children's criteria for research-based practices. Finally, they caution that the sample sizes for video-modeling studies are typically small and that more research is needed. The following review of the research will address video-modeling use in various formats with people on the autism spectrum.

Others As Models

Adult Models

In a review of literature on all forms of video modeling, McCoy and Hermansen (2007) identified eight studies that used adults as models for people with autism. Six of the eight studies dealt with developing social skills, one targeted functional skills (purchasing), and one focused on teaching spelling skills.

Charlop-Christy and Daneshvar (2003) attempted to train three boys ages 6 to 9 in perspective-taking skills. Short videos were made of adults simulating a perspective-taking task, and these were shown to the children. A multiple-baseline design across individuals was used to evaluate results. Two of the three participants made substantial improvements in their perspective-taking. Charlop-Christy and other colleagues (Charlop-Christy et al., 2000) also attempted to compare video modeling to live modeling in teaching functional, social, and language skills to five children with ASDs. Targeted behaviors were chosen on the basis of each child's needs. A multiple-baseline design across individuals was used to evaluate results, along with a multiple-baseline, within-child design addressing the two conditions. The authors found that the behaviors taught using video modeling were acquired more rapidly, and that these learned behaviors generalized across similar conditions (as measured on specific generalization probes); these results were not seen in the live model condition. The PND rate was 82% for intervention and 100% for generalization.

In another study that examined teaching perspective-taking skills to three boys with autism, ages 7–13 (LeBlanc et al., 2003), the authors arranged three perspective-taking tasks for the children to complete. The tasks involved puppets hiding objects (e.g., a bean) and having the children identify where a particular puppet should look for it. A multiple-baseline design across two tasks was used for evaluation purposes. The third task was not trained and served as an indicator of generalization. None of the children responded correctly to these tasks during baseline. Videos of adults completing the tasks were made. The videos showed the models, but also zoomed in on salient clues to help the child. After watching the videos, the children mastered the two tasks but did not transfer their skill to the untrained task. Two of the three participants needed repeated trials on the first task (three and four sessions, respectively) before improvement was seen. Mastery of a second task was almost immediate for all three children.

One study that addressed video modeling by adults had positive acquisition outcomes but poor generalization outcomes (MacDonald, Clark, Garrigan, & Vangala, 2005). The researchers used adult models to train two boys ages 4 and 7 in pretend play using play "scripts." The children improved at scripted play but showed no changes in other forms of play, despite the fact that PND effect sizes for intervention and maintenance were almost 100%. A similar outcome was found in another study that investigated scripted play sessions (D'Ateno, Mangiapanello, & Taylor, 2003). Both verbal and physical interaction increased in scripted play sessions (PND = 92%) following the viewing of adults modeling appropriate behaviors; however, responses in novel play situations did not change (PND = 22%).

Maione and Mirenda (2006) were more successful when they used adults to model verbal initiations in social settings for a 5-year-old boy with autism. A multiple-baseline design across behaviors was used for evaluation. Videotapes were made of two adults playing and talking in three play scenarios. The boy then played with one of two peers known to him in the same settings and with the same materials. In two of the three activities the boy increased his social language use. In the third activity the video modeling alone was not effective, although gains were seen when video feedback (videos of the previous play sessions with the peer) and verbal prompting were applied.

Conversational skill was also the dependent variable in a study by Scattone (2008). The author used two adults to model appropriate conversation skills based on passages created using Social Stories™. The single participant, a 9-year-old with Asperger syndrome, viewed videos of two adults interacting using social conversation skills such as eye contact, smiling, and initiations. Following introduction of the video modeling, rapid improvement was seen in eye contact and initiations in sessions with the researcher, but little gain was seen in smiling. Pairing video modeling and Social Stories in the manner done in this study precludes analysis of the relative strength of these methods.

A similar study involving Social Stories and computer-based modeling was conducted by Sansosti and Powell-Smith (2008). Three children with Asperger syndrome ages 6 to 10 were shown movies of adults modeling Social Stories that were prescribed to meet their social and communication needs. Data on their specific skill performance were collected on the playground during recess and at other times when unstructured activities occurred. A multiple-baseline design across participants was used for evaluation purposes. The authors found that the students' rates of social communication increased following their viewing the videos; however, a social reinforcement system had to be initiated for two of the participants. A 2-week follow-up indicated that all three students maintained their increased performance.

Peers and Siblings as Models

Several studies have incorporated the use of age-similar peers and/or siblings as models. A common dependent variable in these studies is verbalization during play. Charlop and Milstein (1989) worked with three young children to facilitate their conversation skills using a multiple-baseline design across participants. The three individually watched videos of two other children having a conversation about toys with which they were playing. The results were positive and indicated that the new skills generalized across related situations (PND = 87%). The children's progress was monitored for 15 months following the end of the intervention and all behaviors were maintained over that time (PND = 100%).

Taylor, Levin, and Jasper (1999) used a combination of peer and adult modeling to train verbal skills used with siblings during play. A multiple-baseline design across participants was used for evaluation purposes. The children watched a movie of their brothers verbally interacting with an adult and then they practiced scripted play sessions with the same adult. Evaluation was carried out across three separate play activities, and it was found that the scripted comments were made in all three activities.

Reagon, Higbee, and Endico (2006) also used a sibling as a model for a 4-year-old with autism. In the baseline phase of this study, the participant and his sibling were given play equipment for four scenarios—cowboy, firefighter, teacher, and doctor—and told to play without further instruction. Videos were taken of the sibling engaged in play with a typically developing peer in the same situations and then shown to the child with autism. In play sessions in a university preschool setting, the child and sibling successfully engaged in pretend play across all four scenarios. Probes were conducted in the home to test for generalization and maintenance, with positive outcomes for both.

Nikopoulos and Keenan (2003) also used a peer interacting with an adult during play to create videos aimed at stimulating verbal behavior in seven children with autism (ages 9 to 15). The children individually watched videotapes depicting a peer interacting with one of the experimenters in a simple play activity. The results of the multiple-baseline design across participants revealed that four of the seven students increased their rate of social interaction during play. The new behavior generalized across various settings, peers, and toys and was maintained at a 2-month reevaluation session. When all students were evaluated, the effect size for the intervention stage was not strong (PND = 29%); however, maintenance and generalization had better effect sizes (PND = 80% and 100%, respectively). The authors completed a second study (Nikopoulos & Keenan, 2007) in which they tried to train more complex social initiations with three children with autism ages 6½ to 7. Along with the video modeling, verbal instructions and behavior rehearsing were also used. The results replicated the previous study; however, all three children made substantial gains in engagement, social initiations, and responding in this study, generating an effect size of greater than 80% PND. As in the first study, the changes in behavior were maintained over a 2-month span.

Nikopoulos and Keenan (2004) authored a third study in which video modeling was used with three children with autism to stimulate social initiations and play behaviors. The methods used were very similar to those of the study described above (Nikopoulos & Keenan, 2003). The authors found that all three children made gains in reciprocal play and social initiations (PND = 71% during intervention and PND = 100% during maintenance).

Apple, Billingsley, Schwartz, and Carr (2005) worked with two 5-year-olds with high-functioning autism to train compliment giving and responding. Children watched three videos with peers modeling responses to compliments and one in which the peers modeled compliment initiations. Adults narrated the video and embedded rules for giving and responding to compliments within it. The researchers found that video modeling alone was effective (PND = 71%) in training responses to compliments; however, the addition of reinforcement contingencies was needed for the child to produce initiations. More modest results were found for maintenance (PND = 58%).

Much of the research on video modeling deals with facilitating social skills. Little research exists that addresses academic or functional skill instruction. Haring, Kennedy, Adams, and Pitts-Conway (1987) looked at three 20-year-old adults (two male, one female) with autism and their ability to generalize purchasing skills from a classroom environment to three stores located in the surrounding area. The participants were trained using conventional techniques and then were evaluated during trips to the store. The young adults acquired the skill successfully during instruction; however, there was no evidence of generalization to the stores. The initial training was supplemented by the introduction of 1- to 3-min peer-modeling videos that illustrated a complete purchasing sequence. Following the viewing of the videos, the participants increased their purchasing skills in terms of the social interactions and the actual transactions (PND = 97% during intervention; PND =100% during maintenance).

Computer-Based Modeling Programs

The common modes for viewing videos are DVD/VCR players and computers. Computers offer the advantage of being interactive and programmable, and some researchers have created software programs that take full advantage of these attributes.

Simpson, Langone, and Ayres (2004) worked with a teacher-made computer program that allowed the user to embed video clips. Four children with autism participated in this study. Videos of peers showing examples of sharing, following directions, and greetings were placed in the program. Following the viewing of these clips the children were observed participating in group activities. The researchers reported rapid increases in the use of the three target behaviors after children began viewing their videos (PND = 97% during intervention).

Many children with autism use visual schedules to help them build predictability into their daily routines. When photographs of the children are used to illustrate steps or sequences, it becomes a form of self-modeling. Several researchers have used the computer to enhance the visual schedules with videos. Kimball, Kinney, Taylor, and Stromer (2004) described how they used PowerPoint to create activity schedules with pictures, sounds, and videos for a preschooler with autism. Five-second videos were made in which peers were depicted engaged in the selected activity and inviting the child to join in ("Let's play!"). The response to this multimedia activity schedule were impressive, as the boy was able to follow the schedule, and he even started imitating the teacher's recorded prompts. Interestingly, he applied these verbalizations to another notebook-type visual schedule. The skill had generalized. Several of the authors of this study collaborated on another study (Dauphin et al., 2004) that examined the use of embedded videos in activity schedules to teach sociodramatic play to children with autism.

Dauphin and colleagues (2004) embedded video models in computer-based activity schedules to assist a 4-year-old with autism in participating in sociodramatic play (playing with toy figures with others). The video models were peers who stated what to say and do in sociodramatic play situations. In addition, a 3 x 3 matrix was introduced depicting three figurines and three possible actions. These were used to plan the videos and to evaluate results. The authors reported that the child mastered three activities in the original matrix and an additional nine in three other matrices that were subsequently introduced. The authors reported that for every activity learned, the child initiated two additional and unique activities, demonstrating the power of video modeling to promote generalization.

Animated Models

In what might be considered a form of peer modeling, animations of cartoon-like characters have been used for skill training with children with autism. Keen, Brannigan, and Cuskelly (2007) used an animated urination-focused toileting video, along with operant conditioning techniques, with five preschool boys with autism.

Commercially Available Video-Modeling Materials

The success and popularity of video modeling have led to the development of several commercial products.

> The Kennedy/Krieger Center in Baltimore has produced a series of social-skills training videos specifically targeted to children and youth with autism. The series is called Model Me Kids.
> http://www.modelmekids.com/autism-video-samples.html

> Watch Me Learn is another video-modeling product; it delves into the area of academic as well as social skills instruction.
> http://www.watchmelearn.com/

> Social Skill Builder offers a range of peer-modeling videos for children ages 3–18. There are DVDs on community and school social and safety issues plus one focusing on birthday parties.
> http://www.socialskillbuilder.com/

> Coulter Videos has produced one video entitled *Manners for the Real World* that features peers modeling appropriate behaviors, along with instructions for the viewer.
> http://www.coultervideo.com/manners.htm

> Carol Gray and Mark Shelley have produced Storymovies, a series of videos that take the popular Social Stories theme into the realm of video and peer modeling.
> http://www.specialminds.org/story.html/

> The Activity Trainer from Accelerations Educational Software provides more than 170 videos and still photos that can be individualized and provides activities to help generalize new skills to everyday life by providing visual schedules and worksheets. This software also allows the addition of movies taken from home or school so that self-modeling is possible.
> http://www.dttrainer.com/jos

A control group was established that received operant conditioning only. In-toilet urination was the dependent variable in the study. The experimental group made substantially more progress than the control group after they viewed the animated video. However, only three of the five maintained the gains when assessment was done 6 weeks after withdrawal of the intervention, and only two were noted to have generalized the skill to new situations.

Research conducted at the Autism Research Center at the University of Cambridge is suggesting that people with autism can learn to read and identify emotions of others by watching videos with animated characters illustrating the emotions (Golan & Baron-Cohen, 2006). The authors created a DVD that had trolleys with human faces that illustrated 14 emotions. The imagery used was similar to that in the popular TV program *Thomas the Tank Engine* except that the faces on the front of the trolleys were lifelike. Nineteen young adults with milder autism were matched against a control group of similar peers who received no training. Acquisition of the identification of the 14 emotions presented was significantly higher for the adults with autism than for the control group. It was also significantly higher than for another group of typically developing peers. There were some limitations with generalization, however, and the authors suggested that an instructional supplement was needed in this area.

Self As Model

Video self-modeling differs from other forms of modeling in that the observer and the model are the same person. What causes self-modeling to be slightly more technologically challenging than other forms of modeling is that the models have to be seen as having more advanced skills or more appropriate behavior than they presently have. Videos must be creatively edited so that children appear to be functioning beyond present levels or in a more adaptive manner. In the past, the editing demands of this type of modeling probably served as a deterrent to both research and practical applications. However, with the advent of user-friendly video editing software, such as iMovie for the Macintosh and Movie Maker for the PC, editing videos has become a relatively simple process. Collecting footage to use in the editing process does require some creative thinking; however, footage can be obtained by having children imitate or role-play behaviors or situations. For people with autism who do not comply with requests or demands, it might be necessary to film over time in order to capture rare behaviors or to employ peers to elicit behaviors. For an example of a self-modeling video created with iMovie, see the DVD that accompanies this book.

Dowrick (1983) defined two forms of self-modeling: 1) **feedforward** and 2) **positive self-review.** In the feedforward method of video self-modeling, a person is shown video of him- or herself performing a new, yet developmentally appropriate behavior. Feedforward allows children to see themselves as they will probably be at some time in the future. Hopefully, this vision of the future serves as a magnet accelerating the growth toward that future. It is important to be very careful not to project too far ahead, so that the images represent reasonable expectations for the child.

The second form of video self-modeling defined by Dowrick (1983) is positive self-review. This method involves watching videos of oneself to build fluency or proficiency in a skill already learned. Laura Wilkinson, a U.S. gold medal winner in platform diving, uses this method prior to each meet. She watches videos of her best dives that also include images of her coach and parents giving her encouragement. This is positive self-review. Laura already has the skill but is working to improve it. Results of self-review tend not to be as dramatic as those from feedforward. To a large extent, this is because the beginning or baseline rate of behavior tends to be higher than with feedforward because there is less room for improvement. Not surprisingly, there are few researchers investigating in this area.

Video self-modeling has been slowly growing in popularity as an intervention since the early 1970s. The use of video self-modeling has expanded more rapidly as video-editing software has become more available and user-friendly. Likewise, research into the effects of self-modeling has also accelerated, especially with children with autism.

Use of Virtual Self-Modeling with People with Autism Spectrum Disorders

The bulk of the research in video modeling seems aimed at some form of social skill, often in the areas of play or language use. In one of the few studies addressing academic skills (Delano, 2007), written language skills were the focus with three students aged 13, 15, and 17—all with Asperger syndrome. Specifically, the writing rate, or fluency, and the number of elements contained in an essay were measured. A multiple-baseline design across responses was used to evaluate results. It was found that both number of words and number of essay elements increased for all students. All students maintained the word-writing gains as measured on follow-up probes administered 1 week and 3 months following withdrawal of the videos. Maintenance for the essay elements, however, was not noted.

In a study involving three adolescents with moderate to severe autism (Buggey et al., 1999), the researchers focused on teaching verbal responding. During play sessions, a list of 10 play-related questions was asked. Although responses were rare, with the play sessions occurring two nights a week for more than a month, a sufficient number of responses was collected to make 2-min videos. All of the children increased their responses after watching their own videos. Analysis by question revealed that two of the participants went from never responding to a specific question during baseline to 100% responding during intervention. Students maintained gains for a month after the videos were withdrawn. The authors stated that the time commitment for capturing rare behaviors might make this form of video self-modeling too cumbersome for teachers and therapists.

The author of this chapter conducted several studies with preschoolers who ranged in age from 3½ to 5 years old. One study involved a boy with autism who had just turned 4 (Buggey, 2005). A multiple-baseline design across three behaviors—namely, not pushing, verbal responding, and initiating conversation without prompting—was used in this study. The pushing behavior virtually ceased following the student viewing a tape showing positive interactions and appropriate touching. The two language behaviors also showed significant improvement following viewing of the tapes. The effect size (PND) for each of the behaviors was 88% for pushing, 90% for responding, and 100% for verbal initiations. The language movies were created by videotaping individual words spoken by the child and editing them into multiword sentences.

Buggey and colleagues (2011) conducted a study with four preschoolers with autism to determine if social initiations could be facilitated. The 4-year-olds had not responded to Social Stories and a buddy system introduced in their classrooms aimed at promoting social interactions. The participants, along with one or two peers, were taken to the playground for filming. The peers were coached and prompted to interact with the children with autism. Segments of the video illustrating the best examples of social interactions were extracted and combined into 3-min videos. The children watched their movies in the morning and data were recorded when they went onto the playground about an hour later. Three of the four children made substantial gains in social initiations with peers, and two displayed a variety of new behaviors such as swinging, sliding, and verbalizing to adults. One child exhibited no gains, although he watched his videos with enthusiasm. This child was slightly younger than the others, raising the question of whether age or maturity was a critical factor in this case. The age at which self-modeling begins to be effective is unknown. Although the effect of age is likely to depend on a child's development and type of disability, we know very little about the effect of video self-modeling with children under age 3.

Wert and Neisworth (2003) used video self-modeling to train spontaneous requesting in four preschoolers with autism. A multiple-baseline design across children was used to evaluate results. The children were trained to request items via a discrete trial method; however, the resulting requests were rote and there was no generalization to spontaneous requesting. The prompted requests were included in the video self-modeling tapes with the prompts and any negative behaviors edited out. Results for all four participants showed substantial gains. The gains in mean production of spontaneous requests ranged from 800% to 1200%.

In another study that examined the effect of video self-modeling effect on preschoolers with ASDs, Bellini and colleagues (2007) addressed social engagement skills with the children while simultaneously evaluating teachers' ability to implement the intervention. The two 4-year-olds in the study had sufficient social skills to establish a baseline and to permit direct filming of the children at play without any undue manipulation of events. Scenes of the children engaged in play were cut and pasted into 2-min videos. The dependent variable in this study was the percentage of time the children spent engaged in play with others. The children watched the videos in a private setting just before free-play time and then returned to the classroom to play. The results indicated a steep increase in the percentage of time the children spent engaged in play. The teachers found video self-modeling to be easy to implement and reported little disruption to regular classroom routines. Measures of maintenance indicated that the behaviors did not decrease over time.

Comparison Studies

It is somewhat surprising that there is not more research comparing modeling formats. In one of the only such studies, Sherer and colleagues (2001) attempted to compare peer and self-modeling strategies with five children with autism between ages 4 and 11. The dependent variable was responding to a series of verbal questions. A combination of multiple-baseline and alternating treatment designs was used for the evaluation. Three of the five children reached 100% accuracy on the task, while the other two children exhibited very limited improvement. When the rate of acquisition was evaluated across methods, it was determined that there were no differences between self- and peer modeling. The authors stated that the three children who made the greatest gains were those considered to be strong visual learners.

In the only other study comparing two video modeling procedures, Gena and colleagues (2005) sought to compare the effects of peer video modeling with traditional teacher modeling in training affective skills with three preschoolers with autism. The two methods were supplemented with verbal praise and tokens for correct responding and a correction protocol that differed between treatments. The in vivo (live) modeling required a therapist to model the correct behavior and issue verbal prompts. The video-modeling procedure made use of videos of peers exhibiting the correct response and of therapist prompts. The researchers found that both treatment methods were equally well suited for promoting affective response and that these results generalized to different situations and across people.

Point-of-View Modeling

There is a form of video modeling that is just beginning to be researched. Point-of-view modeling takes people through a task as seen from their vantage point. This is accomplished by holding the camera at the eye level of the observer and navigating through a task. This method is related to self-modeling; however, it differs in that the children never see themselves. Rather they must imagine that what they are seeing is viewed from their vantage point. This requirement may negate some of the positive aspects of self-modeling addressed previously regarding self-efficacy and the excitement generated from seeing oneself as the star of a video.

Point-of-view modeling does have the advantage of not requiring the model to be manipulated and filmed. This advantage would be very useful when working with children who do not readily imitate. Hine and Wolery (2006) used this method to teach toy-play skills to two young girls with autism. The ages of the children were 30 and 43 months, making them some of the youngest to participate in a video-modeling study. Gardening and cooking tasks were chosen as the dependent variables. These tasks were broken down into six and five action steps, respectively, and the evaluation consisted of determining how many of the steps were exhibited during observation sessions. A multiple-probe design was used to evaluate results. The children showed considerable improvement in the number of actions during each play session, except for the second child on the cooking task. Here prompting and reinforcement was subsequently used and results improved.

Schreibman, Whalen, and Stahmer (2000) used what they termed "video priming" to facilitate appropriate transition behaviors with three children with autism who were described as severely disruptive during transitions. In video priming, children were shown point-of-view movies of task-analyzed transitions prior to similar transitions taking place. A multiple-baseline design across the participants was used to evaluate results. The authors reported that, following the viewing of videos, the students' disruptive behaviors were severely reduced or completely eliminated. Transitions other than those depicted in the video were also observed and evaluated, and the improvement in behavior had generalized across situations.

The only other study that addressed children with autism using point-of-view modeling was carried out by Shipley-Benamou, Lutzker, and Taubman (2002) to teach functional living skills to three 5-year-old children with autism. The children were shown point-of-view videos related to community outings that had proven difficult for them in the past, including trips to the mall, pharmacy, and grocery store. Verbal instruction was included at the beginning of the video. Only the hands of the filmer were visible. The children were directed to watch what their "friends" were doing. In addition a short clip of the child's favorite cartoon was placed at the front of the video to attract attention. The authors concluded that this form of video modeling was effective in promoting the acquisition of the target skills, which were maintained upon withdrawal of videos and at a 1-month follow-up assessment. Because of the ease of filming and the minimal editing necessary using point-of-view modeling, this method warrants additional research. It would also seem to warrant trials with children with autism at school, home, and clinic. One thing that could be said about most applications of video modeling is that there is potentially much to gain and very little to lose. Even if ineffective, there is little chance of adverse results.

PRACTICAL REQUIREMENTS

In addition to the variety of behaviors that can be addressed with video modeling, the method has the advantage that it can be used by almost anyone with the basic equipment, the minimum of which would be a video camera and VCR or DVD player. If a computer is available with video editing software such as iMovie for the Macintosh or Movie Maker for the PC, users can produce adequate videos with little training. The time commitment necessary to produce a video varies because of a range of factors, including the type of behavior being addressed, the cooperation level of the "stars" of the movie, and the type of video modeling used. If typically developing peers are used as models, the complete video could be shot in one take following a short rehearsal period. In addition, little editing is necessary in this situation. The video could be transferred directly to tape or DVD through a VCR or DVD player, or it could be downloaded onto a computer for minor editing.

Likewise, a point-of-view modeling video can be produced in a short time. Only one person is necessary for the creation of this form of video. A tripod or another cameraperson would be needed if manipulation of objects is to be depicted in the video, such as carrying out the steps in a math computation problem. Here the hands of the model would need to be visible. Point-of-view modeling cannot be used with the same range of behaviors as peer, adult, or self-modeling. Most language behaviors would require a visible model. Social and academic behaviors and many functional skills, however, would fit well with the point-of-view method. A good example would be the modeling of a job interview. A person opens the door to an office, extends his or her hand, politely greets the interviewer, and so forth, continuing to the point of thanking the interviewer and leaving. Of course, in this case a second person would be needed to act as the interviewer.

Self-modeling is more complex to carry out, especially when working with a child who doesn't follow directions well and/or cannot imitate. Use of this method with such a child may require longer filming sessions to capture rare behavior and/or much more intense editing of the footage.

Video modeling is a very democratic form of intervention. Because there is no training necessary other than reading user manuals for the equipment, anyone can be the primary implementer. Likewise, anyone with the necessary skills can serve as the model or models. Thus, video modeling provides a good avenue for involving family members in the education process.

Some possible exceptions exist that may require therapists to take the central role in planning and editing the videos. Occupational and physical therapists may require the video to emphasize specific positioning or muscle movements. Likewise, language and speech skills may require a speech-language pathologist's expertise. At a minimum, these professionals and teachers should be consulted for information on developmental sequences and developmentally appropriate behaviors that could be addressed via video modeling. Professional evaluations may also be needed in these specialized areas to determine potential target behaviors. Functional behavioral assessment (Hanley, Iwata, & McCord, 2003; Sturmey, 1994) should be tied to video modeling when social behaviors are addressed and should be part of a positive behavioral support plan. Roles in the video modeling process can be determined at the positive behavioral support meetings if there is an established protocol and/or a designated video expert is not available on staff.

One of the major assets of video modeling that could offset the time needed to complete a video is that a portable, visual product of correct behavior is created. While the video-modeling movie can be used to teach the individual, it can also be used to demonstrate what is expected to other professionals and parents who work with a child. Many therapists—especially those in school systems—now have consultative duties. Modeling videos can serve the dual purpose of delivering direct instruction to the child as well as providing a format for accurate communication among the teacher, the family, and related service providers.

Like the videos, the equipment for capturing videos (typically a video camera) is also portable. Footage of desired behaviors can be taken in almost any environment, including natural environments such as classrooms, homes, job sites, and playgrounds. Footage would be transferred to the computer for editing. Both PC and Macintosh computers provide easy-to-use software for editing videos. Macintosh computers come ready to be used for video editing: Everything needed for editing and writing videos to discs comes built in. Some modifications and further expense may be needed to establish similar usability with a PC, for example, installing a video card and downloading or buying software that allows writing of DVDs or CDs. One

Table 14.1. Advantages and disadvantages of forms of video modeling

Form	Advantages	Disadvantages
Peer/adult	Easily staged Strong maintenance	Models may not generate high interest Mixed results for generalization
Self	Good for situations in which lack of confidence is an issue May generate higher interest than other forms Strong generalization results	May be difficult to stage More complex editing
Point-of-view	Easily staged Real-life depictions Limited editing needed	Limited range of behaviors Few studies as yet
Animation	Popular format for children Usually professionally produced	Models may lack relevance Range and specificity of behaviors is limited

necessity for either platform is plenty of hard disk storage capability. Removable hard disk drives are relatively inexpensive, and it would be wise to dedicate one of these to the storage of videos. Even 3-min videos require substantial memory. With the addition of this hard drive, any newer computer can become a video-modeling center. As with other technology associated with video modeling, having a hard disk drive dedicated to storage of videos will facilitate user flexibility. A drive can be disconnected and carried to a classroom, where it can then be connected to another computer for downloading the movie. This approach would negate the need for burning DVDs or CDs, because the movie will be on the classroom (or home) computer.

One precaution necessary for any creators of video modeling (except for parents working only with their own children) is to obtain informed consent of all participants. All parties should not only be in agreement about implementing video modeling but also share a clear understanding of who will be viewing the videos and what will happen to the videos once the intervention is completed. Clear protocols about every step of the process should be established if video modeling becomes a regular part of the therapy or instruction.

KEY COMPONENTS

The possible behaviors that can be addressed with video modeling are almost limitless. Any skills or behaviors that are observable can be addressed through video modeling. Skills typically taught or learned in sequences such as math computation or language acquisition can be addressed by a series of video; however, there is no research addressing longitudinal or ongoing applications of video modeling with the same children except several studies that used multiple-baseline designs across behaviors (Buggey, 2005; Maione & Mirenda, 2006). One example of how developmental sequences could be taught with video modeling is the use of morphemes such as past tense endings, articles, and plurals in expressive language. The developmental sequence of morpheme acquisition was outlined by Brown (1973). Between 28 and 36 months, children typically develop present progressive endings, use the prepositions *in* and *on,* and will learn that *s* produces plurals. An assessment of morpheme use would indicate where children are developmentally. Next steps in the sequence could be shown being spoken by their peers or, if children can imitate the more advanced morphemes, they can serve as their own models. It might be possible to provide models who are one step ahead of the children's development and so continue to provide peer modeling over the course of a series of developmental steps.

Maladaptive social skills can be addressed in similar fashion even though there is no developmental sequence for this type of behavior. A child with multiple challenging behaviors could be shown video models of people performing adaptive behaviors in situations that typically trigger his or her negative ones. If the child can role-play these situations, the child can once again serve as his or her own model. If successful, one could use the same technique with another behavior. Because of the dearth of research, it is not known whether children would reach a saturation point with these videos beyond which the method was ineffective, nor do we know whether the novelty of the intervention (especially video self-modeling) wears thin.

DATA COLLECTION TO SUPPORT DECISION MAKING

Data collection for video-modeling interventions should follow the same format as that used in single-subject designs (Kazdin, 1982) and curriculum-based measurements (Salvia & Hughes, 1990). This type of data collection requires the establishment of baseline rates or durations of behaviors, tracking these rates or durations through the intervention phase, and monitoring maintenance. This type of data collection is also often used with functional behavioral assessments, with various members of a team recording data to establish baselines and with some team members carrying through with data collection to measure the efficacy of intervention. If this process of data collection is already in place, it would be sufficient to measure the impact of the video-modeling intervention. Graphic representations could be kept to provide visual evidence of the effect and to help communicate progress to other stakeholders. In curriculum-based measurement, the child is often tasked with charting progress. This would be unacceptable in a research project, because one would be trying to control the variables that might be affecting behavior; however, it might serve as an effective supplement in practical applications. One should be aware at all times of other variables that might be affecting behavior, such as medical issues, the presence of other instruction, and changes in environmental conditions, so these can be considered during data interpretation.

Parents can be instrumental in data collection and may need to be the primary recorders if intervention is carried out in the home. If the intervention is carried out at school, the parents can still collect data to determine whether effects are generalizing across settings.

APPLICATION TO A CHILD

In this case study, self-modeling was chosen as the intervention. Video peer or adult modeling could also have been used, but this illustration of video self-modeling will provide an example of video modeling at its most complex. Scott, presently 8 years old, was diagnosed with Asperger syndrome by school district personnel at the age of 5. Scott perseverated on some tasks and tended to be distractible during academics. He was an avid *Star Trek* fan and could talk about any of the episodes. He often tried to steer conversation to *Star Trek*. The principal arranged a meeting with Scott's parents to find a solution to one of his disruptive behaviors. Both Scott's parents and teachers noted tantrums, which occurred when he was faced with criticism and frustration, as his most serious problem. This disruptive behavior often took the form of hysterical tantrums in which he would flail his arms and legs and weep for long periods. These full-blown episodes could last for half an hour, followed by pouting that lasted up to half a school day. There was a progression or warning prior to the tantrum beginning, which consisted of Scott folding his arms and looking downward. A behavior modification plan to address this challenging behavior was in place and was practiced at home and school for several months with little effect.

It was agreed that the team would collaborate in carrying out a functional behavioral assessment (FBA) to determine exactly what triggered the tantrums and to make some hypotheses regarding why they occurred. This assessment was to precede the development of a positive behavioral support plan. All members of the team were charged with collecting data on the tantrums, including time of onset, duration, and environmental antecedents that might be related to the behavior. After a week of observation, the team members met again to review the results. The team decided to focus first on school-specific behavior and, if improvements were seen, to then turn their attention to the home. Several specific events were found to trigger Scott's tantrums in school: 1) not being called on when he knew an answer, 2) another child jumping in line, 3) missing items on his homework or on seat work when working in small groups, and 4) not receiving permission to do something when he asked. These four situations were depicted in a **storyboard** composed with the cooperation of Scott, who was told that he would be starring in a movie about good behavior. The four frames of the storyboard (illustrated in Figure 14.1) would serve as the scenes in the movie.

Two of Scott's classmates were asked to costar in the movie. For the filming of the video, the students and their teacher came to the classroom while their classmates were at the library. The guidance counselor, who was trained in video self-modeling, served as the producer and cameraperson. The students and teacher followed the storyboard and were given lines and direction by the counselor. Similarly, Scott was fed a line to say concerning each situation. Everyone enjoyed the filming, although at one point Scott began his tantrum aura. When he was reminded that they were making a movie, he stopped.

Figure 14.1. Storyboard for Scott's movie of good behavior.

The teacher and counselor collaborated in making the movie using the Apple iMovie software. The footage was downloaded from the camera into iMovie. Because role-playing had been used, little editing was needed. Transitions were put in between the scenes, and a still frame showing Scott smiling and raising his hand was added to the beginning. The counselor added her own voice labeling the behavior ("Here's Scott's movie. Let's watch Scott handle these tough situations"). This introduction was followed by children cheering (a sound clip included in the iMovie software). The same cheering was added to the end of the movie, along with the counselor saying, "Good job, Scott!"

Because Scott was participating in a study, there was a delay before he was allowed to watch the video so that it could be determined if the role-playing and filming had any effect on behavior. Scott averaged about 20 min per day in tantrums prior to watching his video. Following his first viewing of the tape, which took place upon his arrival at school and before classes began, he never had another tantrum during that school year—a follow-up period of 6 months. Interestingly, he did begin his tantrum aura on several occasions, but in each of these he seemed to control himself and stopped short of a tantrum.

> *I've never used the term "life-changing" about any type of treatment or instruction...until now. It hit me at the end of the day after he starting watching his tape: No tantrums today...hmm. The second day I was quietly shouting for joy.*
>
> —Scott's teacher

APPLICATION TO AN ADOLESCENT OR ADULT

Sara was a 19-year-old with more severe autism. She used picture symbols for most of her communication. She was verbal, but most of her expressive language was echolalic. She was being trained in functional life skills as part of her transition plan. One of her objectives was to learn how to make her bed. Sara's teacher and parents decided to use a peer-modeling video to train this skill. One of Sara's classmates who was typically developing served as the model. The act of making the bed was task analyzed and broken down into eight steps, from gathering the right linen to fluffing the pillows. The classmate came to Sara's home and was filmed making Sara's bed. The classmate gave verbal directions as well as physically completing each step (e.g. "Now we need to fold back the blanket and sheet so we can put the pillows up here."). Sara watched the movie upon returning home from school. She was also allowed to watch it if she indicated she wanted to do so. The day after watching the videos Sara attempted to make the bed without being prompted. She was not able to complete all of the steps without assistance, but she had never even attempted it before. Her mother was able to provide some prompts and completed several steps with which Sara was having difficulty. The mother was told to keep her involvement to a minimum and intervene only when necessary. Within 1 week, Sara had mastered making her bed. She enjoyed the video and watching her friend and continued requesting to view the video for several weeks. After she lost interest in the video and stopped viewing it, her bed-making ability did not change. Sara's parents decided to try video modeling to address other skills.

CONSIDERATIONS FOR CHILDREN FROM CULTURALLY AND LINGUISTICALLY DIVERSE BACKGROUNDS

Because sensitivity to cultural and language diversity is almost inherent in video modeling, little adaptation should be necessary. This is especially true with self-modeling, for the obvious reason that the child serves as his or her own model. For peer or adult modeling, it will be necessary to choose models who are as close as possible to the observer in terms of culture and language. This approach not only is sensitive to cultural diversity but aligns with Bandura's (1969) findings on who makes the best models.

FUTURE DIRECTIONS

Research in video modeling is a relatively recent development with a small yet growing database of studies. Therefore, many questions of efficacy and use remain unanswered. Although a lower age limit for effective use is becoming evident, the studies with this young population have focused on social skills. It could very well be that different behaviors have different age limitations. Research should be done with 3-year-olds focusing on language and functional behaviors.

Likewise, little is known of cognitive development as a factor in efficacy. Is there a point of cognitive delay beyond which video modeling has no effect? Are there differences among the forms of video modeling related to age and cognitive ability?

Almost no information exists concerning the long-term use of video modeling. Does interest in the video medium wane over time? Do people become immune to these methods? We also do not know how the various forms of video modeling compare in sustaining interest. To this point, studies comparing the effectiveness of self-, peer-, point-of-view, and adult modeling have focused on specific behaviors. We do not know if differences exist related to generalization or maintenance of learned behaviors. For that matter, only a handful of studies have been done comparing the various forms for video modeling in any manner. Knowing the comparative strengths of these methods would help practitioners make informed choices about their use.

Almost no studies have addressed training in video-modeling techniques. Even though editing software has made it much easier to create videos, do parents and professionals have the skills and time to create them? In clinical and school settings, which professionals are best suited for creating and showing the videos?

Finally, more research needs to be carried out to determine the range of behaviors that can be addressed across the various forms of video modeling and whether there are advantages to matching these specific forms to specific behaviors.

SUGGESTED READINGS

Buggey, T. (2009). *Seeing is believing: Self-modeling applications with children with autism and other developmental disabilities.* Bethesda, MD: Woodbine House.

Buggey has produced the only book to date specifically addressing video self-modeling. He provides a how-to guide for selecting behaviors, constructing storyboards, capturing appropriate footage, and editing the video. He also provides supporting information on theories and research specific to children with autism. The book is relatively inexpensive and is designed for both parents and professionals.

Grandin, T. (2010). *Thinking in pictures and other reports from my life with autism.* New York, NY: Vintage Books.

In her landmark book, Grandin explains her thinking process and how she converts language to visual images that she can interpret. Although the book does not deal directly with video modeling, Grandin provides insight into why this approach might be effective for those on the autism spectrum who are strong visual learners.

Kehle, T., & Bray, M. (Eds.) (2012). *Psychology in the Schools* [entire issue], *49*(1), 1–103.

This issue of *Psychology in the Schools* was entirely devoted to video self-modeling. Articles by leaders in the field such as Melissa Bray, Tom Buggey, Peter Dowrick, and Thomas Kiehl cover a gamut of topics from theories driving self-modeling to general self-modeling techniques to use of the method with children with autism.

Nikopoulus, C. (2006). *Video modelling and behaviour analysis: A guide for teaching social skills to children with autism.* London, UK: Jessica Kingsley Publishers.

Nikopoulus provides a practical guide to combining two research-based techniques: applied behavior analysis and video (peer) modeling. He explains how to create videos and incorporate them into a treatment plan and also provides background on the theories and research that support this method.

Sigafoos, J. (2007). *How to use video modeling and video prompting.* Austin, TX: PRO-ED.

This and Nikopoulus' book are the only books devoted to the use of video-modeling with children with autism. Sigafoos describes the use of video-modeling instruction, which he defined as the video that contains the complete model of a behavior. Video prompting is a method of breaking the full-length video into smaller sections that prompt very specific steps of a task. This is a how-to guide for parents and professionals with additional information on selecting behaviors, task analysis, obtaining baselines, data collection, and choosing equipment.

Learning Activities

Projects

1.   *Create a movie.* Use video editing software to create a video of any type: Vacation or birthday videos will work. The point of this exercise is to get used to the editing software. The ease of use of commonly used software will surprise those unfamiliar with the process.

2.   *Create two storyboards.* One could be based on teaching a new behavior and the other on a replacement behavior. For teaching a new behavior, choose a skill, do a task analysis of the steps, and then convert each step into a simple picture that can be placed in a grid. For teaching a replacement behavior, first conduct a functional behavior assessment to determine the triggers of the unwanted behavior (this could also be simulated). Then select appropriate ways

to act that could replace the unwanted behaviors. Convert the appropriate reactions into simple pictures and place them on a storyboard grid.

Topics for Further Discussion

1. Specifically for self-modeling, discuss the pros and cons of allowing people to watch unedited videos where both positive and negative behaviors appear.
2. Discuss the strengths and weaknesses of the three main forms of video modeling (self, peer, and point of view) in terms of ease of use. This discussion could be expanded to include the potential power each method would have, allowing for analysis of cost efficiency (mainly in time and efficiency).
3. Peer-modeling videos could be created that address the most common behaviors that need to be modified. Create a list of behaviors for which you feel videos should be created first (those that would have the most widespread usage or that address critical skills often lacking in children with autism).

Questions

1. Why might video modeling be especially effective for people with autism?
2. What would be the steps in creating a peer-modeling video, and how would they differ from the steps for self- or point-of-view-modeling videos?
3. What theories support the use of video modeling? Which apply to all forms and which apply to only one or two of the common video-modeling formats?

REFERENCES

Apple A.L., Billingsley, F., Schwartz, I.S., & Carr, E.G. (2005). Effects of video modeling alone and with self-management on compliment-giving behaviors of children with high-functioning ASD. *Journal of Positive Behavior Interventions, 7*(1), 33–46.

Bandura, A. (1969). *Principles of behavior modification.* New York, NY: Holt, Rinehart & Winston.

Bandura, A. (1997). *Self-efficacy: The exercise of control.* New York, NY: Freeman.

Bauman, M.L. (1999). Autism: Clinical features and neurobiological observations. In H. Tager-Flusberg (Ed.), *Neurodevelopmental Disorders* (pp. 383–399). Cambridge, MA: MIT Press.

Bellini, S., & Akullian, J. (2007). A meta-analysis of video modeling and video self-modeling interventions for children and adolescents with autism spectrum disorders. *Exceptional Children, 73,* 261–284.

Bellini, S., Akullian, J., & Hopf, A. (2007). Increasing social engagement in young children with autism spectrum disorders using video self-modeling. *School Psychology Review, 36,* 80–90.

Brown, R. (1973). *A first language: The early stages.* London, UK: George Allen & Unwin.

Bryan, L.C., & Gast, D.L. (2000). Teaching on-task and on-schedule behaviors to high-functioning children with autism via picture activity schedules. *Journal of Autism and Developmental Disorders, 30*(6), 553–567.

Buggey, T. (2005). Applications of video self-modeling with children with autism in a small private school. *Focus on Autism and Other Developmental Disabilities, 20,* 180–204.

Buggey, T. (2009). *Seeing is believing: Self-modeling applications with children with autism and other developmental disabilities.* Bethesda, MD: Woodbine House.

Buggey, T., Ayers, P., Morris, C., Wichlinski, A., Decker, M., Smith, A., & Vanderpool, B. (2005). A picture is worth...Improving reader's self-efficacy through self-modeling. *Tennessee Reading Teacher, 33.*

Buggey, T., Hoomes, G., Sherberger, M.E., & Williams, S. (2011). Facilitating social initiations of preschoolers with autism spectrum disorders using video self-modeling. *Focus on Autism and Other Developmental Disabilities, 26,* 25–36.

Buggey, T., Toombs, K., Gardner, P., & Cervetti, M. (1999). Self-modeling as a technique to train response behaviors in children with autism. *Journal of Positive Behavior Intervention, 1,* 205–214.

Charlop-Christy, M., & Daneshvar, S. (2003). Using video modeling to teach perspective taking to children with autism. *Journal of Positive Behavior Interventions, 36*(2), 12–21.

Charlop-Christy, M., Le, L., & Freeman, K. (2000). A comparison of video modeling with in vivo modeling for teaching children with autism. *Journal of Autism and Developmental Disorders, 30,* 537–552.

Charlop, M.H., & Milstein, J.P. (1989). Teaching autistic children conversational speech using video modeling. *Journal of Applied Behavior Analysis, 22*(3), 275–285.

Clark, E., Beck, D., Sloane, H., Jenson, W., & Bowen, J. (1993). Self-modeling with preschoolers: Is it different? *School Psychology International, 14,* 83–89.

D'Ateno, P., Mangiapanello, K., & Taylor, B.A. (2003). Using video modeling to teach complex play sequences to a preschooler with autism. *Journal of Positive Behavior Interventions, 5*(1), 5–11.

Dauphin, M., Kinney, E.M., Stromer, R., & Koegel, R.L. (2004). Using video-enhanced activity schedules and matrix training to teach sociodramatic play to a child with autism. *Journal of Positive Behavior Interventions, 6*(4), 238–50.

Delano, M.E. (2007). Improving written language performance of adolescents with Asperger syndrome. *Journal of Applied Behavior Analysis, 40*(2), 342–351.

Dowrick, P.W. (1983). Self-modeling. In P.W. Dowrick & J. Biggs (Eds.), *Using video: Psychological and social applications* (pp. 105–124). New York, NY: Wiley.

Gena, A., Couloura, S., & Kymissis, E. (2005). Modifying the affective behavior of preschoolers with autism using *in-vivo* or video modeling and reinforcement contingencies. *Journal of Autism and Developmental Disorders, 35*(5), 545–546.

Golan, O., & Baron-Cohen, S. (2006). Systemizing empathy: Teaching adults with Asperger syndrome or high-functioning autism to recognize complex emotions using interactive multimedia. *Development and Psychopathology, 18*(2), 591–617.

Grandin, T. (2010). *Thinking in pictures and other reports from my life with autism.* New York, NY: Vintage Books.

Hanley, G.P., Iwata, B.A., & McCord, B.E. (2003). Functional analysis of problem behavior: A review. *Journal of Applied Behavior Analysis, 36,* 147–185.

Haring, T.G., Kennedy, C.H., Adams, M.J., & Pitts-Conway, V. (1987). Teaching generalization of purchasing skills across community settings to autistic youth using videotape modeling. *Journal of Applied Behavior Analysis, 20*(1), 89–96.

Hine, J.F., & Wolery, M. (2006). Using point-of-view video modeling to teach play to preschoolers with autism. *Topics in Early Childhood Special Education, 26*(2), 83–93.

Kazdin, A.E. (1982). *Single-case research designs: Methods for clinical and applied settings.* New York, NY: Oxford University Press.

Keen, D., Brannigan, K.L., & Cuskelly, M. (2007). Toilet training for children with autism: The effects of video modeling. *Journal of Developmental and Physical Disabilities, 19*(4), 291–303.

Kehle, T.J., Bray, M.A., Margiano, S.G., Theodore, L.A., & Zhou, Z. (2002). Self-modeling as an effective intervention for students with serious emotional disturbance: Are we modifying children's memories? *Psychology in the Schools, 39*(2), 203–207.

Kimball, J.W., Kinney, E.M., Taylor, B.A., & Stromer, R. (2004). Video enhanced activity schedules for children with autism: A promising package for teaching social skills. *Education and Treatment of Children, 27,* 280–298.

Kircher, T.T., Senior, C., Phillips, M.L., Benson, P.J., Bullmore, E.T., Brammer, M.,...David, A.S. (2000). Towards a functional neuroanatomy of self-processing: Effects of faces and words. *Cognitive Brain Research, 10,* 133–144.

LeBlanc, L.A., Coates, A.M., Daneshvar, S., Charlop-Christy, M.H., Morris, C., & Lancaster, B.M. (2003). Using video modeling and reinforcement to teach perspective-taking skills to children with autism. *Journal of Applied Behavior Analysis, 36,* 253–257.

Lewis, M., & Brooks-Gunn, J. (1979). *Social cognition and the acquisition of self.* New York, NY: Plenum Press.

MacDonald, R., Clark, M., Garrigan, E., & Vangala, M. (2005). Using video modeling to teach pretend play to children with autism. *Behavioral Interventions, 20*(4), 225–238.

Maione, L., & Mirenda P. (2006). Effects of video modeling and video feedback on peer-directed social language skills of a child with autism. *Journal of Positive Behavior Interventions, 8*(2), 106–118.

McCoy K., & Hermansen, E. (2007). Video modeling for individuals with autism: A review of model types and effects. *Education and Treatment of Children, 30*(4), 183–213.

McCurdy, B.L., & Shapiro, E.S. (1988). Self-observation and the reduction of inappropriate classroom behavior. *Journal of School Psychology, 26,* 371–378.

Neumann, L. (1994). *A visual teaching method for children with autism* (2nd ed.). Croton, MD: Willerik Publishing.

Neumann, L. (1999). *A visual teaching method for children with autism.* Crofton, MD: Willerik Publishing.

Nikopoulos, C.K., & Keenan, M. (2003). Promoting social initiation in children with autism. *Behavioral Interventions, 18*(2), 87–108.

Nikopoulos, C.K., & Keenan, M. (2004). Effects of video modeling on training and generalisation of social initiation and reciprocal play by children with autism. *European Journal of Behaviour Analysis, 5*(1), 1–13.

Nikopoulos, C.K., & Keenan, M. (2007). Using video modeling to teach complex social sequences to children with autism. *Journal of Autism and Developmental Disorders, 37*(4), 678–693.

Piersel, W.C., & Kratochwill, T.R. (1979). Self-observation and behavior change: Applications to academic and adjustment problems through behavioral consultation. *Journal of School Psychology, 17*(2), 151–61.

Reagon, T.S., Higbee, K.A., & Endico, K. (2006). Teaching pretend play skills to a student with autism using video modeling with a sibling as model and play partner. *Education and Treatment of Children, 29*(3), 1–12.

Salvia, J., & Hughes, C.A. (1990). *Curriculum-based assessment: Testing what is taught.* New York, NY: Macmillan.

Sansosti, F.J., & Powell-Smith, K.A. (2008). Using computer-presented Social Stories™ and video models to increase the social communication skills of children with high-functioning autism spectrum disorders. *Journal of Positive Behavior Interventions, 10*(3), 162–178.

Scattone, D. (2008). Enhancing the conversation skills of a boy with Asperger's disorder through Social Stories™ and video modeling. *Journal of Autism and Developmental Disorders, 38*(2), 395–400.

Schreibman L., Whalen, C., & Stahmer, A.C. (2000). The use of video priming to reduce disruptive transition behavior in children with autism. *Journal of Positive Behavior Interventions, 2*(1), 3–11.

Schunk, D.H., & Hanson, A.R. (1989). Self-modeling and children's cognitive skill learning. *Journal of Educational Psychology, 81,* 155–163.

Sherer, M., Pierce, K.L., Paredes, S., Kisacky, K.L., Ingersoll, B., & Schreibman, L. (2001). Enhancing conversation skills in children with autism via video technology: Which is better, "self" or "other" as a model? *Behavior Modification, 25*(1), 140–158.

Shipley-Benamou, R., Lutzker, J.R., & Taubman, M. (2002). Teaching daily living skills to children with autism through instructional video modeling. *Journal of Positive Behavior Interventions, 4*(3), 166–177.

Simpson, A., Langone, J., & Ayres, K.M. (2004). Embedded video and computer based instruction to improve social skills for students with autism. *Education and Training in Developmental Disabilities, 39*(3), 240–252.

Sturmey, P. (1994). Assessing the functions of aberrant behaviors: A review of psychometric instruments. *Journal of Autism and Developmental Disorders, 24*(3), 293–304.

Taylor, B.A., Levin, L., & Jasper, S. (1999). Increasing play-related statements in children with autism toward their siblings: Effects of video modeling. *Journal of Developmental and Physical Disabilities, 11*(3), 253–264.

Wert, B.Y., & Neisworth, J.T. (2003). Effects of video self-modeling on spontaneous requesting in children with autism. *Journal of Positive Behavior Interventions, 5,* 300–305.

Wright, C., & Smith, D. (2009). The effect of PETTLEP imagery on strength performance. *International Journal of Sports and Exercise Psychology, 7,* 18–31.

Future Directions

Rebecca J. McCauley and Patricia A. Prelock

This final chapter is about next steps for our readers, for the researchers whose interventions have been described in this book, and for the larger community of current and future researchers and professionals needed to develop and implement effective communication and social interaction interventions for children, adolescents, and adults with autism spectrum disorders (ASDs). In the first part of the chapter, we review future directions for researchers, initially by summarizing those identified by the authors in this book, then by placing them in the larger context of ongoing discussions in the literature. In the last part of the chapter, Future Directions, we consider future directions for each of our three main audiences (i.e., families, professionals, students and their professors), offering suggestions about how they might advance their ongoing decision making for addressing the needs of individuals with ASDs and how they might continue their quest for information and support about the nature and treatment of autism.

FUTURE DIRECTIONS FOR RESEARCHERS

A reader might see this heading and believe this section is relevant only for researchers—current or future. However, we hope all readers will take the time to review it. If you are a parent of a child with an ASD diagnosis, or if you are a current professional and *not* a researcher, gaps in the existing research literature have at least three claims of relevance for you. First, your interest and your ability to spark the interest of others can be crucial to the success of future research efforts. Research depends on families and individuals with ASDs who are willing to participate in research studies, as well as on the clinicians who recruit participants and intimately observe interventions as they adopt them in their practice. Without these contributions to research endeavors, interventions cannot improve in more than local fits and starts, with benefits available only to those who are geographically close to a treatment center or to interventionists who are achieving great results. In addition, larger numbers of participants permit researchers to undertake more powerful research designs (e.g., randomized controlled trials); for those designs and most others as well, larger numbers of participants help yield more solid findings about what works and why it works. Finally, through efforts at increasing awareness and fundraising, families and professionals can generate the more widespread support necessary for obtaining the monetary and physical resources on which intervention research depends.

Second, for families and practicing clinicians, learning about voids in the research literature may help them view their own experience in a slightly different light. For example, it may help some family members experience the wider community of support represented by the many researchers who are working toward brighter futures for individuals with ASDs and their families. Families may also experience less frustration with currently available interventions and with the professionals who provide them if they recognize the limitations of the available knowledge base—and the ways in which those limitations are being addressed. Similarly, practitioners may experience less frustration with those same interventions if they recognize that improvements are actively being sought.

Third and finally, individual family members and practitioners may find a research question so compelling that they take it on more directly—either by becoming a researcher or by partnering with an existing researcher. Science is thought to flourish when fresh perspectives are brought to bear on research questions. In particular, the perspective of those who see the strengths as well as the hardships associated with ASDs may offer a welcome balance to the scientific conversation. As we discuss later in this chapter, such partnerships are not being seen simply as politically advantageous but are being recognized as vital if high-quality interventions for people with ASDs are to become the norm rather than the exception.

In short, we believe that all readers of this book can benefit from at least a brief exposure to possible paths for future research designed to produce and perfect effective interventions for communication and social interaction for people with ASDs. Regardless of their perspectives going into this reading task, readers will come away from it feeling more understood, we hope, and more energized about their own relationship to the research endeavor.

Summary of Future Directions for Reviewed Interventions

Because the authors of the treatment chapters in this book were carefully chosen for their expertise on the intervention they addressed, their comments regarding research needs offer potentially keen insights. Consequently, we summarize their observations here—identifying common themes, as well as needs unique to particular intervention approaches. Four themes permeated the authors' discussions of future directions: 1) improving the measurements used to study intervention outcomes, 2) tailoring interventions to more effectively meet the needs of individuals for whom they are currently recommended, 3) broadening the populations with whom the interventions can be used effectively, and 4) improving the methods used to initiate and support implementation of the interventions by professionals and by families.

Improving Measurements Used to Study Outcomes In initial studies of an intervention, a limited number of short-term outcomes are examined under relatively ideal circumstances (Fey & Finestack, 2009). Although the measurement of limited outcomes has been viewed as necessary for the integrity of the research designs capable of documenting that an intervention actually makes a difference, many questions remain unanswered—a result as frustrating to researchers as it is to practitioners and families. Among the most important types of measures needed for these unanswered questions are those that can richly reflect the quality of social interactions participants have with peers as well as with adults (e.g., Wegner, Chapter 3, Augmentative and Alternative Communication [AAC] Strategies; Wilczynski, Rue, Hunter, & Christian, Chapter 4, Elementary Behavioral Intervention Strategies; Gerber, Chapter 5, Developmental, Individual-Difference, Relationship-Based (DIR) Model; Durand, Chapter 6, Functional Communication Training [FCT]). Despite the high level of interest in improving social interactions for those individuals with ASDs who are being treated, identifying reasonable measures with which to chart such gains has proved elusive.

In addition to identifying measures to chart gains in the quality of social interactions, other types of measures that chapter authors identified as being needed were raised in the context of individual interventions, yet the potential value of the broader application of those measures seems evident. For example, in Chapter 6, on FCT, Durand commented that more information was needed about how to assess environments that can help support developing skills and how to determine which communication strategies (e.g., behaviors used as alternatives to negative behaviors) are seen as acceptable by potential communication partners. With respect to AAC strategies, Wegner, in Chapter 3, also noted that measuring the impact of such interventions on language development is needed. The need for increasing examination of language development in AAC strategies seems understandable, given the primary focus of such interventions on facilitating communication. Working at the earliest stages of development, Woods, Wetherby, Kashinath, and Holland (Chapter 9, Early Social Interaction Project) called for measures allowing earlier identification of ASDs as a means of facilitating earlier intervention, which, readers will recall, has been widely recommended as a best practice for ASD interventions (National Research Council [NRC], 2001). In short, the kinds of improved measures being called for by authors in this book are intended to result in earlier and broader impacts on the communication and social interaction of individuals with ASDs.

More Effectively Tailoring Interventions to Meet Individual Needs The authors readily acknowledged that participants in their studies varied widely in the degree to which they were helped by the intervention and that additional research was needed to produce more uniformly positive outcomes. One strategy for achieving this goal that was suggested by several authors included research aimed at identifying personal characteristics that might predict better responses to treatment (e.g., Wegner, Chapter 3, AAC Strategies; Wilczynski et al., Chapter 4, Elementary Behavioral Intervention Strategies; Simpson & Ganz, Chapter 11, Picture Exchange Communication System [PECS]; Bruinsma & McNerney, Chapter 12, Pivotal Response Treatment [PRT]). Another suggested research strategy involved the identification of mediating variables (e.g., delivery conditions, the nature of generalization planning, intensity) that could be adjusted in existing interventions to improve their effectiveness (e.g., Wilczynski et al., Chapter 4, Elementary Behavioral Intervention Strategies; Hutchins, Chapter 13, Social Stories™). Given the heterogeneity of individuals with ASDs, this attention to methods by which individuals' needs can be better met is likely to be a continuing research need for some time to come, even as researchers work toward broadly effective methods.

Broadening the Populations with Whom an Intervention Can Be Used Effectively   As another theme in the chapter authors' discussions of future directions, we noted their frequent voicing of suspicions that the intervention they were studying might be useful for a broader range of individuals. In particular, authors identified ASD subgroups that had not yet been studied in terms of their responsiveness, such as individuals with Asperger syndrome (Wilczynski et al., Chapter 4, Elementary Behavioral Intervention Strategies). Other groups that were identified included those who differ in age from existing participant groups, including younger participants (e.g., Hancock & Kaiser, Chapter 8, Implementing Enhanced Milieu Teaching [EMT]) as well as older ones, particularly adolescents and adults (Carter, Sisco, & Chung, Chapter 10, Peer-Mediated Support Interventions; Bruinsma & McNerney, Chapter 12, PRT; Hutchins, Chapter 13, Social Stories). Finally, two more groups that authors identified as yet unstudied but potentially benefiting from studied interventions consisted of 1) individuals who were either at risk for ASDs because of suggestive patterns of difficulties or because their older siblings had the diagnosis (e.g., Hancock & Kaiser, Chapter 8, EMT) and 2) those with communication and/or social interaction challenges associated with an identified neurodevelopmental disorder other than ASDs (e.g., Kasari, Kasambira Fannin, & Stickles Goods, Chapter 7, Joint Attention [JA] Intervention; Buggey, Chapter 14, Video Modeling). Although this theme is closely related to tailoring interventions to the needs of individuals, it seeks to capitalize on subgroups that share at least some important characteristics affecting intervention goals and potential methods.

Improving Methods Used to Initiate and Support Implementation of the Intervention by Professionals and by Families   Obviously, the ultimate success of any intervention approach rests critically on how effectively it can be implemented by those who live with it rather than those who just study it. Research, therefore, should address the needs of the parents and professionals who are charged with day-to-day use of an intervention to assist one or more individuals with an ASD in reaching their fullest potential in communication and social interaction. Unlike research settings, the everyday contexts in which an intervention is routinely used are never "pure." Managing many goals in their professional and personal relationships with the individual being helped, the actual users of an intervention are necessarily less focused on by-the-book methods than the intervention's developers. In addition, they often come to a new intervention with relatively little relevant background or theoretical or procedural knowledge. An obvious barrier to implementation is that interventions for communication and social interaction are made manifest through the actions and decision-making processes of those who use them. This makes the process of implementation far more complex than a simple handoff of a fail-safe manual by the researcher to the person(s) who will implement the intervention. Efficacy results, those demonstrated in a controlled laboratory setting, cannot ensure what is called fidelity of implementation as it is translated from the laboratory to schools, homes, and clinics. Those settings are the context in which true effectiveness is demonstrated.

Not surprisingly then, several chapter authors identified implementation as a major research need—one that requires explicit attention if intended benefits for individuals with ASDs are to be realized. Among the steps seen as needed are the development of teaching methods appropriate to the parents, teachers, and others who will implement an intervention (see Wegner, Chapter 3, AAC Strategies; Gerber, Chapter 5, DIR Model; Durand, Chapter 6, FCT; Kasari et al., Chapter 7, JA; Woods et al., Chapter 9, Early Social Interaction Project; Bruinsma & McNerney, Chapter 12, PRT). The difficulties associated with implementation of evidence-based interventions relate not only to the special circumstances of adult learners but also to the need for learning to occur at a level that would help preserve critical procedural elements while enlisting learners' highest levels of engagement and troubleshooting.

Some approaches may require mastery and then maintenance of extensive techniques during lengthy and sometimes lifelong courses of intervention (e.g., situations in which FCT is needed to help address recurring problem behaviors). Especially for these approaches, effective strategies must address the motivational and memory demands facing those who use them. Offering an example of such research, Durand (Chapter 6) points to beginning work on the implementation of FCT, an approach designed to help minimize problem behaviors. Because of research indicating that the optimism of those who implement an intervention affects the success of its implementation (Durand, 2007), Durand and his colleagues have begun developing ways to help families and teachers become more optimistic (Durand, 2011; Durand & Hieneman, 2008; Durand, Hieneman, Clarke, & Zona, 2009). Improving optimism among families and teachers, then, is seen as a means of supporting their ongoing use of techniques, thus giving the intervention an opportunity to work. Efforts such as these may help intervention researchers and clinicians who use the intervention over time to share responsibility for successful implementation. As in so many arenas, alliances create the strongest defenses—in this case, against the undermining effects of ASDs on individuals' communication and social interaction development and function.

Broader View on the Challenges Involved in Implementing Evidence-Based Interventions

The challenges of implementation that were identified by the chapter authors have elicited additional reflections from many other researchers interested in this problem. Therefore, we decided to pursue discussion of implementation a little further in this section. In particular, we'd like to call readers' attention to two major developments that may have a profound impact on the future of intervention research focusing on social and behavioral manifestations of ASDs. The first involves the examination of actual practices of in-place professionals and families in the home communities of individuals with ASDs. The second involves a reexamination of the paths by which researchers typically move from the initial testing of ideas about how to modify behaviors and improve communication and social interaction skills through to the point of their actual use (e.g., Fey & Finestack, 2009; Smith et al., 2007). These two developments may lead researchers to introduce user-friendly methods and materials at earlier points in the intervention development process than has traditionally been the case.

As a first change in how implementation is being viewed, research examining actual assessment and intervention practices has been gaining interest in a variety of fields (Delprato, 2001; Gresham, Beebe-Frankenberger, & MacMillan, 1998; Heflin & Simpson, 1998; Reichow, Volkmar, & Cicchetti, 2008). This trend can be seen as a natural offshoot of evidence-based practice, which acknowledges not only the intrinsic merit of research to the clinical decision-making process but also the considerable value of the expert clinical judgments and the opinions, preferences, and values of treated individuals and family members (e.g., Dollaghan, 2007; Sackett, Richardson, Rosenberg, & Haynes, 1997).

The ASD literature related to communication and social interaction skills has thus far reported very little research directed toward ascertaining what speech-language pathologists know about ASDs and how they actually assess and treat the individuals with ASDs with whom they come in contact, despite the important role these professionals play in providing services to individuals with ASDs (Filipek et al., 1999). For example, no more than a handful of studies have examined speech-language pathologists' knowledge (Cascella & Colella, 2004; Schwartz & Drager, 2008) and practice (Felderhoff, Gonzales, & Wendel, 2008). Similarly, only a few studies have examined parents' use of the many interventions vying for their attention (e.g., Goin-Kochel, Myers, & Mackintosh, 2007; Green et al., 2006). Even as this work is beginning in Western cultures, such as the United States, parallel steps are being taken to address this issue in various non-Western cultures, such as India and China (e.g., Deshmukh & McCauley, 2010; McCabe, 2010).

In addition to research examining how individuals are handling treatment decisions and implementation, parallel research is under way to examine how organizations are handling these decisions on a grand scale. For example, Downs and Downs (2010) surveyed educational service districts, school districts, and neuro-developmental centers in the Pacific Northwest to compare the actual practices of these groups against those recommended by the NRC (2001). Advances in this type of research may help clarify the complexities of the implementation process and thereby produce potential benefits for individuals with ASDs.

Whereas the first step in changing ideas about the process of implementation involves understanding the nature of missteps that can occur between development and implementation, the second entails a reconsideration of how interventions are developed in the first place. In an article published in 2011, Dingfelder and Mandell discuss a "diffusion of innovation theory" (p. 597), in which an emphasis is placed on the social systems into which new technologies (e.g., new interventions for ASDs) are disseminated and implemented. In so doing, they highlight the importance of research such as that of Downs and Downs (2010). Beginning their discussion on a relatively grim note, Dingfelder and Mandell state that their purpose is to describe "reasons why efficacious interventions for autism are rarely adopted, implemented, and maintained in community settings, all revolving around the perceived fit between the intervention and the needs and capacities of the setting" (p. 597). They go on to suggest that by considering the needs and capacities of those settings at a much earlier point in the process of intervention development, such disappointing outcomes may not need to be a chronic problem.

In their 2011 article, Dingfelder and Mandell describe the diffusion of innovation theory, a theory based largely on work examining the speed and success with which new public mental and preventive health measures are disseminated to potential adopters in a particular setting, then adopted, implemented, and finally maintained by those individuals (e.g., Rogers, 2003). To illustrate some of the challenges facing evidence-based interventions, these authors describe questions that might be raised by administrators in public schools concerning the adoption of discrete trial instruction (DTI; see Wilczynski et al., Chapter 4, Elementary Behavioral Intervention Strategies) versus PRT (see Bruinsma & McNerney, Chapter 12). Although it is beyond the scope of this chapter to summarize the results of that comparison, Table 15.1 lists the questions Dingfelder and Mandell suggest are implicit in the decision making of administrators who will compare novel interventions against existing practices and/or other interventions that might be adopted. We call your attention to these questions because Dingfelder and Mandell would recommend that researchers keep them in mind throughout their development of new interventions. In addition, they provide explicit recommendations that include the following: earlier involvement of end users of an intervention, greater attention to early development of materials that will be used during everyday application of the intervention, improved documentation of what demands and benefits may actually be associated with implementation, and the placing of greater value on studies examining feasibility. Although many of their recommendations simply amplify and extend the work of others addressing the question of implementation (e.g., Lord et al., 2005; Smith et al., 2007), their arguments make clear that what is at stake is not simply the surmounting of annoying barriers to successful outcomes, but the potential removal of what may otherwise be insurmountable obstacles.

An Additional Challenge to Ongoing Intervention Research

The chapter authors did not highlight in their closing comments that most of the intervention research described in this book was conducted primarily with participants who were from monolingual English-speaking homes. One might expect that as a neurodevelopmental disorder, ASDs would have similar effects on children regardless of their cultural and linguistic environment. In fact, however, there may be sizable differences in how those effects of ASDs are perceived across cultures (Dyches, Wilder, Sudweeks, Obiakor, & Algozzine, 2004; Wilder, Dyches, Obiakor, & Algozzine, 2004). For example, cultures and linguistic groups differ on which effects of ASDs are seen as more penalizing or more glaring departures from age-appropriate patterns of communication and social interaction (Daley & Sigman, 2002). Further, the appropriate roles of family members and professionals in relation to the person with an ASD and his or her family differ substantially from culture to culture (e.g., Daley, 2004; Daley & Sigman, 2002; Kalra, Seth, & Sapra, 2005), as can their goals for intervention (Wilder et al., 2004). Because, by definition, interventions for communication and social interaction focus on the very substance of

Table 15.1. Guiding questions applied to decisions about intervention dissemination, adoption, implementation, and maintenance

Which intervention works better...
...based on what evidence?
...for what children?
...for what outcomes?
Is the cost of changing worth the relative advantage offered by the new program?
Does this program have all of the components that I need for full implementation?
Can my staff carry out this program with the resources available to the team?
Will important constituencies (e.g., parents, teachers) accept this program?

Source: Dingfelder and Mandell (2011).

culture, a better understanding of how the linguistic and cultural backgrounds of all parties (families, people with ASDs, professionals) affect interventions is warranted. At the same time, however, resources exist to assist many different groups of professionals and family members in avoiding at least some of the pitfalls caused when members of different cultures and language groups join to improve the communication and social interaction of individuals with ASDs (e.g., American Speech-Language-Hearing Association [ASHA], 2004; Richmond, 2011).

FUTURE DIRECTIONS FOR READERS

Parents and Families of Individuals with Autism Spectrum Disorders

Continuing Decision Making   We hope that readers who are parents and family members of individuals with ASDs have reached this point in their reading with at least an impression that we lived up to the promise we made in earlier parts of the book—to try to add a few useful ideas and interpretable readings to the syllabus you've been required to create as part of a never-ending crash course on ASDs. Understanding that every moment of reading represents time away from your many obligations, including simply being with people you care about, among them, those who may have an ASD, we offer just a few additional thoughts about the ongoing decisions you make concerning how best to seek help in the areas of communication and social interaction. First, although no intervention will have perfect evidence or be a perfect fit for a given child, there are better and worse interventions out there. Second, interventions such as those that are described in this book represent good starting points for consideration. These interventions have been scrutinized from a variety of perspectives, largely by individuals who do not have a vested financial interest in the outcome. Moreover, they are open to additional scrutiny by virtue of their scientific roots. Although they do not constitute a complete list of interventions representing potentially valuable components of your child's program, many of the characteristics they demonstrate will also be evident in any intervention worthy of your consideration. Finally, professionals who work with you as you make ongoing decisions about interventions should value your perspective as the closest observer of your child's difficulties and hard-earned advances in communication and social interaction. Valuing your perspective represents a core ideal that unites most, if not all, professionals working in the area of ASDs today. Based on the additional knowledge you have already sought and gained concerning how interventions are developed by researchers and used by professionals, you are likely to increase the capacity of those working with your child to benefit from your special knowledge.

Additional Resources   As you are well aware, the information and perspectives shared in this book represent just a fraction of dealing with interventions for ASDs. In keeping with our desire to provide valuable information in practical amounts, we've selected just a few resources to support your continuing access to information and to help you evaluate the available research and try out some key strategies. Although we have not formally vetted these specific resources, we believe, based on our years of talking with families about the information they find most valuable, that the content should be useful to you. (Further, we look to our parent readers of this book to advise us about other resources that should be included in subsequent editions). Table 15.2 lists and describes the resources we've selected: two books, two organizations, and two web sites. Some of you may want to explore an even greater number of resources. For that group of eager readers, we recommend that you examine the two remaining tables in this chapter; although the resources in Tables 15.3 and 15.4 were chosen with professionals or students and professors in mind, they may be as relevant to your interests and needs as those in Table 15.2.

Professionals Who Work with Individuals with Autism Spectrum Disorders

Continuing Decision Making We acknowledge that professionals can find themselves in situations similar to what we have described as befalling parents whose children are diagnosed with an ASD. There is so much information of varying quality and so much competition for what needs to be learned, yet there is so little guidance and so little time available for learning. We hope that the descriptions of interventions in this book advanced your learning in a practical fashion by helping you find out a bit more about how the interventions have been developed thus far and what additional refinements are needed. Some of these interventions may be well known to you from past experience or education; others may be novel. Because the chapter authors presented the interventions using the same framework, we hope that both familiar and novel interventions may appear in sharper focus and in a broader context than usual. In addition, if you have accepted the challenge we offered of considering the family perspective as well as your own, we hope that you will find your reading has helped fuel your ongoing journey to achieve more effective work with people with ASDs as they tackle their core difficulties with communication and social interaction.

Additional Resources Table 15.3 provides several additional general sources of information that may prove helpful to teams supporting people and families affected by ASDs, along with sources that have been developed for specific professionals in addressing their work with people with ASDs. Although readers from each profession may be very familiar with resources provided by their own professional organization, they may be less familiar with those of other professions. Thus, we suggest that readers investigate not only those resources provided by their own profession but also resources offered to members of professions with whom they frequently work on ASD-related issues. All readers who work with children, adults, and families affected by ASDs may also benefit from exploring the lay-friendly resources described in Table 15.1.

Students and Their Professors

Continuing Decision Making Whereas the other groups of readers addressed in this book have come to it with actual individuals firmly in mind (their child, sibling, client, student, etc.), students, and even their professors, may have grappled with the issue of interventions for communication and social interaction at a far more abstract level. Thus, we hope and expect that student readers will have gained a basic sense of how such interventions are developed and studied and how they may fit the needs of subgroups with ASDs. However, we recognize that your

Table 15.2.   Recommended resources for parents and families

Resource	Description
Books	
Moor, J. (2008). *Playing, laughing, and learning with children on the autism spectrum: A practical resource of play ideas for parents and carers* (2nd ed.). Philadelphia, PA: Jessica Kingsley Publishers.	This book demonstrates how to break down activities into manageable stages and gain a child's attention and motivation by building on small achievements and by using technology (e.g., computers, the Internet, digital cameras). It also lists web sites to facilitate access to the latest resources for parents.
Organization for Autism Research. (2003). *Life journey through autism: A parent's guide to research.* Arlington, VA: Author.	This guide provides basic information about what autism is and how a diagnosis is made. It also provides an overview of the state of autism research and strategies for reading and evaluating research.
Organizations	
Autism Speaks (http://www.autismspeaks.org)	Founded in 2005, this organization has grown to be the largest science and advocacy organization for autism in the nation. Its goal is to advocate for the needs of individuals with autism and their families; fund research on the causes, prevention, and treatments for autism; and to increase autism awareness.
Autism Society of America (ASA) (http://www.autism-society.org)	ASA is the largest grassroots organization in the nation dedicated to improving the lives of all those affected by autism. Their grassroots efforts include increasing public awareness on the day-to-day and life-span issues faced by individuals with autism, advocating for appropriate services, and providing up-to-date information on intervention, education, advocacy, and research.
Web sites	
http://www.nationalautismcenter.org	The National Autism Center (NAC) is a nonprofit organization serving children and adolescents with ASDs and the May Institute's Center, which promotes evidence-based practice. The NAC offers reliable information about ASDs, promotes best practices, and offers comprehensive resources for families, providers, and communities. In 2009, the NAC published a report on a multiyear treatment evaluation project, the National Standards Project, to establish standards for effective, research-validated educational and behavioral interventions for children with ASDs. This project provides the most comprehensive analysis regarding treatments for children with ASDs to date.
http://www.thegraycenter.org	The Gray Center for Social Learning and Understanding is a nonprofit organization that offers coaching and consulting services for those affected by ASDs and works to cultivate the strengths of individuals with ASDs and those who interact with them. This web site provides access to treatment information related to Social Stories™, including descriptions of what they are, how to write them, and how to use them. Sample Social Stories, Social Story books, story movies, and descriptions of available workshops are provided. The web site also offers an educational tool, the Social Response Pyramid, and related resources to support understanding of social effectiveness.

Table 15.3. Additional resources for professional groups working with individuals with autism spectrum disorders (ASDs)

Group	Resources	Description
Professionals working directly with children, youth, and adults with ASDs	Autism Internet Modules (AIM) prepared by the Ohio Center for Autism and Low Incidence (OCALI)	These 37 modules include visual graphics as well as video examples for topics ranging from antecedent-based interventions to prompting, response interruption/redirection, time delay, and visual supports. Users of these modules sign in to make use of the materials and may also sign up for participation in research on this project.
	http://autismpdc.fpg.unc.edu/	This web site includes EBP Briefs on relevant topics as well as a link to AIM and OCALI (see the first table entry).
	Vargas, C.M., & Prelock, P.A. (Eds.), (2004). *Caring for children with neurodevelopmental disabilities and their families: An innovative approach to interdisciplinary practice.* Mahwah, NJ: Erlbaum.	This book provides an interdisciplinary, family-centered, strengths-based, and culturally competent approach to community-based assessment and intervention planning for children and youth with a variety of neurodevelopmental disorders, including autism.
Educators	Larkey, S. (2005). *Making it a success: Practical strategies and worksheets for teaching students with ASD.* Philadelphia, PA: Jessica Kingsley Publishers.	This books presents strategies to help children with ASDs improve their social skills as well as their academic performance, play, and overall behavior.
	MacKenzie, H. (2008). *Reaching out and teaching the child with autism spectrum disorder: Using learning preference and strengths.* Philadelphia, PA: Jessica Kingsley Publishers.	This book explores how a child's learning preferences, strengths, and interests can be used to enhance motivation and foster learning. The authors provide a comprehensive model for developing independent learning skills in children with ASDs between 3 and 12 years of age.
	Magnusen, C.L. (2005). *Teaching children with autism and related spectrum disorders: An art and a science.* Philadelphia, PA: Jessica Kingsley Publishers.	This book highlights practical strategies for teachers to address everyday problems and adapt to the situations that face them when teaching children with ASDs.
	Ruble, L.A., & Dalrymple, N.J. (2002). COMPASS: A parent–teacher collaborative model for students with autism. *Focus on Autism and Other Developmental Disabilities, 17,* 76–83.	This article describes a model designed to facilitate parent and teacher cooperation and joint work for students with ASDs.
	Simpson, R.L., & Smith Myles, B. (2007). *Educating children and youth with autism–2nd edition: Strategies for effective practice.* Austin, TX: PRO-ED.	This book guides educators on current practice in diagnosis, assessment, instructional strategies, curriculum, behavior management, communication, and inclusion.
Physicians	Myers, S.M., & Johnson, C.P. (2007). Management of children with autism spectrum disorders. *Pediatrics, 120*(5), 1161–1182.	This article summarizes best practices as these were viewed in 2007 by the American Academy of Pediatrics. Such clinical reports are described as expiring automatically 5 years after publication (i.e., in 2012).

continued

Table 15.3.   *(continued)*

Group	Resources	Description
	Perez, J.M., Gonzalez, P.M., Comi, M.L., & Nieto, C. (Eds.). (2006). *New developments in autism: The future is today*. Philadelphia. PA: Jessica Kingsley Publishers.	This edited book provides a comprehensive overview of ASD research by internationally known experts, highlighting the value of early identification and collaboration among parents and professionals in service delivery.
	Stoddart, K.P. (Ed.). (2004). *Children, youth, and adults with Asperger syndrome: Integrating multiple perspectives*. Philadelphia, PA: Jessica Kingsley Publishers.	This edited book represents a range of disciplines and provides an overview of clinical, research, and personal perspectives on Asperger syndrome.
Occupational therapists	Janzen, J.E. (2002). *Understanding the nature of autism: A guide to the autism spectrum disorders* (2nd ed.). Austin, TX: PRO-ED.	This book provides an integrated approach to supporting students with ASDs that matches recognized interventions to a child's specific needs.
	Tomchek, S.D., & Case-Smith, J. (2009) *Occupational therapy practice guidelines for children and adolescents with autism*. Bethesda, MD: AOTA Press.	These guidelines represent an important document for occupational therapists engaged in work with individuals with ASDs.
Physical therapists	Bhat, A.N., Landa, R.J., & Galloway, J.C. (2011). Current perspectives on motor functioning in infants, children, and adults with autism spectrum disorders. *Physical Therapy, 91,* 1116–1129.	This article represents an interdisciplinary approach to this topic that appears in a physical therapy journal but includes a well-known speech-language pathologist as the second author.
	Kurtz, L. (2007). *Understanding motor skills in children with dyspraxia, ADHD, autism and other learning disabilities: A guide to improving coordination*. Philadelphia, PA: Jessica Kingsley Publishers.	This book provides suggestions on ways to recognize typical and atypical motor development and how to seek help or support for motor difficulties. In addition, the author offers teaching strategies to support co-ordination of students on the playground, in the classroom, and at home.
Psychologists	Hewitt, S. (2005). *Specialist support approaches to ASD in mainstream settings*. Philadelphia, PA: Jessica Kingsley Publishers.	This book demonstrates the need for and value of providing specialist support in schools so that students with ASDs and associated behavioral difficulty can be included in mainstream classes.
	Miller, L. (2009). *Practical behaviour management solutions for children and teens with autism: The 5P approach*. Philadelphia, PA: Jessica Kingsley Publishers.	This book offers a framework for behavior intervention that promotes and encourages skill development in independence through the 5 Ps: profiling, prioritizing, problem analysis, problem solving, and planning.
Social workers	Forrester-Jones, R., & Broadhurst, S. (2007). *Autism and loss*. Philadelphia, PA: Jessica Kingsley Publishers.	This book addresses the range of loss that individuals with ASDs might experience over time, including bereavement, family or friends, possessions or health.

continued

Table 15.3. *(continued)*

Group	Resources	Description
	Paxton, K., & Estay, I.A. (2007). *Counseling people on the autism spectrum: A practical manual.* Philadelphia, PA: Jessica Kingsley Publishers.	Individuals with autism often have notable challenges in emotional expression, regulation, and recognition and are at risk for depression and anxiety. This book demonstrates ways individuals on the spectrum can cope with their emotions and anxieties.
Speech-language pathologists	American Speech-Language-Hearing Association (ASHA). (2006). *Guidelines for speech-language pathologists in diagnosis, assessment, and treatment of autism spectrum disorders across the life span.* Available from http://www.asha.org/policy	This document is an official statement of ASHA, the national association of speech-language pathologists in the United States. It is intended to guide the implementation of ASHA's knowledge and skills document (see the table entry that immediately follows).
	American Speech-Language-Hearing Association. (2006). *Knowledge and skills needed by speech-language pathologists for diagnosis, assessment, and treatment of autism spectrum disorders across the life span.* Available from http://www.asha.org/policy	This document is an official statement of ASHA, the national association of speech-language pathologists. It was prepared by an ad hoc committee of experts in ASDs.
	Bogdashina, O. (2004). *Theory of mind and the triad of perspectives on autism and Asperger syndrome: A view from the bridge.* Philadelphia, PA: Jessica Kingsley Publishers.	This books provides an innovative look of how stepping into another's shoes can provide greater perspective to the individual with an ASD as well as the providers with whom he or she is working.
	Potter, C., & Whitaker, C. (2001). *Enabling communication in children with autism.* Philadelphia, PA: Jessica Kingsley Publishers.	The authors argue for encouraging spontaneous communication as a primary educational goal, and they demonstrate ways that children with ASDs and limited verbal skills can and do communicate in environments that enable them to do so with the support of targeted, research-based strategies.
	Tantam, D. (2009). *Can the world afford people with autistic spectrum disorders?* Philadelphia, PA: Jessica Kingsley Publishers.	This book explores the role of nonverbal communication in shaping social behavior and the importance of understanding this impairment in individuals with ASDs. The author describes how knowledge of differences in nonverbal communication can help to shape more positive development.

continuing growth in decision making depends on the application of information provided about how interventions are developed as well as about the interventions described in this book. Therefore, in this section of the chapter, we offer four exercises that might move your thinking further.

1. Read the section Application to a Child or Application to an Adolescent or Adult for one of the interventions that you found particularly interesting or that you had already known something about. Then consider whether one of the other intervention approaches might have been selected as an alternative or an

additional one to use for that individual. What advantages and disadvantages might have been anticipated had the other approach been used or added to the individual's program?

2.   Identify an intervention that seemed especially intriguing to you, looking carefully at what research had already been conducted to support its potential efficacy and what the authors described as needed areas of additional study. Considering what you've learned about how interventions are developed, work in a group to design a study that would constitute a reasonable next step for that approach.

3.   In this chapter, we introduced the idea that researchers may want to consider modifying the process by which interventions are developed so that approaches can become more practical for families and clinicians who conduct them on a day-to-day basis. Because parents and peers are crucial communication partners who will be enlisted in the intervention, reexamine the treatment chapters in this book, looking for ways in which researchers have already begun to consider these clinical partners. Develop a list of these ways, along with ideas about how each of them can be pursued.

4.   A number of firsthand accounts have been written by individuals with ASDs who describe in rich detail their past and continuing challenges in communication and social interaction. Among our favorites are *Thinking in Pictures and Other Reports from My Life with Autism* by Temple Grandin (1996); *Look Me in the Eye: My Life with Asperger's* by John Elder Robison (2007); and *Send in the Idiots: Stories from the Other Side of Autism* by Kamran Nazeer (2006). Read one of these books, making note of the continuing challenges reported by these very successful adults. Which of these challenges might have been, or still could be, addressed by the interventions described in this book? Which could not be? What do these authors write that helps you appreciate why they would, or wouldn't, take part in such interventions if they had access to them?

Additional Resources   Table 15.4 points you to a variety of web sites, books, and organizations that may prove to be avenues for further exploration of information about ASDs. Although much of the investigation we imagine you will undertake consists of gathering further information, we have also listed organizations that you may want to investigate as a means of taking more concrete steps—such as providing support for families of people with ASDs, serving as aides, and so forth—in ways that are the most respectful and productive possible.

CONCLUDING THOUGHTS

ASDs are frequently characterized as a puzzle, especially to those of us who are outsiders to the lived experience of people with ASDs—even when we are their parents, family members, friends, or daily acquaintances. Difficulties in communication and social interaction are among the core features of this puzzle and thus are a focus of ever-increasing efforts to develop and disseminate effective interventions intended to alleviate the core impairments in autism. Knowledgeable collaborations of all of the groups addressed in this book and participating in its preparation—family members, professionals, students and their instructors, and researchers—will be needed

Table 15.4.   Resources for students and their instructors

Resource	Description
Print resources	
National Research Council. (2001). *Educating children with autism*. Washington, DC: National Academy Press.	In this book, nationally and internationally renowned clinical researchers in autism from a variety of disciplines reviewed the literature on the general program needs for young children with autism spectrum disorders (ASDs).
Prelock, P.A. (2006). *Autism spectrum disorders: Issues in assessment and intervention*. Austin, TX: PRO-ED.	This book offers a comprehensive look at assessment and intervention for autism, with a particular focus on understanding and addressing communication, play, and social interaction in individuals with ASDs.
Reichow, B., Doehring, P., Cicchetti, D.V., & Volkmar, F.R. (Eds.). (2011). *Evidence-based practices and treatments for children with autism*. New York, NY: Springer.	This book examines the range of available treatments for children with ASDs used to address the core impairments of the disorder, including educational, pharmacological, sensory, behavioral, communication, social, and other health-related intervention approaches. Each chapter provides a summary of the most frequently used intervention strategies and the scientific evidence currently available to support their use.
Volkmar, F., Paul, R., Cohen, D., & Klin, A. (2005). *Handbook of autism and pervasive developmental disorders–Third edition*. Hoboken, NJ: Wiley.	This book brings together internationally renowned researchers and clinicians to define critical areas of need in the diagnosis, assessment, and intervention of individuals with ASDs across the life span.
Web sites	
http://www.ninds.nih.gov/disorders/autism/detail_autism.htm	This web site through the National Institutes of Health (NIH) provides an autism fact sheet.
http://www.cdc.gov/ncbddd/autism/	This Centers for Disease Control (CDC) site serves as a repository or autism information center.
http://www.firstsigns.org/	First Signs is a web site that highlights the early markers or developmental indicators that are potential red flags for a possible diagnosis of an ASD.
http://www.osepideasthatwork.org/	The Office of Special Education Programs in the U.S. Department of Education created this web site to provide easy access to "research-based products, publications and resources" to help insure the best possible intervention programs for students with disabilities, including those with ASDs.
http://www.ncepmaps.org/Autism-Spectrum-Disorders.php	The American Speech-Language-Hearing Association (ASHA) has developed evidence-based maps for autism to provide easy access to relevant research, including systematic reviews, guidelines, and technical reports related to autism, and autism resources.
Organizations not listed in Table 15.1	
Organization for Autism Research (OAR) (http://www.researchautism.org/)	OAR is the only organization whose primary focus is on applied research, especially in providing answers to critical questions posed by those affected by ASDs.
Autism Speaks (http://events.autismspeaks.org/site/c.nuLTJ6MPKrH/b.4385867/k.BF59/Home.htm)	Student chapters of Autism Speaks have been in existence only since about 2008. Through local chapters, college students host awareness, advocacy, and fundraising events in their community while supporting their local autism communities.

to solve this puzzle in the many forms presented by individuals with ASDs. Their individual and group efforts will surely culminate in better outcomes for individuals, families, and communities affected by ASDs.

REFERENCES

American Speech-Language-Hearing Association. (2004). *Knowledge and skills needed by speech-language pathologists and audiologists to provide culturally and linguistically appropriate services.* Available from http://www.asha.org/policy

American Speech-Language-Hearing Association. (2006). *Guidelines for speech-language pathologists in diagnosis, assessment, and treatment of autism spectrum disorders across the life span.* Available from http://www.asha.org/policy

American Speech-Language-Hearing Association. (2006). *Knowledge and skills needed by speech-language pathologists for diagnosis, assessment, and treatment of autism spectrum disorders across the life span.* Available from http://www.asha.org/policy

Bhat, A.N., Landa, R.J., & Galloway, J.C. (2011). Current perspectives on motor functioning in infants, children, and adults with autism spectrum disorders. *Physical Therapy, 91,* 1116–1129.

Bogdashina, O. (2004). *Theory of mind and the triad of perspectives on autism and Asperger syndrome: A view from the bridge.* Philadelphia, PA: Jessica Kingsley Publishers.

Cascella, P.W., & Colella, C.S. (2004). Knowledge of autism spectrum disorders among school speech-language pathologists. *Focus on Autism and Other Developmental Disabilities, 19*(4), 245–252.

Daley, T.C. (2004). From symptom recognition to diagnosis: Children with autism in urban India. *Social Science and Medicine, 58,* 1323-1335.

Daley, T.C., & Sigman, M.D. (2002). Diagnostic conceptualization of autism among Indian psychiatrists, psychologists and pediatricians. *Journal of Autism and Developmental Disorders, 32*(1), 13-23.

Delprato, D.J. (2001). Comparisons of discrete-trial and normalized behavioral language intervention for young children with autism. *Journal of Autism and Developmental Disorders, 31,* 315–325.

Deshmukh, R., & McCauley, R.J. (2010, November). *Speech-language pathologists' practices for autism in India.* Poster presented at the annual conference of the American Speech-Language-Hearing Association, Philadelphia, PA.

Dingfelder, H.E., & Mandell, D.S. (2011). Bridging the research-to-practice gap in autism intervention: An application of diffusion of innovation theory. *Journal of Autism and Developmental Disorders, 41,* 597–609.

Dollaghan, C.A. (2007). *The handbook for evidence-based practice in communication disorders.* Baltimore, MD: Paul H. Brookes Publishing Co.

Downs, R.C., & Downs, A. (2010). Practices in early intervention for children with autism: A comparison with the National Research Council recommended practices. *Education and Training in Autism and Developmental Disabilities, 45*(1), 150–159.

Durand, V.M. (2007). Positive family intervention: Hope and help for parents with challenging children. *Psychology in Mental Retardation and Developmental Disabilities, 32*(3), 9–13.

Durand, V.M. (2011). *Optimistic parenting: Hope and help for you and your challenging child.* Baltimore, MD: Paul H. Brookes Publishing Co.

Durand, V.M., & Hieneman, M. (2008). *Helping parents with challenging children: Positive family intervention. Facilitator guide.* New York, NY: Oxford University Press.

Durand, V.M., Hieneman, M., Clarke, S., & Zona, M. (2009). Optimistic parenting: Hope and help for parents with challenging children. In G.D.W. Sailor, G. Sugai, & R. Horner (Eds.), *Handbook of positive behavior support* (pp. 233–256). New York, NY: Springer.

Dyches, T., Wilder, L.K., Sudweeks, R.R., Obiakor, F.E., & Algozzine, B. (2004). Multicultural issues in autism. *Journal of Autism and Developmental Disorders, 34*(2), 211–222.

Felderhoff, J., Gonzales, M.D., & Wendel, R.M. (2008, February). *Assessment methods used in Texas elementary schools for diagnosing pervasive developmental disorders*

(PDDs). Poster presented at the annual convention of the Texas Speech, Language, and Hearing Association, San Antonio, TX.

Fey, M.E., & Finestack, L.H. (2009). Research and development in child language intervention: A five-phase model. In R.G. Schwartz (Ed.), *Handbook of child language disorders* (pp. 513–531). New York, NY: Psychology Press.

Filipek, P.A., Accardo, P.J., Baranek, G.T., Cook Jr., E.H., Dawson, G., Gordon, B.,...Vokmar, F.R. (1999). The screening and diagnosis of autistic spectrum disorders. *Journal of Autism and Developmental Disorders, 29*(6), 439–484.

Forrester-Jones, R., & Broadhurst, S. (2007). *Autism and loss.* Philadelphia, PA: Jessica Kingsley Publishers.

Goin-Kochel, R.P., Myers, B.J., & Mackintosh, V.H. (2007). Parental reports on the use of treatments and therapies for children with autism spectrum disorders. *Research in Autism Spectrum Disorders, 1*, 195–209.

Grandin, T. (1996). *Thinking in pictures: And other reports from my life with autism.* New York, NY: Vintage Books.

Green, V.A., Pituch, K.A., Itchon, J., Choi, A., O'Reilly, M., & Sigafoos, J. (2006). Internet survey of treatments used by parents of children with autism. *Research in Developmental Disabilities, 27*, 70–84.

Gresham, F.M., Beebe-Frankenberger, M.E., & MacMillan, D.L. (1999). A selective review of treatments for children with autism: Description and methodological considerations. *School Psychology Review, 28*, 559–575.

Heflin, L.J., & Simpson, R.L. (1998). Interventions for children and youth with autism: Prudent choices in a world of exaggerated claims and empty promises. Part I: Intervention and treatment option review. *Focus on Autism and Other Developmental Disabilities, 13*, 194–211.

Hewitt, S. (2005). *Specialist support approaches to ASD in mainstream settings.* Philadelphia, PA: Jessica Kingsley Publishers.

Janzen, J.E. (2002). *Understanding the nature of autism: A guide to the autism spectrum disorders* (2nd ed). Austin, TX: PRO–ED.

Kalra, V., Seth, R., & Sapra, S. (2005). Autism—Experiences in a tertiary care hospital. *Indian Journal of Pediatrics, 72*(3), 227–230.

Kurtz, L. (2007). *Understanding motor skills in children with dyspraxia, ADHD, autism, and other learning disabilities: A guide to improving coordination.* Philadelphia, PA: Jessica Kingsley Publishers.

Larkey, S. (2005). *Making it a success: Practical strategies and worksheets for teaching students with ASD.* Philadelphia, PA: Jessica Kingsley Publishers.

Lord, C., Wagner, A., Rogers, S., Szatmari, P., Aman, M., Charman, T.,...Yoder, P. (2005). Challenges in evaluating psychosocial interventions for autistic spectrum disorders. *Journal of Autism and Developmental Disorders, 35*(6), 695–708.

MacKenzie, H. (2008). *Reaching out and teaching the child with autism spectrum disorders: Using learning preference and strengths.* Philadelphia, PA: Jessica Kingsley Publishers.

Magnusen, C.L. (2005). *Teaching children with autism and related spectrum disorders: An art and a science.* Philadelphia, PA: Jessica Kingsley Publishers.

McCabe, H. (2010). Employment experiences, perspectives, and wishes of mothers of children with autism in the People's Republic of China. *Journal of Applied Research in Intellectual Disabilities, 23*, 122–131.

Miller, L. (2009). *Practical behaviour management solutions for children and teens with autism: The 5P approach.* Philadelphia, PA: Jessica Kingsley Publishers.

Moor, J. (2008). *Playing, laughing, and learning with children on the autism spectrum: A practical resource of play ideas for parents and carers* (2nd ed.). Philadelphia, PA: Jessica Kingsley Publishers.

Myers, S.M., & Johnson, C.P. (2007). Management of children with autism spectrum disorders. *Pediatrics, 120* (5), 1162–1176.

National Research Council. (2001). *Educating children with autism.* Washington, DC: National Academy Press.

Nazeer, K. (2006). *Send in the idiots: Stories from the other side of autism.* New York, NY: Bloomsbury USA.

Organization for Autism Research. (2003). *Life journey through autism: A parent's guide to research.* Arlington, VA: Author.

Paxton, K., & Estay, I.A. (2007). *Counseling people on the autism spectrum: A practical manual.* Philadelphia, PA: Jessica Kingsley Publishers.

Perez, J.M., Gonzalez, P.M., Comi, M.L., & Nieto, C. (Eds.). (2006). *New developments in autism: The future is today.* Philadelphia, PA: Jessica Kingsley Publishers.

Potter, C., & Whitaker, C. (2001). *Enabling communication in children with autism.* Philadelphia, PA: Jessica Kingsley Publishers.

Prelock, P.A. (2006*). Autism spectrum disorders: Issues in assessment and intervention.* Austin, TX: PRO-ED.

Reichow, B., Doehring, P., Cicchetti, D.V., & Volkmar, F.R. (Eds.). (2011). *Evidence-based practices and treatments for children with autism.* New York, NY: Springer.

Reichow, B., Volkmar, F.R., & Cicchetti, D.V. (2008). Development of the evaluative methods for evaluating and determining evidence-based practices in autism. *Journal of Autism and Developmental Disorders, 38,* 1311–1319.

Richmond, A.S. (2011). Autism spectrum disorder: A global perspective. *Perspectives on Global Issues in Communication Sciences and Related Disorders, 1,* 39–46. doi:10.1044/gics1.2.39

Robison, J.E. (2007). *Look me in the eye: My life with Asperger's.* New York, NY: Crown / Random House.

Rogers, E.M. (2003). *Diffusion of innovations* (5th ed.). New York, NY: Free Press.

Ruble, L.A., & Dalrymple, N.J. (2002). COMPASS: A parent–teacher collaborative model for students with autism. *Focus on Autism and Other Developmental Disabilities, 17,* 76–83.

Sackett, D.L., Richardson, W.S., Rosenberg, W., & Haynes, R.B. (1997). *Evidence-based medicine: How to practice and teach EBM.* New York, NY: Churchill Livingstone.

Schwartz, H., & Drager, K.D.R. (2008). Training and knowledge in autism among speech-language pathologists: A survey. *Language, Speech, and Hearing Services in Schools, 39,* 66–77.

Simpson, R.L., & Smith Myles, B. (2007). *Educating children and youth with autism: Strategies for effective practice* (2nd ed.). Austin, TX: PRO-ED.

Smith, T., Scahill, L., Dawson, G., Guthrie, D., Lord, C., Odom, S.,…Wagner, A. (2007). Designing research studies on psychosocial interventions in autism. *Journal of Autism and Developmental Disorders, 37,* 354–366.

Stoddart, K.P. (Ed.). (2004). *Children, youth, and adults with Asperger syndrome: Integrating multiple perspectives.* Philadelphia, PA: Jessica Kingsley Publishers.

Tantam, D. (2009). *Can the world afford autistic spectrum disorder? Nonverbal communication, Asperger syndrome, and the interbrain.* Philadelphia, PA: Jessica Kingsley Publishers.

Tomchek, S.D., & Case-Smith, J. (2009). *Occupational therapy practice guidelines for children and adolescents with autism.* Bethesda, MD: AOTA Press.

Vargas, C.M., & Prelock, P.A. (Eds.). (2004). *Caring for children with neurodevelopmental disabilities and their families: An innovative approach to interdisciplinary practice.* Mahwah, NJ: Erlbaum.

Volkmar, F., Paul, R., Cohen, D., & Klin, A. (2005). *Handbook of autism and pervasive developmental disorders–Third edition.* Hoboken, NJ: Wiley.

Wilder, L.K., Dyches, T.T., Obiakor, F.E., & Algozzine, B. (2004). Multicultural perspectives on teaching students with autism. *Focus on Autism and Other Developmental Disabilities, 19*(2), 105–113.

White, S.W., Keonig, K., & Scahill, L. (2007). Social skills development in children with autism spectrum disorders: A review of the intervention research. *Journal of Autism and Developmental Disorders, 37,* 1858–1868.

Glossary

||||||||||||||||||||||||||||||||||||||||||||||||||||||||||||||||||||||||||||||||||||||||||||||

adult learning   Study of how adults learn that is applied to the consulting with and coaching of caregivers to be teachers and communication partners with their children. (Chapter 9)

adult modeling   Viewing a person over 21 demonstrating a task. (Chapter 14)

aggression   Behaviors that are directed at other people and that frequently result in pain and/or injury to them. (Chapter 6)

aided AAC [augmentative and alternative communication] system   A form of AAC that requires the use of a tool or equipment external to the individual to replace or supplement oral communication. This includes a way to represent meaning, a way to access the meaning represented, and a way to share that meaning with others (Beukelman & Mirenda, 2005). Aided AAC systems can be low tech, such as communication books with symbols, or high-tech, such as speech-generating devices. (Chapters 3, 10, and 11)

alternative assessment   Alternative approaches to assessing achievement standards for students with significant disabilities (e.g., life skills portfolio, work samples) who are unable to respond to the content and format of standardized statewide assessments. (Chapter 10)

applied behavior analysis (ABA)   A field of study in which the basic principles of behavior change are applied in order to improve socially significant behavior in children and adults. ABA involves the systematic examination of the environment to identify variables that are critical for producing improved outcomes for any person. (Chapter 4)

augmentative and alternative communication (AAC)   The use of aided or unaided systems as a supplement or alternative to oral speech. Such systems are used to assist people with autism or other disabilities in replacing or supplementing deficient or inadequate communication skills. (Chapters 3, 10, and 11)

autism spectrum disorders (ASDs)   Disorders that emerge in early childhood, characterized by deficits in social relatedness, nonverbal and verbal communication, and various interests and behaviors. These deficits can cause pervasive impairment in thinking, language, feeling, and the ability to relate to others. ASDs range from a severe form called autistic disorder, through pervasive developmental disorder–not otherwise specified (PDD-NOS), and finally to the mildest form, called Asperger syndrome. (Chapters 1 and 7)

challenging behaviors   Behaviors, such as physical aggression toward self or others, tantrums, verbal aggression, and self-stimulatory behavior, that in some form interfere with social interaction and a student's ongoing educational and/or social progress. (Chapter 6)

communication   The various means by which individuals interact and share information with others. Forms of communication may be verbal or nonverbal. (Chapter 11)

communicative form   The means by which an individual communicates. Forms of communication may include gestures, vocalizations, and words as well as aberrant behavior. (Chapter 11)

communicative function   The purposes for which an individual communicates. Common communicative functions include requesting desired items, protesting, commenting, and socially interacting with others. (Chapter 11)

consultative coaching approach   The Early Interventionist (EI) consults with rather than provides direct service to the caregiver by sharing information, coaching the caregiver to learn intervention strategies and problem-solving with the caregiver to develop an individualized plan for the parent-child dyad. (Chapter 9)

contemporary behavioral interventions   Interventions in which children are given choices, teaching opportunities are shared between the interventionist and the child, and preferred activities and materials are used. (Chapter 1)

cooperative learning groups   An intervention approach that entails establishing small learning or work groups and restructuring activities to promote positive interdependence among students. (Chapter 10)

core vocabulary   Vocabulary that is used frequently and by a variety of people. Core vocabulary can be obtained from word lists based on individual characteristics such as age, AAC use, and contexts. (Chapter 3)

Developmental, Individual-Difference, Relationship-Based (DIR) Model   An interdisciplinary approach to working with children with developmental disorders that addresses the child's functional emotional developmental level, the child's individual processing profile, and the relationship between the child and his or her caregivers. (Chapter 5)

discrete trial instruction (DTI)   In the field of applied behavior analysis, a method of teaching new skills that consists of an interventionist-provided instruction or stimulus, a behaviorally defined response from the child, and an interventionist-provided consequence that either identifies an incorrect response or rewards the correct response. The main components of this highly directive style of teaching are instruction, prompting, response, consequence, and intertrial interval. Massed trials are said to occur when the sequence of novel tasks presented to a learner are identical across multiple discrete trials. Varied trials are said to occur when the sequence of tasks presented to a learner reflect the broad curriculum but the novel tasks are interspersed. Both massed trials and varied trials are demonstrated in the video accompanying Chapter 4. (Chapters 4 and 7)

discriminative stimulus A stimulus that can lead to reinforcement when responses of some type are present and that does not lead to reinforcement when responses of other types are present. In the context of a discrete trial, the discriminative stimulus is often in the form of an instruction, which, if complied with, will result in reinforcement. (Chapter 4)

emerging treatments A category of treatments for children with ASDs. Although there is some evidence for the effectiveness of these treatments, there is not enough to consider them established treatments. This terminology has been adopted by the National Standards Project. (National Autism Center, 2009) (Chapter 5)

enhanced milieu teaching (EMT) A third generation of naturalistic teaching strategies, building on the principles of milieu teaching and systematically adding principles for responsive conversational skills and language modeling in everyday communication contexts. (Chapter 8)

environmental arrangement One of four core components of EMT, environmental arrangement includes procedures for organizing and managing the child's environment to increase requesting behavior and provide adults with language prompting and scaffolding opportunities. (Chapter 8)

family-centered services and supports Services and supports that strengthen the capacity of parents to enhance their children's development and embrace the family's active involvement in service planning and intervention decision making for the children and family as a whole. (Chapter 9)

feedforward An aspect of self-modeling in which children view themselves performing new behaviors in an adaptive way, simulating how they might be performing at a future time. (Chapter 14)

Floortime A type of therapeutic interaction that involves spontaneous, developmentally appropriate, often one-to-one interactions during which functional emotional development is mobilized. (Chapter 5)

fringe vocabulary Vocabulary to be used in an AAC system that is specific to the individual. This might include names of people, pets, or activities. (Chapter 3)

functional behavioral assessment A class of techniques used to assess the variables that appear to be influencing a behavior or behaviors. It usually involves assessing immediate antecedents and consequences as well as more distant events (setting events). (Chapters 6 and 13)

functional communication training (FCT) An intervention strategy for addressing challenging behavior that relies on replacing problem behavior with functionally equivalent alternative communication. (Chapter 6)

Functional Emotional Assessment Scale (FEAS) The primary assessment tool used in the DIR approach. The FEAS is used to determine the child's FEDLs and the nature of the interactions between the child and his or her caregivers. This, in turn, leads to creating a treatment plan based on the child's individual profile and provides a baseline for measuring the child's progress. (Chapter 5)

functional emotional developmental levels (FEDLs) Six levels of social-emotional-symbolic functioning that describe the foundations of typical child development from birth through the preschool years. This system is used within the DIR approach. (Chapter 5)

functional equivalence The concept that describes how two behaviors can serve the same function for a student and therefore can replace each other in a student's behavioral repertoire. (Chapter 6)

generalization The application of a skill or behavior to a number of related behaviors or across different environments. (Chapter 7)

graphic symbols A way to represent meaning in an aided AAC system. This representation can include pictures, photographs, line drawings, Blissymbols, printed words, and traditional orthography. (Chapter 3)

inclusive education Providing students with disabilities quality educational services and supports in the same classrooms, activities, and schools they would attend if they did not have a disability. (Chapter 10)

individualized education program (IEP) A written statement that identifies and organizes the educational and related services for students with disabilities. (Chapter 10)

individual processing profile A description of a child's sensory modulation, sensory processing, sensory-affective processing, and motor planning and sequencing abilities. (Chapter 5)

initiation An unsolicited verbal or nonverbal behavior directed toward another person to begin a social or verbal interaction. (Chapter 12)

joint attention/joint engagement Behaviors or signals (e.g., pointing, showing, giving, eye gaze) used to direct another's attention to objects or events of interest for the purpose of sharing with others, not necessarily to obtain those objects or events; when a child attends to an object to which a language partner (caregiver, peer, teacher) is also attending. (Chapter 7)

language The rules that govern the use and meaning of symbols, words, and phrases, including their form and function. Language can be expressed in verbal and written form. (Chapter 11)

language modeling One of the four core components of EMT, language modeling includes specific procedures for providing the child with more complex models of language by using targeted language forms in ongoing interactions and when expanding the child's utterances. (Chapter 8)

maintenance interspersal The intermingling of novel, unmastered tasks with mastered tasks within a DTI session. (Chapter 4)

milieu teaching A naturalistic approach to teaching communication skills in everyday communication contexts. The approach uses environmental arrangement, specific natural prompts for language, and functional consequences to increase the frequency and complexity of children's communication. (Chapter 8)

modalities In the language paradigm of the ICDL-DMIC (ICDL, 2005), aspects of early development that are considered central to the process of acquiring language and being a successful communicator. The modalities are shared attention, affective engagement, reciprocity, shared intentions, shared forms and meanings, emerging discourse, sensory processing and audition, and motor planning. These modalities are considered extensively in the DIR approach. (Chapter 5)

motivational operation (MO) An environmental variable that increases the reinforcer effectiveness of a particular stimulus and temporarily results in increased responding for all behaviors that have been reinforced in the presence of a discriminative stimulus. (Chapter 4)

motivational strategies Teaching strategies (interspersing maintenance, shared control, natural reinforcement, reinforcement of attempts, etc.) that increase the likelihood a child will want to interact, respond, and learn new skills. (Chapter 12)

Motivation Assessment Scale A form of functional behavior assessment. The scale includes 16 questions about the antecedents and consequences of the target behavior. (Chapter 6)

multiple cues Environmental stimuli that people must attend to and filter in order to respond appropriately. (Chapter 12)

natural communities of reinforcement The concept that behaviors can be taught to gain access to reinforcers that are naturally occurring in the environment (e.g., praise from teachers). (Chapter 6)

natural environments The everyday routines, activities, and places that are typical or natural for the family; these usually include locations (e.g., the home, child care, family and friends' homes, or other community locations) as well as the activities that occur regularly (e.g., play, caregiving, meals, and family chores). (Chapter 9)

naturalistic language interventions A broad range of developmental and contemporary behavioral strategies that are child directed, interest based, the intrinsically reinforced and that support functional communication when intentionally embedded within everyday activities. (Chapter 9)

naturalistic teaching A teaching method delivered in the child's natural environments in which learning occurs. The intervention uses reinforcers and intrinsic to the child, capitalizes on the child's communication initiations, and focuses on providing intervention in pragmatically functional social interactions. The form and the content of language are taught during naturally occurring exchanges, the interventionist follows the child's lead, and the trials are dispersed throughout the session intermittently. (Chapter 12)

neurodevelopmental disorders of relating and communicating Four types of profiles related to the child's level of functioning within and across developmental domains and individual differences. The range includes the less challenged child, who shows intermittent capacities for relating, reciprocity, and shared problem-solving, and the more challenged child, who shows fleeting capacities for engagement and reciprocity and may experience regression in language, social-emotional development, or adaptive skills. (Chapter 5)

parent implemented intervention   Parents and other caregivers embed naturalistic intervention strategies throughout their typical activities to promote active engagement and learning of functional goals. (Chapter 9)

peer-mediated support interventions   Interventions that involve equipping one or more peers without disabilities to provide ongoing social and/or academic support to their similar-age peers with disabilities under the supervision of adults. Such interventions can increase the quality and quantity of social interactions with their classmates with disabilities. (Chapter 10)

peer interaction training   Information and/or strategies taught to peers without disabilities to increase the quality and quantity of social interactions with their classmates with disabilities. (Chapter 10)

peer modeling   Viewing a person of approximately one's own age demonstrating a task. (Chapter 14)

peer network strategies   Establishing and supporting cohesive social groups around a particular focus student with disabilities in order to help him or her participate more fully in the academic and social life of the school. (Chapter 10)

peer support arrangements   Arranging for one or two peers from within the same classroom to provide academic *and* social support to their classmates with severe disabilities. (Chapter 10)

peer tutoring   Equipping and arranging for students to provide instructional support to their peers on an individual, small group, or classwide basis. (Chapter 10)

pivotal areas   Areas that, when targeted, lead to collateral changes in untargeted areas of functioning and responding. (Chapter 12)

Pivotal Response Treatment (PRT)   An empirically validated, play-based intervention approach, which utilizes applied behavior analysis (ABA) techniques and a developmental approach to target the core deficits of autism (PRT also refers to Pivotal Response Training, Pivotal Response Teaching, Pivotal Response Therapy, and Pivotal Response Intervention. (Chapter 12)

play routines   A plan for how to play with a toy or use objects in a play activity. Play routines have steps that are repeated and a predicable sequence of events. Although the steps, the sequence of the steps, and the language used during the routine are consistent, new steps and acts can be added to the routine. New steps and some unpredictability are necessary to keep the routine from becoming boring and to keep the child engaged. (Chapter 7)

point-of-view modeling   A form of video modeling with all footage of the modeled behavior taken from the observer's eye level and perspective. (Chapter 14)

positive self-review A form of self-modeling used for honing already-learned skills by looking at the best performances. (Chapter 14)

pragmatics The accepted rules of language and communication for social purposes. For example, many cultures have accepted rules for the distance that one person should stand from another when conversing. (Chapter 11)

problem behaviors See *challenging behaviors.*

prompt Supplemental stimulus, or cue, that is presented with the goal of increasing the likelihood that the learner will respond correctly. (Chapter 4)

regulation The ability to maintain a calm, alert, attentive state of arousal. (Chapter 5)

reinforcement When a learner's response yields a stimulus change (e.g., presentation of desirable outcome or removal of undesirable situation) that results in an increased likelihood that the response will occur in the future under similar circumstances. Differential reinforcement is said to occur when a reinforcer is available under one set of conditions and unavailable under all other conditions. (Chapter 4)

related services Developmental, corrective, and other supportive services (e.g., speech-language, audiology, occupational therapy, social work) that may be required to assist a child with a disability to benefit from special education. (Chapter 10)

response A single demonstration of a behavior. In the context of a discrete trial, all actions taken by the learner are considered responses. That is, failure to take a specific action— for example, by sitting and staring off—is considered a response that requires a consequence. (Chapter 4)

responsive interaction One of the four core components of EMT, responsive interaction is a set of strategic behaviors, including following the child's lead, mirroring and mapping, responding to initiations, and providing meaningful semantic feedback that maintains the child's interest in conversations. (Chapter 8)

scaffolding Temporary and adjustable support structures (e.g., visual prompts, verbal prompts, modeling of skills, physical prompts) provided by a teacher that are used to support a child's learning. As the child makes progress in learning the skill being taught, the scaffolding is progressively decreased. The reduction in scaffolding eventually leads to the child's mastering the concepts or task independently. (Chapter 7)

SCERTS® A child-centered, activity-based, developmentally grounded, and family-centered curricular-based assessment and intervention approach (Prizant, Wetherby, Rubin, Laurent, & Rydell, 2006). It targets the most significant challenges faced by children with ASDs in the domains of social communication (SC) and emotional regulation (ER). Goals and objectives in the domain of transactional supports (TS) are targeted for the communication partners (i.e., parents, siblings, peers) to support learning in the natural environment. (Chapter 9)

schema (plural: schemata or schemas) A conceptual framework for understanding events, thoughts, and behaviors. (Chapter 13)

scripted language   Imitated segments of dialogue or discourse from movies, television shows, songs, and books that can be used to communicate meanings and intentions. (Chapter 5)

self-efficacy   The confidence felt by people regarding their ability to successfully carry out a task. (Chapter 14)

self-injurious behavior   Behaviors that are directed at oneself and that often result in injury to the person. (Chapter 6)

self-management   The ability to recognize a desired behavior or response, perform the desired behavior, and administer self-reinforcement. (Chapter 12)

self-modeling   A form of video modeling that is edited so that the observer watches him- or herself performing beyond present levels. (Chapter 14)

self-observation   Viewing of unedited videos of behavior or performance that contain both positive and negative elements. (Chapter 14)

shaping   The process of teaching a correct response by reinforcing responses that more closely approximate the correct response. (Chapter 4)

sign language   An unaided form of AAC, in that the user has no external equipment or tool. There are several different sign language systems, including American Sign Language and Signing Exact English. (Chapter 3)

social cognition   The process by which people make sense of the self and others, and acquire, use, and understand social knowledge. (Chapter 13)

social-pragmatic developmental interventions   Interventions in which the interventionist follows the child's lead, fosters initiation and spontaneity, and reinforces contingent responses. (Chapter 1)

Social Story   A short story that adheres to a specific format and guidelines to objectively describe a person, skill, event, concept, or social situation. (Chapter 13)

speech   The production of meaningful oral sounds and syllables. Voices, used to produce a sound, and articulation, used to shape sounds, are the basic elements of speech. (Chapter 11)

speech-generating device (SGD)   An aided form of AAC that provides voice output when activated. These systems provide synthesized or digitized voice and are computer based. (Chapter 3)

storyboard   A graphic representation of the scenes and sequence of a movie; an area in video editing software where "keeper" video clips are stored and edited. (Chapter 14)

tantrums   A combination of behaviors, such as screaming, running around, and a variety of other behavioral disruptions. (Chapter 6)

theory of mind   The ability to reason about the inner mental worlds of self and others and to understand that others may have perspectives that differ from our own. It is one aspect of social cognition. (Chapter 13)

traditional behavioral interventions   Interventions in which skills are taught one-to-one and which have a predetermined correct response and a highly prescribed teaching structure. (Chapter 1)

unaided AAC system   A form of AAC that requires no external tool or equipment. Unaided forms of AAC include sign language, gestures, vocalizations, and facial expressions. (Chapters 3 and 11)

verbal behavior   Verbal and nonverbal communicative behavior that is reinforced by a listener. B.F. Skinner identified a number of verbal behaviors that currently are used to guide the curricular goals of many children on the autism spectrum. (Chapter 4)

video modeling   Use of videos depicting adults, peers, self, or animated characters performing adaptive skills and behaviors needed by an observer. (Chapter 14)

visual scene display   A picture or scene that represents an activity, an experience, or a situation. Specific objects or people in the scene are programmed to speak a word or message when they are activated. (Chapter 3)

weak central coherence   A cognitive style, believed to be present in ASDs, in which the processing of parts takes precedence over the processing of wholes. (Chapter 13)

REFERENCES

Beukelman, D., & Mirenda, P. (2005). *Augmentative and alternative communication: Supporting children and adults with complex communication needs* (3rd ed.). Baltimore, MD: Paul H. Brookes Publishing Co.

National Autism Center. (2009). *National Standards Project—findings and conclusions: Addressing the needs for evidence-based practice guidelines for autism spectrum disorders.* Randolph, MA: Author. Retrieved from http://www.nationalautismcenter.org

Index

|||||||||||||||||||||||||||||||||||||||||||||||||||||||||||||||||||||||||||||||||||||

Tables, figures, and notes are indicated by *t, f,* and *n,* respectively.